AUDIT & ACCOUNTING GUIDE

Employee Benefit Plans

WITH CONFORMING CHANGES AS OF
JANUARY 1, 2011

This edition of the AICPA Audit and Accounting Guide *Employee Benefit Plans*, which was originally issued in 1991, has been modified by the AICPA staff to include certain changes necessary because of the issuance of authoritative pronouncements since the guide was originally issued and other changes necessary to keep the guide current on industry and regulatory matters. The schedule of changes appendix identifies all changes made in this edition of the guide. The changes do *not* include all those that might be considered necessary if the guide was subjected to a comprehensive review and revision.

Preface

About AICPA Audit and Accounting Guides

This AICPA Audit and Accounting Guide has been developed by the AICPA Employee Benefit Plans Committee to assist management of employee benefit plans in the preparation of financial statements in conformity with U.S. generally accepted accounting principles (GAAP) and to assist auditors in auditing and reporting on such financial statements.

The financial accounting and reporting guidance contained in this guide, when developed by the original committee, was approved by the affirmative vote of at least two-thirds of the members of the Accounting Standards Executive Committee (AcSEC), now the Financial Reporting Executive Committee (FinREC). FinREC is the senior technical body of the AICPA authorized to speak for the AICPA in the areas of financial accounting and reporting. Conforming updates made to the financial accounting and reporting guidance contained in this guide in years subsequent to the original development are reviewed by select FinREC members, among other reviewers where applicable.

This guide does the following:

- Identifies certain requirements set forth in Financial Accounting Standards Board (FASB) *Accounting Standards Codification*™ (ASC).

- Describes FinREC's understanding of prevalent or sole industry practice concerning certain issues. In addition, this guide may indicate that FinREC expresses a preference for the prevalent or sole industry practice, or it may indicate that FinREC expresses a preference for another practice that is not the prevalent or sole industry practice; alternatively, FinREC may express no view on the matter.

- Identifies certain other, but not necessarily all, industry practices concerning certain accounting issues without expressing FinREC's views on them.

- Provides guidance that has been supported by FinREC on the accounting, reporting, or disclosure treatment of transactions or events that are not set forth in FASB ASC.

Accounting guidance for nongovernmental entities included in an AICPA Audit and Accounting Guide is a source of nonauthoritative accounting guidance. As discussed in this preface, FASB ASC is the authoritative source of U.S. accounting and reporting standards for nongovernmental entities, in addition to guidance issued by the Securities and Exchange Commission (SEC). AICPA members should be prepared to justify departures from U.S. GAAP as discussed in Rule 203, *Accounting Principles* (AICPA, *Professional Standards*, ET sec. 203 par. .01).

Auditing guidance included in an AICPA Audit and Accounting Guide is recognized as an interpretive publication pursuant to AU section 150, *Generally Accepted Auditing Standards* (AICPA, *Professional Standards*). Interpretive publications are recommendations on the application of Statements on Auditing Standards (SASs) in specific circumstances, including engagements for entities in specialized industries. An interpretive publication is issued under the authority of the Auditing Standards Board (ASB) after all ASB members have been provided an opportunity to consider and comment on whether the proposed interpretive publication is consistent with the SASs. The members of the ASB have found this guide to be consistent with existing SASs.

The auditor should be aware of and consider interpretive publications applicable to his or her audit. If an auditor does not apply the auditing guidance included in an applicable interpretive publication, the auditor should be prepared to explain how he or she complied with the SAS provisions addressed by such auditing guidance.

Purpose and Applicability

This guide applies to employee benefit plans, including defined benefit plans, defined contribution plans and health and welfare plans, that are subject to the financial reporting requirements of the Employee Retirement Income Security Act of 1974 (ERISA), as well as those that are not. Appendix A, "ERISA and Related Regulations," identifies and summarizes relevant ERISA requirements and regulations.

Generally accepted auditing standards (GAAS) and accounting principles are applicable in general to employee benefit plans.[1] The broad application of those standards and principles is not discussed here. Rather, the guide focuses on the special problems in auditing and reporting on financial statements that are unique to employee benefit plans.

The guide contains certain suggested auditing procedures, but detailed internal control questionnaires and audit programs are not included. The nature, timing, and extent of auditing procedures are a matter of professional judgment and will vary depending on the size, organizational structure, internal control, and other factors in a specific engagement.

The guide also includes information regarding statutory rules and regulations applicable to employee benefit plans and illustrations of plan financial statements and auditors' reports. The Department of Labor Employee Benefits Security Administration strongly encourages the use of this guide in meeting the requirements contained in ERISA Section 103 that a plan have an audit conducted in accordance with GAAS.

The guidance in this audit guide is in certain respects more detailed than that generally included in other AICPA audit guides. To facilitate reference, paragraphs have been numbered.

---

[1] Subject to the Securities and Exchange Commission (SEC) oversight, Section 103 of the Sarbanes-Oxley Act of 2002 authorizes the Public Company Accounting Oversight Board (PCAOB) to establish auditing and related attestation, quality control, ethics, and independence standards to be used by registered public accounting firms in the preparation and issuance of audit reports as required by the act or the rules of the SEC. Accordingly, public accounting firms registered with the PCAOB are required to adhere to all PCAOB standards in the audits of issuers, as defined by the act and other entities when prescribed by the rules of the SEC. Generally, plans that are required to file Form 11-K would be considered issuers.

Recognition

Jay D. Hanson
Chair, FinREC

Darrel R. Schubert
Chair, ASB

Employee Benefit Plans Committee (1990–1991)

Andrew J. Capelli, *Chair*

Steven A. Cook

Rick Covert

Michael J. Fitzpatrick

Gary T. Gray

Mannon Kaplan

Ben B. Korbly

Gilbert K. Reeves

Richard Schwartz

Randi L. Starr

Richard M. Steinberg

David M. Walker

Employee Benefit Plans Audit Guide Revision Task Force (2009–2010)

Lawrence R. Beebe

Judy Goldberg

Josie Hammond

Ann Joda

Marilee P. Lau

Diane Marotta

James E. Merklin

Becky Miller

Kevin Murphy

Kathryn Petrillo

Dennis M. Polisner

Deborah Smith

Michele M. Weldon

Alice Wunderlich

AICPA Staff

Linda C. Delahanty
Technical Manager
Audit and Attest Standards

Diana G. Krupica
Technical Manager
Accounting and Auditing Publications

The Employee Benefit Plans Committee gratefully acknowledges the contributions of Melissa A.R. Krause, former committee member; Susan W. Hicks; Daniel J. Cronin; The Office of Chief Accountant, Employee Security Benefits Administration; and the Office of the Inspector General, U.S. Department of Labor. The AICPA gratefully acknowledges Cathleen Finneran who reviewed and otherwise contributed to the development of this guide. The AICPA staff would also like to acknowledge the Employee Benefit Plans Expert Panel (2009–2010), and the invaluable assistance of JulieAnn Verrekia provided in updating and maintaining the guidance in this guide.

Guidance Considered in This Edition

This edition of the guide has been modified by the AICPA staff to include certain changes necessary due to the issuance of authoritative guidance since the guide was originally issued. Authoritative guidance issued through January 1, 2011, has been considered in the development of this edition of the guide. Authoritative guidance discussed in the text of the guide (as differentiated from the temporary footnotes, which are denoted by a symbol rather than a number) is effective for entities with fiscal years ending on or before January 1, 2011. Authoritative guidance discussed only in temporary footnotes is not yet effective as of January 1, 2011, for entities with fiscal years ending after that same date.

This includes relevant guidance issued up to and including the following:

- FASB Accounting Standards Update (ASU) No. 2010-29, *Business Combinations (Topic 805): Disclosure of Supplementary Pro Forma Information for Business Combinations (a consensus of the FASB Emerging Issues Task Force)*
- SAS No. 120, *Required Supplementary Information* (AICPA, *Professional Standards*, AU sec. 558)
- Interpretation No. 19, "Financial Statements Prepared in Conformity With International Financial Reporting Standards as Issued by the International Accounting Standards Board," of AU section 508, *Reports on Audited Financial Statements* (AICPA, *Professional Standards*, AU sec. 9508 par. .93–.97)
- Revised interpretations issued through January 1, 2011, including Interpretation Nos. 1–4 of AU section 325, *Communicating Internal Control Related Matters Identified in an Audit* (AICPA, *Professional Standards*, AU sec. 9325 par. .01–.13)
- Statement of Position 09-1, *Performing Agreed-Upon Procedures Engagements That Address the Completeness, Accuracy, or Consistency of XBRL-Tagged Data* (AICPA, *Technical Practice Aids*, AUD sec. 14,440)
- Statement on Standards for Attestation Engagements (SSAE) No. 16, *Reporting on Controls at a Service Organization* (AICPA, *Professional Standards*, AT sec. 801)
- Public Company Accounting Oversight Board (PCAOB) Auditing Standard No. 7, *Engagement Quality Review* (AICPA, *PCAOB Standards and Related Rules*, Auditing Standards)

Users of this guide should consider guidance issued subsequent to those items listed previously to determine their effect on entities covered by this guide. In determining the applicability of recently issued guidance, its effective date should also be considered.

The changes made to this edition of the guide are identified in the schedule of changes appendix. The changes do not include all those that might be considered necessary if the guide were subjected to a comprehensive review and revision.

References to Professional Standards

In citing GAAS and its related interpretations, references use section numbers within the codification of currently effective SASs and not the original statement number, as appropriate. For example, SAS No. 54, *Illegal Acts by Clients*, is referred to as AU section 317, *Illegal Acts by Clients* (AICPA, *Professional Standards*). In those sections of the guide that refer to specific auditing standards of the PCAOB, references are made to the AICPA's *PCAOB Standards and Related Rules* publication.

FASB *Accounting Standards Codification*™

Overview

Released on July 1, 2009, FASB ASC is a major restructuring of accounting and reporting standards designed to simplify user access to all authoritative U.S. GAAP by topically organizing the authoritative literature. FASB ASC disassembled and reassembled thousands of nongovernmental accounting pronouncements (including those of FASB, the Emerging Issues Task Force, and the AICPA) to organize them under approximately 90 topics.

FASB ASC also includes relevant portions of authoritative content issued by the SEC, as well as selected SEC staff interpretations and administrative guidance issued by the SEC; however, FASB ASC is not the official source of SEC guidance and does not contain the entire population of SEC rules, regulations, interpretive releases, and SEC staff guidance. Moreover, FASB ASC does not include governmental accounting standards.

FASB published a notice to constituents that explains the scope, structure, and usage of consistent terminology of FASB ASC. Constituents are encouraged to read this notice to constituents because it answers many common questions about FASB ASC. FASB ASC, and its related notice to constituents, can be accessed at http://asc.fasb.org/home and are also offered by certain third party licensees, including the AICPA. FASB ASC is offered by FASB at no charge in a Basic View and for an annual fee in a Professional View.

Issuance of New Standards

New standards are now issued by FASB through ASUs and will serve only to update FASB ASC. FASB does not consider the ASUs authoritative in their own right; new standards become authoritative when they are incorporated into FASB ASC.

New standards will be in the form of ASU No. 20YY-XX, in which "YY" is the last two digits of the year and "XX" is the sequential number for each update. For example, ASU No. 2010-01 is the first update in the calendar year 2010. New standards will include the standard and an appendix of FASB ASC update instructions. ASUs will also provide background information about the standards and provide the basis for conclusions on changes made to FASB ASC.

Pending Content in FASB ASC

New guidance from ASUs (or other authoritative accounting guidance issued prior to the release date of FASB ASC) issued that are not yet fully effective, or became effective within the last six months, for all entities or transactions within its scope are reflected as "Pending Content" in FASB ASC. This pending content is shown in text boxes following the paragraphs being amended in FASB ASC and includes links to the transition information. The pending content boxes are meant to provide users with information about how a paragraph will change when new guidance becomes authoritative. When an amended paragraph has been fully effective for six months, the outdated guidance will be removed, and the amended paragraph will remain without the pending content box. FASB will keep any outdated guidance in the applicable archive section of FASB ASC for historical purposes.

Because not all entities have the same fiscal year-ends, and certain guidance may be effective on different dates for public and nonpublic entities, the pending content will apply to different entities at different times. As such, pending content will remain in place within FASB ASC until the "roll-off" date. Generally, the roll-off date is six months following the latest fiscal year end for which the original guidance being amended or superseded by the pending content could be applied as specified by the transition guidance. For example, assume an ASU has an effective date for fiscal years beginning after November 15, 2010. The latest possible fiscal year end of an entity still eligible to apply the original guidance being amended or superseded by the pending content would begin November 15, 2010, and end November 14, 2011. Accordingly, the roll-off date would be May 14, 2012.

Entities cannot disregard the pending content boxes in FASB ASC. Instead, all entities must review the transition guidance to determine if and when the pending content is applicable to them. This Audit and Accounting Guide identifies pending content where applicable. As explained in the section of the preface "Guidance Considered in This Edition," pending content discussed in the text of the guide (as differentiated from the temporary footnotes, which are denoted by a symbol rather than a number) is effective for entities with fiscal years ending on or before January 1, 2011. Pending content discussed only in temporary footnotes is not yet effective as of January 1, 2011, for entities with fiscal years ending after that same date.

Employee Benefit Plan Sections of FASB ASC

Plan accounting may be found in the following sections of FASB ASC:

- FASB ASC 960, *Plan Accounting—Defined Benefit Pension Plans*
- FASB ASC 962, *Plan Accounting—Defined Contribution Pension Plans*
- FASB ASC 965, *Plan Accounting—Health and Welfare Benefit Plans*

New AICPA.org Website

The AICPA encourages you to visit the new website at www.aicpa.org. It was launched in 2010 and provides significantly enhanced functionality and content critical to the success of AICPA members and other constituents. Certain content on the AICPA's website referenced in this guide may be restricted to AICPA members only.

Select Recent Developments Significant to This Guide

ASB's Clarity Project

In an effort to make GAAS easier to read, understand, and apply, the ASB launched the Clarity Project. When completed, clarified auditing standards will be issued as one SAS that will supersede all prior SASs. The new audit standards are expected to apply to audits of financial statements for periods ending on or after December 15, 2012.

The foundation of the ASB's Clarity Project is the establishment of an objective for each auditing standard. These objectives will better reflect a principles-based approach to standard setting. In addition to having objectives, the clarified standards will reflect new drafting conventions that include

- adding a definitions section, if relevant, in each standard.
- separating requirements from application and other explanatory material.
- numbering application and other explanatory material paragraphs using an A prefix and presenting them in a separate section (following the requirements section).
- using formatting techniques, such as bulleted lists, to enhance readability.
- adding special considerations relevant to audits of smaller, less complex entities.
- adding special considerations relevant to audits of governmental entities.

The project also has an international convergence component. The ASB expects that, upon completion of the project, the requirements of U.S. GAAS will be converged with those of the International Auditing and Assurance Standards Board. AICPA Audit and Accounting Guides, as well as other AICPA publications, will be conformed to reflect the new standards resulting from the Clarity Project after issuance and as appropriate based on the effective dates.

Service Organizations and SAS No. 70 Reports

The ASB has issued SAS *Audit Considerations Relating to an Entity Using a Service Organization* and SSAE No. 16. These two standards will replace SAS No. 70, *Service Organizations* (AICPA, *Professional Standards*, AU sec. 324).

The SAS will supersede the requirements and guidance for user auditors in SAS No. 70 and address the user auditor's responsibility for obtaining sufficient appropriate audit evidence in an audit of the financial statements of an entity that uses one or more service organizations. This SAS has been released but not yet issued as authoritative. Upon the finalization of all remaining SASs to be issued as part of the Clarity Project (that is, "clarified" SASs), one SAS will be issued containing all clarified SASs in codified format. The effective date will be the same as the other clarified standards, which is no earlier than for periods ending after December 15, 2012 (early implementation is not permitted). Until the new SAS is effective, user auditors will still use the guidance currently contained in AU section 324.

SSAE No. 16 addresses examination engagements undertaken by a service auditor to report on controls at organizations that provide services to user entities when those controls are likely to be relevant to user entities' internal control over financial reporting. It is effective for service auditors' reports for periods ending on or after June 15, 2011. Early implementation is permitted.

To help practitioners make the transition from SAS No. 70 to SSAE No. 16, the AICPA has developed the new alert *Service Organizations: New Reporting Options*, which provides practitioners with an overview of the changes to SAS No. 70 and alerts them to reporting options when examining controls at a service organization other than those relevant to financial reporting by user entities. It is intended to help practitioners understand the requirements of SSAE No. 16 and to provide professional guidelines that will enhance both consistency and quality in the performance of attest services. This new alert can be purchased by visiting www.cpa2biz.com/AST/Main/CPA2BIZ_Primary/ AuditAttest/IndustryspecificGuidance/PRDOVR~PC-0224811/PC-0224811.jsp.

In addition, a task force of the ASB is revising the existing Audit Guide *Service Organizations: Applying SAS No. 70, as Amended* (the SAS No. 70 guide) to reflect the requirements and guidance in SSAE No. 16. Also, the Audit Guide *Reporting on Controls at a Service Provider Relevant to Security, Availability, Processing Integrity, Confidentiality, or Privacy*, will address reporting on a service provider's controls over subject matter other than financial reporting. Both Audit Guides are expected to be available for sale in 2011.

International Financial Reporting Standards

International Financial Reporting Standards (IFRSs) consist of accounting standards and interpretations developed and issued by the International Accounting Standards Board (IASB), a London-based independent accounting standard-setting body. IASB began operations in 2001, when it succeeded the International Accounting Standards Committee (IASC). IASC was formed in 1973, soon after the formation of FASB. In 2001, when the IASB replaced the IASC, a new, independent oversight body, the IASC Foundation, was created to appoint the members of the IASB and oversee its due process. The IASC Foundation's oversight role is very similar to that of the Financial Accounting Foundation in its capacity as the oversight body of FASB.

The term *IFRSs* has both a narrow and a broad meaning. Narrowly, IFRSs refer to the new numbered series of pronouncements issued by the IASB, as differentiated from International Accounting Standards (IASs) issued by its predecessor, the IASC. More broadly, however, IFRSs refer to the entire body of authoritative IASB pronouncements, including those issued by the IASC and their respective interpretive bodies. Therefore, the authoritative IFRS literature, in its broadest sense, includes the following:

- Standards, whether labeled IFRSs or IASs
- Interpretations, whether issued by the IFRS Interpretations Committee (the interpretive body of the IFRS Foundation), the International Financial Reporting Interpretations Committee (IFRIC, predecessor to the IFRS Interpretations Committee), or the Standing Interpretations Committee (the predecessor to IFRIC)
- IFRS framework

As of March 31, 2010, IFRIC formally changed its name to the IFRS Interpretations Committee and on July 1, 2010, the IASC Foundation formally changed its name to the IFRS Foundation.

The preface to the IFRS 2010 bound volume states that IFRSs are designed to apply to the general purpose financial statements and other financial reporting of all profit-oriented entities including commercial, industrial, and financial entities regardless of legal form or organization. Included within the scope of profit-oriented entities are mutual insurance entities and other mutual cooperative entities providing dividends or other economic benefits to their owners, members, or participants.

IFRSs are not designed to apply to not-for-profit entities or those in the public sector, but these entities may find IFRSs appropriate in accounting for their activities. In contrast, U.S. GAAP is designed to apply to all nongovernmental entities, including not-for-profit entities, and includes specific guidance for not-for-profit entities, development stage entities, limited liability entities, and personal financial statements.

The AICPA governing council voted in May 2008 to recognize the IASB as an accounting body for purposes of establishing international financial accounting and reporting principles. This amendment to appendix A, *Council Resolution Designating Bodies to Promulgate Technical Standards*, of Rule 202, *Compliance With Standards* (AICPA, *Professional Standards*, ET sec. 202 par. .01), and Rule 203 gives AICPA members the option to use IFRSs as an alternative to U.S. GAAP. As a result, private entities in the United States can prepare their financial statements in accordance with U.S. GAAP as promulgated by FASB; an other comprehensive basis of accounting, such as cash- or tax-basis; or IFRSs, among others. However, domestic issuers are currently required to follow U.S. GAAP and rules and regulations of the SEC. In contrast, foreign private issuers may present their financial statements in accordance with IFRSs as issued by the IASB without a reconciliation to U.S. GAAP, or in accordance with non-IFRS home-country GAAP reconciled to U.S. GAAP as permitted by Form 20-F.

The growing acceptance of IFRSs as a basis for U.S. financial reporting could represent a fundamental change for the U.S. accounting profession. Acceptance of a single set of high quality accounting standards for worldwide use by public companies has been gaining momentum around the globe for the past few years.

TABLE OF CONTENTS

Contents

Contents

Contents

Contents

————————————————

Contents

Chapter 1

*Introduction and Background**

1.01 The purpose of this guide is to provide guidance on accounting, auditing, and reporting on the financial statements of employee benefit plans (plans). This guide applies to defined benefit pension plans, defined contribution plans, and defined benefit and defined contribution health and welfare benefit plans. In the United States, there are nearly 2.8 million health plans, a similar number of other welfare plans, and nearly 708,000 private pension plans. The private pension plans alone cover more than 124 million participants and, at the end of the first quarter of 2010, held assets with an estimated value of nearly $5.6 trillion. The Employee Retirement Income Security Act of 1974 (ERISA) covers roughly 150 million workers, retirees, and dependents of private sector pension and welfare plans.

1.02 This guide applies to audits of financial statements and supplemental schedules, as applicable, of plans that are subject to the financial reporting requirements of ERISA, as well as to those that are not. The recommendations contained in this guide apply to the financial statements of plans sponsored by commercial or not-for-profit private sector entities. The accounting provisions of this guide are not intended to apply to governmental employee benefit plans. The accounting for those plans is prescribed by Governmental Accounting Standards Board (GASB) Statement No. 25, *Financial Reporting for Defined Benefit Pension Plans and Note Disclosures for Defined Contribution Plans*, as amended, and GASB Statement No. 43, *Financial Reporting for Postemployment Benefit Plans Other Than Pension Plans*, as amended; however, portions of the guide may be useful to auditors of those plans. The guide discusses accounting, auditing, and reporting for ongoing and terminated plans. A plan is the reporting entity as defined under ERISA and Financial Accounting Standards Board (FASB) *Accounting Standards Codification* (ASC) 960, *Plan Accounting—Defined Benefit Pension Plans*. Although this guide does not specifically discuss accounting, auditing, and reporting for employee benefit trusts as separate entities, it may be useful to auditors reporting on employee benefit trusts.

1.03 The guidance presented is not all-inclusive, but rather is limited generally to matters that warrant special emphasis or that experience has indicated may be useful. This guide is based on the assumption that the readers are generally expert in accounting and auditing and focuses on specific problems of auditing, accounting, and reporting with respect to the financial statements of employee benefit plans. Accordingly, the guide does not discuss the application of all accounting principles generally accepted in the United States of America (U.S. GAAP)[1] and auditing standards as they pertain to the auditing of such financial statements. The nature, timing, and extent of auditing procedures are matters of professional judgment and will vary according to the size of the plan, the plan operations and administrative structure, the auditor's assessment of

---

* Refer to the preface of this guide for important information about the applicability of the professional standards to audits of issuers and nonissuers.

[1] All references made in this guide to generally accepted accounting principles in the United States of America (U.S. GAAP) relate to U.S. GAAP as promulgated by the Financial Accounting Standards Board (FASB).

the level of risk, and other factors. The independent auditor is also expected to be familiar with applicable governmental laws and regulations.

1.04 The Securities and Exchange Commission (SEC) requires employee stock purchase, savings and similar plans with interests that constitute securities registered under the Securities Act of 1933 to file Form 11-K[†] pursuant to Section 15(d) of the Securities Exchange Act of 1934. Plans that are required to file Forms 11-K are deemed to be *issuers* under the Sarbanes-Oxley Act of 2002 and must submit to the SEC an audit in accordance with the auditing and related professional practice standards promulgated by the Public Company Accounting Oversight Board (PCAOB).[‡] The PCAOB had adopted as interim standards, on an initial, transitional basis, the AICPA generally accepted auditing standards (GAAS) in existence on April 16, 2003. Certain of these interim standards have been subsequently amended by various PCAOB releases. [‖]

1.05 Form 11-K does not require a Sarbanes-Oxley Act of 2002 Section 302 (*Corporate Responsibility for Financial Reports*) certification. Although the rule is silent regarding Section 404 (*Management Assessment of Internal Controls*) reports on Form 11-K, the SEC staff has agreed that because Form 11-K filers are not subject to Item 308 of Regulation S-K, the Form 11-K need not include a 404 report.[#] Accordingly, this guide does not reflect PCAOB Auditing Standard No. 5, *An Audit of Internal Control Over Financial Reporting That Is Integrated with An Audit of Financial Statements* (AICPA, *PCAOB Standards and Related Rules*, Auditing Standards), except to reflect certain conforming amendments found in PCAOB Release 2004-008, *Conforming Amendments to PCAOB Interim Standards Resulting From the Adoption of PCAOB Auditing Standard No. 2, "An Audit of Internal Control Over Financial Reporting Performed in Conjunction With An Audit Of Financial Statements,"* and PCAOB Release 2007-005A, *Auditing Standard No. 5, An Audit of Internal Control Over Financial Reporting That Is Integrated With An Audit of Financial Statements, and Related Independence Rule and Conforming Amendments* (AICPA, *PCAOB Standards and Related Rules*, Select PCAOB Releases). Certain of the provisions in PCAOB Release 2004-008 and PCAOB Release 2007-005A are relevant to situations in which an auditor is engaged solely to audit an entity's financial statements and not just when performing an integrated audit of financial statements and internal control over financial reporting. Therefore, certain of the conforming amendments are reflected in this guide. This guide will discuss if PCAOB standards are more restrictive than GAAS. See paragraph 12.34 for a summary of where PCAOB auditing standards are discussed in this guide.

1.06 See the PCAOB website www.pcaobus.org for a complete listing of PCAOB auditing standards and related conforming amendments. Also, consider PCAOB standards issued subsequent to those covered in the guide.

[†] Or other applicable Securities and Exchange Commission (SEC) filings, such as the Form 10-K/A.

[‡] The December 1, 2005, SEC *Accounting and Disclosure Issues* (page 59) provides guidance regarding the preapproval of audits of employee benefit plans. To view the entire document, see the website www.sec.gov/divisions/corpfin/acctdis120105.pdf.

[‖] See the Public Company Accounting Oversight Board (PCAOB) website at www.pcaobus.org for information about PCAOB auditing standards and related conforming amendments.

[#] This information was taken from the Center for Audit Quality SEC Regulations Committee highlights. Be alert to changes in this position by monitoring the SEC Regulations Committee website at http://thecaq.org/resources/secregs.htm.

1.07 According to FASB ASC 960-10-05-4, *defined benefit pension plans* provide a promise to pay to participants specified benefits that are determinable and are based on such factors as age, years of service, and compensation. These plans, which are discussed in more detail in chapter 2, "Accounting and Reporting by Defined Benefit Pension Plans," include cash balance plans and pension equity plans.

1.08 As stated in the FASB ASC glossary, *defined contribution pension plans* provide an individual account for each participant and provide benefits that are based on (*a*) amounts contributed to the participant's account by the employer or employee, (*b*) investment experience, and (*c*) any forfeitures allocated to the account, less any administrative expenses charged to the plan. These plans, which are discussed in more detail in chapter 3, "Accounting and Reporting by Defined Contribution Plans," include (*a*) profit-sharing plans, (*b*) money purchase pension plans, (*c*) stock bonus and employee stock ownership plans, (*d*) thrift or savings plans including 401(k) and 403(b) arrangements, and (*e*) certain target benefit plans.

1.09 As stated in the FASB ASC glossary, *health and welfare benefit plans*, which are discussed in more detail in chapter 4, "Accounting and Reporting by Health and Welfare Benefit Plans," include plans that provide (*a*) medical, dental, visual, psychiatric, or long-term health care; severance benefits; life insurance; accidental death or dismemberment benefits; (*b*) unemployment, disability, vacations or holiday benefits; and (*c*) other benefits, such as apprenticeships, tuition assistance, day-care, housing subsidies, or legal services benefits. Health and welfare benefit plans may be either defined-benefit or defined-contribution plans, as explained in the following paragraphs and in more detail in chapter 4:

> *a.* Defined-benefit health and welfare plans specify a determinable benefit, which may be in the form of a reimbursement to the covered plan participant or a direct payment to providers or third party insurers for the cost of specified services.
>
> *b.* Defined-contribution health and welfare plans maintain an individual account for each plan participant. They have terms that specify the means of determining the contributions to participants' accounts, rather than the amount of benefits the participants are to receive.

Financial Accounting and Reporting Standards

1.10 FASB ASC 960 provides standards of financial accounting and reporting for financial statements of defined benefit pension plans. FASB ASC 962, *Plan Accounting—Defined Contribution Pension Plans*, and FASB ASC 965, *Plan Accounting—Health and Welfare Benefit Plans*, provide standards for defined contribution and health and welfare plans, respectively.

1.11 Employee benefit plans that are subject to ERISA are required to report certain information annually to federal government agencies—that is, U.S. Department of Labor (DOL), IRS, Pension Benefit Guaranty Corporation (PBGC)—and to provide summarized information to plan participants. For many plans, the information is reported to the DOL on Form 5500, *Annual Return/Report of Employee Benefit Plan*, which includes financial statements prepared in conformity with U.S. GAAP and certain supplemental schedules (for example, Schedule H, line 4i—Schedule of Assets (Held at End of Year) and Schedule H, line 4j—Schedule of Reportable Transactions).

Governmental Regulations

1.12 Various provisions of the Internal Revenue Code (IRC) affect employee benefit plans and trusts established pursuant to employee benefit plans. If an employee benefit plan and its underlying trust qualify under Section 401(a) of the IRC, certain tax benefits are available, including (a) current tax deductions by plan sponsors for contributions, subject to certain limitations; (b) deferment of income to participants until the benefits are distributed; (c) exemption of the trust from income taxes, other than tax on unrelated business income; and (d) favorable tax treatment of certain benefit distributions to participants or their estates. Special rules apply to nonqualified plans and trusts depending on whether the plan is funded or unfunded. Generally, qualified plans provide benefits to relatively broad groups of employees, whereas nonqualified plans provide benefits to only a few key employees and may not be currently funded. Generally, ERISA preempts state laws and regulations (see discussion of ERISA in appendix A, "ERISA and Related Regulations").

Reporting and Disclosure Requirements

1.13 ERISA provides for substantial federal government oversight of the operating and reporting practices of employee benefit plans. In addition to establishing extensive reporting requirements for covered plans, ERISA establishes minimum standards for participation, vesting, and funding for defined benefit and defined contribution plans sponsored by private entities. It also establishes standards of fiduciary conduct and imposes specific restrictions and responsibilities on fiduciaries.

1.14 Under ERISA, the DOL and the IRS have the authority to issue regulations covering reporting and disclosure requirements and certain administrative responsibilities. The PBGC guarantees participants in most defined benefit pension plans against the loss of certain pension benefits if the plan terminates, and it administers terminated plans in certain circumstances.

1.15 Appendix A describes which plans are covered by ERISA and pertinent provisions of ERISA and related reporting and disclosure regulations issued by the DOL. Additional guidance concerning the effects of the IRC, ERISA, and related regulations on the operating and reporting practices of employee benefit plans is discussed throughout this guide.

1.16 Section 104(a)(4) of ERISA describes the power of the DOL to reject reports, and Section 104(a)(5) of the statute grants the Secretary of Labor the authority to retain an independent auditor, if necessary, after having rejected a filing. Additionally, Section 107 of ERISA requires "persons" who have to file any report or certify any information required under ERISA to maintain records (for example, vouchers, worksheets, receipts and applicable resolutions) on matters of which disclosures are required and keep such records available for examination for a period of not less than 6 years. The DOL interprets this section of ERISA to include all working papers supporting audits of employee benefit plans. Section 502(c)(2) of ERISA describes the substantial penalties that may be assessed by the DOL (see appendix A).

Audit Requirements

1.17 ERISA contains a requirement for annual audits of plan financial statements by an independent qualified public accountant. Generally, plans with 100 or more participants (see appendix A) are subject to the audit requirement. The independent auditor's objective and responsibility, under GAAS, are to express an opinion on whether the financial statements are fairly presented in conformity with generally accepted accounting principles (GAAP),[2] and that the related supplemental information is presented fairly, in all material respects, when considered in conjunction with the financial statements taken as a whole. The opinion should include an identification of the United States of America as the country of origin of the accounting principles used to prepare the financial statements and of the auditing standards the auditor followed in performing the audit. Although the audit requirement under ERISA is an important part of the total process designed to protect plan participants, a GAAS audit is not designed to ensure compliance with ERISA's provisions. Under the law, plan administrators, the IRS and the DOL have responsibility to ensure such compliance. The annual report and the financial statements prepared by the plan administrator and the independent auditor's report all contribute to the monitoring activities of these parties and agencies. An audit is an important discipline on the financial information reported by the plan administrator, but it does not ensure compliance with all legislative and regulatory requirements.

1.18 Subject to the SEC oversight, Section 103 of the Sarbanes-Oxley Act of 2002 authorizes the PCAOB to establish auditing and related attestation, quality control, ethics, and independence standards to be used by registered public accounting firms in the preparation and issuance of audit reports as required by the act or the rules of the SEC. Accordingly, public accounting firms registered with the PCAOB are required to adhere to all PCAOB standards in the audits of issuers, as defined by the act, and other entities when prescribed by the rules of the SEC. Generally, plans that are required to file Form 11-K would be considered issuers. See the "Securities and Exchange Commission Reporting Requirements" section in chapter 12, "Other Auditing Considerations," of this guide for guidance on Form 11-K filings.

Operation and Administration

1.19 Employee benefit plans vary by basic type (defined benefit pension plans, defined contribution plans, and defined benefit and defined contribution health and welfare benefit plans) and by basic operating and administrative characteristics. Employee benefit plans may be single employer plans or multiemployer plans.[3] The most distinguishing characteristic between single employer plans and multiemployer plans is administration. Single employer plans are generally established by the management of one employer (or a controlled

---

[2] All references made in this guide to generally accepted accounting principles (GAAP) relate to U.S GAAP as promulgated by FASB and International Financial Reporting Standards as promulgated by the International Accounting Standards Board, among others as designated in Rule 203, *Accounting Principles* (AICPA, *Professional Standards*, ET sec. 203 par. .01).

[3] The Employee Retirement Income Security Act of 1974 defines the term *multiemployer plan* as a plan to which more than one employer is required to contribute, that is maintained pursuant to one or more collective bargaining agreements between one or more employee organizations and more than one employer, and that satisfies other requirements that may be prescribed by U.S. Department of Labor regulations. As used in this guide, the term *single employer plan* may include plans with more than one employer under common control.

group of corporations) either unilaterally or through collective bargaining. In a single employer plan, the employer is the plan sponsor. By contrast, multiemployer plans are normally negotiated and established pursuant to a collective bargaining agreement between an associated group of employers, such as in the construction trades, and the union representing the employees. The plan sponsor of a multiemployer plan, with whom ultimate administrative responsibility rests, is a joint employer or union board of trustees.

1.20 Contributions may be required from both employers and participants (contributory plans) or from employers only (noncontributory plans). Noncontributory plans may contain provisions for payment of contributions or premiums by participants to maintain their eligibility during periods of unemployment; they may also provide for voluntary contributions by participants.

1.21 Plans may be funded through accumulated contributions and investment income (self-funded plans), funded through insurance contracts (insured plans), or funded through a combination of both (split-funded plans).

1.22 Employee benefit plans are normally established and maintained by plan sponsors pursuant to plan instruments. The provisions of plan instruments normally deal with such matters as eligibility to participate, entitlement to benefits, funding, plan amendments, operation and administration of plan provisions, identification of the plan's named fiduciary and allocation of responsibilities among those who also serve in the capacity as fiduciaries for control and management of the plan, and delegation by fiduciaries of duties in connection with administration of the plan. A plan subject to ERISA is required to be in writing. The IRS has prepared and updated standard (master or prototype) plans that are available to plan sponsors and may be qualified by simplified procedures. In addition, standardized (or pattern) plans that have IRS approval are available from various sources.

1.23 The named fiduciary is responsible for the operation and administration of a plan including the identification of a plan administrator. This individual is usually an officer or other employee of the plan sponsor and typically reports to the plan sponsor's board of directors or management. Sometimes the named fiduciary is a trustee and a union representative. The named fiduciary has continuing responsibility for operation of the plan in accordance with the terms of the plan instrument, any trust instrument or insurance contracts, and government laws and regulations. Generally, the named fiduciary makes policy decisions concerning such matters as interpretation of the plan provisions, determination of the rights of participants under the plan, management of investments, and delegation of operational and administrative duties.

1.24 Although the named fiduciary retains responsibility for oversight of the plan, the plan's day-to-day administration (for example, collection of contributions, payment of benefits, management of cash and investments, maintenance of records, and preparation of reports) generally is allocated to one or more of the following: (*a*) the plan sponsor; (*b*) a trustee, such as a bank trust department; (*c*) an insurance company; (*d*) an investment adviser; or (*e*) the person or persons designated as the plan administrator or administrative agent.

1.25 In self-funded plans, the plan assets typically are managed in accordance with a trust instrument that sets forth, among other matters, the authority and responsibilities of the trustees and any investment advisers and managers. In insured plans, the plan assets typically are managed in accordance with an agreement that sets forth the duties and responsibilities of the insurance company.

Accounting Records[4]

1.26 As with other entities, the accounting records of employee benefit plans ordinarily contain information necessary for effective management and reliable financial reporting. The complexity of a plan's accounting records will vary with such factors as the type of plan, number of employer contributors, complexity of the benefit formula, variety of benefit payment options, and delegation of administrative duties.

1.27 The accounting and other plan records of employee benefit plans often are maintained at several locations. Depending on the type of plan, the allocation of fiduciary responsibilities, and the delegation of administrative duties, records may be maintained by trustees, insurance companies, consulting actuaries, service bureaus, the plan administrator, contract administrators, and plan sponsors. The records of plans including, among others, the basic accounting records generally include the following, as applicable:

a. *Investment asset records.* ERISA requires detailed reporting of investment assets including reportable transactions, party in interest transactions, and leases and loans in default.

b. *Participants' records.* Records maintained to determine each employee's eligibility to participate in the plan and receive benefits. Eligibility for participation and benefits may be based on such factors as length of service, earnings, production, and contributions, and can be affected by age or breaks in service. These records are generally part of or derived from the personnel and payroll records maintained by the employer or the plan. These records are often made available to the plan's actuary to be used in computing various amounts including amounts to be funded.

c. *Contribution records.* Separate contribution records maintained for each plan contributor to record payments and accumulated contributions and to determine delinquencies and errors. These records provide sufficient detail to record contributions and payments received from a number of employers according to pertinent agreements or from individual participants.

d. *Claim records.* Claim records for health and welfare plans are generally extensive. They are used for such purposes as determining when benefit limits, if any, are reached by individual claimants and accumulating various historical data regarding types and amounts of claims, amounts paid, and timing of claims.

e. *Distribution records.* Records maintained to support distributions. These records identify entitlements, amounts, payment commencement data, terminations, forfeitures, transfers, and information to determine the tax consequences of distributions.

---

[4] Many plans outsource their processing of transactions to a third-party administrator or to an outside service organization. Often, the plan sponsor does not maintain independent accounting records of transactions initiated through these media. See the section "Understanding Internal Control" in chapter 6, "Internal Control," of this guide for further guidance.

f. *Individual participants' account information.* ERISA requires information that reflects each plan participant's share of the total net assets of the plan to be maintained. Changes in the value of net assets are allocated to the participants' accounts in accordance with the terms of the plan instrument. This information, which is not part of the basic books and records of a defined contribution plan, ordinarily should be in agreement with the aggregate participant account information contained in the basic books and records.

g. *Administrative expenses.* Expenses supported by invoices, contracts, agreements, or other written evidence.

h. *General accounting records.* Plans are required to maintain records of their receipts and disbursements; however, in many cases they are prepared by the trustee or recordkeeper. General ledgers are also generally maintained by the trustee.

i. *Reconciliations.* The plan administrators ordinarily reconcile the entity's records for the plan to the data obtained from third party administrators and the information provided by the trustee and investigates any differences.

Chapter 2

Accounting and Reporting by Defined Benefit Pension Plans

2.01 This chapter describes accounting principles generally accepted in the United States of America (U.S. GAAP) for accounting and financial reporting for defined benefit pension plans as provided in Financial Accounting Standards Board (FASB) *Accounting Standards Codification* (ASC) 960, *Plan Accounting—Defined Benefit Pension Plans*. FASB ASC 960 prescribes the general form and content of financial statements of those plans.

2.02 U.S. GAAP other than those discussed in this chapter may also apply to defined benefit pension plans.

Exhibit 2-1

Quick Reference for Defined Benefit Pension Plans

This guide has been organized so that the accounting and reporting guidance for defined benefit pension plans is contained in this chapter. Auditing guidance for defined benefit, defined contribution, and health and welfare benefit plans is contained throughout the guide. The following table has been developed to help you locate the areas in this guide that may pertain to an audit of a defined benefit pension plan. Not every area listed will be applicable to a particular client and the nature, timing, and extent of auditing procedures are matters of professional judgment.

Chapter 2	"Accounting and Reporting by Defined Benefit Pension Plans"
Chapter 5	"Planning and General Auditing Considerations"
Chapter 6	"Internal Control"
Chapter 7	"Auditing Investments and Loans to Participants"
Chapter 8	"Auditing Contributions Received and Related Receivables"
Chapter 9	"Auditing Benefit Payments"
Chapter 10	"Auditing Participant Data, Participant Allocations, and Plan Obligations" in particular: 10.12–.14 10.25–.33 10.41 Exhibit 10-1, "Illustrative Letter to Plan Actuary" Exhibit 10-2, "Illustrative Letter to Plan Actuary"
Chapter 11	"Party in Interest Transactions"
Chapter 12	"Other Auditing Considerations"
Chapter 13	"The Auditor's Report" in particular: 13.03–.05 Standard reports for defined benefit plans 13.08–.46 Various other reporting situations that may apply
Appendix A	"ERISA and Related Regulations"
Appendix B	"Examples of Controls"
Appendix D	"Illustrative Financial Statements: Defined Benefit Pension Plans"
Appendix G	"Consideration of Fraud in a Financial Statement Audit"

Cash Balance Plans

2.03   Traditional defined benefit pension plans provide benefits that are defined in terms of a percentage of final average compensation or career average compensation, or as a flat dollar benefit per year of service. Other types of benefit formulas have become more popular, including

    a. *cash balance plans.* A cash balance plan is a special form of career average compensation plan. Typically, a cash balance defined benefit pension plan maintains hypothetical *accounts* for participants. The employer credits participants' *accounts* with a certain number of dollars each plan year, and promises earnings at a specified rate. Interest on the *account* balance is credited at a stated rate, which may be and is often different from the plan's actual rate of investment return. The interest rate may be modified prospectively, so long as there are no reductions in the participant's benefit accrued to date. The formula for determining the amount to be credited to participants' *accounts* can be varied from year to year, if the employer properly amends the plan prior to the beginning of the year and complies with notice requirements under the Employee Retirement Income Security Act of 1974 (ERISA). A change in interest rate would also require a plan amendment and compliance with notice requirements under ERISA. The principal advantage to participants of a cash balance plan is the ability to watch their hypothetical *account balances* grow (similar to a defined contribution plan) while providing certainty about the interest to be credited. The participants bear no investment risk. The employer bears the risk that the plan's actual rate of return may fall below the stated rate of interest to be credited to participants' accounts. Additionally, if a vested participant switches careers or retires, the lump sum payment equals the hypothetical *account balance* and in some cases may be taken as a distribution prior to retirement; in a traditional plan a participant would not be able to compute the lump sum he or she is entitled to and generally would not have access until normal or early retirement.

    b. *pension equity plans.* A pension equity plan is a defined benefit pension plan that has many of the advantages of the cash balance plan, but the benefit formula is similar to a final pay program rather than a career average cash balance program. Under this arrangement, a participant is credited with *points* based on age, service or both. On termination of employment, a participant's final average compensation is multiplied by his or her accumulated points to determine a hypothetical account balance. This balance normally may be distributed as a lump sum or converted to an annuity.

Regulatory Reporting Requirements

2.04 In addition to the reporting requirements of FASB ASC 960, defined benefit pension plans have reporting requirements under ERISA.[1] The financial statements required by ERISA are a statement of assets and liabilities and a statement of changes in net assets available for benefits. The schedules required by ERISA, if applicable, include Schedule H, line 4a—Schedule of Delinquent Participant Contributions;[2] Schedule H, line 4i—Schedule of

---

[1] The Employee Retirement Income Security Act of 1974 (ERISA) annual reporting requirements, as well as the common exemptions, are described in appendix A, "ERISA and Related Regulations."

[2] Schedule H, line 4a—Schedule of Delinquent Participant Contributions, is only applicable for defined benefit pension plans that permit participant contributions.

Assets (Held at End of Year) and Schedule of Assets (Acquired and Disposed of Within Year); Schedule H, line 4j—Schedule of Reportable Transactions; Schedule G, Part I—Schedule of Loans or Fixed-Income Obligations in Default or Classified as Uncollectible; Schedule G, Part II—Schedule of Leases in Default or Classified as Uncollectible; and Schedule G, Part III, Nonexempt Transactions. The ERISA reporting requirements are described in appendix A. For guidance on how to report delinquent participant contributions, see the frequently asked questions about reporting delinquent participant contributions on the Form 5500 at the Employee Benefits Security Administration website at www.dol.gov/ebsa/faqs/faq_compliance_5500.html.

2.05 In accordance with the requirements of ERISA Sections 105 and 209, the plan administrator must furnish to any participant who so requests in writing—but not more than once a year—a statement of the participant's total accrued benefit and the earliest date on which he or she will become vested.

Financial Statements

2.06 FASB ASC 960-205-10-1 states that the primary objective of a pension plan's financial statements is to provide financial information that is useful in assessing the plan's present and future ability to pay benefits when due. Per FASB ASC 960-205-10-3, to accomplish its primary objective a plan's financial statements should provide information about all of the following:

   a. Plan resources and how the stewardship responsibility for those resources has been discharged

   b. The accumulated plan benefits of participants

   c. The results of transactions and events that affect the information regarding those resources and benefits

   d. Other factors necessary for users to understand the information provided

2.07 Per FASB ASC 960-30-25-1, the accrual basis[3] of accounting should be used in preparing information regarding the net assets available for benefits. Per FASB ASC 960-205-45-1, the annual financial statements of a defined benefit pension plan should include the following:[4]

   a. A statement that includes information regarding the net assets available for benefits as of the end of the plan year[5]

   b. A statement that includes information regarding the changes during the year in net assets available for benefits

---

[3] The accrual basis requires that purchases and sales of securities be recorded on a trade-date basis. If the settlement date is after the financial statement date, however, and (a) the fair value of the securities purchased or sold immediately before the financial statement date does not change significantly from the trade date to the financial statement date and (b) the purchases or sales do not significantly affect the composition of the plan's assets available for benefits, accounting on a settlement-date basis for such sales and purchases is acceptable.

[4] Financial Accounting Standards Board (FASB) *Accounting Standards Codification* (ASC) 230-10-15-4 states that a statement of cash flows is not required to be provided by a defined benefit pension plan that presents financial information in accordance with the provisions of FASB ASC 960, *Plan Accounting—Defined Benefit Pension Plans*. Employee benefit plans are encouraged to include a statement of cash flows with their annual financial statements when that statement would provide relevant information about the ability of the plan to meet future obligations (for example, when the plan invests in assets that are not highly liquid or obtains financing for investments).

[5] ERISA requires that this statement be presented in comparative form.

    c. Information regarding the actuarial present value of accumulated plan benefits as of either the beginning or end of the plan year

    d. Information regarding the effects, if significant, of certain factors affecting the year-to-year change in actuarial present value of accumulated plan benefits

2.08 FASB ASC 960 gives guidance on the form and content of the required financial statements and specifies that they be presented in sufficient detail to assist readers of plan financial statements in assessing the plan's present and future ability to pay benefits when due. Information regarding the actuarial present value of accumulated plan benefits and changes therein, however, may be presented in the financial statements or in the notes.

Fair Value Measurements

2.09 FASB ASC 820, *Fair Value Measurements and Disclosures*, defines fair value, sets out a framework for measuring fair value, and requires certain disclosures about fair value measurements. The following paragraphs summarize FASB ASC 820 but are not intended as a substitute for reviewing FASB ASC 820 in its entirety.

2.10 Meeting the requirements of FASB ASC 820 requires coordination among plan management, custodians, investment fiduciaries, and plan auditors. Plan sponsors and plan administrators will need to determine whether they have the appropriate valuation processes in place and sufficient data to determine the fair value of the plan's investments using the framework provided and to present the disclosures about the use of fair value measurements required. Although plan management can outsource the mechanics of the valuation process, they need to retain responsibility for the oversight of the final valuations, including determining the adequacy of the related footnote disclosures.

Definition of *Fair Value*

2.11 FASB ASC 820-10-20 defines *fair value* as the price that would be received to sell an asset or paid to transfer a liability in an orderly transaction between market participants at the measurement date.

Valuation Techniques

2.12 Paragraphs 24–35 of FASB ASC 820-10-35 describe the valuation techniques that should be used to measure fair value. Valuation techniques consistent with the market approach, income approach, or cost approach should be used to measure fair value, as follows:

- The market approach uses prices and other relevant information generated by market transactions involving identical or comparable assets or liabilities. Valuation techniques consistent with the market approach include matrix pricing and often use market multiples derived from a set of comparables.

- The income approach uses valuation techniques to convert future amounts (for example, cash flows or earnings) to a single present amount (discounted). The measurement is based on the value indicated by current market expectations about those future amounts. Valuation techniques consistent with the income approach include present value techniques, option-pricing models, and the multi-period excess earnings method.

- The cost approach is based on the amount that currently would be required to replace the service capacity of an asset (often referred to as current replacement cost). Fair value is determined based on the cost to a market participant (buyer) to acquire or construct a substitute asset of comparable utility, adjusted for obsolescence.

2.13 FASB ASC 820-10-35-24 states that valuation techniques that are appropriate in the circumstances and for which sufficient data are available should be used to measure fair value.

2.14 As explained in paragraphs 25–26 of FASB ASC 820-10-35, valuation techniques used to measure fair value should be consistently applied. However, a change in a valuation technique or its application is appropriate if the change results in a measurement that is equally or more representative of fair value in the circumstances. Such a change would be accounted for as a change in accounting estimate in accordance with the provisions of FASB ASC 250, *Accounting Changes and Error Corrections*.

The Fair Value Hierarchy

2.15 The fair value hierarchy in FASB ASC 820-10-35 prioritizes the inputs to valuation techniques used to measure fair value into three broad levels. The three levels are as follows:

- Paragraphs 40–41 of FASB ASC 820-10-35 state that level 1 inputs are quoted prices (unadjusted) in active markets for identical assets or liabilities that the reporting entity has the ability to access at the measurement date. An *active market*, as defined by the FASB ASC glossary, is a market in which transactions for the asset or liability occur with sufficient frequency and volume to provide pricing information on an ongoing basis. A quoted price in an active market provides the most reliable evidence of fair value and should be used to measure fair value whenever available, except as discussed in FASB ASC 820-10-35-43. FASB ASC 820-10-35-44 provides guidance on how the quoted price should not be adjusted because of the size of the position relative to trading volume (blockage factor) but rather would be measured within level 1 as the product of the quoted price for the individual instrument times the quantity held.

- Paragraphs 47–51 of FASB ASC 820-10-35 explain that level 2 inputs are inputs other than quoted prices included within level 1 that are observable for the asset or liability, either directly or indirectly. If the asset or liability has a specified (contractual) term, a level 2 input must be observable for substantially the full term of the asset or liability. Adjustments to level 2 inputs will vary depending on factors specific to the asset or liability. Those factors include the condition and location of the asset or liability, the extent to which the inputs relate to items that are comparable to the asset or liability, and the volume and level of activity in the markets within which the inputs are observed. An adjustment that is significant to the fair value measurement in its entirety might render the measurement a level 3 measurement, depending on the level in the fair value hierarchy within which the inputs used to determine the adjustment fall. As discussed in paragraph 48 of FASB ASC 820-10-35, level 2 inputs include

- quoted prices for similar assets or liabilities in active markets.

- quoted prices for identical or similar assets or liabilities in markets that are not active.

- inputs other than quoted prices that are observable for the asset or liability (for example, interest rates and yield curves observable at commonly quoted intervals, volatilities, prepayment speeds, loss severities, credit risks, and default rates).

- inputs that are derived principally from or corroborated by observable market data by correlation or other means (market-corroborated inputs).

- As discussed in paragraphs 52–55 of FASB ASC 820-10-35, level 3 inputs are unobservable inputs for the asset or liability. Unobservable inputs should be used to measure fair value to the extent that relevant observable inputs are not available, thereby allowing for situations in which there is little, if any, market activity for the asset or liability at the measurement date. Unobservable inputs should be developed based on the best information available in the circumstances, which might include the entity's own data. In developing unobservable inputs, the reporting entity need not undertake all possible efforts to obtain information about market participant assumptions. Unobservable inputs should reflect the reporting entity's own assumptions about the assumptions that market participants would use in pricing the asset or liability (including assumptions about risk). Assumptions about risk include the risk inherent in the inputs to the valuation technique. A measurement (for example, a mark-to-model measurement) that does not include an adjustment for risk would not represent a fair value measurement if market participants would include one in pricing the related asset or liability. The reporting entity should not ignore information about market participant assumptions that is reasonably available without undue cost and effort. Therefore, the entity's own data used to develop unobservable inputs should be adjusted if information is readily available without undue cost and effort that indicates that market participants would use different assumptions. "Pending Content" in FASB ASC 820-10-55-22 discusses level 3 inputs for particular assets and liabilities.

As explained in FASB ASC 820-10-35-37, in some cases the inputs used to measure fair value might fall in different levels of the fair value hierarchy. The level in the fair value hierarchy within which the fair value measurement in its entirety falls should be determined based on the lowest level input that is significant to the fair value measurement in its entirety.

Fair Value Measurements of Investments in Certain Entities That Calculate Net Asset Value per Share (or Its Equivalent)

2.16 Paragraphs 59–62 of FASB ASC 820-10-35 provide additional guidance on the fair value measurements of investments in certain entities that calculate net asset value (NAV) per share (or its equivalent). This guidance permits, as a practical expedient, a reporting entity to estimate the fair value of an investment, that is within the scope of the guidance, using the NAV per share of the investment (or its equivalent) if the NAV is calculated in a manner consistent with the measurement principles of FASB ASC 946, *Financial Services—Investment Companies*, as of the reporting entity's measurement date.[6]

Fair Value Determination When the Volume or Level of Activity Has Significantly Decreased

2.17   Paragraphs 51A–H of FASB ASC 820-10-35 clarifies the application of FASB ASC 820 in determining fair value when the volume and level of activity for the asset or liability has significantly decreased. Guidance is also included in identifying transactions that are not orderly. In addition, select paragraphs of paragraphs 59A–I of FASB ASC 820-10-55 provide illustrations on the application of this guidance.

Fair Value Disclosures[*]

Recurring Measurements[7]

2.18   "Pending Content" in FASB ASC 820-10-50 discusses the disclosures required for assets and liabilities measured at fair value. "Pending Content" in FASB ASC 820-10-50-1 requires the reporting entity to disclose certain information that enables users of its financial statements to assess the valuation techniques and inputs used to develop those measurements. For assets and liabilities that are measured at fair value on a recurring basis in periods subsequent to initial recognition, the disclosures required by FASB ASC 820-10-50 in the tabular format as shown in example 8 (paragraphs 60–63) of "Pending Content" in FASB ASC 820-10-55 should be made. For recurring fair value measurements using significant unobservable inputs (level 3), the reporting entity is required to disclose certain information to help users assess the effect of the measurements on earnings (or changes in net assets) for the period.

2.19   "Pending Content" in FASB ASC 820-10-50-2 requires the following disclosures to be made for each class of assets and liabilities. The reporting entity should provide sufficient information to permit reconciliation of the fair

---

[6] The AICPA issued a series of Technical Questions and Answers (TISs) to provide nonauthoritative guidance that is intended to assist reporting entities with the provisions of FASB ASC 820, *Fair Value Measurements and Disclosures* (specifically, FASB Accounting Standards Update [ASU] No. 2009-12, *Fair Value Measurements and Disclosures [Topic 820]: Investments in Certain Entities That Calculate Net Asset Value per Share [or Its Equivalent]*), to estimate the fair value of investments in certain entities that calculate net asset value per share of the investment. TIS sections 2220.18–.27 (AICPA, *Technical Practice Aids*) apply to investments that are required to be measured and reported at fair value and are within the scope of paragraphs 4–5 of FASB ASC 820-10-15.

[*] In January 2010, FASB issued ASU No. 2010-06, *Fair Value Measurements and Disclosures (Topic 820): Improving Disclosures about Fair Value Measurements*. FASB ASU No. 2010-06, among other things, changes the requirement to show purchases, sales, issuances, and settlements on a net basis to require separate disclosure for each type. The separate disclosure requirement of purchases, sales, issuances, and settlements activity are effective for fiscal years beginning after December 15, 2010, and for interim periods within those fiscal years. Examples related to the guidance in this ASU are included in FASB ASC 820-10-55. Readers are encouraged to review the ASU in its entirety.

[7] "Pending Content" in FASB ASC 820-10-50-5 provides the required disclosures for nonrecurring measurements.

value measurement disclosures for the various classes of assets and liabilities to the line items in the net assets available for benefits:[8]

    a. The fair value measurement at the reporting date.

    b. The level within the fair value hierarchy in which the fair value measurement in its entirety falls, segregating the fair value measurement using any of the following:

        i. Quoted prices in active markets for identical assets or liabilities (level 1).

        ii. Significant other observable inputs (level 2).

        iii. Significant unobservable inputs (level 3).

    c. The amounts of significant transfers between level 1 and level 2 of the fair value hierarchy and the reasons for the transfers. Significant transfers into each level should be disclosed separately from transfers out of each level. A reporting entity should disclose and consistently follow its policy for determining when transfers between levels are recognized.

    d. For fair value measurements using significant unobservable inputs (level 3), a reconciliation of the beginning and ending balances, separately presenting changes during the period attributable to any of the following:

        i. Total gains and losses for the period (realized and unrealized), separately presenting gains or losses included in earnings (or changes in net assets) and gains or losses recognized in other comprehensive income, and a description of where those gains or losses included in earnings (or changes in net assets) are reported in the statement of income (or activities) or in other comprehensive income.

        ii. Purchases, sales, issuances, and settlements.[*]

        iii. Transfers in/out of level 3 and the reasons for those transfers. Significant transfers into level 3 should be disclosed separately from significant transfers out of level 3. A reporting entity should disclose and consistently follow its policy for determining when transfers between levels are recognized. The policy about the timing of recognizing transfers should be the same for transfers into level 3 as that for transfers out of level 3.

    e. The amount of the total gains and losses.

    f. For fair value measurements using significant other observable inputs (level 2) and significant unobservable inputs (level 3), a description of the valuation technique (or multiple valuation techniques) used, and the inputs used in determining the fair values of each class of assets or liabilities. If there has been a change in the valuation technique(s), the reporting entity should disclose that change and the reason for making it.

---

[8] For derivative assets and liabilities, the disclosures listed in paragraph 2.19(*a*)–(*c*) should be made on a gross basis. The disclosures listed in paragraph 2.19(*d*)–(*e*) should be made on either a gross or net basis. See footnote * for further guidance on paragraph 2.19(*d*)(ii).

[*] See footnote * in the heading above paragraph 2.18.

2.20 "Pending Content" in FASB ASC 820-10-50-2A states that for equity and debt securities, class should be determined on the basis of the nature and risks of the investments in a manner consistent with the guidance in FASB ASC 320-10-50-1B even if the equity securities or debt securities are not within the scope of FASB ASC 320-10-50-1B. Major security types are based on the nature and risks of the security. In determining whether disclosure for a particular security type is necessary and whether it is necessary to further separate a particular security type into greater detail, all of the following should be considered:

a. The activity or business sector

b. Vintage

c. Geographic concentration

d. Credit quality

e. Economic characteristic

For all other assets and liabilities, judgment is needed to determine the appropriate classes of assets and liabilities for which disclosures about fair value measurements should be provided.

2.21 Fair value measurement disclosures for each class of assets and liabilities often will require greater disaggregation than the reporting entity's line items in the statement of financial position. A reporting entity should determine the appropriate classes for those disclosures on the basis of the nature and risks of the assets and liabilities and their classification in the fair value hierarchy (that is, levels 1, 2, and 3). In determining the appropriate classes for fair value measurement disclosures, the reporting entity should consider the level of disaggregated information required for specific assets and liabilities under other FASB ASC topics. For example, under FASB ASC 815, *Derivatives and Hedging*, disclosures about derivative instruments are presented separately by type of contract such as interest rate contracts, foreign exchange contracts, equity contracts, commodity contracts, and credit contracts. (Also, see paragraph 2.48.) The classification of the asset or liability in the fair value hierarchy also should affect the level of disaggregation because of the different degrees of uncertainty and subjectivity involved in level 1, level 2, and level 3 measurements. For example, the number of classes may need to be greater for fair value measurements using significant unobservable inputs (that is, level 3 measurements) to achieve the disclosure objectives because level 3 measurements have a greater degree of uncertainty and subjectivity.

Fair Value Measurements of Investments in Certain Entities That Calculate NAV per Share (or Its Equivalent)

2.22 "Pending Content" in FASB ASC 820-10-50-6A requires disclosures for each class of investment about the attributes of investments within the scope of paragraphs 4–5 of FASB ASC 820-10-15, such as the nature of any restrictions on the investor's ability to redeem its investments at the measurement date, any unfunded commitments, and the investment strategies of the investees. These disclosures are required for all investments within the scope of paragraphs 4–5 of FASB ASC 820-10-15 regardless of whether the practical expedient in FASB ASC 820-10-35-59 has been applied.

Fair Value Option

2.23 For assets and liabilities not currently required to be reported at fair value, FASB ASC 825, *Financial Instruments*, creates a fair value option under which an entity may irrevocably elect fair value as the initial and subsequent measure for many financial instruments and certain other items, with changes in fair value recognized in the statement of activities as those changes occur. An election is made on an instrument-by-instrument basis (with certain exceptions), generally when an instrument is initially recognized in the financial statements. Most financial assets and financial liabilities are eligible to be recognized using the fair value option, as are firm commitments for financial instruments and certain nonfinancial contracts. See FASB ASC 825 for further guidance, including presentation and disclosure requirements.

Net Assets Available for Benefits

Investments

2.24 According to FASB ASC 960-325-35-1, plan investments should be presented at their fair value at the reporting date (see paragraphs 2.09–.22 for fair value measurement guidance and paragraph 2.25 for special provisions concerning the valuation of investment contracts). Per FASB ASC 960-325-50-3, the historical cost of plan investments presented at fair value is neither required nor proscribed.[9] (The accounting for assets used in the administration of the plan is discussed in paragraph 2.36–.37.)

Investment Contracts

2.25 A defined benefit plan should report investment contracts at fair value. FASB ASC 960-325-35-3 states that whether or not the plan is subject to ERISA, *insurance contracts* (as defined in the FASB ASC glossary), should be presented in the same manner as specified in the annual report filed by a plan with certain governmental agencies pursuant to ERISA, consistent with the requirements of Form 5500. The current Form 5500 permits unallocated insurance contracts to be reported at either current value or as determined on the Schedule A, "Insurance Information," which is contract value. This is an exception to the general requirement of FASB ASC 960 that plan investments be presented at fair value. A plan not subject to ERISA should present its insurance contracts as if the plan were subject to the reporting requirements of ERISA.

Presentation of Plan Investments

2.26 FASB ASC 960-325-45-1 states that information regarding a plan's investments should be presented in enough detail to identify the types of investments and should indicate whether reported fair values have been measured by quoted prices in an active market or are fair values otherwise determined.[10]

2.27 The presentation of plan investments in the statement of net assets available for benefits detailed by general type may include the following: government securities, short-term securities, corporate bonds, common stocks, mortgages, real estate, investments in bank common or collective trust funds, registered investment companies (for example, mutual funds), master trusts, and investments in contracts with insurance companies, including separate accounts, deposit administration, and immediate participation guarantee contracts.

---

[9] Historical cost is not required to be disclosed in the financial statements; however, supplemental schedules to the Form 5500 require historical cost. See appendix A.

[10] The disclosures required by FASB ASC 820 may typically satisfy these disclosures.

> **Practice Tip**
>
> In addition to the requirement in paragraph 2.27 for plan investments to be detailed by general type, FASB ASC 820 requires disclosures about fair value to be made for each class of assets and liabilities. The disclosures required by FASB ASC 820 (see paragraph 2.18–.22) would typically satisfy the disclosures required by this paragraph.

Securities Lending

2.28 Securities custodians commonly carry out securities lending activities on behalf of their employee benefit plan clients. The borrowers of securities generally are required to provide collateral to the lender (the plan). This collateral is typically cash but sometimes it may be other securities or standby letters of credit, with a value slightly higher than that of the securities borrowed. If the collateral is cash, the lender typically earns a return by investing that cash at rates higher than the rate paid or rebated to the borrower. If the collateral is other than cash, the lender typically receives a fee. FASB ASC 860, *Transfers and Servicing*, provides accounting and reporting guidance for transfers of financial assets, including accounting for securities lending activities. FASB ASC 860 addresses

- whether the transaction is a sale of the loaned securities for financial reporting purposes.
- if the transaction is not a sale, how the lender should report the loaned securities.
- whether and how the lender should report the collateral.
- how the lender should record income earned as a result of securities lending transactions.

2.29 If the securities lending transaction includes an agreement that entitles and obligates the plan (the transferor) to repurchase the transferred securities under which the plan maintains effective control over those securities, then the plan must account for those transactions as secured borrowings (not sales) and continue to report the securities on the statement of net assets. Typically in a securities lending arrangement the transferee has the right by custom or contract to sell or repledge the security loaned. In these instances the securities loaned should be reclassified and reported by the plan (the transferor) separately from other assets not so encumbered (for example, as security pledged to creditors) pursuant to FASB ASC 860-30-25-5. Alternatively, if the transferee does not have the right by custom or contract to sell or repledge the security loaned, the plan should disclose in the notes to the financial statements the carrying amount and classification of any assets pledged as collateral, associated liabilities, and qualitative information about the relationship between those assets and associated liabilities as of the date of the latest statement of net assets presented pursuant to "Pending Content" in FASB ASC 860-30-50-1A. The plan should record the cash collateral received as an asset—and any investments made with that cash, even if made by agents or in pools with other securities lenders—along with the obligation to return the cash (considered the amount borrowed).

2.30 Generally, if the plan receives securities (instead of cash) that may be sold or repledged, the plan accounts for those securities in the same way as it would account for cash received, that is, the plan recognizes in the statement of net assets the securities received as collateral and the obligation to return that collateral. However, pursuant to "Pending Content" in FASB ASC 860-30-50-1A, the plan must also disclose the fair value as of the date of each statement of net assets presented of that collateral and of the portion of that collateral that it has sold or repledged, and information about the sources and uses of that collateral. Because FASB ASC 860-30-25-5 requires that only the lender recognize securities collateral received in its statement of net assets, it is important to accurately identify the lender and borrower in securities lending transactions. One indicator that the plan is the lender is that the collateral received by the lender generally has a value slightly higher (for example, 2 percent) than that of the securities being borrowed.

2.31 The plan must disclose its policy for requiring collateral or other security in accordance with "Pending Content" in FASB ASC 860-30-50-1A.

2.32 According to FASB ASC 960-30-25-2, the interest income earned and rebate interest paid as a result of securities lending activity should be recorded on the statement of changes in net assets available for benefits.

Contributions Receivable

2.33 According to the FASB ASC glossary, *contributions receivable* are amounts due as of the date of the financial statements to the plan from employers, participants, and other sources of funding. Per FASB ASC 960-310-25-2, contributions receivable include those pursuant to formal commitments as well as legal or contractual requirements. For a single employer plan, this would also include obligations resulting from a formal commitment. Evidence of a formal commitment may include (a) a formal resolution by the sponsor, (b) amounts relating to an established funding policy, (c) a deduction on the federal tax return, or (d) the employer's recognition, as of the reporting date, of a contribution payable to the plan.[11] According to FASB ASC 960-310-25-3, contributions receivable should include an adequate allowance for estimated uncollectible amounts.

2.34 The Form 5500 Schedule B may provide useful information in determining the contribution receivable at year-end. See paragraph 8.06 for guidance on auditing the contributions of a defined benefit pension plan.

2.35 A multiemployer plan may also have a receivable for a withdrawing employer's share of the plan's unfunded liability. The plan should record the receivable, net of any allowance for an amount deemed uncollectible, when entitlement has been determined.

Operating Assets

2.36 Assets used in the administration of the plan (for example, buildings, equipment, furniture and fixtures, and leasehold improvements) are to be stated at cost less accumulated depreciation or amortization.

2.37 FASB ASC 360, *Property, Plant, and Equipment*, addresses accounting for the impairment of long-lived assets for assets to be held and used and assets to be disposed of. FASB ASC 360-10-35-21 requires that long-lived assets

---

[11] Per item (d) of FASB ASC 960-310-25-2, the existence of accrued pension costs does not, by itself, provide sufficient support for recognition of a contribution receivable by the plan.

to be held and used by the plan, such as real estate owned by the plan for plan operations, be tested for recoverability whenever events or changes in circumstances indicate that the carrying amount may not be recoverable. Long-lived assets to be abandoned or exchanged for a similar productive asset should be considered held and used until disposed of. FASB ASC 360-10-35-43 states that long-lived assets classified as held for sale should be measured at the lower of its carrying amount or fair value less cost to sell. A long-lived asset should not be depreciated while it is held for sale. See FASB ASC 360 for further accounting and disclosure requirements.[12]

Accrued Liabilities

2.38 A plan may have liabilities (other than for benefits) that should be accrued. Such liabilities may be for amounts owed for securities purchased, income taxes payable by the plan or other expenses (for example, third-party administrator fees). These liabilities should be deducted to arrive at net assets available for benefits. Benefit amounts should not be accrued as liabilities.

Changes in Net Assets Available for Benefits

2.39 According to FASB ASC 960-30-45-1, information regarding changes in net assets available for benefits should be presented in enough detail to identify the significant changes during the year. FASB ASC 960-30-45-2 states that minimum disclosure should include all of the following:

    a. the net appreciation (depreciation) in fair value for each significant class of investments (see paragraph 2.26–.27), segregated between investments whose fair values have been measured by quoted prices in an active market and those whose fair values have been otherwise determined. Realized gains and losses on investments that were both bought and sold during the year should be included. Such information may be useful in assessing the relative degree of objectivity or subjectivity in measuring the plan's investments and the relationship thereof to investment performance during the year. (Separate disclosure of realized gains and losses on investments sold during the year is neither required nor proscribed.)

    b. investment income, exclusive of changes in fair value described in (*a*) preceding.

    c. contributions from employers segregated between cash and noncash contributions. A noncash contribution should be recorded at fair value. The nature of noncash contributions should be described either parenthetically or in a note.

    d. contributions from participants, including those transmitted by the sponsor.

    e. contributions from other identified sources (for example, state subsidies or federal grants).

    f. benefits paid to participants.

---

[12] See also TIS section 6931.03, "Should the Sale of Real Estate Investments Held by Employee Benefit Plans Be Treated as Discontinued Operations?," and TIS section 6931.04, "Depreciation of a Real Estate Investment Owned by a Defined Benefit Pension Plan" (AICPA, *Technical Practice Aids*), for additional nonauthoritative guidance.

g. payments to insurance entities to purchase contracts that are excluded from plan assets.

h. administrative expenses. (See Department of Labor Advisory Opinion No. 2001-01A for guidance on reasonable expenses of administering the plan.)

i. other changes (for example, transfers of assets to or from other plans) should also be presented if they are significant.

Accumulated Plan Benefits

2.40 Accumulated plan benefits are to be presented as the present value of future benefits attributable, under the plan's provisions, to service rendered to the date of the actuarial valuation. The accumulated benefit information may be presented as of the beginning or the end of the plan year. Under FASB ASC 960-205-45-4, however, an end-of-year benefit information date is considered preferable. If the benefit information date is the beginning of the year, a statement that includes information regarding the net assets available for benefits as of that date and a statement that includes information regarding the changes during the preceding year in the net assets available for benefits should also be presented. (See exhibit D-7 in appendix D for an illustration of appropriate financial statement presentation when beginning-of-year benefit information is selected.)

2.41 Per the FASB ASC glossary, *accumulated plan benefits* include benefits to be paid to (*a*) retired or terminated employees or their beneficiaries, (*b*) beneficiaries of deceased employees, and (*c*) present employees or their beneficiaries. FASB ASC 960-20-25-3 states, to the extent possible, plan provisions should apply in recognizing accumulated plan benefits. When the plan does not specify the benefits earned in each year, a general method for measurement is provided in FASB ASC 960-20-25-4. Per FASB ASC 960-20-25-5, projected years of service should be a factor only in determining employees' expected eligibility for particular benefits. Automatic benefit increases specified by the plan (for example, automatic cost-of-living increases) that are expected to occur after the benefit information date should be recognized. Plans providing death and disability benefits should consider these factors in the calculation. Retroactive plan amendments adopted before the date of the calculation should be given effect in the calculation, even if some provisions take effect only in future periods. Plan amendments adopted after the benefit information date should not be recognized. As in the presentation of plan assets, allocated contracts should be excluded. An *allocated contract* is defined in the FASB ASC glossary as a contract with an insurance entity under which related payments to the insurance entity are currently used to purchase immediate or deferred annuities for individual participants.

2.42 The assumptions used in calculating accumulated plan benefits are to be based on the premise of an ongoing plan. According to FASB ASC 960-20-35-1, the assumed rates of return should reflect the expected rates of return during the periods for which the payment of benefits is deferred and should be consistent with returns realistically achievable on the types of assets held by the plan and the plan's investment policy. An appropriate allowance for future employee mortality and turnover should be provided. The significant assumptions used in that determination should reflect the best estimate of the plan's future experience solely with respect to that individual assumption.

These assumptions may differ from those used in the determination of the plan's funding and the plan sponsor's pension costs.

2.43 As noted previously, the benefit information may be presented in a separate statement, combined with other information in a financial statement, or presented in a note to the financial statements. The information, however, must all be located in one place and should be classified as follows (in accordance with FASB ASC 960 20 45 3):

        a. Vested benefits of participants currently receiving payments, including benefits due and payable as of the benefit information date

        b. Other vested benefits

        c. Nonvested benefits

If the plan is contributory, accumulated contributions of active employees including, if applicable, interest credited on those contributions, should be disclosed. If interest is credited on the contributions, the interest rate should also be disclosed.

Changes in Accumulated Plan Benefits

2.44 Information regarding the change in accumulated benefits from the beginning to the end of the year should be presented to identify significant factors affecting the comparability of the year-to-year accumulated benefits. As with the accumulated benefit information, the changes may be presented in the body of the financial statements or in the notes; they may be presented in either a reconciliation or a narrative format. Per FASB ASC 960-20-50-3, minimum disclosure should include the significant effects of factors such as (*a*) plan amendments, (*b*) changes in the nature of the plan, and (*c*) changes in actuarial assumptions. Changes in actuarial assumptions are to be viewed as changes in accounting estimates, and, therefore, previously reported amounts should not be restated. Per FASB ASC 960-20-45-9, if only the minimum required disclosure is presented, presentation in a statement format will necessitate an additional unidentified *other* category to reconcile the beginning and ending amounts.

Additional Financial Statement Disclosures

2.45 FASB ASC 235, *Notes to Financial Statements*, requires the disclosure of significant accounting policies, and FASB ASC 960 requires disclosure of (*a*) the method and significant assumptions used to value investments and contracts with insurance entities (FASB ASC 960-325-50-1) and (*b*) the method and significant assumptions used in determining the actuarial present value of accumulated plan benefits, including any significant changes in the method or assumptions during the year (paragraphs 8–9 of FASB ASC 960-20-50).

2.46 Unless otherwise noted, FASB ASC 960-205-50-1 also requires disclosure of

        a. a brief general description of the plan agreement, including its vesting and benefit provisions.[13]

---

[13] Per item (*a*) of FASB ASC 960-205-50-1, if a plan agreement or a description thereof providing this information is otherwise published and made available, this description may be omitted provided that reference to such other source is made.

b. a description of significant plan amendments adopted during the year. If the amendments were adopted after the date of the accumulated benefit information, and accordingly their effect was not included in the calculation, this fact should be stated.

c. a brief description of the benefit priority and Pension Benefit Guaranty Corporation coverage in the event of plan termination.

d. the funding policy and any changes in the policy during the year. If significant costs of plan administration are being absorbed by the employer(s), that fact should be disclosed. When applicable, the method of determining employee contributions should be disclosed. ERISA plans should disclose their status with respect to any applicable minimum funding requirements. If a minimum funding waiver has been granted by the IRS or if a request for a waiver is pending before the IRS, that fact should be disclosed.

e. the policy regarding the purchase of insurance contracts that have been excluded from plan assets and the income from those contracts for the year. The plan's dividend income for the year that is related to excluded contracts should be disclosed, and, as stated in FASB ASC 960-30-45-2, may be netted against payments to insurance entities related to such contracts as provided in (g) of that paragraph.

f. the federal income tax status of the plan[14] if a favorable determination letter from the IRS has not been obtained or maintained. Note that reports filed in accordance with the requirements of ERISA must include disclosure of "information concerning whether or not a tax ruling or determination letter has been obtained," which is more than is required by FASB ASC 960.

g. per FASB ASC 960-325-50-2, investments that represent 5 percent or more of total net assets. Listing all investments in Schedule H, line 4i—Schedule of Assets (Held at End of Year) required by ERISA does not eliminate the requirement to include this disclosure in the financial statements.

h. significant related-party transactions (see chapter 11 for a discussion of related-party transactions and appendix A for disclosures related to parties in interest).

i. unusual or infrequent events or transactions occurring after the latest benefit information date but before the financial statements are issued or are available to be issued (as discussed in FASB ASC 855-10-25) that might significantly affect the usefulness of the financial statements in an assessment of the plan's present and future ability to pay benefits. For example, a plan amendment adopted after the

---

[14] A plan's tax exempt status is a position that may be subject to uncertainty. In September 2009, FASB issued ASU No. 2009-06, *Income Taxes (Topic 740)—Implementation Guidance on Accounting for Uncertainty in Income Taxes and Disclosure Amendments for Nonpublic Entities*. FASB ASU No. 2009-06 provides implementation guidance on accounting for uncertainty in income taxes and eliminates the disclosure requirements of paragraphs 15(a)–15(b) of FASB ASC 740-10-50 for nonpublic entities, as defined in FASB ASC 740-10-20. The implementation guidance in FASB ASU No. 2009-06 also expands the FASB ASC glossary definition of a *tax position*. In addition, TIS section 5250.15, "Application of Certain FASB Interpretation No. 48 (codified in FASB ASC 740-10) Disclosure Requirements to Nonpublic Entities That Do Not Have Uncertain Tax Positions" (AICPA, *Technical Practice Aids*), clarified that the description of open tax years that remain subject to examination is a required disclosure for a nonpublic entity even if the entity has no uncertain tax positions. Also, see paragraph 12.07 of this guide for further information.

latest benefit information date that significantly increases future benefits that are attributable to employees' service rendered before that date should be disclosed. If such effects are not quantified, the reasons why they are not reasonably determinable should be disclosed. This does not contemplate disclosure of normal changes after the benefit information date, such as benefits attributable to service rendered after that date.

j. subsequent events disclosures as required by FASB ASC 855, *Subsequent Events* (see chapter 12 for a discussion of subsequent events).[†]

This list is not intended to modify the disclosure requirements in FASB ASC 960 but, rather, to serve as a reference to the major requirements. Nor does this list include information required by ERISA to be disclosed in the schedules filed as part of a plan's annual report. In this connection, it is important to note that any information required by ERISA to be disclosed in the schedules must be disclosed in the schedules; disclosure of the information on the face of the financial statements or in the notes to the financial statements but not in the schedules is not acceptable.

Fair Value Measurements

2.47 See paragraphs 2.18–.22 for required disclosures related to fair value measurements.

Derivatives and Hedging

2.48 FASB ASC 815 provides accounting and reporting for derivative instruments, including certain derivative instruments embedded in other contracts (collectively referred to as *derivatives*), and for hedging activities. It requires that an entity recognize all derivatives as either assets or liabilities in the statement of financial position and measure those instruments at fair value. FASB ASC 815 applies to certain contracts that meet the definition of *derivative instrument*, as defined in FASB ASC 815-10-15-83. See FASB ASC 815-10-15 for further information on certain contracts that are not subject to the requirements of FASB ASC 815. (See paragraph 7.59–.66 for further guidance.)[‡]

[†] In February 2010, FASB issued ASU 2010-09, *Subsequent Events (Topic 855): Amendments to Certain Recognition and Disclosure Requirements*. This ASU amends the guidance in FASB ASC 855, *Subsequent Events*, to require entities (except Securities and Exchange Commission [SEC] filers and conduit debt obligors [CDOs]) to evaluate subsequent events through the date that the financial statements are available to be issued. Entities other than SEC filers should disclose the date through which subsequent events have been evaluated. SEC filers and CDOs should evaluate subsequent events through the date the financial statements are issued. An entity that is an SEC filer is not required to disclose the date through which subsequent events have been evaluated.

[‡] In March 2010, FASB issued ASU No. 2010-11, *Derivatives and Hedging (Topic 815): Scope Exceptions Related to Embedded Credit Derivatives*. The amendments in this ASU, among other things, clarify the scope exception under paragraphs 8–9 of FASB ASC 815-15 for embedded credit derivative features related to the transfer of credit risk in the form of subordination of one financial instrument to another. Further, the amendments address how to determine which embedded credit derivatives, including those in collateralized debt obligations and synthetic collateralized debt obligations, are considered to be embedded derivatives that should not be analyzed under FASB ASC 815-15-25 for potential bifurcation and separate accounting.

The amendments in FASB ASU No. 2010-11 are effective for each reporting entity at the beginning of its first fiscal quarter beginning after June 15, 2010. Early adoption is permitted at the beginning of each entity's first fiscal quarter beginning after issuance of this ASU.

The guidance is located in FASB ASC 815-10 and FASB ASC 815-15.

Master Trusts

2.49 As indicated in FASB ASC 960-30-45-11, investments in master trusts are presented in a single line item in the statement of net assets available for benefits. In addition, paragraphs 1–3 of FASB ASC 960-30-50 state that in the notes[15] to the financial statements the investments of the master trust should be detailed by general type, such as government securities, short-term securities, corporate bonds, common stocks, mortgages and real estate, as of the date of each statement of net assets available for benefits presented. The net change in the fair value of each significant type of investment of the master trust and total investment income of the master trust by type, for example, interest and dividends, should also be disclosed in the notes for each period for which a statement of changes in net assets available for benefits is presented. The notes to the financial statements should also include a description of the basis used to allocate net assets, net investment income, gains and losses to participating plans, and the plan's percentage interest in the master trust as of the date of each statement of net assets available for benefits presented.

Financial Instruments

2.50 FASB ASC 825 requires all entities except for those covered by an exemption[16] for which the disclosure is optional, to disclose within the body of the financial statements or in the accompanying notes, the fair value of financial instruments for which it is practicable to estimate fair value.[17] An entity should also disclose the method(s) and significant assumptions used to estimate the fair value of financial instruments. According to FASB ASC 825-10-50-8, financial instruments of a pension plan other than (a) *obligations for pension benefits* as defined in FASB ASC 960 and (b) insurance contracts, other than financial guarantees and investment contracts, as discussed in FASB ASC 944-20, generally are included in the scope of FASB ASC 825 and are subject to its disclosure requirements. In addition, the disclosure requirements of FASB ASC 820 may also apply.[18]

---

[15] The AICPA issued a TIS section to provide guidance on the required fair value measurement disclosures to be made when a plan holds investments in a master trust: TIS section 6931.11, "Fair Value Measurement Disclosures for Master Trusts" (AICPA, *Technical Practice Aids*). This practice aid assists with the implementation of FASB ASC 820 for employee benefits plans that have investments in a master trust. This guidance states that the disclosure requirements of FASB ASC 820 should be made for each major category of master trust assets and liabilities. In addition, consideration should be given to combining, or reconciling, or both, the master trust FASB ASC 820 disclosures with the master trust disclosures as required by paragraphs 1–3 of FASB ASC 960-30-50.

[16] According to FASB ASC 825-10-50-3, the disclosures are optional for plans that meet all of the following criteria:

    a. The plan is a nonpublic entity.

    b. The plan's total assets are less than $100 million on the date of the financial statements.

    c. The plan has no instrument that, in whole or in part, is accounted for as a derivative instrument under FASB ASC 815, *Derivatives and Hedging*, during the reporting period.

[17] Per FASB ASC 825-10-50-11, fair value disclosed in the notes should be presented together with the related carrying amount in a form that makes it clear whether the fair value and carrying amount represent assets or liabilities and how the carrying amounts relate to what is reported in the statement of net assets available for benefits.

[18] In June 2010, the AICPA issued TIS section 1800.05, "Applicability of Fair Value Disclosure Requirements and Measurement Principles in Financial Accounting Standard Board (FASB) *Accounting Standards Codification* (ASC) 820, *Fair Value Measurements and Disclosures*, to Certain

(continued)

2.51 FASB ASC 825-10-50-21 requires disclosure of all significant concentrations of credit risk arising from all financial instruments. The following information should be disclosed about each significant concentration:

- Information about the (shared) activity, region, or economic characteristic that identifies the concentration

- The maximum amount of loss due to credit risk that, based on the gross fair value of the financial instrument, the entity would incur if parties to the financial instruments that make up the concentration failed completely to perform according to the terms of the contracts and the collateral or other security, if any, for the amount due proved to be of no value to the entity

- The entity's policy of requiring collateral or other security to support financial instruments subject to credit risk, information about the entity's access to that collateral or other security, and the nature and a brief description of the collateral or other security supporting those financial instruments

- The entity's policy of entering into master netting arrangements to mitigate the credit risk of financial instruments, information about the arrangements for which the entity is a party, and a brief description of the terms of those arrangements, including the extent to which they would reduce the entity's maximum amount of loss due to credit risk

2.52 *401(h) accounts.* Some defined benefit pension plans provide a postretirement medical-benefit component in addition to the normal retirement benefits of the plan, pursuant to Section 401(h) of the Internal Revenue Code (IRC). Employers may fund a portion of their postretirement medical-benefit obligations related to their health and welfare benefit plans through a health benefit account (401(h) account) in their defined benefit pension plans, subject to certain restrictions and limitations. Funding can be accomplished through a qualified transfer of excess pension plan assets or through additional contributions. Any assets transferred to a 401(h) account in a qualified transfer of excess pension plan assets (and any income allocable thereto) must be used only to pay qualified current retiree health benefits for the taxable year of the transfer (whether directly or through reimbursement). Any assets transferred to a 401(h) account in a qualified transfer of excess pension plan assets (and any income allocable thereto) that are not used in the year must be transferred out of the account to the pension plan.

2.53 The IRC allows employers to allocate up to 25 percent of total contributions to the plan, subject to certain limitations, to the 401(h) account. If the full amount of these contributions is not used during the year, they may be accumulated for future retiree medical expenses in the 401(h) account. The deductibility of employer contributions to a 401(h) account is subject to separate limitations, and, therefore, such contributions have no effect on the amount of deductible contributions an employer can make to fund pension benefits under

---

(footnote continued)

Financial Instruments" (AICPA, *Technical Practice Aids*). This TIS section addresses whether the fair value measurement principles and disclosure requirements in FASB ASC 820 apply to financial instruments that are not recognized at fair value in the statement of financial positions, but for which fair value is required to be disclosed in the notes to financial statements in accordance with paragraphs 10–19 of FASB ASC 825-10-50.

the plan. The earnings on the 401(h) account are ignored for minimum funding purposes. Additionally, under the IRC, qualified transfers are not treated as prohibited transactions for purposes of Section 4975.

2.54 The plan sponsor has discretion in making contributions to the 401(h) account. A pension or annuity plan may provide for payment of medical benefits for retired employees, their spouses, and their dependents if all of the following conditions are met:

a. Benefits are subordinate (as defined in Section 401(h) of the IRC) to the retirement benefits provided by the plan.

b. A separate account is established and maintained for such benefits.

c. The employer's contributions to the separate account are reasonable and ascertainable.

d. It is impossible, at any time prior to the satisfaction of all obligations under the plan to provide such benefits, for any part of the corpus or income of the separate account to be (within the taxable year or thereafter) used for, or diverted to, any purpose other than the providing of such benefits.

e. Notwithstanding the provisions of certain IRC sections, upon satisfaction of all obligations under the plan to provide such benefits, any amount remaining in the separate account must, under the terms of the plan, be returned to the employer.

f. In the case of an employee who is a key employee (as defined in Section 416[i]), a separate account is established and maintained for such benefits which are payable to such employee (and the spouse and dependents), and such benefits (to the extent attributable to plan years beginning after March 31, 1984, for which the employee is a key employee) are payable only to that employee (and the spouse and dependents) from the separate account.

2.55 The 401(h) assets may be used only to pay current retiree health benefits, which generally are obligations of a separate health and welfare benefit plan or health benefit arrangement. They may not be used to satisfy pension obligations. Although the assets may be invested together with assets that are available to pay pension benefits, a separate accounting must be maintained for all qualified transfers, contributions, distributions or expenses, and income earned thereon.

2.56 As stated in paragraphs 4–10 of FASB ASC 960-30-45, because the 401(h) net assets may not be used to satisfy pension obligations, the total of net assets available for pension benefits should not include net assets held in the 401(h) account related to obligations of the health and welfare benefit plan. The 401(h) account assets less liabilities (net assets of the 401(h) account) are required to be shown in defined benefit pension plan financial statements as a single line item on the face of the statements (as illustrated in exhibits D-9–D-11 in appendix D). Those net assets related to the 401(h) account also should be deducted before arriving at the total of net assets available for pension benefits. In deducting those net assets, the amount related to the 401(h) features should be presented as a separate line item in the liabilities section of the statement of net assets available for pension benefits. The financial statement caption should clearly denote that the net assets held in the 401(h) account relate to obligations of the health and welfare plan or arrangement. The statement of changes in net assets should show only the changes in net assets of the pension plan and not any of the components of the changes in the net assets in the 401(h) account. The only amounts that should be reported in the statement of changes in net assets are qualified transfers to the 401(h) account and any unused or unspent amounts (including allocated income) in the 401(h) account at the end of the year that were qualified transfers of excess pension plan assets that should have been, but were not, transferred back to the defined benefit pension plan.

2.57 Information regarding accumulated plan benefits should relate only to pension obligations. Even in situations in which separate financial statements are not prepared for the health and welfare benefit plan, obligations related to retiree health benefits should not be reported in the statement of accumulated plan benefits of the defined benefit pension plan financial statements.

2.58 FASB ASC 960-205-50-4 states that defined benefit pension plans should disclose in the notes to the financial statements the nature of the assets related to the 401(h) account and the fact that the assets are available only to pay retiree health benefits.

2.59 Per FASB ASC 960-205-50-5, because ERISA requires 401(h) accounts to be reported as assets of the pension plan, a reconciliation of the net assets reported in the financial statements to those reported in Form 5500 is required. Additionally, any assets held for investment purposes in the 401(h) account should be shown on Schedule H, line 4i—Schedule of Assets (Held at End of Year) and Schedule H, line 4j—Schedule of Reportable Transactions for the pension plan.

Risks and Uncertainties

2.60 FASB ASC 275, *Risks and Uncertainties*, requires plans to include in their financial statements disclosures about (*a*) the nature of their operations, and (*b*) use of estimates in the preparation of financial statements. In addition, if specified criteria are met, FASB ASC 275 requires plans to include in their financial statements disclosures about (*a*) certain significant estimates, and (*b*) current vulnerability due to certain concentrations.

2.61 Certain significant estimates should be disclosed when known information available prior to the financial statements being issued or being available to be issued (appropriate date determined in accordance with FASB ASC 855-10-25)[†] indicates that (*a*) it is at least reasonably possible that the estimate of the effect on the financial statements of a condition, situation, or set of circumstances that existed at the date of the financial statements will change in the near term due to one or more future confirming events, and (*b*) the effect of the change would be material to the financial statements. For example, the present value of accumulated plan benefits could be subject to a material change when

- employees covered by the plan work in an industry that experienced a significant economic downturn in the previous year and it is reasonably possible that in the subsequent period a significant number of employees will retire early without a monetary incentive to do so in order to avoid being laid-off with nominal benefits.

[†] See footnote † in paragraph 2.46.

This could significantly increase the present value of accumulated plan benefits and possibly cause the plan to be underfunded.

- employees covered by the plan are party to a collective bargaining agreement which was up for renegotiation at year-end and it is reasonably possible that management's offer to significantly increase pension benefits in lieu of granting the union's request for a significant increase in cash compensation will be accepted within the next year. This could significantly increase the present value of accumulated plan benefits.

- prior to year-end the employer announced a planned downsizing but had not decided on the number of employees to be terminated, and it is reasonably possible that when the decision is made during the next year, it will result in employees receiving pension benefits earlier than expected and in an amount greater than originally projected.

- it is reasonably possible that there will be a significant decline in the fair value of investments (that is, financial instruments) during the next year which would change the assumed rates of return used to discount the benefit obligation and therefore could significantly affect the present value of accumulated plan benefits.

2.62 Vulnerability from concentrations arises when a plan is exposed to risk of loss greater than it would have had it mitigated its risk through diversification. Many plan's participants may be concentrated in a specific industry that carries with it certain risks. Plans may also hold investments and other assets (other than financial instruments for which concentrations are covered by FASB ASC 825, rather than FASB ASC 275) that are concentrated in a single industry or in a single geographic area. Concentrations should be disclosed if based on known information prior to the financial statements being issued or being available to be issued (appropriate date determined in accordance with FASB ASC 855-10-25)[†] (a) the concentration exists at the date of the financial statements, (b) the concentration makes the plan vulnerable to the risk of a near-term severe impact, and (c) it is at least reasonably possible that the events that could cause the severe impact will occur in the near term. For example, if the plan owns several investment properties (that is, apartment buildings) located in a geographic area that has only one significant employer and that employer announced last year that it is considering leaving the area and it is reasonably possible that it will do so within the next year, this could significantly affect the plan's future cash flows from rents and the value of the investment properties.

2.63 Because the disclosure requirements of FASB ASC 275 in many circumstances are similar to or overlap the disclosure requirements in certain other FASB ASC topics (for example, FASB ASC 450, *Contingencies*), the disclosures required by FASB ASC 275 may be combined in various ways, grouped together, or placed in diverse parts of the financial statements or included as part of the disclosures made pursuant to the requirements of other FASB ASC topics.

[†] See footnote † in paragraph 2.46.

Terminating Plans

2.64 FASB ASC 960-40 provides guidance for terminating plans that are defined benefit plans. Terminating plans include any plan about which a decision to terminate has been made, regardless of whether the terminated plan will be replaced.

2.65 When the decision to terminate a plan has been made,[19] or a wasting trust (that is, a plan under which participants no longer accrue benefits but that will remain in existence as long as necessary to pay already accrued benefits) exists, the relevant circumstances should be disclosed in all subsequent financial statements issued by the plan.

2.66 If the decision to terminate a plan is made before the end of the plan year, the plan's year-end financial statements should be prepared on the *liquidation* basis of accounting.[20]

2.67 For plan assets, changing to the liquidation basis will usually cause little or no change in values, most of which are current market values. Assets that may not be carried at market values include operating assets, insurance contracts carried at *contract values*, or large blocks of stock or other assets that cannot be readily disposed of at their quoted market prices.

2.68 Accumulated plan benefits should be determined on a liquidation basis, and their value may differ from the actuarial present value of accumulated plan benefits reported for an ongoing plan. In general, upon termination all benefits should be reported as vested.

---

[19] Refer to paragraph 12.28, which states that the auditor should obtain written representations from management as part of an audit of financial statements. Such representations may include whether there is a present intention to terminate the plan. Refer also to paragraph 10.41*h*, which states that the auditor may consider confirming with the plan's actuary knowledge of an intent on the part of the employer to terminate the plan.

[20] Interpretation No. 8, "Reporting on Financial Statements Prepared on a Liquidation Basis of Accounting," of AU section 508, *Reports on Audited Financial Statements* (AICPA, *Professional Standards*, AU sec. 9508 par. .33–.38), contains applicable guidance regarding the auditor's reporting responsibilities for terminating plans.

Chapter 3

Accounting and Reporting by Defined Contribution Plans

3.01 This chapter describes accounting principles generally accepted in the United States of America (U.S. GAAP) for accounting and financial reporting for defined contribution plans as provided in Financial Accounting Standards Board (FASB) *Accounting Standards Codification* (ASC) 962, *Plan Accounting—Defined Contribution Pension Plans*. FASB ASC 962 prescribes the general form and content of financial statements of those plans. U.S. GAAP other than those discussed in this chapter may also apply to defined contribution plans.

Exhibit 3-1

Quick Reference for Defined Contribution Plans

This guide has been organized so that the accounting and reporting guidance for defined contribution plans is contained in this chapter. Auditing guidance for defined benefit, defined contribution, and health and welfare benefit plans is contained throughout the guide. The following table has been developed to help you locate the areas in this guide that may pertain to an audit of a defined contribution plan. Not every area listed will be applicable to a particular client and the nature, timing, and extent of auditing procedures are matters of professional judgment.

Chapter 3	"Accounting and Reporting by Defined Contribution Plans"
Chapter 5	"Planning and General Auditing Considerations"
Chapter 6	"Internal Control"
Chapter 7	"Auditing Investments and Loans to Participants"
Chapter 8	"Auditing Contributions Received and Related Receivables"
Chapter 9	"Auditing Benefit Payments"
Chapter 10	"Auditing Participant Data, Participant Allocations, and Plan Obligations" in particular: 10.15–.21
Chapter 11	"Party in Interest Transactions"
Chapter 12	"Other Auditing Considerations"
Chapter 13	"The Auditor's Report" in particular: 13.06 Standard reports for defined benefit plans 13.08–.46 Various other reporting situations that may apply"
Appendix A	"ERISA and Related Regulations"
Appendix B	"Examples of Controls"
Appendix E	"Illustrative Financial Statements: Defined Contribution Plans"
Appendix G	"Consideration of Fraud in a Financial Statement Audit"

3.02 Defined contribution plans require an individual account for each participant and provide benefits based on (a) amounts contributed to the participant's account by the employer or employee, (b) investment experience on such amounts, (c) expenses, and (d) any forfeitures allocated to the account.

3.03 Under a defined contribution plan, the employer contribution rate is generally determined periodically at the discretion of the employer or by contractual agreement, or both. When a participant retires or withdraws from the plan, the amount allocated to the participant's account (if fully vested) represents the participant's accumulated benefits. That amount may be paid to the participant or used to purchase a retirement annuity, as defined by the plan agreement. The amount of benefits a participant will ultimately receive is generally not determined until the time of payment. By contrast, in a defined benefit plan, benefits are determinable and the contribution necessary to provide those benefits is actuarially determined. In other respects, defined contribution plans are similar to defined benefit plans.

3.04 Three general types of defined contribution plans exist: profit-sharing plans, money purchase pension plans, and stock bonus plans.

a. A *profit-sharing plan* is a defined contribution plan that is not a pension plan (as defined in the Internal Revenue Code [IRC]) or a stock bonus plan. Employer contributions may be discretionary or may be based on a fixed formula related to profits, compensation, or other factors. A profit-sharing plan must be designated as such in the plan document.

b. A *money purchase pension plan* is a defined contribution plan under which employer contributions are based on a fixed formula that is not related to profits and that is designated as a pension plan by the plan sponsor.

c. A *stock bonus plan* is a defined contribution plan under which distributions are normally made in stock of the employer, unless the participant elects otherwise.

3.05 A number of more specialized plans exist that are included in the three general types of plans. These include the following:

- A *cash-or-deferred arrangement* (also called a *Section 401(k) plan*) may be incorporated into a profit-sharing or stock bonus plan (a few money purchase pension plans established before the Employee Retirement Income Security Act of 1974 [ERISA] also incorporate cash-or-deferred arrangements). Under such an arrangement, a participant is permitted to elect to receive amounts in cash or have them contributed to the plan as employer contributions on the participant's behalf. A plan may also include a Roth 401(k) feature.

- A 403(b) plan* is a retirement savings arrangement sponsored by certain not for profit organizations (such as hospitals and private colleges) and public schools. They are defined contribution plans with individual salary deferral limits that are similar, but not identical to, 401(k) programs. See paragraphs 3.62–.65 for further guidance.

- A *thrift plan* (also called a *savings plan*) is a profit-sharing or stock bonus plan under which participants make after-tax employee contributions that are usually matched, in whole or in part, by employer contributions.

---

* In November 2007 the Department of Labor, IRS, and Pension Benefit Guarantee Corporation published in the *Federal Register*, final rules for amending the 2009 Form 5500 annual return or report. Among the revisions to the 2009 Form 5500 is a realignment of the reporting rules of 403(b) plans (subject to Title I) to be compatible with those of 401(k) plans. This would mean that starting with the 2009 plan year the Employee Retirement Income Security Act of 1974 (ERISA) audit requirement for annual audits of plan financial statements by independent qualified public accountants will also pertain to 403(b) plans.

- An *employee stock ownership plan* (ESOP) is a stock bonus plan that may borrow money from, or on the guarantee of, a related party (a *party in interest* as defined in Section 3(14) of ERISA) for the purpose of acquiring securities issued by the plan sponsor and that invests primarily in such securities (a *leveraged ESOP*). The term *employee stock ownership plan* is also generally applied to (*a*) nonleveraged stock bonus plans that satisfy various requirements set forth in Section 4975(e)(7) of the IRC and (*b*) profit-sharing plans (and certain pre-ERISA money purchase pension plans) that invest primarily in securities issued by the plan sponsor (see illustrated ESOP financial statements in appendix E).

- A *tax credit employee stock ownership plan* is a profit-sharing or stock bonus plan established before 1987 that satisfies the requirements of Section 409 of the IRC. The sponsor of such a plan is allowed a tax credit, rather than a deduction, for its contributions. Before 1982, these plans were commonly known as TRASOPs (for Tax Reduction Act stock ownership plans), and the maximum allowable credit was based on the plan sponsor's investments that qualified for the investment tax credit. In 1982, TRASOPs were succeeded by payroll stock ownership plans, under which the credit was based on the plan sponsor's payroll.

- A *target benefit plan* is a form of money purchase pension plan under which the employer's annual contribution on behalf of each participant is the actuarially determined amount required to fund a target benefit established by a plan formula. The target benefit is usually based on compensation and length of service. For some target benefit plans, the substance of the plan may be to provide a defined benefit. For such plans, accounting and reporting as defined benefit plans, as discussed in chapter 2, "Accounting and Reporting by Defined Benefit Pension Plans," of this guide, may be more appropriate.

- A *Keogh plan* (also called an *HR 10 plan*) is any defined benefit or defined contribution plan that covers one or more self-employed individuals.

- A *Simple Plan or Savings Incentive Match Plan for Employees* is a tax-favored retirement plan available to employers that have no more than 100 employees who earned more than $5,000 or more in compensation during the preceding calendar year. The employer's only required contribution is dollar-for-dollar matching contribution of 3 percent of employee's compensation or a limited profit-sharing type contribution. Employer contributions are fully vested at all times.

Regulatory Reporting Requirements

3.06 ERISA established annual reporting requirements for employee benefit plans, including defined contribution plans. Those requirements, including financial statement and schedule requirements, are described in appendix A. (See exhibit A-1, "Examples of Form 5500 Schedules," in appendix A of this guide for examples of Form 5500 schedules). The financial statements required by ERISA are a comparative statement of net assets available for benefits and a statement of changes in net assets available for benefits. The schedules required by ERISA, if applicable, include Schedule H, line 4a—Schedule of Delinquent Participant Contributions; Schedule H, line 4i—Schedule of Assets (Held at End of Year) and Schedule of Assets (Acquired and Disposed of Within Year); Schedule H, line 4j—Schedule of Reportable Transactions; Schedule G, Part I—Schedule of Loans or Fixed Income Obligations in Default or Classified as Uncollectible; Schedule G, Part II—Schedule of Leases in Default or Classified as Uncollectible; and Schedule G, Part III—Nonexempt Transactions. For guidance on how to report delinquent participant contributions, see the frequently asked questions about reporting delinquent participant contributions on the Form 5500 at the EBSA website at www.dol.gov/ebsa/faqs/faq_compliance_5500.html.

3.07 Some defined contribution plans are required to register and report to the Securities and Exchange Commission (SEC). Regulation S-X prescribes the form of the statements of financial position and statements of income and changes in plan equity that those plans must file with the SEC. The SEC has amended its rules for Form 11-K to permit plans subject to ERISA to file financial statements in accordance with ERISA rather than in accordance with Regulation S-X.

3.08 In accordance with the requirements of ERISA Sections 105 and 209, the plan administrator must furnish to any participant a statement of the account balance at least once each calendar quarter to a participant or beneficiary who has the right to direct the investment of assets in his or her account under the plan, at least once each calendar year to a participant or beneficiary who has his or her own account under the plan but does not have the right to direct the investment of assets in that account, and upon written request to a plan beneficiary who is not in either of the first two categories.

Financial Statements

3.09 The primary objective of a defined contribution plan's financial statements is to provide information that is useful in assessing the plan's present and future ability to pay benefits. To accomplish that objective, a plan's financial statements should provide information about (a) plan resources and how the stewardship responsibility for those resources has been discharged, (b) the results of transactions and events that affect the information about those resources, and (c) other factors necessary for users to understand the information provided. In a defined contribution plan, the plan's net assets available to pay benefits equal the sum of participants' individual account balances. Accordingly, the plan's ability to pay benefits relates to the plan's ability to pay individual participants the then current value of their account balances when due. It should be recognized that (a) information in addition to that contained in a plan's financial statements is needed in assessing the plan's present and future ability to pay benefits when due and (b) financial statements for several plan years can provide more useful information for assessing the plan's future ability to pay benefits than can financial statements for a single plan year. FASB ASC 230, *Statement of Cash Flows*, exempts certain benefit plans from the requirement to provide a statement of cash flows. Plans should consider providing a statement of cash flows when that statement would provide relevant information about the ability of the plan to pay benefits (for example, when the plan invests in assets that are not highly liquid or obtains financing for investments).

3.10 FASB ASC 962-205-45-1 states that the financial statements of a defined contribution plan prepared in accordance with U.S. GAAP should be prepared on the accrual basis of accounting[1] and include both (a) a statement of net assets available for benefits as of the end of the plan year[2] and (b) a statement of changes in net assets available for benefits for the year then ended.

3.11 Appendix E provides illustrative financial statements for a defined contribution plans. The information should be presented in sufficient detail to assist readers of plan financial statements in assessing the plan's present and future ability to pay benefits.

Fair Value Measurements

3.12 FASB ASC 820, *Fair Value Measurements and Disclosures*, defines fair value and sets out a framework for measuring fair value, and requires certain disclosures about fair value measurements. The following paragraphs summarize FASB ASC 820 but are not intended as a substitute for reviewing FASB ASC 820 in its entirety.

3.13 Meeting the requirements of FASB ASC 820 requires coordination among plan management, custodians, investment fiduciaries, and plan auditors. Plan sponsors and plan administrators will need to determine whether they have the appropriate valuation processes in place and sufficient data to determine the fair value of the plan's investments using the framework provided and to present the disclosures about the use of fair value measurements required. Although plan management can outsource the mechanics of the valuation process, they need to retain responsibility for the oversight of the final valuations, including determining the adequacy of the related footnote disclosures.

Definition of *Fair Value*

3.14 FASB ASC 820-10-20 defines *fair value* as the price that would be received to sell an asset or paid to transfer a liability in an orderly transaction between market participants at the measurement date.

Valuation Techniques

3.15 Paragraphs 24–35 of FASB ASC 820-10-35 describe the valuation techniques that should be used to measure fair value. Valuation techniques consistent with the market approach, income approach, or cost approach should be used to measure fair value, as follows:

- The market approach uses prices and other relevant information generated by market transactions involving identical or comparable assets or liabilities. Valuation techniques consistent with the market approach include matrix pricing and often use market multiples derived from a set of comparables.

- The income approach uses valuation techniques to convert future amounts (for example, cash flows or earnings) to a single present

---

[1] The accrual basis requires that purchases and sales of securities be recorded on a trade-date basis. If the settlement date is after the financial statement date, however, and (a) the fair value of the securities purchased or sold immediately before the financial statement date does not change significantly from the trade date to the financial statement date and (b) the purchases or sales do not significantly affect the composition of the plan's assets available for benefits, accounting on a settlement-date basis for such sales and purchases is acceptable.

[2] ERISA requires that this statement be presented in comparative form.

amount (discounted). The measurement is based on the value indicated by current market expectations about those future amounts. Valuation techniques consistent with the income approach include present value techniques, option-pricing models, and the multi-period excess earnings method.

- The cost approach is based on the amount that currently would be required to replace the service capacity of an asset (often referred to as current replacement cost). Fair value is determined based on the cost to a market participant (buyer) to acquire or construct a substitute asset of comparable utility, adjusted for obsolescence.

3.16 FASB ASC 820-10-35-24 states that valuation techniques that are appropriate in the circumstances and for which sufficient data are available should be used to measure fair value.

3.17 As explained in paragraphs 25–26 of FASB ASC 820-10-35, valuation techniques used to measure fair value should be consistently applied. However, a change in a valuation technique or its application is appropriate if the change results in a measurement that is equally or more representative of fair value in the circumstances. Such a change would be accounted for as a change in accounting estimate in accordance with the provisions of FASB ASC 250, *Accounting Changes and Error Corrections*.

The Fair Value Hierarchy

3.18 The fair value hierarchy in FASB ASC 820-10-35 prioritizes the inputs to valuation techniques used to measure fair value into three broad levels. The three levels are as follows:

- Paragraphs 40–41 of FASB ASC 820 10 35 state that level 1 in puts are quoted prices (unadjusted) in active markets for identical assets or liabilities that the reporting entity has the ability to access at the measurement date. An *active market*, as defined by the FASB ASC glossary, is a market in which transactions for the asset or liability occur with sufficient frequency and volume to provide pricing information on an ongoing basis. A quoted price in an active market provides the most reliable evidence of fair value and should be used to measure fair value whenever available, except as discussed in FASB ASC 820-10-35-43. FASB ASC 820-10-35-44 provides guidance on how the quoted price should not be adjusted because of the size of the position relative to trading volume (blockage factor) but rather would be measured within level 1 as the product of the quoted price for the individual instrument times the quantity held.

- Paragraphs 47–51 of FASB ASC 820-10-35 explain that level 2 inputs are inputs other than quoted prices included within level 1 that are observable for the asset or liability, either directly or indirectly. If the asset or liability has a specified (contractual) term, a level 2 input must be observable for substantially the full term of the asset or liability. Adjustments to level 2 inputs will vary depending on factors specific to the asset or liability. Those factors include the condition and location of the asset or liability, the extent to which the inputs relate to items that are comparable to the asset or liability, and the volume and level of activity in the markets within which the inputs are observed. An adjustment that is significant to the fair value measurement in its entirety might render the measurement a level 3 measurement, depending on the level in the fair value hierarchy within which the inputs used to determine the adjustment fall. As discussed in paragraph 48 of FASB ASC 820-10-35, level 2 inputs include

- quoted prices for similar assets or liabilities in active markets.
- quoted prices for identical or similar assets or liabilities in markets that are not active.
- inputs other than quoted prices that are observable for the asset or liability (for example, interest rates and yield curves observable at commonly quoted intervals, volatilities, prepayment speeds, loss severities, credit risks, and default rates).
- inputs that are derived principally from or corroborated by observable market data by correlation or other means (market-corroborated inputs).

- As discussed in paragraphs 52–55 of FASB ASC 820-10-35, level 3 inputs are unobservable inputs for the asset or liability. Unobservable inputs should be used to measure fair value to the extent that relevant observable inputs are not available, thereby allowing for situations in which little, if any, market activity for the asset or liability at the measurement date. Unobservable inputs should be developed based on the best information available in the circumstances, which might include the entity's own data. In developing unobservable inputs, the reporting entity need not undertake all possible efforts to obtain information about market participant assumptions. Unobservable inputs should reflect the reporting entity's own assumptions about the assumptions that market participants would use in pricing the asset or liability (including assumptions about risk). Assumptions about risk include the risk inherent in the inputs to the valuation technique. A measurement (for example, a mark-to-model measurement) that does not include an adjustment for risk would not represent a fair value measurement if market participants would include one in pricing the related asset or liability. The reporting entity should not ignore information about market participant assumptions that is reasonably available without undue cost and effort. Therefore, the entity's own data used to develop unobservable inputs should be adjusted if information is readily available without undue cost and effort that indicates that market participants would use different assumptions. "Pending Content" in FASB ASC 820-10-55-22 discusses level 3 inputs for particular assets and liabilities.

As explained in FASB ASC 820-10-35-37, in some cases the inputs used to measure fair value might fall in different levels of the fair value hierarchy. The level in the fair value hierarchy within which the fair value measurement in its entirety falls should be determined based on the lowest level input that is significant to the fair value measurement in its entirety.

Fair Value Measurements of Investments in Certain Entities That Calculate Net Asset Value per Share (or Its Equivalent)

3.19 Paragraphs 59–62 of FASB ASC 820-10-35 provide additional guidance on the fair value measurements of investments in certain entities that calculate net asset value per share (NAV) (or its equivalent). This guidance permits, as a practical expedient, a reporting entity to estimate the fair value of an investment, that is within the scope of the guidance, using the NAV (or its equivalent) if the NAV is calculated in a manner consistent with the measurement principles of FASB ASC 946, *Financial Services—Investment Companies*, as of the reporting entity's measurement date.[3]

Fair Value Determination When the Volume or Level of Activity Has Significantly Decreased

3.20 Paragraphs 51A–H of FASB ASC 820-10-35 clarifies the application of FASB ASC 820 in determining fair value when the volume and level of activity for the asset or liability has significantly decreased. Guidance is also included in identifying transactions that are not orderly. In addition, select paragraphs of paragraphs 59A–I of FASB ASC 820-10-55 provide illustrations on the application of this guidance.

Fair Value Disclosures[†]

Recurring Measurements[4]

3.21 "Pending Content" in FASB ASC 820-10-50 discusses the disclosures required for assets and liabilities measured at fair value. "Pending Content" in FASB ASC 820-10-50-1 requires the reporting entity to disclose certain information that enables users of its financial statements to assess the valuation techniques and inputs used to develop those measurements. For assets and liabilities that are measured at fair value on a recurring basis in periods subsequent to initial recognition, the disclosures required by FASB ASC 820-10-50 in the tabular format as shown in example 8 (paragraphs 60–63) of "Pending Content" in FASB ASC 820-10-55 should be made. For recurring fair value measurements using significant unobservable inputs (level 3), the reporting entity is required to disclose certain information to help users assess the effect of the measurements on earnings (or changes in net assets) for the period.

---

[3] The AICPA issued a series of Technical Questions and Answers (TISs) to provide nonauthoritative guidance that is intended to assist reporting entities with the provisions of Financial Accounting Standards Board (FASB) *Accounting Standards Codification* (ASC) 820, *Fair Value Measurements and Disclosures* (specifically, FASB Accounting Standards Update [ASU] No. 2009-12, *Fair Value Measurements and Disclosures [Topic 820]: Investments in Certain Entities That Calculate Net Asset Value per Share [or Its Equivalent]*), to estimate the fair value of investments in certain entities that calculate net asset value per share of the investment. TIS sections 2220.18–.27 (AICPA, *Technical Practice Aids*) apply to investments that are required to be measured and reported at fair value and are within the scope of paragraphs 4–5 of FASB ASC 820-10-15.

[†] In January 2010, FASB issued ASU No. 2010-06, *Fair Value Measurements and Disclosures (Topic 820): Improving Disclosures about Fair Value Measurements*. FASB ASU No. 2010-06, among other things, changes the requirement to show purchases, sales, issuances, and settlements on a net basis to require separate disclosure for each type. The separate disclosure requirement of purchases, sales, issuances, and settlements activity are effective for fiscal years beginning after December 15, 2010, and for interim periods within those fiscal years. Examples related to the guidance in this ASU are included in FASB ASC 820-10-55. Readers are encouraged to review the ASU in its entirety.

[4] "Pending Content" in FASB ASC 820-10-50-5 provides the required disclosures for nonrecurring measurements.

3.22 "Pending Content" in FASB ASC 820-10-50-2 requires the following disclosures to be made for each class of assets and liabilities. The reporting entity should provide sufficient information to permit reconciliation of the fair value measurement disclosures for the various classes of assets and liabilities to the line items in the net assets available for benefits:[5]

    a. The fair value measurement at the reporting date.

    b. The level within the fair value hierarchy in which the fair value measurement in its entirety falls, segregating the fair value measurement using any of the following:

        i. Quoted prices in active markets for identical assets or liabilities (level 1).

        ii. Significant other observable inputs (level 2).

        iii. Significant unobservable inputs (level 3).

    c. The amounts of significant transfers between level 1 and level 2 of the fair value hierarchy and the reasons for the transfers. Significant transfers into each level should be disclosed separately from transfers out of each level. A reporting entity should disclose and consistently follow its policy for determining when transfers between levels are recognized.

    d. For fair value measurements using significant unobservable inputs (level 3), a reconciliation of the beginning and ending balances, separately presenting changes during the period attributable to any of the following:

        i. Total gains and losses for the period (realized and unrealized), separately presenting gains or losses included in earnings (or changes in net assets) and gains or losses recognized in other comprehensive income, and a description of where those gains or losses included in earnings (or changes in net assets) are reported in the statement of income (or activities) or in other comprehensive income.

        ii. Purchases, sales, issuances, and settlements.[†]

        iii. Transfers in/out of level 3 and the reasons for those transfers. Significant transfers into level 3 should be disclosed separately from significant transfers out of level 3. A reporting entity should disclose and consistently follow its policy for determining when transfers between levels are recognized. The policy about the timing of recognizing transfers should be the same for transfers into level 3 as that for transfers out of level 3.

    e. The amount of the total gains and losses.

    f. For fair value measurements using significant other observable inputs (level 2) and significant unobservable inputs (level 3), a description of the valuation technique (or multiple valuation techniques) used, and the inputs used in determining the fair values of each class of assets or liabilities. If there has been a change in

---

[5] For derivative assets and liabilities, the disclosures listed in paragraph 3.22(*a*)–(*c*) should be made on a gross basis. The disclosures listed in paragraph 3.22(*d*)–(*e*) should be made on either a gross or net basis. See footnote † for further guidance on paragraph 3.22(*d*)(ii).

† See footnote † in the heading above paragraph 3.21.

the valuation technique(s), the reporting entity should disclose that change and the reason for making it.

3.23 "Pending Content" in FASB ASC 820-10-50-2A states that for equity and debt securities, class should be determined on the basis of the nature and risks of the investments in a manner consistent with the guidance in FASB ASC 320-10-50-1B even if the equity securities or debt securities are not within the scope of FASB ASC 320-10-50-1B. Major security types are based on the nature and risks of the security. In determining whether disclosure for a particular security type is necessary and whether it is necessary to further separate a particular security type into greater detail, all of the following should be considered:

a. The activity or business sector

b. Vintage

c. Geographic concentration

d. Credit quality

e. Economic characteristic

For all other assets and liabilities, judgment is needed to determine the appropriate classes of assets and liabilities for which disclosures about fair value measurements should be provided.

3.24 Fair value measurement disclosures for each class of assets and liabilities often will require greater disaggregation than the reporting entity's line items in the statement of financial position. A reporting entity should determine the appropriate classes for those disclosures on the basis of the nature and risks of the assets and liabilities and their classification in the fair value hierarchy (that is, levels 1, 2, and 3). In determining the appropriate classes for fair value measurement disclosures, the reporting entity should consider the level of disaggregated information required for specific assets and liabilities under other FASB ASC topics. For example, under FASB ASC 815, *Derivatives and Hedging*, disclosures about derivative instruments are presented separately by type of contract such as interest rate contracts, foreign exchange contracts, equity contracts, commodity contracts, and credit contracts. (Also, see paragraph 3.52.) The classification of the asset or liability in the fair value hierarchy also should affect the level of disaggregation because of the different degrees of uncertainty and subjectivity involved in level 1, level 2, and level 3 measurements. For example, the number of classes may need to be greater for fair value measurements using significant unobservable inputs (that is, level 3 measurements) to achieve the disclosure objectives because level 3 measurements have a greater degree of uncertainty and subjectivity.

Fair Value Measurements of Investments in Certain Entities That Calculate NAV per Share (or Its Equivalent)

3.25 "Pending Content" in FASB ASC 820-10-50-6A requires disclosures for each class of investment about the attributes of investments within the scope of paragraphs 4–5 of FASB ASC 820-10-15, such as the nature of any restrictions on the investor's ability to redeem its investments at the measurement date, any unfunded commitments, and the investment strategies of the investees. These disclosures are required for all investments within the scope of paragraphs 4–5 of FASB ASC 820-10-15 regardless of whether the practical expedient in FASB ASC 820-10-35-59 has been applied.

Fair Value Option

3.26 For assets and liabilities not currently required to be reported at fair value, FASB ASC 825, *Financial Instruments*, creates a fair value option under which an entity may irrevocably elect fair value as the initial and subsequent measure for many financial instruments and certain other items, with changes in fair value recognized in the statement of activities as those changes occur. An election is made on an instrument-by-instrument basis (with certain exceptions), generally when an instrument is initially recognized in the financial statements. Most financial assets and financial liabilities are eligible to be recognized using the fair value option, as are firm commitments for financial instruments and certain nonfinancial contracts. See FASB ASC 825 for further guidance, including presentation and disclosure requirements.

Net Assets Available for Benefits

Investments

3.27 According to FASB ASC 962-325-35-1, plan investments should generally be presented at their fair value at the reporting date (see paragraphs 3.12–.25 for fair value measurement guidance, paragraph 3.28 for special provisions concerning the valuation of insurance contracts, and paragraphs 3.30–.33 for special provisions concerning the valuation of fully benefit-responsive investment-contracts). Original cost of investments is not required to be disclosed.

3.28 According to FASB ASC 962-325-35-6, *insurance contracts*, as defined by FASB ASC 944-20, should be presented in the same manner as specified in the annual report filed by the plan with certain governmental agencies pursuant to ERISA (that is, either at fair value or at amounts determined by the insurance enterprise [contract value]). Plans not subject to ERISA should present insurance contracts as if the plans were subject to the reporting requirements of ERISA.

3.29 Defined-contribution plans provide benefits based on the amounts contributed to employees' individual accounts plus or minus forfeitures, investment experience, and administrative expenses. In such plans, plan participants have a vested interest in monitoring the financial condition and operations of the plan because they bear investment risk under these plans, and plan transactions can directly affect their benefits (for example, investment mix, and risk and return).

Accounting for Fully Benefit-Responsive Investment Contracts

3.30 In accordance with FASB ASC 962-325-35-5, defined-contribution pension plans should report all investments (including derivative contracts) at fair value. However, contract value is the relevant measurement attribute for that portion of the net assets available for benefits of a defined-contribution plan attributable to fully benefit-responsive investment contracts. The contract value of a fully benefit-responsive investment contract held by a plan is the amount a participant would receive if he or she were to initiate transactions under the terms of the ongoing plan. The statement of net assets available for benefits of the plan should present amounts for (*a*) total assets, (*b*) total liabilities, (*c*) net assets reflecting all investments at fair value, and (*d*) net assets available for benefits. The amount representing the difference between (*c*) and (*d*) should be presented on the face of the statement of net assets available for benefits as a single amount, calculated as the sum of the amounts necessary to adjust the portion of net assets attributable to each fully benefit-responsive investment contract from fair value to contract value. The statement of changes in net assets available for benefits should be prepared on a basis that reflects income credited to participants in the plan and net appreciation or depreciation in the fair value of only those investment contracts that are not deemed to be fully benefit-responsive.

3.31 An investment contract is considered fully benefit-responsive, if all of the following criteria are met for that contract, analyzed on an individual basis:

a. The investment contract is effected directly between the plan and the issuer and prohibits the plan from assigning or selling the contract or its proceeds to another party without the consent of the issuer.

b. Either (i) the repayment of principal and interest credited to participants in the plan is a financial obligation of the issuer of the investment contract or (ii) prospective interest crediting rate adjustments are provided to participants in the plan on a designated pool of investments held by the plan or the contract issuer, whereby a financially responsible third party, through a contract generally referred to as a wrapper, must provide assurance that the adjustments to the interest crediting rate will not result in a future interest crediting rate that is less than zero. If an event has occurred such that realization of full contract value for a particular investment contract is no longer probable (for example, a significant decline in creditworthiness of the contract issuer or wrapper provider), the investment contract should no longer be considered fully benefit-responsive.

c. The terms of the investment contract require all permitted participant-initiated transactions with the plan to occur at contract value with no conditions, limits, or restrictions. Permitted participant-initiated transactions are those transactions allowed by the plan, such as withdrawals for benefits, loans, or transfers to other funds within the plan.

d. An event that limits the ability of the plan to transact at contract value with the issuer (for example, premature termination of the contracts by the plan, plant closings, layoffs, plan termination, bankruptcy, mergers, and early retirement incentives) and that also limits the ability of the plan to transact at contract value with the participants in the plan must be probable of not occurring.

e. The plan itself must allow participants reasonable access to their funds.

3.32 If access to funds is substantially restricted by plan provisions, investment contracts held by those plans may not be considered to be fully benefit-responsive. For example, if plan participants are allowed access at contract value to all or a portion of their account balances only upon termination of their participation in the plan, it would not be considered reasonable access and, therefore, investment contracts held by that plan would generally not be deemed to be fully benefit-responsive. However, in plans with a single investment fund that allow reasonable access to assets by inactive participants, restrictions on access to assets by active participants consistent with the objective of the plan (for example, retirement or health and welfare benefits) will not affect the benefit responsiveness of the investment contracts held by those single-fund plans. Also, if a plan limits participants' access to their account balances to certain specified times during the plan year (for example, semiannually or quarterly) to control the administrative costs of the plan, that limitation generally would not affect the benefit responsiveness of the investment contracts held by that plan. In addition, administrative provisions that place short-term restrictions (for example, three or six months) on transfers to competing fixed-rate investment options to limit arbitrage among those investment options (*equity wash* provisions) would not affect a contract's benefit responsiveness.

3.33 According to paragraphs 9–10 of FASB ASC 962-325-35, if a plan holds multiple contracts, each contract should be evaluated individually for benefit responsiveness. If a plan invests in pooled funds that hold investment contracts, each contract in the pooled fund should be evaluated individually for benefit responsiveness. However, if the pooled fund places any restrictions on access to funds for the payment of benefits, the underlying investment contracts should not be considered fully benefit-responsive. Contracts that provide for prospective interest adjustments may still be fully benefit-responsive provided that the terms of the contracts specify that the crediting interest rate cannot be less than zero.

Participant-Directed Investments

3.34 In accordance with FASB ASC 962-325-45-3, participant-directed plan investments may be shown in the aggregate, as a one-line item, in the statement of net assets available for benefits. Participant-directed plan investments, including self-directed investments held in brokerage accounts, that individually exceed 5 percent of net assets available for benefits must be separately disclosed pursuant to paragraph 3.50*h*.

3.35 According to paragraphs 5–6 of FASB ASC 962-325-45, the presentation of nonparticipant-directed investments in the statement of net assets available for benefits or in the notes should be detailed by general type, such as registered investment companies (for example, mutual funds), government securities, common-collective trusts, pooled separate accounts, short-term securities, corporate bonds, common stocks, mortgages, and real estate. The presentation should indicate whether the fair values of the investments have been measured by quoted market prices in an active market or were determined otherwise.

Securities Lending

3.36 Securities custodians commonly carry out securities lending activities on behalf of their employee benefit plan clients. The borrowers of securities generally are required to provide collateral to the lender (the plan). This collateral is typically cash but sometimes it may be other securities or standby letters of credit, with a value slightly higher than that of the securities borrowed. If the collateral is cash, the lender typically earns a return by investing that cash at rates higher than the rate paid or *rebated* to the borrower. If the collateral is other than cash, the lender typically receives a fee. FASB ASC 860, *Transfers* *and Servicing*, provides accounting and reporting guidance for transfers of financial assets, including accounting for securities lending activities. FASB ASC 860 addresses

- whether the transaction is a sale of the loaned securities for financial reporting purposes.
- if the transaction is not a sale, how the lender should report the loaned securities.
- whether and how the lender should report the collateral.
- how the lender should record income earned as a result of securities lending transactions.

With respect to defined contribution plans, examples of plans and investment holdings in which securities lending activities occur most often include profit sharing plans or plans that hold separately managed funds or funds in a master trust.

3.37 If the securities lending transaction includes an agreement that entitles and obligates the plan (the transferor) to repurchase the transferred securities under which the plan maintains effective control over those securities, then the plan must account for those transactions as secured borrowings (not sales) and continue to report the securities on the statement of net assets. Typically in a securities lending arrangement the transferee has the right by custom or contract to sell or repledge the security loaned. In these instances the securities loaned should be reclassified and reported by the plan (the transferor) separately from other assets not so encumbered (for example, as security pledged to creditors) pursuant to FASB ASC 860-30-25-5. Alternatively, if the transferee does not have the right by custom or contract to sell or repledge the security loaned, the plan should disclose in the notes to the financial statements the carrying amount and classification of any assets pledged as collateral, associated liabilities, and qualitative information about the relationship between those assets and associated liabilities as of the date of the latest statement of net assets presented pursuant to "Pending Content" in FASB ASC 860-30-50-1A. The plan should record the cash collateral received as an asset—and any investments made with that cash, even if made by agents or in pools with other securities lenders—along with the obligation to return the cash (considered the amount borrowed).

3.38 Generally, if the plan receives securities (instead of cash) that may be sold or repledged, the plan accounts for those securities in the same way as it would account for cash received, that is, the plan recognizes in the statement of net assets the securities received as collateral and the obligation to return that collateral. However, pursuant to "Pending Content" in FASB ASC 860-30-50-1A, the plan should also disclose the fair value as of the date of each statement of net assets presented of that collateral and of the portion of that collateral that it has sold or repledged, and information about the sources and uses of that collateral. Because FASB ASC 860-30-25-5 requires that only the lender recognize securities collateral received in its statement of net assets, it is important to accurately identify the lender and borrower in securities lending transactions. One indicator that the plan is the lender is that the collateral received by the lender generally has a value slightly higher (for example, 2 percent) than that of the securities being borrowed.

3.39 The plan should disclose its policy for requiring collateral or other security in accordance with "Pending Content" in FASB ASC 860-30-50-1A.

3.40 According to FASB ASC 962-325-45-9, the interest income earned and rebate interest paid as a result of securities lending activity should be recorded on the statement of changes in net assets available for benefits.

Contributions Receivable

3.41 According to the FASB ASC glossary, *contributions receivable* are the amounts due, as of the date of the financial statements, to the plan from employers, participants, and other sources of funding (for example, state subsidies or federal grants, which should be separately identified). Per FASB ASC 962-310-25-1, contributions receivable include those pursuant to formal commitments as well as legal or contractual requirements. With respect to an employer's contributions, evidence of a formal commitment may include (*a*) a resolution by the employer's governing body approving a specified contribution, (*b*) a consistent pattern of making payments after the plan's year-end pursuant to an established contribution policy that attributes such subsequent payments to the preceding plan year, (*c*) a deduction of a contribution for federal tax purposes for periods ending on or before the financial statement date, or (*d*) the employer's recognition as of the financial statement date of a contribution payable to the plan.[6] According to FASB ASC 962-310-35-1, contributions receivable should include an allowance for estimated uncollectible amounts.

Loans to Participants

3.42 Certain defined contribution plans allow participants to borrow against their vested account balance. Such participant loans are an extension of credit to a plan participant by the plan, in accordance with the plan document or the plan's written loan policy. The loan is secured by the participant's vested account balance. In accordance with "Pending Content" in FASB ASC 962-310-45-2, for reporting purposes, participant loans should be classified as notes receivable from participants. Participant loans should be measured at their unpaid principal balance plus any accrued but unpaid interest in accordance with "Pending Content" in FASB ASC 962-310-35-2. In addition, "Pending Content" in FASB ASC 962-310-50-1 states that the fair value disclosures prescribed in paragraphs 10–16 of FASB ASC 825-10-50 are not required for participant loans.[‡]

Operating Assets

3.43 Plan assets used in plan operations (for example, buildings, equipment, furniture and fixtures, and leasehold improvements) should be reported at cost less accumulated depreciation or amortization. This is in contrast to the Form 5500 reporting requirement that calls for plan assets to be reported at fair value. Resulting differences should be presented in a note to the financial statements that reconciles the differences between amounts reported in the financial statements and Form 5500.

---

[6] According to FASB ASC 962-310-25-1, the existence of an accrued contribution payable in the employer's financial statements does not, by itself, provide sufficient support for recognition of a contribution receivable by the plan.

[‡] In September 2010, FASB issued ASU 2010-25, *Plan Accounting—Defined Contribution Pension Plans (Topic 962): Reporting Loans to Participants by Defined Contribution Pension Plans (a consensus of the FASB Emerging Issues Task Force)*, to clarify how loans to participants should be classified and measured. The amendments in this ASU should be applied retrospectively to all prior periods presented and is effective for fiscal years ending after December 15, 2010, with early adoption permitted.

3.44 FASB ASC 360, *Property, Plant, and Equipment*, addresses accounting for the impairment of long-lived assets for assets to be held and used and assets to be disposed of. FASB ASC 360-10-35-21 requires that long-lived assets to be held and used by the plan, such as real estate owned by the plan for plan operations, be tested for recoverability whenever events or changes in circumstances indicate that the carrying amount may not be recoverable. Long-lived assets to be abandoned or exchanged for a similar productive asset should be considered held and used until disposed of. FASB ASC 360-10-35-43 states that long-lived assets classified as held for sale should be measured at the lower of its carrying amount or fair value less cost to sell. A long-lived asset should not be depreciated while it is held for sale. See FASB ASC 360 for further accounting and disclosure requirements.[7]

Accrued Liabilities

3.45 A plan may have liabilities (other than for benefits) that should be accrued. Such liabilities may be for amounts owed for securities purchased, refund of excess contributions, income taxes payable by the plan or other expenses (for example, third-party administrator fees). These liabilities should be deducted to arrive at net assets available for benefits. The plan should not reflect as liabilities amounts allocated to accounts of persons who have elected to withdraw from the plan but have not yet been paid (see paragraph 3.50*m*).

Changes in Net Assets Available for Benefits

3.46 According to FASB ASC 962-205-45-7, information regarding changes in net assets available for benefits is intended to present the effects of significant changes in net assets during the year and should present, at a minimum, all of the following:

a. The change in fair value (or estimated fair value) of each significant type of investment including participant directed and self-directed investments held in brokerage accounts (see paragraphs 3.34–.35). Gains and losses from investments sold need not be segregated from unrealized gains and losses relating to investments held at year-end.[8] This information may be presented in the accompanying footnotes. (See exhibit E-3, "XYZ Company 401(k) Plan: Notes to Financial Statements," note C, in appendix E, for an illustration.)

b. Investment income, exclusive of changes in fair value described in item (*a*) of this paragraph.

c. Contributions from employers, segregated between cash and noncash contributions. A noncash contribution should be recorded at fair value; the nature of noncash contributions should be described either parenthetically or in a note.

d. Contributions from participants, including those transmitted by the sponsor. See paragraph 9.06 in chapter 9 of this guide for a discussion of corrective distributions disclosures.

e. Contributions from other identified sources (for example, state subsidies or federal grants).

---

[7] See also TIS section 6931.03, "Should the Sale of Real Estate Investments Held by Employee Benefit Plans Be Treated as Discontinued Operations?" (AICPA, *Technical Practice Aids*).

[8] Realized gains and losses on investments that were both bought and sold during the period should be included.

 f. Nenefits paid to participants. See paragraph 7.58*f* in chapter 7 of this guide for a discussion of delinquent loans and related deemed distributions.

 g. Payments to insurance entities to purchase contracts that are excluded from plan assets.

 h. Administrative expenses. (See Department of Labor [DOL] Advisory Opinion No. 2001-01A for guidance on reasonable expenses of administering the plan.)

3.47 The minimum disclosures should be made to the extent that they apply to the plan. Per FASB ASC 962-205-45-8, the list of minimum disclosures is not intended to limit the amount of detail or the manner of presenting the information, and subclassifications or additional classifications may be useful.

3.48 According to FASB ASC 962-205-45-8, other changes in net assets available for benefits (for example, transfers of assets to or from other plans or proceeds from demutualization) should also be presented separately in the financial statements if they are significant.

Additional Financial Statement Disclosures

3.49 According to FASB ASC 962-325-50-1, disclosure of the plan's accounting policies should include a description of the methods and significant assumptions used to determine the fair value of investments and the reported value of insurance contracts (if any).[9]

3.50 Unless otherwise noted, according to FASB ASC 962-205-50-1, the financial statements should disclose, if applicable, all of the following:

 a. A brief, general description of the plan agreement including, but not limited to, vesting and allocation provisions and the disposition of forfeitures.[10]

 b. A description of significant plan amendments adopted during the period, and the effects of such amendments on net assets if significant either individually or in the aggregate.

 c. The amount of unallocated assets, as well as the basis used to allocate asset values to participants' accounts if that basis differs from the one used to record assets in the financial statements.

 d. The basis for determining contributions by employers and, for a contributory plan, the method of determining participants' contributions. Plans subject to the minimum funding requirements of ERISA, such as money purchase pension plans, should disclose whether those requirements have been met. If a minimum funding waiver has been granted by the IRS, or if a request for waiver is pending before the IRS, that fact should be disclosed.

 e. If significant costs of plan administration are being absorbed by the employers, that fact should be disclosed in the notes to the financial statements.

---

[9] See FASB ASC 235, *Notes to Financial Statements.*

[10] If a plan agreement or a description providing this information is otherwise published and made available, this description may be omitted from the financial statement provided that reference to the other source is made.

f. The policy regarding the purchase of contracts with insurance entities that are excluded from plan assets.

g. The federal income tax status of the plan[11] if a favorable determination letter has not been obtained or maintained. Note that reports filed in accordance with the requirements of ERISA must include disclosure of "information concerning whether a tax ruling or determination letter has been obtained," which is more than is required by FASB ASC 960, *Plan Accounting—Defined Benefit Pension Plans.*

h. Per FASB ASC 962-325-45-7, identification of any investments (including self-directed and participant directed investments) that represent 5 percent or more of the net assets available for benefits. If any of those investments are nonparticipant-directed, they should be identified as such. Listing all investments in Schedule H, line 4i—Schedule of Assets (Held at End of Year) required by ERISA does not eliminate the requirement to include this disclosure in the financial statements.

i. Per FASB ASC 962-325-45-8, if a defined contribution plan provides for participant-directed and nonparticipant-directed investment programs, the plan should disclose information in the financial statements about the net assets and significant components of the changes in net assets relating to the nonparticipant-directed program with such reasonable detail, either in the financial statements or accompanying notes, as is necessary to identify the types of investments and changes therein. (See paragraphs 3.34–.35 and exhibit E-3 notes C and D, in appendix E, for an illustration.)

A plan provides for participant-directed investment programs if it allows participants to choose among various investment alternatives. The available alternatives are usually pooled fund vehicles, such as registered investment companies or commingled funds of banks, that provide varying kinds of investments (for example, equity funds and fixed income funds). The participant may select among the various available alternatives and periodically change that selection.

j. Significant related-party transactions (see chapter 11 for a discussion of related-party transactions and appendix A for disclosures related to parties in interest).

k. Investments pledged to secure debt of the plan as well as a description of the provisions regarding the release of such investments from the pledge and the amounts of investments released from the pledge in the last period.

---

[11] A plan's tax exempt status is a position that may be subject to uncertainty. In September 2009, FASB issued ASU No. 2009-06, *Income Taxes (Topic 740)—Implementation Guidance on Accounting for Uncertainty in Income Taxes and Disclosure Amendments for Nonpublic Entities.* FASB ASU No. 2009-06 provides implementation guidance on accounting for uncertainty in income taxes and eliminates the disclosure requirements of paragraphs 15(a)–15(b) of FASB ASC 740-10-50 for nonpublic entities, as defined in FASB ASC 740-10-20. The implementation guidance in FASB ASU No. 2009-06 also expands the FASB ASC glossary definition of a *tax position.* In addition, TIS section 5250.15, "Application of Certain FASB Interpretation No. 48 (codified in FASB ASC 740-10) Disclosure Requirements to Nonpublic Entities That Do Not Have Uncertain Tax Positions" (AICPA, *Technical Practice Aids*), clarified that the description of open tax years that remain subject to examination is a required disclosure for a nonpublic entity even if the entity has no uncertain tax positions. Also, see paragraphs 12.07–.10 of this guide for further information.

    l. Guarantees by others of debt of the plan.

    m. Amounts allocated to accounts of persons who have elected to withdraw from the plan but have not yet been paid. These amounts should not be reported as a liability on the statement of net assets available for benefits, in financial statements prepared in conformity with U.S. GAAP. A note to the financial statements to reconcile the audited financial statements to the Form 5500 may be necessary to comply with ERISA (see paragraphs A.51*a* and A.52*c* in appendix A).

    n. The amount and disposition of forfeited nonvested accounts. Specifically, identification of those amounts that are used to reduce future employer contributions, expenses, or reallocated to participant's accounts, in accordance with plan documents.

    o. Subsequent event disclosures as required by FASB ASC 855, *Subsequent Events* (see chapter 12 for a discussion of subsequent events).[||]

    p. Per FASB ASC 962-325-50-3, for fully benefit-responsive investment contracts, in the aggregate,

         i. a description of the nature of those investment contracts, how they operate, and the methodology for calculating the interest crediting rate, including the key factors that could influence future average interest crediting rates, the basis for and frequency of determining interest crediting rate resets, and any minimum interest crediting rate under the terms of the contracts. This disclosure should explain the relationship between future interest crediting rates and the amount reported on the statement of net assets available for benefits representing the adjustment for the portion of net assets attributable to fully benefit-responsive investment contracts from fair value to contract value.

         ii. the average yield earned by the plan for all fully benefit-responsive investment contracts (which may differ from the interest rate credited to participants in the plan) for each period for which a statement of net assets available for benefits is presented. This average yield should be calculated by dividing the annualized earnings of all fully benefit-responsive investment contracts in the plan (irrespective of the interest rate credited to participants in the plan) by the fair value of all fully benefit-responsive investment contracts in the plan.

         iii. the average yield earned by the plan for all fully benefit-responsive investment contracts with an adjustment to reflect the actual interest rate credited to participants in

---

[||] In February 2010, FASB issued ASU 2010-09, *Subsequent Events (Topic 855): Amendments to Certain Recognition and Disclosure Requirements.* This ASU amends the guidance in FASB ASC 855, *Subsequent Events,* to require entities (except Securities and Exchange Commission [SEC] filers and conduit debt obligors [CDOs]) to evaluate subsequent events through the date that the financial statements are available to be issued. Entities other than SEC filers should disclose the date through which subsequent events have been evaluated. SEC filers and CDOs should evaluate subsequent events through the date the financial statements are issued. An entity that is an SEC filer is not required to disclose the date through which subsequent events have been evaluated.

the plan for each period for which a statement of net assets available for benefits is presented. This average yield should be calculated by dividing the annualized earnings credited to participants in the plan for all fully benefit-responsive investment contracts in the plan (irrespective of the actual earnings of those investments) by the fair value of all fully benefit-responsive investment contracts in the plan.

iv. a description of the events that limit the ability of the plan to transact at contract value with the issuer (for example, premature termination of the contracts by the plan, plant closings, layoffs, plan termination, bankruptcy, mergers, and early retirement incentives), including a statement about whether the occurrence of those events that would limit the plan's ability to transact at contract value with participants in the plan is probable or not probable. (The term *probable* is consistent with its use in FASB ASC 450, *Contingencies.*)

v. a description of the events and circumstances that would allow issuers to terminate fully benefit-responsive investment contracts with the plan and settle at an amount different from contract value.

q. Per FASB ASC 962-325-50-4, for ERISA-covered plans, if a fully benefit-responsive investment contract does not qualify for contract-value reporting in the U.S. DOL Form 5500, but is reported in the financial statements at contract value, and the contract value does not approximate fair value, the DOL's rules and regulations require that a statement explaining the differences between amounts reported in the financial statements and Form 5500 be added to the financial statements.

This list does not include information required by ERISA to be disclosed in the schedules filed as part of a plan's annual report. In this connection, it is important to note that disclosure of this information only on the face of the financial statements or in the notes to the financial statements but not in the schedules is not acceptable under ERISA reporting standards.

Fair Value Measurements

3.51 See paragraphs 3.21–.25 for required disclosures related to fair value measurements.

Derivatives and Hedging

3.52 FASB ASC 815 provides accounting and reporting for derivative instruments, including certain derivative instruments embedded in other contracts (collectively referred to as *derivatives*), and for hedging activities. It requires that an entity recognize all derivatives as either assets or liabilities in the statement of financial position and measure those instruments at fair value. FASB ASC 815 applies to certain contracts that meet the definition of *derivative instrument*, as defined in FASB ASC 815-10-15-83. See FASB ASC 815-10-15 for further information on certain contracts that are not subject to the requirements of FASB ASC 815. (See paragraphs 7.59–.66 for further guidance.)[#]

Master Trusts

3.53 Investments in a master trust should be presented in accordance with paragraphs 6–8 of FASB ASC 962-325-50. In the notes[12] to the financial statements the investments of the master trust should be detailed by general type, such as government securities, short-term securities, corporate bonds, common stocks, mortgages and real estate, as of the date of each statement of net assets available for benefits is presented. The net change in the fair value of each significant type of investment of the master trust and total investment income of the master trust by type, for example, interest, and dividends, should also be disclosed in the notes for each period for which a statement of changes in net assets available for benefits is presented. The notes to the financial statements should also include a description of the basis used to allocate net assets, net investment income, gains and losses to participating plans, and the plan's percentage interest in the master trust as of the date of each statement of net assets available for benefits presented.

Financial Instruments

3.54 FASB ASC 825 requires all entities, except for those covered by an exemption[13] for which the disclosure is optional, to disclose within the body of the financial statements or in the accompanying notes, the fair value of financial instruments, for which it is practicable to estimate fair value.[14] An entity should also disclose the method(s) and significant assumptions used to estimate the fair

---

[#] In March 2010, FASB issued ASU No. 2010-11, *Derivatives and Hedging (Topic 815): Scope Exceptions Related to Embedded Credit Derivatives*. The amendments in this ASU, among other things, clarify the scope exception under paragraphs 8–9 of FASB ASC 815-15 for embedded credit derivative features related to the transfer of credit risk in the form of subordination of one financial instrument to another. Further, the amendments address how to determine which embedded credit derivatives, including those in collateralized debt obligations and synthetic collateralized debt obligations, are considered to be embedded derivatives that should not be analyzed under FASB ASC 815-15-25 for potential bifurcation and separate accounting.

The amendments in FASB ASU No. 2010-11 are effective for each reporting entity at the beginning of its first fiscal quarter beginning after June 15, 2010. Early adoption is permitted at the beginning of each entity's first fiscal quarter beginning after issuance of this ASU.

The guidance is located in FASB ASC 815-10 and FASB ASC 815-15.

[12] The AICPA issued a TIS section to provide guidance on the required fair value measurement disclosures to be made when a plan holds investments in a master trust: TIS section 6931.11, "Fair Value Measurement Disclosures for Master Trusts" (AICPA, *Technical Practice Aids*). This practice aid assists with the implementation of FASB ASC 820 for employee benefits plans that have investments in a master trust. This guidance states that the disclosure requirements of FASB ASC 820 should be made for each major category of master trust assets and liabilities. In addition, consideration should be given to combining, or reconciling, or both, the master trust FASB ASC 820 disclosures with the master trust disclosures as required by paragraphs 6–8 of FASB ASC 962-325-50.

[13] According to FASB ASC 825-10-50-3, the disclosures are optional for plans that meet all of the following criteria:

    a. The plan is a nonpublic entity.

    b. The plan's total assets are less than $100 million on the date of the financial statements.

    c. The plan has no instrument that, in whole or in part, is accounted for as a derivative instrument under FASB ASC 815, *Derivatives and Hedging*, during the reporting period.

[14] Per FASB ASC 825-10-50-11, fair value disclosed in the notes should be presented together with the related carrying amount in a form that makes it clear whether the fair value and carrying amount represent assets or liabilities and how the carrying amounts relate to what is reported in the statement of net assets available for benefits.

value of financial instruments. Generally, financial instruments of a defined-contribution pension plan are included in the scope of FASB ASC 825 and are subject to the disclosure requirements FASB ASC 825-10-50.[15] In addition, the disclosure requirements of FASB ASC 820 may also apply.[16]

3.55 FASB ASC 825-10-50-21 requires disclosure of all significant concentrations of credit risk arising from all financial instruments. The following information should be disclosed about each significant concentration:

- Information about the (shared) activity, region, or economic characteristic that identifies the concentration

- The maximum amount of loss due to credit risk that, based on the gross fair value of the financial instrument, the entity would incur if parties to the financial instruments that make up the concentration failed completely to perform according to the terms of the contracts and the collateral or other security, if any, for the amount due proved to be of no value to the entity

- The entity's policy of requiring collateral or other security to support financial instruments subject to credit risk, information about the entity's access to that collateral or other security, and the nature and a brief description of the collateral or other security supporting those financial instruments

- The entity's policy of entering into master netting arrangements to mitigate the credit risk of financial instruments, information about the arrangements for which the entity is a party, and a brief description of the terms of those arrangements, including the extent to which they would reduce the entity's maximum amount of loss due to credit risk

Risks and Uncertainties

3.56 FASB ASC 275, *Risks and Uncertainties*, requires plans to include in their financial statements disclosures about (*a*) the nature of their operations, and (*b*) use of estimates in the preparation of financial statements. In addition, if specified criteria are met, FASB ASC 275 requires plans to include in their financial statement disclosures about (*a*) certain significant estimates, and (*b*) current vulnerability due to certain concentrations.

3.57 Certain significant estimates should be disclosed when known information available prior to the financial statements being issued or being available to be issued (appropriate date determined in accordance with FASB ASC 855-10-25)[II] indicates that both (*a*) it is at least reasonably possible that the estimate of the effect on the financial statements of a condition, situation, or

---

[15] According to "Pending Content" in FASB ASC 962-310-50-1, the fair value disclosures prescribed in paragraphs 10–16 of FASB ASC 825-10-50 are not required for participant loans. See paragraph 3.44 for a discussion of the financial accounting for participant loans.

[16] In June 2010, the AICPA issued TIS section 1800.05, "Applicability of Fair Value Disclosure Requirements and Measurement Principles in Financial Accounting Standard Board (FASB) *Accounting Standards Codification* (ASC) 820, *Fair Value Measurements and Disclosures*, to Certain Financial Instruments" (AICPA, *Technical Practice Aids*). This TIS section addresses whether the fair value measurement principles and disclosure requirements in FASB ASC 820 apply to financial instruments that are not recognized at fair value in the statement of financial positions, but for which fair value is required to be disclosed in the notes to financial statements in accordance with paragraphs 10–19 of FASB ASC 825-10-50.

[II] See footnote II in paragraph 3.50.

set of circumstances that existed at the date of the financial statements will change in the near term due to one or more future confirming events, and (b) the effect of the change would be material to the financial statements.

3.58 Vulnerability from concentrations arises when a plan is exposed to risk of loss greater than it would have had it mitigated its risk through diversification. Many plan's participants may be concentrated in a specific industry that carries with it certain risks. Plans may also hold investments and other assets (other than financial instruments for which concentrations are covered by FASB ASC 825, rather than FASB ASC 275) that are concentrated in a single industry or in a single geographic area. Concentrations should be disclosed if based on known information prior to the financial statements being issued or being available to be issued (appropriate date determined in accordance with FASB ASC 855-10-25 ‖) (a) the concentration exists at the date of the financial statements, (b) the concentration makes the plan vulnerable to the risk of a near-term severe impact, and (c) it is at least reasonably possible that the events that could cause the severe impact will occur in the near term. For example, if the plan owns several investment properties (that is, apartment buildings) located in a geographic area that has only one significant employer and that employer announced last year that it is considering leaving the area and it is reasonably possible that it will do so within the next year, this could significantly affect the plan's future cash flows from rents and the value of the investment properties.

3.59 Because the disclosure requirements of FASB ASC 275 in many circumstances are similar to or overlap the disclosure requirements in certain FASB ASC sections (for example, FASB ASC 450), the disclosures required by FASB ASC 275 may be combined in various ways, grouped together, or placed in diverse parts of the financial statements, or included as part of the disclosures made pursuant to the requirements of other FASB ASC sections.

Employee Stock Ownership Plans

3.60 An ESOP is a unique form of defined contribution plan. Under the prohibited transaction statutory exemptions, an ESOP has the ability to borrow money and to concentrate plan investments in *qualifying employer securities*. (See paragraph A.90 in appendix A.) Frequently these securities are not publicly traded. These circumstances can increase the auditor's risk of material misstatement on the financial statements.

3.61 The following items are unique to ESOPs:

- Typically, the plan obtains an annual appraisal of the securities. (Chapter 7 provides audit guidance regarding the testing of the fair value of investments. FASB ASC 820-10-35-44 provides guidance for when the use of a blockage factor is prohibited.[17] This could result in a difference between what is recorded on Form 5500 and what is recorded for U.S. GAAP purposes and accordingly, the resulting difference would be presented in a note to

---

‖ See footnote ‖ in paragraph 3.50.

[17] Fair value disclosed in the notes should be presented together with the related carrying amount in a form that makes it clear whether the fair value and carrying amount represent assets or liabilities and how the carrying amounts relate to what is reported in the statement of net assets available for benefits.

the financial statements that reconciles the difference between amounts reported in the financial statements and Form 5500.)

- Leveraged ESOPs will have obligations to a financial institution or a related party lender. (Consider testing debt payments, interest accruals, and loan covenants.) In accordance with FASB ASC 820, the guidance in paragraphs 3.12–.25 is applicable if the ESOP debt is reported at fair value.

- ESOP documents frequently reflect specific tax code restrictions, such as on the use of dividends. Paragraphs 12.01–.10 discuss general tax compliance procedures.

403(b) Plans or Arrangements

3.62 These are retirement savings arrangements sponsored by certain nonprofit organizations (such as hospitals and private colleges) and public schools. They are defined contribution plans with individual salary deferral limits that are similar, but not identical to 401(k) programs. Contributions typically include employee salary deferrals. Nonprofit organizations often establish a 401(a) plan that funds employer-matching contributions to a 403(b) plan. Auditors should obtain an understanding of the deferrals made under the 403(b) plan in order to determine if the employer match under the 401(a) plan is properly determined.

3.63 Investments held in these arrangements are typically restricted by law to annuity contracts or custodial accounts holding units of participation of regulated investment companies (for example, mutual funds).

3.64 Beginning with the 2009 Form 5500 filings, 403(b) plans became subject to the same Form 5500 reporting and audit requirements that currently exist for Section 401(k) plans. These requirements eliminate a previous exemption granted to 403(b) plans from the annual Form 5500 reporting, disclosure, and audit requirements of ERISA. For *large* 403(b) plans, as defined by ERISA, the 2009 reporting requirements include not only the completion of the entire Form 5500 but also the engagement of an independent qualified public accountant to conduct an independent audit of the plan.

3.65 On July 20, 2009, the DOL issued Field Assistance Bulletin (FAB) No. 2009-02, *Annual Reporting Requirements for 403(b) Plans*, to provide certain transition relief for administrators of 403(b) plans that make good faith efforts to transition for the 2009 plan year to ERISA's generally applicable annual reporting requirements. Provided that certain conditions are met, DOL FAB 2009-02 indicates that certain inactive contracts will not be required to be part of the employer's Title I plan or as plan assets for purposes of the annual report (Form 5500). If the plan administrator elects to exclude some or all of those contracts or accounts meeting the conditions of DOL FAB No. 2009-02 from the plan's financial statements or instructs the auditor not to perform procedures on certain or all pre-2009 contracts, or both, the auditor will need to consider the effect of the exclusions on the completeness of the financial statement presentation and restrictions on the scope of the audit.

Terminating Plans

3.66 FASB ASC 962-40 provides guidance for terminating plans that are defined contribution plans. A terminating plan includes any plan about which a decision to terminate has been made regardless of whether the terminating plan will be replaced.

3.67 When the decision to terminate a plan has been made,[18] or a wasting trust (that is, a plan under which participants no longer accrue benefits but that will remain in existence as long as necessary to pay already accrued benefits) exists, the relevant circumstances should be disclosed in all subsequent financial statements issued by the plan.

3.68 If the decision to terminate a plan is made before the end of the plan year, the plan's year-end financial statements should be prepared on the *liquidation* basis of accounting.[19]

3.69 For plan assets, changing to the liquidation basis will usually cause little or no change in values, most of which are at current market values. Assets that may not be carried at market values include operating assets, insurance contracts carried at *contract values*, or large blocks of stock or other assets that cannot be readily disposed of at their quoted market prices.

---

[18] See paragraph 12.28, which states that the auditor should obtain written representation from management as part of an audit of financial statements. Such representations may include whether there is a present intention to terminate the plan. Refer also to paragraph 10.41*h*, which states that the auditor may consider confirming with the plan's actuary knowledge of an intent on the part of the employer to terminate the plan.

[19] Interpretation No. 8, "Reporting on Financial Statements Prepared on a Liquidation Basis of Accounting," of AU section 508, *Reports on Audited Financial Statements* (AICPA, *Professional Standards*, AU sec. 9508 par. .33–.38), contains applicable guidance regarding the auditor's reporting responsibilities for terminating plans.

Chapter 4

Accounting and Reporting by Health and Welfare Benefit Plans

4.01 This chapter describes accounting principles generally accepted in the United States of America (U.S. GAAP) for accounting and financial reporting for health and welfare benefit plans as provided in Financial Accounting Standards Board (FASB) *Accounting Standards Codification* (ASC) 965, *Plan Accounting—Health and Welfare Benefit Plans*. FASB ASC 965 prescribes the general form and content of financial statements of those plans. U.S. GAAP other than those discussed in this chapter may also apply to health and welfare benefit plans.

Exhibit 4-1

Quick Reference for Health and Welfare Benefit Plans

This guide has been organized so that the accounting and reporting guidance for health and welfare benefit plans is contained in this chapter. Auditing guidance for defined benefit, defined contribution, and health and welfare benefit plans is contained throughout the guide. The following table has been developed to help you locate the areas in this guide that may pertain to an audit of a health and welfare benefit plan. Not every area listed will be applicable to a particular client and the nature, timing, and extent of auditing procedures are matters of professional judgment.

Chapter 4	"Accounting and Reporting by Health and Welfare Benefit Plans"
Chapter 5	"Planning and General Auditing Considerations"
Chapter 6	"Internal Control"
Chapter 7	"Auditing Investments and Loans to Participants"
Chapter 8	"Auditing Contributions Received and Related Receivables"
Chapter 9	"Auditing Benefit Payments"
Chapter 10	"Auditing Participant Data, Participant Allocations, and Plan Obligations" in particular: 10.22–.23 10.34–.41
Chapter 11	"Party in Interest Transactions"
Chapter 12	"Other Auditing Considerations"
Chapter 13	"The Auditor's Report" in particular: 13.07 Standard reports for health and welfare benefit plans 13.08–.46 Various other reporting situations that may apply"
Appendix A	"ERISA and Related Regulations"
Appendix B	"Examples of Controls"
Appendix F	"Illustrative Financial Statements: Employee Health and Welfare Benefit Plans"
Appendix G	"Consideration of Fraud in a Financial Statement Audit"

Scope

4.02 Health and welfare benefit plans include plans that provide

    a. medical, dental, visual, psychiatric, or long-term health care; life insurance (offered separately from a pension plan); certain severance benefits; or accidental death or dismemberment benefits.

    b. benefits for unemployment, disability, vacations, or holidays.

    c. other benefits such as apprenticeships, tuition assistance, day care, dependent care, housing subsidies, or legal services.

This chapter applies to both defined-benefit and defined-contribution health and welfare benefit plans (referred to hereafter as *health and welfare benefit plans*).

4.03 Defined-benefit health and welfare plans specify a determinable benefit, which may be in the form of a reimbursement to the covered plan participant or a direct payment to providers or third-party insurers for the cost of specified services. Such plans may also include benefits that are payable as a lump sum, such as death benefits. The level of benefits may be defined or limited based on factors such as age, years of service, and salary. Contributions may be determined by the plan's actuary or be based on premiums, actual claims paid, hours worked or other factors determined by the plan sponsor. Even when a plan is funded pursuant to agreements that specify a fixed rate of employer contributions (for example, a collectively bargained multiemployer plan), such a plan may nevertheless be a defined-benefit health and welfare plan if its substance is to provide a defined benefit.

4.04 Defined-contribution health and welfare plans maintain an individual account for each plan participant. Such plans may include flexible spending arrangements, vacation plans, and health savings accounts (HSAs). They have terms that specify the means of determining the contributions to participants' accounts, rather than the amount of benefits the participants are to receive. The benefits a plan participant will receive are limited to the amount contributed to the participant's account, investment experience, expenses, and any forfeitures allocated to the participant's account.

4.05 *Health Savings Accounts and Health Reimbursement Arrangements.* The Medicare Prescription Drug, Improvement and Modernization Act of 2003 created the HSA, effective January 1, 2004. Individuals enrolled in certain high-deductible health plans (HDHPs) can establish HSAs to receive tax-favored contributions (from either the employee or employer). The contribution made to the HSA is distributed on a tax-free basis to pay or reimburse qualifying[*] health expenses, may be used for future expenses, or may be used (on a taxable basis) for nonhealth purposes. Funds held in the HSA can be used to pay premiums for long-term care insurance, and can be used to pay for health insurance premiums while receiving unemployment benefits or continuation benefits under the Consolidated Omnibus Budget Reconciliation Act (COBRA). The HSA's funds are required to be held by an insurance company or trustee (bank). HSAs generally will not constitute *employee welfare benefit plans* for purposes of the provisions of Title I of the Employee Retirement Income Security Act of 1974 (ERISA).[†] However, unless exempt under Title I (for example, governmental and church plans), an employer-sponsored HDHP that underlies a HSA would be within the meaning of ERISA Section 3(1) and subject to Title I. HSAs' popularity is expected to increase, given that they can be funded on a pretax basis, they can pay most medical expenses on a tax-free basis, unused amounts can be rolled forward to future years (or can be withdrawn at age 65 as supplemental retirement income), and they are portable.

---

[*] This refers to qualified health expenses as defined under Section 213(d) of the Internal Revenue Code.

[†] See U.S Department of Labor Field Assistance Bulletin 2004-1.

4.06 A health reimbursement arrangement (HRA) is similar to an HSA; however, HRAs are funded solely through employer contributions and may not be funded by the employee through a voluntary salary reduction agreement. No requirement exists for the arrangement to be part of an HDHP, and the funds can be held by the employer or a voluntary employees' beneficiary association (VEBA) trust. Employees are reimbursed tax free for qualified medical expenses up to a maximum dollar amount for a coverage period. Amounts remaining at the end of the year can generally be carried over to the next year. The employer is not permitted to refund any part of the balance to the employee, the account cannot be used for anything other than reimbursements for qualified medical expenses, and remaining amounts are not portable upon termination once the employee leaves the employer. HRAs are employer-established benefit plans and may be offered as a component of other health plans, including flexible spending accounts.

4.07 When HSAs or HRAs are standalone, they have no audit requirement. However, HSAs and HRAs that are a component of a health and welfare plan are subject to audit, as are the other components of that health and welfare plan.

4.08 As stated in FASB ASC 965-10-05-10, health and welfare benefit plans generally are subject to certain of the reporting and other requirements of ERISA. Plans that are unfunded (that is, those whose benefits are paid solely and directly out of the general assets of the employer), are fully insured (through the direct payment of premiums to the insurance company by the employer; see paragraphs 4.17–.18), or are certain combinations thereof (for example, self-funded plans with stop-loss coverage; see paragraph 4.20) may not be required to include financial statements in their ERISA filings (see appendix A paragraph A.26). An understanding of the health and welfare benefit plan is needed to determine its accounting and reporting requirements. It is also important to consider the new forms of funding vehicles that are emerging, particularly with respect to postretirement health benefits.

4.09 This chapter describes U.S. GAAP that is particularly important to defined-benefit and defined-contribution health and welfare plans. U.S. GAAP other than those discussed in this chapter may also apply. This chapter does not address the preparation of financial statements on a comprehensive basis of accounting other than U.S. GAAP, however, the financial statements may be prepared on such bases as the cash basis or modified cash basis, as defined by the requirements of financial reporting to the Department of Labor (DOL). If the financial statements are prepared on a comprehensive basis of accounting other than U.S. GAAP, disclosure of the plan's benefit obligation information as described in paragraph 4.23 is required.

4.10 FASB ASC 715, *Compensation—Retirement Benefits*, provides standards of financial accounting and reporting by employers for health and welfare benefits expected to be provided to a participant during retirement. Although FASB ASC 715 does not apply to health and welfare benefit plans, this chapter adopts certain of its measurement concepts (see paragraphs 4.75–.83). Terminology used in discussing postretirement benefits in this chapter is intended to follow usage and definitions provided in FASB ASC 715.

4.11 FASB ASC 712, *Compensation—Nonretirement Postemployment Benefits*, provides standards of financial accounting and reporting by employers for certain postemployment benefits provided to former or inactive employees after employment but before retirement. Benefits provided may include salary continuation, supplemental unemployment benefits, severance, disability-related job training and counseling, and continuation of health care and life insurance. Although FASB ASC 712 does not apply to health and welfare plans, this chapter adopts certain of its measurement concepts (see paragraphs 4.85–.87). Terminology used in discussing postemployment benefits in this chapter is intended to follow usage and definitions provided in FASB ASC 712.

Background

4.12 Plan participants may be active or terminated employees (including retirees), as well as covered dependents and beneficiaries, of a single employer or group of employers. Employer contributions may be voluntary or required under the terms of a collective bargaining agreement negotiated with one or more labor organizations. Plans may require contributions from employers and participants (contributory plans) or from employers only (noncontributory plans). During periods of unemployment, a noncontributory plan may require contributions by participants to maintain their eligibility for benefits. Benefits may be provided through insurance contracts paid for by the plan (an insured plan), from net assets accumulated in a trust established by the plan (a self-funded plan), or both.

4.13 As noted previously and as stated in FASB ASC 965-10-05-5, a plan may establish a trust to hold assets to pay all or part of the covered benefits. The assets may be segregated and legally restricted under a trust arrangement (such as a VEBA or a 501(c)(9) trust, a 401(h) account, or other funding vehicles). Generally, if a separate trust exists, financial statements are required under ERISA. A trust always exists for a multiemployer plan. Such trusteed plans with more than 100 participants generally will require an audit. For ERISA filings, the DOL will not accept an accountant's report that covers the assets of more than one plan. For example, when the assets of more than one plan are held in a 501(c)(9) VEBA trust, separate reports must be prepared for each plan. Some plans may pay only a portion of the plan's benefit payments and other expenses through the VEBA (FASB ASC 965-205-45-10). Plan transactions, including contributions, benefit payments, and expenses whether paid through the VEBA trust or otherwise, should be recorded in a plan's financial statements and subject to audit procedures. Per FASB ASC 965-10-05-6, if the trustee of the VEBA is a bank or trust company, and the trust holds the assets of more than one plan sponsored by a single employer or by a group of companies under common control, it is a master trust subject to the DOL's master trust filing requirements.

4.14 FASB ASC 965-30-25-1 states that a health and welfare plan may process benefit payments directly or it may retain a third-party administrator (see paragraph 4.21). In either case, a plan that is fully or partially self-funded is obligated for the related benefits (see paragraphs 4.67–.89).

4.15 *COBRA.* Many health and welfare plans are required to provide continuation of benefits upon termination of employment through COBRA. In many cases, the collection of COBRA contributions and payment of COBRA benefits are performed by third-party administrators. The administration of these features should be understood so that accounting for all COBRA activity is included in the financial statements of the plan.[1]

Arrangements With Insurance Companies

4.16 According to FASB ASC 965-10-05-7, the nature of, and method of accounting for, the assets and benefit obligations of a health and welfare benefit plan may be determined by the arrangement with the insurance entity. The insurance entity may assume all or a portion of the financial risk (see paragraphs 4.17–.20), or it may provide only administrative services (see paragraph 4.21) or investment management services (see chapter 7). It is important to have an understanding of the insurance arrangement to determine whether any or all of the risks associated with benefit payments or claims have been transferred to the insurance entity. Also, other arrangements are being developed that may involve new types of contracts that involve other parties, including those involving payments to providers, risk sharing of administrative expense with carriers, and so on. Details of these arrangements must also be reviewed carefully.

4.17 In a fully insured, pooled arrangement, specified benefits are covered by the insurance company. The insurance company pools the experience of the plan with that of other similar businesses and assumes the financial risk of adverse experience. In such an arrangement, a plan generally has no obligation for benefits covered by the arrangement other than the payment of premiums due to the insurance company (see paragraph 4.71).

4.18 In a fully insured experience-rated arrangement, specified benefits are paid by the insurance company that assumes all the financial risk. Contract experience is monitored by the insurance company. Contract experience may or may not include the experience of other similar contract holders. To the extent that benefits incurred plus risk charges and administration costs are less than premiums paid, the plan is entitled to an experience-rating refund or dividend (see paragraphs 4.59–.60). If the total of benefits incurred, risk charges, and administrative costs exceeds premiums, the accumulated loss is generally borne by the insurance company but may be carried over to future periods until it has been recovered (see paragraphs 4.72–.73). The plan often has no obligation to continue coverage or to reimburse the carrier for any accumulated loss, although certain types of contracts require additional payments by the plan.

4.19 In a minimum premium plan arrangement, specified benefits are also paid by the insurance company. The insurance contract establishes a dollar limit, or *trigger point*. All claims paid by the insurance company below the trigger point are reimbursed by the plan to the insurance company. The insurance company is not reimbursed for benefits incurred that exceed the trigger point. This type of funding arrangement requires the plan to fund the full claims experience up to the trigger point. Minimum premium plan arrangements may have characteristics of both self-funded and fully insured experience-rated arrangements. Details of each arrangement must be reviewed carefully to determine the specific benefit obligations assumed by the insurance company.

---

[1] The AICPA issued a Technical Question and Answers (TIS) section to provide information on how the effects of the Consolidated Omnibus Budget Reconciliation Act (COBRA) premium subsidy should be reflected when calculating a health and welfare plan's postemployment benefit obligation. See TIS section 6931.12, "Accounting and Disclosure Requirements for Health and Welfare Plans Related to the COBRA Premium Subsidy Included in the American Recovery and Reinvestment Act of 2009" (AICPA, *Technical Practice Aids*), for additional nonauthoritative guidance.

4.20 In a stop-loss insurance arrangement, a plan's obligation for any plan participant's claims may be limited to a fixed dollar amount, or the plan's total obligation may be limited to a maximum percentage (for example, 125 percent) of a preset expected claims level. These arrangements are commonly used with administrative service arrangements. The insurance company assumes the benefit obligation in excess of the limit. Stop-loss insurance arrangements may have characteristics of both self-funded and fully insured arrangements. According to FASB ASC 965-30-35-14, stop-loss arrangements of this type may be described by a variety of terms; therefore, details of all insurance or administrative arrangements should be reviewed carefully to determine if stop-loss provisions are included and to determine the specific benefit obligations assumed by the insurance entity.

4.21 In an administrative service arrangement, the plan retains the full obligation for plan benefits. The plan may engage an insurance company or other third party to act as the plan administrator. The administrator makes all benefit payments, charges the plan for those payments, and collects a fee for the services provided.

Financial Statements of Defined-Benefit Health and Welfare Plans

4.22 FASB ASC 965-205-10-1 states that the objective of financial reporting by defined-benefit health and welfare plans is the same as that of defined-benefit pension plans; both types of plans provide a determinable benefit. Accordingly, the primary objective of the financial statements of a defined-benefit health and welfare plan is to provide financial information that is useful in assessing the plan's present and future ability to pay its benefit obligations when due. To accomplish that objective, a plan's financial statements should provide information about (a) plan resources and the manner in which the stewardship responsibility for those resources has been discharged, (b) benefit obligations, (c) the results of transactions and events that affect the information about those resources and obligations, and (d) other factors necessary for users to understand the information provided.[2]

4.23 In accordance with paragraphs 1–2 of FASB ASC 965-205-45, the financial statements of a defined-benefit health and welfare plan prepared in accordance with U.S. GAAP[3] should be prepared on the accrual basis of accounting[4] and include all of the following:

---

[2] It should be recognized that (a) information in addition to that contained in a plan's financial statements is needed in assessing the plan's present and future ability to pay its benefit obligations when due and (b) financial statements for several plan years may provide more useful information in assessing the plan's future ability to pay benefit obligations than can financial statements for a single year.

[3] Financial statements prepared on a comprehensive basis of accounting other than generally accepted accounting principles should disclose information regarding benefit obligations (see paragraphs 13.20–.23, which discuss auditor's report considerations).

[4] As stated in Financial Accounting Standards Board (FASB) *Accounting Standards Codification* (ASC) 965-320-25-1, the accrual basis of accounting requires that purchases and sales of securities be recorded on a trade-date basis. If the settlement date is after the financial statement date, however, and (a) the fair value of the securities purchased or sold immediately before the financial statement date does not change significantly from the trade date to the financial statement date and (b) the purchases or sales do not significantly affect the composition of the plan's assets available for benefits, accounting on a settlement-date basis for such sales and purchases is acceptable.

- A statement of net assets available for benefits as of the end of the plan year (see paragraphs 4.43–.64)
- A statement of changes in net assets available for benefits for the year then ended (see paragraphs 4.65–.66)
- Information regarding the plan's benefit obligations as of the end of the plan year (see paragraphs 4.67–.87)
- Information regarding the effects, if significant, of certain factors affecting the year-to-year change in the plan's benefit obligations (see paragraphs 4.88–.89)

Information about the benefit obligations should be presented in a separate statement, combined with other information on another financial statement, or presented in the notes to financial statements. Regardless of the format selected, the plan financial statements should present the benefit obligations information in its entirety in the same location. The information should be presented in such reasonable detail as is necessary to identify the nature and classification of the obligations.[5]

4.24 FASB ASC 230, *Statement of Cash Flows*, provides that a statement of cash flows is not required to be provided by a defined benefit pension plan that presents financial information in accordance with the provisions of FASB ASC 960, *Plan Accounting—Defined Benefit Pension Plans*. Other employee benefit plans that present financial information similar to that required by FASB ASC 960 (including the presentation of plan investments at fair value) also are not required to provide a statement of cash flows. However, employee benefit plans are encouraged to include a statement of cash flows with their annual financial statements when that statement would provide relevant information about the ability of the plan to meet future obligations (for example, when the plan invests in assets that are not highly liquid or obtains financing for investments).

Financial Statements of Defined-Contribution Health and Welfare Plans

4.25 According to FASB ASC 965-205-10-2, the objective of financial reporting by a defined-contribution health and welfare plan is to provide financial information that is useful in assessing the plan's present and future ability to pay its benefits. To accomplish that objective, a plan's financial statements should provide information about (*a*) plan resources and the manner in which the stewardship responsibility for those resources has been discharged, (*b*) the results of transactions and events that affect the information about those resources, and (*c*) other factors necessary for users to understand the information provided.[6] For example vacation, holiday, and legal are typical plans whose benefits are limited to the balance in the participant's accounts.

4.26 Per paragraphs 3–4 of FASB ASC 965-205-45, the financial statements of a defined-contribution health and welfare plan prepared in accordance with U.S. GAAP[7] should be prepared on the accrual basis of accounting[8] and include both of the following:

---

[5] Appendix F, "Illustrative Financial Statements: Employee Health and Welfare Benefit Plans," provides illustrative financial statements of four health and welfare benefit plans.

[6] See footnote 2.

[7] See footnote 3.

[8] See footnote 4.

- A statement of net assets available for benefits of the plan as of the end of the plan year (see paragraphs 4.43–.64)

- A statement of changes in net assets available for benefits of the plan for the year then ended (see paragraphs 4.65–.66)

Because a plan's obligation to provide benefits is limited to the amounts accumulated in an individual's account, information regarding benefit obligations is not applicable.

Regulatory Reporting Requirements

4.27 ERISA established annual reporting requirements for employee benefit plans, including health and welfare benefit plans.[9] The financial statements required by ERISA are comparative statements of assets and liabilities and a statement of changes in net assets available for benefits. The schedules required by ERISA include Schedule H, line 4a—Schedule of Delinquent Participant Contributions; Schedule H, line 4i—Schedule of Assets (Held at End of Year) and Schedule of Assets (Acquired and Disposed of Within Year); Schedule H, line 4j—Schedule of Reportable Transactions; Schedule G, Part I—Schedule of Loans or Fixed Income Obligations in Default or Classified as Uncollectible; Schedule G, Part II—Schedule of Leases in Default or Classified as Uncollectible; and Schedule G, Part III, Nonexempt Transactions. The ERISA reporting requirements are described in appendix A. For guidance on how to report delinquent participant contributions, see the frequently asked questions about reporting delinquent participant contributions on the Form 5500 at the Employee Benefits Security Administration website at www.dol.gov/ebsa/faqs/faq_compliance_5500.html.

Fair Value Measurements

4.28 FASB ASC 820, *Fair Value Measurements and Disclosures*, defines fair value, sets out a framework for measuring fair value, and requires certain disclosures about fair value measurements. The following paragraphs summarize FASB ASC 820 but are not intended as a substitute for the reviewing FASB ASC 820 in its entirety.

4.29 Meeting the requirements of FASB ASC 820 requires coordination among plan management, custodians, investment fiduciaries, and plan auditors. Plan sponsors and plan administrators will need to determine whether they have the appropriate valuation processes in place and sufficient data to determine the fair value of the plan's investments using the framework provided and to present the disclosures about the use of fair value measurements required. Although plan management can outsource the mechanics of the valuation process, they need to retain responsibility for the oversight of the final valuations, including determining the adequacy of the related footnote disclosures.

---

[9] The Employee Retirement Income Security Act of 1974 annual reporting requirements, as well as the common exemptions, are described in appendix A, "ERISA and Related Regulations."

Definition of *Fair Value*

4.30 FASB ASC 820-10-20 defines *fair value* as "the price that would be received to sell an asset or paid to transfer a liability in an orderly transaction between market participants at the measurement date."

Valuation Techniques

4.31 Paragraphs 24–35 of FASB ASC 820-10-35 describe the valuation techniques that should be used to measure fair value. This statement does not introduce new valuation techniques but provides a summary of available techniques. Valuation techniques consistent with the market approach, income approach, or cost approach should be used to measure fair value, as follows:

- The market approach uses prices and other relevant information generated by market transactions involving identical or comparable assets or liabilities. Valuation techniques consistent with the market approach include matrix pricing and often use market multiples derived from a set of comparables.

- The income approach uses valuation techniques to convert future amounts (for example, cash flows or earnings) to a single present amount (discounted). The measurement is based on the value indicated by current market expectations about those future amounts. Valuation techniques consistent with the income approach include present value techniques, option-pricing models, and the multiperiod excess earnings method.

- The cost approach is based on the amount that currently would be required to replace the service capacity of an asset (often referred to as current replacement cost). Fair value is determined based on the cost to a market participant (buyer) to acquire or construct a substitute asset of comparable utility, adjusted for obsolescence.

4.32 FASB ASC 820-10-35-24 states that valuation techniques that are appropriate in the circumstances and for which sufficient data are available should be used to measure fair value.

4.33 As explained by paragraphs 25–26 of FASB ASC 820-10-35, valuation techniques used to measure fair value should be consistently applied. However, a change in a valuation technique or its application is appropriate if the change results in a measurement that is equally or more representative of fair value in the circumstances. Such a change would be accounted for as a change in accounting estimate in accordance with the provisions of FASB ASC 250, *Accounting Changes and Error Corrections*.

The Fair Value Hierarchy

4.34 The fair value hierarchy in FASB ASC 820-10-35 prioritizes the inputs to valuation techniques used to measure fair value into three broad levels. The three levels are

- paragraphs 40–41 of FASB ASC 820-10-35 state that level 1 inputs are quoted prices (unadjusted) in active markets for identical assets or liabilities that the reporting entity has the ability to access at the measurement date. An *active market*, as defined by the FASB ASC glossary, is a market in which transactions for the asset or liability occur with sufficient frequency and volume to provide pricing information on an ongoing basis. A quoted price in an active market provides the most reliable evidence of fair value and should be used to measure fair value whenever available, except as discussed in FASB ASC 820-10-35-43. FASB ASC 820-10-35-44 provides guidance on how the quoted price should not be adjusted because of the size of the position relative to trading volume (blockage factor) but rather would be measured within level 1 as the product of the quoted price for the individual instrument times the quantity held.

- paragraphs 47–51 of FASB ASC 820-10-35 explain that level 2 inputs are inputs other than quoted prices included within level 1 that are observable for the asset or liability, either directly or indirectly. If the asset or liability has a specified (contractual) term, a level 2 input must be observable for substantially the full term of the asset or liability. Adjustments to level 2 inputs will vary depending on factors specific to the asset or liability. Those factors include the condition and location of the asset or liability, the extent to which the inputs relate to items that are comparable to the asset or liability, and the volume and level of activity in the markets within which the inputs are observed. An adjustment that is significant to the fair value measurement in its entirety might render the measurement a level 3 measurement, depending on the level in the fair value hierarchy within which the inputs used to determine the adjustment fall. As discussed in paragraph 48 of FASB ASC 820-10-35, level 2 inputs include

  - quoted prices for similar assets or liabilities in active markets.

  - quoted prices for identical or similar assets or liabilities in markets that are not active.

  - inputs other than quoted prices that are observable for the asset or liability (for example, interest rates and yield curves observable at commonly quoted intervals, volatilities, prepayment speeds, loss severities, credit risks, and default rates).

  - inputs that are derived principally from or corroborated by observable market data by correlation or other means (market-corroborated inputs).

- as discussed in paragraphs 52–55 of FASB ASC 820-10-35, level 3 inputs are unobservable inputs for the asset or liability. Unobservable inputs should be used to measure fair value to the extent that relevant observable inputs are not available, thereby allowing for situations in which there is little, if any, market activity for the asset or liability at the measurement date. Unobservable inputs should be developed based on the best information available in the circumstances, which might include the entity's own data. In developing unobservable inputs, the reporting entity need not undertake all possible efforts to obtain information about market participant assumptions. Unobservable inputs should reflect the reporting entity's own assumptions about the assumptions that market participants would use in pricing the asset or liability (including assumptions about risk). Assumptions about risk include the risk inherent in the inputs to the valuation technique. A measurement (for example, a mark-to-model measurement) that does not include an adjustment for risk would not represent a fair value measurement if market participants would include one in pricing the related asset or liability. The reporting entity should not ignore information about market participant assumptions that is reasonably available without undue cost and effort. Therefore, the entity's own data used to develop unobservable inputs should be adjusted if information is readily available without undue cost and effort that indicates that market participants would use different assumptions. "Pending Content" in FASB ASC 820-10-55-22 discusses level 3 inputs for particular assets and liabilities.

As explained in FASB ASC 820-10-35-37, in some cases, the inputs used to measure fair value might fall in different levels of the fair value hierarchy. The level in the fair value hierarchy within which the fair value measurement in its entirety falls should be determined based on the lowest level input that is significant to the fair value measurement in its entirety.

Fair Value Measurements of Investments in Certain Entities That Calculate Net Asset Value per Share (or Its Equivalent)

4.35 Paragraphs 59–62 of FASB ASC 820-10-35 provides additional guidance on the fair value measurements of investments in certain entities that calculate net asset value (NAV) per share (or its equivalent). This guidance permits, as a practical expedient, a reporting entity to estimate the fair value of an investment, that is within the scope of the guidance, using the NAV per share of the investment (or its equivalent) if the NAV is calculated in a manner consistent with the measurement principles of FASB ASC 946, *Financial Services—Investment Companies*, as of the reporting entity's measurement date.[10]

Fair Value Determination When the Volume or Level of Activity Has Significantly Decreased

4.36 Paragraphs 51A–H of FASB ASC 820-10-35 clarifies the application of FASB ASC 820 in determining fair value when the volume and level of activity for the asset or liability has significantly decreased. Guidance is also included in identifying transactions that are not orderly. In addition, select paragraphs of paragraphs 59A–I of FASB ASC 820-10-55 provide illustrations on the application of this guidance.

---

[10] The AICPA issued a series of TISs to provide nonauthoritative guidance that is intended to assist reporting entities with the provisions of FASB ASC 820 (specifically, FASB Accounting Standards Update [ASU] No. 2009-12, *Fair Value Measurements and Disclosures [Topic 820]: Investments in Certain Entities That Calculate Net Asset Value per Share [or Its Equivalent]*), to estimate the fair value of investments in certain entities that calculate net asset value per share. TIS sections 2220.18–.27 (AICPA, *Technical Practice Aids*) apply to investments that are required to be measured and reported at fair value and are within the scope of paragraphs 4–5 of FASB ASC 820-10-15.

Fair Value Disclosures‡

Recurring Measurements[11]

4.37 "Pending Content" in FASB ASC 820-10-50 discusses the disclosures required for assets and liabilities measured at fair value. "Pending Content" in FASB ASC 820-10-50-1 requires the reporting entity to disclose certain information that enables users of its financial statements to assess the valuation techniques and inputs used to develop those measurements. For assets and liabilities that are measured at fair value on a recurring basis in periods subsequent to initial recognition, the disclosures required by FASB ASC 820-10-50 in the tabular format as shown in example 8 (paragraphs 60–63) of "Pending Content" in FASB ASC 820-10-55 should be made. For recurring fair value measurements using significant unobservable inputs (level 3), the reporting entity is required to disclose certain information to help users assess the effect of the measurements on earnings (or changes in net assets) for the period.

4.38 "Pending Content" in FASB ASC 820-10-50-2 requires the following disclosures to be made for each class of assets and liabilities. The reporting entity should provide sufficient information to permit reconciliation of the fair value measurement disclosures for the various classes of assets and liabilities to the line items in the net assets available for benefits.[12]

   a. The fair value measurement at the reporting date.

   b. The level within the fair value hierarchy in which the fair value measurement in its entirety falls, segregating the fair value measurement using any of the following:

      i. Quoted prices in active markets for identical assets or liabilities (level 1).

      ii. Significant other observable inputs (level 2).

      iii. Significant unobservable inputs (level 3).

   c. The amounts of significant transfers between level 1 and level 2 of the fair value hierarchy and the reasons for the transfers. Significant transfers into each level should be disclosed separately from transfers out of each level. A reporting entity should disclose and consistently follow its policy for determining when transfers between levels are recognized.

   d. For fair value measurements using significant unobservable inputs (level 3), a reconciliation of the beginning and ending balances, separately presenting changes during the period attributable to any of the following:

---

‡ In January 2010, FASB issued ASU No. 2010-06, *Fair Value Measurements and Disclosures (Topic 820): Improving Disclosures about Fair Value Measurements.* FASB ASU No. 2010-06, among other things, changes the requirement to show purchases, sales, issuances, and settlements on a net basis to require separate disclosure for each type. The separate disclosure requirement of purchases, sales, issuances, and settlements activity are effective for fiscal years beginning after December 15, 2010, and for interim periods within those fiscal years. Examples related to the guidance in this ASU are included in FASB ASC 820-10-55. Readers are encouraged to review the ASU in its entirety.

[11] "Pending Content" in FASB ASC 820-10-50-5 provides the required disclosures for nonrecurring measurements.

[12] For derivative assets and liabilities, the disclosures listed in paragraph 4.38(*a*)–(*c*) should be made on a gross basis. The disclosures listed in paragraph 4.38(*d*)–(*e*) should be made on either a gross or net basis. See footnote ‡ for further guidance on paragraph 4.38(*d*)(ii).

      i. Total gains and losses for the period (realized and unrealized), separately presenting gains or losses included in earnings (or changes in net assets) and gains or losses recognized in other comprehensive income, and a description of where those gains or losses included in earnings (or changes in net assets) are reported in the statement of income (or activities) or in other comprehensive income.

      ii. Purchases, sales, issuances, and settlements.[‡]

      iii. Transfers in/out of level 3 and the reasons for those transfers. Significant transfers into level 3 should be disclosed separately from significant transfers out of level 3. A reporting entity should disclose and consistently follow its policy for determining when transfers between levels are recognized. The policy about the timing of recognizing transfers should be the same for transfers into level 3 as that for transfers out of level 3.

    e. The amount of the total gains and losses.

    f. For fair value measurements using significant other observable inputs (level 2) and significant unobservable inputs (level 3), a description of the valuation technique (or multiple valuation techniques) used, and the inputs used in determining the fair values of each class of assets or liabilities. If there has been a change in the valuation technique(s), the reporting entity should disclose that change and the reason for making it.

4.39 "Pending Content" in FASB ASC 820-10-50-2A states that for equity and debt securities, class should be determined on the basis of the nature and risks of the investments in a manner consistent with the guidance in FASB ASC 320-10-50-1B even if the equity securities or debt securities are not within the scope of FASB ASC 320-10-50-1B. Major security types are based on the nature and risks of the security. In determining whether disclosure for a particular security type is necessary and whether it is necessary to further separate a particular security type into greater detail, all of the following should be considered:

    a. The activity or business sector

    b. Vintage

    c. Geographic concentration

    d. Credit quality

    e. Economic characteristic

For all other assets and liabilities, judgment is needed to determine the appropriate classes of assets and liabilities for which disclosures about fair value measurements should be provided.

4.40 Fair value measurement disclosures for each class of assets and liabilities often will require greater disaggregation than the reporting entity's line items in the statement of financial position. A reporting entity should determine the appropriate classes for those disclosures on the basis of the nature and risks of the assets and liabilities and their classification in the fair value hierarchy (that is, levels 1, 2, and 3). In determining the appropriate classes for fair value measurement disclosures, the reporting entity should consider the

---

‡ See footnote ‡ in the heading above paragraph 4.37.

level of disaggregated information required for specific assets and liabilities under other FASB ASC topics. For example, under FASB ASC 815, *Derivatives and Hedging*, disclosures about derivative instruments are presented separately by type of contract such as interest rate contracts, foreign exchange contracts, equity contracts, commodity contracts, and credit contracts. (Also see paragraph 4.93.) The classification of the asset or liability in the fair value hierarchy also should affect the level of disaggregation because of the different degrees of uncertainty and subjectivity involved in level 1, level 2, and level 3 measurements. For example, the number of classes may need to be greater for fair value measurements using significant unobservable inputs (that is, level 3 measurements) to achieve the disclosure objectives because level 3 measurements have a greater degree of uncertainty and subjectivity.

Fair Value Measurements of Investments in Certain Entities That Calculate NAV per Share (or Its Equivalent)

4.41 "Pending Content" in FASB ASC 820-10-50-6A requires disclosures for each class of investment about the attributes of investments within the scope of paragraphs 4–5 of FASB ASC 820-10-15, such as the nature of any restrictions on the investor's ability to redeem its investments at the measurement date, any unfunded commitments, and the investment strategies of the investees. These disclosures are required for all investments within the scope of paragraphs 4–5 of FASB ASC 820-10-15 regardless of whether the practical expedient in FASB ASC 820-10-35-59 is applied.

Fair Value Option

4.42 For assets and liabilities not currently required to be reported at fair value, FASB ASC 825, *Financial Instruments*, creates a fair value option under which an entity may irrevocably elect fair value as the initial and subsequent measure for many financial instruments and certain other items, with changes in fair value recognized in the statement of activities as those changes occur. An election is made on an instrument-by-instrument basis (with certain exceptions), generally when an instrument is initially recognized in the financial statements. Most financial assets and financial liabilities are eligible to be recognized using the fair value option, as are firm commitments for financial instruments and certain nonfinancial contracts. See FASB ASC 825 for further guidance, including presentation and disclosure requirements.

Net Assets Available for Benefits

Investments

4.43 According to FASB ASC 965-325-35-1, plan investments, whether they are in the form of equity or debt securities, real estate, or other investments (excluding insurance contracts and fully benefit-responsive investment contracts held by defined-contribution health and welfare plans), should be reported at their fair value at the financial statement date.[13] Fair value of plan

---

[13] The accrual basis of accounting requires that purchases and sales of securities be recorded on a trade-date basis. However, if the settlement date is later than the financial statement date and (*a*) the fair value of the securities purchased or sold just before the financial statement date does not change significantly from the trade date to the financial statement date and (*b*) the purchases or sales do not significantly affect the composition of the plan's assets available for benefits, accounting on a settlement-date basis for such sales and purchases is acceptable (FASB ASC 965-320-25-1).

investments is the price that would be received to sell an asset or paid to transfer a liability in an orderly transaction between market participants at the measurement date. See paragraphs 4.28–.41 for guidance on how to determine fair value when an active market is not available.

Insurance Contracts

4.44 FASB ASC 965-325-35-3 states that *insurance contracts*, as defined by FASB ASC 944-20, should be presented in the same manner as specified in the annual report filed by the plan with certain governmental agencies pursuant to ERISA; that is, either at fair value or at amounts determined by the insurance enterprise (contract value). Plans not subject to ERISA should present insurance contracts as if the plans were subject to the reporting requirements of ERISA.[14]

Investment Contracts

4.45 Investment contracts held by defined-benefit health and welfare benefit plans should be reported at their fair values in accordance with FASB ASC 965-325-35-2.

4.46 FASB ASC 965-325-05-2 states that defined-contribution health and welfare benefit plans provide benefits based on the amounts contributed to employees' individual accounts plus or minus forfeitures, investment experience, and administrative expenses. In such plans, plan participants have a vested interest in monitoring the financial condition and operations of the plan because they bear investment risk under these plans, and plan transactions can directly affect their benefits (for example, investment mix, and risk and return) according to FASB ASC 965-325-05-3.

Accounting for Fully Benefit-Responsive Investment Contracts

4.47 Net assets available for benefits of defined-contribution health and welfare benefit plans should be measured and reported at values that are meaningful to financial statement users including plan participants. The contract value of a *fully benefit-responsive* investment contract held by a defined-contribution health and welfare benefit plan is the amount a participant would receive if he or she were to initiate transactions under the terms of the ongoing plan.

4.48 Defined-contribution health and welfare benefit plans should report all investments (including derivative contracts) at fair value. However, FASB ASC 965-325-35-8 states that contract value is the relevant measurement attribute for that portion of the net assets available for benefits of a defined-contribution health and welfare benefit plan attributable to fully benefit-responsive investment contracts. FASB ASC 965-20-45-1 states that the statement of net assets available for benefits of the plan should present amounts for (*a*) total assets, (*b*) total liabilities, (*c*) net assets reflecting all investments at fair value, and (*d*) net assets available for benefits. In accordance with FASB ASC 965-20-45-2, the amount representing the difference between (*c*) and (*d*) should be presented on the face of the statement of net assets available for benefits as a single amount. This amount is calculated as the sum of

---

[14] The AICPA issued TIS section 6930.02, "Defined Benefit Plan Measurement of a Life Insurance Policy" (AICPA, *Technical Practice Aids*), to provide guidance on how to value life insurance policies.

the amounts necessary to adjust the portion of net assets attributable to each fully benefit-responsive investment contract from fair value to contract value. In addition, FASB ASC 965-20-45-5 states that the statement of changes in net assets available for benefits should be prepared on a basis that reflects income credited to participants in the plan and net appreciation or depreciation in the fair value of only those investment contracts that are not deemed to be fully benefit responsive.

4.49 In accordance with the FASB ASC glossary, an investment contract is considered fully benefit-responsive, if all of the following criteria are met for that contract, analyzed on an individual basis:

a. The investment contract is effected directly between the plan and the issuer and prohibits the plan from assigning or selling the contract or its proceeds to another party without the consent of the issuer.

b. Either (1) the repayment of principal and interest credited to participants in the plan is a financial obligation of the issuer of the investment contract or (2) prospective interest crediting rate adjustments are provided to participants in the plan on a designated pool of investments held by the plan or the contract issuer, whereby a financially responsible third party, through a contract generally referred to as a wrapper, must provide assurance that the adjustments to the interest crediting rate will not result in a future interest crediting rate that is less than zero. If an event has occurred such that realization of full contract value for a particular investment contract is no longer probable (for example, a significant decline in creditworthiness of the contract issuer or wrapper provider), the investment contract should no longer be considered fully benefit responsive.

c. The terms of the investment contract require all permitted participant-initiated transactions with the plan to occur at contract value with no conditions, limits, or restrictions. Permitted participant-initiated transactions are those transactions allowed by the plan, such as withdrawals for benefits, loans, or transfers to other funds within the plan.

d. An event that limits the ability of the plan to transact at contract value with the issuer (for example, premature termination of the contracts by the plan, plant closings, layoffs, plan termination, bankruptcy, mergers, and early retirement incentives) and that also limits the ability of the plan to transact at contract value with the participants in the plan must be probable of not occurring.

e. The plan itself must allow participants reasonable access to their funds.

4.50 If access to funds is substantially restricted by plan provisions, investment contracts held by those plans may not be considered to be fully benefit-responsive. For example, if plan participants are allowed access at contract value to all or a portion of their account balances only upon termination of their participation in the plan, it would not be considered reasonable access and, therefore, investment contracts held by that plan would generally not be deemed to be fully benefit-responsive. However, in plans with a single investment fund that allow reasonable access to assets by inactive participants, restrictions on access to assets by active participants consistent with the objective of the plan (for example, retirement or health and welfare benefits) will not affect the benefit responsiveness of the investment contracts held by those single-fund plans. Also, if a plan limits participants' access to their account balances to certain specified times during the plan year (for example, semiannually or quarterly) to control the administrative costs of the plan, that limitation generally would not affect the benefit responsiveness of the investment contracts held by that plan. In addition, administrative provisions that place short-term restrictions (for example, three or six months) on transfers to competing fixed-rate investment options to limit arbitrage among those investment options (*equity wash* provisions) would not affect a contract's benefit responsiveness.

4.51 Per FASB ASC 965-325-35-6, if a plan holds multiple contracts, each contract should be evaluated individually for benefit responsiveness. If a plan invests in pooled funds that hold investment contracts, each contract in the pooled fund should be evaluated individually for benefit responsiveness. However, if the pooled fund places any restrictions on access to funds for the payment of benefits, the underlying investment contracts would not be considered fully benefit-responsive. Contracts that provide for prospective interest adjustments may still be fully benefit-responsive provided that the terms of the contracts specify that the crediting interest rate cannot be less than zero.

Presentation of Plan Investments

4.52 In accordance with FASB ASC 965-325-45-1, information regarding a plan's investments should be presented in enough detail to identify the types of investments and should indicate whether reported fair values have been measured by quoted prices in an active market or have been determined otherwise (paragraph 4.91 specifies additional disclosures related to investments).

Securities Lending

4.53 Securities custodians commonly carry out securities lending activities on behalf of their employee benefit plan clients. The borrowers of securities generally are required to provide collateral to the lender (the plan). This collateral is typically cash but sometimes it may be other securities or standby letters of credit, with a value slightly higher than that of the securities borrowed. If the collateral is cash, the lender typically earns a return by investing that cash at rates higher than the rate paid or "rebated" to the borrower. If the collateral is other than cash, the lender typically receives a fee. FASB ASC 860, *Transfers and Servicing*, provides accounting and reporting guidance for transfers of financial assets, including accounting for securities lending activities. FASB ASC 860 addresses

- whether the transaction is a sale of the loaned securities for financial reporting purposes.
- if the transaction is not a sale, how the lender should report the loaned securities.
- whether and how the lender should report the collateral.
- how the lender should record income earned as a result of securities lending transactions.

4.54 If the securities lending transaction includes an agreement that entitles and obligates the plan (the transferor) to repurchase the transferred securities under which the plan maintains effective control over those securities, then the plan must account for those transactions as secured borrowings (not sales) and continue to report the securities on the statement of net assets. Typically in a securities lending arrangement the transferee has the right by custom or contract to sell or repledge the security loaned. In these instances the securities loaned should be reclassified and reported by the plan (the transferor) separately from other assets not so encumbered (for example, as security pledged to creditors) pursuant to FASB ASC 860-30-25-5. Alternatively, if the transferee does not have the right by custom or contract to sell or repledge the security loaned, the plan should disclose in the notes to the financial statements the carrying amount and classification of any assets pledged as collateral, associated liabilities and qualitative information about the relationship between those assets, and associated liabilities as of the date of the latest statement of net assets presented pursuant to "Pending Content" in FASB ASC 860-30-50-1A. The plan should record the cash collateral received as an asset—and any investments made with that cash, even if made by agents or in pools with other securities lenders—along with the obligation to return the cash (considered the amount borrowed).

4.55 Generally, if the plan receives securities (instead of cash) that may be sold or repledged, the plan accounts for those securities in the same way as it would account for cash received, that is, the plan recognizes in the statement of net assets the securities received as collateral and the obligation to return that collateral. However, pursuant to "Pending Content" in FASB ASC 860-30-50-1A, the plan must also disclose the fair value as of the date of each statement of net assets presented of that collateral and of the portion of that collateral that it has sold or repledged, and information about the sources and uses of that collateral. Because FASB ASC 860-30-25-5 requires that only the lender recognize securities collateral received in its statement of net assets, it is important to accurately identify the lender and borrower in securities lending transactions. One indicator that the plan is the lender is that the collateral received by the lender generally has a value slightly higher (for example, 2 percent) than that of the securities being borrowed.

4.56 The plan must disclose its policy for requiring collateral or other security in accordance "Pending Content" in FASB ASC 860-30-50-1A.

4.57 The interest income earned and rebate interest paid as a result of securities lending activity should be recorded on the statement of changes in net assets available for benefits.

Contributions Receivable

4.58 According to the FASB ASC glossary, *contributions receivable* are the amounts due, as of the date of the financial statements, to the plan from employers, participants, and other sources of funding (for example, state subsidies or federal grants). Contributions receivable include amounts due pursuant to firm commitments, as well as legal or contractual requirements (for example, collective bargaining agreements). Per FASB ASC 965-310-25-1, with respect to employers' contributions, evidence of a formal commitment may include (*a*) a resolution by the employer's governing body approving a specified contribution; (*b*) a consistent pattern of making payments after the end of the plan year, pursuant to an established funding policy that attributes such subsequent payments to the preceding plan year; (*c*) a deduction of a contribution for federal income tax purposes for periods ending on or before the financial statement date; or (*d*) the employer's recognition as of the financial statement date of a contribution payable to the plan.[15] According to FASB ASC 965-310-35-1, contributions receivable should include an allowance for estimated uncollectible amounts.

Deposits With and Receivables From Insurance Companies and Other Service Providers

4.59 According to paragraphs 2–3 of FASB ASC 965-310-25, whether a premium paid to an insurance entity represents payment for the transfer of risk or merely represents a deposit will depend on the circumstances of the arrangement. The nature of payments made to an insurance entity should be analyzed to determine the extent to which financial risk has been transferred from the plan to the insurance entity. Insurance entities may require that a deposit be maintained that can be applied against possible future losses in excess of current premiums. These deposits should be reported as plan assets until such amounts are used to pay premiums. Similarly, premium stabilization reserves, which exist when premiums paid to an insurance entity exceed the total of claims paid and other charges, are held by an insurance entity and used to reduce future premium payments. Premium stabilization reserves generally should be reported as assets of the plan until such amounts are used to pay premiums. Disclosure of the nature of this type of deposit or reserve should be made in accordance with FASB ASC 965-310-50-1. If such reserves are forfeitable when the insurance contract terminates, this possibility should be considered in recognizing this asset.

4.60 Certain group insurance contracts covering health and welfare benefit plans include a provision for a refund, at the end of the policy year, of the excess of premiums paid over the total of paid claims, required reserves, and the fee charged by the insurance entity. Often such experience-rating refunds (or dividends) are not determined by the insurance entity for several months after the end of the policy year (FASB ASC 965-10-05-8). In this event, and in cases when the policy year does not coincide with the plan's fiscal year, the refund due as of the financial statement date should be reported as a plan asset if it is probable that a refund is due and the amount can be reasonably estimated (FASB ASC 965-310-25-3). If the amount of the refund cannot be reasonably estimated, that fact should be disclosed (FASB ASC 965-310-50-2).

4.61 According to FASB ASC 965-310-40-1, service providers may require that deposits by the plan be applied against claims paid on behalf of plan participants. Such deposits should be reported as plan assets until the deposit is applied against paid claims.

Operating Assets

4.62 Plan assets used in plan operations (for example, buildings, equipment, furniture and fixtures, and leasehold improvements) should be reported at cost less accumulated depreciation or amortization (FASB ASC 965-360-35-1).

---

[15] Per item (*d*) of FASB ASC 965-310-25-1 the existence of an accrued liability in the employer's statement of financial position or a plan's benefit obligations exceeding its net assets available for benefit obligations does not, by itself, provide sufficient support for recognition of a contribution receivable by the plan.

4.63 FASB ASC 360, *Property, Plant, and Equipment*, addresses accounting for the impairment of long-lived assets for assets to be held and used and assets to be disposed of. FASB ASC 360-10-35-21 requires that long-lived assets to be held and used by the plan, such as real estate owned by the plan for plan operations, be tested for recoverability whenever events or changes in circumstances indicate that the carrying amount may not be recoverable. Long-lived assets to be abandoned or exchanged for a similar productive asset should be considered held and used until disposed of. FASB ASC 360-10-35-43 states that long-lived assets classified as held for sale should be measured at the lower of its carrying amount or fair value less cost to sell. A long-lived asset should not be depreciated while it is held for sale. See FASB ASC 360 for further accounting and disclosure requirements.[16]

Accrued Liabilities

4.64 Per FASB ASC 965-20-25-1, a plan may have liabilities (other than for benefits) that should be accrued. Such liabilities may be for amounts owed for securities purchased, income taxes payable by the plan, or other expenses (for example, third-party administrator fees). These liabilities should be deducted to arrive at net assets available for benefits.

Changes in Net Assets Available for Benefits

4.65 Unless otherwise noted, according to paragraphs 3–4 of FASB ASC 965-20-45, the statement of changes in net assets available for benefits should be presented in enough detail to identify the significant changes during the year including, as applicable

   a. contributions from employers, segregated between cash and noncash contributions. A noncash contribution should be reported at fair value at the date of the contribution (FASB ASC 965-20-30-1).

   b. the nature of noncash contributions described either parenthetically or in a note.

   c. contributions from participants, including those collected and remitted by the sponsor.

   d. contributions from other identified sources (for example, state subsidies or federal grants).

   e. the net appreciation or depreciation[17] in fair value for each significant class of investments, segregated between investments whose fair values have been measured by quoted prices in an active market and those whose fair values have been otherwise determined.

   f. investment income, excluding the net appreciation or depreciation.

   g. income taxes paid or payable, if applicable.

   h. payments of claims, excluding payments made by an insurance entity pursuant to contracts that are excluded from plan assets.

---

[16] See also TIS section 6931.03, "Should the Sale of Real Estate Investments Held by Employee Benefit Plans Be Treated as Discontinued Operations?" (AICPA, *Technical Practice Aids*).

[17] Net appreciation or depreciation includes realized gains and losses on investments that were both purchased and sold during the period. Ordinarily, information regarding the net appreciation or depreciation in the fair value of investments is found in the notes to the financial statements.

    i. payments of premiums to insurance entities to purchase contracts that are excluded from plan assets.[18]

    j. operating and administrative expenses. (See DOL Advisory Opinion No. 2001-01A for guidance on reasonable expenses of administering the plan.)

    k. other changes (such as transfers of assets to or from other plans), if significant.

4.66 The list of minimum disclosures is not intended to define the degree of detail or the manner of presenting the information, and subclassifications or additional classifications may be useful.

Benefit Obligations

4.67 According to paragraphs 1–5 of FASB ASC 965-30-35, benefit obligations[19] for single-employer, multiple-employer, and multiemployer defined-benefit health and welfare benefit plans should include the actuarial present value, as applicable, for all of the following:

- Claims payable, claims incurred but not reported (IBNR),[20] and premiums due to insurance entities

- Accumulated eligibility credits and postemployment benefits, net of amounts currently payable

- Postretirement benefits for the following groups of participants:[21]

  — Retired plan participants, including their beneficiaries and covered dependents, net of amounts currently payable and claims IBNR[22]

  — Other plan participants fully eligible for benefits

  — Plan participants not yet fully eligible for benefits

Aggregating claims payable and claims IBNR is often appropriate if adequate time has passed to provide sufficient data on costs incurred and the actuarially determined expected cost of long-term medical claims is insignificant. Benefits expected to be earned for future service by active participants (for example, vacation benefits) during the term of their employment should not be included. Benefit obligations should be reported as of the end of the plan year.[23] In

---

[18] Refer to paragraphs 7.36–.37 for further discussion of allocated insurance contracts.

[19] Administrative expenses expected to be paid by the plan (but not those paid directly by the plan's participating employer[s]) that are associated with providing the plan's benefits should be reflected either by including the estimated costs in the benefits expected to be paid by the plan or by reducing the discount rate(s) used in measuring the benefit obligation. If the latter method is used, the resulting reduction in the discount rate(s) should be disclosed.

[20] Per FASB ASC 965-30-35-1, claims incurred but not reported (IBNR) may be computed in the aggregate for active participants and retirees. Alternatively, if claims IBNR are not calculated in the aggregate for active participants and retirees, the claims IBNR for retirees are included in the postretirement benefit obligation.

[21] See footnote 20.

[22] See footnote 20.

[23] The financial status of the plan considers assets and obligations as of the same date. Because plan assets are required to be presented as of the plan's year end, the benefit obligations also should be measured and presented as of the plan's year end. That requirement does not, however, preclude the plan from using the most recent benefit obligations valuation rolled forward to the plan's year end

(continued)

addition, FASB ASC 965-30-35-7 states that the effect of plan amendments should be included in the computation of the expected and accumulated postretirement benefit obligations once they have been contractually agreed to, even if some provisions take effect only in future periods. For example, if a plan amendment grants a different benefit level for employees retiring after a future date, that increased or reduced benefit level should be included in current-period measurements for employees expected to retire after that date.

4.68 Per FASB ASC 965-30-45-1, to the extent they exist, the amounts of benefit obligations in each of the three major classifications identified previously should be shown as separate line items in the financial statements or notes to financial statements. Regardless of the format selected, the plan financial statements should present the benefit obligations information in its entirety in the same location. For negotiated plans, benefit obligations due during a plan's contract period may, but need not, be disclosed.

Claims

4.69 According to paragraph 2–3 of FASB ASC 965-30-45, in an insured health and welfare benefit plan, claims payable and currently due and claims incurred but not yet reported to the plan will be paid by the insurance entity. Consequently, they should be excluded from the benefit obligations of the plan. Benefit obligations of a self-funded plan should present the amount of claims payable and currently due for active and retired participants, dependents, and beneficiaries and IBNR claims for active participants. IBNR claims for retired participants is included in the postretirement benefit obligation.[24]

4.70 For a self-funded plan, the cost of IBNR should be measured at the present value, as applicable, of the estimated ultimate cost to the plan of settling the claims. Estimated ultimate cost should reflect the plan's obligation to pay claims to or for participants, regardless of status of employment, beyond the financial statement date pursuant to the provisions of the plan or regulatory requirements. For example, an individual contracts a terminal disease or has a catastrophic accident in December. The claim is reported to the plan subsequent to year-end. Treatment is ongoing and is expected to continue throughout the next year. The plan does not require any return to work and will fully cover all services. The actuarial present value of the obligation for all future payments to be made as of the plan year end should be included as a benefit obligation in IBNR.

Premiums Due Under Insurance Arrangements

4.71 Benefits to participants may be provided through insurance arrangements that transfer the risks of loss or liability to an insurance company (see paragraphs 4.16–.21). Group insurance contracts for health and welfare plans

---

(footnote continued)

to account for subsequent events (such as employee service and benefit payments), provided that it is reasonable to expect that the results will not be materially different from the results of an actuarial valuation as of the plan's year end. In rolling forward the benefit obligations to the plan's measurement date, the discount rates should be adjusted as appropriate to reflect current rates of return on high-quality fixed-income investments. For example, if a valuation was performed at September 30 and the plan has a calendar year end, the benefit obligations as of September 30 should be rolled forward to December 31, by making appropriate adjustments, such as for additional employee service; the time value of money; benefits paid; and changes in the number of participants, actuarial assumptions, discount rates, per capita claims costs, and plan terms.

[24] See footnote 20.

are usually written for a one-year period, although the contract may provide for annual renewal. The contract generally specifies, among other things, the schedule of benefits, eligibility rules, premium rate per eligible participant, and the date that premiums are due. Per FASB ASC 965-30-25-2, the benefit obligations should include any obligation for premiums due but not paid.

4.72 According to FASB ASC 965-30-35-13, if the insurance contract requires payment of additional premiums (for example, retrospective premiums) when the loss ratio exceeds a specified percentage, an obligation for the estimated additional premiums should be included in the benefit obligations.

4.73 Also, according to FASB ASC 965-30-25-5, experience ratings determined by the insurance entity or by estimates (see paragraph 4.18) may result in a premium deficit. Premium deficits should be included in the benefit obligations if (a) it is probable that the deficit will be applied against the amounts of future premiums or future experience-rating refunds[25] and (b) the amount can be reasonably estimated. Per FASB ASC 965-30-50-4, if no obligation is included for a premium deficit because either or both of the conditions are not met, or if an exposure to loss exists in excess of the amount accrued, disclosure of the premium deficit should be made if it is reasonably possible that a loss or an additional loss has been incurred.

Accumulated Eligibility Credits

4.74 As stated in FASB ASC 965-30-35-12, plans may provide for the payment of insurance premiums or benefits for a period of time for those participants who have accumulated a sufficient number of eligibility credits or hours (that is, bank of hours). Eligible participants are provided with insurance coverage during periods of unemployment, when employer contributions to the plan would not otherwise provide coverage or benefits. At the financial statement date, such accumulated eligibility credits represent an obligation of the plan arising from prior employee service for which employer contributions have been received. This benefit obligation is generally determined by applying current insurance premium rates to accumulated eligibility credits or, for a self-funded plan, by applying the average cost of benefits per eligible participant to accumulated eligibility credits. In either case, the obligation for accumulated eligibility credits should consider assumptions for mortality and expected employee turnover or other appropriate adjustments, to reflect the obligation at the amount expected to be paid.

Postretirement Benefit Obligations

4.75 Paragraphs 15–22 of FASB ASC 965-30-35 state that health and welfare benefit plans may continue to provide benefits to participants after retirement (postretirement benefits). Those benefits may commence immediately upon termination of service or payment may be deferred until the participant attains a specified age. If a plan provides postretirement benefits to participants, an estimated amount for those benefits, as described subsequently should be included in the benefit obligations.

4.76 The postretirement benefit obligation as of the measurement date is the actuarial present value of all future benefits attributed to plan participants'

---

[25] This determination should consider (a) the extent to which the insurance contract requires payment of such deficits and (b) the plan's intention, if any, to transfer coverage to another insurance company.

services rendered to that date, assuming the plan continues in effect and all assumptions about future events are fulfilled. Postretirement benefits comprise benefits expected to be paid to or on behalf of any retired or active participant, terminated participant, beneficiary, or covered dependent who is expected to receive benefits under the health and welfare benefit plan. Postretirement benefits expected to be paid to or for an active participant, beneficiary, or covered dependent who is still earning his or her postretirement benefits (that is, one who is not yet fully eligible) should be measured over the participant's credited period of service up to the date when full eligibility for benefits is attained.[26]

4.77 If a multiemployer health and welfare benefit plan provides postretirement benefits, the benefit obligations should include the postretirement benefit obligation. Consideration should be given to the promises currently made to employees and the history of making such payments to retirees. The fact that benefits may be reduced or even potentially eliminated would not ordinarily affect the promise made as of the end of the plan year unless the change meets the substantive plan criteria of FASB ASC 715 (for example, an amendment is in place or has been communicated to employees). The fact that the contributing employers of a multiemployer plan do not record a similar obligation under FASB ASC 715 does not affect the accounting for the obligations by the plan.

4.78 The postretirement benefit obligation should be measured using the plan's written provisions to the extent possible, as well as the substantive plan if it differs from the written plan. In many health and welfare benefit plans, postretirement benefits are not defined as a specified amount for each year of service. FASB ASC 715-60-35 describes the measurement of the postretirement benefit obligation. For multiemployer plans that do not have date-of-hire information as required by FASB ASC 715-60-35-66, reasonable estimates thereof should be used to measure the obligation. Death or disability benefits provided outside of a pension plan (when the employee is considered to be retired) should also be included in the calculation of the postretirement benefit obligation. Benefits that are provided through an insurance contract should be excluded.[27]

4.79 In measuring the postretirement benefit obligation explicit assumptions should be used, each of which represents the best estimate of a particular future event. All assumptions should presume that the plan will continue in its present form, unless there is evidence to the contrary. Principal actuarial assumptions used should include all of the following:

- Discount rates, used to reflect the time value of money in determining the present value of future cash outflows currently expected to be required to satisfy the liability in the due course of business
- The timing and amount of future postretirement benefit payments (taking into consideration per capita claims cost by age, health care cost-trend rates, current Medicare reimbursement rates, retirement age, dependency status, and mortality)

---

[26] Per FASB ASC 965-30-35-18, for example, if a participant has worked 8 years and must work another 16 to be fully eligible for benefits after retirement, one-third of the postretirement benefits have been earned and should be included in the postretirement benefit obligation if it is probable that the employee will work the remaining 16 years.

[27] Per FASB ASC 965-30-35-20, insured plans should be reviewed carefully to determine the extent to which postretirement benefits are insured. Currently, except for single-premium life insurance contracts, few, if any, insurance contracts unconditionally obligate an insurance company to provide most forms of postretirement benefits.

- Salary progression (for pay-related plans)

- The probability of payment (considering turnover, retirement age, dependency status, and mortality)

- Participation rates (for contributory plans)

4.80 The postretirement benefit obligation information should include the following classifications:

- Obligations related to retired plan participants, including their beneficiaries and covered dependents

- Obligations related to active or terminated participants who are fully eligible to receive benefits

- Obligations related to other plan participants not yet fully eligible for benefits

Per FASB ASC 965-30-50-1, separate disclosure for each classification for each significant benefit (for example, medical and death) may be appropriate.

4.81 Certain retiree health benefits may be funded through a 401(h) account in a defined benefit pension plan, pursuant to Section 401(h) of the Internal Revenue Code (IRC). Refer to paragraphs 2.52–.59 of this guide for a detailed discussion of 401(h) accounts. According to FASB ASC 965-205-45-6, the 401(h) account assets and liabilities used to fund retiree health benefits, and the changes in those assets and liabilities, should be reported in the financial statements of the health and welfare benefit plan. Per paragraphs 7–8 of FASB ASC 965-205-45, the 401(h) account assets and liabilities and changes in them can be shown in the health and welfare benefit plan financial statements in one of two ways. An entity can present that information either as a single line item on the face of the statements or included in individual line items with separate disclosure in the footnotes about the 401(h) amounts included in those individual line items. If the assets and liabilities are shown as a single line item in the statement of net assets, the changes in net assets also should be shown as a single line item in the statement of changes in net assets. If the assets and liabilities are included in individual asset and liability line items in the statement of net assets, the changes in individual 401(h) amounts should be included in the changes in the individual line items in the statement of changes in net assets, with separate disclosure in the footnotes about the 401(h) amounts included in those individual line items. The notes to the financial statements should disclose the significant components of net assets and changes in net assets of the 401(h) account in accordance with FASB ASC 965-205-50-2. The 401(h) obligations are reported in the health and welfare benefit plan's statement of benefit obligations. Likewise, the health and welfare benefit plan's statement of changes in benefit obligations should include claims paid through the 401(h) account.

4.82 Per FASB ASC 965-205-50-3, if retiree health benefit obligations are funded partially through a 401(h) account of the defined benefit pension plan, the plan should also disclose the fact that the assets are available only to pay retiree health benefits. The notes to the financial statements should disclose the significant components of net assets and changes in net assets of the 401(h) account. Additionally, the notes should include a reconciliation of amounts reported in the financial statements to the amounts reported in the Form 5500 (see paragraph 12.40).

4.83 Per FASB ASC 965-205-50-4, because ERISA requires 401(h) accounts to be reported as assets of the pension plan, a reconciliation of the net assets reported in the financial statements to those reported in Form 5500 is required for the health and welfare benefit plan. Additionally, any assets held for investment purposes in the 401(h) account should be shown on Schedule H, line 4i—Schedule of Assets (Held at End of Year) and Schedule H, line 4j—Schedule of Reportable Transactions for the pension plan.

Medicare Prescription Drug, Improvement and Modernization Act of 2003

4.84 FASB ASC 715 addresses when and how an employer that provides postretirement prescription drug coverage should recognize the effects of the Medicare Prescription Drug, Improvement and Modernization Act of 2003 but does not address the accounting for the subsidy by the health and welfare plan itself. Two Technical Questions and Answers (TIS) address the accounting and disclosures for single employer and multiemployer employee benefit plans related to the Medicare Prescription Drug, Improvement and Modernization Act of 2003.

- TIS section 6931.05, "Accounting and Disclosure Requirements for Single-Employer Employee Benefit Plans Related to the Medicare Prescription Drug, Improvement and Modernization Act of 2003" (AICPA, *Technical Practice Aids*)
- TIS section 6931.06, "Accounting and Disclosure Requirements for Multiemployer Employee Benefit Plans Related to the Medicare Prescription Drug, Improvement and Modernization Act of 2003" (AICPA, *Technical Practice Aids*)

The TIS sections can be found in appendix H, "Accounting and Disclosure Requirements for Single Employer and Multiemployer Employee Benefit Plans Related to the Medicare Prescription Drug, Improvement and Modernization Act of 2003," of this guide or in the AICPA publication *Technical Practice Aids*.

Postemployment Benefits

4.85 According to FASB ASC 965-30-25-3, plans that provide postemployment benefits should recognize a benefit obligation for current participants, based on amounts expected to be paid in subsequent years, if all the following conditions are met:

   a. The participants' rights to receive benefits are attributable to services already rendered.

   b. The participants' benefits vest or accumulate.[28]

   c. Payment of benefits is probable.

   d. The amount can be reasonably estimated.

Per FASB ASC 965-30-35-9, the postemployment benefit obligation should be measured as the actuarial present value of the future benefits attributed to

---

[28] Per item (*b*) of FASB ASC 965-30-25-3, for example, the supplemental unemployment benefit is 52 weeks' pay if a participant worked 3 years, 78 weeks' pay if a participant worked 5 years, and 104 weeks' pay if a participant worked 7 years. In this situation, the benefits would be considered accumulating. Benefits that increase solely as a function of wage or salary increases are not considered accumulating.

plan participants' services rendered to the measurement date, reduced by the actuarial present value of future contributions expected to be received from the current plan participants. That amount represents the benefit obligation that is to be funded by contributions from the plan's participating employer(s) and from existing plan assets. The obligation is to be measured assuming the plan continues in effect and all assumptions about future events are met. Any anticipated forfeitures or integration with other related programs (for example, state unemployment benefits) should be considered. The benefit obligation should be discounted using rates of return on high-quality fixed-income investments currently available with cash flows that match the timing and amount of expected benefit payments and expected participant contributions.

4.86 FASB ASC 965-30-25-4 states that for postemployment benefits that do not meet conditions (*a*) and (*b*) of paragraph 4.85, the plan should recognize a benefit obligation if the event that gives rise to a liability has occurred and the amount can be reasonably estimated. For example, if all participants receive the same medical coverage upon disability regardless of length of service (the benefits do not accumulate) and the benefits do not vest, medical benefits for disabled participants should be accrued at the date of disability and not over the participants' working lives. According to FASB ASC 965-30-35-10, when participant contributions are required after the event triggering postemployment benefits occurs, the postemployment benefit obligation should be measured in a manner consistent with the preceding paragraph. As a result, in those situations the benefit obligation should represent the amount that is to be funded by contributions from the participating employer(s) and from existing plan assets.

4.87 FASB ASC 965-30-50-2, if an obligation for postemployment benefits is not recognized in accordance with the two preceding paragraphs only because the amount cannot be reasonably estimated, the financial statements should disclose that fact.

Changes in Benefit Obligations

4.88 In accordance with paragraphs 4–8 of FASB ASC 965-30-45, information regarding changes in the benefit obligations within a plan period should be presented to identify significant factors affecting year-to-year changes in benefit obligations. Changes in each of the three major classifications of benefit obligations should be presented in the body of the financial statements or in the notes to the financial statements; the information may be presented in either a reconciliation or narrative format. Providing such information in the following three categories will generally be sufficient: (*a*) claims payable, claims IBNR, and premiums due to insurance entities; (*b*) accumulated eligibility credits and postemployment benefits, net of amounts currently payable; and (*c*) postretirement benefits for retired plan participants, including their beneficiaries and covered dependents, net of amounts currently payable and claims IBNR; other plan participants fully eligible for benefits; and plan participants not yet fully eligible for benefits.

4.89 Minimum disclosure regarding changes in benefit obligations should include the significant effects of (*a*) plan amendments, (*b*) changes in the nature of the plan (mergers or spinoffs), and (*c*) changes in actuarial assumptions (health care cost-trend rate or interest rate). Changes in actuarial assumptions are to be considered as changes in accounting estimates and, therefore, previously reported amounts should not be restated. The significant effects of other factors may also be identified. These include, for example, benefits accumulated,[29] the effects of the time value of money (for interest), and benefits paid. If presented, benefits paid should not include benefit payments made by an insurance entity pursuant to a contract that is excluded from plan assets. However, amounts paid by the plan to an insurance entity pursuant to such a contract (including purchases of annuities with amounts allocated from existing investments with the insurance entity) should be included in benefits paid.[30] If only the minimum disclosure is presented, presentation in a statement format will necessitate an additional unidentified other category to reconcile the initial and ultimate amounts.

Additional Financial Statement Disclosures

4.90   Disclosure of a health and welfare benefit plan's accounting policies should include[31]

- a description of the methods and significant assumptions used to determine the fair value of investments and the reported value of insurance contracts (FASB ASC 965-325-50-1).

- a description of the methods and significant actuarial assumptions used to determine the plan's benefit obligations. Any significant changes in assumptions made between financial statement dates and their effects should be described (FASB ASC 965-30-50-5).

4.91   Unless otherwise noted, FASB ASC 965-205-50-1, states that the plan's financial statements should also disclose other information.[32] Separate disclosures may be made to the extent that the plan provides both health and other welfare benefits. The disclosures should include, if applicable, all of the following:

a. A brief, general description of the plan agreement, including, but not limited to, participants covered, vesting, and benefit provisions.[33]

b. A description of significant plan amendments adopted during the period, as well as significant changes in the nature of the plan (for example, a plan spin-off or merger with another plan) and changes in actuarial assumptions.

c. The funding policy and any changes in the policy made during the plan year. If the benefit obligations exceed the net assets of the plan, the method of funding this deficit, as provided for in the plan agreement or collective bargaining agreement, also should be disclosed.

---

[29] Per item (a) of FASB ASC 965-30-45-7, actuarial experience gains or losses may be included with the effects of additional benefits accumulated rather than separately disclosed. If the effects of changes in actuarial assumptions cannot be separately determined, those effects should be included in benefits accumulated and described accordingly.

[30] Per FASB ASC 965-30-45-8, because of the use of different actuarial assumptions, the amount paid by the plan to an insurance entity may be different from the previous measure of the actuarial present value of the related accumulated plan benefits. If that information is available, it should be presented as an actuarial experience gain or loss.

[31] See FASB ASC 235, *Notes to Financial Statements*.

[32] Per FASB ASC 965-205-50-1, certain of the disclosures relate to plans with accumulated assets rather than those with trusts that act more as conduits for benefit payments or insurance premiums.

[33] Per item (a) of FASB ASC 965-205-50-1, if a plan agreement or a description thereof providing this information is otherwise published or made available, the description in the financial statement disclosures may be omitted, provided that a reference to the other source is made.

For a contributory plan, the disclosure should state the method of determining participants' contributions. For each year for which a year-end statement of net assets available for benefits is presented, a description of the portion of the plan's estimated cost[34] of providing postretirement benefits funded by retiree contributions. If the plan terms provide that a shortfall in attaining the intended cost sharing in the prior year(s) is to be recovered by increasing the retiree contribution in the current year, that incremental contribution should be separately disclosed. Similarly, if the plan terms provide that participant contributions in the current year are to be reduced by the amount by which participant contributions in prior year exceeded the amount needed to attain the desired cost-sharing, the resulting reduction in the current year contribution should be separately disclosed. The information about retiree contributions should be provided for each significant group of retired participants to the extent their contributions differ.

d. If significant plan administration or related costs are being borne by the employer, that fact should be disclosed.

e. The federal income tax status of the plan.[35] No determination letter program for health and welfare plans exists; however a 501(c)(9) VEBA trust must obtain a determination letter to be exempt from taxation.

f. The policy regarding the purchase of contracts with insurance entities that are excluded from plan assets. Consideration should be given to disclosing the type and extent of insurance coverage, as well as the extent to which risk is transferred (for example, coverage period and claims reported or claims incurred).

g. In accordance with FASB ASC 965-325-50-1, identification of investments that represent 5 percent or more of the net assets available for benefits as of the end of the year. Consideration should be given to disclosing provisions of insurance contracts included as plan assets that could cause an impairment of the asset value upon liquidation or other occurrence (for example, surrender charges and market value adjustments).

h. The amounts and types of securities of the employer and related parties included in plan assets, and the approximate amount of

---

[34] The plan's estimated cost of postretirement benefits is the plan's expected claims cost for the year. It excludes benefit costs paid by Medicare and costs, such as deductibles and copayments, paid directly to the medical provider by participants. The portion of the plan's estimated cost that is funded by retiree contributions is determined at the beginning of the year based on the plan sponsor's cost-sharing policy. In determining that amount, the retirees' required contribution for the year should be reduced by any amounts intended to recover a shortfall (or increased by amounts intended to compensate for an overcharge) in attaining the desired cost-sharing in prior year(s).

[35] A plan's tax exempt status is a position that may be subject to uncertainty. In September 2009, FASB issued ASU No. 2009-06, *Income Taxes (Topic 740)—Implementation Guidance on Accounting for Uncertainty in Income Taxes and Disclosure Amendments for Nonpublic Entities*. FASB ASU No. 2009-06 provides implementation guidance on accounting for uncertainty in income taxes and eliminates the disclosure requirements of paragraphs 15(a)–15(b) of FASB ASC 740-10-50 for nonpublic entities, as defined in FASB ASC 740-10-20. The implementation guidance in FASB ASU No. 2009-06 also expands the FASB ASC glossary definition of a *tax position*. In addition, TIS section 5250.15, "Application of Certain FASB Interpretation No. 48 (codified in FASB ASC 740-10) Disclosure Requirements to Nonpublic Entities That Do Not Have Uncertain Tax Positions" (AICPA, *Technical Practice Aids*), clarified that the description of open tax years that remain subject to examination is a required disclosure for a nonpublic entity even if the entity has no uncertain tax positions. Also, see paragraph 12.07 of this guide for further information.

future annual benefits of plan participants covered by insurance contracts issued by the employer and related parties.

i. Significant real estate or other transactions in which the plan and any of the following parties are jointly involved: the sponsor, the plan administrator, employers, or employee organizations.

j. Unusual or infrequent events or transactions occurring after the financial statement date, but before the financial statements are issued or are available to be issued (in accordance with 855-10-25), that might significantly affect the usefulness of the financial statements in an assessment of the plan's present and future ability to pay benefits. For example, a plan amendment adopted after the latest financial statement date that significantly increases future benefits attributable to an employee's service rendered before that date, a significant change in the market value of a significant portion of the plan's assets, or the emergence of a catastrophic claim should be disclosed. If reasonably determinable, the effects of such events or transactions should be disclosed. If such effects are not reasonably determinable, the reasons why they are not quantifiable should be disclosed.

k. Subsequent events disclosures as required by FASB ASC 855, *Subsequent Events* (see chapter 12 for a discussion of subsequent events). ‖

l. Material lease commitments, other commitments, or contingent liabilities.

m. The assumed health care cost-trend rate(s) used to measure the expected cost of benefits covered by the plan for the next year, a general description of the direction and pattern of change in the assumed trend rates thereafter, the ultimate trend rate(s), and when that rate is expected to be achieved.

n. For health and welfare benefit plans providing postretirement health care benefits, the effect of a 1 percentage point increase in the assumed health care cost-trend rates for each future year on the postretirement benefit obligation.

o. Any modification of the existing cost-sharing provisions that are encompassed by the substantive plan(s) and the existence and nature of any commitment to increase monetary benefits provided by the plan and their effect on the plan's financial statements.

p. Termination provisions of the plan and priorities for distribution of assets, if applicable.

q. Restrictions, if any, on plan assets (for example, legal restrictions on multiple trusts).

‖ In February 2010, FASB issued ASU 2010-09, *Subsequent Events (Topic 855): Amendments to Certain Recognition and Disclosure Requirements*. This ASU amends the guidance in FASB ASC 855, *Subsequent Events*, to require entities (except Securities and Exchange Commission [SEC] filers and conduit debt obligors [CDOs]) to evaluate subsequent events through the date that the financial statements are available to be issued. Entities other than SEC filers should disclose the date through which subsequent events have been evaluated. SEC filers and CDOs should evaluate subsequent events through the date the financial statements are issued. An entity that is an SEC filer is not required to disclose the date through which subsequent events have been evaluated.

r. In a defined contribution health and welfare plan—the accounting policy for, and the amount and disposition of, forfeited nonvested accounts. Specifically, identification of whether those amounts will be used to reduce future employer contributions, employer expenses, or will be allocated to participants accounts.

s. In accordance with FASB ASC 965-325-50-2, for fully benefit-responsive investment contracts, in the aggregate

     i. a description of the nature of those investment contracts, how they operate, and the methodology for calculating the interest crediting rate, including the key factors that could influence future average interest crediting rates, the basis for and frequency of determining interest crediting rate resets, and any minimum interest crediting rate under the terms of the contracts. This disclosure should explain the relationship between future interest crediting rates and the amount reported on the statement of net assets available for benefits representing the adjustment for the portion of net assets attributable to fully benefit-responsive investment contracts from fair value to contract value.

     ii. the average yield earned by the plan for all fully benefit-responsive investment contracts (which may differ from the interest rate credited to participants in the plan) for each period for which a statement of net assets available for benefits is presented. This average yield should be calculated by dividing the annualized earnings of all fully benefit-responsive investment contracts in the plan (irrespective of the interest rate credited to participants in the plan) by the fair value of all fully benefit-responsive investment contracts in the plan.

     iii. the average yield earned by the plan for all fully benefit-responsive investment contracts with an adjustment to reflect the actual interest rate credited to participants in the plan for each period for which a statement of net assets available for benefits is presented. This average yield should be calculated by dividing the annualized earnings credited to participants in the plan for all fully benefit-responsive investment contracts in the plan (irrespective of the actual earnings of those investments) by the fair value of all fully benefit-responsive investment contracts in the plan.

     iv. a description of the events that limit the ability of the plan to transact at contract value with the issuer (for example, premature termination of the contracts by the plan, plant closings, layoffs, plan termination, bankruptcy, mergers, and early retirement incentives), including a statement about whether the occurrence of those events that would limit the plan's ability to transact at contract value with participants in the plan is probable or not probable. [The term *probable* is used in this statement consistent with its use in FASB ASC 450, *Contingencies*.]

   v. a description of the events and circumstances that would allow issuers to terminate fully benefit-responsive investment contracts with the plan and settle at an amount different from contract value.

  t. In accordance with FASB ASC 965-325-50-3, for ERISA-covered plans, if a fully benefit-responsive investment contract does not qualify for contract-value reporting in the DOL Form 5500 but is reported in the financial statements at contract value, and the contract value does not approximate fair value, the DOL's rules and regulations require that a statement explaining the differences between amounts reported in the financial statements and DOL Form 5500 be added to the financial statements.

  u. In accordance with FASB ASC 965-30-50-5, the weighted-average assumed discount rate used to measure the plan's obligation for postemployment benefits.

This list does not include information that, in accordance with ERISA requirements, must be disclosed in the schedules filed as part of a plan's annual report. It is important to note that any information required by ERISA to be disclosed in the schedules must be disclosed in the schedules; disclosure of the information on the face of the financial statements or in the notes to the financial statements but not in the schedules is not acceptable.

Fair Value Measurements

 4.92 See paragraphs 4.37–.41 for required disclosures related to fair value measurements.

Derivatives and Hedging

 4.93 FASB ASC 815 provides accounting and reporting for derivative instruments, including certain derivative instruments embedded in other contracts (collectively referred to as *derivatives*), and for hedging activities. It requires that an entity recognize all derivatives as either assets or liabilities in the statement of financial position and measure those instruments at fair value. FASB ASC 815 applies to certain contracts that meet the definition of derivative instrument, as defined in FASB ASC 815-10-15-83. See FASB ASC 815-10-15 for further information on certain contracts that are not subject to the requirements of FASB ASC 815. (See paragraphs 7.59–.66 for further guidance.)#

 # In March 2010, FASB issued ASU No. 2010-11, *Derivatives and Hedging (Topic 815): Scope Exceptions Related to Embedded Credit Derivatives*. The amendments in this ASU, among other things clarify the scope exception under paragraphs 8–9 of FASB ASC 815-15 for embedded credit derivative features related to the transfer of credit risk in the form of subordination of one financial instrument to another. Further, the amendments address how to determine which embedded credit derivatives, including those in collateralized debt obligations and synthetic collateralized debt obligations, are considered to be embedded derivatives that should not be analyzed under FASB ASC 815-15-25 for potential bifurcation and separate accounting.

 The amendments in FASB ASU No. 2010-11 are effective for each reporting entity at the beginning of its first fiscal quarter beginning after June 15, 2010. Early adoption is permitted at the beginning of each entity's first fiscal quarter beginning after issuance of this ASU.

 The guidance is located in FASB ASC 815-10 and FASB ASC 815-15.

Financial Instruments

4.94 FASB ASC 825 requires all entities except for those covered by an exemption[36] for which the disclosure is optional, to disclose, within the body of the financial statements or in the accompanying notes, the fair value of financial instruments for which it is practicable to estimate fair value.[37] An entity should also disclose the method(s) and significant assumptions used to estimate the fair value of financial instruments. Generally, financial instruments of a health and welfare plan are included in the scope of FASB ASC 825 and are subject to the disclosure requirements of FASB ASC 825-10-50. In addition, the disclosure requirements of FASB ASC 820 may also apply.[38]

4.95 FASB ASC 825-10-50-21 requires disclosure of all significant concentrations of credit risk arising from all financial instruments. The following information should be disclosed about each significant concentration:

- Information about the (shared) activity, region, or economic characteristic that identifies the concentration

- The maximum amount of loss due to credit risk that, based on the gross fair value of the financial instrument, the entity would incur if parties to the financial instruments that make up the concentration failed completely to perform according to the terms of the contracts and the collateral or other security, if any, for the amount due proved to be of no value to the entity

- The entity's policy of requiring collateral or other security to support financial instruments subject to credit risk, information about the entity's access to that collateral or other security, and the nature and a brief description of the collateral or other security supporting those financial instruments

- The entity's policy of entering into master netting arrangements to mitigate the credit risk of financial instruments, information about the arrangements for which the entity is a party, and a brief description of the terms of those arrangements, including the extent to which they would reduce the entity's maximum amount of loss due to credit risk

---

[36] According to FASB ASC 825-10-50-3, the disclosures are optional for plans that meet the following criteria:

    a. The plan is a nonpublic entity.

    b. The plan's total assets are less than $100 million on the date of the financial statements.

    c. The plan has no instrument that, in whole or in part, is accounted for as a derivative instrument under FASB ASC 815, *Derivatives and Hedging*, during the reporting period.

[37] Per FASB ASC 825-10-50-11 fair value disclosed in the notes should be presented together with the related carrying amount in a form that makes it clear whether the fair value and carrying amount represent assets or liabilities and how the carrying amounts relate to what is reported in the statement of net assets available for benefits.

[38] In June 2010, the AICPA issued TIS section 1800.05, "Applicability of Fair Value Disclosure Requirements and Measurement Principles in Financial Accounting Standard Board (FASB) *Accounting Standards Codification* (ASC) 820, *Fair Value Measurements and Disclosures*, to Certain Financial Instruments" (AICPA, *Technical Practice Aids*). This TIS section addresses whether the fair value measurement principles and disclosure requirements in FASB ASC 820 apply to financial instruments that are not recognized at fair value in the statement of financial positions, but for which fair value is required to be disclosed in the notes to financial statements in accordance with paragraphs 10–19 of FASB ASC 825-10-50.

Risks and Uncertainties

4.96 FASB ASC 275, *Risks and Uncertainties*, requires plans to include in their financial statements disclosures about (*a*) the nature of their operations, and (*b*) use of estimates in the preparation of financial statements. In addition, if specified criteria are met, FASB ASC 275 requires plans to include in their financial statements disclosures about (*a*) certain significant estimates, and (*b*) current vulnerability due to certain concentrations.

4.97 Certain significant estimates should be disclosed when known information available prior to the financial statements being issued or being available to be issued (appropriate date determined in accordance with FASB ASC 855-10-25 [ll]) indicates that (*a*) it is at least reasonably possible that the estimate of the effect on the financial statements of a condition, situation, or set of circumstances that existed at the date of the financial statements will change in the near term due to one or more future confirming events, and (*b*) the effect of the change would be material to the financial statements. For example, the present value of accumulated plan benefits of a defined benefit health and welfare benefit plan could be subject to a material change when

   a. employees covered by the plan work in an industry that experienced a significant economic downturn in the previous year and it is reasonably possible that in the subsequent period a significant number of employees will retire early without a monetary incentive to do so in order to avoid being laid-off with nominal benefits. This could significantly increase the present value of accumulated plan benefits and possibly cause the plan to be underfunded.

   b. employees covered by the plan are party to a collective bargaining agreement which was up for renegotiation at year-end and it is reasonably possible that management's offer to significantly increase pension benefits in lieu of granting the union's request for a significant increase in cash compensation will be accepted within the next year. This could significantly increase the present value of accumulated plan benefits.

   c. prior to year-end the employer announced a planned downsizing but had not decided on the number of employees to be terminated, and it is reasonably possible that when the decision is made during the next year, it will result in employees receiving pension benefits earlier than expected and in an amount greater than originally projected.

   d. it is reasonably possible that there will be a significant decline in the fair value of investments (that is, financial instruments) during the next year which would change the assumed rates of return used to discount the benefit obligation and therefore could significantly affect the present value of accumulated plan benefits.

4.98 Vulnerability from concentrations arises when a plan is exposed to risk of loss greater than it would have had it mitigated its risk through diversification. Many plan's participants may be concentrated in a specific industry that carries with it certain risks. Plans may also hold investments and other assets (other than financial instruments for which concentrations are covered by FASB ASC 825 rather than FASB ASC 275) that are concentrated in a single

---

[ll] See footnote ll in paragraph 4.91.

industry or in a single geographic area. Concentrations should be disclosed if based on known information prior to the financial statements being issued or being available to be issued (appropriate date determined in accordance with FASB ASC 855-10-25 [II]) (a) the concentration exists at the date of the financial statements, (b) the concentration makes the plan vulnerable to the risk of a near-term severe impact, and (c) it is at least reasonably possible that the events that could cause the severe impact will occur in the near term. For example, if the plan owns several investment properties (that is, apartment buildings) located in a geographic area that has only one significant employer and that employer announced last year that it is considering leaving the area and it is reasonably possible that it will do so within the next year, this could significantly affect the plan's future cash flows from rents and the value of the investment properties.

4.99 Because the disclosure requirements of FASB ASC 275 in many circumstances are similar to or overlap the disclosure requirements in certain other FASB ASC topics (for example, FASB ASC 450), the disclosures required by FASB ASC 275 may be combined in various ways, grouped together, or placed in diverse parts of the financial statements, or included as part of the disclosures made pursuant to the requirements of other FASB ASC topics.

Terminating Plans

4.100 FASB ASC 965-40 provides guidance for terminating plans that are health and welfare plans. Terminating plans include any plan about which a termination decision has been made regardless of whether the terminating plan will be replaced.

4.101 When the decision has been made to terminate a plan,[39] or a wasting trust (that is, a plan under which participants no longer accrue benefits but that will remain in existence as long as necessary to pay already accrued benefits) exists, the relevant circumstances should be disclosed in all subsequent financial statements issued by the plan.

4.102 If the decision to terminate a plan is made before the end of the plan year, the plan's year-end financial statements should be prepared on the *liquidation* basis of accounting.[40]

4.103 For plan assets, changing to the liquidation basis will usually cause little or no change in values, most of which are current market values. Assets that may not be carried at market values include operating assets, insurance and certain investment contracts carried at *contract value*, or large blocks of stock or other assets that cannot be readily disposed of at their quoted market prices.

[II] See footnote II in paragraph 4.91.

[39] See paragraph 12.28, which states that the auditor should obtain written representations from management as part of an audit of financial statements. Such representations may include whether there is a present intention to terminate the plan. Refer also to paragraph 10.41*h*, which states that the auditor may consider confirming with the plan's actuary knowledge of an intent on the part of the employer to terminate the plan.

[40] Interpretation No. 8, "Reporting on Financial Statements Prepared on a Liquidation Basis of Accounting," of AU section 508, *Reports on Audited Financial Statements* (AICPA, *Professional Standards*, AU sec. 9508 par. .33–.38), contains applicable guidance regarding the auditor's reporting responsibilities for terminating plans.

4.104 Benefit obligations should be determined on a liquidation basis, and their value may differ from the actuarial present value of benefit obligations reported for an ongoing plan. Consideration should be given upon termination to whether any or all benefits become vested.

Voluntary Employee Beneficiary Associations

4.105 The audit requirement with respect to a health and welfare plan that utilizes a VEBA trust, applies to the plan not the VEBA trust. A trust may be established to hold the assets of an employee welfare benefit plan; it may or may not be tax-exempt. A common form of tax-exempt trust is a IRC Section 501(c)(9) trust, referred to as a voluntary employee beneficiary association or VEBA. VEBA trusts generally have no language covering the plan's operations. The governing instrument is limited to the investment and management of plan assets. Disbursements are made as authorized by the plan administrator. Operational attributes of the related plan must still be audited in accordance with this chapter. However, the tax status is unique to the VEBA and the tax requirements of the IRC must be satisfied for the trust to be tax-exempt.

4.106 Paragraph 4.13 explains that a VEBA is one of several arrangements available to hold plan assets of an employee welfare plan. Key considerations in auditing VEBAs arise from the distinct tax regulations associated with VEBAs and oftentimes assets of several welfare plans are commingled into a single VEBA.

4.107 The audit and reporting issues for a VEBA that holds the assets of a single plan of a single sponsor are discussed fully in this chapter and related paragraphs of this guide. When the VEBA holds the assets of several plans of a single employer additional audit issues are present. If the VEBA qualifies as a master trust, the master trust rules discussed in paragraph 4.13 will apply. When the underlying welfare plans have no assets other than those held by the VEBA, Form 5500 schedules are attached to the master trust filing and need not be included with the separate filing of each participating plan. (See the Instructions to Form 5500 for guidance on master trust filings.) If the VEBA does not qualify as a master trust, Form 5500 schedules should be prepared for each plan. (See appendix A for a discussion of Form 5500 schedules.)

Chapter 5

Planning and General Auditing Considerations[*]

Overview

5.01 In accordance with AU section 150, *Generally Accepted Auditing Standards* (AICPA, *Professional Standards*), an independent auditor plans, conducts, and reports the results of an audit in accordance with generally accepted auditing standards (GAAS). Auditing standards provide a measure of audit quality and the objectives to be achieved in an audit. This section of the guide provides guidance, primarily on the application of the standards of fieldwork. Specifically, this section provides guidance on the risk assessment process (which includes, among other things, obtaining an understanding of the plan and its environment, including its internal control) and general auditing considerations for employee benefit plans.

Planning and Other Auditing Considerations

5.02 The objective of an audit of an employee benefit plan is to express an opinion on whether its financial statements are presented fairly, in all material respects, and in conformity with generally accepted accounting principles (GAAP) or an other comprehensive basis of accounting. To accomplish that objective, the independent auditor's responsibility is to plan and perform the audit to obtain reasonable assurance (a high, but not absolute, level of assurance) that material misstatements, whether caused by error or fraud, are detected. For example, when planning an employee benefit plan audit, the auditor may want to consider that

- investments are properly valued at fair value (including hard to value investments, such as real estate, limited partnerships, and private placement equities.)

- the completeness objective has been achieved with respect to employer and employee contributions.

- pensions and annuities paid and benefits paid have been accurately calculated and have been properly shown on the plan's financial statements.

- the benefit obligations determined by the plan's actuary appear reasonable and significant changes are understood by the auditor.

- expenses paid by the plan are appropriate.

5.03 This section addresses general planning considerations and other auditing considerations relevant to employee benefit plans.

---

[*] Refer to the preface of this guide for important information about the applicability of the professional standards to audits of issuers and nonissuers.

Audit Scope

5.04 Information about the nature of the employee benefit plan and scope of the audit is critical in planning the engagement. Matters that affect the scope of the audit to be considered include the following:

- Whether the audit will be a full scope or a limited scope
- The type of trust arrangement and nature of investment options
- Involvement of third-party service organizations and other key service providers
- Whether the audit is an initial audit, merged plan, or final audit

In accordance with AU section 311, *Planning and Supervision* (AICPA, *Professional Standards*), for each audit engagement, the auditor should establish an understanding with the client regarding the services to be performed including the scope of the audit and the auditor's responsibilities regarding any supplemental schedules accompanying the basic financial statements. This understanding should be documented through a written communication with the plan in the form of an engagement letter. The understanding should include the objectives of the engagement, management's responsibilities, the auditor's responsibilities (including any supplemental schedules accompanying the basic financial statements), and limitations of the engagement. This understanding with the client generally includes, among other matters, management's responsibility for adjusting the financial statements to correct material misstatements and for representing to the auditors that the effects of any uncorrected misstatements are immaterial, both individually and in the aggregate. (See paragraph 5.20 for further guidance on such communications and exhibit 5-5 for an illustrative engagement letter.)

Communication With Those Charged With Governance

5.05 AU section 380, *The Auditor's Communication With Those Charged With Governance* (AICPA, *Professional Standards*), states the auditor should communicate with those charged with governance an overview of the planned scope and timing of the audit. However, it is important for the auditor not to compromise the effectiveness of the audit, particularly where some or all of those charged with governance are involved in managing the plan. For example, communicating the nature and timing of detailed audit procedures may reduce the effectiveness of those procedures by making them too predictable.

5.06 AU section 380 defines *those charged with governance* as the person(s) with responsibility for overseeing the strategic direction of the plan and obligations related to the accountability of the plan. The auditor should determine the appropriate person(s) within the plan's governance structure with whom to communicate. When the appropriate person(s) are not clearly identifiable, the auditor and the engaging party should agree on the relevant person(s) within the plan's governance structure with whom the auditor will communicate (see AU section 380 paragraphs .12–.16 for further guidance). For a single-employer employee benefit plan the individual charged with governance may include the audit committee of the plan sponsor or the appropriate committee overseeing the activities of the employee benefit plan, such as the employee benefit committee, administrative committee, investment committee, plan administrator or responsible party. For a multiemployer plan those charged with governance will ordinarily be the board of trustees.

5.07 The auditor may consider communicating planning matters early in an audit engagement, and for an initial engagement, as part of the terms of the engagement. The auditor should communicate with those charged with governance

    a. the auditor's responsibilities under GAAS (see paragraph 5.08)

    b. an overview of the planned scope and timing of the audit (see paragraph 5.10)

    c. significant findings from the audit (see paragraph 12.44).

The Auditor's Responsibilities Under GAAS

5.08 The auditor should communicate with those charged with governance the auditor's responsibilities under GAAS, including that

    a. the auditor is responsible for forming and expressing an opinion about whether the financial statements that have been prepared by management with the oversight of those charged with governance are presented fairly, in all material respects, in conformity with GAAP.

    b. the audit of the financial statements does not relieve management or those charged with governance of their responsibilities.

5.09 These responsibilities may be communicated through the engagement letter, or other form of contract that records the terms of the engagement, if that letter or contract is provided to those charged with governance. See AU section 380 paragraphs .27–.28 for discussion of additional items the auditor may also communicate.

Planned Scope and Timing of the Audit

5.10 As noted earlier, the auditor should communicate with those charged with governance an overview of the planned scope and timing of the audit. This communication may be oral or in writing. The following lists matters that may be communicated:

- How the auditor proposes to address the significant risks of material misstatement, whether due to fraud or error
- The auditor's approach to internal control relevant to the audit
- The concept of materiality in planning and executing the audit, focusing on the factors considered rather than on specific thresholds or amounts
- Where the plan sponsor has an internal audit function that assists on the plan audit, the extent to which the auditor will use the work of internal audit, and how the external and internal auditors can best work together

5.11 Other planning matters that the auditor may consider discussing with those charged with governance include

- the views of those charged with governance about
  - the appropriate person(s) in the plan's governance structure with whom to communicate.

— the allocation of responsibilities between those charged with governance and management.

— the plan's objectives and strategies, and the related business risks that may result in material misstatements.

— matters those charged with governance consider warrant particular attention during the audit, and any areas where they request additional procedures to be undertaken.

— significant communications with regulators.

— other matters those charged with governance believe are relevant to the audit of the financial statements.

- the attitudes, awareness, and actions of those charged with governance concerning (a) the plan's internal control and its importance in the plan, including how those charged with governance oversee the effectiveness of internal control, and (b) the detection or the possibility of fraud.

- the actions of those charged with governance in response to developments in financial reporting, laws, accounting standards, corporate governance practices, and other related matters.

- the actions of those charged with governance in response to previous communications with the auditor.

5.12   Although communication with those charged with governance may assist the auditor in planning the scope and timing of the audit, it does not change the auditor's sole responsibility to determine the overall audit strategy and the audit plan, including the nature, timing, and extent of procedures necessary to obtain sufficient appropriate audit evidence. The auditor should communicate in writing with those charged with governance significant findings from the audit when, in the auditor's professional judgment, oral communication would not be adequate. Other communications may be oral or in writing. For further guidance on the communication process, including the form, timing, adequacy, and documentation of the communication, see AU section 380.

Limited-Scope Audit Exemption

5.13   The auditor may be engaged to perform a full-scope audit of the financial statements of an employee benefit plan in accordance with GAAS. Alternatively, the Employee Retirement Income Security Act of 1974 (ERISA) Section 103(a)(3)(c) allows the plan administrator to instruct the auditor not to perform any auditing procedures with respect to investment information prepared and certified by a bank or similar institution or by an insurance carrier that is regulated, supervised, and subject to periodic examination by a state or federal agency who acts as trustee or custodian. The election is available, however, only if the trustee, custodian, or insurance company certifies both the *accuracy and completeness* of the information submitted. Certifications that address only accuracy or completeness, but not both, do not comply with the Department of Labor's (DOL) regulation, and therefore are not adequate to allow plan administrators to limit the scope of the audit. This *limited-scope* audit exemption does not apply to information about investments held by a broker or dealer or an investment company. In addition, if a limited-scope audit is to be performed on a plan funded under a master trust arrangement or other similar vehicle then separate individual plan certifications from the trustee or the custodian need to be obtained by the plan administrator for the allocation of the assets and the related income activity to the specific plan. The exemption applies only to the *investment* information certified by the qualified trustee, custodian, or insurance company and does not extend to participant data, contributions, benefit payments or other information whether or not it is certified by the trustee or custodian. Thus, except for the investment related functions performed by the trustee or custodian, an auditor conducting a limited-scope audit would need to include in the scope of the audit functions performed by the plan sponsor or other third-party service organizations, such as third-party welfare plan claims administrators or third-party savings plan administrators, as applicable.

5.14 The nature and scope of testing will depend on a variety of factors including the nature of the functions being performed by the third-party service organization, whether a Statement on Auditing Standards (SAS) No. 70 report[1] that addresses areas other than investments is available, if deemed necessary, and, if so, the type of report and the related results. (See chapter 6, "Internal Control," for a discussion of AU section 324, *Service Organizations* [AICPA, *Professional Standards*].) The limited-scope audit exemption is implemented by Title 29 U.S. *Code of Federal Regulations* (CFR) Part 2520.103-8, which outlines the DOL's rules and regulations for reporting and disclosure under ERISA. The limited-scope exemption does not exempt the plan from the requirement to have an audit. Guidance on the auditor's report and responsibilities for the limited-scope audit is provided in paragraphs 7.72 and 13.26–.31. Exhibit 5-1, "Conditions Generally Allowing a Limited-Scope Audit Versus a Full-Scope Audit for Employee Benefit Plans Subject to ERISA," summarizes the conditions that generally allow for limited-scope audits in decision tree format.

Other Applicable Auditing Guidance

5.15 See the following exhibits for guidance on audit requirements under ERISA:

- Exhibit 5-2, "Pension Plan Audit Decision Tree," summarizes the conditions that generally require audits of pension plan financial statements and schedules under ERISA in decision tree format.
- Exhibit 5-3, "Welfare Benefit Plans Audit: Decision Flowchart," summarizes the conditions that generally require audits of welfare benefit plans under ERISA in decision tree format.
- Exhibit 5-4, "Small Pension Plan Audit Waiver (SPPAW) Summary," summarizes the small pension plan audit waiver in decision tree format.

---

[1] The Auditing Standards Board (ASB) has issued Statement on Standards for Attestation Engagements (SSAE) No. 16, *Reporting on Controls at a Service Organization* (AICPA, *Professional Standards*, AT sec. 801), which will replace the guidance contained in AU section 324, *Service Organizations* (AICPA, *Professional Standards*), for a service auditor when reporting on controls at an organization that provides service to user entities when those controls are likely to be relevant to user entities' internal controls over financial reporting. It is effective for service auditors' reports for periods ending on or after June 15, 2011. Early implementation is permitted; therefore, if adopting SSAE No. 16 early, refer directly to the standard as certain guidance in this guide may not be applicable. Also, refer to the preface of this guide for additional information about the changes related to Statement on Auditing Standards (SAS) No. 70, *Service Organizations* (AICPA, *Professional Standards*, AU sec. 324).

5.16 An auditor must have adequate technical training and proficiency to perform the audit; therefore, the auditor only accepts an audit when he or she will be able to meet the responsibilities and requirements related to the engagement. Factors to be considered include expertise in the benefit plan area, ability to meet the engagement's time requirements and deadlines, and ability to meet ERISA audit requirements. AU section 150 states that when the auditor departs from a presumptively mandatory requirement,[2] the auditor must document in the working papers his or her justification for the departure and how the alternative procedures performed in the circumstances were sufficient to achieve the objectives of the presumptively mandatory requirement. AU section 150 states the auditor should be aware of and consider interpretive publications applicable to his or her audit.

---

[2] AU section 120, *Defining Professional Requirements in Statements on Auditing Standards* (AICPA, *Professional Standards*), defines presumptively mandatory requirements. See AU sections 120 and 150, *Generally Accepted Auditing Standards* (AICPA *Professional Standards*), for further guidance.

Exhibit 5-1³

Conditions Generally Allowing a Limited-Scope Audit Versus a Full-Scope Audit for Employee Benefit Plans Subject to ERISA

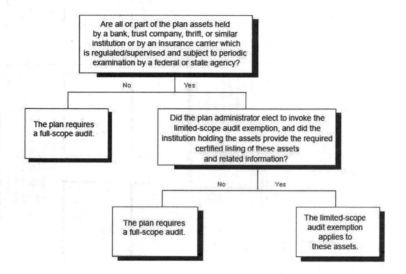

---

³ See paragraph 13.27 for guidance on the effect on the independent auditor's report when only a portion of the plan's investments are certified by a qualified custodian or trustee.

Exhibit 5-2[4]

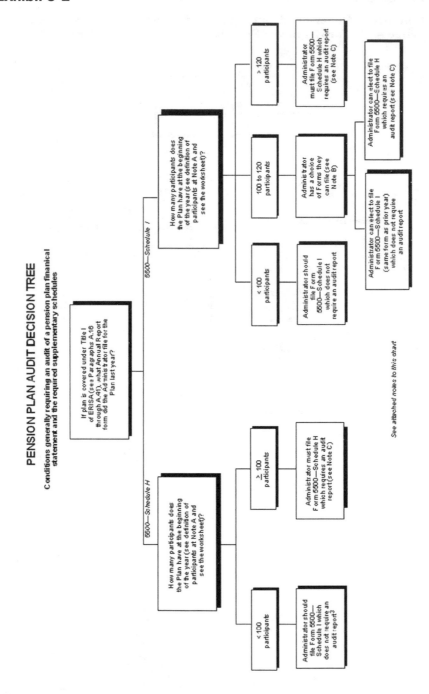

PENSION PLAN AUDIT DECISION TREE

Conditions generally requiring an audit of a pension plan financial statement and the required supplementary schedules

If plan is covered under Title I of ERISA (see Paragraphs A.16 through A.41), what Annual Report form did the Administrator file for the Plan last year?

5500—Schedule H

How many participants does the Plan have at the beginning of the year (see definition of participants at Note A and see the worksheet)?

< 100 participants
Administrator should file Form 5500—Schedule I which does not require an audit report[3]

≥ 100 participants
Administrator must file Form 5500—Schedule H which requires an audit report (see Note C)

5500—Schedule I

How many participants does the Plan have at the beginning of the year (see definition of participants at Note A and see the worksheet)?

< 100 participants
Administrator should file Form 5500—Schedule I which does not require an audit report

100 to 120 participants
Administrator has a choice of Forms they can file (see Note B)

Administrator can elect to file Form 5500—Schedule I (same form as prior year) which does not require an audit report

Administrator can elect to file Form 5500—Schedule H which requires an audit report (see Note C)

> 120 participants
Administrator must file Form 5500—Schedule H which requires an audit report (See Note C)

See attached notes to this chart

---

[4] See the small pension plan audit waiver summary in exhibit 5-4, "Small Pension Plan Audit Waiver (SPPAW) Summary."

Note A—Participants are defined by the DOL as follows:

Active participants

- Any individuals who are currently in employment covered by a plan and who are earning or retaining credited service under a plan;
- Any individuals who are currently below the integration level in a plan that is integrated with social security or eligible to have the employer make payments to a 401(k) or Section 125 arrangements (participants only have to be eligible for the plan, not necessarily participating in a 401(k) or Section 125 arrangement);
- Any nonvested individuals who are earning or retaining credited service under a plan.

The term *active participants* does not refer to nonvested former employees who have incurred the break in service period specified in the plan.

Inactive participants

- Any individuals who are retired or separated from employment covered by a plan and who are receiving or entitled to receive benefits.

The term *inactive participants* does not refer to any individual to whom an insurance company has made an irrevocable commitment to pay all the benefits to which the individual is entitled under the plan.

Deceased participants include:

- Any deceased individuals who have beneficiaries who are receiving or are entitled to receive benefits under the plan.

The term *deceased participants* does not refer to any individual to whom an insurance company has made an irrevocable commitment to pay all the benefits to which the beneficiaries of the individual are entitled under the plan.

Note B—*80–120 Rule*

Under 29 CFR 2520.103-1d, if a plan has between 80 and 120 participants (inclusive) as of the beginning of a plan year, it may elect to file the same category of form it filed the year before (for example, Form 5500, Schedule I, "Financial Information—Small Plans") and avoid the audit requirement. This means that plans with between 80 and 120 participants at the beginning of the plan year that filed a Form 5500, Schedule I, "Financial Information—Small Plans," in the prior year may elect in the current year to complete the Form 5500 following the requirements for a small plan. There is no limit to the number of years this election can be made. DOL officials have indicated that health and welfare plans with 100 or more participants which involve employee contributions generally are required to have an audit unless employee contributions are used to purchase insurance from a third-party insurer or forwarded to a health maintenance organization within prescribed timeframes, even if the sponsor does not maintain a trust and considers the assets to be subject to the rights of general creditors (29 CFR 2520.104-44). In these circumstances, it is important for careful consideration to be given as to whether an audit is required.

This rule does not apply to entities that choose to file using Form 5500-SF in the prior year.

Note C—*Audit Requirement*

If a Form 5500 is filed, an audit of the financial statements generally is required except that (*a*) plans that have a short plan year of seven months or less may elect to defer (but not eliminate) the audit requirement, and (*b*) plans whose sole assets are insurance contracts that fully guarantee benefit payments are not required to be audited (see appendix A, "ERISA and Related Regulations").

Exhibit 5-3

WELFARE BENEFIT PLANS AUDIT:
DECISION FLOWCHART

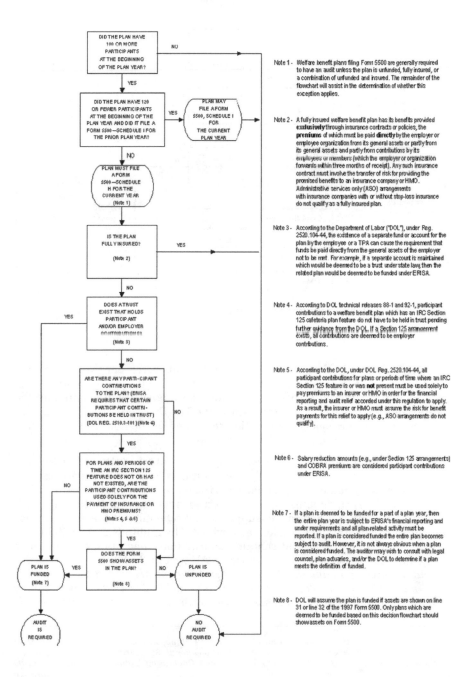

Note 1 - Welfare benefit plans filing Form 5500 are generally required to have an audit unless the plan is unfunded, fully insured, or a combination of unfunded and insured. The remainder of the flowchart will assist in the determination of whether this exception applies.

Note 2 - A fully insured welfare benefit plan has its benefits provided **exclusively** through insurance contracts or policies, the **premiums** of which must be paid **directly** by the employer or employee organization from its general assets or partly from its general assets and partly from contributions by its employees or members (which the employer or organization forwards within three months of receipt). Any such insurance contract must involve the transfer of risk for providing the promised benefits to an insurance company or HMO. Administrative services only (ASO) arrangements with insurance companies with or without stop-loss insurance do not qualify as a fully insured plan.

Note 3 - According to the Department of Labor ("DOL"), under Reg. 2520.104-44, the existence of a separate fund or account for the plan by the employee or a TPA can cause the requirement that funds be paid directly from the general assets of the employer not to be met. For example, if a separate account is maintained which would be deemed to be a trust under state law, then the related plan would be deemed to be funded under ERISA.

Note 4 - According to DOL technical releases 88-1 and 92-1, participant contributions to a welfare benefit plan which has an IRC Section 125 cafeteria plan feature do not have to be held in trust pending further guidance from the DOL. If a Section 125 arrangement exists, all contributions are deemed to be employer contributions.

Note 5 - According to the DOL, under DOL Reg. 2520.104-44, all participant contributions for plans or periods of time where an IRC Section 125 feature is or was **not** present must be used solely to pay premiums to an insurer or HMO in order for the financial reporting and audit relief accorded under this regulation to apply. As a result, the insurer or HMO must assume the risk for benefit payments for this relief to apply (e.g., ASO arrangements do not qualify).

Note 6 - Salary reduction amounts (e.g., under Section 125 arrangements) and COBRA premiums are considered participant contributions under ERISA.

Note 7 - If a plan is deemed to be funded for a part of a plan year, then the entire plan year is subject to ERISA's financial reporting and under requirements and all plan-related activity must be reported. If a plan is considered funded the entire plan becomes subject to audit. However, it is not always obvious when a plan is considered funded. The auditor may wish to consult with legal counsel, plan actuaries, and/or the DOL to determine if a plan meets the definition of funded.

Note 8 - DOL will assume the plan is funded if assets are shown on line 31 or line 32 of the 1997 Form 5500. Only plans which are deemed to be funded based on this decision flowchart should show assets on Form 5500.

Exhibit 5-4

Small Pension Plan Audit Waiver (SPPAW) Summary
(Applies to Plan Years Beginning on or after April 18, 2001)

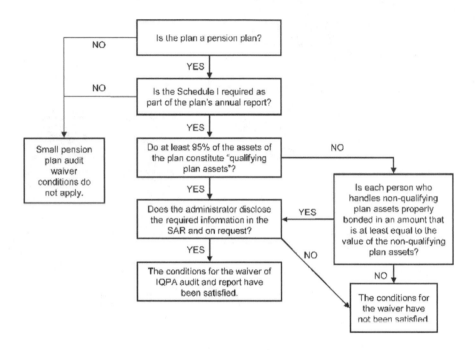

5.17 Generally, the plan's financial statements accompany the Form 5500 that is filed by the plan administrator. The Form 5500 requires footnote disclosure of any differences between the audited financial statements and the statements included as part of the Form 5500. The DOL may reject a filing that does not properly reconcile information contained in the financial statements with information contained in the Form 5500.

5.18 ERISA requires that certain supplemental schedules accompany the basic financial statements. Usually the auditor is engaged to report on such supplemental schedules only in relation to the basic financial statements taken as a whole. In such circumstances, the auditor's measure of materiality with regard to the information in the supplemental schedules is the same as that for the financial statements taken as a whole. The auditor's responsibility for reporting on a document that contains information in addition to the client's basic financial statements is described in AU section 551A, *Reporting on Information Accompanying the Basic Financial Statements in Auditor-Submitted Documents* (AICPA, *Professional Standards*),[†] and is described in paragraphs 13.08–.18. If the auditor is separately engaged to express an opinion on the

---

[†] In February 2010, the AICPA issued SAS No. 119, *Supplementary Information in Relation to the Financial Statements as a Whole* (AICPA, *Professional Standards*, AU sec. 551), which, along with SAS No. 118, *Other Information in Documents Containing Audited Financial Statements*

(continued)

supplementary information, as described in AU section 623, *Special Reports* (AICPA, *Professional Standards*), the measurement of materiality must be related to each individual element, account, or item reported on rather than to the aggregate thereof on the basic financial statements taken as a whole.

5.19 In addition, plans with fewer than 100 participants that elect to file the Form 5500, Schedule H, "Financial Information," under the 80–120 participant rule, rather than a Form 5500, Schedule I, are also required to engage an independent auditor. Under this rule, if a plan has between 80 and 120 participants (inclusive) at the beginning of the plan year, the plan may elect to file the same financial information schedule that was filed for the previous year. Exhibit 5-2 summarizes the conditions that generally require audits of pension plan financial statements and schedules under ERISA in decision tree format. Exhibit 5-3 summarizes the conditions that generally require audits of welfare benefit plans under ERISA in decision tree format.

Engagement Letter

5.20 The understanding with the client concerning the scope of services should be communicated in the form of an engagement letter. Generally, this understanding would be obtained during the planning phase of an engagement (prior to fieldwork). If this understanding changes during the course of the engagement, the auditor may obtain an updated engagement letter that documents such changes. In addition to the matters listed in AU section 311 paragraph .09, the auditor may include the following in an engagement letter for an employee benefit plan audit:

    a. Whether the engagement represents a full-scope or a limited scope audit (see paragraph 5.13).

        i. If the engagement is to be a limited-scope audit, the plan administrator's responsibilities as they relate to the completeness and accuracy of the trustee certification (see 29 CFR 2520.103-5).

    b. Management's responsibility for establishing an accounting and financial reporting process for determining fair value measurements.

    c. The auditor's responsibility with respect to supplemental schedules accompanying the basic financial statements (see paragraph 5.18).

    d. The auditor's responsibility with respect to consideration of the plan's qualification for tax-exempt status, with sufficient specificity to make clear that the audit does not contemplate an opinion on plan tax qualification (see paragraphs 12.01–.10).

    e. The auditor's responsibility with respect to information in the Form 5500 (see paragraphs 12.36–.38). The letter might address the fact that, where the auditor's report is to be included in the Form 5500

(footnote continued)

(AICPA, *Professional Standards*, AU sec. 550), supersedes AU section 551A, *Reporting on Information Accompanying the Basic Financial Statements in Auditor-Submitted Documents* (AICPA, *Professional Standards*). SAS No. 119 addresses the auditor's responsibility when engaged to report on whether supplementary information is fairly stated, in all material respects, in relation to the financial statements as a whole. This SAS is effective for periods beginning on or after December 15, 2010. Early application is permitted and therefore, if adopting SAS No. 119 early, refer to the standard for further guidance.

filing, the auditor's report will not be attached to the financial statements included with the Form 5500 until the auditors have read the completed Form 5500.

f. The auditor's responsibility with respect to reporting matters that come to the auditor's attention regarding lack of compliance with ERISA requirements, making it clear that the audit does not encompass procedures specifically directed at determining such compliance (see paragraph 1.17).

g. Whether, due to the complex or subjective nature of the subject matter, the audit may require the special skills and knowledge of a specialist (for example, use of actuaries for defined benefit pension plans and health and welfare plans; or a valuation professional for investments whose valuations are subjective, such as derivative financial instruments, nonpublicly held stock and real estate).

h. If applicable, the auditor's responsibilities with respect to electronic filings (such as the Form 5500 or Securities and Exchange Commission Form 11-K).

i. The effects of other regulations or laws, such as Sarbanes-Oxley Act of 2002 and the Health Insurance Portability and Accountability Act of 1996 (HIPAA).

j. If applicable, the involvement of third party service providers or affiliates of the public accounting firm (such as the use of staff from a foreign office or location) on the audit engagement.

k. The auditor's responsibilities under GAAS in accordance with AU section 380 (see paragraph 5.08 for further discussion).

Exhibit 5-5

Following is an illustrative engagement letter for a full-scope defined benefit employee benefit plan audit engagement. This letter may not contain all matters that pertain to the engagement and therefore should be modified, as appropriate, for the individual circumstances of each engagement. For example, if the engagement is a Form 11-K audit or is for other than a full scope audit, the letter should be modified accordingly.

[*Date*]

Plan Administrator,[5] Sample Company Employee Benefit Plan or
President or Chief Financial Officer, Sample Company
[*Address*]

This letter will confirm our understanding of our engagement to audit the financial statements and supplemental schedules of Sample Company Employee Benefit Plan (the Plan) as of December 31, 20X1, and for the year then ended, all of which are to be included in the Plan's Form 5500 filing with the Department of Labor (DOL).

We will audit the Plan's financial statements for the year ended December 31, 20X1 for the purpose of expressing an opinion on the fairness with which they present, in all material respects, the financial status of the plan and changes in financial status of the plan[6] in conformity with accounting principles generally accepted in the United States of America, and whether the supplemental schedules are fairly stated in all material respects in relation to the basic financial statements taken as a whole and in conformity with the DOL's Rules and Regulations for Reporting and Disclosure under ERISA.[7]

We will conduct our audit in accordance with auditing standards generally accepted in the United States of America. Those standards require that we obtain reasonable, rather than absolute, assurance about whether the financial statements are free of material misstatements, whether caused by error or fraud. Accordingly, a material misstatement may remain undetected. Also, an audit is not designed to detect error or fraud that is immaterial to the financial statements; therefore, the audit will not necessarily detect misstatements that might exist due to error, fraudulent financial reporting, misappropriation of assets, prohibited transactions with parties in interest, or other violations of ERISA rules and regulations. The Plan Administrator is responsible for establishing and maintaining an effective system of internal control over financial reporting, which is the best means of preventing or detecting such matters. Our report will be addressed to the Plan Administrator and participants.[8]

---

[5] Typically in a multiemployer plan the engagement letter is addressed to the board of trustees because the board of trustees is the administrator of the plan.

[6] Financial status is used for defined benefit pension or health and welfare plans. Defined contribution or health and welfare plans use net assets available for benefits and changes in net assets available for benefits.

[7] If a limited scope audit is to be performed, this paragraph should be deleted.

[8] If a limited scope audit is to be performed, this paragraph and the preceding paragraph should be replaced with the following:

We will conduct the audit in accordance with auditing standards generally accepted in the United States of America except that, as permitted by Regulation 2520.103-8 of the Department of Labor's (DOL's) Rules and Regulations for Reporting and Disclosure under the Employee Retirement Income Security Act of 1974 (ERISA) and as instructed by you, we will not perform

(continued)

We cannot provide assurance that an unqualified [limited scope opinion as permitted by Regulation 2520.103-8 of the DOL's Rules and Regulations for Reporting and Disclosure under ERISA] opinion will be rendered. Circumstances may arise in which it is necessary for us to modify our report or withdraw from the engagement. In such circumstances, our findings or reasons for withdrawal will be communicated to [*the Trustees of the Plan or the members of the Plan Sponsor's Audit Committee*].

The financial statements are the responsibility of the Plan Administrator. Management is also responsible for (*a*) establishing and maintaining effective internal control over financial reporting, (*b*) identifying and ensuring that the plan complies with the laws and regulations applicable to its activities, (*c*) making all financial records and related information available to us, (*d*) properly recording transactions in the accounting records, (*e*) making appropriate accounting estimates, (*f*) safeguarding assets, and (*g*) providing to us at the conclusion of the engagement a representation letter that, among other things, will confirm management's responsibility for the preparation of the financial statements in conformity with accounting principles generally accepted in the United States of America and the supplemental schedules in conformity with the DOL *Rules and Regulations for Reporting and Disclosure under ERISA*, the availability of financial records and related data, the completeness and availability of all minutes of the Board and committee meetings, an acknowledgment of its responsibility for the design and implementation of programs and controls to prevent and detect fraud, an acknowledgment of the absence of any knowledge of fraud or suspected fraud affecting the plan involving (*a*) management, (*b*) employees who have significant roles in the plan's internal control, or (*c*) others where the fraud could have a material effect on the financial statements, and the acknowledgment of the absence of knowledge of any allegations of fraud or suspected fraud affecting the plan received in communications from employees, former employees, participants, regulators, beneficiaries, service providers, third-party administrators or others.

The Plan Administrator has responsibility for the financial statements and all representations contained therein. The Plan Administrator also has responsibility for the adoption of sound accounting policies and the implementation of record keeping and internal control to maintain the reliability of the financial statements and to provide reasonable assurance against the possibility of misstatements that are material to the financial statements.

The Plan Administrator is responsible for adjusting the financial statements to correct material misstatements and for affirming to us in the representation

---

(footnote continued)

any auditing procedures with respect to information prepared and certified to by [name of trustee or custodian], the trustee (or custodian), other than comparing that information with the related information included in the financial statements and supplemental schedules. Because of the significance of the information that we will not audit, we will not express an opinion on the financial statements and supplemental schedules taken as a whole. The form and content of the information included in the financial statements and supplemental schedules, other than that derived from the information certified to by the trustee (or custodian), will be audited by us in accordance with auditing standards generally accepted in the United States of America, and will be subjected to tests of your accounting records and other procedures as we consider necessary to enable us to express an opinion as to whether they are presented in compliance with the DOL's Rules and Regulations for Reporting and Disclosure under ERISA. Our report will be addressed to the Plan Administrator and participants.

letter that the effects of any uncorrected misstatements aggregated by us during the current engagement and pertaining to the latest period presented are immaterial, both individually and in the aggregate, to the financial statements taken as a whole.

An audit is planned and performed to obtain reasonable assurance that material misstatements, whether caused by error or fraud, are detected. Absolute assurance is not attainable because of the nature of audit evidence and the characteristics of fraud. Therefore, there is a risk that material errors or fraud (including fraud that may be an illegal act) may exist and not be detected by an audit performed in accordance with generally accepted auditing standards.

To the extent that they come to our attention, we will inform management about any material errors, any instances of fraud and, unless clearly inconsequential, any illegal acts. If we become aware of information indicating that an instance of fraud or an illegal act may have occurred which in our judgment would have a material effect on the financial statements of the Plan, we will communicate such information to [*the Trustees of the Plan or the member of the Plan Sponsor's Audit Committee*].

Although we are not being engaged to report on the Plan's internal control, we will communicate to you any recommendations for operational or administrative efficiency. In addition, any deficiencies identified during the audit that upon evaluation are considered significant deficiencies or material weaknesses will be communicated, in writing, to you, or to those charged with governance.[9]

The Plan and Sample Company (the Plan Sponsor) agree that all records, documentation, and information we request in connection with our audit will be made available to us, that all material information will be disclosed to us, and that we will have the full cooperation of the Plan's and the Plan Sponsor's personnel.

As a part of our audit, we will perform certain procedures, as required by generally accepted auditing standards, directed at considering the Plan's compliance with applicable Internal Revenue Code requirements for tax exempt status, including inspecting the Plan's latest tax determination letter from the IRS. As we conduct our audit, we will be aware of the possibility that events affecting the Plan's tax status may have occurred. Similarly, we will be aware of the possibility that events affecting the Plan's compliance with the requirements of ERISA may have occurred. We will inform you of any instances of tax or ERISA noncompliance that come to our attention during the course of our audit. You should recognize, however, that our audit is not designed to nor is it intended to determine the Plan's overall compliance with applicable provisions of the Internal Revenue Code or ERISA.

You have not engaged us to prepare or review the Plan's Form 5500 filing with the Department of Labor. Because the audited financial statements are required to be filed with the Form 5500, professional standards require that we

---

[9] For audits of issuers, such as Form 11-K, the guidance in AU section 325, *Communications About Control Deficiencies in an Audit of Financial Statements* (AICPA, *PCAOB Standards and Related Rules*, Interim Standards), should be followed.

read the Form 5500 prior to its filing. The purpose of this procedure is to consider whether information, or the manner of its presentation in the Form 5500, is materially inconsistent with the information, or the manner of its presentation, appearing in the financial statements. These procedures are not sufficient nor are they intended to ensure that the form is completely and accurately prepared. In the event that our report is issued prior to our having read the Form 5500, you agree not to attach our report to the financial statements included with the Form 5500 filing until we have read the completed Form 5500.[10]

The working papers for this engagement are the property of [*name of CPA firm*] and constitute confidential information. Except as discussed below, any requests for access to our working papers will be discussed with you prior to making them available to requesting parties.[11]

- We may be requested to make certain working papers available to the Department of Labor (DOL) pursuant to authority given to it by law or regulation. If requested, access to such working papers will be provided under the supervision of [*name of audit firm*] personnel. Furthermore, upon request, we may provide photocopies of selected working papers to the DOL. We will mark all information as confidential and maintain control over the duplication of all such information. However, the DOL may intend, or decide, to distribute the photocopies or information contained therein to others, including other governmental agencies. You will be billed for additional fees as a result of the aforementioned work.

Our fees will be billed as work progresses and are based on the amount of time required at various levels of responsibility, plus actual out-of-pocket expenses. Invoices are payable upon presentation. We will notify you immediately of any circumstances we encounter that could significantly affect our initial estimate of total fees of $_____.

---

[10] This paragraph should be deleted or revised if the auditor has, in fact, been engaged to prepare or review the plan's Form 5500 filing. The auditor may issue a separate engagement letter, or add the following paragraph if they have been engaged to prepare the Form 5500:

> Our engagement will also include preparation *(or review)* of the Plan's Form 5500 filing for the DOL. With the completion of these services, we will authorize the Plan to include our reports on the financial statements and supplemental schedules in the Plan's Form 5500 filing. In order to perform this nonaudit service, the Plan Administrator in conjunction with management of the Plan Sponsor must agree to perform the following functions:
>
> - make all management decisions and perform all management functions with respect to the Form 5500
> - designate a competent employee, preferably within the Plan Sponsor's senior management, to oversee the services
> - evaluate the adequacy and the results of the services performed
> - accept responsibility for the results of the services
> - establish and maintain internal controls, including monitoring on-going activities.

Any other nonaudit services that you request will be covered in a separate engagement letter.

[11] If the auditors participate in a peer review program they may add the following paragraph:

> Our firm, as well as other accounting firms, participate in a peer review program, covering our audit and accounting practices. This program requires that once every three years we subject our system of quality control to an examination by another accounting firm. As part of this process, the other firm will review a sample of our work. It is possible that the work we perform for you may be selected for their review. If it is, they are bound by professional standards to keep all information confidential.

We shall be pleased to discuss this letter with you at any time. If this letter correctly expresses your understanding, please sign the enclosed copy where indicated and return it to us.

We appreciate the opportunity to serve you.

Very truly yours,

_____

[*Partner's Signature*]

_____

[*Firm Name*]

Accepted and agreed to:[12]

_____
[*Plan Administrator's Signature*][13]

_____
[*Sample Company—Chief Financial Officer's Signature*]

_____
[*Title*]

_____
[*Title*]

_____
[*Date*]

_____
[*Date*]

Audit Planning

5.21 The first standard of field work states, "The auditor must adequately plan the work and must properly supervise any assistants." AU section 311 establishes requirements and provides guidance on the considerations and activities applicable to planning and supervision of an audit conducted in accordance with GAAS, including appointment of the independent auditor; preliminary engagement activities; establishing an understanding with the client; developing and documenting a detailed audit plan; determining the extent of involvement of professionals with specialized skills; and communicating with those charged with governance. Audit planning also involves developing an overall audit strategy for the expected conduct, organization, and staffing of the audit. The nature, timing, and extent of planning will vary according to the type of employee benefit plan, size and complexity of the plan's operations, the auditor's experience with the plan and understanding of the plan and its environment, including its internal control (and any restrictions placed on the audit see paragraph 5.13).

5.22 AU section 311 paragraph .03 states that the auditor must plan the audit so that it is responsive to the assessment of the risks of material misstatement based on the auditor's understanding of the plan and its environment, including its internal control. Planning is not a discrete phase of the audit, but rather an iterative process that begins with engagement acceptance and continues throughout the audit as the auditor performs audit procedures and accumulates sufficient appropriate audit evidence to support the audit opinion.

5.23 If the auditor of the plan's financial statements is also the auditor of the financial statements of the sponsoring employer, it may be more efficient

---

[12] For multiemployer plans, the engagement letter generally is signed by a trustee or the plan administrator (if the plan trustees vote for the plan administrator to do so.)

[13] A copy of the signed letter is generally sent to the audit committee, if one exists.

for the auditor to coordinate the audits, particularly with regard to the testing of payroll and participant data provided to the plan's actuary. Although testing of the payroll area may have been performed in conjunction with the corporate audit, the relevant assertions related to payroll for the plan audit may or may not have been tested. When determining the scope of testing for the plan audit, the plan auditor may consider gaining an understanding of the assertions relevant to payroll that were tested during the corporate audit. For example, payroll testing performed for a corporate audit may not place any emphasis on individual amounts withheld and may be insufficient to satisfy the payroll testing requirements for a plan audit. Often payroll processing is outsourced to an outside service provider that may or may not have an appropriate SAS No. 70 report (see chapter 6 for further discussion of SAS No. 70 reports).

5.24 If the plan sponsor has an internal audit department that has performed work on payroll data that is relevant to the audit, and it would be effective to incorporate their work into the audit, AU section 322, *The Auditor's Consideration of the Internal Audit Function in an Audit of Financial Statements* (AICPA, *Professional Standards*), provides guidance on what the auditor needs to consider when making use of the internal auditors' work in the plan audit.

5.25 In accordance with paragraph .22 of AU section 311, the auditor should consider whether specialized skills are needed in performing the audit. For example, the auditor may need special skill or knowledge to plan and perform auditing procedures for an employee benefit plan that has securities that do not have a readily determinable market value. If specialized skills are needed, the auditor should seek the assistance of a professional possessing such skills, who may be either on the auditor's staff or an outside professional. If the use of such a professional is planned, the auditor should determine whether that professional will effectively function as a member of the audit team. If such a professional is part of the audit team, the auditor's responsibilities for supervising that professional are equivalent to those for other assistants. In such circumstances, the auditor should have sufficient knowledge to communicate the objectives of the other professional's work; to evaluate whether the specified audit procedures will meet the auditor's objectives; and to evaluate the results of the audit procedures applied as they relate to the nature, timing, and extent of further planned audit procedures. AU section 311 provides guidance on the use of individuals who serve as members of the audit team and assist the auditor in planning and performing auditing procedures. The auditor also may plan to use the work of a specialist. AU section 336, *Using the Work of a Specialist* (AICPA, *Professional Standards*), provides guidance on the use of the work of specialists as audit evidence.

5.26 Management ordinarily should have procedures for ensuring accurate financial reporting for the plan's financial statements. Employee benefit plan sponsors typically use third-party service providers in some capacity to assist in administering their plans. It is not uncommon for the third-party service provider reports to be used as the basis for the plan's financial statements as typically there is no general ledger maintained for the plan. Although the plan sponsor may have outsourced administrative functions to a third party, the plan sponsor still has a fiduciary duty under ERISA to ensure accurate financial reporting. Plan sponsors need to be cognizant that service provider reports may not be prepared in accordance with U.S. GAAP and may need adjustments to conform to U.S. GAAP. Plan sponsor personnel responsible for plan financial reporting ordinarily should be familiar with U.S. GAAP and ERISA requirements for employee benefit plans. Review of service provider reports, used to compile financial statements, for reasonableness and appropriate accrual adjustments made by the plan sponsor is recommended. For additional guidance on management's responsibilities with respect to controls over financial reporting refer to AU section 314, *Understanding the Entity and Its Environment and Assessing the Risks of Material Misstatement* (AICPA, *Professional Standards*).

Communication and Coordination

5.27 Communication and coordination considerations are a particularly important aspect in planning and performing an audit of a plan because of the many parties who are involved in the administration of the plan, such as the plan sponsor, trustees, custodian, recordkeeper, administrator, investment trustee, insurance company, other independent auditors, actuary, and attorney.

Audit Risk

5.28 AU section 312, *Audit Risk and Materiality in Conducting an Audit* (AICPA, *Professional Standards*), states that audit risk is a function of the risk that the financial statements prepared by management are materially misstated and the risk that the auditor will not detect such material misstatement. A few areas presenting particular risks of material misstatement when auditing employee benefit plans are (*a*) the fair market value of investments with no readily ascertainable market, (*b*) new types of investments, (*c*) benefit amounts, (*d*) transactions initiated by telephone or electronic means (such as the Internet or intranet), and (*e*) contributions are accurately calculated and remitted on a timely basis. The auditor should consider audit risk in relation to the relevant assertions related to individual account balances, classes of transactions, and disclosures and at the overall financial statement level.

5.29 At the account balance, class of transactions, relevant assertion, or disclosure level, audit risk consists of (*a*) the risks of material misstatement (consisting of inherent risk and control risk) and (*b*) the detection risk. AU section 312 paragraph .23 states that auditors should assess the risk of material misstatement at the relevant assertion level as a basis for further audit procedures (tests of controls or substantive procedures). It is not acceptable to simply deem risk to be "at the maximum." This assessment may be in qualitative terms such as high, medium, and low, or in quantitative terms such as percentages.

5.30 In considering audit risk at the overall financial statement level, the auditor should consider risks of material misstatement that relate pervasively to the financial statements taken as a whole and potentially affect many relevant assertions. Risks of this nature often relate to the plan's control environment and are not necessarily identifiable with specific relevant assertions at the class of transactions, account balance, or disclosure level. Such risks may be especially relevant to the auditor's consideration of the risks of material misstatement arising from fraud, for example, through management override of internal control.

5.31 The following considerations may be useful when assessing the risks of material misstatement in an employee benefit plan audit:

- Determining an overall materiality level for the plan. The determination of what is material to the users is a matter of professional judgment.

- The effect of current developments in the financial markets as they relate to the valuation of plan investments.

- Whether the risk of material misstatement would be high for areas such as investments, contributions, and benefits paid.

Planning Materiality

5.32 The auditor's consideration of materiality is a matter of professional judgment and is influenced by the auditor's perception of the needs of users of financial statements. Materiality judgments are made in light of surrounding circumstances and necessarily involve both quantitative and qualitative considerations.

5.33 In accordance with AU section 312 paragraph .27, the auditor should determine a materiality level for the financial statements taken as a whole when establishing the overall audit strategy for the audit. The auditor often may apply a percentage to a chosen benchmark as a step in determining materiality for the financial statements taken as a whole. Benchmarks for employee benefit plans may include

- net assets.

- beginning of the year net assets for a plan that was merged out of existence during the audit period.

- total contributions or total benefits paid (for a health and welfare plan with a small amount of net assets).

- benefit payments (for a terminating plan).

- allocated net assets or outstanding loan balance (for an employee stock ownership plan [ESOP] with negative net assets).

Tolerable Misstatement

5.34 The initial determination of materiality is made for the financial statement taken as a whole. However, the auditor should allow for the possibility that some misstatements of lesser amounts than the materiality levels could, in the aggregate, result in a material misstatement of the financial statements. To do so, the auditor should determine one or more levels of tolerable misstatement. AU section 312 paragraph .34 defines *tolerable misstatement* (or *tolerable error*) as the maximum error in a population (for example, the class of transactions or account balance) that the auditor is willing to accept. Such levels of tolerable misstatement are normally lower than the materiality levels.

Qualitative Aspects of Materiality

5.35 As indicated in the preceding paragraphs, judgments about materiality include both quantitative and qualitative information. As a result of the interaction of quantitative and qualitative considerations in materiality judgments, misstatements of relatively small amounts that come to the auditor's attention could have a material effect on the financial statements. For example, the effect of an incorrect contribution amount to a participant's account in a defined contribution plan which is otherwise immaterial could be material if there was a systematic error in the process of determining the contribution for many participants occurring over several years. An immaterial error in one year affects a participant's investment return for all future years, and to correct it may require a material contribution from the plan sponsor to reinstate participant account balances to the level they would have been had the errors not occurred. Another aspect is that the error is operational, where the plan is not being operated consistent with the plan document, which could affect the plan's tax-exempt status.

5.36 Qualitative considerations also influence the auditor in reaching a conclusion about whether misstatements are material. Paragraph .60 of AU section 312 provides qualitative factors that the auditor may consider relevant in determining whether misstatements are material. Such qualitative factors for employee benefit plan financial statements may include

- a misstatement that changes the financial status of a plan from overfunded to underfunded.

- a misstatement that changes the regulatory funding requirements of a defined benefit pension plan.

- the potential effect of the misstatement on a plan's compliance with ERISA regulations or tax-qualified status.

- whether the misstatement is an indication of a potential prohibited transaction.

5.37 The following areas are typically the most material areas in a benefit plan's financial statements:

- Investments (and cash in a health and welfare plan)

- Benefits paid (in a health and welfare plan)

- Pensions and annuities paid (in a pension plan)

- Contributions

5.38 Other balances in an employee benefit plan (for example, cash in a pension plan) are not normally material to a plan's financial statements; therefore, errors might be significant in relation to the account balance but still would be below the tolerable error established for that account.

Use of Assertions in Obtaining Audit Evidence

5.39 Paragraphs .14–.19 of AU section 326, *Audit Evidence* (AICPA, *Professional Standards*), discuss the use of assertions in obtaining audit evidence. In representing that the financial statements are fairly presented in accordance with GAAP, management implicitly or explicitly makes assertions regarding the recognition, measurement, and disclosure of information in the financial statements and related disclosures. Assertions used by the auditor fall into the following categories.

Categories of Assertions

| | *Description of Assertions* | | |
	Classes of Transactions and Events During the Period	*Account Balances at the End of the Period*	*Presentation and Disclosure*
Occurrence or Existence	Transactions and events that have been recorded have occurred and pertain to the plan. Example: All investment transactions are recorded during the period pertain to the plan. Example: Participants earning benefits during the year were eligible under the terms of the plan.	Assets, liabilities, and equity interests exist. Example: Investments exist at the end of the period. Example: Plan obligations exist at the end of the period.	Disclosed events and transactions have occurred. Example: Information about investments is properly presented and disclosed. Example: Information about benefit obligations is properly presented and disclosed
Rights and Obligations	—	The plan holds or controls the rights to assets, and liabilities are the obligations of the plan. Example: Investments are owned by the plan and are free of liens, pledges and other security interests or, if not, whether the security interests are identified.	Disclosed events and transactions pertain to the plan. Example: Information about investments is properly presented and disclosed.

(continued)

Categories of Assertions—(continued)

	Description of Assertions		
	Classes of Transactions and Events During the Period	*Account Balances at the End of the Period*	*Presentation and Disclosure*
Completeness	All transactions and events that should have been recorded have been recorded. Example: All participant contributions that should have been recorded under the terms of the plan have been recorded. Example: All eligible participants that should have earned benefits under the terms of the plan have been recorded.	All assets, liabilities, and equity interests that should have been recorded have been recorded. Example: All assets relating to participant contributions that should have been recorded under the terms of the plan have been recorded. Example: Benefit obligations due under the plan relating to eligible participants have been recorded.	All disclosures that should have been included in the financial statements have been included. Example: All disclosures relating to participant contributions that should have been included in the financial statements have been included. Example: All disclosures relating to benefit obligations under the plan have been included.
Accuracy or Valuation and Allocation	Amounts and other data relating to recorded transactions and events have been recorded appropriately. Example: Investment principal and income transactions are recorded and	Assets, liabilities, and equity interests are included in the financial statements at appropriate amounts and any resulting valuation or allocation adjustments are recorded appropriately.	Financial and other information is disclosed fairly and at appropriate amounts. Example: Investment information is properly disclosed and in the appropriate amount.

(continued)

Categories of Assertions—(continued)

	Description of Assertions		
	Classes of Transactions and Events During the Period	*Account Balances at the End of the Period*	*Presentation and Disclosure*
	investment transactions are properly valued in conformity with U.S. GAAP. Example: Benefit payments have been calculated in accordance with the plan document.	Example: Investments are valued at period end in conformity with U.S. GAAP. Example: Plan obligations are included in the financial statements at appropriate amounts.	Example: Plan obligations are properly disclosed and at appropriate amounts.
Cut-off	Transactions and events have been recorded in the correct accounting period. Example: Employer contributions receivable have been properly recorded.	—	—
Classification and Understandability	Transactions and events have been recorded in the proper accounts. Example: Changes to participant data have been properly recorded during the period.	—	Financial information is appropriately presented and described and information in disclosures is expressed clearly. Example: Plan obligations information (for example, vested, nonvested) is appropriately presented.

5.40 The auditor should use relevant assertions for classes of transactions, account balances, and presentation and disclosures in sufficient detail to form a basis for the assessment of risks of material misstatement and the design and performance of further audit procedures. The auditor should use relevant assertions in assessing risks by considering the different types of potential misstatements that may occur, and then designing further audit procedures that are responsive to the assessed risks.

5.41 Risks of misstatement at the assertion level for an employee benefit plan may include the following:

- Investments do not exist, are not valued at fair value, and are not shown properly by investment type in the statement of net assets available for benefits and are not properly disclosed.

- Claims and benefit payments have not been paid in accordance with the plan document.

- Employer contribution income is not properly recognized and is not complete with respect to accruals, including amounts due at the end of the period, a valuation for amounts deemed uncollectible, and the present value of any employer withdrawal liability (for multiemployer plans).

- Participant data used to calculate plan benefit obligations are not complete.

- Transactions with parties in interest have not been properly shown in the plan's financial statements.

- Plan expenses have not been recorded in the proper amount, in the proper accounting period and in accordance with the plan document.

Understanding the Entity, Its Environment, Including Its Internal Control

5.42 AU section 314 establishes requirements and provides guidance about implementing the second standard of field work, as follows:

> The auditor must obtain a sufficient understanding of the plan and its environment, including its internal control, to assess the risks of material misstatement of the financial statements whether due to error or fraud, and to design the nature, timing, and extent of further audit procedures.

5.43 Obtaining an understanding of the plan and its environment, including its internal control, is a continuous, dynamic process of gathering, updating, and analyzing information throughout the audit. Throughout this process, the auditor should also consider the guidance in AU section 316, *Consideration of Fraud in a Financial Statement Audit* (AICPA, *Professional Standards*). See paragraphs 5.91–.114 for additional guidance pertaining to AU section 316.

5.44 This section addresses the unique aspects of employee benefit plans that may be helpful in developing the required understanding of the plan, its environment, and its internal control.

Risk Assessment Procedures

5.45 As described in AU section 326, audit procedures performed to obtain an understanding of the plan and its environment, including its internal control, to assess the risks of material misstatement at the financial statement and relevant assertion levels are referred to as *risk assessment procedures*. AU section 326 paragraph .21 states that the auditor must perform risk assessment procedures to provide a satisfactory basis for the assessment of risks at the financial statement and relevant assertion levels. Risk assessment procedures by themselves do not provide sufficient appropriate audit evidence on which to base the audit opinion and must be supplemented by further audit procedures in the form of tests of controls, when relevant or necessary, and substantive procedures.

5.46 In accordance with AU section 314 paragraph .06, the auditor should perform the following risk assessment procedures to obtain an understanding of the plan and its environment, including its internal control:

   a. Inquiries of management and others involved with the plan

   b. Analytical procedures

   c. Observation and inspection

See paragraphs .06–.13 of AU section 314 for additional guidance on risk assessment procedures.

Inquiries of Management and Others

5.47 Inquiry of plan management and others is performed throughout the audit planning process and can be an effective procedure in identifying risks. Inquiry includes asking questions or requesting further information on a matter, evaluating the response and following up to obtain additional information as needed. When the auditor intends to use information about the plan and its environment obtained in prior periods, the auditor should inquire of management to determine if there were any changes that may affect the relevance of such information in the current audit. In response to inquiries made, additional inquiries may be made to determine whether other risk assessment procedures are necessary. An auditor may want to inquire of external parties involved with the plan such as the service providers including the third party administrator, custodian, investment adviser, payroll processor, valuation experts, and actuary. The auditor may find it necessary to also make inquiries of other knowledgeable internal parties involved with the plan including treasury, finance, payroll, and human resources or those charged with governance. Often individuals in human resources are the auditor's primary contact and therefore the auditor may find it necessary to inquire of other knowledgeable parties depending on the circumstances. Also see paragraph 5.58 for typical inquiries of plan management during information gathering that pertain to benefit plans.

Analytical Procedures

5.48 AU section 329, *Analytical Procedures* (AICPA, *Professional Standards*), provides guidance on the use of analytical procedures and requires the use of analytical procedures in the planning and overall review stages of all audits. For planning purposes, these procedures should focus on (*a*) enhancing the auditor's understanding of the plan and the transactions and events that have occurred since the last audit date and (*b*) identifying areas that may represent specific risks relevant to the audit. These procedures can help to identify such things as the existence of unusual transactions and events and amounts, ratios, and trends that might indicate matters that have financial statement and audit planning ramifications. In accordance with AU section 314 paragraph .09, the auditor should apply analytical procedures in planning the audit to assist in understanding the plan and its environment and to identify areas that may represent specific risks relevant to the audit. In performing analytical procedures as risk assessment procedures, the auditor should develop expectations about plausible relationships that are reasonably expected to exist. When comparison of those expectations with recorded amounts or ratios developed from recorded amounts yields unusual or unexpected relationships, the auditor should consider those results in identifying risks of material misstatement. However, when such analytical procedures use data aggregated at a high level (which is often the situation), the results of those analytical procedures provide only a broad initial indication about whether a material misstatement may exist. Accordingly, the auditor should consider the results of such analytical procedures along with other information gathered in identifying the risks of material misstatement.

5.49 The following are examples of preliminary analytical procedures that the auditor may find useful in obtaining an understanding of an employee benefit plan:

- Comparison of investment balances and rates of return with prior-period amounts

- Analysis of changes in contributions and benefit payments during the current period based on statistical data (for example, number of participants eligible to receive benefits in the current period and number of terminations)

- Review fluctuations of various account balances for reasonableness

Observation and Inspection

5.50 Auditors may also use observation and inspection procedures to obtain an understanding of the plan and its environment, including its internal control. The auditor may use the results of his or her inquires of plan management and others to determine observation and inspection procedures to be performed to corroborate the inquiries made. For example, in response to an inquiry related to plan investments, the auditor was informed of new investments that are considered to be hard to value; as a result, the auditor may want to review the investment committee minutes or investment policy statement to identify risks related to potential misstatements due to improper investment valuation.

5.51 Observation and inspection procedures are effective when responses to inquiries indicate potential risks for a significant account and when responses to inquires are conflicting. Observation and inspection procedures are also effective in recurring engagements when changes have occurred, such as significant amendments affecting plan provisions, changes to personnel or service providers or changes at the sponsor that affect the plan.

5.52 The following table provides some examples of inquiries that may be made and the possible inspection or observation procedures that may be performed related to management's response to the inquiry (if the auditor concludes that additional risk assessment procedures or further audit procedures are necessary).

[**Note:** This table is not all inclusive and may be tailored to specific circumstances of the plan engagement.]

Inquiries	Inspection or Observation
An auditor may ask about changes during the year and be informed of a change in custodians. The auditor would then evaluate the response and determine if a potential risk exists. In this example, the auditor is concerned about investment valuation with the new investment mix with the transfer of assets.	Inspect the custodian's investment statement or an investment agreement. Inspect the investment committee minutes or investment policy statementInspect the reconciliation of the transfer to see that it was done.
An auditor may inquire as to a change in recordkeeper.	Compare the beginning balances to the ending balances between recordkeepers.
An auditor may inquire about plan investments and be informed of new hard to value investments. The auditor would then evaluate the response and determine the risk related to investment valuation.	Inspect the custodian's investment statement or an investment agreement. Inspect the investment committee minutes or investment policy statement.
An auditor may ask about staff turnover in the benefits department and be informed that certain positions were eliminated thus creating lack of segregation of duties for contribution and benefit payment processing. In this example, the auditor would evaluate the response and determine the risk related to proper revenue recognition with respect to contributions and that the benefit payments were computed properly and in accordance with the plan document.	Observe and inspect the internal control documentation related to the transaction processing or observe the process and individuals involved.
An auditor may inquire about SAS No. 70 user controls that the plan sponsor ordinarily should have in place for the SAS No. 70 controls to be effective. The auditor may be informed that one of the user controls, the approval process for rollover contributions, is not currently in place. In this example the auditor would evaluate the response and determine the risk related to the rights and obligations.	Inspect the rollover listing or observe how rollovers are processed.

(continued)

Inquiries	Inspection or Observation
Upon inquiry, an auditor may be informed that the plan is now paying expenses. The auditor would need to evaluate the response and determine the risk related to rights and obligations, cut-off and classification. In this example, the auditor is concerned that the plan allows for payment of plan expenses and that the expenses are allowable under the plan, in the proper amount and period.	Inspect invoices, schedule of expenses, plan amendment or board resolution.
The auditor may inquire about any changes to the plan document (plan amendments) for plan mergers, terminations, or the freezing of accounts.	Observe or inspect the board resolution or minutes, and communications to participants.

5.53 The nature and extent of risk assessment procedures to be performed to determine the risks of material misstatement will vary based on the auditor's prior experience with the client and or service provider(s), changes in the plan's operating environment, type and complexity of the plan, financial sophistication of the client, and new accounting pronouncements or new DOL, IRS or Pension Benefit Guaranty Corporation (PBGC) regulations.

5.54 The information obtained by applying risk assessment procedures is an integral part of the planning process as it provides the auditor with an understanding of the plan and its environment and internal control. The information obtained will be used determining materiality levels and assessing risks of material misstatement at the financial statement and relevant assertion levels. The information obtained as part of the risk assessment procedures may be used in conjunction with the testing of controls or in determining the scope of substantive procedures to be performed.

Discussion Among the Audit Team

5.55 In obtaining an understanding of the plan and its environment, including its internal control, AU section 314 states that there should be discussion among the audit team. In accordance with paragraph .14 of AU section 314, the members of the audit team, including the auditor with final responsibility for the audit, should discuss the susceptibility of the plan's financial statements to material misstatements. Members of the audit team should also discuss the potential for material misstatements due to fraud in accordance with the requirements of paragraphs .14–.18 of AU section 316. This discussion could be held concurrently with the discussion among the audit team that is specified by AU section 314. See paragraph 5.95 for further guidance on the discussion among the engagement personnel regarding the risks of material misstatement due to fraud.

Understanding of the Plan and Its Environment

5.56 AU section 314 states the auditor must obtain an understanding of the plan and its environment, including its internal control. In accordance with

AU section 314 paragraph .04, the auditor should use professional judgment to determine the extent of the understanding required of the plan and its environment, including its internal control. The auditor's primary consideration is whether the understanding that has been obtained is sufficient (*a*) to assess risks of material misstatement of the financial statements and (*b*) to design and perform further audit procedures (tests of controls and substantive tests).

5.57 The auditor's understanding of the plan and its environment consists of an understanding of the following aspects:

a. Industry, regulatory, and other external factors

b. Nature of the plan

c. Objectives and strategies and the related business risks that may result in a material misstatement of the financial statements

d. Measurement and review of the plan's financial performance

e. Internal control, which includes the selection and application of accounting policies (see the following section for further discussion)

Refer to appendix A of AU section 314 for examples of matters that the auditor may consider in obtaining an understanding of the plan and its environment relating to categories (*a*)–(*d*) of this paragraph.

Information Gathering

5.58 The auditor may consider applying the following procedures to gather information needed to plan the audit and obtain an understanding of the plan and its environment:

a. Discuss with trustees, plan administrator, or other appropriate representative of the plan the scope of the audit. Determine whether the scope of the audit will be restricted (limited-scope audit), for example, to exclude financial information certified by a bank or insurance carrier (paragraph 5.13). Discuss the types of reports and other services to be rendered, including the supplementary information, if any, required by ERISA and DOL regulations. Determine what supplementary information will be reported on, as required by ERISA and DOL regulations, and on what information he or she will disclaim an opinion.

b. Make inquiries of plan management whether

    i. the plan's financial statements will be prepared in conformity with U.S. GAAP or with another basis of accounting permitted by ERISA or DOL regulations (see paragraphs 13.20–.23).

    ii. investment assets are held by outside custodians. If investment assets are held by outside custodians, the auditor may (1) determine the location of the investments; (2) determine the nature of safekeeping arrangements; or (3) determine the nature and type of investments, whether there are any unusual or hard to value investments, or any changes in the types of investments or investment arrangements.

    iii. the plan's accounting records and participant data are maintained by the plan sponsor, by a bank, by an insurance carrier, or by other outside parties; and how they are maintained.

    iv. periodic financial statements are prepared.

    v. the plan maintains a list of *parties in interest*, as defined by ERISA Section 3(14).

    vi. the plan has procedures for identifying reportable transactions as defined by ERISA and applicable DOL regulations.

    vii. the plan maintains a list of entities whose employees are participants in the plan.

    viii. the plan has either an audit committee or a group equivalent to an audit committee that has been formally designated with responsibility for oversight of the financial reporting process.

    ix. there is a present intention to terminate the plan or merge or transfer assets in or out of the plan.

    x. they have knowledge of fraud or suspected fraud affecting the plan involving, (1) management (2) employees who have significant roles in internal control, or (3) others where the fraud could have a material effect on the financial statements.

    xi. they acknowledge their responsibilities for the design and implementation of programs and controls to prevent and detect fraud.

    xii. they have knowledge of any allegations of fraud or suspected fraud affecting the plan received in communications from employees, former employees, participants, trustees and or custodians, regulators, beneficiaries, service providers, third-party administrators, or others.

    xiii. the frequency at which transactions are processed and the frequency at which they are valued are the same (for example daily).

    xiv. the plan allows participants to initiate transactions by telephone or in an electronic means (such as the Internet or intranet).

    xv. there were any significant amendments or changes to the plan operations during the year or subsequent to year-end.

    xvi. they acknowledge their responsibilities for unrecorded adjustments.

    xvii. whether there have been any changes in service providers.

    xviii. whether there have been significant changes in the number of participants.

  c. Read the plan instrument, including amendments, to determine, among other things, whether the plan is (i) a single employer, multiemployer, or multiple employer plan, (ii) a contributory or noncontributory plan, and (iii) required to be funded or not, and (iv) the nature of the benefits promised.

  d. Read agreements with trustees, investment advisers, and insurance companies to determine whether the plan is a self-funded, insured, or split-funded plan. If the plan is an insured or split-funded plan, determine the type of insurance contract (for example, deposit administration, immediate participation guarantee, or individual policy).

e. Review the prior-year financial statements and Form 5500, filings with the DOL and related correspondence, and the status of IRS determination letters and DOL advisory or exemption opinions, if any. Consider the tax-exempt status of the plan, including whether the plan has procedures for assuring compliance with applicable Internal Revenue Code (IRC) plan qualification requirements.

f. Determine the extent of involvement, if any, of specialists, internal auditors, and other independent auditors.

g. Read reports from the plan's actuary, bank or trustee, insurance company, service auditors, other independent auditors, and internal auditors. After reading these reports, communications may be necessary with the preparer of these reports to determine the extent of audit procedures or the ability to rely on the content of any of these reports.

h. Consider discussing with actuaries their use of participant and other data that is significant to the actuarial computations. Determine the extent of testing of participant data that is necessary by the auditor.

i. Read minutes of trustee, benefits committee, or board of directors meetings applicable to the plan.

5.59 The auditor may use his or her knowledge of matters affecting employee benefit plans, including ERISA, applicable sections of the IRC, and related DOL and IRS regulations to assist in obtaining an understanding of the plan and its environment. For further discussion of applicable laws and regulations, see appendix A.

Understanding Health and Welfare Plans

5.60 Health and welfare plans present unique challenges. Before performing a health and welfare plan audit, it is critical for the auditor to establish a clear understanding of the plan. Under ERISA, the audit requirement is of the plan, not the trust. Therefore, before conducting each audit, gaining an understanding of the benefits offered by the plan is important. For those benefits offered, consider the following:

- Which benefits are fully insured versus self-insured
- Who the providers are and the elements of the contractual arrangement with the plan
- For self-insured claims, how the various claims are administered
- What information systems are used to support the plan operations, and which of those are in-house systems or outsourced
- Understanding management's process for financial reporting

When answering these questions, it is important that the responses be considered with regard to all covered participants (such as, active, those covered by the Consolidated Omnibus Budget Reconciliation Act,[14] and retirees).

---

[14] Refer to paragraph 4.15 for additional information on the Consolidated Omnibus Budget Reconciliation Act.

Understanding areas such as the various benefits offered, the providers, and the control environment are key to developing the audit approach.

HIPAA Considerations

5.61 HIPAA requires that plan sponsors enter into a "Business Associates Agreement" with any of their service providers that have access to any protected health information (PHI). Accordingly, an auditor is considered a business associate, and after entering into a business associates agreement would be permitted access to the necessary information required by professional standards to opine on a plan's financial statements. HIPAA regulations allow for the auditors' working papers to contain PHI; however, PHI in working papers obligates the auditing firm to comply with the HIPAA privacy laws and business associates agreement provisions to maintain the privacy of the PHI, which includes

- restricting access to the working papers,
- providing an accounting of disclosures of PHI, and
- reporting to the sponsor any misuse of PHI by the accounting firm.

PHI includes such information as: name, dates (such as birth date, admission date, discharge date or date of death), age (if 90 or over), social security numbers (block out all except last four digits), telephone and fax numbers, e-mail addresses, medical record numbers, health plan beneficiary numbers, and account numbers.

AU section 339, *Audit Documentation* (AICPA, *Professional Standards*), provides guidance to auditors on documentation requirements. See paragraphs 5.80–.87 for guidance.

Understanding of Internal Control

5.62 AU section 314 states that the auditor should obtain an understanding of the five components of internal control sufficient to assess the risks of material misstatement of the financial statements whether due to error or fraud, and to design the nature, timing, and extent of further audit procedures. AU section 314 describes the components of internal control, explains how an auditor should consider controls in assessing the risks of material misstatement, and provides guidance about how the plan's use of information technology affects the auditor's understanding of internal control. In obtaining this understanding, the auditor should obtain an understanding of the internal controls in place at the plan administrator (for example, participant data, payroll, and oversight of outside service providers) as well as the controls in place at outside service providers (for example, payroll, investments, and recordkeeping). Internal control of employee benefit plans is discussed in chapter 6.

5.63 The following lists examples of controls (see appendix B, "Examples of Controls," for additional controls to consider) that an employee benefit auditor may consider assessing to gain an understanding of

- the plan's management has controls in place to maintain compliance with applicable rules and regulations (for example, DOL, PBGC, IRS, or Public Company Accounting Oversight Board [PCAOB]) and provisions of the plan document.
- the plan has controls over a system for paying and denying pensions or health claims.

- the plan has controls over the appropriate receipt and recording of investment transactions and investment income.
- the plan actuary and recordkeeper have controls to ensure the appropriate data has been used in calculating the plan obligations.
- the plan has controls to ensure that the participant data or payroll information provided to the actuary or recordkeeper for the provision of benefits is accurate.
- the plan has controls to ensure that plan personnel have the capability to prepare the plan's financial statements.
- the plan has controls to ensure the employer and employee contributions are complete and accurate.
- the plan has controls to ensure securities lending activity has been appropriately accounted for.
- the plan administrator has controls to monitor the activities of their outside service providers.

Assessment of Risks of Material Misstatement and the Design of Further Audit Procedures

5.64 As discussed in the preceding paragraph, risk assessment procedures allow the auditor to gather the information necessary to obtain an understanding of the plan and its environment, including its internal control. This knowledge provides a basis for assessing the risks of material misstatement of the financial statements. These risk assessments are then used to design further audit procedures, such as tests of controls, substantive tests, or both. This section provides guidance on assessing the risks of material misstatement and how to design further audit procedures that effectively respond to those risks.

Assessing the Risks of Material Misstatement

5.65 AU section 314 paragraph .102 states that the auditor should identify and assess the risks of material misstatement at the financial statement level and at the relevant assertion level related to classes of transactions, account balances, and disclosures. For this purpose, the auditor should

- a. identify risks throughout the process of obtaining an understanding of the plan and its environment, including relevant controls (for example, controls at the plan sponsor and outside service provider) that relate to the risks, and considering the classes of transactions, account balances, and disclosures in the financial statements.
- b. relate the identified risks to what could go wrong at the relevant assertion level.
- c. consider whether the risks are of a magnitude that could result in a material misstatement of the financial statements.
- d. consider the likelihood that the risks could result in a material misstatement of the financial statements.

5.66 Reading and gaining an understanding of a SAS No. 70 report from an outside service provider may help the auditor to assess the risks of material misstatement and to design further audit procedures to respond to risks.

5.67 The auditor should use information gathered by performing risk assessment procedures, including the audit evidence obtained in evaluating the design of controls and determining whether they have been implemented, as audit evidence to support the risk assessment. The auditor should use the assessment of the risks of material misstatement at the relevant assertion level as the basis to determine the nature, timing, and extent of further audit procedures to be performed.

Identification of Significant Risks

5.68 As part of the assessment of the risks of material misstatement, the auditor should determine which of the risks identified are, in the auditor's judgment, risks that require special audit consideration (such risks are defined as *significant risks*). The determination of significant risks, which arise on most audits, is a matter for the auditor's professional judgment. In exercising this judgment, the auditor should consider inherent risk to determine whether the nature of the risk, the likely magnitude of the potential misstatement including the possibility that the risk may give rise to multiple misstatements, and the likelihood of the risk occurring are such that they require special audit consideration. Risks for employee benefit plan audits include the following risks:

- For all plans:
  - Hard-to-value investments (that is, securities that do not have a readily determinable market value for which estimates are based on unobservable inputs that are not corroborated by observable market data) are not valued at fair value.
  - The disclosure of the basis for valuation of hard-to-value investments (that is, securities that do not have a readily determinable market value for which estimates are based on unobservable inputs that are not corroborated by observable market data) is not sufficient.
  - Investments that use net asset value (NAV) (or its equivalent) as a practical expedient to estimate fair value and NAV (or its equivalent) is not as of the plan's reporting date or NAV (or its equivalent) is not calculated in a manner consistent with the measurement principles of Financial Accounting Standards Board (FASB) *Accounting Standards Codification* (ASC) 946, *Financial Services— Investment Companies.*
  - New accounting guidance is not presented and disclosed in accordance with U.S. GAAP.
  - Derivatives are not accounted for or disclosed in accordance with U.S. GAAP.
  - Securities lending is not presented or disclosed in accordance with U.S. GAAP.
  - In plans which receive a transfer of assets from another plan, that the transfer of assets is not complete.
  - Significant transactions are processed by an outside service provider and no SAS No. 70 report is available.
  - Significant transactions are processed by an outside service provider and the SAS No. 70 report has qualifications, exceptions or carve-outs.

- For defined contribution plans:

  — Employee and employer contributions are incorrect due to the use of a definition of compensation different than specified in the plan document.

  — Employee contributions are not remitted to the trustee and or custodian in accordance with DOL regulations, causing a prohibited transaction.

  — The integrity of the individual account balances are not maintained when the recordkeeper has changed or where there is a transfer of assets received from another plan.

  — In a private company ESOP, the trustee's valuation determination of fair market value or current value may not be consistent with the U.S. GAAP definition of fair value.

- For health and welfare benefit plans:

  — Not all activity of a health and welfare plan is reflected in the financial statements.

  — Incurred but not reported claims have not been properly recorded.

- For defined benefit plans:

  — In an ongoing cash balance defined benefit pension plan, the activity of the hypothetical balances is not appropriate because of the application of an incorrect interest rate, incorrect service credits, or use of incorrect beginning balance.

  — In the year of conversion of a defined benefit pension plan to a cash balance benefit formula, the beginning balance of the hypothetical accounts is misstated.

  — In a frozen defined benefit pension plan, the demographic information is incorrect.

  — Benefit payments, including lump-sum benefit payments, in a defined benefit pension plan are not properly calculated.

  — Benefit payments are not calculated in the correct amounts when the plan has different benefit formulas for different time periods for employee groups (this may occur as a result of numerous plan mergers over the history of the plan) or when the plan has terminated.

  — In a defined benefit pension plan for which the sponsor is having financial difficulty, a contribution receivable is recorded at greater than the collectable amount.

5.69 Refer to paragraphs .45 and .53 of AU section 318, *Performing Audit Procedures in Response to Assessed Risks and Evaluating the Audit Evidence Obtained* (AICPA, *Professional Standards*), for further audit procedures pertaining to significant risks.

Designing and Performing Further Audit Procedures

5.70 AU section 318 provides guidance about implementing the third standard of field work, as follows:

> The auditor must obtain sufficient appropriate audit evidence by performing audit procedures to afford a reasonable basis for an opinion regarding the financial statements under audit.

5.71 To reduce audit risk to an acceptably low level, the auditor (a) should determine overall responses to address the assessed risks of material misstatement at the financial statement level and (b) should design and perform further audit procedures whose nature, timing, and extent are responsive to the assessed risks of material misstatement at the relevant assertion level. The purpose is to provide a clear linkage between the nature, timing, and extent of the auditor's further audit procedures and the assessed risks. The overall responses and the nature, timing, and extent of the further audit procedures to be performed are matters for the professional judgment of the auditor.

Overall Responses

5.72 The auditor's overall responses to address the assessed risks of material misstatement at the financial statement level may include emphasizing to the audit team the need to maintain professional skepticism in gathering and evaluating audit evidence, assigning more experienced staff or those with specialized skills or using specialists, providing more supervision, or incorporating additional elements of unpredictability in the selection of further audit procedures to be performed. Additionally, the auditor may make general changes to the nature, timing, or extent of further audit procedures as an overall response, for example, performing substantive procedures at period end instead of at an interim date.

Further Audit Procedures

5.73 Further audit procedures provide important audit evidence to support an audit opinion. These procedures consist of tests of controls and substantive tests. The nature, timing, and extent of the further audit procedures to be performed by the auditor should be based on the auditor's assessment of risks of material misstatement at the relevant assertion level. Whether tests of controls or substantive tests are appropriate will be based on auditor judgment considering the most effective audit approach. For some plans where reliance on controls (whether at plan sponsor or outside service provider) is not feasible, an auditor may determine that performing only substantive procedures is appropriate. For other plans, the auditor may find that tests of controls can be performed at the plan sponsor and or the service provider or that a Report on Controls Placed in Operation and Tests of Operating Effectiveness (SAS No. 70 type 2 report) exists for the service provider. The auditor often will determine that in these circumstances a combined audit approach using both tests of the operating effectiveness of controls and substantive procedures is an effective audit approach. See further discussion in chapter 6.

5.74 The auditor should perform tests of controls when the auditor's risk assessment includes an expectation of the operating effectiveness of controls or when substantive procedures alone do not provide sufficient appropriate audit evidence at the relevant assertion level.

5.75 Regardless of the audit approach selected, the auditor should design and perform substantive procedures for all relevant assertions related to each material class of transactions, account balance, and disclosure.

5.76 The auditor's substantive procedures should include the following audit procedures related to the financial statement reporting process:

- Agreeing the financial statements, including their accompanying notes, to the underlying accounting records

- Examining material journal entries and other adjustments made during the course of preparing the financial statements. The nature and extent of the auditor's examination of journal entries and other adjustments depend on the nature and complexity of the plan's financial reporting system and the associated risks of material misstatement. The following list includes examples of adjustments that may be found in employee benefit plan audits:

  — Accrual of contribution receivables

  — Accrual of expenses payable

  — Adjustments for valuation of hard to value investments

  — Accrual for unrelated business income tax relating to voluntary employees' beneficiary association trusts or limited partnership investments (see paragraph 12.04)

  — Accruals relating to operational defects

5.77 Refer to chapters 7–12 for specific guidance on auditing procedures that the independent auditor may consider in the audits of employee benefit plans.

Evaluating Misstatements

5.78 Based on the results of substantive procedures, the auditor may identify misstatements in accounts or notes to the financial statements. AU section 312 paragraph .42 states that auditors must accumulate all known and likely misstatements identified during the audit, other than those that the auditor believes are trivial and communicate them to the appropriate level of management. AU section 312 further states that auditors must consider the effects, both individually and in the aggregate, of misstatements (known and likely) that are not corrected by the plan. This consideration includes, among other things, the effect of misstatements related to prior periods.

5.79 For detailed guidance on evaluating audit findings and audit evidence, refer to AU sections 312 and 326, respectively.

Audit Documentation

5.80 The auditor must prepare audit documentation in connection with each engagement in sufficient detail to provide a clear understanding of the work performed (including the nature, timing, extent, and results of audit procedures performed), the audit evidence obtained and its source, and the conclusions reached. Audit documentation

a. provides the principal support for the representation in the auditor's report that the auditor performed the audit in accordance with GAAS, and

b. provides the principal support for the opinion expressed regarding the financial information or the assertion to the effect that an opinion cannot be expressed.

5.81 Audit documentation is an essential element of audit quality. Although documentation alone does not guarantee audit quality, the process of preparing sufficient and appropriate documentation contributes to the quality of an audit.

5.82 Audit documentation is the record of audit procedures performed, relevant audit evidence obtained, and conclusions the auditor reached. Audit documentation, also known as working papers, may be recorded on paper or on electronic or other media. When transferring or copying paper documentation to another media, the auditor should apply procedures to generate a copy that is faithful in form and content to the original paper document.[15]

5.83 Audit documentation includes, for example, audit programs,[16] analyses, issues memoranda, summaries of significant findings or issues, letters of confirmation[17] and representation, checklists, abstracts or copies of important documents, correspondence (including e-mail) concerning significant findings or issues, and schedules of the work the auditor performed. Abstracts or copies of the plan's records (for example, significant and specific contracts and agreements) should be included as part of the audit documentation if they are needed to enable an experienced auditor to understand the work performed and conclusions reached. The audit documentation for a specific engagement is assembled in an audit file.[18]

5.84 The auditor need not retain in audit documentation superseded drafts of working papers or financial statements, notes that reflect incomplete or preliminary thinking, previous copies of documents corrected for typographical or other errors, and duplicates of documents.

5.85 In addition to the objectives set out in paragraph 5.80, audit documentation serves a number of other purposes, including

- assisting the audit team to plan and perform the audit;
- assisting auditors who are new to an engagement and review the prior year's documentation to understand the work performed as an aid in planning and performing the current engagement;

---

[15] There may be legal, regulatory, or other reasons to retain the original paper document.

[16] See AU section 311, *Planning and Supervision* (AICPA, *Professional Standards*), for guidance regarding preparation of audit programs.

[17] Interpretation No. 1, "Use of Electronic Confirmations," of AU section 330, *The Confirmation Process* (AICPA, *Professional Standards*, AU sec. 9330 par. .01–.08), states that if the auditor is satisfied that an electronic confirmation process is secure and properly controlled and the confirmation is directly from a third party who is a bona fide authorized respondent, electronic confirmations may be considered as sufficient, valid confirmation responses. See Interpretation No. 1 of AU section 330 for further guidance.

[18] The audit documentation contained within the audit file may consist of cross-references to documentation for audit engagements with related entities. For example, the documentation for an audit of the financial statements of an employee benefit plan may consist partly of cross-references to the documentation of dual-purpose payroll-related tests performed in connection with the audit of the financial statements of the plan's sponsor.

- assisting members of the audit team responsible for supervision to direct and supervise the audit work, and to review the quality of work performed;

- demonstrating the accountability of the audit team for its work by documenting the procedures performed, the audit evidence examined, and the conclusions reached;

- retaining a record of matters of continuing significance to future audits of the same plan;

- assisting quality control reviewers (for example, internal inspectors) who review documentation to understand how the engagement team reached significant conclusions and whether there is adequate evidential support for those conclusions;

- enabling an experienced auditor to conduct inspections or peer reviews in accordance with applicable legal, regulatory, or other requirements; and

- assisting a successor auditor who reviews a predecessor auditor's audit documentation.

5.86 For the purposes of this guide, *experienced auditor* means an individual (whether internal or external to the firm) who possesses the competencies and skills that would have enabled him or her to perform the audit. These competencies and skills include an understanding of (*a*) audit processes, (*b*) the SASs and applicable legal and regulatory requirements, (*c*) the business environment in which the entity operates, and (*d*) auditing and financial reporting issues relevant to the entity's industry.

5.87 AU section 339 provides guidance on the form, content, and extent of audit documentation. It also discusses how to document significant findings or issues. This SAS states that in documenting the audit procedures performed, the auditor should record who performed the audit work and who reviewed the specific audit documentation. In addition, it provides guidance on audit documentation of specific items tested, documentation requirements when the auditor departs from a presumptively mandatory requirement of a SAS, revisions to audit documentation made after the date of the auditor's report, and the ownership and confidentiality of audit documentation. See AU section 339 for specific guidance.

Audit Documentation (PCAOB Auditing Standard No. 3)

5.88 (*This section pertains to audits of issuers only, such as Form 11-K filers.*) PCAOB Auditing Standard No. 3, *Audit Documentation* (AICPA, *PCAOB Standards and Related Rules*, Auditing Standards), establishes general requirements for documentation the auditor should prepare and retain in connection with engagements conducted pursuant to PCAOB standards.[19] Audit documentation is the written record of the basis for the auditor's conclusions that provides the support for the auditor's representations, whether those representations are contained in the auditor's report or otherwise. Audit documentation facilitates the planning, performance, and supervision of the engagement, and is the basis for the review of the quality of the work because it provides the

---

[19] PCAOB Auditing Standard No. 3, *Audit Documentation* (AICPA, *PCAOB Standards and Related Rules*, Auditing Standards), supersedes SAS No. 96, *Audit Documentation* (this applies to audits of issuers only).

reviewer with written documentation of the evidence supporting the auditor's significant conclusions. This standard provides specific audit document requirements, provides guidance on documentation of specific matters, and retention of and subsequent changes to audit documentation. See PCAOB Auditing Standard No. 3 for further guidance.

Initial Audits of the Plan

5.89 If the auditor did not audit the plan's financial statements or if they have not been previously audited, the auditor should apply procedures that are practicable and reasonable in the circumstances to assure himself that the accounting principles used by the plan in the current and the preceding year are consistent. See paragraphs .24–.25 of AU section 420, *Consistency of Application of Generally Accepted Accounting Principles* (AICPA, *Professional Standards*), for further guidance.

5.90 Areas of special consideration in an initial audit of a plan's financial statements[20] may include (a) the completeness and accuracy of participant data and records of prior years, especially as they relate to participant eligibility; (b) the amounts and types of benefits; (c) the eligibility for benefits; and (d) account balances. The nature, timing, and extent of auditing procedures applied by the auditor are a matter of judgment and will vary with such factors as the adequacy of past records, the significance of beginning balances, and the complexity of the plan's operations. Because ERISA requires that audited plan financial statements present comparative statements of net assets available for benefits, the current year statements should be audited and the prior year presented for comparative purposes may be either compiled, reviewed, or audited. Appropriate reference in the audit report should be made to describe the level of responsibility assumed (see paragraphs 13.43–.46). However, although a compilation or review of prior year is acceptable, the auditor would apply sufficient auditing procedures on the beginning balance of net assets available for benefits, to provide reasonable assurance that there are no material misstatements to these beginning balances that may affect the current year's statement of changes in net assets available for benefits (see paragraph 10.07).

Consideration of Fraud in a Financial Statement Audit

5.91 AU section 316 is the primary source of authoritative guidance about an auditor's responsibilities concerning the consideration of fraud in a financial statement audit. AU section 316 provides guidance to auditors in fulfilling their responsibility to plan and perform the audit to obtain reasonable assurance about whether the financial statements are free of material misstatement, whether caused by error or fraud as stated in AU section 110, *Responsibilities and Functions of the Independent Auditor* (AICPA, *Professional Standards*).

5.92 There are two types of misstatements relevant to the auditor's consideration of fraud in a financial statement audit:

---

[20] For additional nonauthoritative guidance pertaining to initial audits of employee benefit plan financial statements, refer to Technical Questions and Answers section 6933.01, "Initial Audit of a Plan" (AICPA, *Technical Practice Aids*), issued in March 2007.

- Misstatements arising from fraudulent financial reporting
- Misstatements arising from misappropriation of assets

5.93 Three conditions generally are present when fraud occurs. First, management or other employees have an *incentive* or are under *pressure,* which provides a reason to commit fraud. Second, circumstances exist—for example, the absence of controls, ineffective controls, or the ability of management to override controls—that provide an *opportunity* for a fraud to be perpetrated. Third, those involved are able to *rationalize* committing a fraudulent act.

The Importance of Exercising Professional Skepticism

5.94 Because of the characteristics of fraud, the auditor's exercise of professional skepticism is important when considering the risk of material misstatement due to fraud. Professional skepticism is an attitude that includes a questioning mind and a critical assessment of audit evidence. The auditor should conduct the engagement with a mindset that recognizes the possibility that a material misstatement due to fraud could be present, regardless of any past experience with the plan and regardless of the auditor's belief about management's honesty and integrity. Furthermore, professional skepticism requires an ongoing questioning of whether the information and evidence obtained suggests that a material misstatement due to fraud has occurred.

Discussion Among Engagement Personnel Regarding the Risks of Material Misstatement Due to Fraud[21]

5.95 Members of the audit team should discuss the potential for material misstatement due to fraud in accordance with the requirements of paragraphs .14–.18 of AU section 316. The discussion among the audit team members about the susceptibility of the plan's financial statements to material misstatement due to fraud should include a consideration of the known external and internal factors affecting the plan that might (*a*) create incentives and or pressures for management and others to commit fraud, (*b*) provide the opportunity for fraud to be perpetrated, and (*c*) indicate a culture or environment that enables management to rationalize committing fraud. Communication among the audit team members about the risks of material misstatement due to fraud also should continue throughout the audit. See appendix G, "Consideration of Fraud in a Financial Statement Audit," of this guide for a discussion of fraud risk factors specific to employee benefit plans.

Obtaining the Information Needed to Identify the Risks of Material Misstatement Due to Fraud

5.96 AU section 314 establishes standards and provides guidance about how the auditor obtains an understanding of the plan and its environment, including its internal control for the purpose of assessing the risk of material misstatement. In performing that work, information may come to the auditor's

---

[21] The brainstorming session to discuss the entity's susceptibility to material misstatements due to fraud could be held concurrently with the brainstorming session required under AU section 314, *Understanding the Entity and Its Environment and Assessing the Risks of Material Misstatement* (AICPA, *Professional Standards*), to discuss the potential of the risks of material misstatement.

attention that should be considered in identifying risks of material misstatement due to fraud. As part of this work, the auditor should perform the following procedures to obtain information that is used (as described in paragraphs .35–.42 of AU section 316) to identify the risks of material misstatement due to fraud:

a. Make inquiries of management and others within the plan to obtain their views about the risks of fraud and how they are addressed. (See paragraphs .20 .27 of AU section 316.)

b. Consider any unusual or unexpected relationships that have been identified in performing analytical procedures in planning the audit. (See paragraphs .28–.30 of AU section 316.)

c. Consider whether one or more fraud risk factors exist. (See paragraphs .31–.33 of AU section 316, the appendix to AU section 316, and paragraph 5.99 that follows.)

d. Consider other information that may be helpful in the identification of risks of material misstatement due to fraud. (See paragraph .34 of AU section 316.)

In planning the audit, the auditor also should perform analytical procedures relating to revenue with the objective of identifying unusual or unexpected relationships involving revenue accounts that may indicate a material misstatement due to fraudulent financial reporting, for example, for employee benefit plans investment returns that vary from industry benchmarks for the investment type.

5.97 *Considering fraud risk factors.* As indicated in item (c) in the preceding list, the auditor may identify events or conditions that indicate incentives and or pressures to perpetrate fraud, opportunities to carry out the fraud, or attitudes and or rationalizations to justify a fraudulent action. Such events or conditions are referred to as *fraud risk factors*. Fraud risk factors do not necessarily indicate the existence of fraud; however, they often are present in circumstances where fraud exists.

5.98 AU section 316 provides fraud risk factor examples that have been written to apply to most enterprises. Appendix G of this guide contains a list of fraud risk factors specific to employee benefit plans. Remember that fraud risk factors are only one of several sources of information an auditor considers when identifying and assessing risk of material misstatement due to fraud.

Identifying Risks That May Result in a Material Misstatement Due to Fraud[22]

5.99 In identifying risks of material misstatement due to fraud, it is helpful for the auditor to consider the information that has been gathered in accordance with the requirements of paragraphs .19–.34 of AU section 316. The auditor's identification of fraud risks may be influenced by characteristics such as the

---

[22] AU section 314 paragraph .102 states the auditor should identify and assess the risks of material misstatement at the financial statement level and at the relevant assertion level related to classes of transactions, account balances and disclosures. This requirement provides a link between the auditor's consideration of fraud and the auditor's assessment of risk and the auditor's procedures in response to those assessed risks.

size, complexity, and investment attributes of the plan. In addition, the auditor should evaluate whether identified risks of material misstatement due to fraud can be related to specific financial statement account balances or classes of transactions and related assertions, or whether they relate more pervasively to the financial statements as a whole. Certain accounts, classes of transactions, and assertions that have high inherent risk because they involve a high degree of management judgment and subjectivity also may present risks of material misstatement due to fraud because they are susceptible to manipulation by management. For employee benefit plans, such accounts include valuation of investments that do not have a readily determinable market value; for pension plans the accumulated plan benefit obligation; for health and welfare plans the benefit obligations, including those for postretirement, postemployment, claims incurred but not reported, and claims payable. For multiemployer plans, estimates also include the amount and collectability of contributions receivable and withdrawal liabilities.

A Presumption That Improper Revenue Recognition Is a Fraud Risk

5.100 Material misstatements due to fraudulent financial reporting often result from an overstatement of revenues (for example, through premature revenue recognition or recording fictitious revenues) or an understatement of revenues (for example, through improperly shifting revenues to a different period). Therefore, the auditor should ordinarily presume that there is a risk of material misstatement due to fraud relating to revenue recognition. (See paragraph .41 of AU section 316.) For employee benefit plans, this risk of misstatement due to fraudulent financial reporting primarily includes investment income resulting from inappropriate investment valuation and the inappropriate recognition of contributions.

Misappropriation of Assets

5.101 For employee benefit plans, the risk of misstatement due to misappropriation of assets is primarily related to the theft of plan assets, as well as, the improper recording of contributions, distributions, or other income. (See part 2, "Misappropriation of Assets," of appendix G of this guide.)

A Consideration of the Risk of Management Override of Controls

5.102 Even if specific risks of material misstatement due to fraud are not identified by the auditor, there is a possibility that management override of controls could occur, and accordingly, the auditor should address that risk (see paragraph .57 of AU section 316) apart from any conclusions regarding the existence of more specifically identifiable risks. Specifically, the procedures described in paragraphs .58–.67 of AU section 316 should be performed to further address the risk of management override of controls. These procedures include (a) examining journal entries and other adjustments for evidence of possible material misstatement due to fraud, (b) reviewing accounting estimates for biases that could result in material misstatement due to fraud, and (c) evaluating the business rationale for significant unusual transactions.

Assessing the Identified Risks After Taking Into Account an Evaluation of the Plan's Programs and Controls That Address the Risks

5.103 Auditors should comply with the requirements of paragraphs .43– .45 of AU section 316 concerning a plan's programs and controls that address identified risks of material misstatement due to fraud. Examples of programs and controls for employee benefit plans include those examples detailed in appendix B of this guide and also may include the following:

a. Board of directors or committee oversight of the plan with qualified and stable members

b. Identification and education of the individuals who have fiduciary responsibility for the plan

c. Access to qualified ERISA counsel

d. Use of reputable outside service providers, such as investment custodians, investment managers, recordkeepers, claims administrators, or paying agents

e. Appropriate oversight and monitoring of outside service providers

f. Plan administrator-maintained independent records; periodic checks of information provided to the investment custodian

g. Preparation and review of reconciliations of trust assets to participant accounts or accounting records of the plan

h. Segregation of duties related to benefit payments, contributions, investment transactions, and loans

i. Process for approval of transactions with parties-in-interest

j. Periodic audit of methodology and assumptions used in actuarial valuations

k. In multiemployer plans, payroll audits of contributing employers to verify employer contributions receivable

5.104 The auditor should consider whether such programs and controls mitigate the identified risks of material misstatement due to fraud. After the auditor has evaluated whether the entity's programs and controls have been suitably designed and placed in operation, the auditor should assess these risks, taking into account that evaluation. This assessment should be considered when developing the auditor's response to the identified risks of material misstatement due to fraud.

Responding to the Results of the Assessment[23]

5.105 AU sections 316 paragraphs .46–.67 provide requirements and guidance about an auditor's response to the results of the assessment of the risks of material misstatement due to fraud. The auditor responds to risks of material misstatement due to fraud in the following three ways:

a. A response that has an overall effect on how the audit is conducted—that is, a response involving more general considerations apart from the specific procedures otherwise planned (see AU section 316 paragraph .50).

---

[23] Paragraph .03 of AU section 318, *Performing Audit Procedures in Response to Assessed Risks and Evaluating the Audit Evidence Obtained* (AICPA, *Professional Standards*), states that to reduce audit risk to an acceptably low level, the auditor should determine overall responses to address the assessed risks of material misstatement at the financial statement level and should design and perform further audit procedures whose nature, timing and extent are responsive to the assessed risks of material misstatement at the relevant assertion level. See paragraphs .04 and .07 of AU section 318. This requirement provides a link between the auditor's consideration of fraud and the auditor's assessment of risk and the auditor's procedures in response to those assessed risks.

b. A response to identified risks involving the nature, timing, and extent of the auditing procedures to be performed (see AU section 316 paragraphs .51–.56).

c. A response involving the performance of certain procedures to further address the risk of material misstatement due to fraud involving management override of controls, given the unpredictable ways in which such override could occur (see AU section 316 paragraphs .57–.67).

Paragraph G.08 in appendix G of this guide describes specific auditor procedures that could be performed for employee benefit plans.

Evaluating Audit Evidence

5.106 AU sections 316 paragraphs .68–.78 provide requirements and guidance for evaluating audit evidence. The auditor should evaluate whether analytical procedures that were performed as substantive tests or in the overall review stage of the audit indicate a previously unrecognized risk of material misstatement due to fraud. The auditor also should consider whether responses to inquiries throughout the audit about analytical relationships have been vague or implausible, or have produced evidence that is inconsistent with other audit evidence accumulated during the audit.

5.107 At or near the completion of fieldwork, the auditor should evaluate whether the accumulated results of auditing procedures and other observations affect the assessment of the risks of material misstatement due to fraud made earlier in the audit. As part of this evaluation, the auditor with final responsibility for the audit should ascertain that there has been appropriate communication with the other audit team members throughout the audit regarding information or conditions indicative of risks of material misstatement due to fraud. (The engagement team for the plan may need to consult with the engagement team for the sponsor to complete the evaluation.)

Responding to Misstatements That May Be the Result of Fraud

5.108 When audit test results identify misstatements in the financial statements, the auditor should consider whether such misstatements may be indicative of fraud. See paragraphs .75–.78 of AU section 316 for requirements and guidance about an auditor's response to misstatements that may be the result of fraud. If the auditor believes that misstatements are or may be the result of fraud, but the effect of the misstatements is not material to the financial statements, the auditor nevertheless should evaluate the implications, especially those dealing with the organizational position of the person(s) involved.

5.109 If the auditor believes that the misstatement is or may be the result of fraud, and either has determined that the effect could be material to the financial statements or has been unable to evaluate whether the effect is material, the auditor should

a. attempt to obtain additional audit evidence to determine whether material fraud has occurred or is likely to have occurred and, if so, its effect on the financial statements and the auditor's report thereon.[24]

---

[24] See AU section 508, *Reports on Audited Financial Statements* (AICPA, *Professional Standards*), for guidance on auditors' reports issued in connection with audits of financial statements.

    b. consider the implications for other aspects of the audit (see paragraph .76 of AU section 316).

    c. discuss the matter and the approach for further investigation with an appropriate level of management that is at least one level above those involved, and with senior management and the audit committee.[25]

    d. if appropriate, suggest that the client consult with legal counsel.

5.110 The auditor's consideration of the risks of material misstatement and the results of audit tests may indicate such a significant risk of material misstatement due to fraud that the auditor should consider withdrawing from the engagement and communicating the reasons for withdrawal to the audit committee or others with equivalent authority and responsibility. The auditor may wish to consult with legal counsel when considering withdrawal from an engagement.

Communicating About Possible Fraud to Management, the Plan Administrative Committee, the Audit Committee, and Others

5.111 Whenever the auditor has determined that there is evidence that fraud may exist, that matter should be brought to the attention of an appropriate level of management. See paragraphs .79–.82 of AU section 316 for further requirements and guidance about communications with management, the audit committee, and others.[26]

Documenting the Auditor's Consideration of Fraud

5.112 AU section 910 paragraph .83 requires certain items and events to be documented by the auditor.

Practical Guidance

5.113 The AICPA practice aid *Fraud Detection in a GAAS Audit—Revised Edition* provides a wealth of information and help on complying with the provisions of AU section 316. This practice aid is an *other auditing publication* as defined in AU section 150. Other auditing publications have no authoritative status; however, they may help the auditor understand and apply SASs.

5.114 Auditors need to consider the unique characteristics of employee benefit plans when applying AU section 316 in a plan audit. The auditor may need to determine who is the governing body or person responsible for oversight of a plan, which could vary by plan sponsor, in order to direct inquiries regarding fraud. In addition, the auditor may want to consider management's

---

[25] If the auditor believes senior management may be involved, discussion of the matter directly with the audit committee may be appropriate.

[26] PCAOB Release 2004-008 replaces the phrase "the auditor should consider whether these risks represent reportable conditions relating to the entity's internal control that should be communicated to senior management and the audit committee" with "the auditor should consider whether these risks represent significant deficiencies that must be communicated to senior management and the audit committee" in paragraph .80 of AU section 316, *Consideration of Fraud in a Financial Statement Audit* (AICPA, *PCAOB Standards and Related Rules*, Interim Standards). See the PCAOB website at www.pcaob.org for information about the effective date of these conforming amendments.

146 Employee Benefit Plans

monitoring controls over its service providers or third party administrators in implementing the SAS.

Transactions Processed by Outside Service Organizations

5.115 Many employers outsource certain aspects of the administration of their employee benefit plans. Examples include record-keeping or benefit payments processed by outside service organizations such as bank trust departments, data processing service bureaus, insurance companies and benefits administrators. Many plans allow participants to initiate transactions by telephone or electronic means (such as the Internet or intranet). Often, the plan sponsor does not maintain independent accounting records supporting these transactions. AU section 324 provides guidance on the factors an independent auditor should consider when auditing the financial statements of a plan that obtains services from another organization that are part of its information system (see chapter 6 for further discussion of SAS No. 70 reports).

Party in Interest and Related Party Transactions

5.116 Section 3(14) of ERISA defines a party in interest to include, among others, fiduciaries or employees of the plan, any person who provides services to the plan, an employer whose employees are covered by the plan, an employee organization whose members are covered by the plan, a person who owns 50 percent or more of such an employer or employee organization, or relatives of such persons just mentioned. Although not identical, ERISA defines *parties in interest* in much the same way as FASB ASC 850, *Related Party Disclosures*, defines the term *related parties*.

5.117 Certain plan transactions with parties in interest are prohibited under ERISA Sections 406 and 407 and are required, without regard to their materiality, to be disclosed in the plan's annual report to the DOL (see paragraph 11.19 for a discussion of the effect of management's failure to properly disclose prohibited party in interest transactions on the auditor's report and appendix A for a discussion of DOL reporting requirements). Prohibited transactions are also of interest from the perspective of the plan's financial statements because they can give rise to significant receivables; a plan fiduciary is liable to make good on losses to the plan resulting from a breach of fiduciary duty and restore to the plan any profits that the fiduciary made through the use of the plan's assets. The potential effects of any contingencies on the plan as a result of engaging in prohibited transactions may need to be disclosed in the plan's financial statements in accordance with the requirements of FASB ASC 450, *Contingencies*.

5.118 Prohibited transactions have an effect on the other party to the transactions as well as on the plan. ERISA provides for the levy of an excise tax on the other party up to the full amount of the prohibited transaction. Also, the fiduciary generally must reverse the transaction, compensate the plan for any losses, and return any profits made using plan assets.

5.119 Transactions between a plan and a party in interest that are generally prohibited under Section 406(a) of ERISA include

    a. a sale, exchange, or lease of property.

    b. a loan or other extension of credit (including late deposits of employee deferrals to the trust).

    c. the furnishing of goods, services, or facilities.

    d. a transfer of plan assets to a party in interest for the use or benefit of a party in interest.

    e. an acquisition of employer securities or real property in violation of the 10 percent limitation.

5.120 There are certain exceptions dealing with party in interest transactions that do not prevent a plan fiduciary from receiving reasonable compensation for services to a plan, or receiving benefits from a plan as a participant or beneficiary, as long as such benefits are in accordance with the terms of a plan as applied to all other participants and beneficiaries. In addition, payments to parties in interest for reasonable compensation for office space and legal, accounting, and other services necessary for the operation of a plan are permitted.

5.121 An audit performed in accordance with GAAS cannot be expected to provide assurance that all related party and party in interest transactions will be discovered. Nevertheless, during the course of his or her audit, the auditor should be aware of the possible existence of material related party and party in interest transactions that are required to be disclosed. Procedures directed toward identifying related party and party in interest transactions that are ordinarily performed during the planning phase of the audit are listed in paragraph 11.09.

5.122 Chapter 11, "Party in Interest Transactions," and appendix A discuss additional procedures and considerations related to party in interest transactions.

Illegal Acts

5.123 AU section 317, *Illegal Acts by Clients* (AICPA, *Professional Standards*), sets forth the nature and extent of the consideration an auditor should give to the possibility of illegal acts by a client. The term *illegal acts*, for purposes of that section, relates to violations of laws or government regulations. For those illegal acts that are defined in AU section 317 as having a direct and material effect on the determination of financial statement amounts, the auditor's responsibility to detect misstatements resulting from such illegal acts is the same as that for errors or fraud (see AU section 312).

Accounting Estimates

5.124 Certain areas of employee benefit plans operations require accounting estimates that may be material in the preparation and presentation of financial statements. AU section 342, *Auditing Accounting Estimates* (AICPA, *Professional Standards*), provides guidance on obtaining and evaluating sufficient appropriate audit evidence to support significant accounting estimates. Although the responsibility for making estimates is that of management, the auditor is responsible for evaluating reasonableness of estimates made by management in the context of the financial statements taken as a whole. When planning and performing procedures to evaluate accounting estimates, the auditor should consider both subjective and objective factors.

5.125 Although significant accounting estimates may affect many elements of an employee benefit plan's financial statements, they often affect the asset values for investments that do not have a readily determinable market value. In health and welfare plans, estimates may also affect the obligation for incurred but not reported benefit obligations, the obligation for accumulated eligibility credits, accrued experience-rating adjustments, and postretirement benefit obligations.

Going Concern Considerations

5.126 AU section 341, *The Auditor's Consideration of an Entity's Ability to Continue as a Going Concern* (AICPA, *Professional Standards*), provides guidance to the auditor with respect to evaluating whether there is substantial doubt about the plan's ability to continue as a going concern. For financial reporting purposes, continuation of a plan as a going concern is assumed in the absence of significant information to the contrary. Ordinarily, information that significantly contradicts the going concern assumption relates to the plan's ability to continue to meet its obligations as they become due without an extraordinary contribution by the sponsor or substantial disposition of assets outside the ordinary course of business, externally forced revision of its operations, or similar actions. During the course of the audit, the auditor may become aware of information that raises substantial doubt about the plan sponsor's ability to continue as a going concern. Although employee benefit plans are not automatically and necessarily affected by the plan sponsor's financial adversities, this situation may result in the auditor determining it to be a condition or event sufficient to evaluate whether there is substantial doubt about the plan's ability to continue as a going concern.

5.127 AU section 341 states that the auditor has a responsibility to evaluate whether there is substantial doubt about the plan's ability to continue as a going concern for a reasonable period of time, not to exceed one year beyond the date of the financial statements being audited. The auditor considers the results of the procedures performed in planning, gathering audit evidence relative to the various audit objectives, and completing the audit to identify conditions and events that, when considered in the aggregate, create substantial doubt about the plan's ability to continue as a going concern for a reasonable period of time. If the auditor determines that substantial doubt about the plan's ability to continue as a going concern does exist, an explanatory paragraph is required regardless of the auditor's assessment of asset recoverability and amount and classification of liabilities. For example, if the sponsoring employer intends to terminate the plan within twelve months of the date of the financial statements, the auditor should include an explanatory paragraph in his or her report that discloses that fact. The auditor is precluded from using conditional language in expressing a conclusion concerning the existence of substantial doubt about the plan's ability to continue as a going-concern explanatory paragraph.

Chapter 6

*Internal Control**

6.01 The second standard of fieldwork states that the auditor must obtain a sufficient understanding of the entity and its environment, including its internal control, to assess the risks of material misstatement of the financial statements whether due to error or fraud, and to design the nature, timing, and extent of further audit procedures. This is not to be confused with Public Company Accounting Oversight Board (PCAOB) Auditing Standard No. 5, *An Audit of Internal Control Over Financial Reporting That Is Integrated with An Audit of Financial Statements* (AICPA, *PCAOB Standards and Related Rules*, Auditing Standards) (see the "Securities and Exchange Commission Reporting Requirements" section in paragraphs 12.31–.35 for further guidance). The following paragraphs summarize the auditor's consideration of internal control under AU section 314, *Understanding the Entity and Its Environment and Assessing the Risks of Material Misstatement* (AICPA, *Professional Standards*).[1]

6.02 AU section 314 states that the auditor should obtain an understanding of the five components of internal control sufficient to assess the risks of material misstatement of the financial statements whether due to error or fraud, and to design the nature, timing, and extent of further audit procedures. This understanding may encompass controls placed in operation by the plan and by the service organization whose services are part of the plan's information system.

6.03 The auditor should obtain a sufficient understanding by performing risk assessment procedures to

     a. evaluate the design of controls relevant to an audit of financial statements.

     b. determine whether they have been implemented.

6.04 In obtaining this understanding, the auditor considers how an entity's use of IT[2] and manual procedures may affect controls relevant to the audit. The auditor should use the understanding to

- identify types of potential misstatements.
- consider factors that affect the risks of material misstatement.
- design tests of controls, when applicable, and substantive procedures.

6.05 The following are examples of IT related matters that the auditor may decide to further understand in an employee benefit plan audit:

---

  * Refer to the preface of this guide for important information about the applicability of the professional standards to audits of issuers and nonissuers.

  [1] For additional nonauthoritative guidance pertaining to internal control and the risk assessment standards (Statement on Auditing Standards [SAS] Nos. 104–111), refer to Technical Questions and Answers sections 8200.05–.16 (AICPA, *Technical Practice Aids*), issued in March and April 2008.

  [2] IT encompasses automated means of originating, processing, storing, and communicating information and includes recording devices, communication systems (including hardware and software components and data), and other electronic devices. An entity's use of IT may be extensive; however, the auditor is primarily interested in the entity's use of IT to initiate, authorize, record, process, and report transactions or other financial data.

- Whether the client's IT system is being properly utilized to determine participant data (for example, payroll and employee information) and pension and health benefit payments
- Whether a database system is being properly utilized to check for duplicate payments, improper utilization, and other payments made in the health care payment system
- Whether pension credits earned are being properly accounted for and utilized in calculating the payment of benefits
- Whether passwords are utilized by the plan and appropriate restrictions exist to prevent or detect fraud
- Whether the IT system is accurately allocating shared expenses between plans that share facilities and other expenses

6.06 Obtaining an understanding of internal controls is distinct from testing the operating effectiveness of controls. The objective of obtaining an understanding of internal control is to evaluate the design of controls and determine whether they have been implemented for the purpose of assessing the risks of material misstatement. In contrast, the objective of testing the operating effectiveness of controls is to determine whether the controls, as designed, are operating effectively to prevent or detect and correct a material misstatement.

6.07 AU section 314 paragraph .41 defines *internal control* as "a process—effected by those charged with governance, management, and other personnel—designed to provide reasonable assurance about the achievement of the entity's objectives with regard to reliability of financial reporting, effectiveness and efficiency of operations, and compliance with applicable laws and regulations." Internal control consists of five interrelated components:

a. The control environment

b. Risk assessment

c. Information and communication systems

d. Control activities

e. Monitoring

Refer to paragraphs .40–.101 of AU section 314 for a detailed discussion of the internal control components.

Understanding Internal Control

6.08 In obtaining an understanding of the control environment, the auditor should obtain sufficient knowledge of the control environment to understand the attitudes, awareness, and actions of those charged with governance (for example, the plan administrator, the administrative committee or board of trustees, and others) concerning the plan's internal control and its importance in achieving reliable financial reporting. Accordingly, the auditor considers management's philosophy and operating style, the plan's organizational structure, methods of assigning authority and responsibility, management's integrity and ethical values, management's commitment to competence, and other factors related to the control environment. This understanding would also include consideration of the attitudes, awareness, and actions of the plan administrator and others involved in plan operations, related to the Employee Retirement Income Security Act of 1974 (ERISA) or other compliance matters (for example, ERISA's prohibited transaction rules) that might affect the plan's financial statements and schedules. The control environment is normally enhanced by the existence of an audit committee; however, many employee benefit plans do not have audit committees and, therefore, the auditor may consider whether the plan's investment or administrative committee has been formally designated with responsibility for oversight of the financial reporting process and, in effect, functions as an audit committee.

6.09 The auditor's understanding of the accounting system and control activities is ordinarily obtained through discussion with plan personnel and review of documents in the office of the plan administrator (appendix B, "Examples of Controls," contains examples of certain controls a plan might establish). The understanding of the accounting system and relevant control activities, along with information about the control environment, is used to assess the risks of material misstatement in financial statement assertions.

6.10 In some cases, a third-party administrator or service organization, such as a bank trustee, custodian, insurance company, or contract administrator (hereafter referred to collectively as service organization), processes certain transactions on behalf of the plan administrator. A service organization's services are part of a plan's information system if they affect any of the following:

a. The classes of transactions in the plan's operations that are significant to the plan's financial statements

b. The procedures, both automated and manual, by which the plan's transactions are initiated, authorized, recorded, processed, and reported from their occurrence to their inclusion in the financial statements

c. The related accounting records, whether electronic or manual, supporting information, and specific accounts in the plan's financial statements involved in initiating, authorizing, recording, processing, and reporting the plan's transactions

d. How the plan's information system captures other events and conditions that are significant to the financial statements

e. The financial reporting process used to prepare the plan's financial statements including significant accounting estimates and disclosures

Many plans offer their participants direct access to the service organization by telephone or electronic means (such as the Internet or intranet). Often, the plan sponsor does not maintain independent accounting records supporting these transactions. The auditor's consideration of components of internal control maintained by the service organization will depend on the nature of the relationship between the plan and service organization.

6.11 If a service organization executes and processes transactions initiated by the plan, there may be a high degree of interaction between the activities at the plan and those at the service organization and, in these circumstances, it may be practicable for the plan to implement effective controls for those transactions. Accordingly, the plan may be able to maintain independent records of transactions authorized and executed by the service organization. In those circumstances, the auditor may be able to obtain a sufficient understanding of internal control relevant to transactions executed by the service organization to assess the risks of material misstatement and to determine the nature, timing, and extent of further audit procedures without considering those components of internal control maintained by the service organization. An example of such a service organization is a bank trust department that invests and services assets for a plan under a nondiscretionary or directed trust arrangement. However, even in such circumstances, the auditor may still find it more efficient to seek a reduction in the assessed level of control risk for assertions related to transactions executed by the service organization by considering internal control maintained by the service organization.

6.12 If the service organization is authorized by the plan to initiate, execute, and account for the processing of transactions without specific authorization of individual transactions, a lower degree of interaction exists and it may not be practicable for the plan to implement effective controls for those transactions. The plan therefore may not have independent records of the transactions executed by the service organization. In those circumstances, the auditor may not be able to obtain an understanding of the components of internal control, relevant to such transactions, sufficient to assess the risks of material misstatement and to determine the nature, timing, and extent of further audit procedures without considering those components of internal control maintained by the service organization.

Service Organizations and Using Statement on Auditing Standards No. 70 Reports[3]

6.13 Internal control of a benefit plan consists of the controls at the sponsor as well as the controls at applicable service organizations who perform significant plan functions including but not limited to processing of participant-level transactions such as contributions and distributions, investment custody and valuation, and execution of investment transaction. For a further discussion of internal control as it relates to investments, see the "Internal Control" section in chapter 7, "Auditing Investments and Loans to Participants," of this guide. Statement on Auditing Standards (SAS) No. 70, *Service Organizations* (AICPA, *Professional Standards*, AU sec. 324), as amended, provides guidance on the factors an independent auditor should consider when auditing the financial statements of an entity, such as an employee benefit plan that uses a service organization to process certain transactions that are part of the plan's information system. SAS No. 70, as amended, also provides guidance for independent auditors who issue reports on the processing of transactions by service organizations, such as bank trust departments, third-party administrators, or data processing service organizations, for use by other auditors. A report prepared in accordance with SAS No. 70, as amended, may be useful in providing user auditors with a sufficient understanding of controls at the service organization to assess the risks of material misstatement in accordance with AU section 314. See the AICPA Audit Guide *Service Organizations: Applying SAS No. 70, as Amended*, for additional guidance for user auditors engaged to audit the

---

[3] The Auditing Standards Board has issued Statement on Standards for Attestation Engagements (SSAE) No. 16, *Reporting on Controls at a Service Organization* (AICPA, *Professional Standards*, AT sec. 801), which will replace the guidance contained in AU section 324, *Service Organizations* (AICPA, *Professional Standards*), for a service auditor when reporting on controls at an organization that provides service to user entities when those controls are likely to be relevant to user entities' internal controls over financial reporting. It is effective for service auditors' reports for periods ending on or after June 15, 2011. Early implementation is permitted; therefore, if adopting SSAE No. 16 early, refer directly to the standard as certain guidance in this guide may not be applicable. Also, refer to the preface of this guide for additional information about the changes related to SAS No. 70, *Service Organizations* (AICPA, *Professional Standards*, AU sec. 324).

financial statements of entities that use service organizations and for service auditors engaged to issue reports on the controls of service organizations.

6.14 Under SAS No. 70, as amended, two types of reports may be issued by a service auditor:[†]

a. A *Report on Controls Placed in Operation* (type 1 report) is a report on a service organization's description of its controls that may be relevant to a user organization's internal control as it relates to an audit of financial statements. It addresses whether the description presents fairly, in all material respects, the relevant aspects of the service organization's controls that had been placed in operation as of a specified date and whether such controls were suitably designed to provide reasonable assurance that the specified control objectives would be achieved if those controls were complied with satisfactorily. Such reports may be useful in providing user auditors with an understanding of the service organization's controls sufficient to assess the risks of material misstatement and design the nature, timing, and extent of further audit procedures at the user organization. However, they are not intended to provide user auditors with a basis for reducing their assessment of control risk to low or moderate[4] for relevant financial statement assertions affected by the controls.

b. A *Report on Controls Placed in Operation and Tests of Operating Effectiveness* (type 2 report) is a report on a service organization's description of its controls that may be relevant to a user organization's internal control as it relates to an audit of financial statements. It addresses whether the description presents fairly, in all material respects, the relevant aspects of the service organization's controls that had been placed in operation as of a specified date; whether such controls were suitably designed to provide reasonable assurance that the specified control objectives would be achieved if those controls were complied with satisfactorily; and whether the controls that were tested were operating with sufficient effectiveness to provide reasonable, but not absolute, assurance that the related control objectives were achieved during the period specified. Such reports may be useful in providing user auditors with an understanding of the service organization's controls that is sufficient to assess the risks of material misstatement and design the nature, timing, and extent of further audit procedures and may also provide user auditors with a basis for reducing their assessment of control

---

[†] It has come to the AICPA's attention that, in some cases, service auditors' engagements are being performed and reported on by consulting organizations that are not licensed CPA firms. SAS No. 70, which is part of auditing standards generally accepted in the United States of America, is intended for use by licensed CPAs. For a user auditor to use a service auditor's report, it must be issued by a licensed CPA. CPAs may not use a report provided by an unlicensed individual or entity. User auditors should be alert to the possibility that a service auditor's report may not have been prepared by a licensed CPA and should consider contacting a representative of an unfamiliar organization to verify that the organization is properly licensed, peer reviewed, and able to provide its peer review report and letter of comments and response. If the organization is unlicensed, CPAs are advised to convey that finding to the state board of accountancy in the state in which the engagement was performed or to their own state board.

[4] This assessment may be in terms of qualitative terms such as high, medium, low or in quantitative terms such as percentages.

risk to low or moderate for relevant financial statement assertions affected by the controls.

6.15 The type of report (type 1 or type 2) provided by the service organization may affect the nature, timing, and extent of the audit procedures performed by the auditor of an employee benefit plan. For example, a bank trust department may specify the control objective that security prices are received timely from an authorized source and properly used to price securities. If the bank provides a type 1 report, the report may be useful in providing the auditor with sufficient information to assess the risks of material misstatement (in other words, to assess whether any deficiencies are in the design of the controls that could affect relevant financial statement assertions in the user organization's financial statements). However, the auditor would have no basis to conclude that the controls were operating with sufficient effectiveness to achieve the control objective because they have not been tested. Therefore, the auditor may have to expand the testing of prices used at year-end. If, however, the bank provided a type 2 report, the auditor could have a basis to rely on the effective operation of controls and therefore reduce the extent of the price testing.

6.16 A SAS No. 70 report may provide the most efficient means to obtain an understanding of relevant controls at the service organization. Reading the entire SAS No. 70 document could help the auditor to determine if any instances of noncompliance with the service organization's controls are identified in (a) the service auditor's report, (b) the attached service organizations description of controls, and (c) the information provided by the service auditor, which may include a description of tests of operating effectiveness and other information. If the service organization's SAS No. 70 report identifies instances of noncompliance with the service organization's controls, the plan auditor may consider the effect of the findings on the assessed level of control risk for the audit of the plan's financial statements, and as a result the plan auditor may decide to perform additional tests at the service organization or, if possible, perform additional audit procedures at the plan. In certain situations, the SAS No. 70 report may identify instances of noncompliance with the service organization's controls but the plan auditor concludes that no additional tests or audit procedures are required because the noncompliance does not affect the assessment of control risk for the plan. It is important for the user auditor to read and consider both the report and the evidence provided by the tests of operating effectiveness and relate them to the relevant assertions in the user organization's financial statements. Although a type 2 report may be used to reduce substantive procedures, neither a type 1 nor a type 2 report is designed to provide a basis for assessing control risk sufficiently low to eliminate the need for performing any substantive tests for all of the assertions relevant to significant account balances or transaction classes. Paragraph .51 of AU section 318, *Performing Audit Procedures in Response to Assessed Risks and Evaluating the Audit Evidence Obtained* (AICPA, *Professional Standards*), states that regardless of the assessed risk of material misstatement, the auditor should design and perform substantive procedures for all relevant assertions related to each material class of transactions, account balance, and disclosure.

6.17 It may be necessary for the plan auditor to inquire of the plan's management whether the service organization has reported any uncorrected errors to the user organization and evaluate whether such errors will affect the nature, timing, and extent of his or her audit procedures. In certain instances, the plan auditor may need to obtain additional information to make this evaluation by contacting the service organization and the service auditor to obtain the necessary information.

6.18 For a limited-scope audit, the auditor has no responsibility to obtain an understanding of the controls maintained by the certifying institution over assets held and investment transactions executed by the institution. Therefore in a limited-scope audit, to the extent that the service organization is only providing investment transaction services, no SAS No. 70 report is required. However, if the provider is also providing services such as the processing of participant level transactions, a SAS No. 70 report may be obtained, if it is available and covers these activities.

6.19 When the administrator elects a full scope audit, even though a limited scope audit could be performed (see paragraphs 5.13 and 13.26–.31 for a discussion of limited scope audits), or when the trustee or custodian does not qualify for the limited scope audit exemption, the auditor may need to obtain an understanding of controls at the trustee or custodian. A similar understanding may also be obtained for information processed by the trustee or custodian related to financial statement components not subject to the limited scope audit exemption (for example, benefit claims or payments). As previously noted, this understanding can be efficiently achieved by obtaining and reading the entire SAS No. 70 document for the service organization. In determining whether a SAS No. 70 report would be useful, the degree of interaction and the nature and materiality of the transactions processed by the service organization for the user organization are the most important factors to consider. Reading the description of controls may help the auditor to determine whether complementary user organization controls are required and whether they are relevant to the service provided to the plan. If they are relevant to the plan, the plan auditor should consider such information in assessing the risks of material misstatement. See exhibit B-2, "Examples of User Controls When a Service Organization is Utilized," in appendix B of this guide for examples of user controls.

6.20 Service providers are not required to furnish SAS No. 70 reports. If a SAS No. 70 report is not available, information about the nature of the services provided by the service organization that are part of the user organization's information system and the service organization's controls over those services may be available from a wide variety of sources, such as user manuals, system overviews, technical manuals, the contract between the user organization and the service organization, and reports by internal auditors, or regulatory authorities on the service organization's controls. If the services and the service organization's controls over those services are highly standardized, information obtained through the user auditor's prior experience with the service organization may be helpful in assessing the risks of material misstatement. The user auditor may consider utilizing the specific control objectives and selected controls provided in exhibit B-1, "Examples of Selected Controls for Employee Benefit Plans," of appendix B of this guide in obtaining this understanding. If the user auditor concludes that the available information is not adequate to obtain a sufficient understanding of the service organization's controls to assess the risks of material misstatement and design the nature, timing, and extent of further audit procedures, the user auditor may consider contacting the service organization through the user organization, to obtain specific information or request that a service auditor be engaged to perform procedures at the service organization. If the user auditor is unable to obtain sufficient evidence to achieve the audit objectives, the user auditor should qualify the audit opinion or disclaim an opinion on the financial statements because of a scope limitation. (Historically, the Department of Labor has rejected Form 5500 filings that contain either qualified opinions, adverse opinions or disclaimers of opinion on plan financial statements other than those issued in connection with a limited scope audit pursuant to Title 29 U.S. *Code of Federal Regulations* Part 2520.103-8 or 12.)

6.21 A report prepared in accordance with SAS No. 70, as amended, for the service organization, for use by auditors of financial statements of employee benefit plans, will typically address in that report the control objectives that are relevant to the specific objectives of employee benefit plans as set forth in exhibit B-1.

6.22 Benefit plans are increasingly using service providers to initiate, execute and perform the accounting processing of transactions on behalf of the plan administrator. Often the plan does not maintain independent accounting records of such transactions. For example, for 401(k) plans, many plan sponsors no longer maintain participant enrollment forms detailing the contribution percentage and the investment fund allocation option. For health and welfare plans, often claims are submitted electronically from the health care provider directly to a claims administrator for adjudication and payment. In these situations, the auditor may not be able to obtain a sufficient understanding of internal control relevant to such transactions to assess the risks of material misstatement and design the nature, timing, and extent of further audit procedures without considering those components of internal control maintained by the service organization. This understanding can be efficiently achieved by obtaining and reading the entire document prepared in accordance with SAS No. 70 for the service organization. SAS No. 70 reports generally cover the relevant operations of a service organization; however, certain operations of the service organization may not be addressed in the SAS No. 70 report, and those operations may be significant to the plan audit. In these instances, the engagement team will need to obtain an understanding of the controls in the relevant areas excluded from the scope of the SAS No. 70 report.

6.23 In some cases, a provider may choose to engage an auditor to prepare a SAS No. 70 report on a rotating basis instead of annually. A report on controls placed in operation that is as of a date outside the plan's reporting period may be useful in providing the plan auditor with a preliminary understanding of the controls placed in operation at the service organization if the report is supplemented by additional current information. If this occurs, it is important for the service organization to be contacted to discuss any system changes, major changes in controls, or mergers or acquisitions that occurred during the year. If these changes have occurred, it is important for the engagement team to obtain an understanding of the changes and consider the effect of the changes on the audit. If the SAS No. 70 report is unavailable, the auditor should consider other appropriate procedures to obtain sufficient appropriate evidence to achieve the audit objectives. For example, if participant information is unavailable from the plan sponsor, the auditor may confirm the information directly with the participants. Alternatively, the auditor may consider requesting information from the service provider or visiting the service provider to perform the necessary testing. For defined contribution plans, the service provider may be able to provide detailed transaction reports at the plan or participant level, such as telephone or electronic means transaction reports, trade batch reports, distribution summaries, loan ledgers or details of purchases, sales and dividends posted to individual accounts.

6.24 If the independent auditor determines that the service organization had effective controls in place for processing plan transactions during the reporting period, the auditor generally would conclude that it is not necessary to visit or perform additional procedures at the service organization. If, however, the auditor believes that the service auditor's report may not be sufficient to meet his or her objectives, the auditor may supplement his or her understanding of the service auditor's procedures and conclusions by discussing with the service auditor the scope and results of the service auditor's work. Also, if the auditor believes it is necessary, he or she may contact the service organization, through the user organization, to request that the service auditor perform agreed-upon procedures at the service organization or the auditor may perform such procedures. Following are some examples of those situations:

    a. The service organization issued a SAS No. 70 report describing the controls placed in operation ("type 1" report) and the auditor considers whether to reduce the assessed level of control risk at the service organization—Determine whether it is more efficient to attempt to reduce the assessed level of control risk for the relevant assertions affected by the services performed at the service organization that are part of the plan's information system, or to perform additional audit procedures on the plan's financial statements. If the plan auditor decides it is more efficient to assess the operating effectiveness of the service organization's controls placed in operation, perform tests of the service organization's controls, most likely at the service organization.

    b. The service organization's SAS No. 70 report covers a different reporting period than the plan's fiscal year—Inquiry of the service organization or its auditor to determine whether changes existed in the service organization's controls during the period not covered by the SAS No. 70 report. If the period not covered is significant, or changes in the controls have occurred, gain an understanding of the service organization's controls relating to the plan's transactions during the period not covered by the SAS No. 70 report.

    c. The service organization's SAS No. 70 report covers only some of the services used by the plan (for example, the report might cover custodial services but not allocation services) or the report does not cover activities performed by subservice organizations—Gain an understanding of the controls related to the services not covered in the SAS No. 70 report as they relate to the plan's transactions processed by the service organization that are part of the plan's information system. If the user auditor does not have sufficient information to assess control risk as low or moderate, the plan auditor may decide to perform additional tests of the service organization's controls or perform additional audit procedures on the plan's financial statements. Obtain a copy of the subservice organization's SAS No. 70 report, if one was issued. Additionally, a service organization may use another service organization to perform functions or processing that is part of the plan's information system as it relates to an audit of the financial statements. The subservice organization may be a separate entity from the service organization or may be related to the service organization. To assess control risk, the plan auditor may need to consider controls at the service organization and also may need to consider controls at the subservice organization, depending on the functions each performs. The following illustrates typical subservicing situations in a bank trust department that provides services to an employee benefit plan:

  i. *Limited functions.* A bank trust department may use one or more pricing service organizations to determine the current market price of exchange-traded securities held by the plan.

 ii. *Moderate functions.* A bank trust department may use a data processing service organization to record the transactions and maintain the related accounting records for the plan.

iii. *Extensive functions.* A bank trust department may use a service organization to perform essentially all of the transaction execution, recording, and processing for the plan.

Consider the effect of the subservice organization on the internal control of the plan as follows:

 iv. The degree of interaction, as well as the nature and materiality of the transactions processed by the service organization and the subservice organization.

  v. The available information about the service organization's and subservice organization's controls, including (1) information in the plan management's possession, such as user manuals, system overviews, technical manuals, and the contract between the plan and the service organization; and (2) reports on the service organization's and subservice organization's controls, such as reports by service auditors, internal auditors, or regulatory authorities. Because a plan typically does not have any contractual relationship with the subservice organization, the plan may obtain available reports and information about the subservice organization from the service organization.

After considering the preceding factors and evaluating available information, the plan auditor may conclude that he or she has the means to obtain sufficient understanding of a user organization's internal control to assess the risks of material misstatement. If the user auditor concludes that information is not available to obtain a sufficient understanding to assess the risks of material misstatement, he or she may consider contacting the service organization through the user organization or contacting the subservice organization, through the user and service organizations, to obtain specific information or request that a service auditor be engaged to perform procedures that will supply the necessary information. Alternatively, the user auditor may visit the service organization or subservice organization and perform such procedures. (For further guidance on the use of subservice organizations, see chapter 5, "Service Organizations That Use Other Service Organizations," in the AICPA Audit Guide *Service Organizations: Applying SAS No. 70, as Amended.*)

6.25 It is not uncommon for a type 2 SAS No. 70 report to have exceptions in tests of operating effectiveness. Those exceptions may result in a qualification of the report. The auditor may consider the following when a SAS No. 70 report contains exceptions to determine if an expansion of the scope of detailed testing is necessary:

- Whether the exception is related to user organization activities
- The nature of the exception based on details provided in the SAS No. 70 report and inquiries of the user organization personnel or the service auditor or both
- Whether any follow-up procedures and additional testing has been performed by the user organization or service organization to address the exception
- Whether compensating controls exist that would mitigate the effect of the exception

An auditor may consider whether they are able to rely on controls at the service organization if exceptions are noted in the SAS No. 70 report.

6.26 A SAS No. 70 report may be qualified for the following reasons:

- The service organization's controls are not correctly described.
- Controls were not suitably designed to achieve the specified control objectives.
- The controls that were tested were not operating effectively (exceptions in testing).

Auditors may consider the following when a SAS No. 70 report is qualified to determine if an expansion of the scope of detailed testing is necessary.

- Whether the qualification is related to user organization activities
- The nature of the qualification based on details provided in the SAS No. 70 report and inquiries of the user organization personnel or the service auditor or both
- Whether any follow-up procedures and additional testing has been performed by the user organization or the service organization to address the reason for the qualification
- Whether compensating controls exist that would mitigate the effect of the qualification

It is important for an auditor to determine whether or not they can rely on a qualified SAS No. 70 report.

Documentation

6.27 AU section 314 establishes the requirements for documentation of the understanding of internal control and the assessment of control risk. The auditor should document the key elements of the understanding of the five components of the plan's internal control obtained to assess the risks of material misstatement; the sources of information from which the understanding was obtained; and the risk assessment procedures. In addition, the auditor should document the assessment of the risks of material misstatement both at the financial statement level and at the relevant assertion level. The form and extent of the auditor's documentation are influenced by the nature, size, and complexity of the entity's internal control, and nature of the entity's documentation of its internal control.

Communicating Internal Control Related Matters (For Audits of Nonissuers Only)

6.28 AU section 325, *Communicating Internal Control Related Matters Identified in an Audit* (AICPA, *Professional Standards*),[5] provides guidance on communicating matters related to internal control over financial reporting identified in an audit of financial statements and communicating, in writing, to management and those charged with governance,[6] significant deficiencies and material weaknesses identified during the audit. The auditor should evaluate the severity of each deficiency in internal control identified during the audit to determine whether the deficiency, individually or in combination, is a *significant deficiency* or a *material weakness*. A deficiency in internal control exists when the design or operation of a control does not allow management or employees, in the normal course of performing their assigned functions, to prevent or detect misstatements on a timely basis. A *material weakness* is a deficiency, or combination of deficiencies, in internal control, such that there is a reasonable possibility[7] that a material misstatement of financial statements will not be prevented or detected and corrected on a timely basis. A *significant deficiency* is a deficiency, or a combination of deficiencies, in internal control that is less severe than a material weakness, yet important enough to merit attention by those charged with governance.

6.29 Deficiencies identified during the audit that upon evaluation are considered significant deficiencies or material weaknesses should be communicated, in writing, to management and those charged with governance as a part of each audit, including significant deficiencies and material weaknesses that were communicated to management and those charged with governance in previous audits, and have not yet been remediated. This written communication is best made by the report release date, which is the date the auditor grants the plan permission to use the auditor's report in connection with the financial

---

[5] AU section 325, *Communicating Internal Control Related Matters Identified in an Audit* (AICPA, *Professional Standards*), is not applicable if the auditor is engaged to examine the design and operating effectiveness of an entity's internal control over financial reporting that is integrated with an audit of the entity's financial statements under AT section 501, *An Examination of an Entity's Internal Control Over Financial Reporting That Is Integrated With an Audit of Its Financial Statements* (AICPA, *Professional Standards*).

For audits of issuers, such as Form 11-K audits, Public Company Accounting Oversight Board (PCAOB) standards should be followed. See paragraph 6.33 of this guide for further guidance. For an integrated audit of financial statements and internal control over financial reporting, paragraphs 78–84 of PCAOB Auditing Standard No. 5, *An Audit of Internal Control Over Financial Reporting That Is Integrated with An Audit of Financial Statements* (AICPA, *PCAOB Standards and Related Rules*, Auditing Standards) should be followed. (See also AU section 325, *Communication About Control Deficiencies in An Audit of Financial Statements* [AICPA, *PCAOB Standards and Related Rules*, Interim Standards].)

[6] *Those charged with governance* is defined in paragraph .03 of AU section 380, *The Auditor's Communication With Those Charged With Governance* (AICPA, *Professional Standards*), "as the person(s) with responsibility for overseeing the strategic direction of the entity and obligations related to the accountability of the entity. This includes overseeing the financial reporting and disclosure process."

[7] A *reasonable possibility* exists when the likelihood of the event is either reasonably possible or probable as defined by the Financial Accounting Standards Board *Accounting Standards Codification* glossary.

statements, but should be no later than 60 days following the report release date.[8] For further guidance see AU section 325.

6.30 If the auditor, as a result of the assessment of the risks of material misstatement, has identified risks of material misstatement due to fraud that have continuing internal control implications (whether or not transactions or adjustments that could be the result of fraud have been detected), the auditor should consider whether these risks represent significant deficiencies or material weaknesses relating to the entity's internal control that should be communicated to management and those charged with governance.[9] The auditor also should consider whether the absence of or deficiencies in programs and controls to mitigate specific risks of fraud or to otherwise help prevent, deter, and detect fraud represent significant deficiencies or material weaknesses that should be communicated to management and those charged with governance.

6.31 When reading a type 1 or type 2 SAS No. 70 report, the plan auditor may become aware of situations at the service organization that constitute significant deficiencies or material weaknesses for the user organization. Such situations may relate to the design or the operating effectiveness of the service organization's controls and it is important such deficiencies or material weaknesses be communicated to management and those charged with governance, as appropriate.

6.32 For a single employer plan that does not have an audit committee, the individual with the level of authority and responsibility equivalent to an audit committee would normally be the named fiduciary, which is often the plan sponsor, an officer thereof, or the sponsor's board of directors. For a multiemployer plan, authority and responsibility equivalent to that of an audit committee would ordinarily rest with the board of trustees.

Significant Deficiencies (For Audits of Issuers Only, Such as Form 11-K Audits)

6.33 AU section 325, *Communications About Control Deficiencies in An Audit of Financial Statements* (AICPA, *PCAOB Standards and Related Rules*, Interim Standards), states the auditor must communicate in writing to management and the audit committee[10] all significant deficiencies and material weaknesses identified during the audit. The written communication should be made prior to the issuance of the auditor's report on the financial statements. The auditor's communication should distinguish clearly between those matters considered significant deficiencies and those considered material weaknesses. A significant deficiency is a deficiency, or a combination of deficiencies, in internal control over financial reporting, that is less severe than a material weakness yet important enough to merit attention by those responsible for oversight of the plan's financial reporting. A *material weakness* is a deficiency, or a combination of deficiencies, in internal control over financial reporting, such that a reasonable possibility exists that a material misstatement of the plan's financial

---

[8] See paragraph .23 of AU section 339, *Audit Documentation* (AICPA, *Professional Standards*), for additional guidance related to the report release date.

[9] Alternatively, the auditor may decide to communicate solely with those charged with governance.

[10] For audits of issuers, such as Form 11-K audits, if no such committee exists with respect to the entity, all references to the audit committee in this standard apply to the entire board of directors of the entity.

statements will not be prevented or detected on a timely basis. For further guidance on what should be included in the written communication, see PCAOB Release 2004-008, PCAOB Release 2007-005A, *Auditing Standard No. 5,* An Audit of Internal Control Over Financial Reporting That Is Integrated With An Audit of Financial Statements, *and Related Independence Rule and Conforming Amendments* (AICPA, *PCAOB Standards and Related Rules,* Select PCAOB Releases), and AU section 325.

Chapter 7

Auditing Investments and Loans to Participants

Background

7.01 The investments of an employee benefit plan often consist of securities with a readily determinable market value, such as common or preferred stocks, bonds, notes, or shares of registered investment companies. Other investments may include real estate, mortgages or other loans, leases, securities that do not have a readily determinable market value, or units of participation in common or collective trust funds maintained by a bank or similar institution. Investments may also be in the form of deposit administration or immediate participation guarantee contracts and individual or pooled separate accounts maintained by an insurance company. The Audit and Accounting Guide *Investment Companies* and the Audit Guide *Auditing Derivative Instruments, Hedging Activities, and Investments in Securities* may be helpful in understanding and auditing certain financial instruments that may be found in employee benefit plans.

7.02 Within the last decade, many plans have adopted aggressive investment strategies that incorporate a variety of techniques or specialized products to increase investment returns. Use of investment advisers has increased, and their roles are increasingly specialized. It is common for larger plans to use more than one adviser with the intention of increasing diversity in their portfolios through asset allocation. Many of those advisers are specialists selected to invest a portion of the plan's portfolio in a particular product or industry, or to use specialized strategies or techniques.

7.03 Corporate financing strategy has given rise to an increase in the use of debt, and other alternative investment products, which increases the need for financial institutions to maintain adequate capital levels. These and other issues are reflective of the increased inherent risk in many employee benefit plan investment portfolios. This increase is, in part, reflective of the complexity in valuing securities that do not have a readily determinable market value. It is moreover a reflection of the changing nature of pension and benefit plan portfolios that once were considered to follow conservative investment policies and approaches.

7.04 Advisers also are using existing investments for different purposes. Many forms of investments, such as repurchase or reverse repurchase agreements, futures and options, and securities lending arrangements, are now available. Collateralized mortgage obligations, real estate mortgage investment conduits, and myriad securitized portfolio investments are part of the growing list of specialized real estate related investment securities found in plan portfolios.

7.05 Chapter 5, "Planning and General Auditing Considerations," discusses planning and general auditing considerations, including those relevant to auditing investments. Except in the case of a limited-scope audit, the auditor should obtain an understanding of the plan's process for determining fair value measurements and disclosures and of the relevant controls sufficient to develop an effective audit approach. For an employee benefit plan audit, this would include gaining an understanding of the role of the investment manager or adviser (for self-directed plans, the participants themselves) and how that role interrelates to the plan, trustee, administrator, or custodian with respect to investment decisions or plan administration.

7.06 This chapter discusses the auditing objectives and related procedures for the following:

- Paragraphs 7.11–.34—auditing trusteed assets
- Paragraphs 7.35–.56—auditing plan assets held with an insurance company
- Paragraphs 7.57–.58—auditing loans to participants
- Paragraphs 7.59–.66—auditing derivatives and hedging activities
- Paragraphs 7.67–.72—auditing certain other types of plan investments including self-directed accounts and separately managed accounts
- Paragraphs 7.73–.77—auditing procedures to be performed when the audit scope is limited with respect to assets held by a bank or similar institution or insurance company[1]

Internal Control

7.07 Chapter 6, "Internal Control," discusses internal control, including controls relevant to investments. The extent of the understanding of controls over investments obtained by the auditor depends on how much information the auditor needs to identify the types of potential misstatements, consider factors that affect the risks of material misstatement, design tests of controls where appropriate, and design substantive tests. The understanding obtained may include controls over investment transactions from their initiation to their inclusion in the financial statements. It may encompass controls placed in operation by the entity and by service organizations whose services are part of the entity's information system. AU section 314, *Understanding the Entity and Its Environment and Assessing the Risks of Material Misstatement* (AICPA, *Professional Standards*), defines the information system as the procedures, whether automated or manual, and records established to initiate, authorize, record, process, and report plan transactions (as well as events and conditions) and to maintain accountability for the related assets, liabilities, and equity. For further guidance on when a service organization's services are part of an entity's information system for investments, see paragraphs 6.10–.12 in chapter 6 of this guide.

7.08 The auditor should obtain an understanding of the entity's process for determining fair value measurements and disclosures and of the relevant controls sufficient to develop an effective audit approach. Management is responsible for establishing an accounting and financial reporting process for determining fair value measurements. Financial Accounting Standards Board (FASB) *Accounting Standards Codification* (ASC) 820, *Fair Value Measurements and Disclosures*, defines fair value, establishes a framework for measuring fair value, and expands disclosures about fair value measurements. See paragraphs 2.09–.22, 3.12–.25, or 4.28–.41 for applicable guidance.

---

[1] See paragraphs 13.26–.31 for a discussion of the scope of the audit when it is limited with respect to assets held by banks, similar institutions, or insurance carriers.

7.09 Examples of a service organization's services that would be part of an entity's information system include

- the initiation of the purchase or sale of equity securities by a service organization acting as investment adviser or manager.
- services that are ancillary to holding an entity's securities such as
  - collecting dividend and interest income and distributing that income to the entity.
  - receiving notification of corporate actions.
  - receiving notification of security purchase and sale transactions.
  - receiving payments from purchasers and disbursing proceeds to sellers for security purchase and sale transactions.
  - maintaining records of securities transactions for the entity.
- a pricing service providing fair values of derivatives and securities through paper documents or electronic downloads that the entity uses to value its derivatives and securities for financial statement reporting.
- security lending transactions where the service organization records the collateral for the plan exchange for short-term use of certain securities.

7.10 Examples of a service organization's services that would not be part of an entity's information system are the following:

- The execution by a securities broker of trades that are initiated by either the entity or its investment adviser
- The holding of an entity's securities

Trusted Assets

7.11 Although investments are an integral part of the assets and operations of an employee benefit plan, the investment activities ordinarily are administratively distinct from other aspects of the plan because the plan administrator or named fiduciary usually engages a trustee or an investment manager, or both.

7.12 In a *directed trust*, including a participant-directed trust, the trustee acts as custodian of a plan's investments and is responsible for collecting investment income and handling trust asset transactions as directed by the party named as having discretion to make investment decisions, such as the plan administrator, the plan's investment committee, the participant, or the plan's investment adviser. A *discretionary trust* differs in that the trustee has discretionary authority and control over investments and is authorized by the plan or its investment committee to make investment decisions. A discretionary trust gives the trustee authority to purchase and sell investment assets within the framework of the trust instrument. Many variations of investment authority may be given to the trustee, such as a combination of discretionary and directed arrangements within a trust. Furthermore, a plan may have one or more trusts as well as one or more custodial or safekeeping accounts. Many multiemployer plans make use of the services of a third-party administrator (TPA) who contracts to be responsible for plan administration. Although TPAs are not normally considered trustees under the Employee Retirement Income Security Act of 1974 (ERISA), circumstances may exist in which they perform investment income collection or other related functions.

7.13 Trustees generally are responsible for the safekeeping of the investments under their control. Sometimes, however, a plan will not appoint a trustee to maintain custody of the plan's investments but, rather, will self-administer the investments and investment transactions and provide for their safekeeping with a custodian.

7.14 The auditing procedures will vary according to the nature of the trustee arrangement (discretionary or directed) and the physical location and control of the plan's records and investments.

Auditing Objectives

7.15 The objectives of auditing procedures applied to investments and related transactions are to provide the auditor with a reasonable basis for concluding

- a. whether all investments are recorded and exist.
- b. whether investments are owned by the plan and are free of liens, pledges, and other security interests or, if not, whether the security interests are identified.
- c. whether investment principal and income transactions are recorded and investments are properly valued in conformity with generally accepted accounting principles (GAAP).
- d. whether information about investments is properly presented and disclosed.
- e. whether investment transactions are initiated in accordance with the established investment policies.

General Auditing Procedures

7.16 AU section 332, *Auditing Derivative Instruments, Hedging Activities, and Investments in Securities* (AICPA, *Professional Standards*), provides guidance on auditing investments in debt and equity securities, investments accounted for under FASB ASC 323, *Investments—Equity Method and Joint Ventures*, and derivative instruments and hedging activities. Examples of substantive procedures to be applied to the investments of a plan include the following:[2]

- a. Obtaining an understanding of the plan's investment strategy and its effect on the plan's investment portfolio. Generally the risks of material misstatement associated with valuation of securities that do not have a readily determinable market value would also be assessed as would the determination of whether the inherent risk of investments held by the plan had changed. The auditor may need special skill or knowledge to perform auditing procedures for securities that do not have a readily determinable market value or derivatives. The auditor may seek the assistance of employees

---

[2] When deemed appropriate, these procedures can be used for audits of a directed trust.

of the auditor's firm, or others outside the firm, with the necessary skill or knowledge. AU section 311, *Planning and Supervision* (AICPA, *Professional Standards*), provides guidance with respect to the supervision of individuals who serve as members of the audit team and assist the auditor in performing auditing procedures. The auditor also may use the work of a specialist. AU section 336, *Using the Work of a Specialist* (AICPA, *Professional Standards*), provides guidance on the use of the work of a specialist as audit evidence. If plans hold investments then the plan should have investment policy guidelines. Once the auditor has an understanding of these guidelines, the auditor may compare them to what is being done to ascertain whether or not the policy is being followed and if the minimum and maximum percentage range of investments to be invested in are being adhered to (that is, real estate 0 percent to 7 percent of assets).

b. Obtaining an analysis of changes in investments during the period. The analysis ordinarily will include such information as (i) the name of the issuer; (ii) a description of the investment, including the number of shares of stock, par value of bonds, principal amount of mortgages, maturity date, interest rate, and collateral; (iii) cost and fair value at the beginning and end of the period and the basis of determining the fair value; and (iv) cost of investments acquired and proceeds from investments sold during the period.

c. Obtaining evidence regarding the existence and ownership of investments and information about any liens, pledges, or other security interests, either by direct confirmation from the trustee or custodian or by physical count (in the increasingly less common circumstance in which securities are held in the plan or employer's vault or safe deposit box and registered in the name of the plan or its nominee). With respect to the confirmation procedure, the trustee, such as a bank, is legally responsible for assets held in its trust department. Thus, if a plan's investments are held by a bank's trust department, the auditor ordinarily accepts a confirmation from the bank as evidence of the existence and ownership of the investments. The auditor should direct the confirmation request to a third party who the auditor believes is knowledgeable about the information to be confirmed. The auditor may obtain information regarding the trustee's responsibility and financial capability. Procedures that the auditor may consider include

  i. reviewing the trust instrument provision to determine the trustee's responsibilities.

  ii. determining whether the trustee has insurance covering the plan assets under his or her control.

  iii. reading recent financial statements of the trustee.

The auditing procedures in paragraph 7.19 ordinarily will provide additional evidence regarding the existence and ownership of plan assets.

Note: A certification provided by the trustee or custodian regarding the completeness and accuracy of the investment information does not constitute a confirmation as evidence of the existence and ownership of the investments. The confirmation of existence and ownership includes an indication that no liens, pledges, or other encumbrances exist, and is to be received directly from the trustee or custodian.

   d. Reviewing minutes, agreements, and confirmations for evidence of liens, pledges, or other security interest in investments.

   e. Testing investment transactions by

        i. determining that they were properly authorized.

       ii. examining brokers' advices, cash records, and other supporting documentation for the historical cost or selling price, quantity, identification, and dates of acquisition and disposal of the investments.[3]

      iii. comparing prices at which purchases and sales were recorded with published market price ranges on the trade dates.

      iv. checking the computation of realized and unrealized gains and losses when such items are presented in the statement of changes in net assets or in the notes to the financial statements. (See appendix A, "ERISA and Related Regulations," for specific Department of Labor [DOL] rules regarding the computation of realized gains and losses.)

       v. for daily valued plans, comparing the initiated trade to the detail recordkeeping activity. (When a plan is valued daily a single trade is usually executed at the close of business based upon information provided by the recordkeeper. The trade represents the net of all participant directed activity for that day.)

   f. Confirming with the plan's custodian or cotrustee broker the status of any securities that are in transit.

   g. Determining whether income accruing from investments during the period has been properly recorded. If the investment manager's compensation is material and is based on the plan's investment performance or other similar criteria, determine that the investment performance criteria affecting such compensation have been adequately tested to serve both purposes. It may be necessary for the plan administrator to engage a specialist as part of this procedure.

   h. Testing the fair value of investments by reference to market quotations or other evidence of fair value in accordance with AU section 342, *Auditing Accounting Estimates* (AICPA, *Professional Standards*). Obtaining a confirmation from the trustee, custodian, or investment manager that contains fair values does not constitute valuation testing. For further guidance refer to Interpretation No. 1, "Auditing Interests in Trusts Held by a Third-Party Trustee and Reported at Fair Value," of AU section 328, *Auditing Fair Value Measurements and Disclosures* (AICPA, *Professional Standards*,

---

[3] The accrual basis of accounting requires that purchases and sales of securities be recorded on a trade-date basis. If the settlement date is after the financial statement date, however, and (*a*) the fair value of the securities purchased or sold just before the financial statement date does not change significantly from the trade date to the financial statement date and (*b*) the purchases or sales do not significantly affect the composition of the plan's assets available for benefits, accounting on a settlement-date basis for such sales and purchases is acceptable.

AU sec. 9328 par. .01–.04)* Values need to be independently corroborated. If fair value has been determined in good faith by the plan's board of trustees, administrative committee, or other designated party, the plan auditor does not substitute his or her judgment for that of the plan trustees, the plan administrator, or other adviser, because the plan auditor is not an appraiser or investment banker. The auditor's understanding of the reliability of the process used by management to determine fair value is an important element in support of the resulting amounts and therefore affects the nature, timing, and extent of audit procedures. When testing the entity's fair value measurements and disclosures, the auditor evaluates whether (i) management's assumptions are reasonable and reflect, or are not inconsistent with, market information; (ii) the fair value measurement was determined using an appropriate model, if applicable; and (iii) management used relevant information that was reasonably available at the time.[4]

AU section 328 establishes standards and provides guidance on auditing fair value measurements and disclosures contained in financial statements. In particular, this statement addresses audit considerations relating to the measurement and disclosure of assets, liabilities, and specific components of equity presented or disclosed at fair value in financial statements. Fair value measurements of assets, liabilities, and components of equity may arise from both the initial recording of transactions and later changes in value. Changes in fair value measurements that occur over time may be treated in different ways under GAAP. However, this section does not address specific types of assets or liabilities, transactions, or industry specific practices (see AU section 332), nor does it amend or supersede any existing Statements on Auditing Standards (SASs).

The auditor should obtain sufficient appropriate audit evidence to provide reasonable assurance that fair value measurements and disclosures in the financial statements are in conformity with GAAP. The guidance and disclosures contained in FASB ASC 820 are applicable.

---

* For further nonauthoritative guidance, see the AICPA Practice Aid *Alternative Investments—Audit Considerations (A practice aid for auditors)*. This practice aid addresses challenges associated with auditing investments for which a readily determinable fair value does not exist (that is, that are not listed on national exchanges or over-the-counter markets, or for which quoted market prices are not available from sources such as financial publications, the exchanges, or the NASDAQ). Alternative investments can present challenges with respect to obtaining sufficient appropriate audit evidence in support of the existence and valuation assertions, because of the lack of a readily determinable fair value for these investments and the limited investment information generally provided by fund managers.

[4] In December 2007, the Public Company Accounting Oversight Board (PCAOB) issued PCAOB Staff Audit Practice Alert No. 2, *Matters Related to Auditing Fair Value Measurements of Financial Instruments and the Use of Specialists* (AICPA, *PCAOB Standards and Related Rules*, PCAOB Staff Guidance, sec. 400 par. .02). Practice Alert No. 2 reminds auditors of their responsibilities for auditing fair value measurements of financial instruments and provides direction in accordance with the auditing standards for evaluating the application of generally accepted accounting principles (GAAP), specifically Financial Accounting Standards Board (FASB) *Accounting Standards Codification* (ASC) 820, *Fair Value Measurements and Disclosures*. Practice Alert No. 2 focuses on specific matters that are likely to increase the risk of material misstatement related to the fair value of financial instruments in a rapidly changing economic environment.

In establishing the scope of his or her work and when selecting transactions for testing, consideration of the increased complexity inherent in valuing many of the new forms of investments is important. Examples of substantive procedures that the auditor may consider related to the valuation of investments include

    i. reviewing and evaluating the plan's methods and procedures for estimating the fair value of investments.

    ii. determining whether the plan's methods and procedures for estimating fair value were followed.

    iii. testing the underlying documentation supporting the estimates.

    iv. if the investment manager's compensation is material and based on the fair value of plan investments, determining whether the fair value of investments has been adequately tested for this purpose.

    v. inquiring if the plan's board of trustees, administrative committee, or other designated party has reviewed and approved estimates of the fair value of plan investments, and reading supporting minutes or other documentation (see paragraph 13.34).

i. Testing the computation of net change in appreciation or depreciation of fair value of investments.

j. Inquiring of the plan administrator or other appropriate parties if they are aware of any situation where the plan's investments or other transactions violate applicable laws or regulations (see chapter 5, chapter 11, "Party in Interest Transactions," and appendix A for a discussion of prohibited party in interest transactions under ERISA).

k. Once the auditor has obtained the requisite investment information from the plan trustee, consider obtaining the same type of information from the party named as having discretion to make investment decisions, such as the plan administrator, the plan's investment committee, or the plan's investment adviser (the directing party) and reviewing and reconciling the directing party's reports (investment position and activity) with those of the trustee.

l. Review subsequent events and transactions.

m. Evaluate whether the entity has made adequate disclosures about fair value information. If an item contains a high degree of measurement uncertainty, the auditor assesses whether the disclosures are sufficient to inform users of such uncertainty. When disclosure of fair value information under GAAP is omitted because it is not practicable to determine fair value with sufficient reliability, the auditor evaluates the adequacy of disclosures required in these circumstances. If the entity has not appropriately disclosed fair value information required by GAAP, the auditor evaluates whether the financial statements are materially misstated.

Discretionary Trusts

7.17 AU section 314 requires that in all audits the auditor should obtain an understanding of each of the five components of internal control (control environment, risk assessment, control activities, information and communication systems, and monitoring) sufficient to assess the risks of material misstatement of the financial statements whether due to error or fraud, and to design the nature, timing, and extent of further audit procedures. A sufficient understanding is obtained by performing risk assessment procedures to evaluate the design of controls relevant to an audit of financial statements and determining whether they have been implemented. In obtaining this understanding, the auditor considers how a plan's use of IT[5] and manual procedures may affect controls relevant to an audit. The auditor should use the understanding to identify types of potential misstatements:

- Consider factors that affect the risks of material misstatement.
- Design tests of controls, when applicable, and substantive procedures.

(See chapter 6 for a further discussion of internal control.)

7.18 The examples of substantive procedures in paragraph 7.16 are also applicable to records maintained by the plan when investments are maintained in a discretionary trust arrangement (see paragraph 7.12). Under a discretionary trust arrangement, the plan will not have an independent record of investment transactions executed by the trust, and thus the plan auditor may be unable to examine brokers' advices, cash records, and other supporting documentation to verify investment transactions.

7.19 Examples of substantive procedures to be applied when transactions are executed by the discretionary trust include the following:

a. If the trustee has engaged an independent auditor to prepare a report on the processing of transactions by a service organization for use by other auditors (SAS No. 70 report[6]), obtain and read a copy of the latest available report. Ordinarily the auditor will not need to review the trust department auditor's single-audit working papers, provided that the plan auditor is satisfied with the professional reputation and independence of the trust department auditor (see paragraph .10a of AU section 543, *Part of Audit Performed by Other Independent Auditors* [AICPA, *Professional Standards*]).

b. If a special-purpose report on the internal control procedures of the trust department cannot be obtained, the plan auditor would apply appropriate procedures at the trust department. In applying those auditing procedures, the plan auditor may consider using the work

---

[5] IT encompasses automated means of originating, processing, storing, and communicating information, and includes recording devices, communication systems (including hardware and software components and data), and other electronic devices. An entity's use of IT may be extensive; however, the auditor is primarily interested in the entity's use of IT to initiate, authorize, record, process, and report transactions or other financial data.

[6] The Auditing Standards Board has issued Statement on Standards for Attestation Engagements (SSAE) No. 16, *Reporting on Controls at a Service Organization* (AICPA, *Professional Standards*, AT sec. 801), which will replace the guidance contained in AU section 324, *Service Organizations* (AICPA, *Professional Standards*), for a service auditor when reporting on controls at an organization that provides service to user entities when those controls are likely to be relevant to user entities' internal controls over financial reporting. It is effective for service auditors' reports for periods ending on or after June 15, 2011. Early implementation is permitted; therefore, if adopting SSAE No. 16 early, refer directly to the standard as certain guidance in this guide may not be applicable. Also, refer to the preface of this guide for additional information about the changes related to Statement on Auditing Standards (SAS) No. 70, *Service Organizations* (AICPA, *Professional Standards*, AU sec. 324).

of the trust department's independent auditor or internal auditor (see AU section 322, *The Auditor's Consideration of the Internal Audit Function in an Audit of Financial Statements* [AICPA, *Professional Standards*]).

If the plan auditor is unable to apply the auditing procedures discussed in this paragraph, then a limitation on the scope of the audit may exist. Restrictions on the scope of the audit, whether imposed by the client or by circumstances, such as the inability to obtain sufficient appropriate audit evidence, may require the auditor to qualify his or her opinion or to disclaim an opinion (see AU section 508, *Reports on Audited Financial Statements* [AICPA, *Professional Standards*]). The significant number of new and different types of investments generally has increased the inherent risk and the risk of material misstatement related to plan investments. It is the responsibility of the plan auditor to read the report of the service auditor to determine that the tests performed encompass the types of investments held by the plan. If the report is unclear or it does not address such circumstances, it will be necessary for the auditor, as discussed in SAS No. 70, *Service Organizations* (AICPA, *Professional Standards*, AU sec. 324), to supplement his or her understanding of the trust auditor's procedures and conclusions by discussing with the service auditor the scope and results of his or her work.

Investments in Common or Collective Trusts

7.20 A common or collective trust (CCT) may be used to invest some or all of a plan's assets. A plan generally acquires investment units, sometimes referred to as *units of participation*, representing an undivided interest in the underlying assets of the trust. The purchase or redemption price of the units is determined periodically by the trustee, based on the current market values of the underlying assets of the fund. The financial statements of many CCTs are examined and reported on by auditors engaged by the bank.

7.21 The objectives of auditing procedures applied to investments in CCTs are to provide the auditor with a reasonable basis for concluding

   a. whether the units of participation held by the plan exist.

   b. whether the units of participation are owned by the plan and are unencumbered.

   c. whether valuation of units of participation at the plan's year-end has been determined in conformity with GAAP.

   d. whether purchase, redemption, and income transactions of the units held by the plan are properly recorded.

7.22 Examples of substantive procedures for CCTs include

   a. confirming directly with the trustee the units of participation held by the plan. For further guidance refer to Interpretation No. 1 of AU section 328.

   b. examining documents approving and supporting selected investment transactions in units of participation, such as investment committee minutes, trust agreements, or investment guidelines.

   c. inspecting audited financial statements of the CCTs or other evidence supporting fair value, as applicable. If net asset value (NAV) (or its equivalent) is used as a practical expedient to estimate fair value, consult paragraphs 59–62 of FASB ASC 820-10-35 for guidance. AICPA Technical Questions and Answers (TIS) sections 2220.18–.27 (AICPA, *Technical Practice Aids*) and the AICPA Practice Aid *Alternative Investments—Audit Considerations* contain additional nonauthoritative guidance.

If the plan auditor is unable to apply the auditing procedures discussed in this paragraph, then a limitation on the scope of the audit may exist. Restrictions on the scope of the audit, whether imposed by the client or by circumstances, such as the inability to obtain sufficient appropriate audit evidence, may require the auditor to qualify his or her opinion or to disclaim an opinion (see AU section 508 paragraphs .22–.26).

Mutual Funds

7.23 Many employee benefit plans, particularly 401(k) plans and profit sharing plans, hold investments in mutual funds (also known as registered investment companies). Typically, a plan holds units of participation in mutual funds which are valued at quoted market prices (which may fluctuate daily) representing the NAV of the units held by the plan.

7.24 The objectives of auditing procedures applied to investments in mutual funds are to provide the auditor with a reasonable basis for concluding

- *a.* whether the shares held by the plan exist.
- *b.* whether the shares are owned by the plan and are unencumbered.
- *c.* whether valuation of shares at the plan's year-end has been determined in conformity with GAAP.
- *d.* whether purchase, redemption, and income transactions of the shares held by the plan are properly recorded.

7.25 Many of the audit procedures discussed in paragraph 7.16 are applicable for mutual funds. Such procedures may include the following:

- *a.* Confirming transactions (contributions, transfers, and withdrawals) or account balances with individual participants or both.
- *b.* Tracing contributions and withdrawals from the plan recordkeeper's records to the mutual fund's activity statements for the applicable time period.
- *c.* Confirming directly with the mutual fund the number of units of participation held by the plan.
- *d.* Testing the fair value of the investments in mutual funds by comparing per unit values as of year-end to market quotations.
- *e.* Obtaining a copy of the mutual fund's recent financial statements (or alternative source of yield information, such as business journals) and analytically comparing for reasonableness the information in the mutual fund's financial statements to the information recorded by the plan for its units of participation, including market values and the net change in fair value of investments (that is, realized and unrealized gains and losses) for the period under audit. The mutual fund's financial statements need not cover the exact period covered by the plan's financial statements but it is important that they be sufficiently recent to satisfy the plan auditor's objectives. (The financial statements of mutual funds are typically readily available.)

7.26 Difficulties are often incurred in auditing mutual fund investments with daily valuations, participant-directed automated transactions (for example, voice-activated telephone systems) and other paperless transactions. In such circumstances, the plan is often unable to maintain independent records of such transactions necessitating that the auditor obtain an understanding of internal control of the service organization in order to plan the audit in accordance with AU section 314. This understanding can be efficiently achieved by obtaining and reviewing a report prepared in accordance with SAS No. 70 on the relevant controls of the service organization (typically the recordkeeper, which in certain circumstances may be a service division of the mutual fund organization). (See paragraphs 6.13–.26 for a further discussion of SAS No. 70.) Consideration of the areas and findings addressed in the SAS No. 70 report and whether the SAS No. 70 report is a type 1 or type 2 report, should be made by the auditor to determine the extent of substantive procedures to perform. For example, if a type 2 report is obtained, the auditor may be able to limit tests of certain mutual fund transactions such as those described in paragraphs 7.25a–b.

Omnibus Accounts

7.27 An *omnibus account* is an institutional account, often in the name of a custodian bank or an investment adviser, in which transactions are effected on behalf of a number of beneficial owners that are aggregated for trading purposes and are later allocated to those beneficial owners. Traditionally, although the bank or the investment adviser is expected to maintain records that reflect the transactions allocated among the beneficial owners or customers, any information regarding the identity of the customers for whom transactions were executed is frequently maintained by an affiliated recordkeeper. The recordkeeper system is the only record of an individual plan's activity within the investment fund. The following audit steps may be considered when auditing investments in omnibus accounts:

a. Confirm overall values of each investment fund holding at the omnibus level with the transfer agent at period end.

b. Obtain a reconciliation of the aggregated balances of all participating plans for each investment fund held by the plan to the transfer agent's omnibus account (test reconciling items as applicable) for the period end.

c. Agree plan's balances for each investment fund per recordkeeping system to the amounts included in the period end listing of participating plans.

d. Test fair value by comparing the NAV of each investment fund holding at the omnibus level to market quotations or audited financial statements.

e. Perform analytical procedures on changes in fair value of the plan's investment in the omnibus account to the overall investment fund's changes in fair value by reference to financial statements or published sources of information.

f. Obtain a SAS No. 70 type 2 report for recordkeeper or transfer agent. Review, as applicable, for pertinent data relating to omnibus account and reconciliations procedures. If no SAS No. 70 report is available, consider confirming omnibus level transactions directly with each participating plan, tracing transactions from the recordkeeper or transfer agent records to the omnibus account investment fund statements or other tests of transactions at the omnibus account level or both.

Master Trusts and Similar Vehicles

7.28 An entity that sponsors more than one employee benefit plan or a group of corporations under common control may place assets relating to some or all of the plans into one combined trust account, sometimes referred to as a *master trust*. Each plan has an interest in the assets of the trust, and ownership is represented by a record of proportionate dollar interest or by units of participation. A bank ordinarily serves as the trustee for a master trust, acts as custodian, and may or may not have discretionary control over the assets. If a limited scope audit is to be performed on a plan funded under a master trust arrangement or other similar vehicle, separate individual plan certifications from the trustee or the custodian should be obtained for the allocation of the assets, and the related income activity, to the specific plan.

7.29 Plan administrators normally engage an auditor to report only on the financial statements of individual plans. The auditing objectives and procedures described in paragraphs 7.15–.16 also apply to the activities of a master trust in which a plan participates. When the same auditor examines the master trust and the individual plans that have some or all of their assets in the master trust, it will normally be efficient for the auditor first to apply appropriate procedures to the master trust and then to examine how ownership is attributed to individual plans.

7.30 If the master trust is audited by another independent auditor, the plan auditor may obtain the other auditor's report on the master trust's financial statements. The plan auditor uses this report in a manner that is consistent with his or her use of the report of another auditor on the financial statements of a CCT (see paragraph 7.22c). If the master trust is not audited, the plan auditor may perform those procedures necessary to obtain sufficient audit evidence to support the financial statement assertions about plan investments or qualify or disclaim his or her report.

7.31 The plan auditor may review the trust instrument to obtain reasonable assurance that the accounting for the undivided interest is consistent with the instrument. If the instrument does not specify the accounting method, it is important that all administrators of plans participating in the master trust agree with the method of allocation.

7.32 Many limited partnerships, hedge funds and other pooled funds such as group trusts elect to file with the DOL as a 103-12 entity. A 103-12 entity is an arrangement, consisting of two or more plans that are not members of a related group of employee benefit plans that is not a master trust, investment account, CCT, or PSA whose underlying assets include plan assets within the meaning of DOL Regulation Title 29 U.S. *Code of Federal Regulations* (CFR) Part 2510.3-101. A 103-12 designation does not represent a legal form of operation but is merely a term given to an entity once it elects to file a Form 5500 with the DOL as a 103-12 entity.

7.33 Making this determination, as to whether a plan can follow this alternative method of reporting, can be complicated and may necessitate legal or other specialized industry consultation. Generally, a 103-12 entity will operate based on its legal structure (according to its operating agreements) in the form of a financial services product such as a trust or a limited partnership. Typically, audited financial statements are required by the entity's operating agreement and are prepared in accordance with GAAP in a format following industry standards consistent with the entity's operations. For example, a 103-12 entity that operates as a limited partnership would look to GAAP financial statement reporting requirements for limited partnerships. See paragraph A.57 for guidance on the filing requirements for 103-12 entities, as applicable.

7.34 To determine the auditing procedures for a plan's investment in a 103-12 entity, the auditor needs to understand the legal structure (for example, limited partnership or trust) and follow the auditing procedures as described in paragraph 7.67 (limited partnerships) or paragraphs 7.20–.22 (CCTs).

Contracts With Insurance Companies[7]

7.35 A plan may invest assets with an insurance company pursuant to any of a number of different types of contracts. The nature of the contract will determine the related accounting and regulatory reporting requirements.[8]

7.36 The amounts remitted to an insurance company become the assets of the insurance company, for which it, in turn, assumes an obligation to fulfill the contract terms. This differs from a bank trust arrangement in which a bank holds the assets for the plan as a fiduciary and the assets are not included in the bank's financial statements.[9] The extent to which the assets and transactions related to insurance arrangements are recorded in the plan's financial statements, and the extent of auditing procedures to be applied, depend on the terms of the contract with the insurance company.

7.37 For employee benefit plans, the fundamental basis of distinction in classifying contracts for accounting purposes is (a) whether the contributions are currently used to purchase insurance or annuities for the individual participants or (b) whether some or all of the contributions are accumulated in an unallocated fund to be used to meet benefit payments as they come due or to purchase annuities for participants at retirement or on earlier termination of service with a vested right.[10] Contractual arrangements under which funds are currently allocated to purchase insurance or annuities for individual participants are referred to as *allocated* funding arrangements, whereas other arrangements are called *unallocated* funding arrangements. Funds in an unallocated contract may be withdrawn or otherwise invested. Some contractual arrangements may involve both allocated and unallocated funding. Essentially, allocated contracts are excluded from, and unallocated contracts are included in, plan assets.[11]

---

[7] FASB ASC 815, *Derivatives and Hedging*, applies to certain contracts that meet the definition of derivative instrument, as defined in FASB ASC 815-10-15-83. See FASB ASC 815-10-15 for further information on certain contracts that are not subject to the requirements of FASB ASC 815.

[8] As noted in appendix A, "ERISA and Related Regulations," plans funded solely with certain types of insurance contracts are not required under the Employee Retirement Income Security Act of 1974 to prepare financial statements or engage an independent auditor.

[9] See paragraphs 7.44–.47 and 7.54 for a discussion of insurance company separate accounts.

[10] Although the term *allocated account* is used by insurance companies in connection with defined contribution plans when amounts are recorded in separate participant accounts, the term *allocated*, as it is used here, refers to situations in which the obligation to pay defined benefits under the plan is assumed by the insurance company.

[11] See paragraph 2.25 in this guide as well as FASB ASC 960-325-35-3.

7.38 Allocated funding arrangements include insurance or annuity contracts in which the insurer has a legal obligation to make all benefit payments for which it has received the premiums or requested consideration. Allocated funding instruments can be individual insurance or annuity contracts, group permanent insurance contracts, or conventional deferred group annuity contracts. Some of these contracts may also include unallocated side or auxiliary funds, which ordinarily would be considered plan assets.

7.39 Unallocated funding instruments apply to any arrangement under which employer or employee contributions to an employee benefit plan are held in an undivided fund until they are used to meet benefit payments as they come due or to purchase annuities for participants at retirement or on earlier termination of employment with vested benefits. Unallocated funding ordinarily is associated with a group deposit administration contract (DA) and an immediate participation guarantee contract (IPG).[12] For investment purposes, unallocated funds may be commingled in a general or pooled separate account or held in an individual separate account.

7.40 Determining whether contract assets and related obligations should be reported in the plan's financial statements requires a careful review of the contract. Typical DA and IPG contracts are unallocated funding arrangements, and the value of these contracts generally should be included in a plan's financial statements. Assets held in separate accounts are similarly reflected in the plan's financial statements, because they are unallocated amounts held by the insurance company.

Deposit Administration Contracts

7.41 The term *deposit administration* is applied to a type of contract under which contributions are not currently applied to the purchase of single-payment deferred annuities for individual participants. Under a DA contract, payments to the insurance company that are intended to provide future benefits to present employees are credited to an account. For investment purposes, the monies in the account are commingled with other assets of the insurance company. The account is credited with interest at the rate specified in the contract; it is charged with the purchase price of annuities when participants retire and with any incidental benefits (death, disability, and withdrawal) disbursed directly from the account.

7.42 Although the insurance company will guarantee a minimum stipulated interest rate on funds in the *active life fund* and rates at which annuities may be purchased, it does not guarantee that sufficient funds will be available to meet the cost of annuities to be purchased.

7.43 Experience-rated interest credits on funds in the undivided account are determined by the insurance company, but they are not guaranteed. The calculation of these credits is based on internal records kept by the insurance company for each contract and are determined by the actual investment experience of the insurance company. These interest credits may be paid out, added to the balance of funds in the undivided account, or considered in an overall dividend calculation that also takes into account mortality, other actuarial experience, and reserves required by the insurance company. Under DA contracts,

---

[12] The term *group annuity* is frequently applied to a broad category of insurance contracts that provide the vehicle for funding pension benefits. Those include *deferred group annuity* contracts, *deposit administration* contracts, and *immediate participation guarantee* contracts.

amounts of dividend or rate credits are determined solely at the discretion of the insurance company, which has no contractual obligation to pay a dividend. The contract holder has no contractual right to demand an accounting.

Immediate Participation Guarantee Contracts

7.44 The IPG contract is a variation of the DA contract. In an IPG contract, the account is credited with the contributions received during the contract period plus its share of the insurance company's actual investment income. The IPG contract is written in two forms. Under either form the insurance company is obligated to make lifetime benefit payments to retired employees. One form provides for the actual purchase of annuities as employees retire. An annual adjustment to the account reflects the insurance company's experience under the annuities. In the other form, the IPG contract may accomplish the same objective through a different technique. When an employee retires, pension payments are made directly from the account without the purchase of an annuity. However, the balance of the account must be maintained at the amount required, according to a premium schedule in the contract, to provide for the remaining pension benefits for all current retirees. That portion of the account is referred to as the *retired life fund*. Thus, if necessary, the account could always be used to buy all annuities in force.

Investment Arrangements With Insurance Companies

7.45 A separate account may be used independent of, or as an adjunct to, a DA or IPG contract.

7.46 Separate accounts were developed to allow insured plans to compete with trust funds in making investments and in funding variable annuity plans. The assets of a separate account plan are assets of the insurance company but are not commingled with the insurance company's general assets. The purpose of a separate account is to provide flexibility in the investment of the plan's funds. A separate account may be established solely for one plan or, more commonly, may be pooled with the funds of several plans.

7.47 A separate account in which only one plan participates is generally referred to as an *individual separate account* or as a *separate-separate account*. The investments in the account must be separately identified, and the account is operated similarly to a bank trust fund, although it is included in the insurance company's financial statements.

7.48 A separate account in which several plans participate generally is referred to as a *pooled separate account*. Each plan's share of a pooled separate account is determined on a participation-unit or variable-unit basis.[13] The plan's equity account provides a cumulative record of the number of participation units credited to the account and the number of units allocated or withdrawn from the account. The balance of participation units credited to the account multiplied by the current participation-unit value equals the amount of equity account assets held on behalf of the policyholder at any given time.

---

[13] In some separate accounts, a plan receives a guaranteed rate of return on funds held in the separate account. A plan's share would be the value of its units determined in accordance with applicable guidance for valuing investment contracts, and the funds held in the separate account should be viewed as an unallocated funding arrangement. Each investment contract in the pooled account should be evaluated individually for benefit responsiveness. However, if the separate account places any restrictions on access to funds for the payment of benefits, the underlying investment contracts would not be considered fully benefit-responsive.

The participation-unit value is adjusted periodically, usually each business day, to reflect investment results under the separate account.

7.49 Many plans hold guaranteed investment contracts (GICs) in their investment portfolios. Normally issued through the general account, in its simplest form a GIC is a contract between an insurance company and a plan that provides for a guaranteed return on principal invested over a specified time period. Variations include contracts in which the plan is permitted to make deposits or withdrawals during certain windows during the contract life, contracts with multiple maturities (and rates), contracts in which the insurance company guarantees a minimum rate and may credit the contract holder with additional interest, and contracts with floating rates. These contracts are unallocated and are generally to be included as plan assets at their contract value or fair values, as appropriate (see paragraphs 3.30–.33 for further guidance.)

7.50 Defined contribution plans often invest in CCTs that invest in contracts with insurance companies or guaranteed investment contracts or both. Determining whether the fund in which the plan invests is a CCT, as described in paragraph 7.20 (refer to auditing procedures in paragraph 7.22), or an account set up to hold insurance or investment contracts specifically for one plan (refer to auditing procedures in paragraphs 7.55) takes careful consideration.

7.51 For defined contribution plans, another variation of a GIC is commonly referred to as a synthetic GIC. A synthetic GIC is an investment contract that simulates the performance of a traditional GIC through the use of financial instruments. A key difference between a synthetic GIC and a traditional GIC is that the plan owns the assets underlying the synthetic GIC. (With a traditional GIC, the plan owns only the investment contract itself that provides the plan with a call on the contract issuer's assets in the event of default.) Those assets may be held in a trust owned by the plan and typically consist of government securities, private and public mortgage-backed and other asset-backed securities, and investment grade corporate obligations. To enable the plan to realize a specific known value for the assets if it needs to liquidate them to make benefit payments, synthetic GICs utilize a benefit responsive *wrapper* contract issued by a third party that provides market and cash flow risk protection to the plan. (The third-party issuer of the wrapper is an entity other than the plan sponsor, administrator, or trustee and could be the entity that issues the investment contract.) Because the assets underlying a synthetic GIC are owned by the plan, those assets and the wrapper should be separately valued and disclosed in the Form 5500 Schedule H, line 4i—Schedule of Assets (Held at End of Year). (See FASB ASC 962-325-55 and paragraph 7.53*d*.)

Auditing Objectives

7.52 The objectives of auditing procedures applied to plan assets held with an insurance company are to provide the auditor with a reasonable basis for concluding

  a. whether plan assets, represented by contracts with insurance companies, exist.

  b. whether changes in plan assets during the period are properly recorded and valued in conformity with GAAP.

  c. whether the plan has any intention of seeking to dispose of or terminate the contract.

    d. whether the terms of the contract are being complied with and are appropriately disclosed in the plan's financial statements.

Auditing Procedures

7.53 The auditing procedures that may be applied to contracts with insurance companies (to the extent they are applicable to a particular contract) include

    a. reading the contracts between the contract holder and the insurance company and evaluating whether they are investment or insurance contracts, in accordance with paragraphs 1 and 3 of FASB ASC 960-325-35 if applicable.

    b. confirming the following directly with the insurance company, as applicable:

        i. Contributions or premium payments made to the fund or account during the year

        ii. Interest, dividends, refunds, credits, and changes in value and whether such amounts have been charged or credited during the year on an estimated or actual basis

        iii. The value of the funds in the general or separate account at the plan's year-end and the basis for determining such value

        iv. The amount of insurance company fee and other expenses chargeable during the year

        v. For insurance contracts with unallocated funds, annuity purchases or benefits paid from unallocated plan assets during the year

        vi. Transfers between various funds and accounts

    c. evaluating whether the characteristics of the contract that restrict the use of assets require disclosure in the financial statements of the plan. For example, if the plan has indicated an intention to dispose of or terminate the contract or the contract contains a termination clause (for example, a market value determination adjustment), the auditor would perform sufficient procedures either with plan representatives or the insurance company to satisfy the audit objectives identified in the foregoing with respect to proper valuation and appropriate disclosure. Alternatively, if plan management is aware that an event has affected the contract issuer that may require disclosure or, in rare circumstances, may cause plan management to conclude that reporting the investment at a value less than contract value is appropriate, the auditor would perform sufficient procedures to satisfy the audit objectives identified.

    d. for defined contribution plans for which the *wrapper* is benefit responsive, tests of the individual securities or other investments that comprise the assets underlying a synthetic GIC and tests of the related wrapper contract to ascertain the fairness of the values of each to be disclosed by the plan in the Form 5500 Schedule H, line 4i—Schedule of Assets (Held at End of Year).

7.54 For contracts in which assets are held in the insurance company's general account (DAs and IPGs), additional auditing procedures that may be applied include

a. for DA contracts, evaluating the reasonableness of the interest credited to the contracts in relation to any minimum guaranteed interest rate stated in the contract.[14]

b. for IPG contracts, considering the plan administrator's conclusion regarding the basis for recording changes in contract values to recognize investment returns in accordance with the terms of the contract. This conclusion is usually made by referring to investment yield data furnished to the plan by the insurance company. Generally, this evaluation would sufficiently satisfy the auditor regarding the aggregate investment income credited to the contract. If the amount of investment yield credited to the contract, based on current investment returns, does not appear reasonable, the auditor may apply additional procedures, such as making inquiries of the insurance company regarding its compliance with the method required under the terms of the contract for computing investment return. In the event that the plan auditor is unable to obtain assurance concerning the reasonableness of the rate of investment return credited, he or she may consider asking the plan administrator to contact the insurance company to arrange for the insurer's independent auditor to perform agreed-upon procedures and issue a report thereon (see AT section 201, *Agreed-Upon Procedures Engagements* [AICPA, *Professional Standards*]). Those procedures would be applied to the insurance company's determination of investment returns in accordance with the contract.

c. determining that annuity purchases were made on the basis of rates stipulated in the contract. If annuities are not purchased and benefits are paid directly from the fund, benefit payments may be tested in accordance with the auditing procedures discussed in paragraph 9.03.

d. reading the financial statements or obtaining the credit rating of the insurance company.

e. evaluating whether expenses charged to the contract by the insurance company are in accordance with the insurance contract or are otherwise authorized by the plan.

7.55 For insurance contracts in which investments are made in separate accounts, the auditor may apply the following additional procedures:

a. For investments in which assets are held in individual separate accounts, include the individual investment transactions and documents that provide support for those transactions and consider the auditing procedures in paragraph 7.16.

b. For investments in pooled separate accounts, the plan auditor is concerned with the plan's units of participation in the pooled account. Examine documents that provide support for those transactions. To perform those procedures, the plan auditor may do the following:

---

[14] The plan auditor need not apply auditing procedures to the experience fund of a typical group deposit administration contract DA account or to any similar fund that is used by the insurance company to determine a "discretionary" dividend or rate credit under the contract (see paragraph 7.42).

i. If the pooled account's financial statements have been audited by an independent auditor, obtain and read the pooled account's financial statements and the auditor's report. The financial statements need not cover the exact period covered by the plan's financial statements; they should, however, be sufficiently recent to satisfy the plan auditor. Consider the effect that any reported matters have on the carrying amounts of the units of participation held by the plan, such as restrictions on redemption or subjectively determined values. If the auditor believes the carrying amount may be impaired, procedures such as applying analytical procedures to the interim financial information of the pooled account from the date of the account's audited financial statements to determine whether such a loss in value has occurred may be appropriate.

ii. If the pooled separate account's financial statements have not been audited by an independent auditor, then see additional guidance and procedures provided in Interpretation No. 1 of AU section 328 and the AICPA Practice Aid *Alternative Investments—Audit Considerations (A practice aid for auditors)*.

7.56 If the plan auditor is unable to apply the auditing procedures discussed in paragraphs 7.53–.55, then a limitation on the scope of the audit may exist. Restrictions on the scope of the audit, whether imposed by the client or by circumstances, such as the inability to obtain sufficient appropriate audit evidence, may require the auditor to qualify his or her opinion or to disclaim an opinion (see AU section 508 paragraphs .22–.26).

Loans to Participants

7.57 The objectives of auditing procedures applied to loans to participants are to provide the auditor with a reasonable basis for concluding whether the amounts due the plan have been properly valued, recorded, and disclosed in the financial statements in conformity with GAAP and plan documents.

7.58 The auditing procedures to be applied to participant loans may include

a. examining participant loan documentation supporting loans.

b. confirming loans with participants.

c. testing that interest is properly recorded.

d. testing whether the loans were made in conformance with the plan document.

e. reviewing financial statement classification to ascertain that participant loans are properly reported as a receivable on the statement of net assets available for benefits. Participant loans should be measured at their unpaid principal balance plus any accrued but unpaid interest in accordance with "Pending Content" in FASB ASC 962-310-35-2.

Note: Participant loans are to be included on the supplemental Schedule H, line 4i—Schedule of Assets (Held at End of Year) and recorded as an investment on Form 5500, Schedule H. See chapter 3, "Accounting and Reporting by Defined Contribution Plans," for further discussion of participant loans.[†]

> f. determining whether delinquent loans receivable should be reclassified as distributions. This determination is dependent on the terms of the plan document and related plan policies and procedures. The written terms of the plan, the plan sponsor's written provisions concerning participant loans, and the loan documents determine when a loan is in default.
>
> The fact that the participant pays tax on the amount of the loan does not necessarily mean the loan is considered to be canceled and should be recorded as a distribution in the financial statements. A participant may pay tax on a loan balance because the tax rules have been violated. Depending on the nature of the plan and the plan terms, the loan may remain due and payable, interest may still accrue and the loan may continue to be reported as a plan investment on the financial statements and as an obligation in default on the Form 5500 schedule until it is actually repaid, the default cured in some other manner or the loan is considered to be cancelled and therefore is recorded as a distribution.
>
> A plan may call for a previous loan to be considered to be distributed to a participant and considered to be cancelled in the event the participant goes into default or otherwise violates the provisions of the documents. In this case, the loan ceases to exist and should be shown as a distribution. The loan is last reported on the Form 5500, Schedule G, Part I, Schedule of Loans or Fixed Income Obligations in Default or Classified as Uncollectible, if applicable, in the year prior to the year it is canceled and considered to be distributed. Do not report in Form 5500, Schedule G Part I, participant loans under an individual account plan with investment experience segregated for each account, that are made in accordance with 29 CFR 2550.408b-1, and that are secured solely by a portion of the participant's vested accrued benefit.
>
> g. ascertaining that participant loans considered to be delinquent based on the terms of the plan document and related plan policies and procedures are included in the supplemental Schedule G, Part I, Schedule of Loans or Fixed Income Obligations in Default or Classified as Uncollectible. Delinquent loans are considered to be assets held for investment purposes.[†]

Derivatives and Hedging Activities

7.59 FASB ASC 815, *Derivatives and Hedging*, provides accounting and reporting standards for derivative instruments, including certain derivative

---

[†] In February 2010, the AICPA issued SAS No. 119, *Supplementary Information in Relation to the Financial Statements as a Whole* (AICPA, *Professional Standards*, AU sec. 551), which, along with SAS No. 118, *Other Information in Documents Containing Audited Financial Statements* (AICPA, *Professional Standards*, AU sec. 550), supersedes AU section 551A, *Reporting on Information Accompanying the Basic Financial Statements in Auditor-Submitted Documents* (AICPA, *Professional Standards*). SAS No. 119 addresses the auditor's responsibility when engaged to report on whether supplementary information is fairly stated, in all material respects, in relation to the financial statements as a whole. This SAS is effective for periods beginning on or after December 15, 2010. Early application is permitted and therefore, if adopting SAS No. 119 early, refer to the standard for further guidance.

instruments embedded in other contracts (collectively referred to as *derivatives*) and hedging activities. Certain employee benefit plans invest in derivative instruments and participate in hedging activities. Derivatives get their name because they derive their value from movements in an underlying,[15] such as changes in the price of a security or a commodity. Examples of common derivatives are options, forwards, futures and swaps. Employee benefit plans that use derivatives to manage risk are involved in hedging activities. Hedging is a risk alteration activity that attempts to protect the employee benefit plan against the risk of adverse changes in the fair values or cash flows of assets, liabilities, or future transactions. FASB ASC 815 requires that an entity recognize all derivatives as either assets or liabilities in the statement of financial position and measure those instruments at fair value.

7.60 As discussed in FASB ASC 815-10-05-4, if certain conditions are met, an entity may elect to designate a derivative instrument in any one of the following ways:

  a. A hedge of the exposure to changes in the fair value of a recognized asset or liability or an unrecognized firm commitment that are attributable to a particular risk (fair value hedge)

  b. A hedge of the exposure to variability in the cash flows of a recognized asset or liability or of a forecasted transaction that is attributable to a particular risk (cash flow hedge)

  c. A hedge of the foreign currency exposure of a net investment in a foreign operation, an unrecognized firm commitment (a foreign currency fair value hedge), an available-for-sale security (a foreign currency fair value hedge), or a forecasted transaction (a foreign currency cash flow hedge)

7.61 As stated by FASB ASC 815-10-35-2, the accounting for changes in the fair value (that is, gains or losses) of a derivative instrument depends on whether it has been designated and qualifies as part of a hedging relationship and, if so, on the reason for holding it. FASB ASC 815-10-50 also contains extensive disclosure requirements.

7.62 FASB ASC 815-10-50-1 requires enhanced disclosures about the following:

  a. How and why an entity uses derivative instruments (of such nonderivative instruments)

  b. How derivative instruments (or such nonderivative instruments) and related hedged items are accounted for under FASB ASC 815

  c. How derivative instruments (or such nonderivative instruments) and related hedged items affect an entity's financial position, financial performance, and cash flows

7.63 In accordance with paragraphs 1A–B of FASB ASC 815-10-50, an entity that holds or issues derivative instruments (or nonderivative instruments that are designated and qualify as hedging instruments pursuant to FASB ASC

---

[15] The FASB ASC glossary defines an *underlying* as a specified interest rate, security price, commodity price, foreign exchange rate, index of prices, or rates, or other variable (including the occurrence or nonoccurrence of a specified event such as scheduled payment under a contract). An underlying may be a price or rate of an asset or liability, but it is not the asset or liability itself. An underlying is a variable that along with either a notional amount or payment provision determines the settlement of a derivative instrument.

815-20-25-58 and 815-20-25-66) should disclose all of the following for every annual and interim reporting period for which a statement of financial position and statement of financial performance are presented:

    a. Its objectives for holding or issuing those instruments

    b. The context needed to understand those objectives

    c. Its strategies for achieving those objectives

    d. Information that would enable users of its financial statements to understand the volume of its activity in those instruments

For item (*d*) in the preceding paragraph, an entity should select the format and the specifics of disclosures relating to its volume of such activity that are most relevant and practicable for its individual facts and circumstances. Information about the instruments in items (*a–c*) in the preceding paragraph should be disclosed in the context of each instrument's primary underlying risk exposure. Further, those instruments should be distinguished between those used for risk management purposes and those used for other purposes. Derivative instruments (and nonderivative instruments that are designated and qualify as hedging instruments pursuant to FASB ASC 815-20-25-58 and FASB ASC 815-20-25-66) used for risk management purposes include those designated as hedging instruments under FASB ASC 815-20 as well as those used as economic hedges and for other purposes related to the entity's risk exposures.

    7.64 The objectives of auditing procedures applied to derivative instruments and related transactions are to provide the auditor with a reasonable basis for concluding

    a. whether derivatives transactions are initiated in accordance with management's established policies.

    b. whether information relating to derivatives transactions is complete and accurate.

    c. whether derivatives accounted for as hedges meet the designation, documentation, and assessment requirements of GAAP.

    d. whether the carrying amount of derivatives is adjusted to fair value, and changes in the fair value of derivatives are accounted for in conformity with GAAP.

    e. whether derivatives are monitored on an ongoing basis to recognize and measure events affecting related financial statement assertions.

    7.65 Examples of substantive procedures regarding derivative instruments and hedging activities are

    a. confirmation with the counterparty to the derivative.

    b. confirmation of settled and unsettled transactions with the counterparty.

    c. testing the fair value (see paragraph 7.16*h*).

    d. physical inspection of the derivative contract.

    e. reading and inspecting related agreements, underlying agreements, and other forms of documentation for amounts reported, unrecorded repurchase agreements, and other evidence.

    f. inspecting supporting documentation for subsequent realization or settlements after the end of the reporting period.

    g. reading other information such as minutes of committee meetings.

    h. testing to ensure derivative transactions are initiated in accordance with policies established by the plan's management.

7.66 The auditor may need special skills or knowledge to plan and perform auditing procedures for certain assertions about derivatives and securities, especially with the unique characteristics of derivatives instruments and securities, coupled with the relative complexity of the related accounting guidance. AU section 332 is intended to alert auditors to the possible need for such skill or knowledge. Also, see AICPA Audit Guide *Auditing Derivative Instruments, Hedging Activities, and Investments in Securities* for further guidance on auditing such instruments.

Other Investments

7.67 The objectives of auditing procedures applied to other types of investments and related transactions are to provide the auditor with a reasonable basis for concluding

    a. whether all investments are recorded and exist.

    b. whether the investments are owned by the plan and are free of liens, pledges, and other security interests, or if not, whether the security interests are identified.

    c. whether investment transactions are recorded and the investments are properly valued in conformity with GAAP.

7.68 Examples of substantive procedures for other types of investments follow:

For real estate

    a. Examining closing and other documents supporting the cost of ownership.

    b. Examining deeds, title policies, encumbrances, and other evidence related to ownership.

    c. Testing the fair value (see paragraph 7.16*h*). If an outside valuation specialist has been engaged (such as a real estate appraiser) perform appropriate tests of the accounting data provided to the specialist. Review the specialist's professional qualifications, reputation, and relationship to the plan sponsor.

    d. Examining current-year tax bills and relating them to property descriptions under (*b*) preceding.

    e. Testing investment income from real estate, such as rents, and payments of related expenses, such as taxes and maintenance.

    f. Inquiring whether the plan's investments or other transactions violate applicable laws or regulations. (See appendix A for a discussion of party in interest and reportable transactions under ERISA.)

For loans and mortgages (excludes participant loans; see paragraphs 7.57–.58 for a discussion on loans to participants)

    a. Examining documents, including notes, mortgages, deeds, and insurance policies, supporting selected loans and mortgages.

    b. Confirming selected loans and mortgages with borrowers.

    c. Testing the fair value, including the extent of collateral, if any (see paragraph 7.16*h*).

    d. Testing to see that interest is properly recorded.

    e. Inquiring whether the plan's investments or other transactions violate applicable laws or regulations. (See appendix A for a discussion of party in interest and reportable transactions under ERISA.)

For alternative investments, such as limited partnerships, hedge funds, private equity or venture capital funds

    a. Obtain confirmation of the plan's holdings in the alternative investments from the investment manager or adviser (including activity during the year and percentage ownership). ***Note:*** Confirmation does not constitute adequate audit evidence regarding valuation. For further guidance see Interpretation No. 1, "Auditing Investments in Securities Where a Readily Determinable Fair Value Does Not Exist," of AU section 332 (AICPA, *Professional Standards*, AU sec. 9332 par. .01–.04).

    b. Obtain copy of audited financial statements for the alternative investment and year-end capital allocation schedule from investment manager or adviser and relate reasonableness of the alternative investment value reported in the financial statements and allocation schedule to the alternative investment value recorded by the participating plan, including fair value, purchases or sales value, income earned and income accrued. If NAV (or its equivalent) is used as a practical expedient to estimate fair value, consult paragraphs 59–62 of FASB ASC 820-10-35 for guidance. TIS sections 2220.18–.27 and the AICPA Practice Aid *Alternative Investments—Audit Considerations* contain additional nonauthoritative guidance.

    c. Examine documents approving and supporting selected investment purchase and sale transactions (such as subscription or redemption documentation, investment agreement, and minutes of meeting).

    d. If the alternative investment is not audited by an independent auditor, or if the independent auditor's report on the alternative investment is not satisfactory, the plan auditor should apply further auditing procedures (see paragraph 7.16) that may include

        i. obtaining a copy of the alternative investment holdings and inquire of management regarding the methods for valuation.

        ii. obtaining copy of appraisal (refer to AU section 336) or perform valuation procedures.

        iii. obtaining an understanding of the alternative investment controls and assess control risk relating to the alternative investment (may be achieved through review of service auditor's report, if available). Often the trustee or custodian does not have timely or accurate information regarding the amount and valuation of the plan's investment in the alternative investment.

For nonpublicly traded stock and employer securities

    a. Obtain an analysis of changes in investments during the period.

     b. Obtain evidence regarding existence and ownership of investments either through confirmation from trustee or custodian or by physical count.

     c. Review minutes, agreements, and confirmations for evidence of liens, pledges, or other security interest in investments.

     d. Perform tests of investment transactions, including the following:

         i. Determine that they were properly authorized.

         ii. Examine cash records or other supporting documentation for the historical cost or selling price, quantity, identification, and date of acquisition and disposal.

         iii. Agree prices at which purchases and sales were recorded to supporting evidence (including information provided by outside specialist, if applicable) for price ranges on the trade dates.

         iv. Check the computation of the net change in appreciation or depreciation.

     e. Test the fair value of investments in accordance with AU section 342 (paragraph 7.16*h*). If an outside valuation specialist has been engaged, perform appropriate tests of the accounting data provided to the specialist. Review the specialist's professional qualifications, reputation, and relationship to the plan sponsor.

     f. Inquire whether the plan's investments or other transactions violate applicable laws or regulations.

Also see the AICPA Audit Guide *Auditing Derivative Instruments, Hedging Activities, and Investments in Securities* for further guidance on auditing investment values based on an investee's financial results.

Self-Directed Accounts

    7.69 Many defined contribution plans with participant directed investment programs also offer a self-directed program to participants. For the purposes of this discussion, a self-directed program is one that allows participants to invest their account balances in any investment desired, within certain specified limitations. Under this type of arrangement, participants can direct investments into the self-directed program in addition to or in lieu of the various formal investment programs offered by the plan. Some defined contribution plans are completely self-directed and do not offer any formal participant directed investment programs. The self-directed account does not represent a pooled investment vehicle but is an account comprised of individual investments owned by the plan. Often the self-directed accounts contain other investments that are hard-to-value, such as real estate and mortgages. Auditors should obtain an understanding of the nature of the plan. The nature of the plan includes the types of investments that the plan has or will invest in. For self-directed accounts this understanding includes the individual investments that comprise the account to determine appropriate audit procedures. Paragraphs 7.67–.68 provide audit objectives and procedures relating to other investments. Paragraphs 3.34–.35, 3.46*a–b*, 3.49, and 3.50*h* provide financial statement reporting requirements for defined contribution plan investments.

    7.70 Although self-directed accounts are viewed as individual investments for auditing purposes, the instructions to Form 5500 Schedule H, Financial

Information, permit aggregate reporting of certain self-directed accounts (also known as participant-directed brokerage accounts) on the Form 5500 and related schedule of assets. Investments made through participant-directed brokerage accounts may be reported either: (a) as individual investments in the applicable categories in Parts I and II of Schedule H; or (b) by reporting the aggregate amount on the assets line 1c(15), *Other,* and the aggregate investment income (loss) before expenses on line 2c. This aggregate reporting is not available for loans, partnerships or joint-ventures, real property, employer securities, or investments that could result in a loss in excess of the account balance of the individual who directed the transaction.

7.71 Investments made through participant-directed brokerage accounts reported in the aggregate on line 1c(15) of Schedule H are treated as one asset on line 4i schedules of assets, except that investments in tangible personal property continue to be separately reported on this schedule. (See exhibit A-1, "Examples of Form 5500 Schedules," in appendix A of this guide for examples of Form 5500 schedules.)

Separately Managed Accounts

7.72 Some plans have accounts at a trust company or similar institution consisting of individual plan assets that are managed by an investment manager specifically for the plan. Often these separately managed accounts are mistaken for pooled investment vehicles. A review of the underlying investment agreement with the investment manager will typically reveal whether the investment is a pooled or separately managed vehicle. Individual assets of a separately managed account are held in the name of the plan. The auditing objectives and procedures described in paragraphs 7.15–.16 also apply to individual assets and activity for a separately managed account. (Such individual investments are also subject to the reporting requirements in paragraphs 2.26–.27, 3.34–.35, or 4.52. In addition, these investments would be considered individual investments for purposes of reporting on Form 5500, Schedule H, line 4i—Schedule of Assets (Held at End of Year) and line 4j—Schedule of Reportable Transactions.)

Limited-Scope Auditing Procedures

7.73 As discussed in paragraphs 5.13 and 13.26–.31 the audit may be restricted with respect to assets held and transactions executed by certain institutions. In an ERISA limited scope audit, the plan administrator can instruct the auditor to limit the scope of testing on investment information prepared and certified by a qualified trustee, custodian, or insurance company as complete and accurate. The scope limitation and the corresponding limitation of the auditor's work extend only to investments and related investment information certified by the qualified trustee, custodian, or insurance company. Plan investments not held by a qualified trustee, custodian, or insurance company, such as real estate, leases, mortgages, self-directed brokerage accounts, participant loans, and any other investments or assets not covered by such an entity's certification should be subjected to appropriate audit procedures. Moreover, the appropriate audit procedures for all noninvestment related information (for example, benefit payments, employer or employee contributions, and receivables) are the same for a limited scope audit as for a full scope audit.

7.74 When the auditor is instructed by the plan administrator to perform a limited scope audit, the auditor has no responsibility to obtain an understanding of internal control maintained by the certifying institution over investments held and investment transactions executed for the plan or to assess control risk associated with assets held and transactions executed by the institution. The auditor's responsibilities for any investments covered by the limited-scope exception are to (*a*) obtain and read a copy of the certification from the plan administrator, (*b*) determine whether the entity issuing the certification is a qualifying institution under DOL regulations, (*c*) to compare the investment information certified by the plan's trustee or custodian to the financial information contained in the plan's financial statements and related disclosures, (*d*) perform the necessary procedures to become satisfied that any received or disbursed amounts (for example, contributions and benefit payments) reported by the trustee or custodian were determined in accordance with the plan provisions, and (*e*) determine whether the form and content of the financial statement disclosures related to the investment information prepared and certified by the plan's trustee or custodian are in conformity with GAAP and are in compliance with DOL rules and regulations. When performing a limited scope audit, the auditor has no responsibility to test the accuracy or completeness of the investment information certified by the plan's trustee or custodian.

7.75 Although the auditor is not required to audit certain investment information when the limited scope audit exception is applicable, if the auditor becomes aware that the certified information is incomplete, inaccurate, or otherwise unsatisfactory further inquiry may be necessary which might result in additional testing or modification to the auditor's report. In certain instances, a limited scope audit may no longer be appropriate. In addition, if it comes to the auditor's attention that the required supplementary schedules are omitted, do not contain all required information, or contain information that is inaccurate or is inconsistent with the financial statements, the auditor should consider the guidance in paragraph 13.15.

7.76 If, for example, the auditor becomes aware that adequate year-end valuation procedures have not been performed and therefore the financial statements may not be prepared in conformity with GAAP, the auditor would communicate those findings to the plan administrator. It is the plan administrator's responsibility to prepare the financial statements and footnote disclosures in conformity with GAAP and in compliance with DOL rules and regulations. Accordingly, the plan administrator may request the trustee or custodian to

    a. recertify or amend the certification for such investments at their appropriate year-end values, or

    b. recertify or amend the certification to exclude such investments from the certification

If the trustee or custodian amends the certification to exclude such investments from the certification, the plan administrator is responsible for valuing such investments as of the plan year end and engaging the auditor to perform full audit procedures on the investments excluded from the certification.

7.77 If the certification is not amended, it is the plan administrator's responsibility to determine whether the financial statements and footnote disclosures, related to such investment information are prepared in conformity with

GAAP and in compliance with DOL rules and regulations. The following is an illustrative report[16]for when the plan investments have been certified and the plan administrator was unable to determine whether the investment information is valued in conformity with U.S. GAAP. However, this form of report is not appropriate if the plan administrator has information that causes the auditor to believe that the investment information is not valued in conformity with U.S. GAAP.[17]

Independent Auditor's Report

[*Addressee*]

We were engaged to audit the accompanying statement of net assets available for benefits of XYZ Plan (the Plan) as of December 31, 20YY, and 20XX, and the changes in net assets available for benefits for the years then ended and the supplemental schedules of (*a*) Schedule H, line 4i—Schedule of Assets Held (At End of Year) and (*b*) Schedule H, line 4j—Schedule of Reportable Transactions as of or for the year ended December 31, 20YY. These financial statements and supplemental schedules are the responsibility of the Plan's management.

As permitted by 29 CFR 2520.103-8 of the Department of Labor's Rules and Regulations for Reporting and Disclosure under the Employee Retirement Income Security Act of 1974, the plan administrator instructed us not to perform, and we did not perform, any auditing procedures with respect to the investment information summarized in Note 3, which was certified by ABC Trust Company, the trustee of the Plan, except for comparing such information with the related information included in the financial statements. We have been informed by the plan administrator that the trustee holds the Plan's investment assets and executes investment transactions. The plan administrator has obtained a certification from the trustee as of and for the years ended December 31, 20YY, and 20XX, that the information provided to the plan administrator by the trustee is complete and accurate.

Department of Labor Rules and Regulations and generally accepted accounting principles require plan investments to be valued at fair value as of the end of the Plan year. As described in Note X, Plan management does not have adequate procedures to properly value certain investments as of year end and therefore these investments may not be presented in compliance with Department of Labor Rules and Regulations or in conformity with generally accepted accounting principles. The effects on the financial statements and supplemental schedules of not applying adequate procedures to determine the fair value of these investments has not been determined.

Because of the significance of the information that we did not audit, we are unable to, and do not, express an opinion on the accompanying financial statements and supplemental schedules taken as a whole. The form and content of the information included in the financial statements and supplemental schedules taken as a whole, other than that derived from the investment information certified by the trustee, have been audited by us in accordance with auditing standards generally accepted in the United States of America and, in our

---

[16] Historically, the Department of Labor has rejected Form 5500 filings that contain either qualified opinions, adverse opinions, or disclaimers of opinion other than those issued in connection with a limited scope audit pursuant to Title 29 U.S. *Code of Federal Regulations* Part 2520.103-8 or 12.

[17] AU section 508, *Reports on Audited Financial Statements* (AICPA, *Professional Standards*), requires the auditor to disclose any material modifications from GAAP.

opinion, are presented in compliance with the Department of Labor's Rules and Regulations for Reporting and Disclosure under the Employee Retirement Income Security Act of 1974.

Chapter 8

Auditing Contributions Received and Related Receivables

8.01 For all types of employee benefit plans, the basis for determining employer and, if applicable, employee contributions is specified in the plan instrument or related documents. For defined benefit plans covered by Employee Retirement Income Security Act of 1974 (ERISA), employer annual contributions must also satisfy the minimum funding standards of ERISA. (See paragraphs A.10–A.14 of appendix A, "ERISA and Related Regulations," for a discussion of the funding standard account and minimum funding standards of ERISA.) The existence of an accrued liability in the employer's statement of financial position or of a plan's accumulated benefit obligations in excess of its net assets available for benefits do not, by themselves, provide sufficient support for recognition of a contribution receivable by the plan.

Auditing Objectives

8.02 The objectives of auditing procedures applied to contributions received and related receivables of employee benefit plans are to provide the auditor with a reasonable basis for concluding

  a. whether the amounts received or due the plan have been determined and recorded and disclosed in the financial statements in conformity with plan documents and generally accepted accounting principles (GAAP).

  b. whether an appropriate allowance has been made for uncollectible plan contributions receivable in conformity with GAAP.

Auditing Procedures

8.03 Examples of substantive procedures for employer and employee contributions are as follows:

  a. Obtaining a list of participating employers (in a multiemployer plan) and testing its completeness by examining appropriate plan documents (for example, a record of contributing employers and delinquency records could be obtained from the plan administrator).

  b. Obtaining a schedule of contributions received or receivable and relating the contributions to the listing of participating employers obtained in procedure (*a*) of this list and of other plans under reciprocal arrangements.

  c. Testing contribution reports to see that the reports are arithmetically correct and that the contribution rate specified in the plan instrument, including collective bargaining agreements, if applicable, was used.

  d. Reconciling contributions received from the schedule obtained in procedure (*b*) to the plan's cash receipts records and bank statements or trustee reports. Sometimes a central bank account is used for the deposit of employer contributions to several related employee benefit plans. In those circumstances it may be necessary to test the amounts transferred to the bank account of the individual employee benefit plan.

 e. Testing postings from the employer contribution reports to the participant employee or employer records and from participant records to contribution reports.

 f. Confirming directly with contributors amounts received and receivable.

 g. Reviewing criteria used by the plan in accruing employer and employee contributions receivable and determining that the accruals have been recorded in accordance with GAAP.

 h. Evaluating the reasonableness of the plan's allowance for estimated uncollectible amounts based on testing of collections subsequent to the date of the financial statements and reviewing the status of unpaid amounts.

8.04 The auditor may accomplish the foregoing procedures more efficiently by coordinating the auditing procedures for plan contributions with those for participant data (see chapter 10, "Auditing Participant Data, Participant Allocations, and Plan Obligations"). In auditing the financial statements of a multiemployer plan, the auditor may need to make arrangements to examine records of contributing employers. The auditing procedures and related guidance described in paragraph 10.06 may be applicable to those circumstances (see also paragraph 13.32).

8.05 If the auditor is unable to apply the auditing procedures relating to contributions received or related receivables, there may be a limitation on the scope of the audit. Restrictions on the scope of the audit, whether imposed by the client or by circumstances, such as the inability to obtain sufficient appropriate audit evidence, may require the auditor to qualify his or her opinion or to disclaim an opinion. (See paragraphs .22–.26 of AU section 508, *Reports on Audited Financial Statements* [AICPA, *Professional Standards*]).

Defined Benefit Plans

8.06 In addition to the auditing procedures discussed in paragraph 8.03, examples of substantive procedures for the contributions of a defined benefit pension plan or a defined benefit health and welfare plan include

 a. determining that employer contributions are consistent with the report of the plan's actuary, if applicable.

 b. reviewing the amount contributed and, if applicable, determining that it meets the requirements of the funding standard account (see appendix A for a discussion of the funding standard account).

 c. considering the results of the auditing procedures described in chapter 10 for participants' data and using the work of an actuary when examining the amount recorded as contributions in the plan's financial statements. For example, significant errors in participants' data provided to the actuary may have a material effect on the actuarially determined amount of contributions.

 d. reconciling contributions to Schedule B (Form 5500) or with the records of the plan sponsors.

    e. determining that contributions are reflected in the proper period in accordance with GAAP.

See paragraphs 2.33–.35 for the accounting guidance related to defined benefit pension plan contributions receivable.

Defined Contribution Plans

8.07 Besides the auditing procedures discussed in paragraph 8.03, examples of additional substantive procedures for contributions to defined contribution plans include

    a. reviewing the contribution provisions of the plan instrument and testing compliance with the plan instrument. (The plan instrument of a defined contribution plan often specifies the criteria that must be met for the employer and employee to make a contribution, the formula to determine upper and lower contribution limits, or the rates for determining the contribution.)

    b. comparing the amount of employer contributions recorded in the plan's records to the amount approved by the board of directors of the plan sponsor, if the plan instrument requires that the board of directors determine or approve the employer contribution.

    c. considering, whether forfeited nonvested participant accounts, if any, have been properly applied to reduce contributions, if appropriate, under provisions of the plan.

    d. considering, if applicable, the results of the auditing procedures described in chapter 10 for participants' data (including any contributions for salary reduction plans, and employees, retirees and Consolidated Omnibus Budget Reconciliation Act participants for health and welfare plans).

    e. inquiring about the timeliness of employee contribution remittances to the plan and, if necessary, applying additional audit procedures. Failure of the plan sponsor to remit employee contributions to the plan in accordance with Department of Labor regulations may constitute a prohibited transaction. Additional information on remittance rules can be found in paragraph A.15 of appendix A.

See paragraph 3.41 for accounting guidance related to defined contribution plan contributions receivable.

Rollover Contributions

8.08 Many plans allow participants to transfer contributions into the plan from another qualified plan or from an individual retirement account.[1] Such transfers are known as rollover contributions. The auditing procedures applied to rollover contributions may include

    a. review plan document to determine that the rollover was made in accordance with plan provisions.

    b. test asset transfer from the former trustee (custodian) to the current trustee (custodian), including verification of the participant-directed investments, if applicable.

---

[1] The contributions should originate from a qualified plan before being transferred to the individual retirement account.

c. review participant recordkeeping account to determine that the rollover amount is properly reflected.

Health and Welfare Plans—Other Receivables

8.09 If there are rebates receivable from a service provider, the auditor may consider examining those rebates to determine if the correct amount for the appropriate periods of time has been reflected in the proper period. In addition, it is important to gain an understanding of the service contracts and apply procedures to determine if all rebates have been properly accounted for and consider the propriety of the rebates. These include rebates from prescription drug programs or excess premiums paid for claims incurred under certain contractual arrangements with insurance companies. For example, if the payment vehicle for the claims receiving the rebate was the voluntary employees' beneficiary association trust account, receipt of the rebate by the plan sponsor and deposit of such rebate into a nontrust account may not be appropriate. Paragraph 4.20 provides guidance on stop-loss insurance arrangements. See paragraph 4.58 for accounting guidance related to health and welfare benefit plan contributions receivable.

Chapter 9

Auditing Benefit Payments

9.01 The amount, timing, and form of benefits paid or payable to participants and beneficiaries are determined in accordance with the plan instrument or related documents. The plan administrator or his or her agent is responsible for assuring that any disbursements of plan assets satisfy the requirements set forth in the plan instrument and related documents and are otherwise consistent with the Employee Retirement Income Security Act of 1974.

Auditing Objectives

9.02 The objectives of auditing procedures applied to benefit payments for employee benefit plans are to provide the auditor with a reasonable basis for concluding

a. whether the payments are in accordance with plan provisions and related documents.

b. whether the payments are made to or on behalf of persons entitled to them and only to such persons (that is, that benefit payments are not being made to deceased beneficiaries or to persons other than eligible participants and beneficiaries).

c. whether transactions are recorded in the proper account, amount, and period.

Auditing Procedures

9.03 Examples of substantive procedures for benefit payments include

a. for selected participants receiving benefit payments

i. examining the participant's file for type and amount of claim and propriety of required approvals including tracing approval of benefit payments to board of trustees or administrative committee minutes, if applicable. For health and welfare benefit plans, examining service provider statements or other evidence of service rendered.

ii. evaluating the participant's or beneficiary's eligibility (that is, whether the payee meets the plan's eligibility requirements) by examining evidence of age and employment history data; comparing employment dates, credited service, earnings, and any employee contributions to payroll or other appropriate records; and examining the benefit election form and dependent designation to determine appropriateness of payment, including the form of distribution (for example, lump sum, installments, or annuity contract).

iii. for plan benefits, such as death and disability benefits, examining a copy of the death certificate and beneficiary form, physician's statement, and other appropriate documents.

     iv. recomputing benefits based on the plan instrument and related documents, option elected, and pertinent service or salary history. For complex benefit calculations, such as lump sum benefit payments or conversion of an account balance to an annuity, consider using the assistance of an actuary in evaluating the method and assumptions used in the benefit calculation. Verifying that all contributions, income and expenses have been properly posted to participant's account prior to making the distribution.

     v. recomputing forfeited participant balances based on the vesting provisions of the plan and pertinent service history.

     vi. comparing the benefit payment amount to cash disbursement records or trustee reports. Reviewing trade reports to determine that correct investments were liquidated at distribution.

     vii. for health and welfare plans, comparing the payment of premiums to an insurance company, prepaid health plan or similar organization on behalf of a participant to the participant's eligibility records.

     viii. for benefit payments received directly by participants, testing receipt of the benefit payment. This can be accomplished by a number of methods, such as comparing canceled checks with the plan's cash disbursement records, comparing the payee name or account name on electronic funds transfers to the participant or beneficiary name, or confirming payment of benefits by corresponding directly with selected participants, service providers, and beneficiaries and comparing signatures with the application for plan benefits, service provider statements, or other appropriate documents. In addition, the auditor may want to consider inquiring as to the existence and frequency of participant complaints.

  b. evaluating whether procedures exist for determining the continued eligibility of participants or beneficiaries to receive benefits to assure that individuals are removed from the benefit rolls upon death and that payments made to individuals over an unusually long number of years are still appropriate.

  c. evaluating whether procedures exist for investigating long-outstanding benefit checks.

  d. for defined contribution plans, comparing disbursements to participants with individual participant's account records that have been examined in accordance with the auditing procedures in paragraphs 10.15–.17.

  e. for defined contribution plans, reviewing the criteria used by the plan to record benefit payments and determining that the benefit payments have been recorded in accordance with generally accepted accounting principles (GAAP). Refer to paragraph 3.50*m* for guidance in reporting benefit payments on the statement of net assets available for benefits.

  f. for health and welfare plans, reviewing the criteria used by the plan to record benefit payments, and determining that the benefit payments have been recorded in accordance with GAAP. Refer to paragraphs 4.67–.89 for more complete guidance.

g. for cash balance or pension equity plans (paragraph 2.03), reviewing the accumulation of the participants' hypothetical "accounts" including the interest rate credited in accordance with the terms of the plan document.

9.04 In some circumstances, benefit disbursements are determined or made by a third party such as a bank, an insurance company, or other service provider (that is, third-party administrator [TPA]). In these circumstances, the auditor may need to obtain an understanding of the internal control procedures of the TPA. This can be satisfied either through obtaining a service auditor's report in accordance with Statement on Auditing Standards (SAS) No. 70, *Service Organizations* (AICPA, *Professional Standards*, AU sec. 324),[1] or through applying appropriate auditing procedures to the third-party administrator.[2] These procedures are performed irrespective of whether the plan avails itself of the limited-scope audit exemption relating to certain assets held by a bank or similar institution or insurance carrier regulated and supervised and subject to periodic examination by a state or federal agency. The use of such a third party's independent auditor or internal auditors to perform certain of the foregoing procedures may be appropriate in those circumstances. Although a type 2 SAS No. 70 report may be used to reduce substantive procedures, neither a type 1 nor a type 2 SAS No. 70 report is designed to provide a basis for assessing control risk sufficiently low to eliminate the need for performing any substantive tests.

9.05 For plan's that allow transfers to another qualified plan or to an individual retirement account, otherwise known as rollover distributions, review the plan document to determine that the rollover was made in accordance with plan provisions and the rollover account is in the name of the participant or beneficiary.

9.06 Corrective distributions may be required in the event that employee contributions exceed contribution limitations of the plan. These amounts are often recorded as a liability as of the plan's year end and reflected on the statement of changes in net assets available for benefits as an offset to contributions or as a separate line item. If shown as an offset to contributions, a reconciliation to the Form 5500 may be necessary.

9.07 If the auditor is unable to apply the auditing procedures relating to benefit payments there may be a limitation on the scope of the audit. Restrictions on the scope of the audit, whether imposed by the client or by circumstances, such as the inability to obtain sufficient appropriate audit evidence,

---

[1] The Auditing Standards Board has issued Statement on Standards for Attestation Engagements (SSAE) No. 16, *Reporting on Controls at a Service Organization* (AICPA, *Professional Standards*, AT sec. 801), which will replace the guidance contained in AU section 324, *Service Organizations* (AICPA, *Professional Standards*), for a service auditor when reporting on controls at an organization that provides service to user entities when those controls are likely to be relevant to user entities' internal controls over financial reporting. It is effective for service auditors' reports for periods ending on or after June 15, 2011. Early implementation is permitted; therefore, if adopting SSAE No. 16 early, refer directly to the standard as certain guidance in this guide may not be applicable. Also, refer to the preface of this guide for additional information about the changes related to Statement on Auditing Standards (SAS) No. 70, *Service Organizations* (AICPA, *Professional Standards*, AU sec. 324).

[2] If a type 2 SAS No. 70 report is obtained, that specifically covers the testing of benefit payments, the auditor may be able to limit tests of the benefit payments.

may require the auditor to qualify his or her opinion or to disclaim an opinion. (See paragraphs .22–.26 of AU section 508, *Reports on Audited Financial Statements* [AICPA, *Professional Standards*]).

Chapter 10

Auditing Participant Data, Participant Allocations, and Plan Obligations

Participant Data and Allocations

10.01 The nature of plan benefit obligations and the accounting methods and auditing procedures for them differ with the various types of plans; however, each type would entail the testing of certain participant data. The type of participant data to be tested differs according to the type of plan, and from plan to plan within each type. The data used to determine accumulated plan benefits will be identified in the plan instrument or collective bargaining agreement, if applicable. If the plan requires the services of an actuary, an actuarial report may describe or summarize the participant data used by the actuary. The data should be tested by the auditor in accordance with AU section 336, *Using the Work of a Specialist* (AICPA, *Professional Standards*). (See paragraphs 10.28–.33 and 10.40–.41 of this guide.)

10.02 The objectives of auditing procedures applied to participant data are to provide the auditor with a reasonable basis for concluding (*a*) whether all covered employees have been properly included in employee eligibility records and, if applicable, in contribution reports and (*b*) whether accurate participant data for eligible employees were supplied to the plan administrator and, if appropriate, to the plan actuary.

10.03 The period for which the data are tested will depend on the date as of which the related financial information is presented in the financial statements. For example, if the accumulated plan benefits are actuarially valued as of the beginning of the plan year, the data to be tested will be as of or for the period ending as of that date. Similarly, if contributions are determined on the basis of an actuarial valuation as of the beginning of the plan year, data submitted to the actuary and to be tested by the auditor would be as of that date. If the auditor also audits the employer's financial statements, the auditing procedures applied in the prior year's audit of the employer's financial statements generally need not be duplicated in the audit of the plan's financial statements. The auditor may find that he or she can accomplish the work more efficiently by coordinating the auditing procedures for participant data with procedures for plan contributions and plan benefits described in chapter 8, "Auditing Contributions Received and Related Receivables," and chapter 9, "Auditing Benefit Payments." The auditor also may be able to reduce the extent of tests of participant data by relying on a Statement on Auditing Standards (SAS) No. 70, *Service Organizations* (AICPA, *Professional Standards*, AU sec. 324)[1] type 2 report (see paragraph 6.14*b*) because entities issuing such reports for

---

[1] The Auditing Standards Board has issued Statement on Standards for Attestation Engagements (SSAE) No. 16, *Reporting on Controls at a Service Organization* (AICPA, *Professional Standards*, AT sec. 801), which will replace the guidance contained in AU section 324, *Service Organizations* (AICPA, *Professional Standards*), for a service auditor when reporting on controls at an organization that provides service to user entities when those controls are likely to be relevant to user entities' internal controls over financial reporting. It is effective for service auditors' reports for periods ending on or after June 15, 2011. Early implementation is permitted; therefore, if

(continued)

recordkeepers often test certain participant data, such as contribution, income, and forfeiture allocations for participant directed investment fund options.

10.04 The types of participant data that are tested in an audit of a plan's financial statements will vary from plan to plan, depending on the factors on which contributions and benefits are determined. In general, the data tested may include

    a. demographic data, such as sex, marital status, birth date, period of service with the employer, and other service history.

    b. payroll data, such as wage rate, hours worked, earnings, and contributions to the plan, if any.

    c. benefit data for participants receiving benefits, such as benefit levels and benefit options selected.

10.05 Examples of substantive procedures for testing the employer's participant records include

    a. reviewing pertinent sections of the plan instrument and collective bargaining agreement, if applicable, as a basis for considering what participant data to test in the audit of the plan's financial statements.

    b. testing the summarization of the payroll journal and schedules of participant data, if applicable, and tracing postings of gross pay to general or subsidiary ledger accounts.

    c. testing payroll data for one or more pay periods and for a number of participants by

        i. tracing the individual payrolls from the payroll journal to the participants' earnings records.

        ii. for participants paid on an hourly or piecework basis, testing payroll hours, production tickets, or other supporting evidence and testing the computation of hours.

        iii. testing rates of pay to authorizations or union contracts.

        iv. testing calculations of earnings.

        v. reviewing personnel files for hiring notice and employment data, pay rates and rate changes, termination notice, sex, birth date, and so forth.

    d. if participant files are maintained in the custody of the plan administrator or recordkeeper, testing whether the data maintained in those files correspond to the data maintained in employer payroll and personnel files.

10.06 If the auditor is unable to examine the participant records maintained by the employer, which may occur in a multiemployer plan, there may be circumstances, depending on the existing internal control, in which the auditor can obtain the necessary assurance by applying one or more procedures, such as

---

(footnote continued)

adopting SSAE No. 16 early, refer directly to the standard as certain guidance in this guide may not be applicable. Also, refer to the preface of this guide for additional information about the changes related to Statement on Auditing Standards No. 70, *Service Organizations* (AICPA, *Professional Standards*, AU sec. 324).

    a. if the plan administrator maintains records of participant data and maintains internal control to help ensure that data on all participants are included in the records, testing the data on which contributions and actuarially determined amounts are based by direct communication with participants and by comparison with union or other records, if applicable. The auditor may also confirm hours, pay rates, and other appropriate information.

    b. if the plan administrator's normal procedures include periodic visits to employers to test data submitted to him or her, reviewing and testing the plan administrator's procedures.

    c. obtaining a report from the auditor of the employer company stating that agreed-upon procedures (as described in paragraph 10.10) have been performed, and obtaining the auditor's findings regarding the procedures applied. In addition, the plan auditor may apply such other auditing procedures as he or she considers necessary in the circumstances. In this regard, it may be necessary for the plan auditor to request the other auditor to apply additional tests (see AU section 543, *Part of Audit Performed by Other Independent Auditors* [AICPA, *Professional Standards*]).

    10.07 If the auditor is unable to obtain the necessary assurance regarding participant data or participant accounts there may be a limitation on the scope of the audit. Restrictions on the scope of the audit, whether imposed by the client or by circumstances, such as the inability to obtain sufficient appropriate audit evidence, may require the auditor to qualify his or her opinion or to disclaim an opinion. (see AU section 508, *Reports on Audited Financial Statements* [AICPA, *Professional Standards*], paragraphs .22–.26).

    10.08 *Eligible compensation.* Plan documents specify the various aspects of compensation (for example, base wages, overtime, and bonuses) that are considered in the calculation of plan contributions for defined contribution plans and in the determination of benefits in a defined benefit plan. Testing of payroll data includes the determination of eligible compensation for individual employees and comparison of the definition of eligible compensation used in the calculation to the plan document. When this process is not included in the payroll testing of the plan sponsor or in type 2 SAS No. 70 reports, a comparison of eligible compensation per the plan document to eligible compensation used in plan operations may be necessary. It is important to understand the definition of *compensation* to determine that the method used is in accordance with the plan document. An employer may use any definition of *compensation* that satisfies Internal Revenue Code Section 414(s), which does not allow a method of determining compensation if that method discriminates in favor of highly compensated employees.

Multiemployer Plans

    10.09 In addition to the auditing procedures described in paragraphs 10.05–.06 of this chapter, the following auditing procedures may be considered when auditing the financial statements of multiemployer plans:

    a. Comparing the employers' contribution reports with the information shown in participants' earnings records and comparing hours worked and earnings records with the employer's contribution reports to evaluate whether the participants have been properly included in or excluded from the reports *b.* If significant participant data is not available, determining the adequacy of the methods used by the plan administrator or plan actuary to give effect to such missing data

10.10 When auditing participant data in a multiemployer benefit plan, the auditor is often unable to directly test payroll records. Plan sponsors or trustees may engage the employer's auditor, other outside auditors, in-house compliance personnel or internal audit, or others to perform agreed upon procedures to test the completeness of employer contributions. It is important that the employer payroll procedures be designed to test that all employees working for a contributing employer performing covered work (*covered work* is defined under the collective bargaining agreement) and that any subcontracting payments for covered work have been properly reported. A representative group of contributing employers would be tested each year. The number of years the testing of contributing employers will take may vary, but a four year cycle is typical. The auditor performing the payroll procedures will typically issue an agreed-upon procedures report in accordance with AT section 201, *Agreed-Upon Procedures Engagements* (AICPA, *Professional Standards*).

10.11 It is important for the plans independent auditors to review the payroll procedures performed in order to determine that the completeness objective has been achieved. If a multiemployer benefit plan does not have annual employer payroll procedures performed, or if the auditor does not believe that the procedures being performed are acceptable and if the auditor is unable to obtain the necessary assurance by other means, then the auditor may issue a qualified or disclaim an opinion on the financial statements because of the limitation on the scope of the audit[2] or adjust and correct the internal auditor's payroll procedures to the point where the auditor can issue an unqualified opinion on the audited financial statements.

Defined Benefit Plans

10.12 Contributions to a defined benefit plan ordinarily are determined on the basis of an actuarial valuation of the plan carried out by the plan actuary, using participant data received from the plan administrator or the employer company and using actuarial techniques. For multiemployer plans and certain other negotiated plans, contribution levels are normally specified in the plan instrument or collective bargaining agreement, and an actuarial valuation is used to compare accumulated contributions to date with accumulated plan benefits. Paragraph .12 of AU section 336 states, "The auditor should (*a*) obtain an understanding of the methods and assumptions used by the specialist, (*b*) make appropriate tests of data provided to the specialist, taking into account the auditor's assessment of control risk, and (*c*) evaluate whether the specialist's findings support the related assertions in the financial statements." Accordingly, the auditor should satisfy himself or herself that the participant data provided to and used by the actuary were accurate and complete in all material respects.

10.13 In addition to the auditing procedures described in paragraphs 10.04–.06 of this chapter, examples of substantive procedures for auditing the financial statements of defined benefit plans that involve actuarial valuations, include

---

[2] See paragraphs .22–.26 of AU section 508, *Reports on Audited Financial Statements* (AICPA, *Professional Standards*), for further guidance.

   a. tracing the information obtained during tests of participant data to the participant data given by the plan administrator to the actuary.

   b. testing the basic data used by the actuary in his or her calculations (for example, name, sex, birth date, hours worked, employment dates, dates of participation in plan, and salary based on definition of eligible compensation per the plan document) by tracing data from the actuary's report (if the data are shown in the report) or from a confirmation letter obtained from the actuary to the data furnished by the plan. This test would normally include a selection of individuals as well as summary totals (see paragraph 10.30*f*).

Cash Balance Plans

10.14 As further described in paragraph 2.03, cash balance plans and pension equity plans are a type of defined benefit pension plan. Although the benefit formula of a cash balance plan or a pension equity plan is different from that of a traditional defined benefit pension plan, the audit procedures to be performed on the benefit obligation information would be the same as those for a traditional defined benefit pension plan. In addition, because the hypothetical account for each participant is generally credited with a compensation and earnings credits each year, consider applying auditing procedures that include

   a. testing the interest rate used in the current year's interest credit to ensure that it complies with the provision of the plan.

   b. testing a sample of participants' earnings and appropriate factor used for the compensation credit to ensure that it complies with the provisions of the plan.

Defined Contribution Plans

10.15 For defined contribution plans, the types of participant data to test will vary from plan to plan. The data tested may include

   a. covered compensation of individual participants (for example, definition of compensation per plan document, which may include bonuses or other compensation). Misinterpreting the definition of compensation is one of the most common operational errors for defined contribution plans. *Note:* IRS regulations generally require that the nonmatching company contribution be allocated to participants on the basis of the ratio of their covered compensation to total covered compensation for all participants.

   b. individual participants' contributions to the plan.

   c. birth date, date of hire, and other demographic data that determine eligibility and vesting.

10.16 In addition to other uses, these data are used by the auditor to test the validity of terminations and the eligibility of individuals to participate in the plan. Examples of the auditor's procedures in which the data are used are

   a. tracing individuals who have terminated to benefit payments and, if forfeitures are involved, to the record of forfeited amounts.

   b. for individuals who qualify for participation during the year and who elect to participate, evaluating whether the individuals have been properly included in the individual participant accounts.

c. for individuals who qualify for a loan from the plan, determining that the loan is made in accordance with the plan's loan policy and has been properly segregated in the individual's account. (See paragraph 7.57–.58 for loans to participants auditing procedures.)

10.17 The auditing procedures discussed in paragraphs 10.04–.06 (including procedures relating to the use of the work of an actuary, if applicable) may also be applied to the data.

Defined Contribution Plans—Allocation Testing

10.18 The net assets available for benefits for defined contribution plans are normally allocated to individual participant accounts according to procedures set forth in the plan instrument or in a collective bargaining agreement. In some cases the plan instrument may even specify the allocation of individual plan assets.

10.19 Plan assets of defined contribution plans are generally to be presented at their fair value (see paragraphs 3.27 and 3.30–.33 for special provisions concerning the valuation of insurance contracts and the valuation of fully benefit-responsive-investments contracts, see paragraph 3.42 for the valuation of participant loans). Such plans typically permit periodic contributions, withdrawals, participant loans, and changes in investment elections. Transactions can be executed by the plan participant at varying frequencies depending upon the plan's provisions; however, plans that permit transactions on a daily basis are becoming more common. Thus, the determination of the value of plan assets on the dates throughout the year in which the plan permits transactions is important. Where an investment option in a defined contribution plan contains "hard to price" investments such as limited partnerships, periodic valuation is more difficult, but nonetheless important. Failure to properly value plan assets on the date of a participant directed transaction can result in such transactions being executed at inappropriate amounts and consequently either an understatement or overstatement of plan assets and distributions.

10.20 The objective of auditing procedures applied to individual participant accounts of defined contribution plans is to provide the auditor with a reasonable basis for concluding

a. whether net assets have been allocated to the individual participant accounts in accordance with the plan instrument.[3]

b. whether the sum of the participant accounts reconciles with the total net assets available for plan benefits.

c. whether participant transactions are authorized and have been executed at the proper amount in the proper period.

10.21 Procedures that the auditor may apply to individual participant accounts (rather than at the plan level) include

a. obtaining an understanding of how allocations are to be made. This may include reviewing pertinent sections of the plan instrument or collective bargaining agreement and discussion with plan administrator.

---

[3] The effects of misallocation of assets should be considered in relation to the financial statements as a whole rather than in relation to individual accounts.

b. testing the allocation of income or loss, appreciation or depreciation in value of investments, administrative expenses, and amounts forfeited for selected accounts. The testing of internal controls over this area may be addressed in the SAS No. 70 report of the recordkeeper for the plan's investment. To reduce the amount of substantive testing, consider relying on a SAS No. 70 report, if available (provided the SAS No. 70 report covers those areas).

c. testing the allocation of the employer's contribution. (The testing of internal controls over this area may be addressed in the SAS No. 70 report of the recordkeeper for the plan's investment.)

d. for plans with participant contributions, determining whether individual contributions are being credited to the proper participant accounts and to the investment medium selected by the participant, if applicable. Where participants make contribution or investment elections by telephone or electronic means (such as the Internet or intranet), consider confirming contribution percentage and source (pretax or posttax) and investment election directly with the participant or compare to a transaction report, if one is maintained. Determine that contributions are properly classified and invested according to the participants' investment election. (The testing of internal controls over this area may be addressed in the SAS No. 70 report of the recordkeeper for the plan's investment.)

e. determining whether the sum of individual accounts reconciles with the total net assets are available for benefits.

Depending on the existing internal control, nature of SAS No. 70 reports and the results of other auditing procedures, the auditor may also confirm contributions and other pertinent information directly with participants

Health and Welfare Benefit Plans

10.22 The types of participant data that may be tested in the audit of the financial statements of a health and welfare benefit plan differ widely from plan to plan. In general, the data tested may include

a. payroll data, including salary or wage rate and hours worked.

b. demographic data, including sex, birth date, date of hire, and number of dependents.

c. claims history records maintained by the plan administrator.

10.23 The auditing procedures discussed in paragraphs 10.04–.06 (including procedures relating to the use of the work of an actuary, if applicable) may also be applied to the data. The use of the data in evaluating eligibility and benefits is discussed in paragraph 9.03.

Plan Obligations

10.24 As discussed earlier in this chapter and in chapter 2, "Accounting and Reporting by Defined Benefit Pension Plans," chapter 3, "Accounting and Reporting by Defined Contribution Plans," and chapter 4, "Accounting and Reporting by Health and Welfare Benefit Plans," the nature of plan benefit obligations and the methods of valuing and recording those obligations differ significantly among the three types of plans.

Defined Benefit Plans

10.25 The objective of auditing procedures applied to accumulated plan benefits is to provide the auditor with a reasonable basis for concluding whether the actuarial present value of accumulated plan benefits, components of those benefits, and amounts of changes in the actuarial present value of accumulated plan benefits are presented in conformity with Financial Accounting Standards Board (FASB) *Accounting Standards Codification* (ASC) 960, *Plan Accounting—Defined Benefit Pension Plans*. That objective is ordinarily accomplished by applying the auditing procedures described in paragraph 9.03 for benefit payments, paragraphs 10.04–.13 for participant data, and paragraphs 10.28–.33 for using the work of an actuary.

10.26 The actuarial valuation used to determine accumulated plan benefits in accordance with FASB ASC 960 is based on the benefit provisions of the plan and on participant data. For many defined benefit plans the participant data submitted to the actuary are current only as of the beginning of the plan year. The practice of preparing valuations as of the beginning of a plan year developed as a practical expedient to facilitate completion of the valuation on a timely basis. For financial reporting purposes, the information may be presented either as of the beginning or the end of the plan year; FASB ASC 960 states, however, that an end-of-year benefit information date is considered preferable.

10.27 In the event that an actuarial valuation has not been prepared as of the beginning or the end of the plan year, the plan administrator may nevertheless prepare financial statements using estimated accumulated benefit information as contemplated by FASB ASC 960. If the benefit information is so estimated, the auditor should obtain an understanding of how the plan administrator developed the estimate and assure himself or herself that the methods and assumptions used to estimate the accumulated benefit information are reasonable in the circumstances.

Using the Work of an Actuary

10.28 The auditor's qualifications do not encompass actuarial science or the complexities of probability and longevity associated with life contingencies. The auditor may have a general awareness and understanding of actuarial concepts and practices; he or she does not, however, purport to act in the capacity of an actuary. The auditor, therefore, needs to follow the guidance of AU section 336 to obtain assurance regarding the work of an actuary on such matters as plan contributions (see chapter 8) and accumulated benefit valuations.[4]

10.29 An audit of plan financial statements entails cooperation and coordination between the auditor and the plan actuary. The auditor uses the work of an actuary as an audit procedure to obtain sufficient appropriate audit evidence; the auditor does not merely rely on the report of an actuary. Although the appropriateness and reasonableness of the methods and assumptions used,

---

[4] With regard to actuarial services provided to a client by the auditor's firm, a related ethics interpretation under the AICPA Code of Conduct says that a member's independence would not be impaired if a member prepares an actuarial valuation of a client's pension or postemployment benefit liabilities provided all significant assumptions and matters of judgment are determined or approved by the client and the client is in a position to have an informed judgment on, and accepts responsibility for, the results of the actuarial service. (See Interpretation No. 101–3, "Performance of nonattest services," under Rule 101, *Independence* [AICPA, *Professional Standards*, ET sec. 101 par. .05].)

as well as their application, are within the expertise of the actuary, the auditor does not divide responsibility with the actuary for his or her opinion on the financial statements taken as a whole. Thus, the auditor should evaluate the professional qualifications and reputation of the actuary as stated in AU section 336 paragraph .08. The auditor should obtain an understanding of the actuary's methods and assumptions, test accounting data provided to the actuary, and consider whether the actuary's findings support the related representations in the financial statements. Ordinarily, the auditor would use the work of the actuary unless the auditing procedures lead him or her to believe that the findings were unreasonable in the circumstances. Assumptions related to the method of payment of benefits generally should agree to actual results shown in the financial statements (that is, lump sum versus annuity payments). Sometimes it may be necessary for the auditor to obtain the services of an actuary other than the one who prepared the plan's actuarial valuation. This might occur when the plan actuary is related to the plan (see paragraph 10.30*d*) or when the auditor believes that the determinations made by the plan actuary are unreasonable.

10.30 With respect to the actuarial present value of accumulated plan benefits and changes therein (as well as contributions), the auditor may consider the following guidance in AU section 336:

a. Obtaining satisfaction regarding the professional qualifications of the actuary. If the actuary is not known to the auditor, consider other factors that might provide information regarding the actuary's qualifications. Examples of factors to consider are whether the actuary is an *enrolled actuary* under Employee Retirement Income Security Act of 1974 (ERISA) Sections 3041 and 3042; the actuary's membership in a recognized professional organization; and the opinion of other actuaries, whom the auditor knows to be qualified, regarding the actuary's professional qualifications.[5]

b. Obtaining an understanding of the actuary's objectives, scope of work, methods, and assumptions, and their consistency of application. For defined benefit plans ascertain whether the method and assumptions used in the accumulated plan benefit information are in conformity with FASB ASC 960 and whether the funding method and assumptions are in accordance with ERISA.

c. Inquiring whether the actuarial valuation considers all pertinent provisions of the plan, including any changes to the plan or other events affecting the actuarial calculations. For example, amounts contributed by employees and earnings thereon are properly included as vested benefits.

d. Inquiring about the nature of any relationship the actuary may have with the plan or the employer company that may impair objectivity. This can usually be accomplished by asking the client to have the actuary describe in writing the relationship, if any, that may exist and that may appear to impair the objectivity of the actuary's work. The engagement of a consulting actuary to perform valuations on behalf of plan participants or a sponsor company ordinarily is not a relationship that would impair the objectivity of

---

[5] There are no universal standards for establishing the professional qualifications of an actuary. Some actuaries specialize in or concentrate on pension matters; others confine their practice to life or property and liability insurance matters. Qualification, by education and experience, to practice in one of these areas does not necessarily prepare the actuary to practice in other areas.

the actuary. If the actuary is related to the client, or if the auditor is unable to determine that the actuary has no relationship with the client that might impair objectivity, the auditor should perform additional auditing procedures regarding some or all of the actuary's assumptions, methods or findings to determine that the findings are not unreasonable.

c. Testing the reliability and completeness of the census data provided by the plan and used by the actuary in the actuarial valuation. These tests may be coordinated with the auditing procedures described in paragraphs 8.03–.05 for plan contributions and paragraphs 10.01–.13 for participant data. The auditor should make appropriate tests of data provided to the specialist. Accordingly, in the event that data provided to the actuary are significantly incomplete, the auditor may inquire of the actuary in regard to the treatment of the incomplete data and determine if the method used by the actuary to give effect to the missing data in his or her valuation is reasonable in the circumstances. This situation is most likely to occur in multiemployer plans.

f. Confirming aggregate participant data used in the actuarial valuation. (The auditor may include this request as part of the audit inquiry letter to the plan's actuary.) In addition, the auditor may also confirm information related to selected individual participants that is part of the aggregate amounts.

10.31 The auditor may ask the plan administrator to send a letter to the plan's actuary requesting that the actuary (a) provide the auditor with a copy of the actuarial report, Schedule B of Form 5500, or comparable information or (b) confirm to the auditor the actuarial information that has already been obtained from the plan in connection with the audit.

10.32 An illustration of a letter to the plan's actuary requesting a copy of the actuary's report or other information on the plan appears as exhibit 10-1, "Illustrative Letter to Plan Actuary." In situations in which the auditor also audits the financial statements of the sponsor company, he or she may combine the request for this information with a request for information necessary for compliance with FASB ASC 715, *Compensation—Retirement Benefits*.

10.33 An illustration of a letter to the plan's actuary requesting confirmation of information taken from the actuary's report or the plan's or the sponsor company's records appears as exhibit 10-2, "Illustrative Letter to Plan Actuary."

Health and Welfare Benefit Plans

10.34 Plan obligations for health and welfare benefit plans are paid out of a fund of accumulated contributions and income (a self-funded plan), are provided through insurance purchased by the plan from an insurance company (an insured plan), or are provided through some combination of the two. Insured plans may involve several funding arrangements including (a) fully insured, pooled; (b) fully insured, experience-rated; (c) minimum premium plans; and (d) stop-loss arrangements.[6] Insured plans may also encompass a continuum of products including (a) basic indemnity plans; (b) preferred provider plans;

---

[6] See paragraph 4.20 for further guidance on stop-loss arrangements.

(c) point-of-service plans (also known as multioption); and (d) health mainte-nance organization plans. Self-funded plans may take several forms including (a) Administrative Service Only arrangements; (b) Claims Service Only ar-rangements; and (c) unlimited retro-premium arrangements. This significant variety of funding, product, and service arrangements increases the inherent risk in identifying and valuing the benefit obligations of the plan. For example, in an insured plan, obligations for claims reported but not paid and obligations for claims incurred but not reported will be paid, in whole or in part (depending on the funding or product arrangements or both) by the insurance company and, therefore, to such extent would not appear as obligations in the financial statements of the plan. Alternatively, a self-funded plan should include in its financial statements information regarding the plan's obligations for each of these types of claims. With regard to plan obligations, it is important for the auditor to read all relevant provisions of the plan instrument and underlying contracts and determine that they are properly accounted for.

10.35 Procedures auditors may apply to individual participant enrollment and contributions include

    a. reviewing pertinent sections of the plan instrument or collective bargaining agreement to obtain an understanding of eligibility and contribution provisions.

    b. for individuals qualifying for participation during the year and who elect to participate, evaluating whether the individuals have been properly included in the plan records.

    c. for plans that require participant contributions, determining that the proper contribution is being made based upon the partici-pant's elections. Where participants enroll by telephone or elec-tronic means (such as the Internet or Intranet) confirm plan elec-tions directly with the participant.

10.36 For insured plans, the auditor may determine whether the proper dollar amount of premiums has been remitted to the insurance company and whether any obligation for unpaid insurance premiums has been properly recorded. Insurance premium payments are generally determined from the participants' eligibility records and the premium rates in the insurance con-tract. Examples of auditing procedures for testing the premium payments and related obligation include

    a. comparing the number of eligible participants, as shown by the eligibility records, to the premium computation and tracing the ap-plicable premium rates to the insurance contract.

    b. tracing participants listed in the premium computation list to the eligibility records.

    c. comparing premiums paid, including subsequent payments, and investigating the reasons for significant changes.

    d. requesting direct confirmation from the insurance company of the total amount of premiums paid during the year, premiums payable to the insurance company, and other obligations and assets of the plan at year-end.

Any premium payable to the insurance company should be recorded as a benefit obligation. Review of the insurance contracts will help the auditor to determine that the obligation is in accordance with the contract provisions.

10.37 In self-funded plans, claims reported to the plan administrator but not paid are obligations of the plan. Examples of auditing procedures for testing the obligation for claims reported but not paid include

a. comparing individual claims with the trial balance, and reviewing the nature of the claim and the documentary support.

b. reviewing payments made after the date of the financial statements to determine whether all claims reported have been properly included in the trial balance.

c. performing a search of open claim files, an option the auditor may choose, depending on the timing of the audit.

10.38 As of the date of the financial statements, there will be certain claims incurred but not yet reported to the plan, and some of these may not be reported for an extended period of time. Claims of this nature cannot be determined on an individual basis, but the aggregate amount of such claims should be subject to reasonable estimation on the basis of past loss experience and actuarial determination (see paragraph 10.40). If information necessary to make this estimate is not available, the auditor should consider the possible effect on his or her report.

10.39 The eligibility rules for many plans provide for the accumulation of eligibility credits for participants. The obligation arising from eligibility credits is generally determined by applying current insurance premium rates to accumulated eligibility credits or, in the case of a self-funded plan, by applying the average cost of benefits per eligible participant. The accrued obligation may be reviewed and tested for adequacy and reasonableness. Such tests may include a comparison of the employer's contributions with the participants' eligibility records, a test of the arithmetical accuracy of the accumulated credits, and a review of the overall computation of the estimated obligation.

10.40 Many health and welfare benefit plans provide benefits that require an actuarial determination of the plan's benefit obligation. An actuary may also be used to determine contribution rates. If the plan requires the services of an actuary in determining amounts in the financial statements, then the procedures discussed in paragraphs 10.28–.33 for using the work of an actuary would be applicable.

10.41 The types of information the auditor may consider confirming with the actuary include

a. a description of participant groups covered.

b. a brief, general description of the characteristics of the plan used in the actuary's calculations, including, but not limited to, benefit provisions.

c. the number of employees in the actuary's valuation and the number of participants and beneficiaries who are active, terminated with vested benefits, or retired under the plan.

d. the present value of the plan's benefit obligations. (Be careful that the actuarially calculated benefit obligations do not include claims included elsewhere in the statement of net assets. Consider also whether all claims are properly included.)

e. the dates of the valuation of the benefit obligations and of the census data used. (If the date of the census data used is other than the plan year-end, have the actuary indicate the basis for projecting the data to the year-end.)

f. descriptions of the principal assumptions and methods used in determining the present value of plan obligations and of any changes in assumptions or methods (for example, interest rates), and the effect of any changes.

g. the significant effects (either individually or in the aggregate) on the current year of the changes resulting from plan amendments.

h. knowledge of an intent on the part of the employer (sponsor company) to fully or partially terminate the plan.

i. the amount of unbilled or unpaid actuary's fees applicable to the plan's year-end and payable by the plan.

j. ensuring that the postretirement benefit obligations are reduced by the actuarial present value of contributions expected to be received in the future by current plan participants.

k. the adjusted funding target percentage determined in accordance with the Pension Protection Act of 2006.

Exhibit 10-1

Illustrative Letter to Plan Actuary[*]

In connection with an audit of the financial statements of XYZ Pension Plan [*date of statements*], please furnish our auditors [*name and address*], the information described in the following as of [*the more recent benefit information date, either the date of the plan year-end or the date of beginning of plan year*]. For your convenience, you may supply in response to these requests pertinent sections, properly signed and dated, of your actuarial report or Schedule B of Form 5500, if available and if the requested information is contained therein.

a. Please indicate the actuarial present value of accumulated plan benefits as defined in Financial Accounting Standards Board (FASB) *Accounting Standards Codification* (ASC) 960, *Plan Accounting—Defined Benefit Pension Plans*, classified as follows:

       i. Vested benefits of participants and beneficiaries currently receiving payments $ _____

      ii. Other vested benefits $ _____

     iii. Nonvested benefits $ _____

      iv. Total $ _____

b. The date of the preceding valuation of accumulated plan benefits is _____.

c. Describe the principal assumptions used in determining the actuarial present value of accumulated plan benefits.

d. Please indicate the following:

       i. The minimum annual contribution, including the use of any carryover or prefunding balance

      ii. A description of the actuarial assumptions used in computing the minimum required contribution

     iii. The aggregate effect of any change in the method(s) or assumption(s)

e. Briefly describe the employee group covered.

f. Please provide the following:

       i. A brief general description of the benefit provisions of the plan used in the actuarial valuation

      ii. A description of any benefits, as prescribed by FASB ASC 960, not included in the accumulated plan benefits valuation and the reason therefore

     iii. The effective date of the last plan amendment included in this valuation

g. Please provide the following information relating to the employee census data used in performing the actuarial valuation:

       i. The date as of which the census data were collected is _____.

---

[*] The illustrative letter to plan actuary included herein has been updated to reflect the Financial Accounting Standards Board (FASB) *Accounting Standards Codification*™ (ASC) references. However, in FASB's notice to constituents, it suggests the use of plain English to describe broad FASB ASC topic references. For specific information on FASB ASC, please see the preface in this guide.

Compensation Participant	Number of Persons	Compensation (if applicable)
Currently receiving payments	_____	_____
Active with vested benefits	_____	_____
Terminated with deferred vested benefits	_____	_____
Active without vested benefits	_____	_____
Other (describe)	_____	_____
Total	_____	_____

[Note to auditor: If information is not available for each of the preceding categories, indicate which categories have been grouped. Please describe any group or groups of participants not included in the preceding information.]

ii. Information for specific individuals contained in the census:

- Participant's Name or Number
- Age or Birth Date
- Sex
- Salary
- Date Hired or Years of Service

[Note to auditor: Select information from employer records to compare with the census data used by the actuary. In addition, the auditor may consider selecting certain census data from the actuary's files to compare with the employer's records.]

h. Describe, if significant (either individually or in the aggregate), the effects of the following factors on the change in the actuarial present value of accumulated plan benefits from the preceding to the current benefit information date. (Effects that are individually significant should be separately identified.)

    i. Plan amendments

    ii. Changes in the nature of the plan (for example, a plan spin-off or a merger with another plan)

    iii. Changes in actuarial assumptions

i. Describe, for the current year, the effects of the following on changes in the present value of accumulated plan benefits:

    i. Increase in benefits accumulated

    ii. Increase due to the passage of time

    iii. Benefits paid

[Note to auditor: Item (i) generally applies only if the change in actuarial information is being presented in statement format.]

j. If any unpaid minimum required contributions exist, the amount necessary to reduce this amount to zero under the Employee Retirement Income Security Act of 1974.

   k. Have you been notified of a decision by the sponsor company to fully or partially terminate the plan, including a "freeze" of benefit accruals or eligibility to participate? If so, please describe the effect on the plan.

   l. Please describe the nature of the relationship, if any, that you may have with the plan or the sponsor company and that may appear to impair the objectivity of your work.

   m. What is the amount of the unbilled or unpaid actuarial or other fees due your firm applicable to the plan year-end and payable by the plan?

   n. Please supply any additional information that you believe is necessary.

Your prompt attention to this request will be appreciated.

Very truly yours,

_____

Plan Administrator

Exhibit 10-2

Illustrative Letter to Plan Actuary

In connection with their audit of our financial statements as of [*date of plan year-end*], our auditors [*name and address*], have requested that you confirm to them the following information as of [*benefit information date*] with respect to our defined benefit pension plan described in your report dated _____.

[List of information to be confirmed]

Please confirm the preceding information by signing the enclosed copy of this letter in the space provided, and return it directly to our auditors. If the preceding information is not correct, please inform our auditors directly and, if possible, send them full details of the differences.

Your prompt attention to this request will be appreciated.

Very truly yours,

_____

Plan Administrator

The preceding information is correct except as noted in the following.

_____

[*Signature of Actuary*]

_____

Chapter 11

Party in Interest Transactions

11.01   Section 3(14) of the Employee Retirement Income Security Act of 1974 (ERISA) defines a *party in interest* to include fiduciaries or employees of the plan, any person who provides services to the plan, an employer whose employees are covered by the plan, an employee organization whose members are covered by the plan, a person who owns 50 percent or more of such an employer or employee association, or relatives of such persons just listed. Although not identical, ERISA defines *parties in interest* in much the same way as Financial Accounting Standards Board (FASB) *Accounting Standards Codification* (ASC) 850, *Related Party Disclosures*, defines the term *related parties*.

11.02   The following are certain transactions between a plan and a party in interest that are generally prohibited under Section 406(a) of ERISA:

- A sale, exchange, or lease of property
- A loan or other extension of credit (this includes untimely deposits to the trust of employee salary deferral deposits)
- The furnishing of goods, services, or facilities
- A transfer of plan assets to a party in interest for the use or benefit of a party in interest
- An acquisition of employer securities or real property in violation of the 10 percent limitation

Additional information regarding prohibited transactions under ERISA is found in paragraphs A.91–A.93 in appendix A, "ERISA and Related Regulations."

11.03   Certain exceptions deal with party in interest transactions that do not prevent a plan fiduciary from receiving reasonable compensation for services to a plan, or receiving benefits from a plan as a participant or beneficiary, as long as such benefits are in accordance with the terms of a plan as applied to all other participants and beneficiaries. In addition, payments to parties in interest for reasonable compensation for office space and legal, accounting, and other services necessary for the operation of a plan are permitted if certain conditions are met. For example, although transactions with a trustee affiliate also serving as a fund adviser or manager would generally be prohibited transactions, the Department of Labor (DOL) has issued Prohibited Transaction Exemptions (PTE) (Nos. 84-24, 80-51, 78-19, 84-14, and 77-4) relating to these types of transactions. Therefore, they are considered to be *exempt* party in interest transactions and would not have to be reported on the Form 5500 or in the related supplemental schedules. However, in accordance with FASB ASC 850-10-50-1, financial statements should include disclosures of material related party transactions.

In-House Asset Manager Class Exemption

11.04   Managers of many large pensions utilize the services of in-house asset managers (INHAMs). Oftentimes, these managers want to conduct transactions that are prohibited by ERISA. ERISA does provide, however, that the DOL has the authority to grant exemptions from the prohibited transaction restrictions if it can be demonstrated that a transaction is administratively feasible, in the interests of the plan and its participants and beneficiaries, and protective of the rights of the participants and beneficiaries of the plan. The DOL reviews applications for such exemptions and determines whether or not to grant relief. Individual exemptions relate to a particular plan or applicant; class exemptions are applicable to anyone engaging in the described transactions, provided the enumerated conditions are satisfied.

11.05 Related to INHAMs, the DOL issued a class exemption, PTE No. 96-23, effective April 10, 1996, in which plans managed by in-house managers can engage in a variety of transactions with service providers if certain conditions are met. The special exemptions relate to the leasing of office or commercial space, leasing residential space to employees and the use of public accommodations owned by plans. Only large employers whose plans have at least $250 million in assets, with $50 million under direct in-house management can use the exemption, and it also requires that in-house managers be registered investment advisers and make all decisions concerning the affected transactions.

11.06 One of the provisions of the exemption requires that, an independent auditor, who has appropriate technical training or experience and proficiency with ERISA's fiduciary responsibility provisions and so represents in writing, must conduct an exemption audit on an annual basis. Upon completion of the audit, the auditor is required to issue a written report to the plan presenting its specific findings regarding the level of compliance with the policies and procedure adopted by the INHAM.

11.07 The exemption was published in the Federal Register on April 10, 1996, and may be found on the Employee Benefits Security Administration (EBSA) website at www.dol.gov/ebsa/programs/oed/archives/96-23.htm.[*]

Party in Interest Transactions

11.08 An audit performed in accordance with generally accepted auditing standards (GAAS) cannot be expected to provide assurance that all related-party or party in interest transactions will be discovered. Nevertheless, during the course of his or her audit, the auditor should be aware of the possible existence of party in interest and material related-party transactions that could affect the financial statements or for which DOL Reporting Regulations (see appendix A) and FASB ASC 850 require disclosure. Many of the procedures outlined in the following paragraphs are normally performed in an audit in accordance with GAAS, even if the auditor has no reason to suspect that party in interest transactions exist. Other audit procedures set forth in this section are specifically directed to party in interest transactions.

11.09 The existence of certain party in interest relationships, such as plan-sponsor, may be clearly evident. Determining the existence of other parties in interest requires the application of specific audit procedures, which may include the following:

     a. Evaluate the plan administrator's procedures for identifying and properly accounting and reporting for party in interest transactions.

---

[*] An amendment to this class exemption was proposed on June 14, 2010. The proposed revision can be found at www.thefederalregister.com/d.p/2010-06-14-2010-14205. Be alert for the issuance of a final amendment.

  b. Request from appropriate personnel the names of all parties in interest and inquire whether there were any transactions with these parties during the period.

  c. Review filings (for example, Forms 5500 and LM-2) by the reporting entity with the DOL and other regulatory agencies for the names of parties in interest.

  d. Review prior years' working papers for the names of known parties in interest.

  e. Inquire of the predecessor plan auditor, if applicable, concerning his or her knowledge of existing relationships and the extent of management involvement with parties in interest.

  f. Inquire of the plan administrator whether any prohibited transactions have been identified as a result of past DOL, IRS, or other governmental examinations.

  g. Review agreements with service providers.

  11.10 The following procedures are intended to provide guidance for identifying transactions with known parties in interest and for identifying transactions that may be indicative of the existence of previously undetermined party in interest relationships:

  a. Provide audit personnel performing segments of the audit with the names of known parties in interest so that they may become aware of transactions with such parties during the audit.

  b. Review the minutes of the meetings of the board of trustees of the plan and executive or operating committees for information about transactions authorized or discussed at their meetings.

  c. Review correspondence from and material filed with the DOL and other regulatory agencies for information about transactions with parties in interest.

  d. Review conflict-of-interests statements obtained by the plan from its officials.[1]

  e. Review the extent and nature of business transacted with the plan's major investees, suppliers, borrowers, lessees, and lenders for indications of previously undisclosed relationships.

  f. Consider whether transactions are occurring but are not being given accounting recognition, such as receiving or providing accounting management or other services at no charge or a major stockholder of the plan-sponsor absorbing plan expenses.

  g. Review accounting records (plan sponsor or applicable service provider) for large, unusual, or nonrecurring transactions or balances, paying particular attention to transactions recognized at or near the end of the reporting period.

  h. Review confirmations of compensating balance arrangements for indications that balances are or were maintained for or by parties in interest.

---

[1] Conflict-of-interests statements are intended to provide plan officials with information about the existence or nonexistence of relationships between the reporting persons and parties with whom the plan transacts business.

i. Review invoices from law firms that have performed regular or special services for the plan for indications of the existence of parties in interest or party in interest transactions.

j. Review confirmations of loans receivable and payable for indications of guarantees. When guarantees are indicated, determine their nature and the relationships, if any, of the guarantors to the reporting entity.

11.11 The auditor should place emphasis on testing material transactions with parties he or she knows are related to the plan. After identifying related party and party in interest transactions, the auditor should apply the procedures he or she considers necessary to obtain satisfaction concerning the purpose, nature, and extent of these transactions and their effect on the financial statements. The procedures should be directed toward obtaining and evaluating sufficient appropriate audit evidence and should extend beyond inquiry of management. Procedures that should be considered include the following:

a. Obtain an understanding of the business purpose of the transaction.[2]

b. Examine invoices, executed copies of agreements, contracts, and other pertinent documents.

c. Determine whether the transaction has been approved by the board of trustees or other appropriate officials.

d. Test for reasonableness the compilation of amounts to be disclosed or considered for disclosure.

e. Inspect or confirm and obtain satisfaction concerning the transferability and value of collateral.

11.12 When necessary to fully understand a particular related party or party in interest transaction, the following procedures, which might not otherwise be deemed necessary to comply with GAAS, should be considered:[3]

a. Confirm transaction amount and terms, including guarantees and other significant data, with the other party or parties to the transaction.

b. Inspect evidence in possession of the other party or parties to the transaction.

c. Confirm or discuss significant information with intermediaries, such as banks, guarantors, agents, or attorneys, to obtain a better understanding of the transaction.

d. Refer to financial publications, trade journals, credit agencies, and other information sources when there is reason to believe that unfamiliar customers, suppliers, or other business enterprises with which material amounts of business have been transacted may lack substance.

---

[2] Until he or she understands the business sense of material transactions, the auditor cannot complete his or her audit. If the auditor lacks sufficient specialized knowledge to understand a particular transaction, he or she should consult with persons who do have the requisite knowledge.

[3] Arrangements for certain procedures should be made or approved in advance by appropriate plan officials.

e. With respect to material uncollected balances, guarantees, and other obligations, obtain information about the financial capability of the other party or parties to the transaction. Such information may be obtained from audited financial statements, unaudited financial statements, and reports issued by regulatory agencies, taxing authorities, financial publications, or credit agencies. The auditor should decide on the degree of assurance required and the extent to which available information provides such assurance.

f. Review schedule of employee contributions and agree to deposit dates at the trustee to verify timely deposits of employee deferrals.

Prohibited Transactions

11.13 In accordance with the provisions of AU section 317, *Illegal Acts by Clients* (AICPA, *Professional Standards*), the auditor should be aware of the possibility that illegal acts may have occurred. For employee benefit plans, this would include party in interest transactions that may be prohibited by ERISA. When the auditor becomes aware of information concerning a possible prohibited party in interest transaction, the auditor should obtain an understanding of the nature of the transaction, the circumstances in which it occurred, and sufficient other information to evaluate the effect on the financial statements. In doing so, the auditor should inquire of plan management at a level above those involved, if possible. If management does not provide satisfactory information that the transaction is not prohibited, the auditor should

a. consult with the client's legal counsel or other specialists about the application of ERISA to the circumstances and the possible effects on the financial statements. Arrangements for such consultation with the client's legal counsel should be made by the client.

b. if necessary, apply procedures such as those described in paragraphs 11.11–.12 to obtain further understanding of the nature of the transaction.

11.14 If the auditor concludes, based on information obtained and, if necessary, consultation with legal counsel, that a party in interest transaction has resulted in the occurrence of an illegal act, the auditor should consider the effect on the financial statements as well as the implications for other aspects of the audit.

11.15 The auditor should consider the effect of the illegal act or prohibited transaction on the amounts presented in financial statements including contingent monetary effects, such as fines, penalties, and damages. Because a plan fiduciary is liable to make good on losses to the plan resulting from a breach of fiduciary duty and to restore to the plan any profits that the fiduciary made through the use of the plan's assets, prohibited transactions can give rise to significant receivables. Any receivable to be recorded should include an allowance for estimated uncollectible amounts. Contingencies arising from prohibited transactions may also need to be disclosed in accordance with the requirements of FASB ASC 450, *Contingencies*.

11.16 The auditor should evaluate the adequacy of disclosure in the financial statements and required supplementary schedules of the potential effects of prohibited transactions on the plan's operations. If material revenue or earnings are derived from transactions involving illegal acts, or if illegal acts create significant unusual risks associated with material revenue or earnings, that information should be considered for disclosure.

Implications for Audit

11.17 The auditor should consider the implications of prohibited transactions in relation to other aspects of the audit, particularly the reliability of representations of management. The implications of particular prohibited transactions will depend on the relationship of the perpetration and concealment, if any, of the transactions to specific control procedures and the level of management or employees involved.

Effect on the Auditor's Report

11.18 Both ERISA and GAAS require that the auditor's report on financial statements included in an annual report filed with the DOL cover the information in the required supplementary schedules—including Schedule G, Part III—Nonexempt Transactions—presented along with the basic financial statements. Chapter 13, "The Auditor's Report," includes a discussion of auditor's reports on financial statements and information in supplementary schedules as well as examples of such reports.

11.19 ERISA requires that all transactions with parties in interest (excluding any transactions exempted from prohibited transaction rules) be disclosed in the supplementary schedule without regard to their materiality. Only those party in interest transactions that are considered prohibited by ERISA, regardless of materiality, should be included on the Schedule G, Part III—Nonexempt Transactions. It is important to note however that delinquent participant contributions reported on line 4a are no longer required to be reported on line 4d or on Schedule G. See the frequently asked questions about reporting delinquent participant contributions on the Form 5500 at the EBSA website at www.dol.gov/ebsa/faqs/faq_compliance_5500.html. Plan officials faced with prohibited transactions (including late remittances of employee deferrals) ordinarily should consult with legal council to determine if the plan sponsor should apply to the DOL's Voluntary Fiduciary Correction Program (VFCP) with respect to a prohibited transaction. Full compliance with the VFCP will result in the DOL's issuance of a "No-Action Letter" and no imposition of penalties. In addition, applicants that satisfy both the VFCP requirements and the conditions of PTE 2 No. 002-51

- will be eligible for immediate relief from payment of certain prohibited transaction excise taxes imposed by the IRS. For more information, see 67 Fed. Reg. 15062 and 67 Fed. Reg. 70623 (November 25, 2002);
- do not report the *corrected* transaction(s) as nonexempt transactions on line 4d of either Schedule H or Schedule I; and
- do not include such transaction(s) on the supplemental schedule of nonexempt transactions with parties in interest.

The EBSA's website contains useful information about the VFCP and a frequently asked questions section.

11.20 If the auditor concludes that the plan has entered into a prohibited transaction with a party in interest, and the transaction has not been properly disclosed in the required supplementary schedule, the auditor should (*a*) express a qualified opinion or an adverse opinion on the supplementary schedule if the transaction is material to the financial statements or (*b*) modify his or her report on the supplementary schedule by adding a paragraph to disclose the omitted transaction if the transaction is not material to the financial statements (see paragraph 13.17 for examples of reports). If the client refuses to accept the auditor's report as modified, the auditor should withdraw from the engagement and indicate the reasons for withdrawal in writing to the plan administrator or board of trustees.

Communication With Responsible Parties

11.21 The auditor should assure himself or herself that the plan administrator, or others with equivalent authority and responsibility, is adequately informed with respect to prohibited transactions and other illegal acts that come to the auditor's attention (see footnote 6 in paragraph 6.28 for a discussion of individuals with the level of authority and responsibility equivalent to an audit committee). The auditor need not communicate matters that are clearly inconsequential and may reach agreement in advance with the plan administrator on the nature of such matters to be communicated.

Communication With Respondents

Chapter 12

*Other Auditing Considerations**

Plan Tax Status

12.01 A trust established under an employee benefit pension plan ordinarily is qualified under the Internal Revenue Code (IRC) as exempt from federal income taxes. The objective of auditing procedures applied with respect to the tax status of a plan is to permit the auditor to consider

a. whether the trust is qualified under the IRC as being exempt from federal income taxes and whether transactions or events have occurred that might affect the plan's qualified status.[1]

b. whether asserted and unasserted claims and assessments affecting plan assets resulting from the loss of tax exemption have been properly recorded or disclosed in conformity with generally accepted accounting principles (GAAP).

12.02 The financial statements of an employee benefit plan generally have no accrued income tax liability or provision for income tax expense. Plans must be designed and operated in accordance with IRC requirements in order to maintain their qualified status. The existence of a determination letter does not in and of itself serve as evidence that the plan is qualified. Determination letters provide evidence that the plan is designed in accordance with applicable IRC requirements. However, qualified plans must comply with certain operating tests in order to be tax qualified (for example, coverage, discrimination, and maximum benefit limitation tests) Nevertheless, the auditor of an employee benefit plan should be aware of the possibility that violations of tax laws and regulations may have occurred. If specific information comes to the auditor's attention that provides evidence concerning the existence of possible violations affecting the financial statements, the auditor should apply auditing procedures specifically directed to ascertaining whether a violation has occurred (see paragraph .07 of AU section 317, *Illegal Acts by Clients* [AICPA, *Professional Standards*]). The auditor is also expected to inquire of, and obtain representations from, management concerning compliance with the laws and regulations and the prevention of violations that may cause disqualification.

12.03 Examples of substantive procedures for auditing a plan's tax status include

a. reviewing the IRS tax determination letter or an opinion letter from the plan's qualified tax counsel. If the plan has been amended, review any new rulings issued by the IRS regarding the modified plan instrument. If the plan is amended subsequent to the receipt of the

---

* Refer to the preface of this guide for important information about the applicability of the professional standards to audits of issuers and nonissuers.

[1] Note that the Employee Retirement Income Security Act of 1974 requires disclosure of information concerning whether or not a tax ruling or determination letter has been obtained. Financial Accounting Standards Board (FASB) *Accounting Standards Codification* (ASC) 960-205-50-1 items *f*, *g*, and *d* require disclosure of the federal income tax status of a plan only if a favorable tax determination has not been obtained or maintained.

latest determination letter, appropriate disclosure should be made, for example:

> The plan obtained its latest determination letter on [*date*], in which the Internal Revenue Service stated that the plan, as then designed, was in compliance with the applicable requirements of the Internal Revenue Code. The plan has been amended since receiving the determination letter. However, the plan administrator and the plan's tax counsel believe that the plan is currently designed and being operated in compliance with the applicable requirements of the Internal Revenue Code.[2]

If a determination letter has not been requested and an opinion letter from the plan's tax counsel is not available, the auditor may consider reviewing those aspects of the plan document relevant to the determination of its tax-exempt status.

For health and welfare plans, review the IRS tax determination letter for the trust, if applicable. Voluntary employees' beneficiary associations (VEBAs) established since 1984 are required to request exempt status from the IRS using Form 1024. VEBAs established before 1984 do not need a determination letter, if they had previously formally declared exempt status through the filing of Form 990 with the IRS. If the trust has been amended since the original determination letter, the Form 990 procedures require disclosure of the changes; no new application for determination is required.[3]

Currently there is no tax determination letter program for a 403(b) plan. The tax exempt status of a 403(b) plan is different from that of a 401(k) plan because the tax exempt status of a 403(b) plan relates to an exclusion from income for the participant rather than an exemption of tax for the plan. The following is an example of a tax status disclosure for a 403(b) plan:

> The Plan has been designed to qualify under Section 403(b) of the Internal Revenue Code (the Code). The terms of the Plan have been prepared to conform with the sample language provided by the Internal Revenue Service (IRS) in Revenue Procedure 2007-71 [*or the draft Listing of Required Modifications issued April 4, 2009*]. The plan administrator intends to apply for a determination letter on the Plan once the IRS opens such a program. The Plan is required to operate in conformity with the Code to maintain the tax-exempt status for plan participants under Section 403(b).[4]

b. inquiring of the plan administrator, trustee, or other appropriate plan representative about the plan's or trust's operations or changes in plan or trust design that may cause the plan or trust to lose its tax-exempt status. Examples of IRC requirements with which a

---

[2] This is only a portion of the tax status footnote. For an example of a complete tax footnote covering tax status, operations, and uncertain tax positions, refer to the illustrative financial statements in appendix D, "Illustrative Financial Statements: Defined Benefit Pension Plans;" appendix E, "Illustrative Financial Statements: Defined Contribution Plans;" and appendix F, "Illustrative Financial Statements: Employee Health and Welfare Benefit Plans."

[3] It is the trust that is required to get a determination letter and not the plan itself.

[4] See footnote 2.

plan must comply in order to maintain its tax exempt status include the following:

    i. Minimum coverage test (retirement plans only).

    ii. Minimum participation tests (retirement plans only).

    iii. Nondiscrimination test (both retirement and welfare plans).

    iv. Average deferral and contribution percentage limits (both apply to 401(k) plans only; 403(b) plans with employer contributions are subject to the contribution percentage test).

    v. Annual additions limitation (generally retirement plans only, but funded health plans can reduce the allowable benefit for key employees).

    vi. Top heavy test (qualified retirement plans only; not 403(b) plans).

    vii. Exclusive benefit rule (both retirement and welfare plans).

    viii. Diversification of certain employer security holdings.

    c. reviewing the results of auditing procedures applied in other areas of the audit and considering the findings in relation to tax qualification requirements such as those noted in (b) in this list.

As a result of the procedures performed in items (b)–(c) of paragraph 12.03, the auditor may become aware of possible violations of tax laws and regulations that could adversely affect the plan's tax status. In those situations, the auditor should consider the effect on the financial statements as well as implications for other aspects of the audit as described in AU section 317.

Unrelated Business Income Tax

12.04 Although qualified benefit plans are not generally subject to taxation, certain activities of a qualified plan may be taxable. In general, unrelated business taxable income (UBTI) of a tax-exempt entity is subject to taxation. UBTI is

    a. gross income derived from an unrelated trade or business that is regularly carried on, less

    b. allowable deductions directly connected with the trade or business.

With respect to qualified retirement plans, *unrelated trade or business* is defined as any trade or business regularly carried on by the trust or by a partnership or S corporation of which the trust is a member. This means that a qualified plan can have UBTI due to its investments. For tax-exempt welfare plans, UBTI includes the preceding definition. In addition, such plans may be subject to UBTI on their investment income, if their assets exceed certain allowable reserves. (See paragraphs 12.07–.10 for a discussion of Financial Accounting Standards Board [FASB] *Accounting Standards Codification* [ASC] 740, *Income Taxes*.)

12.05 Nonleveraged investments, such as government securities, stocks and debt instruments of noncontrolled corporations, mutual funds and insurance company annuity contracts, do not typically generate UBTI. However, other nonleveraged investments, such as investments in partnerships, real estate investment trusts, loans or mortgages, and options to buy or sell securities such as short sales or repurchase agreements, may generate UBTI. Due to the nature of their investments, the most common plans that generate UBTI are health and welfare plans and defined benefit pension plans. With the increase, however, of such investments held by defined contribution plans, such plans may begin to be subject to UBTI also.

12.06 UBTI may be generated when a plan uses debt to purchase an investment or if the plan purchases a partnership that uses debt to purchase an investment. Passive investments, such as these, may generate UBTI.

Income Taxes

12.07 FASB ASC 740-10 clarifies the accounting and provides implementation guidance for uncertainty in income taxes recognized in an entity's financial statements. In certain situations, uncertain tax positions may be associated with the determination of UBTI (see paragraphs 12.04–.05). The following steps may be considered when auditing UBTI:

  a. Inquire about the procedures applied by the plan administrator in determining UBTI.

  b. To the extent UBTI is generated by investments of the plan or pass-through entities, inquire about the procedures to determine whether any uncertain tax positions have been taken relating to the UBTI either at the trust or at the investment entity level which could have a material impact at the plan level.

  c. Inquire of the plan administrator regarding whether a Form 990-T has been filed.

  d. Obtain a copy of the Form 990-T, UBTI calculations, and supporting detail for the year, and test as necessary.

  e. Determine UBTI for the year and accrual at year-end has been recorded in accordance with GAAP.

12.08 FASB ASC 740-10 prescribes a recognition threshold and measurement attribute for the financial statement recognition and measurement of a tax position taken or expected to be taken in a tax return. FASB ASC 740-10 also provides guidance on derecognition, classification, interest and penalties, accounting in interim periods, disclosure, and transition. According to the FASB ASC glossary, the term *tax position* refers to a position in a previously filed tax return or a position expected to be taken in a future tax return that is reflected in measuring current or deferred income tax assets and liabilities for interim or annual periods. A tax position can result in a permanent reduction of income taxes payable, a deferral of income taxes otherwise currently payable to future years, or a change in the expected realizability of deferred tax assets.

12.09 A plan's status as tax-exempt is a tax position that may be subject to uncertainty.[5] If the plan has entered into a correction program, such as the Employee Plans Compliance Resolution System,[6] such program may aid the plan administrator in assessing that there is no uncertainty with respect to

---

[5] Technical Questions and Answers (TIS) section 9110.17, "Application of Financial Accounting Standards Board (FASB) *Accounting Standards Codification* 740-10 (previously, FASB Interpretation No. 48, *Accounting for Uncertainty in Income Taxes*) to Other Comprehensive Basis of Accounting Financial Statements—Recognition and Measurement Provisions" (AICPA, *Technical Practice Aids*), states that the recognition and measurement provisions of FASB ASC 740-10 would not apply to other comprehensive basis of accounting financial statements because a liability for an uncertain tax position would not be reported on such statements. See TIS section 9110.17 for further nonauthoritative guidance.

[6] See IRS Revenue Procedure No. 2009-50, also known as the Employee Plans Compliance Resolution System.

the plans tax exempt status. Such programs do not apply to tax exempt welfare benefit plans.

12.10 FASB ASC 740-10-50-15 states that all entities[7] should disclose all of the following at the end of each annual reporting period presented:

a. The total amounts of interest and penalties recognized in the statement of operations and the total amounts of interest and penalties recognized in the statement of financial position

b. For positions for which it is reasonably possible that the total amounts of unrecognized tax benefits will significantly increase or decrease within 12 months of the reporting date:

i. The nature of the uncertainty

ii. The nature of the event that could occur in the next 12 months that would cause the change

iii. An estimate of the range of the reasonably possible change or a statement that an estimate of the range cannot be made

c. A description of tax years that remain subject to examination by major tax jurisdiction[8]

See FASB ASC 740-10 for further guidance.

Commitments and Contingencies

12.11 Procedures that the auditor may apply in connection with the commitments and contingencies of an employee benefit plan include

a. discussing possible areas of commitments and contingencies with the sponsoring employer, plan administrator, or other parties performing the plan's management functions.

b. reviewing minutes of various committees of the plan during and subsequent to the period being audited for discussion of possible contingent liabilities or commitments.

c. analyzing legal expenses for the period and reviewing invoices and statements from legal counsel for indications of possible contingencies. The legal expenses of a single employer plan may be paid directly by the employer, in which case the auditor may consider reviewing those expenses.

d. obtaining a representation letter from the appropriate persons, normally the plan's administrator or other parties performing the plan's management function (see AU section 333, *Management Representations* [AICPA, *Professional Standards*], and paragraph 12.28 of this guide).

---

[7] For audits of issuers, such as Form 11-K audits, see FASB ASC 740-10-50-15A for additional disclosures.

[8] TIS section 5250.15, "Application of Certain FASB Interpretation No. 48 (codified in FASB ASC 740-10) Disclosure Requirements to Nonpublic Entities That Do Not Have Uncertain Tax Positions" (AICPA, *Technical Practice Aids*), clarifies that the disclosures required by paragraphs 15C–E of FASB ASC 740-10-50 remain in effect (if applicable), regardless of whether the entity has any uncertain tax positions. Typically, plan tax years will remain open for three years however this may differ depending upon the tax situations of each individual plan. Plan sponsors may consider consulting with their tax specialist to determine the applicable open tax years for their plan.

e. inquiring about any audit or investigation that the Department of Labor (DOL), the IRS, or other regulatory agency has made of the plan's activities or filings since the last audit (such reviews might arise, for example, from enforcement activities, from a request for an advisory opinion, or from a request for a prohibited transaction exemption). Obtain and review for financial statement implications any report of an audit or investigation not reviewed as part of the audit planning process, (see paragraph 5.58e) including the effect of transactions noted therein that give rise to potential receivables arising from breaches of fiduciary duties or prohibited transactions. Consider whether this information obtained from the inquiry should be included in the representation letter.

f. inquiring about any possible mergers or spin-offs affecting the plan.

12.12 An audit inquiry letter to the plan's lawyer is the auditor's primary means of corroborating the information provided by plan management concerning litigation, claims, and assessments (see AU section 337, *Inquiry of a Client's Lawyer Concerning Litigation, Claims, and Assessments* [AICPA, *Professional Standards*]). The American Bar Association (ABA) has approved a "Statement of Policy Regarding Lawyers' Responses to Auditors' Requests for Information," which is set forth in AU section 337C, *Exhibit II—American Bar Association Statement of Policy Regarding Lawyers' Responses to Auditors' Requests for Information* (AICPA, *Professional Standards*). Audit inquiries to plan lawyers should be made in the context of the ABA or AICPA understanding, as discussed in AU section 337. If the plan sponsor has not utilized the services of a lawyer, consider including such a statement in the management representation letter.

12.13 The auditor should request plan management to send an audit inquiry letter to those lawyers who have been consulted regarding litigation, claims, assessments, and qualification matters relating to the plan. AU section 337 paragraph .09 describes the matters that should be covered by the audit inquiry letter, and include a list prepared by management (or a request by management that the lawyer prepare a list) that describes and evaluates pending or threatened litigation, claims, and assessments or unasserted claims with respect to which the lawyer has been engaged and to which he or she has devoted substantial attention on behalf of the plan in the form of legal consultation or representation. The matters described in *(a)–(g)* of paragraph 12.09 may be included in the "pending or threatened litigation" or "unasserted claims and assessments" sections of the attorney's letter. They may not be listed as "other matters," and the letter should refer to specific matters disclosed by management, or expressly state that management has advised the auditor that there are no such matters. Many law firms will not respond if the following matters are not disclosed or if not expressly stated that there are no such matters:

a. Breach of fiduciary responsibilities.

b. Prohibited party in interest transactions and other transactions prohibited by the Employment Retirement Income Security Act of 1974 (ERISA). *Parties in interest* are defined in ERISA Section 3(14) and regulations under that section. See also chapter 11, "Party in Interest Transactions."

    c. Loans or leases in default and reportable to the DOL, including late remittances of employee deferral contributions or loan repayments.

    d. Events reportable to the Pension Benefit Guaranty Corporation.

    e. Events that may jeopardize the plan's tax qualification status.

    f. Legal actions brought against the plan on behalf of plan participants and beneficiaries.

    g. Review or inquiry by the DOL, the IRS, or other regulatory agency of the plan's activities or filings since the last audit. A review or inquiry might arise, for example, from enforcement activities, from a request for an advisory opinion, or from a request for a prohibited transaction exemption.

Cash Balances

12.14 Cash balances of employee benefit plans tend to be very small, representing residual amounts not otherwise invested. When cash balances are held in trust under a trust agreement or under an insurance contract, confirmation of the balance normally is adequate. For a plan that maintains and controls cash accounts that are independent from the trust accounts or insurance contracts, auditing procedures such as those customarily used in audits of other entities are normally appropriate.

Notes Payable—Employee Stock Ownership Plan

12.15 The objective of auditing procedures applied to notes payable is to provide the auditor with a reasonable basis for concluding whether the notes payable exist, are in accordance with debt agreements, are properly classified and disclosed, interest expense is recorded in appropriate amounts and periods, and unallocated shares are properly released.

12.16 Examples of substantive procedures for notes payable include

    a. obtaining or preparing an analysis of notes payable (summarizing the activity) for the year.

    b. determining that the terms and other details are in agreement with the underlying documents.

    c. confirming balances payable from the creditors.

    d. recomputing prepaid or accrued interest or testing for reasonableness.

    e. reviewing restrictive covenants, if any, for compliance (consider existence of covenants at plan sponsor level).

    f. reviewing notes payable for indications of guarantees and determining the nature of the guarantees and the relationships, if any, of the guarantors of the plan.

    g. obtaining or preparing a five year schedule of maturities of debt.

    h. testing the release of shares held as collateral in accordance with plan or loan document provisions and inquire about the consistency of those provisions with the nonexempt transaction requirements.

    i. in addition to other general compliance matters, consider the following for testing and disclosure:

        i. Pass through voting rights.

ii. Dividend handling.

iii. Diversification provisions.

iv. Distributions.

v. Put options.

Administrative Expenses

12.17 The objective of auditing procedures applied to administrative expenses is to provide the auditor with a reasonable basis for concluding whether those expenses are in accordance with agreements, are properly classified, and are recorded in appropriate amounts and periods.

12.18 Examples of substantive procedures for administrative expenses include

a. analyzing the account and examining supporting invoices, documents, and computations.

b. reviewing the terms of the plan instrument and the minutes of the board of trustees or administrative committee to determine that administrative expenses were properly authorized.

c. if the plan employs a contract administrator, reviewing the contract and testing to ascertain that the services contracted were performed and that payments were in accordance with the terms of the contract.

d. if one office functions as a service organization for several plans and administrative expenses are allocated because they are not directly associated with a specific plan, reviewing the allocation to determine that it is appropriate and determining that the method of allocation selected was approved by the board of trustees or administrative committee.

e. determining that fees charged by trustees, investment advisers, and others are in accordance with the respective agreements.

Subsequent Events[†]

12.19 Guidance on the accounting and reporting for subsequent events is provided in FASB ASC 855, *Subsequent Events*. Guidance on the auditor's procedures relating to subsequent events is provided in AU section 560, *Subsequent Events* (AICPA, *Professional Standards*).[9] The following auditing procedures generally should be applied for all employee benefit plans. The list is

---

[†] In February 2010, FASB issued Accounting Standards Update (ASU) 2010-09, *Subsequent Events (Topic 855): Amendments to Certain Recognition and Disclosure Requirements*. This ASU amends the guidance in FASB ASC 855, *Subsequent Events*, to require entities (except Securities and Exchange Commission [SEC] filers and conduit debt obligors [CDOs]) to evaluate subsequent events through the date that the financial statements are available to be issued. Entities other than SEC filers should disclose the date through which subsequent events have been evaluated. SEC filers and CDOs should evaluate subsequent events through the date the financial statements are issued. An entity that is an SEC filer is not required to disclose the date through which subsequent events have been evaluated.

[9] TIS section 8700.01, "Effect of FASB ASC 855 on Accounting Guidance in AU section 560" (AICPA, *Technical Practice Aids*), provides nonauthoritative guidance on the applicability of accounting guidance in AU section 560, *Subsequent Events* (AICPA, *Professional Standards*), for audits of nongovernmental entities.

not all-inclusive and may be modified to suit the circumstances of a specific engagement:

a. Reviewing minutes of committee meetings through the date of the auditor's report.

b. Obtaining supplemental legal representations if there is a significant period between the date of the plan's legal counsel's response and the date of the auditor's report.

c. Obtaining the plan's interim financial statements (trustee and recordkeeper statements) for a period subsequent to the audit date, if they are available, comparing them with the financial statements being audited, and investigating any unusual fluctuations.

d. Inquiring of and discussing with the plan administrator or other parties performing the plan's management function

    i. abnormal disposal or purchase of investments since year-end.

    ii. mergers or spin-offs of plan assets.

    iii. amendments to plan and trust instruments and insurance contracts.

    iv. matters involving unusual terminations of participants, such as termination arising from a sale of a division or layoffs.

    v. changes in plan commitments or contingent liabilities.

    vi. adverse financial conditions of the plan sponsor.

    vii. any review or inquiry by the DOL, the IRS, or other regulatory agency of the plan's activities or filings since the last audit (a review or inquiry might arise, for example, from enforcement activities, from a request for an advisory opinion, or from a request for a prohibited transaction exemption).

Plan Mergers

12.20 Company mergers and acquisitions, or other events may result in employee benefit plan terminations, mergers, or freezing of accrued benefits. The auditing procedures for a merged plan should provide the auditor with reasonable assurance that net assets available for benefits and plan obligations have been properly transferred to the successor plan. Procedures the auditor may consider applying regarding plan mergers are as follows:

Defined contribution and health and welfare benefit plans:

- Reconciling net assets available for benefits per the trustee (custodian) to the recordkeeper immediately prior and subsequent to the merger

- Comparing selected participant accounts immediately prior and subsequent to the merger to determine that accounts were transferred properly

- Testing transfers of assets from the former trustee (custodian) to the current trustee (custodian)

- For multiemployer plans, testing that the contributions are allocated to the proper plan

Defined benefit pension and health and welfare benefit plans:

- Testing selected employee census data immediately prior and subsequent to the merger to determine that employees affected by the merger have been properly included in the data
- Reviewing actuarial report to determine that the effect of the merger on the plan's benefit obligation is properly disclosed in the statement of changes in accumulated benefits
- Testing the transfer of assets from the former trustee (custodian) to the current trustee (custodian)
- For multiemployer plans, testing that the benefits are charged to the proper plan

12.21 Because the effective date of a merger, according to the relevant plan merger documents, often is prior to the actual transfer date of the related plan assets, confusion exists concerning what the last reporting date is for Form 5500 and financial statement purposes.

12.22 Procedures the auditors may consider applying to determine the effective date of the merger include review of plan documents, amendments, minutes of plan meetings, correspondence with service provider, and other pertinent plan information and reviewing the transfer date of assets from the former trustee (custodian) to the current trustee (custodian).

12.23 Auditors need to use judgment in each merger situation based on the procedures previously described to determine the proper merger date for Form 5500 and financial statement purposes. Once the proper merger date is determined, the final Form 5500 is required to be filed 7 months after that merger date.

Terminating Plans

12.24 The procedures for auditing a terminating plan should provide the auditor with a reasonable basis for concluding that

- a. final termination payments are in accordance with the plan provisions, related documents, and applicable regulations.
- b. the payments are made only to or on behalf of persons entitled to them.
- c. transactions are recorded in the proper account, amount, and period.
- d. any plan asset reversions to the plan sponsor, if applicable, are in accordance with the plan provisions, related documents, and applicable regulations.
- e. actuarial valuations are prepared on the liquidation basis of accounting.

See chapter 9, "Auditing Benefit Payments." The auditor may consider increasing the extent of benefit payment testing during the period the termination benefits are paid. Also see paragraphs 2.64–.67, 3.66–.69, and 4.100–.104 for accounting and reporting for a terminating plan.

12.25 Upon full or partial termination of a plan, affected participants become fully vested in accrued benefits at the termination date. A partial termination can occur if approximately 20 percent or more of plan participants are terminated by the plan sponsor as a result of an action, such as a plant closure, a decision to downsize, or the termination of a product line. The reduction can accumulate over 1 or more plan years and still be classified as a partial termination. Judgment is needed to determine whether a partial termination has occurred. Consultation with the IRS or qualified legal counsel may be necessary if questions arise regarding the occurrence of a partial plan termination. Consideration also may be given to determine that terminated participants received their fully vested benefits and that there were no forfeited amounts.

Changes in Service Providers

12.26 Changing service providers (recordkeeper, trustee, and custodian) is fairly common for employee benefit plans. The auditor may want to consider the following procedures when a plan changes service providers:

- Obtain an understanding of the control environment for predecessor and successor service providers.

- Test transaction processing for predecessor and successor service providers during the year.

- For a change in defined contribution plan recordkeepers, agree the sum of the participant accounts per the predecessor recordkeeper prior to the change to the sum recorded by the successor recordkeeper immediately after the change. Select individual participant accounts immediately prior and subsequent to the change to ensure all account information was properly recorded by the successor recordkeeper.

- For a change in trustee or custodian, reconcile assets transferred from predecessor trustee or custodian to successor trustee or custodian. (If a defined contribution plan changes trustees or custodians and recordkeepers simultaneously, reconcile the sum of the participant accounts to the net assets per the trustee or custodian immediately prior and subsequent to the change.)

- Form 5500 requires disclosure for any change in actuaries or independent auditors on Schedule C part II.

Changes in Actuaries

12.27 Employers may change the employee benefit plan's actuary. Before commencing the valuation for the current year, the new actuary usually attempts to replicate the former actuary's last valuation to ensure a consistent understanding of the plan provisions and their effects on the valuation. Paragraphs 10.26–.33 provide audit guidance when using the work of an actuary. It is not unusual, after a change in actuary, for certain demographic assumptions, such as mortality, to change. In that case, the auditor will need to ascertain the reasonableness of the new assumption(s) and their conformity with FASB ASC 960, *Plan Accounting—Defined Benefit Pension Plans*; FASB ASC 715, *Compensation—Retirement Benefits*; and ERISA, as appropriate.

Plan Representations

12.28 The auditor should obtain written representations from management as part of an audit of financial statements performed in accordance with generally accepted auditing standards (GAAS). For employee benefit plans, the written representations are normally obtained from the plan's administrator or other parties performing the plan's management function for all financial statements and periods covered by the auditor's report. AU section 333 lists specific representations that should be included in the written communication. Among them, the representations should relate to management's belief that the effects of any uncorrected misstatements aggregated by the auditor during the current engagement and pertaining to the latest period presented are immaterial, both individually and in the aggregate, to the financial statements taken as a whole. It also states that a summary of the uncorrected misstatements should be included in or attached to the representation letter. The representation letter ordinarily should be tailored to include additional appropriate representations from management relating to matters specific to the entity's business or industry. In addition to the representations included in the illustrative management representation letter in exhibit 12-1, the following is a list of additional representations that may be appropriate in certain situations:

a. Whether financial circumstances are strained, with disclosure of management's intentions and the plan's ability to continue as a going concern[10]

b. Whether the possibility exists that the value of specific significant long-lived assets may be impaired[10]

c. Whether the work of a specialist has been used by the plan[10]

d. Whether receivables have been recorded in the financial statements[10]

e. Whether plan management has apprised the auditor of all communications, whether written or oral, with regulatory agencies concerning the operation of the plan

f. Management's intention to not terminate benefit responsive investment contracts

g. The effect of new accounting standards

h. The adequacy of allowances for receivables, as appropriate

i. The information contained in the notes to the financial statements when the notes are in the opinion of plan management (or plan sponsor)

j. The reasonableness of significant fair value assumptions, including whether they appropriately reflect management's intent and ability to carry out specific courses of action on behalf of the entity where relevant to the use of fair value measurements or disclosures

k. The appropriateness of the measurement methods, including related assumptions, used by management in determining fair value and the consistency in application of the methods

l. The completeness and adequacy of disclosures related to fair values

m. Whether subsequent events require adjustment to the fair value measurements and disclosures included in the financial statements other than normal market fluctuations

---

[10] See appendix B, "Additional Illustrative Representations," of AU section 333, *Management Representations* (AICPA, *Professional Standards*), for sample wording of this representation.

  n. If the engagement is a limited-scope audit, the plan administrator's responsibilities as they relate to the completeness and accuracy of the trustee certification

  o. Whether plan management has obtained and reviewed a Statement on Auditing Standards No. 70 report (if available) and are performing the applicable user controls

12.29 According to AU section 333, if a representation made by management is contradicted by other audit evidence, the auditor should investigate the circumstances and consider the reliability of the representation made. Based on the circumstances, the auditor should consider whether his or her reliance on management's representations relating to other aspects of the financial statements is appropriate and justified. Management's refusal to furnish written representations constitutes a scope limitation sufficient to preclude an unqualified opinion (see "Scope Limitations" section of AU section 508, *Reports on Audited Financial Statements* [AICPA, *Professional Standards*]).

Exhibit 12-1 ‡

Following is an illustrative management representation letter for a full-scope defined benefit pension plan audit engagement, in accordance with AU section 333. This letter should be tailored to the specific type of plan being audited (for example, defined contribution, 403(b), or health and welfare plans). [11] *This letter may not contain all matters that pertain to the engagement and therefore should be modified, as appropriate, for the individual circumstances of each engagement, including if the engagement is for other than a full scope audit.* [12] *This letter should also be modified for special circumstances, such as plan mergers or terminations.*

[Date]

To [Independent Auditor]

We are providing this letter in connection with your audits of the financial statements and supplemental schedules of Sample Company Employee Benefit Plan (the Plan) as of December 31, 20X2 and 20X1, and for the year ended December 31, 20X2. We understand that your audits were made for the purpose of expressing an opinion as to whether the financial statements present fairly, in all material respects, the financial status [13] and changes in financial status [14] of the Plan in conformity with accounting principles generally accepted in the United States of America, and whether the supplemental schedules are fairly stated in all material respects in relation to the basic financial statements taken as a whole.

Certain representations in this letter are described as being limited to matters that are material. Notwithstanding this, items are considered material, regardless of size, if they involve an omission or misstatement of accounting information that, in the light of surrounding circumstances, makes it probable that the judgment of a reasonable person relying on the information would be changed or influenced by the omission or misstatement.

We confirm, to the best of our knowledge and belief, [as of (*date of auditor's report*)] the following representations made to you during your audit.

    1. We are responsible for the fair presentation in the Plan's financial statements of financial status [14] and changes in financial status [14] in conformity with accounting principles generally accepted in the United States of America [or other comprehensive basis of accounting] and for the fair presentation of the accompanying supplemental

---

‡ The illustrative management representation letter included herein has been updated to reflect FASB ASC references. However, in FASB's notice to constituents, it suggests the use of plain English to describe broad FASB ASC topic references. For specific information on FASB ASC, please see the preface in this guide.

[11] For example, defined contribution and health and welfare plan audits would not need to include representations 11–13 regarding actuarial assumptions.

[12] For limited scope engagements, substitute the following for the first paragraph of this letter: We understand that, at our instruction, you did not perform any audit procedures with respect to information prepared and certified to by [*Name of Institution*], the trustee, in accordance with the Department of Labor's Rules and Regulations for Reporting and Disclosure under the Employee Retirement Income Security Act of 1974 (DOL Regulation 2520.103-5), other than comparing such information to the financial statements and supplemental schedules. Because of the significance of the information which you did not audit, we understand that you will not express an opinion on the financial statements and schedules taken as a whole.

[13] Defined contribution and health and welfare plans replace *financial status* with *net assets*.

[14] See footnote 12.

schedules in conformity with the Department of Labor's Rules and Regulations for Reporting and Disclosure under the Employee Retirement Income Security Act of 1974. The financial statements and related notes are fairly presented in conformity with accounting principles generally accepted in the United States of America [or other comprehensive basis of accounting] and the notes include all disclosures required by laws and regulations to which the plan is subject.

2. We have made available to you all—

   a. Financial records and related data.

   b. All minutes of the meetings [*name of plan administrative committee or trustee*], or summaries of actions of recent meetings for which minutes have not yet been prepared.

   c. Amendments made to the plan instrument, the trust agreement, or insurance contracts during the year, including amendments to comply with applicable laws.

   d. Actuarial valuation reports and other reports prepared by the actuary for the Plan and the Plan Sponsor.

3. There have been no communications from regulatory agencies concerning noncompliance with or deficiencies in financial reporting practices, that could have a material effect on the financial statements in the event of noncompliance.

4. We have no—

   a. Plans or intentions that may materially affect the carrying value or classification of assets and liabilities.

   b. Intentions to terminate the plan.

5. There are no material transactions that have not been properly recorded in the accounting records underlying the financial statements.

6. We believe that the effects of the uncorrected financial statement misstatements summarized in the accompanying schedule are immaterial, both individually and in the aggregate, to the financial statements taken as a whole.[15]

7. We recognize that we are responsible for establishing and maintaining effective internal control over financial reporting.

8. We acknowledge our responsibility for the design and implementation of programs and controls to prevent and detect fraud.

9. We have no knowledge of any fraud or suspected fraud affecting the entity involving—

   a. Management,

   b. Employees who have significant roles in internal control, or

   c. Others where the fraud could have a material effect on the financial statements.

---

[15] If management believes that certain of the identified items are not misstatements, management's belief may be acknowledged by adding to the representation, for example, "We do not agree that items XX and XX constitute misstatements because [*description of reasons*]."

10. We have no knowledge of any allegations of fraud or suspected fraud affecting the entity received in communications from employees, former employees, participants, regulators, beneficiaries, service providers, third-party administrators, or others.

11. The following have been properly recorded or disclosed in the financial statements:

    a. Related-party transactions, including transactions with parties-in-interest, as defined in ERISA Section 3(14) and regulations thereunder, including sales, purchases, loans, transfers, leasing arrangements, and guarantees, and amounts receivable from or payable to related parties.

    b. Guarantees, whether written or oral, under which the plan is contingently liable to a bank or other lending institution.

    c. All significant estimates and material concentrations known to management that are to be disclosed in accordance with Financial Accounting Standards Board (FASB) *Accounting Standards Codification* (ASC) 275, *Risks and Uncertainties*. [We understand that the significant estimates covered by this disclosure are estimates at the balance sheet date that are reasonably possible of changing materially within the next year. Concentrations refer to the nature and type of investments held by the plan, or markets for which events could occur which would significantly disrupt normal finances within the next year.]

    d. Amendments to the plan instrument, if any.

12. There are no—

    a. Violations or possible violations of laws or regulations whose effects should be considered for disclosure in the financial statements or as a basis for recording a loss contingency.

    b. Unasserted claims or assessments that our lawyer has advised us are probable of assertion and must be disclosed in accordance with FASB ASC 450, *Contingencies*.

    c. Other liabilities or gain or loss contingencies that are required to be accrued or disclosed by FASB ASC 450.

    d. Transactions that have not been properly recorded in the accounting records underlying the financial statements.

    e. Other matters (for example, breach of fiduciary responsibilities, nonexempt transactions, loans or loans in default, events reportable to the PBGC, or events that may jeopardize the tax status) that legal counsel have advised us that must be disclosed.

13.[16] There were no omissions from the participants' data provided to the plan's actuary for the purpose of determining the actuarial

---

[16] These steps would not apply to defined contribution and health and welfare plans.

present value of accumulated plan benefits and other actuarially determined amounts in the financial statements.[17]

14.[18] The plan administrator agrees with the actuarial methods and assumptions used by the actuary for funding purposes and for determining accumulated plan benefits and has no knowledge or belief that such methods or assumptions are inappropriate in the circumstances. We did not give any, nor cause any, instructions to be given to the Plan's actuary with respect to values or amounts derived, and we are not aware of any matters that have impacted the independence or objectivity of the plan's actuary.

15.[19] There have been no changes in [or the following have been properly recorded or disclosed in the financial statements]—

  a. The actuarial methods or assumptions used in calculating amounts recorded or disclosed in the financial statements.

  b. Plan provisions between the actuarial valuation date and the date of this letter.

16. The plan has complied with all aspects of debt and other contractual agreements that would have a material effect on the financial statements in the event of noncompliance, including the release of unallocated shares held in ESOP plans.

17. The methods and significant assumptions used to estimate fair values of financial instruments are as follows: [*describe methods and significant assumptions used to estimate fair values of financial instruments*]. The methods and significant assumptions used result in a measure of fair value appropriate for financial measurement and disclosure purposes.

18. Financial instruments with off-balance-sheet risk and financial instruments with concentrations of credit risk have been properly recorded or disclosed in the financial statements.

19. All required filings with the appropriate agencies have been made.

20. The plan (and the trust established under the plan) is qualified under the appropriate section of the Internal Revenue Code and intends to continue as a qualified plan (and trust). The plan sponsor(s) has operated the Plan and trust or insurance contract in a manner that did not jeopardize this tax status.

21. The plan has complied with the Department of Labor's regulations concerning the timely remittance of participants contributions to trusts containing assets for the plan.

22. The plan has complied with the fidelity bonding requirements of ERISA.

23. The plan has satisfactory title to all owned assets which are recorded at fair value, [state exceptions, if any] and all liens, encumbrances, or security interest requiring disclosure in the financial statements have been properly disclosed.

---

[17] For health and welfare benefit plans that require the services of an actuary: There were no omissions from the participants' data provided to the plan's actuary for the purpose of determining the liability for claims incurred but not reported and other actuarially determined amounts in the financial statements.

[18] See footnote 16.

[19] See footnote 17.

24. For any securities that do not have a readily determinable market value, we are in agreement with the methods used to estimate fair value or the approach used by the appraiser.

25. There are no—

    a. Nonexempt party-in-interest transactions (as defined in ERISA Section 3(l) and regulations under that section) that were not disclosed in the supplemental schedules or financial statements.

    b. Investments in default or considered to be uncollectible that were not disclosed in the supplemental schedules.

    c. Reportable transactions (as defined in ERISA Section 103(b)(3)(H) and regulations under that section) that were not disclosed in the supplemental schedules.

26. We have apprised you of all communications, whether written or oral, with regulatory agencies concerning the operation of the plan.

27. No events have occurred subsequent to the balance-sheet date and through the date of this letter that would require adjustment to or disclosure in the aforementioned financial statements.

[Name of Plan Administrator and Title][20]

[Name of Plan Financial Officer and Title]

Attachment to Management Representation Letter[21]

Sample Company Employee Benefit Plan
Summary of Unadjusted Differences
Year Ended December 31, 20X1

Proposed Adjustments	Statement of Net Assets Available for Benefits December 31, 20X1		Statement of Changes in Net Assets Available for Benefits December 31, 20X1	
	Assets	*Net Assets*	*Contributions*	*Net Increase*
20X1 contributions made during 20X2 but not accrued at 12/31/X1	($800,000)	($800,000)	($800,000)	($800,000)
Totals[22]	$76,900,000	$76,900,000	$20,000,000	$40,000,000
Percentage effect of adjustments on total[22]	(1.04%)	(1.04%)	(4.00%)	(2.00%)

---

[20] For multiemployer plans, consideration should be given to having the trustees (management or employer and labor or union) sign the management representation letter.

[21] AU section 333 states that a summary of the uncorrected misstatements should be included in or attached to the representation letter. The summary should include sufficient information to provide management with an understanding of the nature, amount, and effect of the uncorrected misstatements. Similar items may be aggregated. The attachment presented here is for illustrative purposes only and is not necessarily the only possible presentation.

[22] This information is not required by paragraphs .06 and .16 of AU section 333.

Confidentiality or Indemnification Agreements

12.30 In certain instances (for example, testing claims at a third party administrator), a third-party administrator will request that the auditor enter into a confidentiality or indemnification agreement signed by the auditor, third-party administrator, and plan sponsor relating to the claims testing. Auditors need to take special care in reviewing these agreements. Often the auditor may not agree with certain language in the agreement, resulting in delays in the audit while mutually agreeable language is determined. Many of the representations are very broad. The agreements generally require that the auditor hold the claim processor harmless from any actual or threatened action arising from the release of information without limitation of liability. In addition, the agreements may require the auditor to hold the client harmless as well. This last indemnification will most likely contradict provisions in the engagement letter between the auditor and the client. Auditors need to keep in mind that the testing of claims at a third-party administrator could be delayed as a result of the request to sign such an agreement and therefore plan the timing of the audit accordingly. Before entering into any confidentiality agreements, the agreement should be reviewed by the auditor's legal counsel. If the auditor is unable to obtain access to records as a result of not signing a confidentiality agreement, a scope limitation could result.

Securities and Exchange Commission Reporting Requirements [23]

12.31 In certain circumstances, interests in plans and related entities are subject to the requirements of the Securities Act of 1933. These requirements mandate registration, typically utilizing Form S-8 for plan securities, and subject the plan to the requirements of annual reporting on Form 11-K under the Securities Exchange Act of 1934. Section 3(a)(2) of the Securities Act of 1933 provides exemptions from registration requirements for defined benefit plans and defined contribution plans not involving the purchase of employer securities with employee contributions. All other plans are subject to the Securities Act of 1933 provided they are both voluntary and contributory.

12.32 Generally, a plan is both voluntary and contributory if the employees are given, at any point, the option to contribute their own funds to the plan knowing that such contributions may or will be used to acquire employer securities. This requirement is not limited to plans sponsored by employers with publicly traded securities. The advent of the 401(k) plan with multiple investment options, including an employer security option, has triggered Securities and Exchange Commission (SEC) filings for many otherwise private entities. Plans that offer to sell employer securities generally are subject to the Securities Act of 1933 in the same manner as employers engaging in similar transactions, although there are specific exemptions. Advice of counsel may be obtained to determine if any of the exemptions apply.

---

[23] The Public Company Accounting Oversight Board (PCAOB) has adopted a registration system for public accounting firms. All U.S. public accounting firms must be registered with the PCAOB if they want to prepare or issue audit reports on U.S. public entities or to play a substantial role in the preparation or issuance of such reports after October 22, 2003. Generally, plans that are required to file Form 11-K would be considered issuers.

12.33　Plans that are required to file Form 11-Ks[24] are deemed to be *issuers*[ll] under the Sarbanes-Oxley Act of 2002 and must submit to the SEC an audit in accordance with the auditing and related professional practice standards promulgated by the Public Company Accounting Oversight Board (PCAOB). The PCAOB adopted as interim standards, on an initial, transitional basis, the GAAS in existence on April 16, 2003. Certain of these interim standards have been subsequently amended by various PCAOB releases.[25] The PCAOB has issued the following auditing standards that should be followed when auditing plans that are required to file Form 11-K. These standards and related conforming amendments can be found in the AICPA's *PCAOB Standards and Related Rules*, Auditing Standards:[26]

- Auditing Standard No. 1, *References in Auditors' Reports to the Standards of the Public Company Accounting Oversight Board*
- Auditing Standard No. 3, *Audit Documentation*
- Auditing Standard No. 4, *Reporting on Whether a Previously Reported Material Weakness Continues to Exist*
- Auditing Standard No. 5, *An Audit of Internal Control Over Financial Reporting That Is Integrated with An Audit of Financial Statements*
- Auditing Standard No. 6, *Evaluating Consistency of Financial Statements*
- Auditing Standard No. 7, *Engagement Quality Review*

Form 11-K does not require a Sarbanes-Oxley Act of 2002 Section 302, "Corporate Responsibility for Financial Reports," certification. Although the rule is silent regarding Section 404, "Management Assessment of Internal Controls," reports on Form 11-K, the SEC staff has agreed that because Form 11-K filers are not subject to Item 308 of Regulation S-K, Form 11-K need not include a Section 404 report.[#] Accordingly, this guide does not reflect the requirements of Auditing Standard No. 5, except to reflect certain conforming amendments

---

[24] Or other applicable SEC filings, such as the Form 10-K\A.

[ll] The December 1, 2005, SEC *Accounting and Disclosure Issues* (page 59) provides guidance regarding the preapproval of audits of employee benefit plans. To view the entire document, see the website www.sec.gov/divisions/corpfin/acctdis120105.pdf.

[25] See the PCAOB website at www.pcaobus.org for information about PCAOB auditing standards and related amendments.

[26] The PCAOB is adopting eight auditing standards related to the auditor's assessment of and response to risk that will supersede six of the PCAOB's interim auditing standards and related amendments to PCAOB standards. The eight auditing standards and related amendments will be applicable to all registered firms conducting audits in accordance with PCAOB standards. PCAOB Release No. 2010-004, *Auditing Standards Related to the Auditor's Assessment of and Response to Risk and Related Amendments to PCAOB Standards* (AICPA, *PCAOB Standards and Related Rules*, Select PCAOB Releases), states that the PCAOB expects that the standards would be effective for audits of fiscal years beginning on or after December 15, 2010.

[#] This information was taken from the Center for Audit Quality's SEC Regulations Committee highlights. The AICPA SEC Regulations Committee meets periodically with the staff of the SEC to discuss emerging technical accounting and reporting issues relating to SEC rules and regulations. The highlights of these meetings have not been considered and acted on by senior technical committees of the AICPA, or by FASB, and do not represent an official position of either organization. In addition, these highlights are not authoritative positions or interpretations issued by the SEC or its staff. They were not transcribed by the SEC and have not been considered or acted upon by the SEC or its staff. Accordingly, they do not constitute an official statement of the views of the SEC or of the staff of the SEC. Be alert to changes in this position by monitoring the SEC Regulation Committee website at www.thecaq.org/resources/secregs.htm.

found in PCAOB Release 2004-008, *Conforming Amendments to PCAOB Interim Standards Resulting From the Adoption of PCAOB Auditing Standard No. 2, "An Audit of Internal Control Over Financial Reporting Performed in Conjunction With An Audit Of Financial Statements,"* and PCAOB Release No. 2007-005A, *Auditing Standard No. 5,* An Audit of Internal Control Over Financial Reporting That Is Integrated With An Audit of Financial Statements, *and Related Independence Rule and Conforming Amendments* (AICPA, *PCAOB Standards and Related Rules*, Select PCAOB Releases). Certain of the provisions in PCAOB Release 2004-008 and PCAOB Release No. 2007-005A are relevant to situations in which an auditor is engaged solely to audit an entity's financial statements and not just when performing an integrated audit of financial statements and internal control over financial reporting. Therefore, certain of the conforming amendments are reflected in this guide as noted in the following table. For information on PCAOB Auditing Standards, Quality Control Standards, and related guidance that may have been issued subsequent to the writing of this guide, please refer to the PCAOB website at www.pcaobus.org (audits of issuers only).

12.34 The following table has been developed to help locate the areas in this guide that pertain to a Form 11-K audit and when it may differ from a GAAS audit. Keep in mind that based on AICPA staff discussions with the SEC and PCAOB staff to seek clarification of the performance and reporting requirements for audits of 11-K filers, firms will need to conduct their audits of these 11-K plans in accordance with two sets of standards and prepare two separate audit reports: an audit report referencing PCAOB standards for Form 11-K filings with the SEC and a separate audit report referencing GAAS for DOL filings. The PCAOB and SEC staff believe that an opinion issued in accordance with Auditing Standard No. 1 does not allow a reference to GAAS, hence a dual standard report is not appropriate and will not be accepted by the SEC.

Paragraph Reference	*Topic*
1.04–.06 and footnotes †, ‡, ‖, and #	To discuss general applicability of PCAOB to 11-K filers and how this guide reflects the PCAOB standards.
1.18	To discuss audit requirements under PCAOB.
Chapters 5–7	Chapters 5–7 of this guide have been updated to reflect the risk assessment standards. These standards differ from the PCAOB interim standards and are in some cases more restrictive.
Exhibit 5-5 footnote 9	To reflect the conforming amendments from PCAOB Release 2004-008 and PCAOB Release No. 2007-005A. The term *reportable condition* is changed to *significant deficiency.*
5.88 and footnote 19	To reflect PCAOB Auditing Standard No. 3.
5.111 footnote 26	To reflect the conforming amendments made to PCAOB AU section 316 by PCAOB Release 2004-008 and PCAOB Release No. 2007-005A.

(continued)

Paragraph Reference	Topic
6.01	To discuss the applicability of PCAOB Auditing Standard No. 5.
6.33 and footnote 10	To reflect conforming amendments from PCAOB Release 2004-008 and PCAOB Release No. 2007-005A to supersede Statement on Auditing Standards No. 60, *Communication of Internal Control Related Matters Noted in an Audit.*
Footnote 23 in the heading before 12.31	To discuss the applicability of PCAOB standards.
12.31–.35 and footnotes 24, ‖, 25, #, and 27	To discuss the applicability of PCAOB standards.
13.01a and footnotes * and †	To reflect PCAOB Auditing Standard No. 1.
13.02	To reflect PCAOB Auditing Standard No. 1.
13.19	To reflect PCAOB Auditing Standard No. 1.

12.35 In lieu of the requirements of the Securities Exchange Act of 1934, plans subject to ERISA may file plan financial statements and schedules prepared in accordance with the financial reporting requirements of ERISA. To the extent required by ERISA, the plan financial statements should be audited by an independent auditor. However, a limited-scope audit report under ERISA will not be accepted by the SEC. Reports on Form 11-K generally should be filed within 90 days after the end of the fiscal year of the plan. Plans subject to ERISA that elect to file ERISA financial statements may file the plan financial statements within 180 days after the plan's fiscal year-end. See the instructions to the Form 11-K and Rule 15d-21 of the Securities Exchange Act of 1934 for filing alternatives.

Form 5500 [**]

12.36 Information in the Form 5500 may be relevant to an independent audit or to the continuing propriety of the auditor's report. The auditor's responsibility for information in the Form 5500 does not extend beyond the financial information identified in his or her report, and the auditor has no obligation to perform any procedures to corroborate other information contained in the Form 5500. However, the auditor should read the other information and consider whether such information, or the manner of its presentation, is materially inconsistent with information, or the manner of its presentation, appearing in

---

[**] Statement on Auditing Standards (SAS) No. 118, *Other Information in Documents Containing Audited Financial Statements,* (AICPA, *Professional Standards,* AU sec. 550), issued in February 2010, addresses and clarifies the auditor's responsibility in relation to other information in documents containing audited financial statements and the auditor's report thereon. The SAS is effective for audits of financial statements for periods beginning on or after December 15, 2010. Early implementation is permitted and, therefore, if adopting SAS No. 118 early, refer to the standard for further guidance. Upon its effective date, SAS No. 118 will supersede the requirements and guidance in AU section 550A, *Other Information in Documents Containing Audited Financial Statements* (AICPA, *Professional Standards*), and, along with SAS No. 119, *Supplementary Information in Relation to the Financial Statements as a Whole* (AICPA, *Professional Standards*), the requirements in AU section 551A, *Reporting on Information Accompanying the Basic Financial Statements in Auditor-Submitted Documents* (AICPA, *Professional Standards*).

the financial statements. If the auditor concludes that there is a material inconsistency, he or she should determine whether the financial statements, the auditor's report, or both require revision. If the auditor concludes that they do not require revision, he or she should ask the client to revise the other information. If the other information is not revised to eliminate the material inconsistency, the auditor should consider other actions such as revising his or her report to include an explanatory paragraph describing the material inconsistency, withholding the use of the auditor's report in the document, and withdrawing from the engagement. The action he or she takes will depend on the particular circumstances and the significance of the inconsistency in the other information.

12.37 If, while reading the other information contained in the Form 5500, the auditor becomes aware of information that he or she believes is a material misstatement of fact that is not a material inconsistency, the auditor should discuss the matter with the client. In connection with this discussion, the auditor should consider that he or she may not have the expertise to assess the validity of the statement, that there may be no standards by which to assess its presentation, and that there may be valid differences of judgment or opinion. If the auditor concludes that he or she has a valid basis for concern, the auditor should propose that the client consult with some other party whose advice might be useful, such as the client's legal counsel.

12.38 If, after discussing the matter, the auditor concludes that a material misstatement of fact remains, the action the auditor takes will depend on his or her judgment in the particular circumstances. The auditor should consider such steps as notifying the plan administrator in writing of his or her views concerning the information and consulting his or her legal counsel regarding further appropriate action in the circumstances.

Reports Issued Prior to Form 5500 Filing

12.39 The auditor may encounter situations in which the financial statements and auditor's report are issued prior to the auditor's review of the Form 5500. If such a situation occurs, the auditor should inform the plan administrator that the financial statements and auditor's report are not to be attached to the filing without the auditor's review of the filing on Form 5500. When the engagement letter is prepared, it may include a statement that if the financial statements and auditor's report are issued prior to the filing of Form 5500, those statements and report should not be attached to the filing without it being reviewed by the auditor. The auditor may also consider including a statement in the transmittal letter to the client indicating that the financial statements and auditor's report, as presented, are not to be attached to the Form 5500 filing without the auditor's review of that filing.

12.40 ERISA requires a plan's financial statements to include a note explaining differences, if any, between amounts reported in the financial statements and the amounts reported in the Form 5500. If, upon review of the Form 5500 subsequent to the issuance of the plan's financial statements, the auditor identifies any such differences, he or she may consider reissuing the auditor's report, dual-dated with respect to the note explaining the differences. If the differences represent a material inconsistency or misstatement of fact in the preparation of the Form 5500, then the guidance in paragraphs 12.36–.38 is appropriate.

Access to Auditors' Working Papers

12.41 The DOL believes that, under ERISA, it has a legal right to access auditor working papers supporting the audited financial statements attached to the Form 5500. Consequently, the DOL may request an on-site or off-site review of auditor working papers as part of its ongoing enforcement activities. See Interpretation No. 1, "Providing Access to or Copies of Audit Documentation to a Regulator," of AU section 339, *Audit Documentation* (AICPA, *Professional Standards*, AU sec. 9339 par. .01–.15), for additional guidance on providing access to working papers.

Communication With Those Charged With Governance

12.42 AU section 380, *The Auditor's Communication With Those Charged With Governance* (AICPA, *Professional Standards*), recognizes the importance of effective two way communication with those charged with governance about certain significant matters related to the audit and also establishes standards and provides guidance on (*a*) which matters should be communicated, (*b*) who they should be communicated to, and (*c*) the form and timing of the communication. AU section 380 uses the term *those charged with governance* to refer to those with responsibility for overseeing the strategic direction of the plan and obligations related to the accountability of the plan, including overseeing the plan's financial reporting process.

12.43 The auditor should communicate with those charged with governance

    a. the auditor's responsibilities under GAAS (see paragraph 5.08).

    b. an overview of the planned scope and timing of the audit (see paragraph 5.10).

    c. significant findings from the audit (see paragraph 12.44).

Significant Findings From the Audit

12.44 The auditor should communicate the following with those charged with governance:

    a. The auditor's views about qualitative aspects of the plan's significant accounting policies, including accounting policies, accounting estimates (see paragraph 12.47), and financial statement disclosures

    b. Significant difficulties, if any, encountered during the audit

    c. Uncorrected misstatements (other than those the auditor believes are trivial), if any (see paragraph 5.04)

    d. Disagreements with management, if any

    e. Other findings or issues, if any, arising from the audit that are, in the auditor's professional judgment, significant and relevant to those charged with governance regarding their oversight of the financial reporting process

12.45 Unless all of those charged with governance are involved in managing the entity, the auditor also should communicate

    a. material, corrected misstatements.

    b. representations that the auditor is requesting of management.

    c. management's consultations with other accountants.

    d. significant issues discussed with management and other significant findings or issues that the auditor believes are significant and relevant to those charged with governance.

12.46 AU section 380 paragraphs .40–.41 states the auditor should communicate with those charged with governance uncorrected misstatements and the effect that they may have on the opinion in the auditor's report, and request their correction. In communicating the effect that material uncorrected misstatements may have on the opinion in the auditor's report, the auditor should communicate them individually. Where there are a large number of small uncorrected misstatements, the auditor may communicate the number and overall monetary effect of the misstatements, rather than the details of each individual misstatement. The auditor should discuss with those charged with governance the implications of a failure to correct known and likely misstatements, if any, considering qualitative as well as quantitative considerations, including possible implications in relation to future financial statements. The auditor should also communicate with those charged with governance the effect of uncorrected misstatements related to prior periods on the relevant classes of transactions, account balances or disclosures, and the financial statements as a whole. Paragraph .81 of AU section 316, *Consideration of Fraud in a Financial Statement Audit* (AICPA, *Professional Standards*), states the auditor also may wish to communicate other risks of fraud identified as a result of the assessment of the risks of material misstatement due to fraud. Such a communication may be a part of an overall communication with those charged with governance and financial statement risks affecting the plan or in conjunction with the auditor communication about the quality of the plan's accounting principles. Communications required by AU section 380 are applicable regardless of a plan's governance structure or size; however, particular considerations apply where all of those charged with governance are involved in managing a plan. Requirements for the auditor to communicate with those charged with governance are included in other standards, including the following:

- AU section 317

- AU section 316

- AU section 325, *Communicating Internal Control Related Matters Identified in an Audit* (AICPA, *Professional Standards*)[27]

---

[27] AU section 325, *Communicating Internal Control Related Matters Identified in an Audit* (AICPA, *Professional Standards*), supersedes AU section 325A, *Communicating Internal Control Related Matters Identified in an Audit*, and is effective for audits of financial statements for periods ending on or after December 15, 2009. Earlier implementation is permitted.

    AU section 325 is not applicable if the auditor is engaged to examine the design and operating effectiveness of an entity's internal control over financial reporting that is integrated with an audit of the entity's financial statements under Statement on Standards for Attestation Engagements No. 15, *An Examination of an Entity's Internal Control Over Financial Reporting That Is Integrated With an Audit of Its Financial Statements* (AICPA, *Professional Standards*, AT sec. 501).

    For audits of issuers, such as Form 11-K audits, auditors would follow the guidance in PCAOB Release 2004-008, *Conforming Amendments to PCAOB Interim Standards Resulting From the Adoption of PCAOB Auditing Standard No. 2,* "An Audit of Internal Control Over Financial Reporting Performed in Conjunction With An Audit Of Financial Statements," and PCAOB Release 2007-005A, *Auditing Standard No. 5,* An Audit of Internal Control Over Financial Reporting That Is Integrated With An Audit of Financial Statements, *and Related Independence Rule and Conforming Amendments* (AICPA, *PCAOB Standards and Related Rules*, Select PCAOB Releases), for audits of financial statements only, or paragraphs 78–84 of PCAOB Auditing Standard No. 5, *An Audit of Internal Control*

(continued)

12.47 As noted in paragraph 12.44*a*, the auditor should communicate with those charged with governance the auditor's views about qualitative aspects of the plan's significant accounting practices, including accounting estimates. Certain accounting estimates are particularly sensitive because of their significance to the financial statements and because of the possibility that future events affecting them may differ markedly from management's current judgments. For significant estimates such communication may include management's identification of accounting estimates, management's process for making accounting estimates, risks of material misstatement, indicators of possible management bias, and disclosure of estimation uncertainty in the financial statements see appendix B, "Qualitative Aspects of Accounting Practices," of AU section 380 for further guidance. For example, the auditor may consider communicating the nature of significant assumptions used in fair value measurements, the degree of subjectivity involved in the development of the assumptions, and the relative materiality of the items being measured at fair value to the financial statements as a whole.

12.48 The auditor should explain to those charged with governance why the auditor considers a significant accounting practice (including accounting estimates) not to be appropriate and, when considered necessary, request changes. If requested changes are not made, the auditor should inform those charged with governance that the auditor will consider the effect of this on the financial statements of the current and future years, and on the auditor's report. See AU section 380 for further guidance.

12.49 Although the communication can be oral, it should be in writing when, in the auditor's judgment, oral communication would not be adequate. AU section 380 also contains information on the communication process, timing of the communication, adequacy of the communication process, and specific examples of what should be communicated. (See AU section 380 paragraphs .23–.44 for examples of items to be communicated.)

12.50 When matters required to be communicated have been communicated orally, the auditor should document them. AU section 339 requires that the audit documentation include documentation of the significant findings or issues discussed, and when and with whom the discussions took place. When matters have been communicated in writing, the auditor should retain a copy of the communication. Documentation of oral communication may include a copy of minutes prepared by the plan if those minutes are an appropriate record of the communication. For further guidance, see AU section 380.

(footnote continued)

Over Financial Reporting That Is Integrated with An Audit of Financial Statements (AICPA, *PCAOB Standards and Related Rules*, Auditing Standards), for an integrated audit of financial statements and internal control over financial reporting. (See AU section 325, *Communicating Internal Control Related Matters Identified in an Audit* [AICPA, *PCAOB Standards and Related Rules*, Interim Standards]). See the PCAOB website at www.pcaobus.org for information about the effective date of these conforming amendments.

Chapter 13

The Auditor's Report

13.01 This chapter provides guidance on the auditor's report on the financial statements of an employee benefit plan when

    a. the auditor expresses an unqualified opinion on financial statements presented in accordance with generally accepted accounting principles (GAAP) (paragraphs 13.03–.07). The opinion should include an identification of the United States of America as the country of origin of those accounting principles (for example, accounting principles generally accepted in the United States of America [U.S. GAAP]).* Form 11-K filers should instead refer to "the standards of the Public Company Accounting Oversight Board (United States)" in accordance with Public Company Accounting Oversight Board (PCAOB) Auditing Standard No. 1, *References in Auditors' Reports to the Standards of the Public Company Accounting Oversight Board* (AICPA, *PCAOB Standards and Related Rules*, Auditing Standards).†

    b. supplemental schedules relating to the Employee Retirement Income Security Act of 1974 (ERISA) and Department of Labor (DOL) regulations accompany the financial statements (paragraphs 13.08–.18).

    c. the financial statements have been prepared on a basis of accounting other than GAAP (paragraphs 13.20–.23).

    d. information regarding accumulated plan benefits is omitted or is not measured in conformity with GAAP (paragraphs 13.24–.25).

    e. limited scope audits (paragraphs 13.26–.31).

    f. the auditor is reporting on the financial statements of a trust established under a plan (paragraph 13.33).

    g. the plan's investments include securities that do not have a readily determinable market value, and either the valuation is appropriate but the range of possible values is significant or the investments are not valued in accordance with GAAP (paragraphs 13.34–.38).

    h. the plan auditor uses the work of other auditors regarding plan investments (paragraph 13.39).

    i. a defined contribution plan provides investment options to participants, and the financial statements for an 11-K filing are presented in accordance with paragraph 3.50*i* of the guide (paragraph 13.40).

---

  * Public Company Accounting Oversight Board (PCAOB) Auditing Standard No. 1, *References in Auditors' Reports to the Standards of the Public Company Accounting Oversight Board* (AICPA, *PCAOB Standards and Related Rules*, Auditing Standards), requires auditors' reports on engagements conducted in accordance with the board's standards to include a reference that the engagement was performed in accordance with the standards of the PCAOB. This replaces the previously required references to generally accepted auditing standards (GAAS). See the PCAOB website at www.pcaobus.org for a complete copy of this standard.

  † Based on AICPA staff discussions with the Securities and Exchange Commission (SEC) and PCAOB staff to seek clarification of the performance and reporting requirements for audits of 11-K filers, firms will need to conduct their audits of these 11-K plans in accordance with two sets of standards and prepare two separate audit reports; an audit report referencing PCAOB standards for Form 11-K filings with the SEC and a separate audit report referencing GAAS for Department of Labor (DOL) filings. The PCAOB and SEC staff believe that an opinion issued in accordance with PCAOB Auditing Standard No. 1 does not allow a reference to GAAS, hence a "dual" standard report is not appropriate and will not be accepted by the SEC.

   j. the employee benefit plan is not expected to continue in existence (paragraphs 13.41–.42).

   k. initial audits of plans (paragraphs 13.43–.46).

The Auditor's Standard Report [1]

13.02 The illustrative auditor's reports presented in this chapter have been prepared to present the standard auditor's reports on financial statements of employee benefit plans in accordance with AU section 508, *Reports on Audited Financial Statements* (AICPA, *Professional Standards*). These reports may be addressed to the plan or the trust whose financial statements are being audited, or to the plan administrator or board of trustees, or to participants and beneficiaries. Historically, the DOL has rejected Form 5500 filings that contain either qualified opinions, adverse opinions, or disclaimers of opinion other than those issued in connection with a limited scope audit pursuant to Title 29 U.S. *Code of Federal Regulations* (CFR) Part 2520.103-8 or 12. For audits of issuers, such as Form 11-K audits, see paragraph 13.19 for an illustrative auditor's report for a Form 11-K audit.

Defined Benefit Plans

13.03 The following are illustrations of an auditor's report with an unqualified opinion on the financial statements of a defined benefit plan. In addition to the statement of net assets available for benefits and the statement of changes during the year in net assets available for benefits required by Financial Accounting Standards Board (FASB) *Accounting Standards Codification* (ASC) 960, *Plan Accounting—Defined Benefit Pension Plans*, the illustrations assume (unless otherwise noted) that information regarding the actuarial present value of accumulated plan benefits and changes therein is presented in separate financial statements. FASB ASC 960 permits variation in the presentation of information regarding the actuarial present value of accumulated plan benefits and changes therein. If such information is not presented in separate financial statements but is presented on the face of one or more financial statements or the notes thereto, the opening paragraph of the auditor's report should refer only to the financial statements that are presented. For example, if information regarding accumulated plan benefits and changes therein is presented in the notes to the financial statements regarding net assets available for benefits and changes therein, the first sentence of the auditor's report might read as follows: "We have audited the accompanying statement of net assets available for benefits of XYZ Pension Plan as of December 31, 20X3, and the related statement of changes in net assets available for benefits for the year then ended." The wording of the opinion paragraph would be the same as in the illustration and would refer to the financial status of the plan. Under an ERISA filing, as discussed in paragraph 13.08, an auditor's report should cover the required supplemental schedules. See paragraph 13.11 for guidance on the reporting on such supplemental schedules.

---

[1] The auditor's report should not be dated earlier than the date on which the auditor has obtained sufficient appropriate audit evidence to support the opinion (paragraph .01 of AU section 530, *Dating of the Independent Auditor's Report* [AICPA, *Professional Standards*]). AICPA Technical Questions and Answers (TIS) section 9100.06, "The Effect of Obtaining the Management Representation Letter on Dating the Auditor's Report," and TIS section 8700.02, "Auditor Responsibilities for Subsequent Events" (AICPA, *Technical Practice Aids*), provide nonauthoritative guidance on dating the auditor's report.

Illustration of Auditor's Report on Financial Statements of Defined Benefit Plan Assuming End-of-Year Benefit Information Date

13.04

Independent Auditor's Report

[Addressee]

We have audited the accompanying statements of net assets available for benefits and of accumulated plan benefits of XYZ Pension Plan as of December 31, 20X2, and 20X1, and the related statements of changes in net assets available for benefits and of changes in accumulated plan benefits for the year ended December 31, 20X2. These financial statements are the responsibility of the Plan's management. Our responsibility is to express an opinion on these financial statements based on our audits.

We conducted our audits in accordance with auditing standards generally accepted in the United States of America. Those standards require that we plan and perform the audit to obtain reasonable assurance about whether the financial statements are free of material misstatement. *[Optional: An audit includes consideration of internal control over financial reporting as a basis for designing audit procedures that are appropriate in the circumstances, but not for the purpose of expressing an opinion on the effectiveness of the Plan's internal control over financial reporting. Accordingly, we express no such opinion.]*‡ An audit includes examining, on a test basis, evidence supporting the amounts and disclosures in the financial statements. An audit also includes assessing the accounting principles used and significant estimates made by management, as well as evaluating the overall financial statement presentation. We believe that our audits provide a reasonable basis for our opinion.

In our opinion, the financial statements referred to above present fairly, in all material respects, the financial status of the Plan as of December 31, 20X2, and 20X1, and the changes in its financial status for the year ended December 31, 20X2, in conformity with accounting principles generally accepted in the United States of America.[2]

[Signature of Firm]

[City and State]

[Date]

---

‡ This optional language may be added to the auditor's standard report to clarify that an audit performed in accordance with GAAS does not require the same level of testing and reporting on internal control over financial reporting as an audit of an issuer when Section 404(b) of the act is applicable. If this optional language is added then the remainder of the paragraph should read as follows:

> An audit also includes examining, on a test basis, evidence supporting the amounts and disclosures in the financial statements, assessing the accounting principles used and significant estimates made by management, as well as evaluating the overall financial statement presentation. We believe that our audits provide a reasonable basis for our opinion.

See Interpretation No. 17, "Clarification in the Audit Report of the Extent of Testing of Internal Control Over Financial Reporting in Accordance With Generally Accepted Auditing Standards," of AU section 508, *Reports on Audited Financial Statements* (AICPA, *Professional Standards*, AU sec. 9508 par. .85–.88), issued in June 2004.

[2] Financial Accounting Standards Board (FASB) *Accounting Standards Codification* (ASC) 960, *Plan Accounting—Defined Benefit Pension Plans*, left unresolved the question of whether accumulated plan benefit information represents a liability of a defined benefit pension plan. Accordingly, because the financial statements of a defined benefit pension plan do not present information on accumulated plan benefits as a liability of the plan, and because they do not present an account comparable to the owners' equity of other types of entities, the auditor's opinion in the illustrative reports does not refer to the presentation of the financial position of the plan. The terms *financial status* and *changes in financial status*, as used here, refer to the presentation of information regarding net assets available for plan benefits and changes therein and information regarding accumulated plan benefits and changes therein as specified in FASB ASC 960.

Illustration of Auditor's Report on Financial Statements of Defined Benefit Plan Assuming Beginning-of-Year Benefit Information Date

13.05

Independent Auditor's Report

[Addressee]

We have audited the accompanying statements of net assets available for benefits of XYZ Pension Plan as of December 31, 20X2, and 20X1, and the related statements of changes in net assets available for benefits for the years then ended and the statement of accumulated plan benefits as of December 31, 20X1, and the related statement of changes in accumulated plan benefits for the year then ended. These financial statements are the responsibility of the Plan's management. Our responsibility is to express an opinion on these financial statements based on our audits.

We conducted our audits in accordance with auditing standards generally accepted in the United States of America. Those standards require that we plan and perform the audit to obtain reasonable assurance about whether the financial statements are free of material misstatement. *[Optional: An audit includes consideration of internal control over financial reporting as a basis for designing audit procedures that are appropriate in the circumstances, but not for the purpose of expressing an opinion on the effectiveness of the Plan's internal control over financial reporting. Accordingly, we express no such opinion.]* ‡ An audit includes examining, on a test basis, evidence supporting the amounts and disclosures in the financial statements. An audit also includes assessing the accounting principles used and significant estimates made by management, as well as evaluating the overall financial statement presentation. We believe that our audits provide a reasonable basis for our opinion.

In our opinion, the financial statements referred to above present fairly, in all material respects, information regarding the Plan's net assets available for benefits as of December 31, 20X2, and changes therein for the year then ended and its financial status as of December 31, 20X1, and changes therein for the year then ended in conformity with accounting principles generally accepted in the United States of America.

[Signature of Firm]
[City and State]
[Date]

Defined Contribution Plans

13.06 The following is an illustration of an auditor's report with an unqualified opinion on the financial statements of a profit-sharing plan:

Independent Auditor's Report

[Addressee]

We have audited the accompanying statements of net assets available for benefits of ABC Company Profit-Sharing Plan as of December 31, 20X2, and 20X1, and the related statement of changes in net assets available for benefits for the year ended December 31, 20X2. These financial statements are the responsibility of the Plan's management. Our responsibility is to express an opinion on these financial statements based on our audits.

---

‡ See footnote ‡ in paragraph 13.04.

We conducted our audits in accordance with auditing standards generally accepted in the United States of America. Those standards require that we plan and perform the audit to obtain reasonable assurance about whether the financial statements are free of material misstatement. [*Optional: An audit includes consideration of internal control over financial reporting as a basis for designing audit procedures that are appropriate in the circumstances, but not for the purpose of expressing an opinion on the effectiveness of the Plan's internal control over financial reporting. Accordingly, we express no such opinion.*] An audit includes examining, on a test basis, evidence supporting the amounts and disclosures in the financial statements. An audit also includes assessing the accounting principles used and significant estimates made by management, as well as evaluating the overall financial statement presentation. We believe that our audits provide a reasonable basis for our opinion.

In our opinion, the financial statements referred to above present fairly, in all material respects, the net assets available for benefits of the Plan as of December 31, 20X2, and 20X1, and the changes in net assets available for benefits for the year ended December 31, 20X2, in conformity with accounting principles generally accepted in the United States of America.

[*Signature of Firm*]

[*City and State*]

[*Date*]

Health and Welfare Benefit Plans

13.07 The following is an illustration of an auditor's report with an unqualified opinion on the financial statements of a health and welfare benefit plan, assuming that the provisions of FASB ASC 965, *Plan Accounting—Health and Welfare Benefit Plans*, have been adopted:

Independent Auditor's Report

[*Addressee*]

We have audited the accompanying statements of net assets available for benefits and of plan benefit obligations of Allied Industries Benefit Plan as of December 31, 20X2, and 20X1, and the related statements of changes in net assets available for benefits and of changes in benefits obligations for the year ended December 31, 20X2. These financial statements are the responsibility of the Plan's management. Our responsibility is to express an opinion on these financial statements based on our audits.

We conducted our audits in accordance with auditing standards generally accepted in the United States of America. Those standards require that we plan and perform the audit to obtain reasonable assurance about whether the financial statements are free of material misstatement. [*Optional: An audit includes consideration of internal control over financial reporting as a basis for designing audit procedures that are appropriate in the circumstances, but not for the purpose of expressing an opinion on the effectiveness of the Plan's internal control over financial reporting. Accordingly, we express no such opinion.*] ‡ An audit includes examining, on a test basis, evidence supporting the amounts and disclosures in the financial statements. An audit also includes assessing the accounting principles used and significant estimates made by management,

---

‡ See footnote ‡ in paragraph 13.04.

as well as evaluating the overall financial statement presentation. We believe that our audits provide a reasonable basis for our opinion.

In our opinion, the financial statements referred to above present fairly, in all material respects, the financial status of the Plan as of December 31, 20X2, and 20X1, and the changes in its financial status for the year ended December 31, 20X2, in conformity with accounting principles generally accepted in the United States of America.

[Signature of Firm]

[City and State]

[Date]

Supplemental Schedules Relating to ERISA and DOL Regulations

13.08 Besides the financial statements and related disclosures, which may conform to the requirements of FASB ASC 960; FASB ASC 962, *Plan Accounting—Defined Contribution Pension Plans*; and FASB ASC 965, ERISA and DOL regulations require additional information to be disclosed. Some of this information is required to be covered by the auditor's report (for example, supplemental schedules; see paragraph A.52(b)), but other required additional information need not be covered by the auditor's report. (The information required by ERISA and by the regulations is described in appendix A, "ERISA and Related Regulations.")

13.09 AU section 551A, *Reporting on Information Accompanying the Basic Financial Statements in Auditor-Submitted Documents* (AICPA, *Professional Standards*),[II] provides guidance on the form and content of reporting when the auditor submits to the client or others a document containing information accompanying the basic financial statements. Paragraph .06 of AU section 551A provides the following guidelines for the auditor's report in those circumstances:

a. The report should state that the audit has been performed for the purpose of forming an opinion on the basic financial statements taken as a whole.

b. The report should identify the accompanying information. (Identification may be by descriptive title or page number of the document.)

c. The report should state that the accompanying information is presented for purposes of additional analysis and is not a required part of the basic financial statements. The report may refer to regulatory agency requirements applicable to the information.

[II] In February 2010, the AICPA issued Statement on Auditing Standards (SAS) No. 119, *Supplementary Information in Relation to the Financial Statements as a Whole* (AICPA, *Professional Standards*, AU sec. 551), which, along with SAS No. 118, *Other Information in Documents Containing Audited Financial Statements* (AICPA, *Professional Standards*, AU sec. 550), supersedes AU section 551A, *Reporting on Information Accompanying the Basic Financial Statements in Auditor-Submitted Documents* (AICPA, *Professional Standards*). SAS No. 119 addresses the auditor's responsibility when engaged to report on whether supplementary information is fairly stated, in all material respects, in relation to the financial statements as a whole. This SAS is effective for periods beginning on or after December 15, 2010. Early application is permitted and therefore, if adopting SAS No. 119 early, refer to the standard for further guidance.

d. The report should include either an opinion on whether the accompanying information is fairly stated in all material respects in relation to the basic financial statements taken as a whole or a disclaimer of opinion, depending on whether the information has been subjected to the auditing procedures applied in the audit of the basic financial statements. The auditor may express an opinion on a portion of the accompanying information and disclaim an opinion on the remainder.

e. The report on the accompanying information may be added to the auditor's standard report on the basic financial statements or appear separately in the auditor-submitted document.

13.10 Although not required by AU section 551A, when reporting on the supplemental schedules, auditor's may include a statement that the supplemental schedules are the responsibility of the plan's management. Because the introductory paragraph of the standard audit report (paragraph .08 of AU section 508) identifies responsibilities between plan management and auditors as they relate to the financial statements only, this additional statement clarifies the responsibilities as they relate to the supplemental schedules. The example reports found throughout this chapter that report on the supplemental schedules include this additional statement.

13.11 An example of an auditor's report on supplemental schedules required by ERISA and DOL regulations, applicable to all types of employee benefit plans, follows:[#]

Independent Auditor's Report

[*Addressee*]

Our audits were performed for the purpose of forming an opinion on the basic financial statements taken as a whole. The supplemental schedules of [*identify title of schedules and period covered*] are presented for the purpose of additional analysis and are not a required part of the basic financial statements but are supplementary information required by the Department of Labor's Rules and Regulations for Reporting and Disclosure under the Employee Retirement Income Security Act of 1974. These supplemental schedules are the responsibility of the Plan's management. The supplemental schedules have been subjected to the auditing procedures applied in the audits of the basic financial statements and, in our opinion, are fairly stated in all material respects in relation to the basic financial statements taken as a whole.

[*Signature of Firm*]
[*City and State*]
[*Date*]

13.12 When additional information is presented on which the auditor does not express an opinion, the information should be marked as unaudited or should refer to the auditor's disclaimer of opinion, and the last sentence of the preceding example paragraph will vary according to the circumstances, for example: "The supplemental schedules have not been subjected to the auditing procedures applied in the audit of the basic financial statements, and, accordingly, we express no opinion on them."

[#] This illustrative auditor's report has been prepared in accordance with AU section 551A. If a plan early adopts SAS No. 119, see the exhibit, "Illustrative Reporting Examples," in AU section 551 for illustrative wording.

13.13 In situations in which a disclaimer arises from the exemption permitted under 29 CFR 2520.103-8 of the DOL's Rules and Regulations for Reporting and Disclosure under ERISA, see paragraph 13.26 in this guide for guidance on the reporting on the supplemental schedules.

13.14 In an audit in accordance with generally accepted auditing standards, the report need not state that the financial statements and schedules comply with the DOL filing requirements. During the audit, however, the auditor may become aware of a departure from such requirements that is not also a departure from GAAP. If the departure is not related to a prohibited transaction with a party in interest, the auditor may consider emphasizing the matter in an explanatory paragraph of the report. If the auditor becomes aware that the plan has entered into a prohibited transaction with a party in interest, and the transaction has not been properly disclosed in the required supplemental schedule, then see the guidance in paragraph 11.19.

13.15 When the auditor concludes that the supplemental schedules do not contain all required information or contain information that is inaccurate or is inconsistent with the financial statements, the auditor should first discuss the matter(s) with the client and propose appropriate revision(s). If the client will not agree to revision, the auditor should consider, depending on the nature of the problem and the type of examination, either (*a*) modifying his or her report on the supplemental schedules by adding a paragraph to disclose the omission of the information or (*b*) expressing a qualified or an adverse opinion on the supplemental schedules, as appropriate. The following table illustrates the report modifications that an auditor might consider to be necessary when a required schedule, or information thereon, is omitted or is materially inconsistent with the financial statements.

| | *Report Modification* | | |
| | | *Limited-Scope Audit (defined in paragraph 7.73)* | |
Error, Omission, or Inconsistency	*Full Scope Audit*	*Exception in Information Certified by Trustee or Custodian*	*Exception in Information Not Certified by Trustee or Custodian But Tested by Auditor (see paragraph 7.75)*
Required information omitted from schedule, for example, historical cost information for nonparticipant directed transactions.	Emphasis of a Matter paragraph	Emphasis of a Matter paragraph	Qualified or adverse as to the form & content of the schedules
Required schedule omitted,** for example, Schedule H, line 4j—Schedule of Reportable Transactions.	Emphasis of a Matter paragraph	Emphasis of a Matter paragraph	Qualified or adverse as to the form & content of the schedules
Required schedule materially inconsistent with financial statements.	Qualified or adverse as to schedules	Emphasis of a Matter paragraph	Qualified or adverse as to the form & content of the schedules

---

** See paragraph 11.20 when Schedule G, Part III—Nonexempt Transactions is omitted.

13.16

Modified Report—Omitted Information or Omitted Schedule Required Under DOL Regulations

Following are examples of paragraphs added to the auditor's report when the auditor modifies his or her report on the supplemental schedules because of omitted information or an omitted schedule, which is required under DOL regulations:

Independent Auditor's Report

[Addressee]

[Same first, second, and third paragraphs as the standard report.]

Our audits were performed for the purpose of forming an opinion on the financial statements taken as a whole. The supplemental schedules of [identify title of schedules and period covered] are presented for the purpose of additional analysis and are not a required part of the basic financial statements, but are supplementary information required by the Department of Labor's Rules and Regulations for Reporting and Disclosure under the Employee Retirement Income Security Act of 1974. These supplemental schedules are the responsibility of the Plan's management. The supplemental schedules have been subjected to the auditing procedures applied in the audits of the basic financial statements and, in our opinion, are fairly stated in all material respects in relation to the basic financial statements taken as a whole.

The supplemental Schedule H, line 4i—Schedule of Assets (Held at End of Year) as of December 31, 20X2 that accompanies the Plan's financial statements does not disclose the historical cost of certain nonparticipant directed plan assets held by the Plan trustee [or custodian]. Disclosure of this information is required by the Department of Labor's Rules and Regulations for Reporting and Disclosure under the Employee Retirement Income Security Act of 1974.

or

The Plan has not presented the supplemental Schedule H, line 4j—Schedule of Reportable Transactions for the year ended December 31, 20X2. Disclosure of this information is required by the Department of Labor's Rules and Regulations for Reporting and Disclosure under the Employee Retirement Income Security Act of 1974.

[Signature of Firm]

[City and State]

[Date]

Qualified Opinion—Omitted or Incomplete Schedule or Material Inconsistency

The following are examples of paragraphs added to the auditor's report when the auditor qualifies his or her opinion on the supplemental schedules because a schedule, or information thereon, was omitted (when the schedules are not covered by a trustee's certification as to completeness and accuracy), or because information in a required schedule is materially inconsistent with the financial statements.

Independent Auditor's Report

[*Addressee*]

[*Same first, second, and third paragraphs as the standard report.*]

The supplemental Schedule H, line 4i—Schedule of Assets (Held at End of Year) as of December 31, 20X2, that accompanies the Plan's financial statements does not disclose that the Plan had loans to participants, which are considered assets held for investment purposes. Disclosure of this information is required by the Department of Labor's Rules and Regulations for Reporting and Disclosure under the Employee Retirement Income Security Act of 1974.

Our audits were performed for the purpose of forming an opinion on the financial statements taken as a whole. The supplemental schedules of [*identify title of schedules and period covered*] are presented for the purpose of additional analysis and are not a required part of the basic financial statements, but are supplementary information required by the Department of Labor's Rules and Regulations for Reporting and Disclosure under the Employee Retirement Income Security Act of 1974. These supplemental schedules are the responsibility of the Plan's management. The supplemental schedules have been subjected to the auditing procedures applied in the audits of the basic financial statements and, in our opinion, except for the omission of the information discussed in the preceding paragraph, are fairly stated in all material respects in relation to the basic financial statements taken as a whole.

[*Signature of Firm*]

[*City and State*]

[*Date*]

Modified Report—Omitted Information or Omitted Schedule Required Under DOL Regulations in a Limited Scope Engagement

In the following illustration, Schedule H, line 4i—Schedule of Assets (Held at End of Year) as of December 31, 20X2, which accompanies the Defined Contribution Plan's financial statements does not disclose that the Plan has loans to participants. Because the omitted participant loan information is information that is not certified by the trustee or custodian, a qualified or adverse opinion as to the form and content of the supplemental schedule(s) should be issued on the applicable supplemental schedules because of an omission of participant loan information (see table in paragraph 13.15).

Independent Auditor's Report

[*Addressee*]

[*Same first and second paragraphs as the limited-scope report.*]

The supplemental Schedule H, line 4i—Schedule of Assets (Held at End of Year) as of December 31, 20X2, that accompanies the Plan's financial statements does not disclose that the Plan has loans to participants, which are considered assets held for investment purposes. Disclosure of this information is required by the Department of Labor's Rules and Regulations for Reporting and Disclosure under the Employee Retirement Income Security Act of 1974.

Because of the significance of the information that we did not audit, we are unable to, and do not, express an opinion on the accompanying financial statements and schedules taken as a whole. The form and content of the information included in the financial statements and schedules, other than that derived from the information certified by the trustee, have been audited by us in accordance with auditing standards generally accepted in the United States of America and, in our opinion, except for the omission of the information discussed in the preceding paragraph, are presented in compliance with the Department of Labor's Rules and Regulations for Reporting and Disclosure under the Employee Retirement Income Security Act of 1974.

[*Signature of Firm*]

[*City and State*]

[*Date*]

or

In the following illustration, the Plan has not presented the supplemental Schedule H, line 4j—Schedule of Reportable Transactions. Because Schedule H, line 4j—Schedule of Reportable Transactions is information that is certified by the trustee or custodian, an omission of the schedule would require that an explanatory paragraph be added to the auditor's report (see table in paragraph 13.15).

Independent Auditor's Report

[*Addressee*]

[*Same first, second, and third paragraphs as the limited-scope report.*]

The Plan has not presented the supplemental Schedule H, line 4j—Schedule of Reportable Transactions for the year ended December 31, 20X2. Disclosure of this information is required by the Department of Labor's Rules and Regulations for Reporting and Disclosure under the Employee Retirement Income Security Act of 1974.

[*Signature of Firm*]

[*City and State*]

[*Date*]

13.17 When the auditor concludes that the plan has entered into a prohibited transaction with a party in interest, and the transaction has not been properly disclosed in the required supplemental schedule, the auditor should (*a*) express a qualified opinion or an adverse opinion on the supplemental schedule[3] if the effect of the transaction is material to the financial statements or (*b*) modify his or her report on the supplemental schedule by adding a paragraph to disclose the omitted transaction if the effect of the transaction is not material to the financial statements. Illustrations of reports modified in those circumstances follow. All of the illustrations are presented assuming that the report on the supplemental schedules is added to the auditor's standard report on the basic financial statements (see paragraph 13.09*c*).

Qualified Opinion—Disclosure of Material Prohibited Transaction With Party in Interest Omitted

The following are examples of paragraphs added to the auditor's report on the plan's financial statements when the auditor qualifies his or her opinion on the

---

[3] If a material party in interest transaction that is not disclosed in the supplemental schedule is also considered a related-party transaction and if that transaction is not properly disclosed in the notes to the financial statements, the auditor should express a qualified or adverse opinion on the financial statements as well as on the supplemental schedule. See paragraph 13.18.

supplemental schedules because disclosure of a material prohibited transaction with a party in interest is omitted:

Independent Auditor's Report

[*Addressee*]

[*Same first, second, and third paragraphs as the standard report.*][4]

The supplemental Schedule G, Part III—Nonexempt Transactions that accompanies the plan's financial statements does not disclose that the Plan [*describe prohibited transaction*]. Disclosure of this information is required by the Department of Labor's Rules and Regulations for Reporting and Disclosure under the Employee Retirement Income Security Act of 1974.

Our audits were performed for the purpose of forming an opinion on the financial statements taken as a whole. The supplemental schedules [*identify title of schedules and period covered*] are presented for the purpose of additional analysis and are not a required part of the basic financial statements, but are supplementary information required by the Department of Labor's Rules and Regulations for Reporting and Disclosure under the Employee Retirement Income Security Act of 1974. These supplemental schedules are the responsibility of the Plan's management. The supplemental schedules have been subjected to the auditing procedures applied in the audits of the basic financial statements and, in our opinion, except for the omission of the information discussed in the preceding paragraph, are fairly stated in all material respects in relation to the basic financial statements taken as a whole.

[*Signature of Firm*]

[*City and State*]

[*Date*]

Adverse Opinion—Disclosure of Material Prohibited Transaction With Party in Interest Omitted

The following are examples of paragraphs added to the auditor's report on the plan's financial statements when the auditor decides that an adverse opinion should be expressed on the supplemental schedules because disclosure of a material prohibited transaction with a party in interest is omitted:

Independent Auditor's Report

[*Addressee*]

[*Same first, second, and third paragraphs as the standard report.*][5]

Schedule G, Part III—Nonexempt Transactions that accompanies the plan's financial statements does not disclose that the Plan [*describe prohibited transaction*]. Disclosure of this information is required by the Department of Labor's Rules and Regulations for Reporting and Disclosure under the Employee Retirement Income Security Act of 1974.

Our audits were performed for the purpose of forming an opinion on the financial statements taken as a whole. The supplemental schedules of [*identify title of schedules and period covered*] are presented for the purpose of additional analysis and are not a required part of the basic financial statements, but are

---

[4] See footnote 3.

[5] See footnote 3.

supplementary information required by the Department of Labor's Rules and Regulations for Reporting and Disclosure under the Employee Retirement Income Security Act of 1974. These supplemental schedules are the responsibility of the Plan's management. The supplemental schedules have been subjected to the auditing procedures applied in the audits of the basic financial statements and, in our opinion, because of the omission of the information discussed in the preceding paragraph are not fairly stated in all material respects in relation to the basic financial statements taken as a whole.

[Signature of Firm]

[City and State]

[Date]

Modified Report—Disclosure of Immaterial Prohibited Transaction With Party in Interest Omitted

The following are examples of paragraphs added to the auditor's report on the plan's financial statements when the auditor decides to modify his or her report on the supplemental schedules because disclosure of a prohibited transaction with a party in interest that is not material to the financial statements has been omitted:

Independent Auditor's Report

[Addressee]

[Same first, second, and third paragraphs as the standard report.]

Our audits were performed for the purpose of forming an opinion on the financial statements taken as a whole. The supplemental schedules of [identify title of schedules and period covered] are presented for the purpose of additional analysis and are not a required part of the basic financial statements, but are supplementary information required by the Department of Labor's Rules and Regulations for Reporting and Disclosure under the Employee Retirement Income Security Act of 1974. These supplemental schedules are the responsibility of the Plan's management. The supplemental schedules have been subjected to the auditing procedures applied in the audits of the basic financial statements and, in our opinion, are fairly stated in all material respects in relation to the basic financial statements taken as a whole.

Schedule G, Part III—Nonexempt Transactions that accompanies the plan's financial statements does not disclose that the Plan [describe prohibited transaction]. Disclosure of this information, which is not considered material to the financial statements taken as a whole, is required by the Department of Labor's Rules and Regulations for Reporting and Disclosure under the Employee Retirement Income Security Act of 1974.

[Signature of Firm]

[City and State]

[Date]

13.18 When the auditor concludes that the plan has entered into a prohibited transaction with a party in interest that is also considered a related-party transaction and is material to the financial statements, and the transaction has not been properly disclosed in the notes to the financial statements and the required supplemental schedule, the auditor should express a qualified or adverse opinion on the financial statements and the supplemental schedule.

The following is an example of a qualified opinion issued on the financial statements of a profit-sharing plan, and the related supplemental schedules, under those circumstances:

Independent Auditor's Report

[*Addressee*]

We have audited the accompanying statement of net assets available for benefits of XYZ Company Profit-Sharing Plan as of December 31, 20X1 and 20X0, and the related statement of changes in net assets available for benefits for the year ended December 31, 20X1. These financial statements are the responsibility of the Plan's management. Our responsibility is to express an opinion on these financial statements based on our audits.

We conducted our audits in accordance with auditing standards generally accepted in the United States of America. Those standards require that we plan and perform the audit to obtain reasonable assurance about whether the financial statements are free of material misstatement. An audit includes examining, on a test basis, evidence supporting the amounts and disclosures in the financial statements. An audit also includes assessing the accounting principles used and significant estimates made by management, as well as evaluating the overall financial statement presentation. We believe that our audits provide a reasonable basis for our opinion.

The Plan's financial statements do not disclose that the Plan [*describe related-party transaction*]. Disclosure of this information is required by accounting principles generally accepted in the United States of America.

In our opinion, except for the omission of the information discussed in the preceding paragraph, the financial statements referred to above present fairly, in all material respects, the net assets available for benefits of the Plan as of December 31, 20X1, and 20X0, and the changes in net assets available for benefits for the year ended December 31, 20X1, in conformity with accounting principles generally accepted in the United States of America.

Schedule G, Part III—Nonexempt Transactions that accompanies the plan's financial statements does not disclose that the plan [*describe prohibited transaction*]. Disclosure of this information is required by the Department of Labor's Rules and Regulations for Reporting and Disclosure under the Employee Retirement Income Security Act of 1974.

Our audits were performed for the purpose of forming an opinion on the financial statements taken as a whole. The supplemental schedules of [*identify title of schedules and period covered*] are presented for the purpose of additional analysis and are not a required part of the basic financial statements, but are supplementary information required by the Department of Labor's Rules and Regulations for Reporting and Disclosure under the Employee Retirement Income Security Act of 1974. These supplemental schedules are the responsibility of the Plan's management. The supplemental schedules have been subjected to the auditing procedures applied in the audits of the basic financial statements and, in our opinion, except for the omission of the information discussed in the preceding paragraph, are fairly stated in all material respects in relation to the basic financial statements taken as a whole.

[*Signature of Firm*]
[*City and State*]
[*Date*]

Form 11-K Filings

13.19 As noted in paragraph 1.18, generally, plans that are required to file Form 11-K would be considered issuers. Accordingly, public accounting firms registered with the PCAOB should adhere to all PCAOB standards in the audits of issuers. PCAOB Auditing Standard No. 1 provides guidance on the auditor's report for an audit of an issuer. The following is an example of an opinion for an 11-K audit:

Report of Independent Registered Public Accounting Firm

[*Addressee*]

We have audited the accompanying statements of net assets available for benefits of the ABC 401(k) plan (the Plan) as of December 31, 20X2, and 20X1, and the related statement of changes in net assets available for benefits for the year ended December 31, 20X2. These financial statements are the responsibility of the Plan's management. Our responsibility is to express an opinion on these financial statements based on our audits.

We conducted our audits in accordance with the standards of the Public Company Accounting Oversight Board (United States). Those standards require that we plan and perform the audit to obtain reasonable assurance about whether the financial statements are free of material misstatement. An audit includes examining, on a test basis, evidence supporting the amounts and disclosures in the financial statements. An audit also includes assessing the accounting principles used and significant estimates made by management, as well as evaluating the overall financial statement presentation. We believe that our audits provide a reasonable basis for our opinion.

In our opinion, the financial statements referred to above present fairly, in all material respects, the net assets available for benefits of the Plan as of December 31, 20X2, and 20X1, and the changes in net assets available for benefits for the year ended December 31, 20X2, in conformity with accounting principles generally accepted in the United States of America.

Non-GAAP-Basis Financial Statements

13.20 Present DOL regulations permit, but do not require, financial statements included in the annual report (Form 5500) to be prepared on a basis of accounting other than GAAP. Also, they do not prohibit variances from GAAP if the variances are described in a note to the financial statements.

13.21 A common example of the use of a basis other than GAAP is financial statements prepared on the modified cash basis of accounting for filing with the DOL. AU section 623, *Special Reports* (AICPA, *Professional Standards*), provides guidance on financial statements prepared in conformity with a comprehensive basis of accounting other than generally accepted accounting principles. AU section 623 is further clarified by Interpretation No. 14, "Evaluating the Adequacy of Disclosure and Presentation in Financial Statements Prepared in Conformity With an Other Comprehensive Basis of Accounting (OCBOA)" (AICPA, *Professional Standards*, AU sec. 9623 par. .90–.95). Included in the definition of a *comprehensive basis of accounting* are the cash basis and modifications thereof having substantial support. Cash basis financial statements that adjust securities investments to fair value are considered to be prepared on a modified cash basis of accounting.

13.22 The following is an illustration of an auditor's report on the financial statements of a defined benefit pension plan prepared on the modified cash basis. The information regarding accumulated plan benefits (as required by OCBOA) is included in the notes to the financial statements:

Independent Auditor's Report

[*Addressee*]

We have audited the accompanying statements of net assets available for benefits (modified cash basis) of XYZ Pension Plan as of December 31, 20X2, and 20X1, and the related statement of changes in net assets available for benefits (modified cash basis) for the year ended December 31, 20X2. These financial statements are the responsibility of the Plan's management. Our responsibility is to express an opinion on these financial statements based on our audits.

We conducted our audits in accordance with auditing standards generally accepted in the United States of America. Those standards require that we plan and perform the audit to obtain reasonable assurance about whether the financial statements are free of material misstatement. [*Optional: An audit includes consideration of internal control over financial reporting as a basis for designing audit procedures that are appropriate in the circumstances, but not for the purpose of expressing an opinion on the effectiveness of the Plan's internal control over financial reporting. Accordingly, we express no such opinion.*] ‡ An audit includes examining, on a test basis, evidence supporting the amounts and disclosures in the financial statements. An audit also includes assessing the accounting principles used and significant estimates made by management, as well as evaluating the overall financial statement presentation. We believe that our audits provide a reasonable basis for our opinion.

As described in Note X, these financial statements and supplemental schedules were prepared on a modified cash basis of accounting, which is a comprehensive basis of accounting other than GAAP.

In our opinion, the financial statements referred to above present fairly, in all material respects, the net assets available for benefits of XYZ Pension Plan as of December 31, 20X2, and 20X1, and the changes in net assets available for benefits for the year ended December 20X2, on the basis of accounting described in Note X.

Our audits were performed for the purpose of forming an opinion on the financial statements taken as a whole. The supplemental schedules (modified cash basis) of [*identify titles of schedules and period covered*] are presented for the purpose of additional analysis and are not a required part of the basic financial statements, but are supplementary information required by the Department of Labor's Rules and Regulations for Reporting and Disclosure under the Employee Retirement Income Security Act of 1974. These supplemental schedules are the responsibility of the Plan's management. The supplemental schedules have been subjected to the auditing procedures applied in the audits of the basic financial statements and, in our opinion, are fairly stated in all material respects in relation to the basic financial statements taken as a whole.

[*Signature of Firm*]

[*City and State*]

[*Date*]

---

‡ See footnote ‡ in paragraph 13.04.

13.23 AU section 623 paragraph .09 states that when reporting on financial statements prepared in conformity with a basis of accounting other than GAAP, the auditor should consider whether the financial statements (including the accompanying notes) include all informative disclosures that are appropriate for the basis of accounting used. Interpretation No. 14 of AU section 623 states that if OCBOA financial statements contain elements, accounts, or items for which GAAP would require disclosure, the statements should either provide the relevant disclosure that would be required for those items in a GAAP presentation or provide information that communicates the substance of that disclosure. That may result in substituting qualitative information for some of the quantitative information required for GAAP presentations. The interpretation states further that if GAAP sets forth requirements that apply to the preparation of financial statements, the OCBOA financial statements should either comply with those requirements or provide information that communicates the substance of those requirements. The substance of GAAP presentation requirements may be communicated using qualitative information and without modifying the financial statement format. If the plan administrator prepares financial statements on a modified cash basis or other basis not in conformity with GAAP, he or she might consider not disclosing or qualitatively disclosing information regarding accumulated plan benefits (such as the amount of the plan's estimated accumulated plan benefits or accumulated benefit obligations, as applicable, and the amount of accumulated benefit obligations by type, for example, claims payable, incurred but not reported, accumulated eligibility credits, and postretirement benefit obligations). Normally the plan would be unable to properly communicate the substance of these disclosures without providing the disclosures quantitatively. It may be acceptable to condense some of the quantitative disclosures (for example, to disclose the total amount currently payable to or for participants, beneficiaries, and dependents without breaking out how much relates to health claims payable versus death and disability benefits payable). If such disclosures are not made, the auditor should express a qualified or an adverse opinion on the financial statements and comment in his or her report on the lack of such disclosures.

Accumulated Plan Benefits—GAAP Departures and Changes in Accounting Estimates

13.24 As noted in paragraph 2.07, the financial statements of a defined benefit pension plan, prepared in conformity with GAAP, should include information regarding the actuarial present value of accumulated plan benefits and the effects, if significant, of certain factors affecting the year-to-year change in accumulated plan benefits. If the benefit information either is omitted or is not appropriately measured in conformity with FASB ASC 960, the auditor should express a qualified or adverse opinion (see paragraph 13.23 regarding omitted disclosures in non-GAAP-basis financial statements).

13.25 The auditor's report need not be modified as to consistency for changes in actuarial assumptions, changes that merely result in presenting new or additional accumulated plan benefits information, a change in the format of presentation of accumulated plan benefit information (for example, from a separate statement to disclosure in the notes to the financial statements) or a change from presenting the accumulated plan benefit information (of a defined benefit pension plan) as of the beginning of the year to presenting it as of the end of the year (see Interpretation No. 10, "Change in Presentation of

Accumulated Benefit Information in the Financial Statements of a Defined Benefit Pension Plan," of AU section 420, *Consistency of Application of Generally Accepted Accounting Principles* [AICPA, *Professional Standards*, AU sec. 9420 par. .64–.65]).

Limited-Scope Audits Under DOL Regulations

13.26 As discussed in paragraph 7.73, under DOL regulations the plan auditor need not examine and report on certain information prepared by banks, similar institutions, or insurance carriers that are regulated, supervised, and subject to periodic examination by a state or federal agency if that information is certified as complete and accurate by the bank or similar institution, or an insurance carrier (see paragraphs A.58–A.59). Thus the plan administrator may restrict the auditor's examination of the assets held and transactions executed by such institutions.

Note that if, however, the auditor is unable to obtain sufficient appropriate audit evidence regarding other noninvestment related information or investment information not covered by the certification then the form of limited scope report illustrated in the following paragraph may not be appropriate. Also, it likely will not be appropriate for the auditor to opine on the form and content of the supplemental schedules as presented in compliance with the DOL's Rules and Regulations for Reporting and Disclosure under the ERISA. See AU section 508 for reporting guidance.

The following is an example of the auditor's report for a defined benefit pension plan, in these circumstances when he or she believes this to be a significant limitation on the scope of the audit:[6]

Independent Auditor's Report

[*Addressee*]

We were engaged to audit the accompanying statements of net assets available for benefits of XYZ Pension Plan as of December 31, 20X2, and 20X1, and the related statement of changes in net assets available for benefits for the year ended December 31, 20X2, and the supplemental schedules of (1) Schedule H, line 4i-Schedule of Assets (Held At End of Year), and (2) Schedule H, line 4j-Schedule of Reportable Transactions as of or for the year ended December 31, 20X2. These financial statements and supplemental schedules are the responsibility of the Plan's management.

As permitted by 29 CFR 2520.103-8 of the Department of Labor's Rules and Regulations for Reporting and Disclosure under the Employee Retirement Income Security Act of 1974, the plan administrator instructed us not to perform, and we did not perform, any auditing procedures with respect to the information summarized in Note X, which was certified by ABC Bank, the trustee (or custodian) of the Plan, except for comparing such information with the related information included in the financial statements and supplemental schedules.

---

[6] This illustration assumes that information regarding accumulated plan benefits and changes therein is included in the notes to the financial statements. If the plan's financial statements are prepared on the cash basis or a modified cash basis of accounting, the auditor's report should also include a paragraph stating the basis of presentation and refers to the note in the financial statements that describes the basis and states that the basis of presentation is a comprehensive basis of accounting other than generally accepted accounting principles. Paragraph 13.22 provides an illustration of the wording of such paragraph.

We have been informed by the plan administrator that the trustee (or custodian) holds the Plan's investment assets and executes investment transactions. The plan administrator has obtained a certification from the trustee (or custodian) as of December 31, 20X2, and 20X1 and for the year ended December 31, 20X2, that the information provided to the plan administrator by the trustee (or custodian) is complete and accurate.

Because of the significance of the information that we did not audit, we are unable to, and do not, express an opinion on the accompanying financial statements and supplemental schedules taken as a whole. The form and content of the information included in the financial statements and supplemental schedules, other than that derived from the information certified by the trustee or custodian, have been audited by us in accordance with auditing standards generally accepted in the United States of America and, in our opinion, are presented in compliance with the Department of Labor's Rules and Regulations for Reporting and Disclosure under the Employee Retirement Income Security Act of 1974.

[*Signature of Firm*]

[*City and State*]

[*Date*]

13.27 As discussed in paragraph 7.73, plan investments not held by a qualified trustee or custodian that meet the limited-scope exemption criteria set forth in the DOL regulations (see paragraphs A.58–A.59 for a discussion of such criteria) should be subjected to appropriate audit procedures. Plans may hold investment assets only a portion of which are covered by a certification by a qualified trustee or custodian. In that case, the balance of the investments are not eligible for the limited-scope exemption and should be subjected to auditing procedures by the plan auditor. In these circumstances, the limited-scope audit report would be required if the plan's assets that are not audited (that is, those assets covered by the trustee or custodian's certification) are material to the plan's financial statements taken as a whole.

Limited-Scope Audit in Prior Year

13.28 An employee benefit plan administrator may elect not to limit the scope of the audit in the current year even though the scope of the audit in the prior year was limited in accordance with DOL regulations.[7] The following illustrates a report on comparative financial statements of a defined benefit pension plan under those circumstances:

Independent Auditor's Report

[*Addressee*]

We have audited the accompanying statements of net assets available for benefits of XYZ Pension Plan as of December 31, 20X2, and 20X1, and the related statement of changes in net assets available for benefits for the year ended December 31, 20X2, and the statements of accumulated plan benefits as of December 31, 20X2, and 20X1, and the related statement of changes in accumulated plan benefits for the year ended December 31, 20X2. These financial

---

[7] Present DOL regulations prescribe that the annual report include a statement of net assets available for benefits on a comparative basis; the statement of changes in net assets available for benefits is required for the current year only.

statements are the responsibility of the Plan's management. Our responsibility is to express an opinion on these financial statements based on our audits.

Except as explained in the following paragraph, we conducted our audit in accordance with auditing standards generally accepted in the United States of America. Those standards require that we plan and perform the audit to obtain reasonable assurance about whether the financial statements are free of material misstatement. An audit includes examining, on a test basis, evidence supporting the amounts and disclosures in the financial statements. An audit also includes assessing the accounting principles used and significant estimates made by management, as well as evaluating the overall financial statement presentation. We believe that our audits provide a reasonable basis for our opinion.

As permitted by 29 CFR 2520.103-8 of the Department of Labor's Rules and Regulations for Reporting and Disclosure under the Employee Retirement Income Security Act of 1974, investment assets held by ABC Bank, the trustee (or custodian) of the Plan, and transactions in those assets were excluded from the scope of our audit of the Plan's 20X1 financial statements, except for comparing the information provided by the trustee (or custodian), which is summarized in Note X, with the related information included in the financial statements.

Because of the significance of the information that we did not audit, we are unable to, and do not, express an opinion on the Plan's financial statements as of December 31, 20X1. The form and content of the information included in the 20X1 financial statements, other than that derived from the information certified by the trustee (or custodian), have been audited by us and, in our opinion, are presented in compliance with the Department of Labor's Rules and Regulations for Reporting and Disclosure under the Employee Retirement Income Security Act of 1974.

In our opinion, the financial statements, referred to above, of XYZ Pension Plan as of December 31, 20X2, and for the year then ended present fairly, in all material respects, the financial status of XYZ Pension Plan as of December 31, 20X2, and changes in its financial status for the year then ended in conformity with accounting principles generally accepted in the United States of America.

Our audit of the Plan's financial statements as of and for the year ended December 31, 20X2, was made for the purpose of forming an opinion on the financial statements taken as a whole. The supplemental schedules of [*identify title of schedules and period covered*] are presented for the purpose of additional analysis and are not a required part of the basic financial statements, but are supplementary information required by the Department of Labor's Rules and Regulations for Reporting and Disclosure under the Employee Retirement Income Security Act of 1974. These supplemental schedules are the responsibility of the Plan's management. The supplemental schedules have been subjected to the auditing procedures applied in the audit of the basic financial statements for the year ended December 31, 20X2, and, in our opinion, are fairly stated in all material respects in relation to the basic financial statements taken as a whole.

[*Signature of Firm*]

[*City and State*]

[*Date*]

Limited-Scope Audit in Current Year

13.29 A plan may exclude from the auditor's examination its assets held by banks or insurance companies in the current year, whereas the scope of the audit in the prior year was unrestricted. When comparative financial statements will be issued in those circumstances, the auditor should report on the prior year's financial statements of the plan. Although the auditor's report should ordinarily be dated no earlier than the date on which the auditor has obtained sufficient appropriate audit evidence to support the opinion for the most recent audit, the procedures performed in an audit that has been restricted, as permitted by 29 CFR 2520.103-8 of the DOL's Rules and Regulations for Reporting and Disclosure, generally are not sufficient to enable the auditor to update the report on the prior year's financial statements. Accordingly, the auditor should consider referring to the date of the previously issued report on the prior year's financial statements in expressing an opinion on that information. The following illustrates a report on comparative financial statements of a defined benefit pension plan in those circumstances:[8]

Independent Auditor's Report

[*Addressee*]

We were engaged to audit the accompanying statement of net assets available for benefits of XYZ Pension Plan as of December 31, 20X2, and the related statement of changes in net assets available for benefits for the year ended December 31, 20X2, and the supplemental schedules of (1) Schedule H, line 4i—Schedule of Assets Held (At End of Year), (2) Schedule H, line 4j—Schedule of Reportable Transactions as of or for the year ended December 31, 20X2. These financial statements and supplemental schedules are the responsibility of the Plan's management.

As permitted by 29 CFR 2520.103-8 of the Department of Labor's Rules and Regulations for Reporting and Disclosure under the Employee Retirement Income Security Act of 1974, the plan administrator instructed us not to perform, and we did not perform, any auditing procedures with respect to the information summarized in Note X, which was certified by ABC Bank, the trustee (or custodian) of the Plan, except for comparing the information with the related information included in the 20X2 financial statements and the supplemental schedules. We have been informed by the plan administrator that the trustee (or custodian) holds the Plan's investment assets and executes investment transactions. The plan administrator has obtained a certification from the trustee (or custodian) as of and for the year ended December 31, 20X2, that the information provided to the plan administrator by the trustee (or custodian) is complete and accurate.

Because of the significance of the information in the Plan's 20X2 financial statements that we did not audit, we are unable to, and do not, express an opinion on the accompanying financial statements and supplemental schedules as of or for the year ended December 31, 20X2. The form and content of the information included in the financial statements and supplemental schedules, other than that derived from the information certified by the trustee (or custodian), have been audited by us in accordance with auditing standards generally accepted

---

[8] This illustration assumes that information regarding accumulated plan benefits and changes therein is included in the notes to the financial statements.

in the United States of America and, in our opinion, are presented in compliance with the Department of Labor's Rules and Regulations for Reporting and Disclosure under the Employee Retirement Income Security Act of 1974.

We have audited the statement of net assets available for benefits of XYZ Pension Plan as of December 31, 20X1, and in our report dated May 20, 20X2, we expressed our opinion that such financial statement presents fairly, in all material respects, the financial status of XYZ Pension Plan as of December 31, 20X1, in conformity with accounting principles generally accepted in the United States of America.

[Signature of Firm]

[City and State]

[Date]

Initial Limited-Scope Audit in Current Year, Prior Year Limited-Scope Audit Performed by Other Auditors

13.30 An example of an initial limited-scope audit in the current year with the prior year limited-scope audit performed by other auditors for a profit sharing plan follows:

Report of Independent Certified Public Accountants

[Addressee]

We were engaged to audit the accompanying statement of net assets available for benefits of ABC Company Profit-Sharing Plan (the Plan) as of December 31, 20X2, and the related statement of changes in net assets available for benefits for the year ended December 31, 20X2, and the supplemental Schedule H, line 4i—Schedule of Assets (Held at End of Year) as of December 31, 20X2. These financial statements and supplemental schedule are the responsibility of the Plan's management. The financial statements of the plan as of December 31, 20X1, were audited by other auditors. As permitted by 29 CFR 2520.103-8 of the Department of Labor's Rules and Regulations for Reporting and Disclosure under the Employee Retirement Income Security Act of 1974 (ERISA), the Plan administrator instructed the other auditors not to perform and they did not perform, any auditing procedures with respect to the information certified by the Trustee. Their report, dated May 20, 20X2, indicated that (*a*) because of the significance of the information that they did not audit, they were unable to, and did not, express an opinion on the financial statements taken as a whole and (*b*) the form and content of the information included in the financial statements other than that derived from the information certified by the Trustee, were presented in compliance with the Department of Labor's Rules and Regulations for Reporting and Disclosure under ERISA.

As permitted by 29 CFR 2520.103-8 of the Department of Labor's Rules and Regulations for Reporting and Disclosure under the Employee Retirement Income Security Act of 1974, the Plan administrator instructed us not to perform, and we did not perform, any auditing procedures with respect to the information summarized in note E, which was certified by Bank & Trust Company, the trustee of the Plan, except for comparing such information with the related information included in the 20X2 financial statements and supplemental schedule. We have been informed by the Plan administrator that the trustee holds the Plan's investment assets and executes investment transactions. The Plan administrator has obtained a certification from the trustee as of and for the year ended December 31, 20X2, that the information provided to the Plan administrator by the trustee is complete and accurate.

Because of the significance of the information in the Plan's 20X2 financial statements and supplemental schedule that we did not audit, we are unable to, and do not, express an opinion on the accompanying 20X2 financial statements and supplemental schedule taken as a whole. The form and content of the information included in the 20X2 financial statements and supplemental schedule, other than that derived from the information certified by the trustee, have been audited by us in accordance with auditing standards generally accepted in the United States of America and, in our opinion, are presented in compliance with the Department of Labor's Rules and Regulations for Reporting and Disclosure under the Employee Retirement Income Security Act of 1974.

[*Signature of Firm*]

[*City and State*]

[*Date*]

Change in Trustee

13.31 An example of an auditor's report reflecting a change in trustee for a pension plan follows:

Report of Independent Certified Public Accountants

[*Addressee*]

We were engaged to audit the accompanying statements of net assets available for benefits and of accumulated plan benefits of XYZ Pension Plan as of December 31, 20X2, and 20X1, and the related statements of changes in net assets available for benefits and of changes in accumulated plan benefits for the year ended December 31, 20X2, and the supplemental schedules of (1) Schedule H, line 4i—Schedule of Assets (Held at End of Year) as of December 31, 20X2, and (2) Schedule H, line 4j—Schedule of Reportable Transactions for the year ended December 31, 20X2. These financial statements and schedules are the responsibility of the Plan's management.

As permitted by 29 CFR 2520.103-8 of the Department of Labor's Rules and Regulations for Reporting and Disclosure under the Employee Retirement Income Security Act of 1974, the plan administrator instructed us not to perform, and we did not perform, any auditing procedures with respect to the investment information summarized in Note X, which was certified by the ABC Bank and XYZ Trust Company, the trustees of the Plan, except for comparing such information with the related information included in the financial statements and supplemental schedules. We have been informed by the plan administrator that XYZ Trust Company held the Plan's investment assets and executed investment transactions from July 1, 20X2, to December 31, 20X2, and that ABC Bank held the Plan's investment assets and executed investment transactions as of December 31, 20X1, and for the period January 1, 20X1, to June 30, 20X2. The plan administrator has obtained certifications from the trustees as of and for the years ended December 31, 20X2, and 20X1, that the information provided to the plan administrator by the trustees is complete and accurate.

Because of the significance of the information that we did not audit, we are unable to, and do not, express an opinion on the accompanying financial statements and supplemental schedules taken as a whole. The form and content of the information included in the financial statements and supplemental schedules, other than that derived from the investment information certified by the trustees, have been audited by us in accordance with auditing standards generally accepted in the United States and, in our opinion, are presented in compliance with the Department of Labor's Rules and Regulations for Reporting and Disclosure under the Employee Retirement Income Security Act of 1974.

[Signature of Firm]

[City and State]

[Date]

Audit of Multiemployer Pension Plan With Scope Limitation

13.32 The following is an example of the auditor's report disclaiming an opinion on the financial statements of a multiemployer defined benefit pension plan when the auditor has been unable to apply all the procedures he or she considers necessary with regard to participants' data maintained by, and contributions from, the sponsor companies:[9]

Independent Auditor's Report

[Addressee]

We were engaged to audit the statements of [identify title of schedules and period covered] of XYZ Multiemployer Pension Plan as of December 31, 20X2, and 20X1, and for the years then ended. These financial statements are the responsibility of the Plan's management.

The Plan's records and procedures are not adequate to assure the completeness of participants' data on which contributions and benefit payments are determined, and the Board of Trustees did not engage us to perform, and we did not perform, any other auditing procedures with respect to participants' data maintained by the sponsor companies or individual participants.

Because of the significance of the information that we did not audit, the scope of our work was not sufficient to enable us to express, and we do not express, an opinion on these financial statements.

[Signature of Firm]

[City and State]

[Date]

Reporting on the Financial Statements of a Trust Established Under a Plan

13.33 Under both FASB ASC 960 and ERISA, the reporting entity is the employee benefit plan. However, the plan administrator may engage an independent auditor to report on the financial statements of a trust established under the plan. The limited scope exemption, as described in paragraph 7.73,

---

[9] Historically, the DOL has rejected Form 5500 filings that contain either qualified opinions, adverse opinions, or disclaimers of opinion other than those issued in connection with a limited scope audit pursuant to Title 29 U.S. *Code of Federal Regulations* Part 2520.103-8 or 12.

applies to employee benefit plans. If the auditor is engaged to report on the financial statements of a trust, the full scope auditing procedures would apply. In such audits, following the applicable auditing guidance contained is this guide would be appropriate. Users of the financial statements of the trust may not be aware of the distinction between the trust and the plan. Therefore, when reporting on such a trust, the auditor's report should explain that the financial statements of the trust do not purport to present the financial status or changes in financial status of the plan in accordance with GAAP and that the financial statements do not purport to satisfy the DOL reporting and disclosure requirements. The following is an example of the auditor's report on the financial statements of a trust established under an employee benefit plan:

Independent Auditor's Report

[*Addressee*]

We have audited the accompanying statement of net assets of ABC Pension Trust as of December 31, 20X2, and the related statement of changes in net assets and trust balance for the year then ended. These financial statements are the responsibility of the Trust's management. Our responsibility is to express an opinion on these financial statements based on our audit.

We conducted our audit in accordance with auditing standards generally accepted in the United States of America. Those standards require that we plan and perform the audit to obtain reasonable assurance about whether the financial statements are free of material misstatement. An audit includes examining, on a test basis, evidence supporting the amounts and disclosures in the financial statements. An audit also includes assessing the accounting principles used and significant estimates made by management, as well as evaluating the overall financial statement presentation. We believe that our audit provides a reasonable basis for our opinion.

In our opinion, the financial statements referred to above present fairly, in all material respects, the net assets of ABC Pension Trust as of December 31, 20X2, and the changes in its net assets and trust balance for the year then ended in conformity with accounting principles generally accepted in the United States of America.

The accompanying statements are those of ABC Pension Trust, which is established under XYZ Pension Plan; the statements do not purport to present the financial status of XYZ Pension Plan. The statements do not contain certain information on accumulated plan benefits and other disclosures necessary for a fair presentation of the financial status of XYZ Pension Plan in conformity with accounting principles generally accepted in the United States of America. Furthermore, these statements do not purport to satisfy the Department of Labor's Rules and Regulations for Reporting and Disclosure under the Employee Retirement Income Security Act of 1974 relating to the financial statements of employee benefit plans.

[*Signature of Firm*]

[*City and State*]

[*Date*]

Investments That Do Not Have a Readily Determinable Market Value

13.34 ERISA defines *current value* as fair market value where available and otherwise the fair value as determined in good faith by a trustee or a named fiduciary. Investments for which fair market value may not be readily determinable include such items as securities that are not readily marketable, private debt placements, and real estate investments.

13.35 A matter involving an uncertainty is one that is expected to be resolved at a future date at which time conclusive audit evidence concerning its outcome would be expected to become available. Conclusive audit evidence concerning the ultimate outcome of uncertainties cannot be expected to exist at the time of the audit because the outcome and related audit evidence are prospective. In these circumstances, management is responsible for estimating the effect of future events on the financial statements, or determining that a reasonable estimate cannot be made and making the required disclosures, all in accordance with GAAP, based on management's analysis of existing conditions. Absence of the existence of information related to the outcome of an uncertainty does not necessarily lead to a conclusion that the audit evidence supporting management's assertion is not sufficient. Rather, the auditor's judgment regarding the sufficiency of the audit evidence is based on the audit evidence that is, or should be, available.

13.36 When the financial statements include securities whose values were estimated by the plan (for example, board of trustees, plan administrator, investment committee, or other named fiduciary) in the absence of readily ascertainable market values, the auditor is responsible for evaluating the reasonableness of accounting estimates made by management in the context of the financial statements taken as a whole. The guidance in AU section 342, *Auditing Accounting Estimates* (AICPA, *Professional Standards*), and AU section 332, *Auditing Derivative Instruments, Hedging Activities, and Investments in Securities* (AICPA, *Professional Standards*), may be helpful in making that evaluation. If, after considering the existing conditions and available evidence supporting the plan's good-faith estimate of value, the valuation principles are acceptable, are being consistently applied, and are reasonably supported by the documentation, an unqualified opinion ordinarily is appropriate. In addition, the AICPA practice aid *Alternative Investments—Audit Consideration* is a source of nonauthoritative guidance that may be helpful when considering the inclusion of an emphasis of a matter paragraph in the auditor's report when the financial statements include securities whose values were estimated in good-faith.

13.37 If the auditor's review discloses that the valuation procedures followed by the plan are inadequate or unreasonable, or if the underlying documentation does not appear to support the valuation, there may be a limitation on the scope of the audit. Restrictions on the scope of the audit, whether imposed by the client or by circumstances, such as the inability to obtain sufficient competent audit evidence, may require the auditor to qualify his or her opinion or to disclaim an opinion. Such an opinion would be appropriate if sufficient audit evidence related to an uncertainty does or did exist but was not available to the auditor for reasons such as management's record retention policies or restrictions imposed by management.

13.38 Scope limitations related to uncertainties differ from situations in which the auditor concludes that the financial statements are materially misstated due to a departure from GAAP due to an uncertainty. Such departures may be caused by inadequate disclosure concerning the uncertainty, the use of inappropriate accounting principles, or the use of unreasonable accounting estimates. The auditor should issue a qualified or an adverse opinion because of a departure from GAAP. The following illustration provides an example of an auditor's report on a defined benefit pension plan qualified for a departure from U.S. GAAP because of inadequate procedures to value investments. The illustration assumes that the auditor cannot reasonably determine the effects of the departure.

Independent Auditor's Report

[*Addressee*]

We have audited the accompanying statements of net assets available for benefits of XYZ Pension Plan as of December 31, 20X2, and 20X1, and of accumulated Plan benefits as of December 31, 20X2, and the related statements of changes in net assets available for benefits and of changes in accumulated plan benefits for the year ended December 31, 20X2. These financial statements are the responsibility of the Plan's management. Our responsibility is to express an opinion on these financial statements based on our audits.

We conducted our audits in accordance with auditing standards generally accepted in the United States of America. Those standards require that we plan and perform the audit to obtain reasonable assurance about whether the financial statements are free of material misstatement. [*Optional: An audit includes consideration of internal control over financial reporting as a basis for designing audit procedures that are appropriate in the circumstances, but not for the purpose of expressing an opinion on the effectiveness of the Plan's internal control over financial reporting. Accordingly, we express no such opinion.*][‡] An audit includes examining, on a test basis, evidence supporting the amounts and disclosures in the financial statements. An audit also includes assessing the accounting principles used and significant estimates made by management, as well as evaluating the overall financial statement presentation. We believe that our audits provide a reasonable basis for our opinion.

As discussed in Note X, investments amounting to $____ (__percent of net assets available for benefits) as of December 31, 20X2, have been valued at estimated fair value as determined by the Board of Trustees. We have reviewed the procedures applied by the trustees in valuing the securities and have inspected the underlying documentation. In our opinion, those procedures are not adequate to determine the fair value of the investments in conformity with accounting principles generally accepted in the United States of America. The effect on the financial statements and supplemental schedules of not applying adequate procedures to determine the fair value of the securities is not determinable.

In our opinion, except for the effects of the procedures used by the Board of Trustees to determine the valuation of investments as described in the preceding paragraph, the financial statements referred to above present fairly, in all material respects, the financial status of XYZ Pension Plan as of December 31,

---

‡ See footnote ‡ in paragraph 13.04.

20X2, and information regarding the Plan's net assets available for benefits as of December 31, 20X1, and the changes in its financial status for the year ended December 31, 20X2, in conformity with accounting principles generally accepted in the United States of America.

Our audits were performed for the purpose of forming an opinion on the financial statements taken as a whole. The supplemental schedules of [*identify title of schedules and period covered*] are presented for the purpose of additional analysis and are not a required part of the basic financial statements, but are supplementary information required by the Department of Labor's Rules and Regulations for Reporting and Disclosure under the Employee Retirement Income Security Act of 1974. These supplemental schedules are the responsibility of the Plan's management. That additional information has been subjected to the auditing procedures applied in the audit of the basic financial statements for the year ended December 31, 20X2; and in our opinion, except for the effects of the valuation of investments, as described above, the additional information is fairly stated in all material respects in relation to the basic financial statements taken as a whole.

_____

[*Signature of Firm*]

[*City and State*]

[*Date*]

Reference to the Work of Other Auditors

13.39 Throughout this guide, circumstances are discussed in which the plan auditor may use the work of another auditor regarding plan investments. For example, the plan auditor may use the report of the independent auditor of the financial statements of a common or commingled trust fund or a separate account to obtain assurance regarding significant amounts of the plan's assets, and the auditor may use a service auditor's report on the processing of transactions by a service organization (see AU section 324, *Service Organizations* [AICPA, *Professional Standards*]) in considering the plan's internal control. Although the amount of the plan's assets covered by the other auditor's report or relating to internal control covered by the service auditor's report may be material in relation to the net assets of the plan, the plan auditor ordinarily would be the principal auditor. The work of the other auditor is used by the plan auditor in obtaining an understanding of internal control relating to plan investments. Because the plan auditor performs procedures with respect to investments, contributions, benefit payments, plan obligations, participants' data, and other elements of the financial statements, the plan auditor is ordinarily the only auditor in a position to express an opinion on the plan's financial statements taken as a whole. The plan auditor may use reports by other auditors in the audit of the plan's financial statements, but the other auditors are not responsible for examining a portion of the plan's financial statements as of any specific date or for any specific period. Thus, there cannot be a meaningful indication of a division of responsibility for the plan's financial statements. If the auditor decides to assume responsibility for the work of the other auditor insofar as that work relates to the principal auditor's expression of an opinion on the financial statements taken as a whole, no reference should be made to the other auditor's work or report.

Reporting Separate Investment Fund Information

13.40 Article 6A of Regulation S-X addresses reporting requirements for profit sharing, stock bonus, thrift or savings, and similar plans, that are required to file reports with the Securities and Exchange Commission (SEC). Those rules allow a plan providing for investment programs with separate funds to present the required information either in columnar form in the financial statements, or by separate financial statements for each fund, or in schedules. The SEC amended its rules for Form 11-K to permit plans subject to ERISA to file financial statements in accordance with ERISA rather than in accordance with Regulation S-X. Accordingly, adherence to the requirements of paragraph 3.50*i* and other pertinent GAAP and ERISA requirements described in this guide may satisfy the SEC rules.

Terminating Plans

13.41 The accounting and reporting by a defined benefit pension plan for which a decision to terminate has been made are described in FASB ASC 960-40 (see also paragraphs 2.64–.68).[10] The auditor may express an unqualified opinion on financial statements prepared on the liquidation basis of accounting, provided the basis has been properly applied and that adequate disclosures are made in the financial statements. The auditor's report may be modified by the addition of an explanatory paragraph that states that the plan is being terminated and that the financial statements (including the benefit information disclosures presented) have been prepared on a liquidation basis. If the financial statements are presented along with financial statements of a period prior to adoption of a liquidation basis that were prepared on the basis of GAAP for ongoing plans, the explanatory paragraph should state that the plan has changed the basis of accounting used to determine the amounts at which assets, liabilities, and benefit information are presented from the ongoing plan basis to a liquidation basis. The following is an illustration of the explanatory paragraph when the auditor wants to emphasize that a defined benefit pension plan is being terminated:

> As further discussed in Notes A and B to the financial statements, the Board of Directors of the XYZ Company, the Plan's sponsor, voted on November 9, 20X2 to terminate the Plan. In accordance with accounting principles generally accepted in the United States of America, the Plan has changed its basis of accounting used to determine the amounts at which investments in insurance contracts and the accumulated benefit information are stated, from the ongoing plan basis used in presenting the 20X1 financial statements to the liquidation basis used in presenting the 20X2 financial statements.

The following is an illustration of the explanatory paragraph when the auditor wants to emphasize that a defined contribution plan is being terminated:

> As further discussed in Notes A and B to the financial statements, the Board of Directors of the XYZ Company, the Plan's sponsor, voted on November 9, 20X2 to terminate the Plan. In accordance with accounting principles generally accepted in the United States of America, the

---

[10] FASB ASC 962-40 contains the accounting and reporting guidance for defined contribution plans that are terminating (see also paragraphs 3.62–.65). FASB ASC 965-40 contains the accounting and reporting guidance for health and welfare plans that are terminating (see also paragraphs 4.98–.102).

Plan has changed its basis of accounting from the ongoing plan basis used in presenting the 20X1 financial statements to the liquidation basis used in presenting the 20X2 financial statements.

13.42 During the audit of a nonterminated employee benefit plan, the auditor may become aware that the plan sponsor may not be able to continue as a going concern. Although employee benefit plans are not automatically and necessarily affected by the plan sponsor's financial adversities, this situation may result in the auditor determining it to be a condition or event sufficient to evaluate whether there is substantial doubt about the plan's ability to continue as a going concern. AU section 341, *The Auditor's Consideration of an Entity's Ability to Continue as a Going Concern* (AICPA, *Professional Standards*), precludes the auditor from using conditional language in expressing a conclusion concerning the existence of substantial doubt about the plan's ability to continue as a going-concern in a going-concern explanatory paragraph.

Initial Audits of Plans

13.43 For initial audits of plans where the plan had assets in the prior year, ERISA requires presenting a comparative statement of net assets available for plan benefits. Comparative statements are not required under U.S. GAAP. Generally, sufficient auditing procedures can be performed on the prior year's balances if the records are complete (paragraph 5.90) so that the auditor can express an unqualified opinion or a limited-scope opinion on the prior year's statement of net assets available for plan benefits. If, however, the auditor is unable to obtain sufficient appropriate audit evidence, there may be a limitation on the scope of the audit. Restrictions on the scope of the audit, whether imposed by the client or by circumstances, such as the inability to obtain sufficient appropriate audit evidence, may require the auditor to qualify his or her opinion or to disclaim an opinion (see AU section 508 paragraphs .22–.26).

13.44 Guidance on the reporting on audited and unaudited financial statements in comparative form is contained in AU section 504, *Association With Financial Statements* (AICPA, *Professional Standards*), and AR section 200, *Reporting on Comparative Financial Statements* (AICPA, *Professional Standards*). When the financial statements of the prior period have not been audited (but a statement of net assets is included for comparative purposes in compliance with the regulations), the report on the current period is to contain a separate paragraph. This paragraph should include (*a*) a statement of the service performed in the prior period, (*b*) the date of the report on that service, (*c*) a description of any material modifications noted in that report, and (*d*) a statement that the service was less in scope than an audit and does not provide the basis for the expression of an opinion on the financial statements taken as a whole (see paragraph .17 of AU section 504).

13.45 The following is an example of the last two paragraphs of the auditor's report for the initial audit of a defined contribution plan when the prior period statement of net assets is compiled. (See paragraphs 5.89–.90 in this guide for a discussion of initial audits of plans.)

> We have compiled the accompanying statement of net assets available for benefits of ABC Company Plan as of December 31, 20X1, in accordance with Statements on Standards for Accounting and Review Services issued by the American Institute of Certified Public Accountants.

A compilation is limited to presenting in the form of financial statements information that is the representation of management. We have not audited or reviewed the accompanying statement of net assets available for benefits and, accordingly, do not express an opinion or any other form of assurance on it.

13.46 If the plan was audited in the prior year by another auditor and the current year auditor is presenting comparative financial statements, the current year auditor should indicate in the introductory paragraph (a) that the financial statements of the prior period were audited by another auditor, (b) the date of his or her report, (c) the type of report issued by the predecessor auditor, and (d) if the report was other than a standard report, the substantive reasons therefore. For example, the following sentence may be added to the first paragraph of the report: "The financial statements of the Plan as of and for the year ended December 31, 20X1, were audited by other auditors whose report dated July 31, 20X2, expressed an unqualified opinion on those financial statements."

Appendix A

ERISA and Related Regulations

Introduction

A.01 The following description, prepared with the assistance of the Employee Benefits Security Administration (EBSA), U.S. Department of Labor (DOL), is intended to enable the auditor to familiarize himself or herself with the important provisions of the Employee Retirement Income Security Act of 1974 (ERISA). This is a summary and is not intended to serve as a substitute for the entire Act, the related regulations, or for the advice of legal counsel. Changes in the statute and related regulations subsequent to publication of this guide also should be considered.

A.02 The primary purpose of ERISA is to protect the interests of workers who participate in employee benefit plans and their beneficiaries. ERISA seeks to attain that objective by requiring financial reporting to government agencies and disclosure to participants and beneficiaries, by establishing standards of conduct for plan fiduciaries, and by providing appropriate remedies, sanctions, and access to the federal courts. Another objective of ERISA is to improve the soundness of employee pension benefit plans[1] by requiring plans (*a*) to vest the accrued benefits of employees with significant periods of service, (*b*) to meet minimum standards of funding, and (*c*) with respect to defined benefit pension plans, to subscribe to plan termination insurance through the Pension Benefit Guaranty Corporation (PBGC).

A.03 ERISA replaced the Welfare and Pension Plans Disclosure Act of 1958, amended certain sections of the Internal Revenue Code (IRC), and generally preempted state laws that related to employee benefit plans.

Coverage Under Title I

A.04 Title I of ERISA generally applies to employee benefit plans established or maintained by employers engaged in interstate commerce or in any industry or activity affecting interstate commerce or by employee organizations representing employees engaged in such activities, or by both employer and employee organizations.[2] Most aspects of ERISA do not apply to

- *a.* governmental plans, including those of state and local governments.
- *b.* church plans unless the plan has made a voluntary election under IRC Section 410(d).
- *c.* plans established and maintained solely for the purpose of complying with applicable workers' compensation, unemployment compensation, or disability insurance laws.

---

[1] Pension plans are broadly defined in the Employee Retirement Income Security Act of 1974 (ERISA) to include all defined benefit and defined contribution plans, including profit-sharing, stock bonus, and employee stock ownership plans.

[2] No correlation exists between coverage under Title I of ERISA and qualification under the Internal Revenue Code (IRC).

    d. plans maintained outside the United States primarily for nonresident aliens.[3]

    e. unfunded excess benefit plans (ERISA Section 3[36]).

Participant Standards for Pension Plans (ERISA Section 202)[4]

A.05 ERISA generally provides that a pension plan cannot exclude an employee from participation because of age or service if he or she has completed 1 year of service and is at least 21 years old. However, a pension plan may defer participation until attainment of age 21 and 2 years of service, provided that benefits vest 100 percent thereafter. In addition, ERISA provides that an individual may not be denied the right to participate in a plan on the basis of having attained a specific age.

Vesting Standards for Pension Plans (ERISA Section 203)

A.06 Pension plan participants' rights to accrued benefits from their own contributions are nonforfeitable. In addition, generally, defined benefit plans are required to provide that the employees' rights to accrued benefits from employer contributions vest in a manner that equals or exceeds either of 2 alternative schedules: (*a*) graded vesting of accrued benefits, with at least 20 percent vesting after 3 years of service, at least 20 percent each year thereafter for 4 years, so that the employee's accrued benefit would be 100 percent vested after 7 years; or (*b*) 100 percent vesting of accrued benefits after 5 years of service, with no vesting required before the end of the 5 year period. Defined contribution (individual account) plans are required to provide that the employees' rights to accrued benefits from employer contributions vest in a manner that equals or exceeds either of 2 faster alternative schedules: (*a*) graded vesting of accrued benefits, with at least 20 percent vesting after 2 years of service, at least 20 percent each year thereafter for 3 years, so that the employee's accrued benefit would be 100 percent vested after 6 years; or (*b*) 100 percent vesting of accrued benefits after 3 years of service, with no vesting required before the end of the 3-year period.

A.07 Tax-qualified plans require more stringent vesting if a termination, partial termination, or discontinuance of contribution to the plan is initiated, or if the plan is top-heavy (IRC Sections 411[d] and 416).

A.08 For computation of years of service as they relate to an employee's vesting rights, a year of service is defined in ERISA as a 12-month period during which the participant has completed at least 1,000 hours of service (ERISA Section 203[b][2]). Regulations that refine that definition are complex. In addition, complex rules apply that define breaks in service.

A.09 Sufficient records must be maintained to determine an employee's benefits. ERISA Section 105 sets forth the requirements applicable to the furnishing of pension benefit statements to plan participants and beneficiaries.

---

[3] The phrase *plans maintained outside the United States* does not include a plan that covers residents of Puerto Rico, the U.S. Virgin Islands, Guam, Wake Island, or America Samoa.

[4] Reorganization Plan No. 4 of 1978 (Title 43 U.S. *Code of Federal Regulations* (CFR) Part 47713, October 17, 1978) generally transferred from the Secretary of Labor to the Secretary of the Treasury regulatory and interpretative authority for Parts 2 and 3 of Title I of ERISA.

Plan administrators of both individual account plans and defined benefit plans are required to automatically furnish pension benefit statements, at least once each quarter, in the case of individual account plans that permit participants to direct their investments; at least once each year, in the case of individual account plans that do not permit participants to direct their investments; and at least once every three years in the case of defined benefit plans. ERISA Section 209 also requires the maintenance of records by employers relating to individual benefit reporting. ERISA Section 107 provides general record retention requirements for employee benefit plans.

Minimum Funding Standards for Pension Plans (ERISA Sections 301–305)

A.10 ERISA requires that pension plans subject to the minimum funding standards maintain an account called the *funding standard account* (FSA). This account is a memorandum account, and it is not included in the plan's financial statements. Defined benefit pension plans are required to maintain an FSA. Certain defined contribution plans (that is, money-purchase and target-benefit plans) must maintain FSAs, but on a more limited basis. The FSA is used to determine compliance with minimum funding standards set forth in ERISA.

A.11 For most defined benefit pension plans, the sponsor's annual contribution to the plan must be sufficient to cover the normal cost for the period, and the amount to amortize initial unfunded past service liability, and increases or decreases in unfunded past service liability resulting from plan amendments, experience gains or losses, and actuarial gains or losses from changes in actuarial assumptions.

A.12 An accumulated funding deficiency is the excess of total charges (required contributions) to the FSA for all plan years (beginning with the first plan year when the funding standards are applicable) over total credits (actual contributions) to the account for those years. Accumulated funding deficiencies, in the absence of a funding waiver issued by the IRS, may result in an excise tax payable by the plan sponsor for failure to meet the minimum funding standards and in possible action by the IRS to enforce the standards. If a deficiency in the FSA exists at the end of the plan year, the auditor should consider whether a receivable from the employer company (and, possibly, a related reserve for uncollectible amounts) should be reflected in the plan's financial statements (see chapter 8, "Auditing Contributions Received and Related Receivables," for a discussion of contributions receivable).

A.13 The IRS may waive all or part of the minimum funding requirements for a plan year in which the minimum funding standard cannot be met without imposing substantial business hardship on the employer. That waiver is issued, however, only if failure to do so would be adverse to the participants' interests. The IRS determines whether a substantial hardship would occur on the basis of various factors, certain of which are stated in ERISA Section 303. This does not change the plan's possible need to record a contribution receivable.

A.14 ERISA Section 305 provides rules for multiemployer plans determined to be in endangered status or critical status. The actuary of a multiemployer defined benefit plan should certify to the Department of Treasury and the plan sponsor whether or not the plan is in endangered status and whether or not the plan is in or will be in critical status, no later than the 90th day of each plan year. In addition, the actuary should certify whether or not the plan is making the scheduled progress in meeting the requirements of the funding improvement plan or rehabilitation plan. Within 30 days of being certified in critical, seriously endangered or endangered status, the plan sponsor should notify in writing the participants and beneficiaries, the bargaining parties, the PBGC and the Department of Labor. Not later than 240 days following the required date for the actuarial certification of endangered status, the plan sponsor should adopt a funding improvement plan if the plan is in endangered or seriously endangered status or a rehabilitation plan if in critical status.

Trust Requirements (ERISA Section 403)

A.15 Generally, tax laws require that qualified pension, profit-sharing, and stock bonus plans be funded through a trust. The IRC does not contain any such requirement for welfare benefit plans or fringe benefit plans. ERISA Section 403 generally requires, however, that the assets of all employee benefit plans, including welfare plans, be held in trust. There are exceptions for certain insurance contracts and 403(b) custodial accounts. Participant contributions, including salary reduction amounts, are considered to be employee contributions under ERISA and generally do constitute *plan assets*. An employer is required to segregate employee contributions from its general assets as soon as practicable, but in no event more than (*a*) ninety days after the contributions are paid by employees or withheld from their wages for a welfare benefit plan or (*b*) the 15th business day following the end of the month in which amounts are contributed by employees or withheld from their wages for a pension benefit plan [ref. DOL Reg. 2510.3-102]. The DOL has announced that it will not presently enforce the trust requirement for cafeteria plans under IRC Section 125 to which employees make contributions. This policy also temporarily relieves these contributory welfare plans from compliance with the trust requirements of ERISA with respect to participant contributions used to pay insurance premiums in accordance with the department's reporting regulations.[5]

Voluntary Employee Benefit Associations

A.16 A Voluntary Employee Benefit Association (VEBA) is a welfare trust under IRC Section 501(c)(9). Generally, plans funded by a Section 501(c)(9) trust must be audited if they have 100 or more participants at the beginning of the plan year (see paragraph A.26).

Reporting and Disclosure for Pension and Welfare Plans (ERISA Sections 101–111 and 1032–1034)

A.17 ERISA generally requires that the administrator of an employee benefit plan prepare and file various documents with the DOL, the IRS, and the PBGC. Under Title I of ERISA, the plan administrator is required to furnish to the DOL, upon request, any documents relating to the employee benefit plan, including but not limited to, the latest summary plan description (including any summaries of plan changes not contained in the summary plan description), and the bargaining agreement, trust agreement, contract, or other instrument under which the plan is established or operated (ERISA Section 104[a][6]). In addition, most plans are required to file an annual report that also satisfies the

---

[5] See 29 CFR 2520.104-20(b)(2)(ii) or (iii) and 29 CFR 2520.104-44(b)(1)(ii) or (iii), as applicable.

annual reporting requirements of Titles I and IV of ERISA (Sections 104[a][1][A], 1031 and 4065) and the IRC. Title I of ERISA also requires that the plan administrator furnish certain information relative to the employee benefit plan to each participant and beneficiary receiving benefits under the plan. These disclosures include summary plan descriptions, including summaries of changes and updates to the summary plan description (Section 104[b][1]), summary annual reports (Section 104[b][3]) (except for defined benefit plans to which ERISA Section 101[f] applies), defined benefit plan funding notices (Section 101[f]), and, in the case of most pension plans, individual benefit reports describing the participant's accrued and vested benefits under the plan (Sections 105 and 209).

Annual Report

A.18 The report of most significance to the auditor is the annual report. The annual report required to be filed for employee benefit plans generally is the Form 5500. The Form 5500 is a joint-agency form developed by the IRS, DOL, and PBGC, that may be used to satisfy the annual reporting requirements of the IRC and Titles I and IV of ERISA. For purposes of Title I of ERISA only, a plan administrator may, in lieu of filing the Form 5500, elect to file the information required by ERISA Section 103. However, almost all plan administrators use the Form 5500. Use of the Form 5500 is required for filings under the IRC and Title IV of ERISA.

Who Must File

A.19 An administrator of an employee benefit plan subject to ERISA, and not otherwise exempt, must file an annual report for each such plan every year. The IRS, DOL, and PBGC have consolidated their requirements into the Form 5500 to minimize the filing burden for plan administrators and employers. Likewise, direct filing entities (DFE), described as follows, are also required to use the Form 5500 when reporting to the DOL. In general, the Form 5500 reporting requirements vary depending on whether the Form 5500 is being filed for a *large plan*, a *small plan*, or a DFE, and on the particular type of plan or DFE involved. Plans with 100 or more participants as of the beginning of the plan year must complete the Form 5500 following the requirements for a *large plan*. Plans with fewer than 100 participants should follow the requirements for a *small plan*. (There are 3 approaches to small plan filings. The first is Form 5500 with all attachments but replacing Schedule H with Schedule I. The second is Form 5500-SF which is limited to small plans whose investments are limited to those with a readily determinable market value and do not include any employer securities. The final choice is Form 5500-EZ which is generally limited to plans covering owners only.) DOL regulations permit plans that have between 80 and 120 participants (inclusive) at the beginning of the plan year to complete the Form 5500 in the same category (*large plan* or *small plan*) as was filed for the previous year. This privilege is limited to small plans that filed Form 5500 with Schedule I and not filers of the other two forms. The Form 5500 and Form 5500-SF is filed with the EBSA in accordance with the instructions to the form.

Participants

A.20 ERISA Section 3(7) defines a participant as any employee or former employee of an employer, or any member or former member of an employee organization, who is or may become eligible to receive a benefit of any type from an employee benefit plan that covers employees of such employer or members of such organization, or whose beneficiaries may be eligible to receive any such benefit.

A.21 For IRC Section 401(k) qualified cash or deferred arrangement, a *participant* means any individual who is eligible to participate in the plan whether or not the individual elects to contribute or has an account under the plan [ref: DOL Regulation Title 29 U.S. *Code of Federal Regulations* (CFR) Part 2510.3-3(d) and the Form 5500 Instructions]. For welfare plans, however, an individual becomes a participant on the earlier of: the date designated by the plan as the date on which the individual begins participation in the plan; the date on which the individual becomes eligible under the plan for a benefit subject only to occurrence of the contingency for which the benefit is provided; or the date on which the individual makes a contribution to the plan, whether voluntary or mandatory [ref: DOL Reg. 29 CFR 2510.2-3(d) and the Form 5500 Instructions].

Stop-Loss Coverage

A.22 Many self-funded plans carry stop-loss coverage to limit either the plan's or employer's loss exposure. Stop-loss coverage is a contract with an insurer that provides that the insurer will pay claims in excess of a specified amount. The coverage may be aggregate (that is, the insurer will pay if total claims exceed the specified amount) or specific (that is, the insurer will pay if an individual claim exceeds the specified amount).

Plans Required to File the Annual Report and Audited Financial Statements

A.23 Generally, plans subject to Part 1 of Title I of ERISA require an audit. Certain plans are not covered by ERISA and accordingly are not subject to the federal audit requirement (see paragraph A.04). In addition, it should be noted that the plan administrator's obligation to retain an accountant to audit the plan continues to remain in effect even when the plan loses its tax-qualified status.

Who Must Engage an Independent Qualified Public Accountant

A.24 Employee benefit plans filing the Form 5500 as a *large plan* (for example, plans with 100 or more participants as of the beginning of the plan year), are generally required to engage an independent qualified public accountant (IQPA) pursuant to ERISA Section 103(a)(3)(A). In counting participants for these purposes, an individual usually becomes a participant under a welfare plan when he or she becomes eligible for a benefit, and under a pension plan when he or she has satisfied the plan's age and service requirements for participation (see paragraph 5.11 and instructions to the Form 5500 Annual Return/Report). An IQPA's opinion, accompanying financial statements and notes, must also be attached to a Form 5500 for a *large plan* unless (*a*) the plan is an employee welfare benefit plan that is unfunded, fully insured, or a combination of unfunded and insured as described in 29 CFR 2520.104-44(b)(1);[6] (b) the plan is an employee pension benefit plan whose sole asset(s) consist of insurance contracts that provide that, upon receipt of the premium payment, the insurance carrier fully guarantees the amount of benefit payments as specified in 29 CFR 2520.104-44(b)(2) and the Form 5500 instructions;[7] or (c) the plan has elected to defer attaching the accountant's opinion for the first of two plan years, one of which is a short plan year of seven months or less as allowed by 29 CFR 2520.104-50[8] (see paragraphs A.62–A.68, 29 CFR 2520.104-50, and the instructions to the Form 5500).

Pension benefit plans filing the Form 5500 as a small plan (for example, those with fewer than 100 participants as of the beginning of the plan year), are exempt from the audit requirement to the extent that at least 95 percent of their assets are *qualifying plan assets*. Plans not satisfying this test may still avoid the audit requirement if the total amount of nonqualifying plan assets are covered by an ERISA Section 412 fidelity bond. Small pension plans seeking to avoid the audit requirement must also make certain required disclosures to plan participants.

Pension Benefit Plans

A.25 An annual report is generally required to be filed even if (a) the plan is not qualified, (b) participants no longer accrue benefits, and (c) contributions were not made for the plan year. The following are among the pension benefit plans for which a Form 5500 Annual Return or Report must be filed:

- Annuity arrangements under IRC Section 403(b)(1)
- Custodial accounts established under IRC Section 403(b)(7) for regulated investment company stock
- Individual retirement accounts established by an employer under IRC Section 408(c)
- Pension benefit plans maintained outside the United States primarily for nonresident aliens if the employer who maintains the plan is a domestic employer, or a foreign employer with income derived from sources within the United States (including foreign subsidiaries of domestic employers) and deducts contributions to the plan on its U.S. income tax return
- Church pension plans electing coverage under IRC Section 410(d)

Pension benefit plans generally provide retirement income and include

- defined benefit plans; and
- defined contribution plans, including profit-sharing plans, money-purchase pension plans, stock-bonus and employee stock-ownership plans, and 401(k), 403(b), and other thrift or savings plans.

---

[6] Single employer welfare plans using an IRC Section 501(c)(9) trust are generally not exempt from the requirement of engaging an independent qualified public accountant. See paragraph A.35 for an explanation of the welfare plans considered to be unfunded, fully insured, or a combination of unfunded and insured.

[7] See paragraph A.69n.

[8] 29 CFR 2520.104-50 permits the administrator of an employee benefit plan to defer the audit requirement for the first of two consecutive plan years, one of which is a short plan year of seven or fewer months' duration, and to file an audited statement for that plan year when the annual report is filed for the immediately following plan year, subject to certain conditions.

General Filing Requirements:

- Plans with 100 or more participants at the beginning of the plan year must file the Form 5500, Form 5500-SF or Form 5500-EZ following the requirements for *large plans.*
- Plans with fewer than 100 participants at the beginning of the plan year must file the Form 5500 following the requirements for *small plans.*

Exception:

Pursuant to DOL Regulation 29 CFR 2520.103-1(d), plans that have between 80 and 120 participants (inclusive) at the beginning of the plan year may complete the Form 5500 in the same category (*large plan* or *small plan*) as was filed for the previous year. Plans that file the Form 5500 as a *small plan* pursuant to the 80/120 rule will not be required to have an audit of their financial statements provided they meet the requirements of DOL Reg. 29 CFR 2520.104.46, as amended (see paragraph A.24). To take advantage if this exception, the plan must have filed using Form 5500 and not Form 5500-SF or 5500-EZ.

General Audit Requirements:

- Plans with 100 or more participants at the beginning of the plan year that file the Form 5500 as a *large plan* are required to have an annual audit of their financial statements.
- Plans with fewer than 100 participants at the beginning of the plan year that file the Form 5500 as a *small plan* may be exempt from the audit requirement provided they meet the requirements of DOL Reg. 29 CFR 2520.104.46, as amended (see paragraph A.24). Plans may only file using Form 5500-SF if they meet the conditions to be exempt from audit.

General Exemptions From Filing and Audit Requirements:

- Plans that are unfunded or fully insured and provide benefits only to a select group of management or highly compensated employees. *Note:* A one-time DOL notification is required for these "top hat" plans [ref: DOL Reg. 29 CFR 2520.104-23].

General Exemptions From Audit Requirement Only:

Plans, irrespective of the number of participants at the beginning of the plan year, that

- provide benefits exclusively through allocated insurance contracts. A contract is considered to be allocated only if the insurance company or organization that issued the contract unconditionally guarantees, upon receipt of the required premium or consideration, to provide a retirement benefit of a specified amount, without adjustment for fluctuations in the market value of the underlying assets of the company or organization, to each participant, and each participant has a legal right to such benefits that is legally enforceable directly against the insurance company or organization;
- are funded solely by premiums paid directly from the general assets of the employer or the employee organization maintaining the plan, or partly from such general assets and partly from contributions from employees;

- forward any participant contributions within three months of receipt; and

- provide for the return of refunds to contributing participants within three months of receipt by the employer or employee organization [ref: DOL Reg. 29 CFR 2520.104-44(b)(2)].

Welfare Benefit Plans

A.26 These plans are described in Section 3(1) of Title I of ERISA. An employee welfare benefit plan includes any plan, fund, or program that provides, through the purchase of insurance or otherwise, medical, surgical, hospital, sickness, accident, disability, severance, vacation, prepaid legal services, apprenticeship, and training benefits for employees.[9]

General Filing Requirements:

- Plans with 100 or more participants at the beginning of the plan year must file the Form 5500 as a *large plan*.

- Plans with fewer than 100 participants at the beginning of the plan year must file the Form 5500 as a *small plan*, as previously described.

Exception:

Pursuant to DOL Reg. 29 CFR 2520.103-1(d), a plan that covers between 80 and 120 participants at the beginning of the plan year may elect to complete the Form 5500 in the same category (*large plan* or *small plan*) as was filed for the previous year. Plans that file the Form 5500 as a *small plan* pursuant to the 80/120 rule are not required to have an audit of their financial statements [ref: DOL Reg. 29 CFR 2520.104-46]. Eligibility for this rule is limited to plans that file a Form 5500, not a Form 5500-SF.

General Audit Requirements:

- Plans with 100 or more participants at the beginning of the plan year that file the Form 5500 as a *large plan* are required to have an annual audit of their financial statements.

- Plans with fewer than 100 participants at the beginning of the plan year that file the Form as a *small plan* are exempt from the audit requirement.

General Exemptions From Filing and Audit Requirements:

- Plans that are unfunded or fully insured and provide benefits only to a select group of management or highly compensated employees. *Note*: The Department of Labor can require that certain information be provided upon request [ref: DOL Reg. 29 CFR 2520.104-24].

- Plans that have fewer than 100 participants at the beginning of the plan year, and

  — (1) pay benefits solely from the general assets of the employer or employee organization maintaining the plan, or (2) provide benefits exclusively through insurance contracts or policies issued by a qualified insurance company

---

[9] In certain cases, a severance plan will be considered a pension plan. See DOL Reg. 29 CFR 2510.3-2(b).

        or through a qualified HMO, the premiums of which are paid directly out of the general assets of the employer or employee organization, or partly from general assets and partly from employee or member contributions, or (3) partly as in (1) and partly as in (2); *AND*

— forward any employee contributions to the insurance company within three months of receipt; *AND*

— pay any employee refunds to employees within three months of receipt [ref: DOL Reg. 29 CFR 2520.104-20].

General Exemption From Audit Requirement Only:

Plans, irrespective of the number of participants at the beginning of the plan year, that

- (1) pay benefits solely from the general assets of the employer or employee organization maintaining the plan, or (2) provide benefits exclusively through insurance contracts or policies issued by a qualified insurance company or through a qualified HMO, the premiums of which are paid directly out of the general assets of the employer or employee organization, or partly from general assets and partly from employee or member contributions, or (3) provide benefits partly from the general assets of the employer or employee organization and partly through insurance (for example, a stop-loss insurance policy purchased or owned by the plan); *AND*

- forward any employee contributions to the insurance company within three months of receipt; *AND*

- pay any employee refunds to employees within three months of receipt [ref: DOL Reg. 29 CFR 2520.104-44(b)(1)].

Plans Covered by IRC Section 6058

A.27 Most retirement and savings plans (for example, pension, profit-sharing, or stock bonus plans) are required to file a Form 5500 series return under IRC Section 6058 as well as ERISA. According to Announcement 82-146, however, church plans that have not made a Section 410(d) election and governmental plans are not required to file a return.

Cafeteria Arrangements (IRC Section 125 Plans)

A.28 In Notice No. 2002-24, the IRS eliminated the filing requirement for cafeteria plans maintained pursuant to Section 125. It is important to note, however, that this notice does not affect the annual reporting requirements of employee benefit plans under Title I of ERISA. This means that cafeteria plans that incorporate welfare benefits are no longer required to complete a Schedule F, but may still be required to file a Form 5500 to report on the plan's welfare benefits covered by Title I of ERISA (see paragraph A.26).

PWBA Technical Release 92-1

A.29 In June 1992, the Pension and Welfare Benefits Administration (PWBA [now known as the EBSA]) issued Technical Release 92-1 announcing the DOL's enforcement policy with respect to welfare benefit plans with participant contributions. Cafeteria plans described in Section 125 of the IRC may not be required to have an audit if the participant contributions used to pay benefits have not been held in trust. An audit may also not be required for other contributory welfare benefit plans where participant contributions are applied to the payment of premiums and such contributions have not been held in trust. The enforcement policy stated in ERISA Technical Release 92-1 will continue to apply until the adoption of final regulations addressing the application of the trust and reporting requirements of Title I of ERISA to welfare plans that receive participant contributions. See exhibit 5-3, "Welfare Benefit Plans Audit: Decision Flowchart," for further guidance.

Plans Excluded From Filing

A.30 Plans maintained only to comply with workers' compensation, unemployment compensation, or disability insurance laws are excluded from filing.

A.31 An unfunded excess benefit plan (Section 3[36]) is excluded from filing.

A.32 A welfare benefit plan maintained outside the United States primarily for persons substantially all of whom are nonresident aliens (see footnote 3) is excluded from filing.

A.33 A pension benefit plan maintained outside the United States is excluded from filing if it is a qualified foreign plan within the meaning of IRC Section 404A(e) that does not qualify for the treatment provided in IRC Section 402(c) (see paragraph A.04*d* in this appendix).

A.34 A church plan not electing coverage under IRC Section 410(d) or a governmental plan is excluded from filing.

A.35 An annuity arrangement described in 29 CFR 2510.3-2(f) is excluded from filing.

A.36 A welfare benefit plan as described in 29 CFR 2520.104-20 is excluded from filing. Such a plan has fewer than 100 participants as of the beginning of the plan year and generally is one of the following:

    a. Unfunded. Benefits are paid as needed directly from the general assets of the employer or the employee organization that sponsors the plan.[10]

    b. Fully insured. Benefits are provided exclusively through insurance contracts or policies, the premiums being paid directly by the employer or employee organization from its general assets or partly from its general assets and partly from contributions by its employees or members.

    c. A combination of unfunded and insured. Benefits are provided partially as needed directly from the general assets of the employer or the employee organization that sponsors the plan and partially through insurance contracts or policies, the premiums being paid directly by the employer or employee organization from its general assets (see paragraph A.69*d* in this appendix).

---

[10] *Directly* means that the plan does not use a trust or separately maintained fund (including a IRC Section 501(c)(9) trust) to hold plan assets or to act as a conduit for the transfer of plan assets.

A.37 An apprenticeship or training plan meeting all of the conditions specified in 29 CFR 2520.104-22 is excluded from filing (see paragraph A.69*f*).

A.38 An unfunded pension benefit plan or an unfunded or insured welfare benefit plan (*a*) whose benefits go only to a select group of management or highly compensated employees and (*b*) that meets the requirements of 29 CFR 2520.104-23 (including the requirement that a notification statement be filed with DOL) or 29 CFR 2520.104-24, respectively, is excluded from filing (see paragraphs A.69*g–h*).

A.39 Day-care centers as specified in 29 CFR 2520.104-25 are excluded from filing (see paragraph A.69*i*).

A.40 Certain dues-financed welfare and pension plans that meet the requirements of 29 CFR 2520.104-26 and 2520.104-27 are excluded from filing (see paragraph A.69*j*).

A.41 A welfare plan that participates in a group insurance arrangement that files a Form 5500 on behalf of the welfare plan is excluded from filing (see 29 CFR 2520.104-43).

A.42 A simplified employee pension (SEP) described in IRC Section 408(k) that conforms to the alternative method of compliance described in 29 CFR 2520.104-48 or -49 is excluded from filing. A SEP is a pension plan that meets certain minimum qualifications regarding eligibility and employer contributions (see paragraphs A.69*p–q*).

Kinds of Filers

A.43 A *single employer plan* is a plan sponsored by one employer.[11]

A.44 A plan for a *controlled group* is a plan for a controlled group of corporations under IRC Section 414(b), a group of trades or businesses under common control under IRC Section 414(c), or an affiliated service group under IRC Section 414(m). For Form 5500 filing purposes, a controlled group is generally considered one employer when benefits are payable to participants from the plan's total assets without regard to contributions by each participant's employer (ref: Form 5500 instructions].

A.45 A *multiemployer plan* is a plan (*a*) in which more than one employer is required to contribute, (*b*) that is maintained pursuant to one or more collective bargaining agreements, and (*c*) that had not made the election under IRC Section 414(f)(5) and ERISA Section 3(37)(E).

A.46 A *multiple-employer plan* is a plan that involves more than one employer, is not one of the plans described in paragraphs A.44–A.45, and includes only plans whose contributions from individual employers are available to pay benefits to all participants.[12] Participating employers do not file individually for these plans. Multiple-employer plans can be collectively bargained and collectively funded, but if covered by PBGC termination insurance, must have properly elected before September 27, 1981, not to be treated as a multiemployer plan under IRC Section 414(f)(5) or ERISA Sections 3(37)(E) and 4001(a)(3).

---

[11] If several employers participate in a program of benefits wherein the funds attributable to each employer are available only to pay benefits to that employer's employees, each employer must file as a sponsor of a single employer plan.

[12] A separate schedule T, for each participating employer that provides pension benefits, must be attached to the plan's Form 5500.

A.47 DFEs include common or collective trusts (CCTs), pooled separate accounts (PSAs), master trust investment accounts (MTIAs), 103-12 investment entities (103-12 IEs) and group insurance arrangements (GIAs). CCTs, PSAs, MTIAs and 103-12 IEs must generally comply with the Form 5500 instructions for large pension plans. GIAs must follow the instructions for large welfare plans.

A.48 A *group insurance arrangement* is an arrangement that provides welfare benefits to the employees of two or more unaffiliated employers (not in connection with a multiemployer plan nor a multiple employer collectively bargained plan), fully insures one or more welfare plans of each participating employer, and uses a trust (or other entity such as a trade association) as the holder of the insurance contracts and the conduit for payment of premiums to the insurance company. If such an arrangement files a Form 5500 in accordance with 29 CFR 2520.103-2, the welfare plans participating in the arrangement need not file a separate report.[13]

When to File

A.49 *Plans and Group Insurance Arrangements*: The annual report is due by the last day of the seventh calendar month after the end of a plan year (not to exceed 12 months in length), including a short plan year (any plan year less than 12 months). A plan year ends upon the date of the change in accounting period or upon the complete distribution of the assets of the plan. *Direct Filing Entities Other than Group Insurance Arrangements*: The annual report is due no later than 9.5 months after the end of the direct filing entity's year. No extension of time is available to these entities for making their Form 5500 filings.

A.50 A one-time extension of time up to 2.5 months may be granted for filing the annual report of a plan or group insurance arrangement if Form 5558, *Application for Extension of Time to File Certain Employee Plan Returns*, is filed with the IRS before the normal due date of the report. In addition, single-employer plans and plans sponsored by a controlled group of corporations that file consolidated federal income tax returns are automatically granted an extension of time to file Form 5500 to the due date of the federal income tax return of the single employer or controlled group of corporations if certain conditions described in the instructions to the forms are met. A copy of the extension is no longer required to be filed with the annual report, but should be retained in the sponsor's records.

Filing Under the Statute Versus the Regulations

A.51 As stated in paragraph A.18, plan administrators may, for purposes of Title I of ERISA, file an annual report containing all of the information required by ERISA Section 103 (that is, the statute) or the information required by the regulations. As also noted in paragraph A.18, however, a filing in accordance with ERISA Section 103 will not satisfy an administrator's annual reporting obligations under the IRC or Title IV of ERISA; the Form 5500 must be filed to comply with those requirements.

---

[13] Also see 29 CFR 2520.104-21 and 2520.104-43.

a. *Regulations.* Filing the Form 5500 is considerably different than filing pursuant to the statute. The regulations require that the accountant's report

 i. disclose any omitted auditing procedures deemed necessary by the accountant and the reasons for their omission.

 ii. state clearly the accountant's opinion of the financial statements and schedules covered by the report and the accounting principles and practices reflected therein.

 iii. state clearly the consistency of the application of the accounting principles between the current year and the preceding year or about any changes in such principles which have a material effect on the financial statements.[14]

 iv. state clearly any matters to which the accountant takes exception, the exception, and to the extent practical, the effect of such matters on the related financial statements. Exceptions are required to be further identified as (*a*) those that are the result of DOL regulations and (*b*) all others.[15]

The regulations also require (1) current value,[16] comparing the beginning and end of the plan year, (2) a description of accounting principles and practices reflected in the financial statements and, if applicable, variances from accounting principles generally accepted in the United States of America (U.S. GAAP) and an explanation of differences, if any, between the information contained in the separate financial statements and the net assets, liabilities, income, expense, and changes in net assets as required to be reported on the Form 5500.

b. *Statute.* In particular, a plan administrator electing to comply with the statute must satisfy all the requirements of ERISA Section 103 and may not rely on regulatory exemptions and simplified methods of reporting or alternative methods of compliance prescribed with respect to the Form 5500. In addition, the statute requires (1) the accountant to express an opinion on whether the financial statements and ERISA Section 103(b) schedules conform with U.S. GAAP on a basis consistent with that of the preceding year and (2) current value, comparing the end of the previous plan year and the end of the plan year being reported.

A.52 The statute and the regulations require that the examination be conducted in accordance with U.S. GAAP.

a. Financial information required under both methods includes plan assets and liabilities (aggregated by categories and valued at their

---

[14] An accountant's report prepared in accordance with AU section 508, *Reports on Audited Financial Statements* (AICPA, *Professional Standards*), which prescribes that no reference be made to the consistent application of GAAP in those cases where there has been no accounting change, will be viewed as consistent with the requirements of ERISA and regulations issued thereunder with regard to the required submission of an accountant's report.

[15] Other requirements are that the report be dated, manually signed, and that it indicate the city and state where it is issued, and that it identify (without necessarily enumerating) the statements and schedules covered.

[16] *Current value*, as used in this document, means fair market value where available and otherwise the fair value as determined in good faith by a trustee or a named fiduciary (as defined in Section 402[a][2]) pursuant to the terms of the plan and in accordance with regulations of the Secretary, assuming an orderly liquidation at the time of such determination (Section 3(26) of ERISA).

current value with the same data displayed in comparative form using the end of the current plan year and either (1) the end of the previous plan year (statute) or (2) beginning of the current plan year (regulations), and information concerning plan income, expenses, and changes in net assets during the plan year).

b. Required supplemental information includes mandatory use of standardized schedules (Form 5500 schedule G) as follows (see paragraph A.77):

    i. Loans or fixed income obligations due in default or uncollectible

    ii. Leases in default or uncollectible

    iii. Nonexempt transactions

Required information also includes the following nonstandardized schedules:

    iv. Schedule H, line 4a—Schedule of Delinquent Participant Contributions

    v. Schedule H, line 4i—Schedule of Assets (Held at End of Year)

    vi. Schedule H, line 4i—Schedule of Assets Held (Acquired and Disposed of Within Year) if filing under the alternative method[17]

    vii. Schedule H, line 4j—Schedule of Reportable Transactions (that is, transactions that exceed 3 percent (statute) or 5 percent (regulations) of the current value of plan assets at the beginning of the year).[18]

c. Notes to the financial statements, when applicable, shall be provided concerning

    i. a description of the plan, including significant changes in the plan and effect of the changes on benefits.

    ii. the funding policy and changes in funding policy (including policy with respect to prior service cost), and any changes in such policies during the year (only applicable under the statutory method for pension plans).

    iii. a description of material lease commitments and other commitments and contingent liabilities.

    iv. a description of any agreements and transactions with persons known to be parties in interest.

    v. a general description of priorities in the event of plan termination.

    vi. whether a tax ruling or determination letter has been obtained.

---

[17] Any assets held for investment purposes in a 401(h) account should be shown on Schedule H, line 4i—Schedule of Assets (Held at End of Year) and Schedule H, line 4j—Schedule of Reportable Transactions for the pension plan.

[18] Plans filing their annual reports under the statutory method are required to report transactions that exceed 3 percent of the fair value of plan assets at the beginning of the year, whereas plans that file pursuant to the alternative method of compliance prescribed in DOL regulations are required to report transactions that exceed 5 percent of the fair value of plan assets at the beginning of the year.

     vii. any other information required for a fair presentation.

    viii. an explanation of differences, if any, between the information contained in the separate financial statements and the net assets, liabilities, income, expense, and changes in net assets as required to be reported on the Form 5500, if filing under the alternative method (see paragraph A.51).

Investment Arrangements Filing Directly With DOL

A.53 Generally, when the assets of two or more plans are maintained in one trust or account or separately maintained fund, all annual report entries, including any attached schedules, shall be completed by including the plan's allocable portion of the trust, account, or fund. Certain exceptions have been made, however, for plans that invest in certain investment arrangements that are either required to, or may elect to, file information concerning themselves and their relationship with employee benefit plans directly with DOL as discussed subsequently. Plans participating in these investment arrangements are required to attach certain additional information to the Form 5500 as specified in subsequent paragraphs. For a definition of plan assets and the look-through provisions, see 29 CFR 2510.3-101.

Common or Collective Trusts and Pooled Separate Accounts

A.54 For reporting purposes, a CCT is a trust maintained by a bank, trust company, or similar institution that is regulated, supervised, and subject to periodic examination by a state or federal agency for the collective investment and reinvestment of assets contributed thereto from employee benefit plans maintained by more than one employer or a controlled group of corporations, as the term is used in IRC Section 1563.

For reporting purposes, a PSA is an account maintained by an insurance carrier that is regulated, supervised, and subject to periodic examination by a state agency for the collective investment and reinvestment of assets contributed thereto from employee benefit plans maintained by more than one employer or controlled group of corporations, as that term is used in IRC Section 1563.

Although CCTs and PSAs are not required to file directly with the Department of Labor, their filing or lack thereof directly affects the participating plan's filing responsibilities. If the CCT or PSA does elect to directly file, participating plans must

    a. file a Form 5500, completing items 1c(9) or 1c(10) and items 2b(6) or (7) on Schedule H, "Financial Information," and

    b. complete Part I of Schedule D, "DFE/Participating Plan Information."

If the CCT or PSA does not file directly with the Department of Labor, plans participating in these arrangements must

    a. file a Form 5500, allocating and reporting the underlying assets of the CCT or PSA in the appropriate categories on a line by line basis on Part I of Schedule H, "Financial Information," and

    b. complete Part I of Schedule D, "DFE/Participating Plan Information."

CCTs and PSAs that elect to file directly with the Department of Labor must do so by filing a Form 5500, including Schedule D, "DFE/Participating Plan Information" and Schedule H, "Financial Information."

See paragraphs A.69*b–c* and 29 CFR 2520.103-3, -4 and -5, and 2520.103-9.[19]

Master Trust

A.55 For reporting purposes, a master trust is a trust for which a regulated financial institution serves as trustee or custodian (regardless of whether such institution exercises discretionary authority or control with respect to the management of assets held in the trust), and in which assets of more than one plan sponsored by a single employer or by a group of employers under common control are held.[20] Participating plans are required to complete item 1c(11) and item 2b(8) on Schedule H, "Financial Information," and Part I of Schedule D, "DFE/Participating Plan Information."

The following information is required to be filed by the plan administrator or by a designee directly with DOL no later than 9.5 months after the end of the master trust's year. The Form 5500 filing of each plan participating in the master trust will not be deemed complete unless all the information is filed within the prescribed time.

   a. Form 5500

   b. Schedule A, "Insurance Information" for each insurance or annuity contract held in the master trust (See paragraph A.74)

   c. Schedule C, "Service Provider Information," Part I, if any service provider was paid $5,000 or more. (See paragraph A.75)

   d. Schedule D, "DFE/Participating Plan Information," Part II. (See paragraph A.76)

   e. Schedule G, "Financial Transaction Schedules." (See paragraph A.77)

   f. Schedule H, "Financial Information." (See paragraph A.78)

See paragraph A.69*a* and 29 CFR 2520.103-1(e).

Plans Versus Trusts

A.56 Under ERISA, the audit requirement is applied to each separate plan and not each separate trust. As a result, each plan funded under a master trust arrangement is subject to a separate Form 5500 and audit requirement, unless otherwise exempt.

103-12 Investment Entities

A.57 For purposes of the annual report, entities described subsequently that file the information directly with DOL as specified subsequently constitute

---

[19] For reporting purposes, a separate account that is not considered to be holding plan assets pursuant to 29 CFR 2510.3-101(h)(1)(iii) shall not constitute a pooled separate account.

[20] A *regulated financial institution* means a bank, a trust company, or a similar institution that is regulated, supervised, and subject to periodic examination by a state or federal agency. Common control is determined on the basis of all relevant facts and circumstances.

"103-12 Investment Entities"(103-12 IEs).[21] Plans may invest in an entity, the underlying assets of which include *plan assets* (within the meaning of 29 CFR 2510.3-101) of two or more plans that are not members of a related group of employee benefit plans. For reporting purposes, a *related group* consists of each group of two or more employee benefit plans (*a*) each of which receives 10 percent or more of its aggregate contributions from the same employer or from a member of the same controlled group of corporations (as determined under IRC Section 1563(a), without regard to IRC Section 1563(a)(4) thereof); or (*b*) each of which is either maintained by, or maintained pursuant to, a collective bargaining agreement negotiated by the same employee organization or affiliated employee organizations. For purposes of this paragraph, an "affiliate" of an employee organization means any person controlling, controlled by, or under common control with such organization.

The following information for the fiscal year of the 103-12 IE ending with or within the plan year must be filed directly with DOL by the sponsor of the 103-12 IE no later than 9.5 months after the end of the 103-12 IE's year:

- *a.* Form 5500
- *b.* Schedule A, "Insurance Information" for each insurance or annuity contract held in the 103-IE (See paragraph A.74)
- *c.* Schedule C, "Service Provider Information," Part I, if any service provider was paid $5,000 or more, and Part II, if the accountant was terminated. (See paragraph A.75)
- *d.* Schedule D, "DFE/Participating Plan Information," Part 2. (See paragraph A.76)
- *e.* Schedule H, "Financial Information." (See paragraph A.78)
- *f.* Schedule G, "Financial Transaction Schedules." (See paragraph A.77)
- *g.* A report of an IQPA regarding the preceding items and other books and records of the 103-12 IE that meets the requirements of 29 CFR 2520.103-1(b)(5)

See 29 CFR 2520.103-12 and paragraph A.61.

Limited-Scope Audit Exemption

A.58 Under DOL regulations, any assets held by a bank or similar institution (for example, a trust company) or insurance company that is regulated and subject to periodic examination by a state or federal agency may be excluded from the annual audit provided the plan administrator exercises this option and the institution holding the assets certifies the required information. The limited-scope audit exemption does not exempt the plan from the requirement to have an audit.[22] All noninvestment activity of the plan, such as contributions, benefit payments, and plan administrative expenses are subject to audit whether or not the assets of the plan have been certified as described previously. See paragraphs 7.73 and 13.26 for limited-scope audit procedures and reporting.

---

[21] The plan administrator cannot use this alternative method of reporting unless the report of the investment entity has been submitted to DOL in accordance with the requirements specified in the Form 5500 instructions.

[22] This limitation on the scope of an auditor's examination applies to plans sponsored by a "regulated" bank or insurance carrier for its own employees, as well as to other plans.

A.59 The limited-scope audit exemption does not apply to assets held by a broker or dealer or an investment company. It also does not extend to benefit payment information [ref: DOL Reg. 29 CFR 2520.103-8; 2520.103-3; and 2520.103-4]. See paragraphs 7.73 and 13.26–13.32 for a discussion of the auditor's responsibilities when the scope of the audit is so restricted.

A.60 The Securities and Exchange Commission will not accept a limited-scope audit report in connection with a Form 11-K filing, even if the plan has elected to file financial statements that are prepared in accordance with the financial reporting requirements of ERISA. (See paragraph 12.28 for a further discussion of SEC reporting requirements.)

103-12 IEs

A.61 If a plan's assets include assets of a 103-12 investment entity, the examination and report of an independent qualified public accountant required by 29 CFR 2520.103-1 need not extend to such assets, if the entity reports directly to DOL pursuant to 29 CFR 2520.103-12 and the instructions to the Form 5500. Under 29 CFR 2520.103-12, the entity is required to include the report of an IQPA.

What to File (See Exhibit A-3)

A.62 File Form 5500 annually for each plan required to file (see 29 CFR 2520.104a-5 and -6 and paragraphs A.30–A.42, A.61, and A.83). Plans with 100 or more participants at the beginning of the plan year must file as a *large plan*. Plans with fewer than 100 participants at the beginning of the year must file as a *small plan*, using either Form 5500, 5500-SF or 5500-EZ, as applicable.

A.63 Exception to A.61: If a plan has between 80 and 120 participants (inclusive) as of the beginning of the plan year, the plan may elect, instead of following paragraph A.62 to complete the current year's return/report in the same category (*large plan* or *small plan*) as was filed for the prior year. (see 29 CFR 2520.104a-5 and paragraph A.66).

A.64 Amended reports should be filed as appropriate; however, they must include an original signature of the plan administrator.

A.65 A final report is required when all assets under a pension plan (including insurance or annuity contracts) have been distributed to the participants and beneficiaries or distributed to another plan or when all liabilities for which benefits may be paid under a welfare benefit plan have been satisfied and all assets, if the plan is not unfunded, have been distributed. A final report is filed on the Form 5500.

Exemptions—Audit

A.66 "Small" pension plans that file the Form 5500 or Form 5500-SF will not be required to have an audit of their financial statements provided they meet the requirements of DOL Reg. 29 CFR 2520.104.46, as amended (see paragraph A.24). "Large" pension plans generally must engage an auditor (see paragraphs A.24 and A.61–A.63, and 29 CFR 2520.104-41 and 2520.104-46).

A.67 Plan years of seven months or less, due to: (1) initial year; (2) merger; or (3) change of plan year can generally postpone (but not eliminate) the audit requirement (but not the requirement to file a Form 5500) until the following year. This rule also applies when a full plan year is followed by a short plan year of seven months or less. The audit report would therefore cover both the short year and the full plan year [ref: DOL Reg. 29 CFR 2520.104-50].

Exemptions—Other Filing Requirements

A.68 Plans that are filing in a short plan year may defer the IQPA's report (see 29 CFR 2520.104-50).

A.69 The following is a list of variances that modify the general annual reporting requirements:

> *a.* 29 CFR 2520.103-1(e) provides the regulatory authority for the reporting of financial information by plans participating in a master trust (see paragraph A.55).
>
> *b.* 29 CFR 2520.103-3 and -4 provide exemptions for plans some or all the assets of which are held in a common or collective trust of a bank or similar institution or a pooled separate account of an insurance carrier from reporting information concerning the individual transactions of the common or collective trusts and pooled separate accounts provided the conditions of the regulation are satisfied (see paragraph A.54).
>
> *c.* 29 CFR 2520.103-9 permits the direct filing of financial information to the DOL by banks and insurance companies of information otherwise required to be submitted to IRS with the Form 5500 when plans hold units of participation in common or collective trusts or pooled separate accounts (see paragraph A.54).
>
> *d.* 29 CFR 2520.104-20 provides a limited exemption for certain small welfare plans (see paragraphs A.36 and A.62).
>
> *e.* 29 CFR 2520.104-21 provides a limited exemption for certain group insurance arrangements.
>
> *f.* 29 CFR 2520.104-22 provides an exemption for apprenticeship and training plans (see paragraph A.37).
>
> *g.* 29 CFR 2520.104-23 provides an alternative method of compliance for pension plans for certain selected employees (see paragraph A.38).
>
> *h.* 29 CFR 2520.104-24 provides an exemption for welfare plans for certain selected employees (see paragraph A.38).
>
> *i.* 29 CFR 2520.104-25 provides an exemption for day-care centers (see paragraph A.39).
>
> *j.* 29 CFR 2520.104-26 provides a limited exemption for certain dues-financed welfare plans maintained by employee organizations (see paragraph A.40).
>
> *k.* 29 CFR 2520.104-27 provides a limited exemption for certain dues-financed pension plans maintained by employee organizations.
>
> *l.* 29 CFR 2520.104-41 prescribes simplified annual reporting requirements for plans with fewer than 100 participants (see paragraph A.63).

m. 29 CFR 2520.104-43 provides an exemption from annual reporting requirements for certain group insurance arrangements (see paragraph A.41).

n. 29 CFR 2520.104-44 provides a limited exemption and alternative method of compliance for the annual report of certain unfunded and insured plans (see paragraphs A.58–A.62).[23]

o. 29 CFR 2520.104-46 provides a waiver of examination and report of an auditor for plans with fewer than 100 participants (see paragraph A.63).

p. 29 CFR 2520.104-47 provides a limited exemption and alternative method of compliance for filing of insurance company financial reports (see Section 103[e]).

q. 29 CFR 2520.104-48 provides an alternative method of compliance for Model Simplified Employee Pensions (see paragraph A.42).

r. 29 CFR 2520.104-49 provides an alternative method of compliance for certain simplified employee pensions (see paragraph A.42).

A.70 *In-house asset manager (INHAM) class exemption.* Managers of many large pensions utilize the services of in-house asset managers, otherwise known as INHAMs. Oftentimes, these managers want to conduct transactions that are prohibited by ERISA. ERISA does provide, however, that the DOL has the authority to grant exemptions from the prohibited transaction restrictions if it can be demonstrated that a transaction is administratively feasible, in the interests of the plan and its participants and beneficiaries, and protective of the rights of the participants and beneficiaries of the plan. The DOL reviews applications for such exemptions and determines whether or not to grant relief. Individual exemptions relate to a particular plan or applicant; class exemptions are applicable to anyone engaging in the described transactions, provided the enumerated conditions are satisfied.

A.71 Related to INHAMs, the DOL issued a class exemption, Prohibited Transaction Exemption (PTE) 96-23, effective April 10, 1996, in which plans managed by in-house managers can engage in a variety of transactions with service providers if certain conditions are met. The special exemptions relate to the leasing of office or commercial space, leasing residential space to employees and the use of public accommodations owned by plans. Only large employers whose plans have at least $250 million in assets, with $50 million under direct in-house management can use the exemption, and it also requires that in-house managers be registered investment advisers and make all decisions concerning the affected transactions.

A.72 One of the provisions of the exemption requires that, an independent auditor, who has appropriate technical training or experience and proficiency with ERISA's fiduciary responsibility provisions and so represents in writing, must conduct an exemption audit on an annual basis. Upon completion of the audit, the auditor is required to issue a written report to the plan presenting

---

[23] For purposes of 29 CFR 2520.104-44, a contract is considered to be "allocated" only if the insurance company or organization that issued the contract unconditionally guarantees, upon receipt of the required premium or consideration, to provide a retirement benefit of a specified amount, without adjustment for fluctuations in the market value of the underlying assets of the company or organization, to each participant, and each participant has a legal right to such benefits that is legally enforceable directly against the insurance company or organization.

its specific findings regarding the level of compliance with the policies and procedure adopted by the INHAM.

A.73 The exemption was published in the Federal Register on April 10, 1996 and may be found on the EBSA website at: www.savingmatters.dol. gov/ebsa/programs/oed/archives/96-23.htm.

Schedules for Form 5500 Series

A.74 Schedule A, *Insurance Information*, must be attached to Form 5500 if any benefits under the plan are provided by an insurance company, insurance service, or other similar organization (such as Blue Cross, Blue Shield, or a health maintenance organization) (see paragraphs A.55, A.57, and A.62).

A.75 Schedule C, *Service Provider Information*, must be attached to Form 5500 (see paragraphs A.55, A.57, A.62, and A.85).

A.76 Schedule D, *DFE/Participating Plan Information*, must be attached to Form 5500 for DFE filings and for plans participating in a DFE.

A.77 Schedule G, *Financial Transaction Schedules*, must be attached to Form 5500 to report certain supplemental information.

A.78 Schedule H, *Large Plan and DFE Financial Information*, generally must be attached to Form 5500 for employee benefit plans that covered 100 or more participants as of the beginning of the plan year, and for DFE filings.

A.79 Schedule I, *Small Plan Financial Information*, generally must be attached to Form 5500 for employee benefit plans that covered less than 100 participants as of the beginning of the plan year. This is for plans that are not choosing to file using Form 5500-SF.

A.80 Schedule MB, *Multiemployer Defined Benefit Plan and Certain Money Purchase Plan Actuarial Information*, must be attached to Form 5500 for multiemployer defined benefit plans that are subject to the minimum funding standards.

A.81 Schedule R, *Retirement Plan Information*, generally must be attached to Form 5500 for both tax qualified and nonqualified pension benefit plans.

A.82 Schedule SB, *Single-Employer Defined Benefit Plan Actuarial Information*, must be attached to Form 5500 for single-employer defined benefit plans (including multiple-employer defined benefit plans) that are subject to the minimum funding standards.

A.83 Additional separate schedules must be attached to Form 5500 only in accordance with the instructions to the form and must always clearly reference the item number that requires this information (see exhibit A-1, "Examples of Form 5500 Schedules").

Termination of Accountant or Actuary

A.84 Terminations of certain service providers must be reported in Part II of Schedule C, which is attached to the Form 5500. In addition, the plan administrator is required to provide terminated accountants and actuaries with a copy of the explanation for the termination as reported on Schedule C and a notice stating that the terminated party has the opportunity to comment directly to the DOL concerning the explanation (see paragraphs A.62 and A.72).

Independence of Independent Qualified Public Accountants

A.85 ERISA Section 103(a)(3)(A) requires that the accountant retained by an employee benefit plan be "independent" for purposes of examining plan financial information and rendering an opinion on the financial statements and schedules required to be contained in the annual report. Under this authority DOL will not recognize any person as an auditor who is in fact not independent with respect to the employee benefit plan upon which that accountant renders an opinion in the annual report.

DOL has issued guidelines (29 CFR 2509.75-9) for determining when an auditor is independent for purposes of auditing and rendering an opinion on the annual report. For example, an accountant will not be considered independent with respect to a plan if

a. during the period of professional engagement to examine the financial statements being reported, at the date of the opinion, or during the period covered by the financial statements the accountant or his or her firm or a member thereof

 i. had, or was committed to acquire, any direct financial interest or any material indirect financial interest in the plan or plan sponsor;

 ii. was connected as a promoter, underwriter, investment adviser, voting trustee, director, officer, or employee of the plan or plan sponsor except that a firm will not be deemed not independent if a former officer or employee of the plan or plan sponsor is employed by the firm and such individual has completely disassociated himself or herself from the plan or plan sponsor and does not participate in auditing financial statements of the plan covering any period of his or her employment by the plan or plan sponsor.

b. An accountant or a member of an accounting firm maintains financial records for the employee benefit plan.

 However, an auditor may permissibly engage in or have members of his or her firm engage in certain activities that will not have the effect of removing recognition of independence. For example, an accountant will not fail to be recognized as independent if

c. at or during the period of his or her professional engagement the accountant or his or her firm is retained or engaged on a professional basis by the plan sponsor. However, the accountant must not violate the prohibitions in (a) and (b) preceding.

d. the rendering of services by an actuary associated with the accountant or his or her firm shall not impair the accountant's or the firm's independence. The auditor should ensure that the provision of these services complies with the prohibited transaction rules of ERISA Section 406(a)(1)(c).

Penalties

A.86 ERISA and the IRC provide for the assessment or imposition of penalties for failures to comply with the reporting and disclosure requirements.

Annual Reporting Penalties

A.87 One or more of the following penalties may be imposed or assessed in the event of a failure or refusal to file reports in accordance with the statutory and regulatory requirements:

    a. Up to $1,100 a day for each day a plan administrator fails or refuses to file a complete annual report (see ERISA Section 502(c)(2) and 29 CFR 2560.502c-2). Any failure of a plan's actuary to certify a plan's status in accordance with ERISA Section 305(b)(3) is considered a failure to file a complete annual report.

    Perfection Penalties for Deficient Filings

    Presently the Department assesses penalties of: (1) $150 a day (up to $50,000) per annual report filing where the required auditor's report is missing or deficient; (2) $100 a day (up to $36,500) per annual report filing that contains deficient financial information (for example, missing required supplemental schedules); and (3) $10 a day (up to $3,650) for information required on the Form 5500 Series reports (that is, failure to answer a question).

    Nonfiler and Late Filer Penalties

    Presently the Department assesses nonfiler penalties of $300 per day, up to $30,000 per annual report, per year. Late filer penalties are assessed at $50 per day.

    Egregious Penalties may be assessed in addition to other penalty amounts.

    b. $25 a day (up to $15,000) by the IRS for not filing returns for certain plans of deferred compensation, certain trusts and annuities, and bond purchase plans by the due dates(s) (see IRC Section 6652[e]). This penalty also applies to returns required to be filed under IRC Section 6039D.

    c. $1 a day (up to $5,000) by the IRS for each participant for whom a registration statement (Schedule SSA [Form 5500]) is required but not filed (see IRC Section 6652[d][1]).

    d. $1 a day (up to $1,000) by the IRS for not filing a notification of change of status of a plan (see IRC Section 6652[d][2]).

    e. $1,000 by the IRS for not filing an actuarial statement (see IRC Section 6692).

These penalties may be waived or reduced if it is determined that there was reasonable cause for the failure to comply.

A.88 The following are other penalties:

    a. Any individual who willfully violates any provision of Part 1 of Title I of ERISA shall be fined not more than $5,000 or imprisoned not more than one year or both (see ERISA Section 501).

    b. A penalty up to $10,000, five years imprisonment, or both, for making any false statement or representation of fact, knowing it to be false, or for knowingly concealing or not disclosing any fact required by ERISA (see Section 1027, Title 18, U.S.C., as amended by ERISA Section 111).

c. Any employer maintaining a plan who fails to meet the notice requirement of Section 101(d) with respect to any participant or beneficiary may in the court's discretion be liable to such participant or beneficiary in the amount of up to $100 a day from the date of such failure, and the court may in its discretion order such other relief as it deems proper (see ERISA Section 502[c][3]).

d. Civil penalties may be assessed against parties in interest or disqualified persons who engage in prohibited transactions (see ERISA Section 502(i). An excise tax also exists for prohibited transactions under IRC Section 4975).

e. ERISA Section 502(l) requires a civil penalty to be assessed by the Secretary of Labor against a fiduciary who breaches his or her fiduciary duty or commits a violation of Part 4 of Title I or any other person who knowingly participates in such breach or violation. The civil penalty is 20 percent of the amount recovered pursuant to a settlement agreement with the Secretary or ordered to be paid by a court.[24]

f. A civil penalty of up to $100 a day may be assessed against a plan administrator for the failure or refusal to furnish notice to participants and beneficiaries of blackout period in accordance with Section 101(i) of ERISA. Also, this civil penalty may be assessed for the failure or refusal to furnish the notice of the right to direct the proceeds from the divestment of employer securities in accordance with Section 101(m) of ERISA. Each violation with respect to any single participant or beneficiary shall be treated as a separate violation. (see ERISA Section 502[c][7]).

g. A civil penalty of not more than $1,000 per day may be assessed for failure or refusal to furnish (see ERISA Section 502[c][4]) the following:

i. Notice of funding-based limits in accordance with Section 101(j) of ERISA

ii. Actuarial, financial or funding information in accordance with Section 101(k) of ERISA

iii. Notice of potential withdrawal liability in accordance with Section 101(l) of ERISA

iv. Notice of rights and obligations under an automatic contribution arrangement in accordance with Section 514(e)(3) of ERISA

v. A failure of refusal to furnish the item with respect to any person entitled to receive such item shall be treated as a separate violation (see ERISA Section 502[c][4])

h. A civil penalty of not more than $1,100 per day may be assessed against the plan sponsor of a multiemployer plan for each violation of the requirement under ERISA Section 305 to adopt by deadline

---

[24] An accountant who knows about a fiduciary breach or violation but chooses not to disclose it may knowingly participate in a breach or violation for purposes of Section 502(l).

established in that Section a funding improvement plan or rehabilitation plan with respect to a multiemployer plan which is in
endangered or critical status. Also, in the case of a plan in endangered status which is not in seriously endangered status, this civil
penalty may be assessed for the failure by the plan to meet the applicable benchmarks under ERISA Section 305 by the end of the
funding improvement period with respect to the plan.

Fiduciary Responsibilities (ERISA Sections 401–414)

A.89 ERISA establishes standards for plan investments and transactions
and imposes restrictions and responsibilities on plan fiduciaries.

A.90 A fiduciary's responsibilities include managing plan assets solely in
the interest of participants and beneficiaries (with the care a prudent person
would exercise) and diversifying investments to minimize the risk of large losses
unless it is clearly not prudent to do so (see ERISA Section 404). Plans are prohibited from acquiring or holding employer securities that are not qualifying
employer securities (QES) or employer real property that is not qualifying employer real property (QERP). Furthermore, plans (other than certain individual
account plans) may not acquire any QES or QERP if immediately after such
acquisition the aggregate fair market value of QES and QERP held by the plan
exceeds 10 percent of the assets of the plan (see ERISA Section 407).

A.91 A plan fiduciary is prohibited from causing the plan to engage in
certain transactions with a party in interest (see ERISA Section 406).[25] The
following transactions between a plan and a party in interest are generally
prohibited (see ERISA Section 406):

   a. A sale, exchange, or lease of property, except to the extent allowed

   b. A loan or other extension of credit

   c. The furnishing of goods, services, or facilities, except as allowed
      under ERISA

   d. A transfer of plan assets to a party in interest for the use or benefit
      of a party in interest

   e. An acquisition of employer securities or real property, except to the
      extent allowed (see ERISA Section 408[e])

However, conditional exemptions from the application of these provisions are
provided by ERISA.

A.92 A fiduciary is also generally prohibited from using the plan assets for
his or her own interest or account, acting in any plan transactions on behalf of
a party whose interests are adverse to those of the plan or its participants, and
receiving consideration for his or her own account from a party dealing with
the plan in connection with a transaction involving the plan assets (see ERISA
Section 406[b]).

A.93 ERISA Section 408 provides for exceptions to the rules on prohibited transactions. Section 408(a) gives authority to the Secretary of Labor to

---

[25] ERISA defines a party in interest generally as any fiduciary or employee of the plan, any
person who provides services to the plan, an employer whose employees are covered by the plan, an
employee association whose members are covered by the plan, a person who owns 50 percent or more
of such an employer or employee association, or a relative of a person described in the foregoing (see
ERISA Section 3[14]).

grant administrative exemptions from the prohibited transaction restrictions of ERISA Sections 406 and 407. Sections 408(b), (c), and (e) provide statutory exemptions from the prohibited transaction rules for various transactions, provided the conditions specified in the statutory exemptions are satisfied. For example, reasonable arrangements can be made with a party in interest to provide services if the one who selects and negotiates with the service provider on behalf of the plan is independent of the service provider. Advice of legal counsel should be obtained when investigating a possible prohibited transaction or a possible breach of fiduciary duty.

A.94 A fiduciary must make good any losses to the plan resulting from a breach of fiduciary duty and must return to the plan any profits he or she made through the use of plan assets (see ERISA Section 409).

Plan Termination Insurance

A.95 The insurance provisions under Title IV of ERISA, as amended, apply to qualified, defined benefit pension plans, with certain statutory exceptions, and do not apply to defined contribution plans or welfare plans (see ERISA Section 4021).

A.96 The PBGC's termination insurance program is funded in part through premiums paid to the PBGC. The designated payor must make annual premium payments to the PBGC (see ERISA Section 4007). For this purpose, the designated payor for a single employer plan is the contributing sponsor or the plan administrator. The designated payor for a multiemployer plan is the plan administrator. For single employer plans, premiums are based on the number of participants in a plan and the amount by which the plan's benefits are underfunded (see ERISA Section 4006). Premiums for multiemployer plans are based solely on the number of participants in the plan. In general, premiums may be paid by the contributing sponsor or by plan funds, whichever is permitted under the terms of the plan; however, premiums for a plan that is undergoing a distress termination or an involuntary termination must be paid by the contributing sponsor (see 29 CFR 2610.26). Each member of the contributing sponsor's controlled group, if any, is jointly and severally liable for the required premiums (see ERISA Section 4007).

A.97 A plan administrator or contributing sponsor must notify the PBGC when a "reportable event" such as bankruptcy of the contributing sponsor or inability of the plan to pay benefits occurs (see ERISA Sections 4041[c] and 4043; 29 CFR Part 2615). Each person who is a contributing sponsor of a single employer pension plan is responsible for quarterly contributions required to meet the minimum funding standards (see ERISA Section 302[e]). If the contributing sponsor is a member of a controlled group, each person who is also a member of the controlled group is jointly and severally liable for the contributions (see ERISA Section 302[c][11]). Failure to make the required contributions may result in a lien upon all property and property rights belonging to such persons, which lien may be enforced by the PBGC. ERISA provides for two types of voluntary single employer plan terminations for defined benefit pension plans: a standard termination and a distress termination (ERISA Section 4041). A plan may be terminated voluntarily in a standard termination only if it can pay all benefit liabilities under the plan. A plan may be terminated in a distress termination only if the contributing sponsor and each member of the contributing sponsor's controlled group meet the necessary distress criteria (for example, undergoing liquidation). In either type of termination, an enrolled actuary's certification of the value of the plan's assets and benefits must be filed with the PBGC. When an underfunded single employer plan terminates in a distress termination, the contributing sponsor and each member of the contributing sponsor's controlled group are liable to the PBGC for the total amount of unfunded benefit liabilities and the total amount of unpaid minimum funding contributions and applicable interest (see ERISA Section 4062). If an employer that contributes to a multiemployer plan withdraws from the plan in a complete or partial withdrawal, the employer is generally liable to the plan for an allocable share of the unfunded vested benefits of the plan (see ERISA Section 4201).

Administration and Enforcement (ERISA Sections 501–514)

A.98 Responsibility for administration of ERISA and enforcement of its provisions rests primarily with the IRS and the DOL. The agencies are empowered to bring suit in federal court in civil actions, criminal actions, or both.

A.99 Failure to meet ERISA's requirements can result in the imposition of substantial fines, excise taxes, and other penalties, including possible loss of tax-exempt status. Although ERISA states that the plan is subject to certain of the penalties, the penalties are likely to fall not on the plan but on the sponsoring employer because Congress, in formulating ERISA, sought to protect plan assets for participants and their beneficiaries, not to protect employers from liability (see paragraphs A.87–A.88).

A.100 ERISA was intended to generally supersede state laws relating to employee benefit plans. Thus, plans subject to Title I of ERISA or Title IV of ERISA are generally not subject to state regulation. Preemption of state laws does not extend, however, to generally applicable criminal statutes or laws regulating insurance, banking, or securities.

A.101 Plans that are multiple employer welfare arrangements (MEWAs) may also be subject to state or local regulation even if the MEWA is also an employee benefit plan covered under Title I of ERISA. A MEWA is any employee welfare benefit plan or other arrangement that provides benefits to the employees of two or more employers but does not include arrangements maintained under or pursuant to one or more collective bargaining agreements, by a rural electric cooperative, or by two or more trades or businesses within the same control group (see ERISA Section 3[40]). If the MEWA is a fully insured plan covered by Title I of ERISA, the state government may only provide standards requiring specified levels of reserves and specified levels of contributions adequate to be able to pay benefits in full when due. If the MEWA is a plan covered by Title I that is not fully insured, any law of a state regulating insurance may apply to the extent that it is not inconsistent with the provisions of Title I of ERISA. On February 11, 2000, the DOL published in the Federal Register (65 CFR 7152) an interim final rule requiring the administrator of a MEWA, or other entity, to file a form with the DOL for the purpose of determining whether the requirements of certain health care laws are being met. MEWAs and those entities claiming exemption from the rule's requirements were required to submit their first forms by May 1, 2000. Subsequent filings are due by the March 1 following any "year to be reported."

Exhibit A-1

Examples of Form 5500 Schedules
Required By the Regulations
[Not Permitted If Filing By the Statutory Method]

The Form 5500 requires that certain supplemental schedules be attached to the annual Form 5500 filing using the Form 5500 series and not Form 5500-SF or 5500-EZ.

Information on all delinquent participant contributions should be reported on line 4a of either Schedule H or Schedule I of the Form 5500, and should not be reported on line 4d of Schedule H or I or on Schedule G. Beginning for 2009 plan years, large plans with delinquent participant contributions should attach a schedule clearly labeled, "Schedule H Line 4a—Schedule of Delinquent Participant Contributions" using the following format.

Participant Contributions Transferred Late to Plan		Total That Constitute Nonexempt Prohibited Transactions		Total Fully Corrected Under Voluntary Fiduciary Correction Program (VCFP) and Prohibited Transaction Exemption 2002-51
Check Here	Contributions	Contributions Corrected	Contributions Pending	
If Late Participant Loan Repayments Are Included	Not Corrected	Outside National Family Caregiver Program	Correction in VCFP	

Participant loan repayments paid to or withheld by an employer for purposes of transmittal to the plan that were not transmitted to the plan in a timely fashion must be reported either on line 4a in accordance with the reporting requirements that apply to delinquent participant contributions or on line 4d. See Advisory Opinion No. 2002-2A at www.dol.gov/ebsa.

Delinquent forwarding of participant loan repayments is eligible for correction under the Voluntary Fiduciary Correction Program and PTE 2002-51 on terms similar to those that apply to delinquent participant contributions.

For further guidance see the instructions to the Form 5500 and the EBSA website frequently asked questions at www.dol.gov/ebsa/faqs/faq_compliance_5500.html.

The following schedule is "Schedule H, line 4i—Schedule of Assets (Held at End of Year)." In column (a), place an asterisk (*) on the line of each identified person known to be a party in interest to the plan. The schedule must use the format shown as follows or a similar format and the same size paper as the Form 5500, and be clearly labeled, "Schedule H, line 4i—Schedule of Assets (Held at End of Year)."

(a)	(b) Identity of issue, borrower, lessor or similar party	(c) Description of investment including maturity date, rate of interest, collateral, par, or maturity value	(d) Cost[26]	(e) Current value[27]

---

[26] *Cost or Cost of Asset* refers to the original or acquisition cost of the asset. The DOL generally will accept any clearly defined and consistently applied method of determining historical cost that is based on the initial acquisition cost of the asset (for example, first in-first out or average cost). The use of revalued cost (the fair value of the asset at the beginning of the current plan year) for these schedules is not acceptable.

[27] *Current Value* means fair market value where available. Otherwise, it means the fair value as determined in good faith under the terms of the plan by a trustee or a named fiduciary, assuming an orderly liquidation at the time of the determination.

Note 1: Participant loans may be aggregated and presented with a general description of terms and interest rates.

Note 2: In column (d), cost information may be omitted with respect to participant or beneficiary directed transactions under an individual account plan.

Note 3: Any assets held for investment purposes in the 401(h) account should be shown on Schedule H, line 4i—Schedule of Assets (Held at End of Year) and Schedule H, line 4j—Schedule of Reportable Transactions for the pension plan.

The following schedule is "Schedule H, line 4i—Schedule of Assets (Acquired and Disposed of within Year)" (see 2520.103-11). This schedule must be clearly labeled, "Schedule H, line 4i—Schedule of Assets (Acquired and Disposed of within Year)" and must use the following format or similar format and the same size paper as the Form 5500:

(a) Identity of issue, borrower, lessor or similar party	(b) Description of investment including maturity date, rate of interest, collateral, par, or maturity value	(c) Costs of acquisitions	(d) Proceeds of dispositions

Note: In column (c), cost information may be omitted with respect to participant or beneficiary directed transactions under an individual account plan.

The following schedule is "Schedule H, line 4j—Schedule of Reportable Transactions." This schedule must be clearly labeled, "Schedule H, line 4j—Schedule of Reportable Transactions" and must use the following format:

(a) Identity of party involved	(b) Description of asset (include interest rate and maturity in case of a loan)	(c) Purchase price	(d) Selling price	(e) Lease rental	(f) Expense incurred with transaction	(g) Cost of asset[26]	(h) Current value of asset on transaction date[27]	(i) Net gain or (loss)

Note 1: Participant or beneficiary directed transactions under an individual account plan should not be taken into account for purposes of preparing this schedule. The current value of all assets of the plan, including those resulting from participant direction, should be included in determining the 5 percent figure for all other transactions.

Note 2: Any assets held for investment purposes in the 401(h) account should be shown on Schedule H, line 4i—Schedule of Assets (Held at End of Year) and Schedule H, line 4j—Schedule of Reportable Transactions for the pension plan.

The following schedule is the "Schedule of Loans or Fixed Income Obligations in Default or Classified as Uncollectible." **This schedule is required to be reported in Schedule G, Part I of the Form 5500.** In column (a), place an asterisk (*) on the line of each identified person known to be a party in interest to the plan. Include all loans that were renegotiated during the plan year. Also, explain what steps have been taken or will be taken to collect overdue amounts for each loan listed. The following are the headings of Schedule G, Part I:

(a)	(b) Identity and address of obligor	(c) Original amount of loan	Amount received during reporting year		(f) Unpaid balance at end of year	(g) Detailed description of loan including dates of making and maturity, interest rate, the type and value of collateral, any renegotiation of the loan and the terms of the renegotiation and other material items	Amount overdue	
			(d) Principal	(e) Interest			(h) Principal	(i) Interest

The next schedule is the "Schedule of Leases in Default or Classified as Uncollectible." **This schedule is required to be reported in Schedule G, Part II of the Form 5500.** In column (a), place an asterisk (*) on the line of each identified person known to be a party in interest to the plan. The following are the headings of Schedule G, Part II:

(a)	(b) Identity of lessor or lessee	(c) Relationship to plan, employer, employee organization or other party-in-interest	(d) Terms and description (type of property, location and date it was purchased, terms regarding rent, taxes, insurance, repairs, expenses, renewal options, date property was leased)	(e) Original cost	(f) Current value at time of Lease	(g) Gross rental receipts during the plan year	(h) Expenses paid during the plan year	(i) Net Receipts	(j) Amount in arrears

The last schedule is the schedule of "Nonexempt Transactions." **This schedule is required to be reported in Schedule G, Part III of the Form 5500.** The following are the headings of Schedule G, Part III:

(a) Identity of party involved	(b) Relationship to plan, employer, or other party-in-interest	(c) Description of transactions including maturity date, rate of interest, collateral, par or maturity value	(d) Purchase price	(e) Selling price	(f) Lease rental	(g) Expenses incurred in connection with transaction	(h) Cost of asset[25]	(i) Current value of asset[26]	(j) Net gain or (loss) on each transaction

Exhibit A-2

Employee Benefits Security Admin., Labor

Part 2520

SUBCHAPTER C—REPORTING AND DISCLOSURE UNDER THE EMPLOYEE RETIREMENT INCOME SECURITY ACT OF 1974

PART 2520—RULES AND REGULATIONS FOR REPORTING AND DISCLOSURE	
Subpart A—General Reporting and Disclosure Requirements	
Section	
2520.101-1	Duty of Reporting and disclosure
Subpart B—Contents of Plan Descriptions and Summary Plan Descriptions	
2520.102-1	Plan description.
2520.102-2	Style and format of summary plan description.
2520.102-3	Contents of summary plan description.
2520.102-4	Option for different summary plan descriptions.
2520.102-5	Limited exemption with respect to summary plan descriptions of welfare plans providing benefits through a qualified health maintenance organization.
Subpart C—Annual Report Requirements	
2520.103-1	Contents of the annual report.
2520.103-2	Contents of the annual report for a group insurance arrangement.
2520.103-3	Exemption from certain annual reporting requirements for assets held in a common or collective trust.
2520.103-4	Exemption from certain annual reporting requirements for assets held in an insurance company pooled separate account.
2520.103-5	Transmittal and certification of information to plan administrator for annual reporting purposes.
2520.103-6	Definition of reportable transaction for Annual Return or Report.
2520.103-7	Special accounting rules for plans filing the annual report for plan years beginning in 1975.
2520.103-8	Limitation on scope of accountant's examination.
2520.103-9	Direct filing for bank or insurance carrier trusts and accounts.
2520.103-10	Annual report financial schedules.
2520.103-11	Assets held for investment purposes.

(continued)

Subpart C—Annual Report Requirements—(continued)	
2520.103-12	Limited exemption and alternative method of compliance for annual reporting of investments in certain entities.

Subpart D—Provisions Applicable to Both Reporting and Disclosure Requirements	
2520.104-1	General.
2520.104-2	Postponing effective date of annual reporting requirements and extending WPPDA reporting requirements.
2520.104-3	Deferral of certain initial reporting and disclosure requirements.
2520.104-4	Alternative method of compliance for certain successor pension plans.
2520.104-5	Deferral of certain reporting and disclosure requirements relating to the summary plan description for welfare plans.
2520.104-6	Deferral of certain reporting and disclosure requirements relating to the summary plan description for pension plans.
2520.104-20	Limited exemption for certain small welfare plans.
2520.104-21	Limited exemption for certain group insurance arrangements.
2520.104-22	Exemption from reporting and disclosure requirements for apprenticeship and training plans.
2520.104-23	Alternative method of compliance for pension plans for certain selected employees.
2520.104-24	Exemption for welfare plans for certain selected employees.
2520.104-25	Exemption from reporting and disclosure for day care centers.
2520.104-26	Limited exemption for certain funded dues financed welfare plans maintained by employee organizations.
2520.104-27	Alternative method of compliance for certain unfunded dues financed pension plans maintained by employee organizations.
2520.104-28	Extension of time for filing and disclosure of the initial summary plan description.
2520.104-41	Simplified annual reporting requirements for plans with fewer than 100 participants. 2520.104-42 Waiver of certain actuarial information in the annual report.
2520.104-43	Exemption from annual reporting requirement for certain group insurance arrangements.

(continued)

Subpart D—Provisions Applicable to Both Reporting and Disclosure Requirements—(continued)	
2520.104-44	Limited exemption and alternative method of compliance for annual reporting by unfunded plans and by certain insured plans.
2520.104-45	Temporary exemption from reporting insurance fees and commissions for insured plans with fewer than 100 participants.
2520.104-46	Waiver of examination and report of an independent qualified public accountant for employee benefit plans with fewer than 100 participants.
2520.104-47	Limited exemption and alternative method of compliance for filing of insurance company financial reports.
2520.104-48	Alternative method of compliance for model simplified employee pensions IRS Form 5305-SEP.
2520.104-49	Alternative method of compliance for certain simplified employee pensions.
2520.104-50	Short plan years, deferral of accountant's examination and report.
Subpart E—Reporting Requirements	
2520.104a-1	Filing with the Secretary of Labor.
2520.104a-2	Plan description reporting requirements.
2520.104a-3	Summary plan description.
2520.104a-4	Material modifications to the plan and changes in plan description information.
2520.104a-5	Annual report filing requirements.
2520.104a-6	Annual reporting for plans which are part of a group insurance arrangement.
2520.104a-7	Summary of material modifications.
Subpart F—Disclosure Requirements	
2520.104b-1	Disclosure.
2520.104b-2	Summary plan description.
2520.104b-3	Summary of material modifications to the plan and changes in the information required to be included in the summary plan description.
2520.104b-4	Alternative methods of compliance for furnishing the summary plan description and summaries of material modifications of a pension plan to a retired participant, a separated participant with vested benefits, and a beneficiary receiving benefits.

(continued)

Subpart F—Disclosure Requirements—(continued)	
2520.104b-5	ERISA Notice.
2520.104b-10	Summary Annual Report.
2520.104b-12	Summary Annual Report for 1975 Plan Year Optional method of distribution for certain multiemployer plans.
2520.104b-30	Charges for documents.
	Authority: Secs. 101, 102, 103, 104, 105, 109, 110, 111(b)(2), 111(c), and 505, Pub. L. 93-406, 88 Stat. 840-52 and 894 (29 U.S.C. 1021-25, 1029-31, and 1135); Secretary of Labor's Order No. 27-74, 13-76, 1-87, and Labor Management Services Administration Order No. 2-6.

Exhibit A-3

QUICK REFERENCE CHART FOR FILING THE FORM 5500[28]

	Large Pension Plan	Small Pension Plan Filing Form 5500 Series, Not Form 5500-SF or 5500-EZ	Large Welfare Plan	Small Welfare Plan Filing Form 5500 Series, Not Form 5500-SF or 5500-EZ	DFE
Form 5500	Must complete.	Must complete.	Must complete.	Must complete.[29]	Must complete.
Schedule A (Insurance Information)	Must complete if plan has insurance contracts.	Must complete if plan has insurance contracts.	Must complete if plan has insurance contracts.	Must complete if plan has insurance contracts.	Must complete if MTIA, 103-12 IE or GIA has insurance contracts.
Schedule C (Service Provider Information)	Must complete Part I if service provider was paid $5,000 or more, Part II if a service provider failed to provide information necessary for the completion of Part I and Part III if an accountant or actuary was terminated.	Not required.	Must complete Part I if service provider was paid $5,000 or more, Part II if a service provider failed to provide information necessary for the completion of Part I, and Part III if an accountant or actuary was terminated.	Not required.	MTIAs, GIAs and 103-12 IEs must complete Part I if service provider paid $5,000 or more, and Part II if a service provider failed to provide information necessary for the completion of Part I. GIAs and 103-12 IEs must complete Part III if accountant was terminated.
Schedule D (DFE/Participating Plan Information)	Must complete Part I if plan participated in a CCT, PSA, MTIA, or 103-12 IE.	Must complete Part I if plan participated in a CCT, PSA, MTIA, or 103-12 IE.	Must complete Part I if plan participated in a CCT, PSA, MTIA, or 103-12 IE.	Must complete Part I if plan participated in a CCT, PSA, MTIA, or 103-12 IE.	All DFEs must complete Part II, and DFEs that invest in a CCT, PSA, or 103-12 IE must also complete Part I.
Schedule G (Financial Schedules)	Must complete if Schedule H, lines 4b, 4c, or 4d are "Yes."[30]	Not required.	Must complete if Schedule H, lines 4b, 4c, or 4d are "Yes."[29,30]	Not required.	Must complete if Schedule H, lines 4b, 4c, or 4d for a GIA, MTIA, or 103-12 IE are "Yes."[30]

(continued)

QUICK REFERENCE CHART FOR FILING THE FORM 5500[28]—(continued)

	Large Pension Plan	Small Pension Plan Filing Form 5500 Series, Not Form 5500-SF or 5500-EZ	Large Welfare Plan	Small Welfare Plan Filing Form 5500 Series, Not Form 5500-SF or 5500-EZ	DFE
Schedule H (Financial Information)	Must complete.[30]	Not required.	Must complete.[29,30]	Not required	All DFEs must complete Parts I, II, & III. MTIAs, 103-12 IEs, and GIAs must also complete Part IV.[30]
Schedule I (Financial Information)	Not required.	Must complete.	Not required.	Must complete.[29]	Not required.
Schedule MB (Actuarial Information)	Must complete if multiemployer defined benefit plan or money purchase plan subject to minimum funding standards.[31]	Must complete if multiemployer defined benefit plan or money purchase plan subject to minimum funding standards.[31]	Not required.	Not required.	Not required.
Schedule R (Pension Plan Information)	Must complete.[32]	Must complete.[32]	Not required.	Not required.	Not required.

(continued)

QUICK REFERENCE CHART FOR FILING THE FORM 5500[28]—(continued)

	Large Pension Plan	Small Pension Plan Filing Form 5500 Series, Not Form 5500-SF or 5500-EZ	Large Welfare Plan	Small Welfare Plan Filing Form 5500 Series, Not Form 5500-SF or 5500-EZ	DFE
Schedule SB (Actuarial Information)	Must complete if single-employer or multiple-employer defined benefit plan, including an eligible combined plan and subject to minimum funding standards.	Must complete if single-employer or multiple-employer defined benefit plan, including an eligible combined plan and subject to minimum funding standards.	Not required.	Not required.	Not required.
Accountant's Report	Must attach.	Not required unless Schedule I, line 4k, is checked "No."	Must attach.	Not required.	Must attach for a GIA or 103-12 IE.

[28] This chart provides only general guidance. Not all rules and requirements are reflected. Refer to specific Form 5500 instructions and regulations for complete information on filing requirements.

[29] Unfunded, fully insured and combination unfunded or insured welfare plans covering fewer than 100 participants at the beginning of the plan year that meet the requirements of 29 CFR 2520.104-20 are exempt from filing an annual report. Such a plan with 100 or more participants must file an annual report, but is exempt under 29 CFR 2520.104-44 from the accountant's report requirement and completing Schedule H, but MUST complete Schedule G, Part III, to report any nonexempt transactions.

[30] Schedules of assets and reportable (5 percent) transactions also must be filed with the Form 5500 if Schedule H, lines 4i or 4j is "Yes," but use of printed form is not required.

[31] Certain money purchase defined contribution plans are required to complete Schedule MB, lines 3, 9, and 10 in accordance with the instructions for Schedule R, line 5.

[32] A pension plan is exempt from filing Schedule R if all of the following five conditions are met:
- The plan is not a multiemployer defined benefit plan.
- The plan is not a defined benefit plan or otherwise subject to the minimum funding standards of IRC Section 412 or ERISA Section 302.
- No in-kind distributions reportable on line 1 of Schedule R were distributed during the plan year.
- No benefits were distributed during the plan year which are reportable on Form 1099-R using an EIN other than that of the plan sponsor or plan administrator.
- In the case of a plan that is not a profit-sharing, employee stock-ownership plan or stock bonus plan, no plan benefits were distributed during the plan year in the form of a single-sum distribution.

Exhibit A-4

Special Rules

"Plan Assets"—Plan Investments

DOL Regulation 29 CFR 2520.103-12 provides an alternative method of reporting for plans that invest in an entity (other than common or collective trusts, pooled separate accounts, and master trusts), the underlying assets of which include "plan assets" (within the meaning of DOL Reg. 29 CFR 2510.3-101) of two or more plans that are not members of a "related group" of employee benefit plans. For reporting purposes, these investment entities (commonly referred to as 103-12 Investment Entities) are required to provide certain information directly to DOL for the fiscal year of the entity ending with or within the plan year for which the plan's annual report is made. This information includes the report of an independent qualified public accountant regarding the *statements* and *schedules* described in DOL Reg. 29 CFR 2520.103-12(b)(2)-(5), which meets the requirements of DOL Reg. 29 CFR 2520.103-1(b)(5).

Fringe Benefit Plans

Fringe benefit plans may also be welfare benefit plans required to file annual reports under Title I of ERISA.

Welfare Benefit Plans

Under ERISA, according to DOL Regulation 29 CFR 2510.3-1, a welfare plan provides medical, surgical, or hospital benefits, or benefits in event of sickness, accident, disability, death, or unemployment, or vacation benefits, apprenticeship or training programs, or day-care centers (distinct from dependent care assistance programs), scholarship funds, prepaid legal services and certain benefits under the Labor Management Relations Act of 1947. Plan sponsors have a great degree of discretion regarding the number of benefits provided through one welfare benefit plan.

Appendix B

Examples of Controls

B.01 This appendix provides guidance for the use of service organization reports (Statement on Auditing Standards [SAS] No. 70, *Service Organizations* [AICPA, *Professional Standards*, AU sec. 324], reports)* and gives examples of selected controls for employee benefit plans (exhibit B-1, "Examples of Selected Controls for Employee Benefit Plans"). The controls included are related to specific control objectives that may be relevant to an audit of a plan's financial statements and, accordingly, control activities concerning the effectiveness, economy, and efficiency of certain management decision-making processes are not included. The examples are not intended to be all-inclusive or to suggest the specific objectives and controls that should necessarily be adopted by employee benefit plans. Some of the illustrated control objectives may not be relevant to particular plans because of the type of plan or the absence of certain types of transactions. When using the objectives in exhibit B-1, auditors may find it useful to keep in mind the assertions set forth in AU section 326, *Audit Evidence* (AICPA, *Professional Standards*).[1] AU section 318, *Performing Audit Procedures in Response to Assessed Risks and Evaluating the Audit Evidence Obtained* (AICPA, *Professional Standards*), states that the auditor should design and perform further audit procedures whose nature, timing, and extent are responsive to the assessed risks of material misstatement at the relevant assertion level. The purpose is to provide a clear linkage between the nature, timing, and extent of the auditor's further audit procedures and the risk assessments. Exhibit B-1 references the chapters in this guide where suggested auditing procedures can be found for each of the control objectives identified.

B.02 Many SAS No. 70 reports include a list of controls that should be in place at the user organization. If effective user controls are not in place, the service organization controls may not compensate for such weaknesses. The user auditor my need to test the user organization controls to ensure that they are in place. Exhibit B-2, "Examples of User Controls When a Service Organization is Utilized," provides examples of user controls that might be implemented when significant plan operations are performed by a service organization.

---

* The Auditing Standards Board has issued Statement on Standards for Attestation Engagements (SSAE) No. 16, *Reporting on Controls at a Service Organization* (AICPA, *Professional Standards*, AT sec. 801), which will replace the guidance contained in AU section 324, *Service Organizations* (AICPA, *Professional Standards*), for a service auditor when reporting on controls at an organization that provides service to user entities when those controls are likely to be relevant to user entities' internal controls over financial reporting. It is effective for service auditors' reports for periods ending on or after June 15, 2011. Early implementation is permitted; therefore, if adopting SSAE No. 16 early, refer directly to the standard as certain guidance in this guide may not be applicable. Also, refer to the preface of this guide for additional information about the changes related to Statement on Auditing Standards (SAS) No. 70, *Service Organizations* (AICPA, *Professional Standards*, AU sec. 324).

[1] AU section 326, *Audit Evidence* (AICPA, *Professional Standards*), recategorizes assertions by classes of transactions, account balances, and presentation and disclosure. See the section titled "Use of Assertions in Obtaining Audit Evidence" in chapter 5 for additional guidance.

Exhibit B-1

Examples of Selected Controls for Employee Benefit Plans

Investments

Specific Objectives	Examples of Selected Controls
Investment transactions are recorded at the appropriate amounts and in the appropriate periods on a timely basis. (chapter 7, "Auditing Investments and Loans to Participants")[2]	• Reports submitted by trustees or asset custodians or investment managers are reviewed. • Detailed subsidiary records are reconciled to trust reports on a regular basis. • Control totals from participant's records are compared to control totals from trust reports on a regular basis. Report of trustee's/asset custodian's independent auditor is reviewed. • Purchases and Sales (as a result of contributions, distributions) of mutual funds are reviewed to determine that the net asset value agrees to published quotations. • Purchases and Sales are reviewed to determine that the appropriate fair value was utilized.
Investment income and expenses are recorded at the appropriate amount and in the appropriate period on a timely basis. (chapter 7)	• Commissions and management fees are reviewed for appropriateness and adherence to the contract. • Interest, dividends, and other sources of income, including securities lending fees, are reviewed for receipt and for accuracy by reference to reliable sources. • If income is allocated to more than one plan or participant accounts, allocation methods of income between plans and participants is documented and reviewed.

(continued)

[2] All chapter references in this appendix refer to where suggested auditing procedures for such objective can be found in this guide.

Examples of Selected Controls for Employee Benefit Plans—(continued)

*Investments—***(continued)**

Specific Objectives	Examples of Selected Controls
Investments (other than insurance contracts with insurance companies and fully benefit responsive investment contracts held by defined contribution and health and welfare plans) are measured at fair value. (chapter 7)	• Quotation sources and appraisal reports are compared with recorded values. • Pooled separate accounts and common collective trusts are compared to net asset values calculated by the issuer. • Financial statements of pooled separate accounts and common collective trusts are obtained and unit information contained in the financial statements is compared for reasonableness to the unit values reported to the plan. • Valuation methods are documented in the trust agreement or plan committee minutes. • Basis for good faith estimates including independent appraisals, if any, is documented. • Good faith estimates are approved by plan committee.
Premiums and interest relating to insurance contracts are recorded at the appropriate amount and in the appropriate period on a timely basis. (chapter 7)	• Premium statements are compared with insurance contracts. • Interest amount calculation is tested. • List of current participants is reviewed.
Investment transactions are initiated in accordance with the established investment policies. (chapter 7)	• Investment criteria or objectives are documented in the plan instrument or plan committee minutes. • Authority to execute transactions is specified in the plan instrument or plan committee minutes. • Investment transactions are reviewed by a plan committee for adherence to investment guidelines.

(continued)

Examples of Selected Controls for Employee Benefit Plans—(continued)

Investments—(continued)

Specific Objectives	Examples of Selected Controls
Investment assets are protected from loss or misappropriation. (chapter 7)	• Responsibility for investment decisions and transactions is segregated from custodian's functions. • Financial stability of financial institutions holding investments is reviewed. • Securities that are physically held (for example by a custodian or depository) are periodically counted or otherwise verified. • Written-off investments are reviewed for possible appreciation. • Documents are controlled in a limited-access, fireproof area. • Securities held by independent custodians are confirmed. • Access to computerized investment records is limited to those with a logical need for such access.
Obligations under insurance companies' insurance contracts can be met. (chapter 7)	• Financial statements of insurance companies are reviewed.
For deposits with insurance companies, terms of insurance contracts are authorized. (chapter 7)	• Terms are specified in the plan instrument. • Modifications of contracts are approved by the plan committee.

Examples of Selected Controls for Employee Benefit Plans—(continued)

Contributions Received and Related Receivables and Participant Loans

Specific Objectives	Examples of Selected Controls
Amounts of contributions by employers and participants meet authorized or required amounts. (chapter 8, "Auditing Contributions Received and Related Receivables")	• Contribution requirements or limitations are described in the plan instrument or collective bargaining agreement.
	• Contributions are determined using approved eligibility lists.
	• Actuary is used to make periodic valuations and reports.
Contributions are recorded at the appropriate amount and in the appropriate period on a timely basis. (chapter 8)	• Sponsor or employer payroll records are compared with contribution calculations. In the case of multiemployer plans, some form of periodic payroll audit is performed.
	• Initial controls are established over contribution records for both employer and participant contributions (for example, salary reduction amounts, after tax and rollovers).
	• Clerical accuracy of contribution forms is checked.
	• Subsidiary contribution records are reconciled to the trustee/asset custodian or third party administrator reports.
	• Contribution forms are reconciled to cash receipts ledger and bank deposits.
	• Control totals for participant and employer contributions are maintained.
	• Contribution receipts are issued to participants containing notices requesting reviews of discrepancies.
	• Participant contributions are remitted to the trust within guidelines prescribed by Department of Labor regulation.

(continued)

Examples of Selected Controls for Employee Benefit Plans—(continued)

Contributions Received and Related Receivables and Participant Loans—(continued)

Specific Objectives	Examples of Selected Controls
Loans receivable from plan participants and related interest income are properly reported. (chapter 7)	• Loans are made only with proper authorization based on guidelines established in the plan instrument in conformance with ERISA and tax requirements. • Entries to detailed loan records are reconciled with cash disbursements and receipts records. • Interest income is calculated periodically in accordance with rates established in the plan instrument and properly accrued. • Detailed records maintained by third party administrator are reconciled with trustee's or asset custodian's reports. • Records are reviewed periodically for past-due amounts.
Access to cash receipts, cash receipts records, and contribution records is suitably controlled to prevent or detect within a timely period the interception of unrecorded cash receipts or the abstraction of recorded cash receipts. (chapter 8)	• Cash is independently controlled upon receipt. • Cash receipts are deposited intact daily. • Checks are restrictively endorsed upon receipt. • Responsibility for receiving and processing contributions is adequately segregated. • Bank accounts are reconciled monthly. • Past-due contributions are investigated on a timely basis. • Access to computerized contribution records is limited to those with a logical need for such access.

Examples of Selected Controls for Employee Benefit Plans—(continued)

Benefit Payments Claims and Distributions

Specific Objectives	*Examples of Selected Controls*
Payments are recorded at the appropriate amount and in the appropriate period on a timely basis. (chapter 9, "Auditing Benefit Payments," and chapter 10, "Auditing Participant Data, Participant Allocations, and Plan Obligations")	• Calculations supporting payments are checked for clerical accuracy. • Benefits and claims payable outstanding for a long period are investigated. • Initial controls are established over applications. • Amounts are compared with plan or insurance company records. • Control totals for monthly pension benefits are maintained. • Participants or beneficiaries are notified of their right to have denied claims reviewed. • Initial controls are established over the maximum contributions allowed under tax regulations and corrective distributions made as required by tax regulations. • Initial controls are established over hardship withdrawals and documentation is maintained that supports the withdrawal request, authorization, amount and adherence to related tax regulations. • If required by the plan agreement, participants making hardship withdrawals do not make any contributions to any plan during the six months following the withdrawal. • Initial controls are established over forfeitures and utilization/allocation of forfeitures is made in accordance with the plan agreement.

(continued)

Examples of Selected Controls for Employee Benefit Plans—(continued)

Benefit Payments Claims and Distributions—(continued)

Specific Objectives	Examples of Selected Controls
Payments are determined and authorized in accordance with the plan instrument. (chapters 9–10)	• Changes in participant eligibility are approved by the plan committee. • Eligibility lists are approved. • Signed application forms or other authorized procedures (that is, endorsed checks) are used. • Applications that provide for review of eligibility, benefit amounts, or plan compliance require approval.
Participant's benefit and cash disbursement records are controlled to prevent or detect on a timely basis unauthorized or duplicate payments. (chapters 9–10)	• Responsibilities for benefit approval, recording of benefits, and maintenance of participant files are adequately segregated. • Blank forms are prenumbered and effectively controlled. • Periodic correspondence with retired beneficiaries is maintained, and correspondence or payments are returnable to plan committee if undeliverable. • Check endorsements are compared with signature in applicable participant records. • Supporting documents are effectively canceled on payment. • Access to computerized benefit payment records is limited to those with a logical need for such access.

Examples of Selected Controls for Employee Benefit Plans—(continued)

Participant Data (and Plan Obligations)

Specific Objectives	Examples of Selected Controls
Participant data are properly recorded on a timely basis. (chapter 10)	• Participant forms (for example, enrollment, transfers, investment allocation) are controlled and are maintained for future reference. • Participants are encouraged to review transactions initiated electronically or directly with the third party administrator. • The number of plan participants is reconciled using enrollment forms. • Subsidiary records are maintained for participants who are active, retired, or terminated with vested benefits. • Plan records maintained by the sponsor are reconciled with information maintained by third party service providers. • Participant data are updated and reconciled to employer's personnel and payroll records (or participating employers in a multiemployer plan). • Account balances and benefit data are furnished to participants on written request.
Actuarial valuation of accumulated benefits or benefit obligations reflects the understanding and agreement of the plan committee or responsible officials. (chapter 10)	• Plan committee or responsible officials discuss with the actuary the actuarial methods and significant assumptions that are the basis for actuarial calculations.
Accumulated benefit or benefit obligation amounts and other actuarially determined information are determined periodically and recorded in the plan's records at the appropriate amounts. (chapter 10)	• Valuation report prepared by an enrolled actuary is reviewed. • Participant data in the actuary's valuation report are reconciled with the participants' subsidiary records. • Incurred but not reported claims are compared to historical claims lag reports on a periodic basis.

(continued)

Examples of Selected Controls for Employee Benefit Plans—(continued)

Participant Data (and Plan Obligations)—(continued)

Specific Objectives	Examples of Selected Controls
Participant eligibility is determined in accordance with authorization. (chapter 10)	• Eligibility is defined in the plan instrument. • Enrollment applications or third party enrollment reports are reviewed by the plan committee or a responsible official.
Employees are notified of their eligibility. (chapter 10)	• Procedures for identifying and contacting eligible employees are established.
Access to participants' data is controlled to prevent unauthorized changes or additions. (chapter 10)	• Employee participation refusals are retained for future reference. • Maintenance of participant data is segregated from responsibility for benefit approval or processing. • In the case of multiemployer plans, participant data on a sample basis are updated and reconciled to the contributing employer's personnel and payroll records during the course of a payroll audit. • All participant-initiated enrollments, transfers, changes in investment allocations, and other change requests must be authorized by the participant by submitting a manually signed request form. The ability to perform these activities electronically or directly with a third party administrator is restricted to authorized participants through the use of specific identification and a personnel identification number. Invalid attempts to access and perform functions are reviewed and investigated. • Written confirmation are sent to participants for participant-initiated account activity.

Examples of Selected Controls for Employee Benefit Plans—(continued)

Administrative Expenses

Specific Objectives	Examples of Selected Controls
Administrative expenses are recorded at the appropriate amount and in the appropriate period on a timely basis. (chapter 12, "Other Auditing Considerations")	• Expenses are compared to contracts and to disbursements. • If expenses are allocated to more than one plan, investment or fund, allocation methods and calculations are reviewed.
Types of administrative services to be offered are authorized. (chapter 12)	• Administrative services are described in the plan instrument. • Expenses are approved by a responsible official.
Access to accounts payable and cash disbursements records is controlled to prevent or detect on a timely basis unauthorized or duplicate payments. (chapters 9 and 12)	• Responsibilities for expense approval and processing are adequately segregated. • Supporting documents are effectively canceled on payment.

Examples of Selected Controls for Employee Benefit Plans—(continued)

Reporting

Specific Objectives	Examples of Selected Controls
Records are maintained in sufficient detail to provide for proper and timely reconciliation. (chapter 1, "Introduction and Background")	• For defined benefit plans, subsidiary ledgers are reconciled with the trustee's or asset custodian's reports on a periodic and timely basis. • For defined contribution plans the total of all participant account balances is reconciled to the net assets in the trustee's or asset custodian's reports on a periodic and timely basis.
Financial statements, actuarial information, disclosures and supplemental schedules as prepared are complete, accurate and in conformity with management's authorization. (chapters 1–6, 10, and appendix A)	• Procedures are established to identify required disclosure items, for example, party in interest transactions and transactions in excess of 5 percent of plan assets. • Accumulating information for disclosure in accordance with the rules and regulations of appropriate authorities. • Review of all financial reports and filings. • Written representations on financial matters are obtained from actuaries, trustees, asset custodians, insurance companies, and others. • Plan committee reviews presentation of, and disclosures in, financial reports. • Procedures are established to identify required supplemental schedules and determine that they are presented in accordance with the rules and regulations of appropriate authorities.

(continued)

Examples of Selected Controls for Employee Benefit Plans—(continued)

Reporting—(continued)

Specific Objectives	Examples of Selected Controls
Journal entries made are authorized. (chapters 1 and 5–6)	• Journal entries are adequately approved by a responsible official.
Accounting policies, including selections from among alternative principles, are adopted as authorized. (chapters 1 and 5–6)	• Responsibility is assigned for approval of accounting policies.
Direct and indirect access to the plan's records is controlled to protect against physical hazards and to prevent or detect on a timely basis unauthorized entries. (chapters 1 and 5–6)	• Critical forms are prenumbered and controlled before and after issuance. • Record files are maintained in a controlled area with a suitable retention program. • Information pertinent to plan activities is identified and prepared for analysis.

Examples of Selected Controls for Employee Benefit Plans—(continued)

General Computer Controls (In-house system or service organization)

Specific Objectives	Examples of Selected Controls
Changes to application system programs are authorized, tested, reviewed and approved prior to implementation in the production environment, and system modifications are properly documented.	• Segregation of duties between end users, programmers, quality assurance, library management and production operations and support personnel is maintained throughout the program change management and development process. • Separate computer environments for application development and maintenance, quality assurance testing, and production processing are maintained. Programmers and quality assurance personnel are restricted from directly modifying production source and executable code. • Program code is moved to the production processing environment by library management personnel after approval by quality assurance and management personnel.
Development, implementation, and maintenance of information systems follow a defined systems development life cycle methodology which contains management's philosophy, guidelines and direction in developing, acquiring and maintaining application systems.	• A system development life cycle methodology exists and is followed.
Physical access to the computer facility containing hardware, peripherals, communications equipment, backup media and sensitive output and forms is restricted to authorized personnel.	• Formal procedures for granting and terminating access to company facilities, including computer center, exist and are followed. • Physical access to blank check stocks, printers, and signature fonts is restricted to authorized personnel. Check logs are used to confirm checks printed and numbers used.

(continued)

Examples of Selected Controls for Employee Benefit Plans—(continued)

General Computer Controls (In-house system or service organization)—(continued)

Specific Objectives	Examples of Selected Controls
Logical access security is administered and maintained according to management's intentions and authorization.	• Access to the system is granted to individuals by security administration personnel based on written request for such authorization. • Access rights to terminated or transferred employees are removed or modified timely by the security administration personnel based upon written request from authorized management.
Access to computer resources such as application programs, data files, sensitive utilities, and system commands is limited to authorized individuals.	• Access to the system is granted to each user via a unique user identification and password. • Access to systems is limited based upon job responsibilities. • The ability to modify application executable programs and production data files is limited to authorized individuals.
Remote access to dial-up system is established for authorized individuals, plan administrators, and participants.	• The voice response system and Internet and intranet access is limited to authorized participants through the use of specific identification and a personnel identification number. Invalid attempts to access and perform functions are rejected and transferred to an assigned representative.
Critical processing activities can be continued or restored to an acceptable level without prolonged delay or loss of service in the event of disruption.	• Master files and transaction files are stored off-site to allow recreation of the master file. • Contingency plans have been developed for alternative processing. • Disaster recovery plans have been developed and tested for adequacy.

Exhibit B-2

Examples of User Controls When a Service Organization is Utilized

Specific Objectives	Examples of Selected Controls
Investments	
Controls should provide reasonable assurance that the appropriate asset purchases or redemptions are made as a result of contributions, disbursements, or other changes	• Quarterly and annual plan reports are sent to the participant. Reports should be reviewed by the participant for accuracy of dividends and capital gains processing. Plan administrators should have procedures in place to timely follow-up on all reconciling items.
Contributions Received and Related Receivables and Participant Loans	
Controls should provide reasonable assurance that contributions are adequately safeguarded upon receipt and processed in a timely manner by authorized individuals.	• Confirmation notices (that is, turnaround documents) and quarterly statements are mailed to plan administrators and participants. These individuals have procedures in place for reviewing these documents on a timely basis for accuracy and completeness. Plan administrators should have procedures in place to timely follow-up on all reconciling items
	• Plan administrators should have policies and procedures in place, which provide reasonable assurance that the confidentiality of their password is maintained and access to the recordkeeping software is limited to authorized personnel.
Controls should provide reasonable assurance that contribution remittances are applied to the appropriate plan and participant accounts and processed accurately and completely by money type (that is, contributions versus loan repayments) according to the investment options selected by the participant.	• Confirmation notices (that is, turnaround documents) and quarterly statements are mailed to plan administrators and participants. These individuals should have procedures in place for reviewing these documents on a timely basis for accuracy and completeness.
	• Plan administrators should have policies and procedures in place, which provide reasonable assurance that their input into the recordkeeping system is accurate and complete. Plan administrators should have procedures in place to timely follow-up on all reconciling items.

(continued)

Examples of User Controls When a Service Organization is Utilized—(continued)

Specific Objectives	Examples of Selected Controls
Benefit Payments, Claims and Distributions:	
Controls should provide reasonable assurance that disbursements and related transactions (for example, redemptions, forfeitures) are authorized and valid.	• The plan administrator should have procedures in place which provide reasonable assurance that disbursement requests are authorized and in compliance with the plan provisions. • The plan administrator informs the recordkeeper in writing if any disbursement amounts are to be forfeited. The plan administrator should have procedures in place, which provide reasonable assurance the information communicated to the recordkeeper is complete and accurate.
Controls should provide reasonable assurance that disbursements and related transactions, including taxes, penalties and forfeitures, are recorded and processed accurately, completely, and on a timely basis.	• The plan administrator informs the recordkeeper in writing if any disbursement amounts are to be forfeited. The plan administrator should have procedures in place, which provide reasonable assurance the information communicated to the recordkeeper is complete and accurate. • Confirmations and quarterly statements are sent to participants and plan administrators. Participants and plan administrators should have procedures in place for reviewing confirmations and quarterly statements on a timely basis for accuracy and completeness. Plan administrators should have procedures in place to timely follow-up on all reconciling items.

(continued)

Examples of User Controls When a Service Organization is Utilized—(continued)

Specific Objectives	Examples of Selected Controls
Participant Data (and Plan Obligations)	
Controls should provide reasonable assurance that all additions and modifications to plan information are authorized and are recorded and processed completely, accurately and on a timely basis.	• Confirmation notices are sent to participants to confirm accuracy of additions and modifications of data. Plan administrators should have procedures in place to timely follow-up on all discrepancies. • Confirmations are reviewed by the participant.
Controls should provide reasonable assurance that participant data is recorded and processed accurately, completely and on a timely basis, and that modifications to participant data are valid and authorized.	• Confirmation notices are generated and mailed to participants to review the completeness and accuracy of information entered into the recordkeeping system. Plan administrators should have procedures in place to timely follow-up on all discrepancies. • Participants have procedures in place for regularly reviewing the completeness and accuracy of information included on the confirmation notices and communicating any discrepancies to the plan administrator or recordkeeper on a timely basis. • Plan administrators should have control policies and procedures in place which provide reasonable assurance that employees are eligible, authorized and valid participants before submitting employee application forms to the recordkeeper or enrolling employees through online access.
Controls should provide reasonable assurance that participants initiated transfers, changes in investment allocations, and other changes are authorized and valid.	• Confirmations and quarterly statements are sent to participants and plan administrators. Participants and plan administrators should have procedures in place for reviewing confirmations and quarterly statements on a timely basis for accuracy and completeness. Plan administrators should have procedures in place to timely follow-up on all reconciling items.

(continued)

Examples of User Controls When a Service Organization is Utilized—(continued)

Specific Objectives	Examples of Selected Controls
Controls should provide reasonable assurance that participant-initiated transfers, changes in investment allocations, and other changes are processed accurately, completely and on a timely basis.	• Confirmations and quarterly statements are sent to participants and plan administrators. Participants and plan administrators should have procedures in place for reviewing confirmations and quarterly statements on a timely basis for accuracy and completeness. Plan administrators should have procedures in place to timely follow-up on all reconciling items.
Reporting	
Controls should provide reasonable assurance that the annual plan reports are complete, accurate and generated on a timely basis.	• Quarterly statements and annual plan reports are sent to plan administrators. Plan administrators should have procedures in place for reviewing these documents on a timely basis for accuracy and completeness and notifying the recordkeeper of errors or discrepancies in a timely manner.
Controls should provide reasonable assurance that accurate plan data is available to provide accurate results when annual testing is performed.	• Plan administrators should have procedures in place, which provide reasonable assurance that plan data (census and compensation) are communicated accurately and on a timely basis to the recordkeeper.
Controls should provide reasonable assurance that access to computer resources such as application programs, data files, sensitive utilities and system commands is limited to authorized individuals.	• Plan administrators should have policies and procedures in place, which provide reasonable assurance that the confidentiality of their password is maintained and access to the software is limited to authorized personnel.
Controls should provide reasonable assurance that remote access to recordkeeping systems are established for authorized individuals and customers.	• Policies and procedures should be designed and implemented at user organizations to provide reasonable assurance that access to the recordkeeping system's hardware, software, voice response system and password is granted only to authorized individuals.

Appendix C

Cross Reference of FASB and AICPA Accounting Pronouncements to the FASB Accounting Standards Codification™

C.01 The Financial Accounting Standards Board (FASB) *Accounting Standards Codification™* (ASC) has disassembled and reassembled thousands of accounting pronouncements (including those of FASB, the Emerging Issues Task Force, and the AICPA) to organize them under approximately 90 topics. Most codified accounting pronouncements were codified into numerous topics; the following list includes the most prevalent and relevant topic(s) discussed in this guide and the specific accounting pronouncement to which it was codified. It is important to remember that the accounting guidance in each of the industry specific topics (in this case 960, 962, and 965) only explain the *industry specific* guidance—for guidance on a topic as it would relate to all entities, consult the appropriate topic in the codification (for example, receivables). As stated in the FASB ASC notice to constituents, "these topics [industries] relate to accounting that is unique to an industry or type of activity."

C.02 This appendix provides a cross reference listing of the more frequently referenced FASB and AICPA accounting pronouncements to FASB ASC.

Pronouncement Reference	Name	FASB ASC Reference	Name
FASB Statement			
No. 5	Accounting for Contingencies	450	Contingencies
No. 35	Accounting and Reporting by Defined Pension Benefit Plans	960	Defined Benefit Pension Plans
No. 102	Statement of Cash Flows—Exemption of Certain Enterprises and Classification of Cash Flows from Certain Securities Acquired for Resale—an amendment of FASB Statement No. 95	230	Statement of Cash Flows
No. 106	Employers' Accounting for Postretirement Benefits Other Than Pensions	715	Compensation—Retirement Benefits
No. 112	Employers' Accounting for Postemployment Benefits—an amendment of FASB Statements No. 5 and 43	712	Compensation—Nonretirement Postemployment Benefits
No. 133	Accounting for Derivative Instruments and Hedging Activities	815	Derivatives and Hedging
No. 140	Accounting for Transfers and Servicing of Financial Assets and Extinguishments of Liabilities—a replacement of FASB Statement No. 125	860	Transfers and Servicing
No. 144	Accounting for the Impairment or Disposal of Long-Lived Assets	360	Property, Plant, and Equipment
No. 154	Accounting Changes and Error Corrections—a replacement of APB Opinion No. 20 and FASB Statement No. 3	250	Accounting Changes and Error Corrections
No. 157	Fair Value Measurements	820	Fair Value Measurements and Disclosures

(continued)

Pronouncement Reference	Name	FASB ASC Reference	Name
No. 159	*The Fair Value Option for Financial Assets and Financial Liabilities—Including an amendment of FASB Statement No. 115*	825	*Financial Instruments*
No. 161	*Disclosures about Derivative Instruments and Hedging Activities—an amendment of FASB Statement No. 133*	815	*Derivatives and Hedging*
No. 165	*Subsequent Events*	855	*Subsequent Events*
No. 166	*Accounting for Transfers of Financial Assets—an amendment of FASB Statement No. 140*	860	*Transfers and Servicing*

AICPA Statement of Position (SOP)

Pronouncement Reference	Name	FASB ASC Reference	Name
SOP 92-6 (as amended by SOP 01-2)	*Accounting and Reporting by Health and Welfare Benefit Plans*	965	*Health and Welfare Benefit Plans*
SOP 94-4 (as amended by FASB Staff Position AAG INV-1 and SOP 94-4-1)	*Reporting of Investment Contracts Held by Health and Welfare Benefit Plans and Defined-Contribution Pension Plans*	962	*Defined Contribution Pension Plans*
		965	*Health and Welfare Benefit Plans*
SOP 94-6	*Disclosure of Certain Significant Risks and Uncertainties*	275	*Risks and Uncertainties*
SOP 99-2	*Accounting for and Reporting of Postretirement Medical Benefit (401(h)) Features of Defined Benefit Pension Plans*	960	*Defined Benefit Pension Plans*
		965	*Health and Welfare Benefit Plans*

(continued)

AAG-EBP APP C

Pronouncement Reference	Name	FASB ASC Reference	Name
SOP 99-3	*Accounting for and Reporting of Certain Defined Contribution Plan Investments and Other Disclosure Matters*	962	*Defined Contribution Pension Plans*
		965	*Health and Welfare Benefit Plans*

Accounting Principles Board (APB) Opinion

No. 22	*Disclosure of Accounting Policies*	235	*Notes to Financial Statements*

FASB Interpretation

No. 48	*Accounting for Uncertainty in Income Taxes—an interpretation of FASB Statement No. 109*	740	*Income Taxes*

Appendix D

Illustrative Financial Statements: Defined Benefit Pension Plans

D.01 These illustrative financial statements were originally derived from Financial Accounting Standards Board (FASB) Statement No. 35, *Accounting and Reporting by Defined Benefit Pension Plans*, which has now been codified in FASB *Accounting Standards Codification* (ASC) 960, *Plan Accounting— Defined Benefit Pension Plans*. These illustrative financial statements have since been modified to include certain changes necessary due to the subsequent issuance of authoritative guidance. This appendix illustrates certain applications of the requirements of FASB ASC 960 that are applicable for the annual financial statements of a hypothetical plan, the C&H Company Pension Plan. It does not illustrate other requirements of FASB ASC 960 as well as other FASB ASC topics that might be applicable in circumstances other than those assumed for the C&H Company Pension Plan. The formats presented and the wording of accompanying notes are illustrative and are not necessarily the only possible presentation. Further, the circumstances assumed for the C&H Company Pension Plan are designed to facilitate illustration of many of the requirements of FASB ASC 960. The illustrative financial statements in this appendix have been amended to conform to FASB ASC 820, *Fair Value Measurements and Disclosures*.[*]

Note: FASB ASC 820 disclosures are limited to the financial instruments contained within this specific example. It is recommended that users consult all the illustrative financial statements within appendixes D–F for FASB ASC 820 examples of different types of financial instruments.

D.02 Included are illustrations of the following alternatives permitted by paragraphs 1–8 of FASB ASC 960-20-45:

    a. An end-of-year versus beginning-of-year benefit information date

    b. Separate versus combined statements for presenting information regarding (*a*) the net assets available for benefits and the actuarial present value of accumulated plan benefits and (*b*) changes in the net assets available for benefits and changes in the actuarial present value of accumulated plan benefits

    c. A separate statement that reconciles the year-to-year change in the actuarial present value of accumulated plan benefits versus presenting the effects of a change in actuarial assumptions on the face of the statement of accumulated plan benefits

---

[*] The illustrative financial statements and footnote disclosures included in this appendix have been updated to reflect FASB ASC references. However, in FASB's notice to constituents, it suggests the use of plain English in financial statement footnotes to describe broad FASB ASC topic references. They suggest a reference similar to "as required by the *Derivatives and Hedging* topic of the FASB *Accounting Standards Codification*." Entities might consider revising their financial statement references to reflect this plain English referencing, rather than the use of specific FASB ASC references. For specific information on FASB ASC, please see the preface in the guide.

D.03 Although not illustrated, FASB ASC 960-20-45-2 permits the information regarding the actuarial present value of accumulated plan benefits and changes therein to be presented as notes to the financial statements.

FASB ASC 960-20-45-2 also permits certain flexibility in presenting the information regarding the actuarial present value of accumulated plan benefits and changes therein. Therefore either or both of these categories of information may be presented on the face of one or more financial statements or the notes thereto. Regardless of the format selected, each category of information should be presented in its entirety in the same location. If a statement format is selected for either category, a separate statement may be used to present that information or, provided the information is as of the same date or for the same period, that information may be presented together with information regarding the net assets available for benefits and the year-to-year changes therein.

D.04 This appendix also illustrates certain applications of the provisions of FASB ASC 960 that apply for the annual financial statements of a hypothetical defined benefit pension plan that has been amended to include a 401(h) account (exhibits D-9–D-11). This appendix does not illustrate other provisions of FASB ASC 960 as well as other FASB ASC topics that might apply in circumstances other than those assumed in the illustration. It also does not illustrate all disclosures required for a fair presentation in conformity with accounting principles generally accepted in the United States of America (U.S. GAAP). The formats presented and the wording of accompanying notes are only illustrative and are not necessarily the only possible presentations.

D.05 The notes to the financial statements are for the illustrative financial statements that use end-of-year benefit information. Modifications to the notes necessary when beginning-of-year benefit information is presented are in brackets.

D.06 U.S. GAAP does not require comparative financial statements unless the beginning-of-year benefit information is used. In this case, a prior-year statement of net assets available for benefits and changes therein must also be presented in order to report on the financial status of the plan. The Employee Retirement Income Security Act of 1974 (ERISA) requires a comparative statement of net assets available for benefits. The illustrative financial statements are intended to comply with the requirements of ERISA.

D.07 ERISA and Department of Labor (DOL) regulations require that certain information be included in supplemental schedules, which are not required under U.S. GAAP, and are reported on by the independent auditor. See appendix A, "ERISA and Related Regulations," for a further discussion of the ERISA and DOL requirements.

D.08 The Statement of Net Assets Available for Benefits assuming a beginning-of-year information date would be the same as that illustrated in exhibit D-1.

CONTENTS

I. Illustrations Assuming an End-of-Year Benefit Information Date

Exhibit D-1

C&H Company Pension Plan
Statement of Net Assets Available for Benefits

	December 31,	
	20X1	20X0
Assets		
Investments, at fair value (notes E, F, G, and H):		
Plan interest in C&H Master Trust	$2,250,000	$1,860,000
C&H Company common stock	690,000	880,000
Guaranteed investment contract with insurance company	1,000,000	890,000
Corporate bonds	3,500,000	3,670,000
U.S. government securities	350,000	270,000
Mortgages	480,000	460,000
Real estate	270,000	240,000
Total investments	8,540,000	8,270,000
Receivables		
Employer's contribution	40,000	35,000
Securities sold	310,000	175,000
Accrued interest and dividends	77,000	76,000
Total receivables	427,000	286,000
Cash	200,000	90,000
Total assets	9,167,000	8,646,000
Liabilities		
Due to broker for securities purchased	—	400,000
Accounts payable	70,000	60,000
Accrued expenses	85,000	40,000
Total liabilities	155,000	500,000
Net assets available for benefits	$9,012,000	$8,146,000

The accompanying notes are an integral part of the financial statements.

Exhibit D-2

C&H Company Pension Plan
Statement of Changes in Net Assets
Available for Benefits

	Year Ended December 31, 20X1
Investment income:	
Net appreciation in fair value of investments (note E)	$ 278,000
Interest	325,000
Dividends	5,000
	608,000
Less investment expenses	39,000
	569,000
Plan interest in C&H Master Trust investment income (note G)	129,000
	698,000
Contributions (note C):	
Employer	780,000
Employees	450,000
	1,230,000
Total additions	1,928,000
Benefits paid directly to participants	740,000
Purchases of annuity contracts (note H)	257,000
	997,000
Administrative expenses	65,000
Total deductions	1,062,000
Net increase	866,000
Net assets available for benefits:	
Beginning of year	8,146,000
End of year	$9,012,000

The accompanying notes are an integral part of the financial statements.

Exhibit D-3

C&H Company Pension Plan
Statement of Accumulated Plan Benefits

	December 31,	
	20X1	20X0
Actuarial present value of accumulated plan benefits (notes B and C)		
Vested benefits:		
Participants currently receiving payments	$3,040,000	$2,950,000
Other participants	8,120,000	6,530,000
	11,160,000	9,480,000
Nonvested benefits	2,720,000	2,400,000
Total actuarial present value of accumulated plan benefits	$13,880,000	$11,880,000

The accompanying notes are an integral part of the financial statements.

Exhibit D-4

C&H Company Pension Plan
Statement of Changes in Accumulated Plan Benefits

	Year Ended December 31, 20X1
Actuarial present value of accumulated plan benefits at beginning of year	$11,880,000
Increase (decrease) during the year attributable to:	
Plan amendment (note I)	2,410,000
Change in actuarial assumptions (note B)	(1,050,500)
Benefits accumulated	895,000
Increase for interest due to the decrease in the discount period (note B)	742,500
Benefits paid	(997,000)
Net increase	2,000,000
Actuarial present value of accumulated plan benefits at end of year	$13,880,000

The accompanying notes are an integral part of the financial statements.

Exhibit D-5

C&H Company Pension Plan
Statement of Accumulated Plan Benefits and Net Assets Available for Benefits
[An alternative for exhibits D-1 and D-3]

	December 31,	
	20X1	20X0
Accumulated Plan Benefits (notes B and C)		
Actuarial present value of vested benefits		
Participants currently receiving payments	$3,040,000	$2,950,000
Other participants	8,120,000	6,530,000
	11,160,000	9,480,000
Actuarial present value of nonvested benefits	2,720,000	2,400,000
Total actuarial present value of accumulated plan benefits	13,880,000	11,880,000
Net Assets Available for Benefits		
Investments, at fair value (notes E, F, G, and H):		
Plan interest in C&H Master Trust	2,250,000	1,860,000
C&H Company common stock	690,000	880,000
Guaranteed investment contract with insurance company	1,000,000	890,000
Corporate bonds	3,500,000	3,670,000
U.S government securities	350,000	270,000
Mortgages	480,000	460,000
Real estate	270,000	240,000
Total investments	8,540,000	8,270,000
Receivables		
Employer's contribution	40,000	35,000
Securities sold	310,000	175,000
Accrued interest and dividends	77,000	76,000
Total receivables	427,000	286,000
Cash	200,000	90,000
Total assets	9,167,000	8,646,000
Due to broker for securities purchased	—	400,000
Accounts payable	70,000	60,000
Accrued expenses	85,000	40,000
Total liabilities	155,000	500,000
Net assets available for benefits	9,012,000	8,146,000
Excess of actuarial present value of accumulated plan benefits over net assets available for benefits	$4,868,000	$3,734,000

The accompanying notes are an integral part of the financial statements.

Exhibit D-6

C&H Company Pension Plan
Statement of Changes in Accumulated Plan Benefits and Net Assets Available for Benefits
[An alternative for exhibits D-2 and D-4]

	Year Ended December 31, 20X1
Net Increase in Actuarial Present Value of Accumulated Plan Benefits	
Increase (decrease) during the year attributable to:	
Plan amendment (note I)	$2,410,000
Change in actuarial assumptions (note B)	(1,050,500)
Benefits accumulated	895,000
Increase for interest due to the decrease in the discount period (note B)	742,500
Benefits paid	(997,000)
Net increase	2,000,000
Net Increase in Net Assets Available for Benefits	
Investment income:	
Net appreciation in fair value of investments (note E)	278,000
Interest	325,000
Dividends	5,000
	608,000
Less investment expenses	39,000
	569,000
Plan interest in C&H Master Trust investment income (note G)	129,000
	698,000
Contributions (note C):	
Employer	780,000
Employees	450,000
	1,230,000
Total additions	1,928,000
Benefits paid directly to participants	740,000
Purchases of annuity contracts (note H)	257,000
	997,000
Administrative expenses	65,000
Total deductions	1,062,000
Net increase	866,000
Increase in excess of actuarial present value of accumulated plan benefits over net assets available for benefits	1,134,000
Excess of actuarial present value of accumulated plan benefits over net assets available for benefits:	
Beginning of year	3,734,000
End of year	$4,868,000

The accompanying notes are an integral part of the financial statements.

II. Illustrations Assuming a Beginning-of-Year Benefit Information Date

Exhibit D-7

C&H Company Pension Plan
Statement of Changes in Net Assets
Available for Benefits

(If a beginning-of-year benefit information date is selected)

	Year Ended December 31,	
	20X1	20X0
Investment income:		
Net appreciation in fair value of investments (note E)	$ 278,000	$ 41,000
Interest	325,000	120,000
Dividends	5,000	90,000
	608,000	251,000
Less investment expenses	39,000	35,000
	569,000	216,000
Plan interest in C&H Master Trust investment income (note G)	129,000	150,000
	698,000	366,000
Contributions (note C):		
Employer	780,000	710,000
Employees	450,000	430,000
	1,230,000	1,140,000
Total additions	1,928,000	1,506,000
Benefits paid directly to participants	740,000	561,000
Purchases of annuity contracts (note H)	257,000	185,000
	997,000	746,000
Administrative expenses	65,000	58,000
Total deductions	1,062,000	804,000
Net increase	866,000	702,000
Net assets available for benefits:		
Beginning of year	8,146,000	7,444,000
End of year	$9,012,000	$8,146,000

The accompanying notes are an integral part of the financial statements.

Exhibit D-8

C&H Company Pension Plan
Statement of Accumulated Plan Benefits
(If a beginning-of-year benefit information date is selected)

	December 31, 20X0
Actuarial present value of accumulated plan benefits (notes B and C),	
Vested benefits:	
Participants currently receiving payments	$2,950,000
Other participants	6,530,000
	9,480,000
Nonvested benefits	2,400,000
Total actuarial present value of accumulated plan benefits	$11,880,000

During 20X0, the actuarial present value of accumulated plan benefits increased $700,000 as a result of a change in actuarial assumptions (note B). Also see note I. The actuarial present value of accumulated plan benefits was $9,890,000 at December 31, 20W9.

The accompanying notes are an integral part of the financial statements.

C&H Company Pension Plan
Notes to Financial Statements[1]

A. Description of Plan

The following brief description of the C&H Company Pension Plan (plan) is provided for general information purposes only. Participants should refer to the plan agreement for more complete information

1. *General.* The plan is a defined benefit pension plan covering substantially all employees of C&H Company (company). It is subject to the provisions of ERISA.

2. *Pension Benefits.* Employees with 5 or more years of service are entitled to annual pension benefits beginning at normal retirement age (65) equal to 1 percent of their final 5-year average annual compensation for each year of service. The plan permits early retirement at ages 55–64. Employees may elect to receive their pension benefits in the form of a joint and survivor annuity. If employees terminate before rendering 5 years of service, they forfeit the right to receive the portion of their accumulated plan benefits attributable to the company's contributions. Employees may elect to receive the value of their accumulated plan benefits as a lump-sum distribution upon retirement or termination, or they may elect to receive their benefits as a life annuity payable monthly from retirement. For each employee electing a life annuity, payments will not be less than the greater of (*a*) the employee's accumulated contributions plus interest or (*b*) an annuity for 5 years.

3. *Death and Disability Benefits.* If an active employee dies at age 55 or older, a death benefit equal to the value of the employee's accumulated pension benefits is paid to the employee's beneficiary. Active employees who become totally disabled receive annual disability benefits that are equal to the normal retirement benefits they have accumulated as of the time they become disabled. Disability benefits are paid until normal retirement age at which time disabled participants begin receiving normal retirement benefits computed as though they had been employed to normal retirement age with their annual compensation remaining the same as at the time they became disabled.

B. Summary of Accounting Policies

The following are the significant accounting policies followed by the plan:

1. *Basis of Accounting.* The accompanying financial statements are prepared on the accrual basis of accounting.

2. *Use of Estimates.* The preparation of financial statements in conformity with accounting principles generally accepted in the United States of America requires management to make estimates and assumptions that affect the reported amounts of assets, liabilities, and changes therein, disclosure of contingent assets and liabilities, and the actuarial present value of accumulated plan benefits at the

---

[1] The notes are for the accompanying illustrative financial statements that use an end-of-year benefit information date. Modifications necessary to accompany the illustrative financial statements that use a beginning-of-year benefit information date are presented in brackets.

date of the financial statements. Actual results could differ from those estimates.

3. *Investment Valuation and Income Recognition.* Investments are reported at fair value. Fair value is the price that would be received to sell an asset or paid to transfer a liability in an orderly transaction between market participants at the measurement date. See note F for a discussion of fair value measurements.

    Purchases and sales of securities are recorded on a trade-date basis. Interest income is recorded on the accrual basis. Dividends are recorded on the ex-dividend date. Net appreciation includes the plan's gains and losses on investments bought and sold as well as held during the year.

4. *Actuarial Present Value of Accumulated Plan Benefits.* Accumulated plan benefits are those future periodic payments, including lump-sum distributions, that are attributable under the plan's provisions to the service employees have rendered. Accumulated plan benefits include benefits expected to be paid to (*a*) retired or terminated employees or their beneficiaries, (*b*) beneficiaries of employees who have died, and (*c*) present employees or their beneficiaries. Benefits under the plan are based on employees' compensation during their last five years of credited service. The accumulated plan benefits for active employees are based on their average compensation during the five years ending on the date as of which the benefit information is presented (the valuation date). Benefits payable under all circumstances—retirement, death, disability, and termination of employment—are included, to the extent they are deemed attributable to employee service rendered to the valuation date. Benefits to be provided via annuity contracts excluded from plan assets are excluded from accumulated plan benefits.

    The actuarial present value of accumulated plan benefits is determined by an actuary from the AAA Company and is that amount that results from applying actuarial assumptions to adjust the accumulated plan benefits to reflect the time value of money (through discounts for interest) and the probability of payment (by means of decrements such as for death, disability, withdrawal, or retirement) between the valuation date and the expected date of payment. The significant actuarial assumptions used in the valuations as of December 31, 20X1 [20X0] and 20X0 were (*a*) life expectancy of participants (the RP 2000 Combined Mortality Table was used), (*b*) retirement age assumptions (the assumed average retirement age was 60), and (*c*) investment return. The 20X1 [20X0] and 20X0 valuations included assumed average rates of return of 7 percent [6.25 percent] and 6.25 percent, respectively, including a reduction of 0.2 percent to reflect anticipated administrative expenses associated with providing benefits. The foregoing actuarial assumptions are based on the presumption that the plan will continue. Were the plan to terminate, different actuarial assumptions and other factors might be applicable in determining the actuarial present value of accumulated plan benefits.

5. *Payment of Benefits.* Benefit payments to participants are recorded upon distribution.

6. *Subsequent Events*. The plan has evaluated subsequent events through [*insert date*], the date the financial statements were available to be issued.

C. Funding Policy

As a condition of participation, employees are required to contribute 3 percent of their salary to the plan. Present employees' accumulated contributions at December 31, 20X1 and 20X0 were $2,575,000 and $2,325,000, respectively, including interest credit on an interest rate of 5 percent compounded annually. The company's funding policy is to make annual contributions to the plan in amounts that are estimated to remain a constant percentage of employees' compensation each year (approximately 5 percent for 20X1 [and 20X0]), such that, when combined with employees' contributions, all employees' benefits will be fully provided for by the time they retire. Beginning in 20X2, the company's contribution is expected to increase to approximately 6 percent to provide for the increase in benefits attributable to the plan amendment effective July, 20X1 (note H). The company's contributions for 20X1 [and 20X0] exceeded the minimum funding requirements of ERISA.

Although it has not expressed any intention to do so, the company has the right under the plan to discontinue its contributions at any time and to terminate the plan subject to the provisions set forth in ERISA.

D. Plan Termination

In the event the plan terminates, the net assets of the plan will be allocated, as prescribed by ERISA and its related regulations, generally to provide the following benefits in the order indicated:

1. Benefits attributable to employee contributions, taking into account those paid out before termination.

2. Annuity benefits that former employees or their beneficiaries have been receiving for at least three years, or that employees eligible to retire for that three-year period would have been receiving if they had retired with benefits in the normal form of annuity under the plan. The priority amount is limited to the lowest benefit that was payable (or would have been payable) during those three years. The amount is further limited to the lowest benefit that would be payable under plan provisions in effect at any time during the five years preceding plan termination.

3. Other vested benefits insured by the Pension Benefit Guaranty Corporation (PBGC) (a U.S. government agency) up to the applicable limitations (discussed subsequently).

4. All other vested benefits (that is, vested benefits not insured by the PBGC).

5. All nonvested benefits.

Benefits to be provided via contracts under which National (note H) is obligated to pay the benefits would be excluded for allocation purposes.

Certain benefits under the plan are insured by the PBGC if the plan terminates. Generally, the PBGC guarantees most vested normal age retirement benefits, early retirement benefits, and certain disability and survivor's pensions. However, the PBGC does not guarantee all types of benefits under the plan, and the amount of benefit protection is subject to certain limitations. Vested benefits under the plan are guaranteed at the level in effect on the date of the plan's termination. However, a statutory ceiling exists, which is adjusted periodically, on the amount of an individual's monthly benefit that the PBGC guarantees. For plan terminations occurring during 20X2 that ceiling is $X,XXX per month. That ceiling applies to those pensioners who elect to receive their benefits in the form of a single-life annuity and are at least 65 years old at the time of retirement or plan termination (whichever comes later). For younger annuitants or for those who elect to receive their benefits in some form more valuable than a single-life annuity, the corresponding ceilings are actuarially adjusted downward. Benefit improvements attributable to the plan amendment effective July 1, 20X1 (note I) may not be fully guaranteed even though total benefit entitlements fall below the aforementioned ceilings. For example, none of the improvement would be guaranteed if the plan were to terminate before July 1, 20X2. After that date, the PBGC would guarantee 20 percent of any benefit improvements that resulted in benefits below the ceiling, with an additional 20 percent guaranteed each year the plan continued beyond July 1, 20X2. If the amount of the benefit increase below the ceiling is also less than $100, $20 of the increase (rather than 20 percent) becomes guaranteed by the PBGC each year following the effective date of the amendment. As a result, only the primary ceiling would be applicable after July 1, 20X6.

Whether all participants receive their benefits should the plan terminate at some future time will depend on the sufficiency, at that time, of the plan's net assets to provide for accumulated benefit obligations and may also depend on the financial condition of the plan sponsor and the level of benefits guaranteed by the PBGC.

E. Investments

The following table presents the fair values of investments.[†] Investments that represent 5 percent or more of the plan's net assets are separately identified.

	December 31,	
	20X1	20X0
C&H Company common stock (25,000 shares)	$ 690,000	$ 880,000
U.S. government securities	350,000	270,000
Corporate bonds	3,500,000	3,670,000
Plan interest in C&H Master Trust	2,250,000	1,860,000
Guaranteed investment contract with National Insurance Company #8041A, 8.0% (note H)	1,000,000	890,000
Mortgages	480,000	460,000
Real estate	270,000	240,000
	$8,540,000	$8,270,000

During 20X1 [and 20X0], the plan's investments (including gains and losses on investments bought and sold, as well as held during the year) appreciated in value by $278,000 [and $41,000, respectively,] as follows:

[†] See note F for discussion of fair value measurements.

Net Appreciation (Depreciation) in Fair Value

	Year Ended December 31,	
	20X1	*20X0*
C&H Company common stock	$208,000	$(59,000)
U.S. government securities	20,000	40,000
Corporate bonds	(40,000)	60,000
Guaranteed investment contract with insurance company	40,000	100,000
Mortgages	100,000	(90,000)
Real estate	(50,000)	(10,000)
	$278,000	$41,000

F. Fair Value Measurements

Financial Accounting Standards Board (FASB) *Accounting Standards Codification* (ASC) 820, *Fair Value Measurements and Disclosures*, provides the framework for measuring fair value. That framework provides a fair value hierarchy that prioritizes the inputs to valuation techniques used to measure fair value. The hierarchy gives the highest priority to unadjusted quoted prices in active markets for identical assets or liabilities (level 1 measurements) and the lowest priority to unobservable inputs (level 3 measurements). The three levels of the fair value hierarchy under FASB ASC 820 are described as follows:

Level 1	Inputs to the valuation methodology are unadjusted quoted prices for identical assets or liabilities in active markets that the plan has the ability to access.
Level 2	Inputs to the valuation methodology include • quoted prices for similar assets or liabilities in active markets; • quoted prices for identical or similar assets or liabilities in inactive markets; • inputs other than quoted prices that are observable for the asset or liability; • inputs that are derived principally from or corroborated by observable market data by correlation or other means. If the asset or liability has a specified (contractual) term, the level 2 input must be observable for substantially the full term of the asset or liability.
Level 3	Inputs to the valuation methodology are unobservable and significant to the fair value measurement.

The asset's or liability's fair value measurement level within the fair value hierarchy is based on the lowest level of any input that is significant to the fair value measurement. Valuation techniques used need to maximize the use of observable inputs and minimize the use of unobservable inputs.

Following is a description of the valuation methodologies used for assets at fair value. There have been no changes in the methodologies used at December 31, 20X1 and 20X0.

> ***Note:*** Information contained herein for fair value disclosures is based upon information for the Illustration of Financial Statements: Defined Benefit Pension Plans (appendix D—C&H Company Pension Plan) as presented in exhibits D-1–D-8. This illustrative disclosure is not representative of all types of investment securities and does not represent the classification for every instance of such investment securities. It should not be assumed that these methodologies are the only appropriate methodologies for these types of assets. As stated in FASB ASC 820-10-35-5, "The principle (or most advantageous) market (and thus, market participants) should be considered from the perspective of the reporting entity, thereby allowing for differences between and among entities with different activities." Plan sponsors will have to evaluate the appropriate classification for each type of investment securities based upon the plan's portfolio and actual fair valuation techniques used.

C&H Company common stock: Valued at the closing price reported on the New York Stock Exchange.

Guaranteed investment contract with the National Insurance Company (National): Valued at fair value by discounting the related cash flows based on current yields of similar instruments with comparable durations considering the credit-worthiness of the issuer (See note H). Funds under the guaranteed investment contract that have been allocated and applied to purchase annuities (that is, National is obligated to pay the related pension benefits) are excluded from the plan's assets.

Corporate bonds: Certain corporate bonds are valued at the closing price reported in the active market in which the bond is traded. Other corporate bonds are valued based on yields currently available on comparable securities of issuers with similar credit ratings. When quoted prices are not available for identical or similar bonds, the bond is valued under a discounted cash flows approach that maximizes observable inputs, such as current yields of similar instruments, but includes adjustments for certain risks that may not be observable, such as credit and liquidity risks.

U.S. government securities: Valued at the closing price reported in the active market in which the individual security is traded.

Mortgages: Valued on the basis of their future principal and interest payments discounted at prevailing interest rates for similar investments.

Real estate: Valued on the basis of a discounted cash flow approach, which includes the future rental receipts, expenses, and residual values as the highest and best use of the real estate from a market participant view as rental property.

The preceding methods may produce a fair value calculation that may not be indicative of net realizable value or reflective of future fair values. Furthermore, although the plan believes its valuation methods are appropriate and consistent with other market participants, the use of different methodologies or assumptions to determine the fair value of certain financial instruments could result in a different fair value measurement at the reporting date.

The following table sets forth by level, within the fair value hierarchy, the plan's assets at fair value as of December 31, 20X1, and 20X0. The following table does not include the plan's interest in the C&H Master Trust because that information is presented in a separate table (See note G):

Practice Tips

The following table illustrates certain disclosure requirements of FASB ASC 820. The disclosures illustrated describe the nature and risks of securities as required by FASB ASC 820-10-50 and are included for illustrative purposes and are NOT intended to represent the ONLY way to disclose such information.

In addition, in January 2010, FASB issued Accounting Standards Update (ASU) No. 2010-06, *Fair Value Measurements and Disclosures (Topic 820): Improving Disclosures about Fair Value Measurements.* FASB ASU No. 2010-06 amends the disclosure requirements of FASB ASC 820 including amendments regarding the level of disaggregation for each class of assets and liabilities. The illustrative financial statements in this appendix have been amended to conform to FASB ASU No. 2010-06 where applicable. The amendments in the level 3 fair value measurement roll forward, related to the separate disclosures requirement of purchases, sales, issuances, and settlements activity are effective for fiscal years beginning after December 15, 2010, and for interim periods within those fiscal years, and therefore these financial statements have not been updated for those amendments. These illustrative financial statements do not contain any significant transfers between fair value levels and therefore, a related disclosure has been included. (See "Changes in Fair Value Levels" note). See paragraph 2.19 for the required disclosures.

Assets at Fair Value as of December 31, 20X1

	Level 1	Level 2	Level 3	Total
C&H Company common stock	$690,000	—	—	$690,000
Guaranteed investment contract with National Insurance Company	—	—	$1,000,000	1,000,000
Corporate bonds:				
Aaa credit rating	1,000,000	—	—	1,000,000
Aa credit rating	—	$2,000,000	—	2,000,000
A credit rating	—	—	500,000	500,000
Total corporate bonds	1,000,000	2,000,000	500,000	3,500,000
U.S. government securities	350,000	—	—	350,000
Mortgages	—	480,000	—	480,000
Real Estate	—	—	270,000	270,000
Total assets, excluding plan interest in C&H Master Trust, at fair value	**$2,040,000**	**$2,480,000**	**$1,770,000**	**$6,290,000**

Assets at Fair Value as of December 31, 20X0

	Level 1	Level 2	Level 3	Total
C&H Company common stock	$880,000	—	—	$880,000
Guaranteed investment contract with National Insurance Company	—	—	$890,000	890,000
Corporate bonds:				
Aaa credit rating	1,200,000	—	—	1,200,000
Aa credit rating	—	$2,250,000	—	2,250,000
A credit rating	—	—	220,000	220,000
Total corporate bonds	1,200,000	2,250,000	220,000	3,670,000
U.S. government securities	270,000	—	—	270,000
Mortgages	—	460,000	—	460,000
Real estate	—	—	240,000	240,000
Total assets, excluding plan interest in C&H Master Trust, at fair value	**$2,350,000**	**$2,710,000**	**$1,350,000**	**$6,410,000**

Level 3 Gains and Losses

The following table sets forth a summary of changes in the fair value of the plan's level 3 assets for the year ended December 31, 20X1.

	Level 3 Assets			
	Guaranteed Investment Contract With National Insurance Company	Corporate Bonds	Real Estate	Total
Balance, beginning of year	$890,000	$220,000	$240,000	$1,350,000
Realized gains/(losses)	—	100,000	25,000	125,000
Unrealized gains/ (losses) relating to assets still held at the reporting date	40,000	(30,000)	(75,000)	(65,000)
Purchases, sales, issuances, and settlements (net)	70,000	210,000	80,000	360,000
Balance, end of year	**$1,000,000**	**$500,000**	**$270,000**	**$1,770,000**
The amount of total gains or losses for the period included in changes in net assets attributable to the change in unrealized gains or losses relating to assets still held at the reporting date	$40,000	$(30,000)	$(75,000)	$(65,000)

Gains and losses (realized and unrealized) included in changes in net assets for the period above are reported in net appreciation in fair value of investments in the Statement of Changes in Net Assets Available for Benefits.

Changes in Fair Value Levels

The availability of observable market data is monitored to assess the appropriate classification of financial instruments within the fair value hierarchy. Changes in economic conditions or model-based valuation techniques may require the transfer of financial instruments from one fair value level to another. In such instances, the transfer is reported at the beginning of the reporting period.

We evaluated the significance of transfers between levels based upon the nature of the financial instrument and size of the transfer relative to total net assets available for benefits. For the year ended December 31, 20X1, there were no significant transfers in or out of levels 1, 2 or 3.

G. Interest in C&H Master Trust

A portion of the plan's investments are in the Master Trust which was established for the investment of assets of the plan and several other C&H Company sponsored retirement plans. Each participating retirement plan has an undivided interest in the Master Trust. The assets of the Master Trust are held by GLC Trust Company (Trustee).

The value of the plan's interest in the C&H Master Trust is based on the beginning of year value of the plan's interest in the trust plus actual contributions and allocated investment income less actual distributions and allocated administrative expenses. At December 31, 20X1, and 20X0, the plan's interest in the net assets of the Master Trust was approximately 9 percent and 11 percent, respectively. Investment income and administrative expenses relating to the Master Trust are allocated to the individual plans based upon average monthly balances invested by each plan.

The following table presents the assets, including investments, of the Master Trust.

| | December 31, | |
	20X1	20X0
Common stocks	$11,900,000	$8,800,000
Corporate bonds	11,800,000	6,700,000
U.S. government securities	867,000	750,000
	24,567,000	16,250,000
Receivable for securities sold	433,000	659,091
	$25,000,000	$16,909,091
Plan interest in C&H Master Trust	$2,250,000	$1,860,000

Investment income for the Master Trust is as follows:

	Year Ended December 31,	
	20X1	20X0
Investment income:		
Net appreciation in fair value of investments:		
Common stocks	$ 300,000	$ 200,000
Corporate bonds	200,000	200,000
U.S. government securities	300,000	200,000
	800,000	600,000
Interest	400,000	300,000
Dividends	230,000	300,000
	$1,430,000	$1,200,000

The closing prices reported in the active markets in which the securities are traded are used to value the investments in the Master Trust. The following table sets forth by level, within the fair value hierarchy, the Master Trust's assets at fair value as of December 31, 20X1, and 20X0:

Practice Tips

The assets of the master trust are classified within level 1 of the fair value hierarchy due to the fact that they are valued using quoted market prices. Note that this is not representative of all master trusts. Accordingly, other master trusts may hold assets that are also classified within levels 2 and 3 of the fair value hierarchy. Presentation in the footnotes to the financial statements should be made accordingly.

***

The following table illustrates certain disclosure requirements of FASB ASC 820. The disclosures illustrated describe the nature and risks of securities as required by FASB ASC 820-10-50 and are included for illustrative purposes and are NOT intended to represent the ONLY way to disclose such information.

In addition, in January 2010, FASB issued FASB ASU No. 2010-06. FASB ASU No. 2010-06 amends the disclosure requirements of FASB ASC 820 including amendments regarding the level of disaggregation for each class of assets and liabilities. The illustrative financial statements in this appendix have been amended to conform to FASB ASU No. 2010-06, where applicable. The amendments in the level 3 fair value measurement roll forward, related to the separate disclosures requirement of purchases, sales, issuances, and settlements activity are effective for fiscal years beginning after December 15, 2010, and for interim periods within those fiscal years, and therefore these financial statements have not been updated for those amendments. These illustrative financial statements do not contain any significant transfers between fair value levels and therefore, a related disclosure has been included. (See "Changes in Fair Value Levels" note.) See paragraph 2.19 for the required disclosures.

	Assets at Fair Value as of December 31, 20X1			
	Level 1	Level 2	Level 3	Total
Common stocks:				
Energy	$5,500,000	—	—	$5,500,000
Healthcare	3,750,000	—	—	3,750,000
Information technology	1,250,000	—	—	1,250,000
Consumer goods	900,000	—	—	900,000
Utilities	500,000	—	—	500,000
Total common stocks	11,900,000	—	—	11,900,000
Corporate bonds	11,800,000	—	—	11,800,000
U.S. government securities	867,000	—	—	867,000
Total assets at fair value	**$24,567,000**	—	—	**$24,567,000**

	Assets at Fair Value as of December 31, 20X0			
	Level 1	Level 2	Level 3	Total
Common stocks:				
Energy	$3,750,000	—	—	$3,750,000
Healthcare	3,000,000	—	—	3,000,000
Information technology	1,000,000	—	—	1,000,000
Consumer goods	750,000	—	—	750,000
Utilities	300,000	—	—	300,000
Total common stocks	8,800,000	—	—	8,800,000
Corporate bonds	6,700,000	—	—	6,700,000
U.S. government securities	750,000	—	—	750,000
Total assets at fair value	**$16,250,000**	—	—	**$16,250,000**

Changes in Fair Value Levels

The availability of observable market data is monitored to assess the appropriate classification of financial instruments within the fair value hierarchy. Changes in economic conditions or model-based valuation techniques may require the transfer of financial instruments from one fair value level to another. In such instances, the transfer is reported at the beginning of the reporting period.

We evaluated the significance of transfers between levels based upon the nature of the financial instrument and size of the transfer relative to total net assets available for benefits. For the year ended December 31, 20X1, there were no significant transfers in or out of levels 1, 2 or 3.

H. Guaranteed Investment Contract With National Insurance Company

In 20W8, the plan entered into a guaranteed investment contract with National Insurance Company (National) under which the plan deposits a minimum of $100,000 a year. National maintains the contributions in an unallocated fund to which it adds interest at a rate of 8 percent. The interest rate is guaranteed through 20X3 but is subject to change for each succeeding five-year period. When changed, the new rate applies only to funds deposited from the date of change. At the direction of the plan's administrator, a single premium to buy an annuity for a retiring employee is withdrawn by National from the unallocated fund. Purchased annuities are contracts under which National is obligated to pay benefits to named employees or their beneficiaries. The premium rates for such annuities to be purchased in the future and maximum administration expense charges against the fund are also guaranteed by National on a five-year basis.

The annuity contracts provide for periodic dividends at National's discretion on the basis of its experience under the contracts. Such dividends received by the plan for the year(s) ended December 31, 20X1 [and 20X0] were $25,000 [and $24,000, respectively]. In reporting changes in net assets, those dividends have been netted against amounts paid to National for the purchase of annuity contracts.

I. Plan Amendment

Effective July 1, 20X1, the plan was amended to increase future annual pension benefits from 1.25 percent to 1.5 percent of final 5-year average annual compensation for each year of service, including service rendered before the effective date. The retroactive effect of the plan amendment, an increase in the actuarial present value of accumulated plan benefits of $2,410,000, was accounted for in the year ended December 31, 20X1. [The actuarial present value of accumulated plan benefits at December 31, 20X0 do not reflect the effect of that plan amendment. The plan's actuary estimates that the amendment's retroactive effect on the actuarial present value of accumulated plan benefits at December 31, 20X0 was an increase of approximately $1,750,000, of which approximately $1,300,000 represents an increase in vested benefits.]

J. Tax Status

The Internal Revenue Service has determined and informed the company by a letter dated June 30, 20XX, that the plan and related trust are designed in accordance with applicable sections of the Internal Revenue Code (IRC). The plan has been amended since receiving the determination letter. However, the plan administrator and the plan's tax counsel believe that the plan is designed and is currently being operated in compliance with the applicable requirements of the IRC.

Accounting principles generally accepted in the United States of America require plan management to evaluate tax positions taken by the plan and recognize a tax liability (or asset) if the organization has taken an uncertain position that more likely than not would not be sustained upon examination by the [identify the taxing authorities]. The plan administrator has analyzed the tax positions taken by the plan, and has concluded that as of December 31, 20X1, there are no uncertain positions taken or expected to be taken that would require recognition of a liability (or asset) or disclosure in the financial statements. The plan is subject to routine audits by taxing jurisdictions; however, there are currently no audits for any tax periods in progress. The plan administrator believes it is no longer subject to income tax examinations for years prior to 20XX.

K. Risks and Uncertainties

The plan invests in various investment securities. Investment securities are exposed to various risks such as interest rate, market, and credit risks. Due to the level of risk associated with certain investment securities, it is at least reasonably possible that changes in the values of investment securities will occur in the near term and that such changes could materially affect the amounts reported in the statement of net assets available for benefits.

Plan contributions are made and the actuarial present value of accumulated plan benefits are reported based on certain assumptions pertaining to interest rates, inflation rates and employee demographics, all of which are subject to change. Due to uncertainties inherent in the estimations and assumptions process, it is at least reasonably possible that changes in these estimates and assumptions in the near term would be material to the financial statements.

L. Related-Party Transactions

Certain plan investments are shares of C&H Company common stock. The plan held 25,000 shares of C&H Company common stock at December 31, 20X1 and 20X0, valued at $690,000 and $880,000, respectively. During the years ended December 31, 20X1 and 20X0, purchases of shares by the plan totaled $1,100,000 and $500,000, respectively, and sales of shares by the plan totaled $1,498,000 and $750,000, respectively. This investment and transactions in this investment qualify as party-in-interest transactions which are exempt from the prohibited transaction rules of ERISA.

III. Illustrative Defined Benefit Pension Plan Financial Statements and Related 401(h) Account Disclosures

Exhibit D-9‡

Note: The following illustrative defined benefit pension plan financial statements are not representative of a complete set of financial statements and notes thereto.

---

‡ The illustrative financial statements example is from FASB ASC 960-205-55-2.

C&H Company Pension Plan
Statement of Net Assets Available for Pension Benefits

	December 31,	
	20X1	*20X0*
Assets		
Investments, at fair value (note A):		
Plan interest in C&H Master Trust	$2,000,000	$1,660,000
C&H Company common stock	600,000	800,000
Guaranteed investment contract with		
insurance company	850,000	800,000
Corporate bonds	3,000,000	3,170,000
U.S. government securities	300,000	200,000
Mortgages	480,000	460,000
Money market fund	270,000	240,000
Total investments	7,500,000	7,330,000
Net assets held in 401(h) account (note I)[2]	1,072,000	966,000
Receivables:		
Employer's contribution	20,000	10,000
Securities sold	310,000	175,000
Accrued interest and dividends	70,000	70,000
Total receivables	400,000	255,000
Cash	180,000	80,000
Total assets	9,152,000	8,631,000
Liabilities		
Due to broker for securities purchased	—	400,000
Accounts payable	70,000	60,000
Accrued expenses	70,000	25,000
Amounts related to obligation of 401(h)		
account	1,072,000	966,000
Total liabilities	1,212,000	1,451,000
Net assets available for pension benefits	$7,940,000	$7,180,000

The accompanying notes are an integral part of the financial statements.

---

[2] Any assets held for investment purposes in the 401(h) account should be shown on Schedule H, line 4i—Schedule of Assets (Held at End of Year) and Schedule H, line 4j—Schedule of Reportable Transactions for the pension plan.

Exhibit D-10[‡]

C&H Company Pension Plan
Statement of Changes in Net Assets Available for
Pension Benefits

	Year Ended December 31, 20X1
Investment income:	
Net appreciation in fair value of investments	$ 233,000
Interest	293,000
Dividends	4,000
	530,000
Less investment expenses	30,000
	500,000
Plan interest in C&H Master Trust investment income (note G)	117,000
	617,000
Contributions (note C):	
Employer	740,000
Employees	450,000
	1,190,000
Total additions	1,807,000
Benefits paid directly to participants	740,000
Purchases of annuity contracts (note H)	257,000
	997,000
Administrative expenses	50,000
Total deductions	1,047,000
Net increase	760,000
Net assets available for pension benefits:	
Beginning of year	7,180,000
End of year	$7,940,000

The accompanying notes are an integral part of the financial statements.

[‡] The illustrative financial statements example is from FASB ASC 960-205-55-2.

Exhibit D-11‡

C&H Company Pension Plan
Notes to Financial Statements

A. 401 (h) Account

Effective January 1, 20X0, the plan was amended to include a medical-benefit component in addition to the normal retirement benefits to fund a portion of the postretirement obligations for retirees and their beneficiaries in accordance with Section 401(h) of the IRC. A separate account has been established and maintained in the plan for the net assets related to the medical-benefit component [401(h) account]. In accordance with IRC Section 401(h), the plan's investments in the 401(h) account may not be used for, or diverted to, any purpose other than providing health benefits for retirees and their beneficiaries. Any assets transferred to the 401(h) account from the defined benefit pension plan in a qualified transfer of excess pension plan assets (and any income allocable thereto) that are not used during the plan year must be transferred out of the account to the pension plan. The related obligations for health benefits are not included in this plan's obligations in the statement of accumulated plan benefits but are reflected as obligations in the financial statements of the health and welfare benefit plan. Plan participants do not contribute to the 401(h) account. Employer contributions or qualified transfers to the 401(h) account are determined annually and are at the discretion of the plan sponsor. Certain of the plan's net assets are restricted to fund a portion of postretirement health benefits for retirees and their beneficiaries in accordance with IRC Section 401(h).

B. Reconciliation of Financial Statements to Form 5500 [3]

The following is a reconciliation of net assets available for pension benefits per the financial statements to the Form 5500:

	December 31,	
	20X1	20X0
Net assets available for pension benefits per the financial statements	$7,940,000	$7,180,000
Net assets held in 401(h) account included as assets in Form 5500	1,072,000	966,000
Net assets available for benefits per the Form 5500	$9,012,000	$8,146,000

The net assets of the 401(h) account included in Form 5500 are not available to pay pension benefits but can be used only to pay retiree health benefits.

---

‡ The illustrative financial statements example is from FASB ASC 960-205-55-2.

[3] The reconciliation of amounts reported in the plan's financial statements to amounts reported in Form 5500 is required by the Employee Retirement Income Security Act of 1974.

The following is a reconciliation of the changes in net assets per the financial statements to the Form 5500:

	For the Year Ended December 31, 20X1		
	Amounts per Financial Statements	401(h) Account	Amounts per Form 5500
Net appreciation in fair value of investments	$233,000	$10,800	$243,800
Interest income	293,000	80,200	373,200
Employer contributions	740,000	40,000	780,000
Benefits paid to retirees	740,000	10,000	750,000
Administrative expenses	50,000	15,000	65,000

Appendix E

Illustrative Financial Statements: Defined Contribution Plans

E.01 This appendix illustrates certain applications of the provisions of the Financial Accounting Standards Board (FASB) *Accounting Standards Codification* (ASC) 962, *Plan Accounting—Defined Contribution Pension Plans*, that apply for the annual financial statements of hypothetical defined contribution plans with participant-directed and nonparticipant-directed investments. Such illustrative plans include the XYZ Company 401(k) Plan (exhibits E-1–E-3), the XYZ Company Profit-Sharing Plan (exhibits E-4–E-6), and the Sponsor Company Employee Stock Ownership Plan (exhibits E-7–E-9). It does not illustrate other provisions of FASB ASC 962 as well as other FASB ASC topics that might apply in circumstances other than those assumed in this example. The formats presented and the wording of accompanying notes are only illustrative and are not necessarily the only possible presentations. In addition, the illustrative financial statements in this appendix have been amended to conform to FASB ASC 820, *Fair Value Measurements and Disclosures.*[*]

> *Note:* FASB ASC 820 disclosures are limited to the financial instruments contained within this specific example. It is recommended that users consult all the illustrative financial statements within appendixes D–F for FASB ASC 820 examples of different types of financial instruments.

E.02 FASB ASC 962-325-35 states that defined-contribution plans should report all investments (including derivative contracts) at fair value. However, contract value is the relevant measurement attribute for that portion of the net assets available for benefits of a defined-contribution plan attributable to fully benefit-responsive investment contracts. According to paragraphs 2–3 of FASB ASC 962-205-45, the statement of net assets available for benefits of the plan should present amounts for (*a*) total assets, (*b*) total liabilities, (*c*) net assets reflecting all investments at fair value, and (*d*) net assets available for benefits. The amount representing the difference between (*c*) and (*d*) should be presented on the face of the statement of net assets available for benefits as a single amount, calculated as the sum of the amounts necessary to adjust the portion of net assets attributable to each fully benefit-responsive investment contract from fair value to contract value. The statement of changes in net assets available for benefits should be prepared on a basis that reflects income credited to participants in the plan and net appreciation or depreciation in the fair value of only those investment contracts that are not deemed to be fully benefit responsive.

---

[*] The illustrative financial statements and footnote disclosures included in this appendix have been updated to reflect the Financial Accounting Standards Board (FASB) *Accounting Standards Codification*™ (ASC) references. However, in FASB's notice to constituents, it suggests the use of plain English in financial statement footnotes to describe broad FASB ASC topic references. They suggest a reference similar to "as required by the *Derivatives and Hedging* topic of the FASB *Accounting Standards Codification*." Entities might consider revising their financial statement references to reflect this plain English referencing, rather than the use of specific FASB ASC references. For specific information on FASB ASC, please see the preface in the guide.

E.03 In addition, FASB ASC 962-310-45-2 states that for reporting purposes participant loans should be classified as notes receivable from participants. Participant loans should be measured at their unpaid principal balance plus any accrued but unpaid interest in accordance with FASB ASC 962-310-35-2. In addition, FASB ASC 962-310-50-1 states that the fair value disclosures for financial instruments prescribed in paragraphs 10–16 of FASB ASC 825-10-50 are not required for participant loans. Participant loans continue however to be considered an investment for Form 5500 reporting purposes.

E.04 Although accounting principles generally accepted in the United States of America do not require comparative financial statements, the Employee Retirement Income Security Act of 1974 (ERISA) requires a comparative statement of net assets available for benefits. The illustrative financial statements are intended to comply with the requirements of ERISA.

E.05 ERISA and Department of Labor (DOL) regulations require that certain information be included in supplemental schedules, which are not required under accounting principles generally accepted in the United States of America, and reported on by the independent auditor. See appendix A, "ERISA and Related Regulations," for a further discussion of the ERISA and DOL requirements.

CONTENTS

I. Illustrative Financial Statements and Disclosures of a Defined Contribution Plan With Participant-Directed and Nonparticipant-Directed Investment Programs

Exhibit E-1

XYZ Company 401(k) Plan
Statements of Net Assets Available for Benefits

	December 31,	
	20X1	*20X0*
Assets		
Investments at fair value (See notes C, D, and E)	$8,892,000	$7,655,000
Receivables:		
Employer contribution	14,000	10,000
Participant contributions	52,000	50,000
Notes receivable from participants	300,000	350,000
Total receivables	366,000	410,000
Total assets	9,258,000	8,065,000
Liabilities:		
Accounts payable	10,000	20,000
Accrued expenses	15,000	—
Total liabilities	25,000	20,000
Net assets reflecting investments at fair value	9,233,000	8,045,000
Adjustment from fair value to contract value for fully benefit-responsive investment contracts	(15,000)	(10,000)
Net assets available for benefits	$9,218,000	$8,035,000

See accompanying notes to the financial statements.

Exhibit E-2

XYZ Company 401(k) Plan
Statement of Changes in Net Assets Available for Benefits

	Year Ended December 31, 20X1
Additions:	
Additions to net assets attributed to:	
Investment income:	
Net appreciation in fair value of investments (see note C)	$279,000
Interest	419,000
Dividends	165,000
	863,000
Less investment expenses	(50,000)
Total assests	813,000
Interest income on notes receivable from participants	20,000
Contributions:	
Participant	900,000
Employer	699,000
	1,599,000
Total additions	2,432,000
Deductions:	
Deductions from net assets attributed to:	
Benefits paid to participants	1,144,000
Administrative expenses (see note G)	105,000
Total deductions	1,249,000
Net increase	1,183,000
Net assets available for benefits:	
Beginning of year	8,035,000
End of year	$9,218,000

See accompanying notes to the financial statements.

Exhibit E-3

XYZ Company 401(k) Plan
Notes to Financial Statements

A. Description of Plan

The following description of the XYZ Company (company) 401(k) Plan (plan) provides only general information. Participants should refer to the plan agreement for a more complete description of the plan's provisions.

1. *General.* The plan is a defined contribution plan covering all full-time employees of the company who have one year of service and are age twenty-one or older. The plan is subject to the provisions of ERISA.

2. *Contributions.* Each year, participants may contribute up to 12 percent of pretax annual compensation, as defined in the plan. Participants who have attained age 50 before the end of the plan year are eligible to make catch-up contributions. Participants may also contribute amounts representing distributions from other qualified defined benefit or defined contribution plans. Participants direct the investment of their contributions into various investment options offered by the plan. The plan currently offers various mutual funds and an insurance investment contract as investment options for participants. The company contributes 25 percent of the first 6 percent of base compensation that a participant contributes to the plan. The matching company contribution is invested directly in XYZ Company common stock. Additional profit sharing amounts may be contributed at the option of the company's board of directors and are invested in a portfolio of investments as directed by the company. Contributions are subject to certain limitations.

3. *Participant Accounts.* Each participant's account is credited with the participant's contribution and allocations of (*a*) the company's contribution and (*b*) plan earnings, and charged with an allocation of administrative expenses. Allocations are based on participant earnings or account balances, as defined. The benefit to which a participant is entitled is the benefit that can be provided from the participant's vested account.

4. *Vesting.* Participants are vested immediately in their contributions plus actual earnings thereon. Vesting in the company's contribution portion of their accounts is based on years of continuous service. A participant is 100 percent vested after five years of credited service.

5. *Notes Receivable From Participants.* Participants may borrow from their fund accounts a minimum of $1,000 up to a maximum equal to the lesser of $50,000 or 50 percent of their account balance. The loans are secured by the balance in the participant's account and bear interest at rates that range from 6 percent to 10 percent, which are commensurate with local prevailing rates as determined quarterly by the plan administrator. Principal and interest is paid ratably through monthly payroll deductions.

6. *Payment of Benefits.* On termination of service due to death, disability, or retirement, a participant may elect to receive either a

lump-sum amount equal to the value of the participant's vested interest in his or her account, or annual installments over a ten-year period. For termination of service for other reasons, a participant may receive the value of the vested interest in his or her account as a lump-sum distribution.

7. *Forfeited Accounts.* At December 31, 20X1 and 20X0 forfeited non-vested accounts totaled $7,500 and $5,000 respectively. These accounts will be used to reduce future employer contributions. Also, in 20X1, employer contributions were reduced by $5,000 from forfeited nonvested accounts.

B. Summary of Accounting Policies

Basis of Accounting

The financial statements of the plan are prepared on the accrual basis of accounting.

Investment contracts held by a defined-contribution plan are required to be reported at fair value. However, contract value is the relevant measurement attribute for that portion of the net assets available for benefits of a defined-contribution plan attributable to fully benefit-responsive investment contracts because contract value is the amount participants would receive if they were to initiate permitted transactions under the terms of the plan. The Statement of Net Assets Available for Benefits presents the fair value of the investment contracts as well as the adjustment of the fully benefit-responsive investment contracts from fair value to contract value. The Statement of Changes in Net Assets Available for Benefits is prepared on a contract value basis.

Use of Estimates

The preparation of financial statements in conformity with accounting principles generally accepted in the United States of America requires management to make estimates and assumptions that affect the reported amounts of assets and liabilities and changes therein, and disclosure of contingent assets and liabilities. Actual results could differ from those estimates.

Investment Valuation and Income Recognition

Investments are reported at fair value. Fair value is the price that would be received to sell an asset or paid to transfer a liability in an orderly transaction between market participants at the measurement date. See note E for discussion of fair value measurements.

Purchases and sales of securities are recorded on a trade-date basis. Interest income is recorded on the accrual basis. Dividends are recorded on the ex-dividend date. Net appreciation includes the plan's gains and losses on investments bought and sold as well as held during the year.

Notes Receivable From Participants

Notes receivable from participants are measured at their unpaid principal balance plus any accrued but unpaid interest. Delinquent participant loans are reclassified as distributions based upon the terms of the plan document.

Payment of Benefits

Benefits are recorded when paid.

Operating Expenses

All expenses of maintaining the plan are paid by the company.

Subsequent Events

The plan has evaluated subsequent events through [*insert date*], the date the financial statements were available to be issued.

C. Investments

The following presents investments[†] that represent 5 percent or more of the plan's net assets.

	December 31,	
	20X1	20X0
XYZ Company common stock, 400,000 and 390,000 shares, respectively	$ 470,000*	$ 420,000*
ABC Corporation common stock, 390,000 and 380,000 shares, respectively	490,000*	450,000*
Prosperity Investments Common Stock Fund, 226,250 and 200,000 shares, respectively	2,262,500*	2,000,000*
Prosperity Investments Balanced Fund, 140,000 and 210,000 shares, respectively	1,422,000	2,100,000
Guaranteed investment contract with National Insurance Company, at contract value #2012A, matures 12/31/X5 (note F)	1,500,000	650,000

* Nonparticipant-directed

During 20X1, the plan's investments (including gains and losses on investments bought and sold, as well as held during the year) appreciated in value by $279,000 as follows:

Mutual funds	$ 229,000
Common stocks	30,000
Corporate bonds	30,000
U.S. government securities	(10,000)
	$ 279,000

D. Nonparticipant-Directed Investments

Information about the net assets and the significant components of the changes in net assets relating to the nonparticipant-directed investments is as follows:

	December 31,	
	20X1	20X0
Net Assets:		
Common stocks	$ 960,000	$ 870,000
Mutual funds	2,262,500	2,000,000
Corporate bonds	307,500	255,000
U.S. government securities	225,000	120,000
	$3,755,000	$3,245,000

[†] See note E for discussion of fair value measurements.

	Year Ended December 31, 20X1
Changes in Net Assets:	
Contributions	$ 699,000
Dividends	165,000
Net appreciation	60,000
Benefits paid to participants	(280,000)
Transfers to participant-directed investments	(134,000)
	$ 510,000

E. Fair Value Measurements

Financial Accounting Standards Board (FASB) *Accounting Standards Codification* (ASC) 820, *Fair Value Measurements and Disclosures,* provides the framework for measuring fair value. That framework provides a fair value hierarchy that prioritizes the inputs to valuation techniques used to measure fair value. The hierarchy gives the highest priority to unadjusted quoted prices in active markets for identical assets or liabilities (level 1 measurements) and the lowest priority to unobservable inputs (level 3 measurements). The three levels of the fair value hierarchy under FASB ASC 820 are described as follows:

Level 1	Inputs to the valuation methodology are unadjusted quoted prices for identical assets or liabilities in active markets that the plan has the ability to access.
Level 2	Inputs to the valuation methodology include
	• quoted prices for similar assets or liabilities in active markets;
	• quoted prices for identical or similar assets or liabilities in inactive markets;
	• inputs other than quoted prices that are observable for the asset or liability;
	• inputs that are derived principally from or corroborated by observable market data by correlation or other means.
	If the asset or liability has a specified (contractual) term, the level 2 input must be observable for substantially the full term of the asset or liability.
Level 3	Inputs to the valuation methodology are unobservable and significant to the fair value measurement.

The asset or liability's fair value measurement level within the fair value hierarchy is based on the lowest level of any input that is significant to the fair value measurement. Valuation techniques used need to maximize the use of observable inputs and minimize the use of unobservable inputs.

Following is a description of the valuation methodologies used for assets measured at fair value. There have been no changes in the methodologies used at December 31, 20X1 and 20X0.

> ***Note:*** Information contained herein for fair value disclosures is based upon information for the Illustrative Financial Statements: Defined Contribution Plans (appendix E) as presented in exhibits E-1–E-3. This illustrative disclosure is not representative of all types of investment securities and does not represent the classification for every instance of such investment securities. It should not be assumed that these methodologies are the only appropriate methodologies for these types of assets. As stated in FASB ASC 820-10-35-5, "The principle (or most advantageous) market (and thus, market participants) should be considered from the perspective of the reporting entity, thereby allowing for differences between and among entities with different activities." Plan sponsors will have to evaluate the appropriate classification for each type of investments securities based upon the plan's portfolio and actual fair valuation techniques used.

Common stocks, corporate bonds and U.S. government securities: Valued at the closing price reported on the active market on which the individual securities are traded.

Mutual funds: Valued at the net asset value (NAV) of shares held by the plan at year end.

Guaranteed investment contract: Valued at fair value by discounting the related cash flows based on current yields of similar instruments with comparable durations considering the credit-worthiness of the issuer (See note F).

The preceding methods described may produce a fair value calculation that may not be indicative of net realizable value or reflective of future fair values. Furthermore, although the plan believes its valuation methods are appropriate and consistent with other market participants, the use of different methodologies or assumptions to determine the fair value of certain financial instruments could result in a different fair value measurement at the reporting date.

The following table sets forth by level, within the fair value hierarchy, the plan's assets at fair value as of December 31, 20X1 and 20X0:

Practice Tips

The following table illustrates certain disclosure requirements of FASB ASC 820. The disclosures illustrated describe the nature and risks of securities as required by FASB ASC 820-10-50 and are included for illustrative purposes and are NOT intended to represent the ONLY way to disclose such information.

In addition, in January 2010, FASB issued Accounting Standards Update (ASU) No. 2010-06, *Fair Value Measurements and Disclosures (Topic 820): Improving Disclosures about Fair Value Measurements*. FASB ASU No. 2010-06 amends the disclosure requirements of FASB ASC 820 including amendments regarding the level of disaggregation for each class of assets and liabilities. The illustrative financial statements in this appendix have been amended to conform to FASB ASU No. 2010-06, where applicable. The amendments in the level 3 fair value measurement roll forward, related to the separate disclosures requirement of purchases, sales, issuances, and settlements activity are effective for fiscal years beginning after December 15, 2010, and for interim periods within those fiscal years, and therefore these financial statements have not been updated for those amendments. These illustrative financial statements do not contain any transfers between fair value levels and therefore no disclosure has been made. See paragraph 3.22 for the required disclosures.

Assets at Fair Value as of December 31, 20X1

	Level 1	Level 2	Level 3	Total
Mutual funds:				
Index funds	$2,262,500	—	—	$2,262,500
Balanced funds	1,422,000	—	—	1,422,000
Growth funds	1,375,000	—	—	1,375,000
Fixed income funds	800,000	—	—	800,000
Other funds	25,000	—	—	25,000
Total mutual funds	5,884,500	—	—	5,884,500
Common stocks:				
Industrials	384,000	—	—	384,000
Telecommunications	240,000	—	—	240,000
Consumer	192,000	—	—	192,000
Other	144,000	—	—	144,000
Total common stocks	960,000	—	—	960,000
Corporate bonds	307,500	—	—	307,500
U.S. government securities	225,000	—	—	225,000
Guaranteed investment contract	—	—	$1,515,000	1,515,000
Total assets at fair value	$7,377,000	—	$1,515,000	$8,892,000

Assets at Fair Value as of December 31, 20X0

	Level 1	Level 2	Level 3	Total
Mutual funds:				
Index funds	$2,000,000	—	—	$2,000,000
Balanced funds	2,100,000	—	—	2,100,000
Growth funds	1,150,000	—	—	1,150,000
Fixed Income	400,000	—	—	400,000
Other funds	100,000	—	—	100,000
Total mutual funds	5,750,000	—	—	5,750,000
Common stocks:				
Industrials	348,000	—	—	348,000
Telecommunications	217,500	—	—	217,500
Consumer	174,000	—	—	174,000
Other	130,500	—	—	130,500
Total common stocks	870,000	—	—	870,000
Corporate bonds	255,000	—	—	255,000
U.S. government securities	120,000	—	—	120,000
Guaranteed investment contract	—	—	$660,000	660,000
Total assets at fair value	$6,995,000	—	$660,000	$7,655,000

Level 3 Gains and Losses

The following table sets forth a summary of changes in the fair value of the plan's level 3 assets for the year ended December 31, 20X1.

| | Level 3 Assets Year Ended December 31, 20X1 | |
	Guaranteed Investment Contract	Total
Balance, beginning of year	$660,000	$660,000
Realized gains/(losses)	—	—
Unrealized gains/(losses) relating to instruments still held at the reporting date	40,000	40,000
Purchases, sales, issuances, and settlements (net)	815,000	815,000
Balance, end of year	$1,515,000	$1,515,000
The amount of total gains or losses for the period attributable to the change in unrealized gains or losses relating to assets still held at the reporting date	$40,000	$40,000

F. Guaranteed Investment Contract With National Insurance Company

In 20X0, the plan entered into a benefit-responsive guaranteed investment contract with National Insurance Company (National). National maintains the contributions in a general account. The account is credited with earnings on the underlying investments and charged for participant withdrawals and administrative expenses. The guaranteed investment contract issuer is contractually obligated to repay the principal and a specified interest rate that is guaranteed to the plan.

Because the guaranteed investment contract is fully benefit-responsive, contract value is the relevant measurement attribute for that portion of the net assets available for benefits attributable to the guaranteed investment contract. The guaranteed investment contract is presented on the face of the statement of net assets available for benefits at fair value with an adjustment to contract value in arriving at net assets available for benefits. Contract value, as reported to the plan by National, represents contributions made under the contract, plus earnings, less participant withdrawals and administrative expenses. Participants may ordinarily direct the withdrawal or transfer of all or a portion of their investment at contract value.

There are no reserves against contract value for credit risk of the contract issuer or otherwise. The fair value of the investment contract at December 31, 20X1 and 20X0 was $1,515,000 and $660,000, respectively. The crediting interest rate is based on a formula agreed upon with the issuer, but it may not be less than 4 percent. Such interest rates are reviewed on a quarterly basis for resetting.

Certain events limit the ability of the plan to transact at contract value with the issuer. Such events include the following: (1) amendments to the plan documents (including complete or partial plan termination or merger with another plan), (2) changes to the plan's prohibition on competing investment options or deletion of equity wash provisions, (3) bankruptcy of the plan sponsor or other plan sponsor events (for example, divestitures or spin-offs of a subsidiary) that cause a significant withdrawal from the plan, or (4) the failure of the trust to qualify for exemption from federal income taxes or any required prohibited transaction exemption under ERISA. The plan administrator does not believe that any events which would limit the plan's ability to transact at contract value with participants are probable of occurring.

The guaranteed investment contract does not permit the insurance company to terminate the agreement prior to the scheduled maturity date.

Average yields:	20X1	20X0
Based on actual earnings	4.68%	4.90%
Based on interest rate credited to participants	4.68%	4.90%

G. Related-Party Transactions

Certain plan investments are shares of mutual funds managed by Prosperity Investments. Prosperity Investments is the trustee as defined by the plan and, therefore, these transactions qualify as party-in-interest transactions. Fees paid by the plan for the investment management services amounted to $105,000 for the year ended December 31, 20X1.

H. Plan Termination

Although it has not expressed any intent to do so, the company has the right under the plan to discontinue its contributions at any time and to terminate the plan subject to the provisions of ERISA. In the event of plan termination, participants would become 100 percent vested in their employer contributions.

I. Tax Status

The IRS has determined and informed the company by a letter dated August 30, 20XX, that the plan and related trust are designed in accordance with applicable sections of the Internal Revenue Code (IRC). Although the plan has been amended since receiving the determination letter, the plan administrator and the plan's tax counsel believe that the plan is designed and is currently being operated in compliance with the applicable requirements of the IRC and therefore believe that the plan is qualified and the related trust is tax-exempt.

Accounting principles generally accepted in the United States of America require plan management to evaluate tax positions taken by the plan and recognize a tax liability (or asset) if the plan has taken an uncertain position that more likely than not would not be sustained upon examination by the [identify applicable taxing authorities]. The plan administrator has analyzed the tax positions taken by the plan, and has concluded that as of December 31, 20X1, there are no uncertain positions taken or expected to be taken that would require recognition of a liability (or asset) or disclosure in the financial statements. The plan is subject to routine audits by taxing jurisdictions; however, there are currently no audits for any tax periods in progress. The plan administrator believes it is no longer subject to income tax examinations for years prior to 20XX.

J. Risks and Uncertainties

The plan invests in various investment securities. Investment securities are exposed to various risks such as interest rate, market, and credit risks. Due to the level of risk associated with certain investment securities, it is at least reasonably possible that changes in the values of investment securities will occur in the near term and that such changes could materially affect participants' account balances and the amounts reported in the statement of net assets available for benefits.

K. Reconciliation of Financial Statements to Form 5500

The following is a reconciliation of net assets available for benefits per the financial statements at December 31, 20X1 and 20X0 to Form 5500:

	20X1	20X0
Net assets available for benefits per the financial statements	$9,218,000	$8,035,000
Amounts allocated to withdrawing participants	(50,000)	(35,000)
Net assets available for benefits per the Form 5500	$9,168,000	$8,000,000

The following is a reconciliation of benefits paid to participants per the financial statements for the year ended December 31, 20X1, to Form 5500:

Benefits paid to participants per the financial statements	$1,144,000
Add: Amounts allocated to withdrawing participants at December 31, 20X1	50,000
Less: Amounts allocated to withdrawing participants at December 21, 20X0	(35,000)
Benefits paid to participants per Form 5500	$1,159,000

Amounts allocated to withdrawing participants are recorded on the Form 5500 for benefit claims that have been processed and approved for payment prior to December 31, 20X1, but not yet paid as of that date.

II. Illustrations of Financial Statements: Profit-Sharing Plan

Exhibit E-4

Profit-Sharing Plan
XYZ Company Profit-Sharing Plan
Statements of Net Assets Available for Benefits

	December 31,	
	20X1	*20X0*
Assets		
Investments:		
At fair value (notes C, D, and F)		
U.S. government securities	$ 455,000	$ 425,000
Corporate bonds	3,900,000	3,730,000
Common stocks	2,822,000	1,931,000
Guaranteed investment contract with		
insurance company (note E)	1,082,000	1,040,000
Certificates of deposit	1,000,000	1,000,000
Total investments	9,259,000	8,126,000
Receivables:		
Employer's contribution	14,000	12,000
Participants' contributions	52,000	47,000
Due from broker for securities sold	403,000	357,000
Accrued interest and dividends	77,000	62,000
	546,000	478,000
Cash	280,000	198,000
Total assets	10,085,000	8,802,000
Liabilities		
Accounts payable	10,000	8,000
Accrued expenses	100,000	150,000
Due to broker for securities purchased	75,000	63,000
Total liabilities	185,000	221,000
Net assets reflecting investments at fair value	9,900,000	8,581,000
Adjustment from fair value to contract value for		
fully benefit-responsive investment contract	(82,000)	(40,000)
Net assets available for benefits	$9,818,000	$8,541,000

The accompanying notes are an integral part of these financial statements.

Exhibit E-5

XYZ Company Profit-Sharing Plan
Statement of Changes in Net Assets Available for Benefits

	Year Ended December 31, 20X1
Additions to net assets attributed to:	
Investment income:	
Net appreciation in fair value of investments (note C)	$ 269,000
Interest	449,000
Dividends	165,000
	883,000
Less investment expenses	(50,000)
	833,000
Contributions:	
Employer's	1,014,000
Participants'	585,000
	1,599,000
Total additions	2,432,000
Deductions from net assets attributed to:	
Benefits paid to participants	1,050,000
Administrative expenses	105,000
Total deductions	1,155,000
Net increase	1,277,000
Net assets available for plan benefits:	
Beginning of year	8,541,000
End of year	$9,818,000

The accompanying notes are an integral part of these financial statements.

Exhibit E-6

XYZ Company Profit-Sharing Plan
Notes to Financial Statements

A. Description of Plan

The following description of the XYZ Company (company) Profit-Sharing Plan (plan) provides only general information. Participants should refer to the plan agreement for a more complete description of the plan's provisions.

1. *General.* The plan is a defined contribution plan covering all full-time employees of the company who have one year of service and are age twenty-one or older. The plan is subject to the provisions of ERISA.

2. *Contributions.* Each year, the company contributes to the plan 10 percent of its current profits before pension and profit-sharing costs and income taxes. Additional amounts may be contributed at the option of the company's board of directors. Participants may contribute up to 10 percent of their annual wages before bonuses and overtime. Contributions are subject to certain limitations.

3. *Participant Accounts.* Each participant's account is credited with the participant's contribution and an allocation of (a) the company's contribution, (b) plan earnings, and (c) forfeitures of terminated participants' nonvested accounts and charged with an allocation of administrative expenses. Allocations are based on participant earnings or account balances, as defined. The benefit to which a participant is entitled is the benefit that can be provided from the participant's vested account.

4. *Vesting.* Participants are immediately vested in their voluntary contributions plus actual earnings thereon. Vesting in the company contributions portion of their accounts plus earnings thereon is based on years of continuous service. A participant is 100 percent vested after 5 years of credited service.

5. *Payment of Benefits.* On termination of service due to death, disability or retirement, a participant may elect to receive an amount equal to the value of the participant's vested interest in his or her account in either a lump-sum amount, or in annual installments over a ten year period. For termination of service due to other reasons, a participant may receive the value of the vested interest in his or her account as a lump-sum distribution.

6. *Forfeited Accounts.* At December 31, 20X1 forfeited nonvested accounts totaled $10,000. These accounts will be reallocated to participants in the same manner as employer contributions.

B. Summary of Accounting Policies

Basis of Accounting

The financial statements of the plan are prepared on the accrual basis of accounting.

Investment contracts held by a defined-contribution plan are required to be reported at fair value. However, contract value is the relevant measurement attribute for that portion of the net assets available for benefits of a defined-contribution plan attributable to fully benefit-responsive investment contracts because contract value is the amount participants would receive if they were to initiate permitted transactions under the terms of the plan. The Statement of Net Assets Available for Benefits presents the fair value of the investment contracts as well as the adjustment of the fully benefit-responsive investment contracts from fair value to contract value. The Statement of Changes in Net Assets Available for Benefits is prepared on a contract value basis.

Use of Estimates

The preparation of financial statements in conformity with accounting principles generally accepted in the United States of America requires management to make estimates and assumptions that affect the reported amounts of assets, liabilities, and changes therein, and disclosure of contingent assets and liabilities. Actual results could differ from those estimates.

Investment Valuation and Income Recognition

The plan's investments are stated at fair value. Fair value is the price that would be received to sell an asset or paid to transfer a liability in an orderly transaction between market participants at the measurement date. See note D for discussion of fair value measurements.

Purchases and sales of securities are recorded on a trade-date basis. Interest income is recorded on the accrual basis. Dividends are recorded on the ex-dividend date. Net appreciation includes the plan's gains and losses on investments bought and sold as well as held during the year.

Payment of Benefits

Benefits are recorded when paid.

Operating Expenses

All expenses of maintaining the plan are paid by the company.

Subsequent Events

The plan has evaluated subsequent events through [*insert date*], the date the financial statements were available to be issued.

C. Investments

Except for its investment contract with an insurance company (note E), the plan's investments are held in a bank-administered trust fund. The following table presents investments. Investments that represent 5 percent or more of the plan's net assets are separately identified.[‡]

	December 31,	
	20X1	*20X0*
U.S. government securities	$ 455,000	$ 425,000
Corporate bonds:		
National Auto 7%, face value of $860,000 and		
$1,000,000, respectively, bonds due 12/31/X5	875,000	1,226,000
Other	3,025,000	2,504,000
Common stocks:		
Bizco Corporation, 100,000 and 90,000 shares,		
respectively	950,000	685,000
Other	1,872,000	1,246,000
Certificates of deposit	1,000,000	1,000,000
Guaranteed investment contract with National		
Insurance Company, at contract value (note E)	1,000,000	1,000,000
	$9,177,000	$8,086,000

[‡] See note D for discussion of fair value measurements.

During 20X1 the plan's investments (including investments bought, sold, and held during the year) appreciated in value by $269,000 as follows:

Net Change in Fair Value

	Year Ended December 31, 20X1
U.S. government securities	$(15,000)
Corporate bonds:	(180,000)
Common stocks	464,000
Net change in fair value	**$269,000**

D. Fair Value Measurements

Financial Accounting Standards Board (FASB) *Accounting Standards Codification* (ASC) 820, *Fair Value Measurements and Disclosures*, provides the framework for measuring fair value. That framework provides a fair value hierarchy that prioritizes the inputs to valuation techniques used to measure fair value. The hierarchy gives the highest priority to unadjusted quoted prices in active markets for identical assets or liabilities (level 1 measurements) and the lowest priority to unobservable inputs (level 3 measurements). The three levels of the fair value hierarchy under FASB ASC 820 are described as follows:

Level 1	Inputs to the valuation methodology are unadjusted quoted prices for identical assets or liabilities in active markets.
Level 2	Inputs to the valuation methodology include • quoted prices for similar assets or liabilities in active markets; • quoted prices for identical or similar assets or liabilities in inactive markets; • inputs other than quoted prices that are observable for the asset or liability; • inputs that are derived principally from or corroborated by observable market data by correlation or other means. If the asset or liability has a specified (contractual) term, the level 2 input must be observable for substantially the full term of the asset or liability.
Level 3	Inputs to the valuation methodology are unobservable and significant to the fair value measurement.

The asset or liability's fair value measurement level within the fair value hierarchy is based on the lowest level of any input that is significant to the fair value measurement. Valuation techniques used need to maximize the use of observable inputs and minimize the use of unobservable inputs.

Following is a description of the valuation methodologies used for assets measured at fair value. There have been no changes in the methodologies used at December 31, 20X1 and 20X0.

> ***Note:*** Information contained herein for fair value disclosures is based upon information for the Illustrative Financial Statements: Defined Contribution Plans (appendix E—XYZ Company Profit-Sharing Plan) as presented in exhibits E-4–E-6. This illustrative disclosure is not representative of all types of investment securities and does not represent the classification for every instance of such investment securities. It should not be assumed that these methodologies are the only appropriate methodologies for these types of assets. As stated in FASB ASC 820-10-35-5, "The principle (or most advantageous) market (and thus, market participants) should be considered from the perspective of the reporting entity, thereby allowing for differences between and among entities with different activities." Plan sponsors will have to evaluate the appropriate classification for each type of investment securities based upon the plan's portfolio and actual fair valuation techniques used.

U.S. government securities: Valued at the closing price reported in the active market in which the individual securities are traded.

Corporate bonds: Certain corporate bonds are valued at the closing price reported in the active market in which the bond is traded. Other corporate bonds are valued based on yields currently available on comparable securities of issuers with similar credit ratings.

Common stocks: Certain common stocks are valued at the closing price reported in the active market in which the individual securities are traded. Investments in certain restricted common stocks are valued at the quoted market price of the issuer's unrestricted common stock less an appropriate discount. If a quoted market price for unrestricted common stock of the issuer is not available, restricted common stocks are valued at a multiple of current earnings less an appropriate discount. The multiple chosen is consistent with multiples of similar companies based on current market prices.

Guaranteed investment contract: Valued at fair value by discounting the related cash flows based on current yields of similar instruments with comparable durations considering the credit-worthiness of the issuer (See note E).

Certificates of deposit: Valued at fair value by discounting the related cash flows based on current yields of similar instruments with comparable durations considering the credit-worthiness of the issuer.

The preceding methods described may produce a fair value calculation that may not be indicative of net realizable value or reflective of future fair values. Furthermore, although the plan believes its valuation methods are appropriate and consistent with other market participants, the use of different methodologies or assumptions to determine the fair value of certain financial instruments could result in a different fair value measurement at the reporting date.

The following table sets forth by level, within the fair value hierarchy, the plan's assets at fair value as of December 31, 20X1 and 20X0.

Assets at Fair Value as of December 31, 20X1

	Level 1	Level 2	Level 3	Total
U. S. government securities	$455,000	—	—	$455,000
Corporate bonds:				
Aaa credit rating	250,000	—	—	250,000
Aa credit rating	—	$3,650,000	—	$3,650,000
Total corporate bonds	250,000	$3,650,000	—	3,900,000
Common stocks	2,447,000	250,000	$125,000	2,822,000
Guaranteed investment contract with insurance company	—	—	1,082,000	1,082,000
Certificates of deposit	—	1,000,000	—	1,000,000
Total assets at fair value	$3,152,000	$4,900,000	$1,207,000	$9,259,000

Assets at Fair Value as of December 31, 20X0

	Level 1	Level 2	Level 3	Total
U. S. government securities	$425,000	—	—	$425,000
Corporate bonds:				
Aaa credit rating	176,000	—	—	176,000
Aa credit rating	—	$3,554,000	—	3,554,000
Total corporate bonds	176,000	3,554,000	—	3,730,000
Common stocks	1,666,000	175,000	$90,000	1,931,000
Guaranteed investment contract with insurance company	—	—	1,040,000	1,040,000
Certificates of deposit	—	1,000,000	—	1,000,000
Total assets at fair value	$2,267,000	$4,729,000	$1,130,000	$8,126,000

Level 3 Gains and Losses

The following table sets forth a summary of changes in the fair value of the plan's level 3 assets for the year ended December 31, 20X1.

	Level 3 Assets Year Ended December 31, 20X1		
	Restricted Common Stock	Guaranteed Investment Contract	Total
Balance, beginning of year	$90,000	$1,040,000	$1,130,000
Realized gains/(losses)	(25,000)	—	(25,000)
Unrealized gains/(losses) relating to instruments still held at the reporting date	40,000	(50,000)	(10,000)
Purchases, sales, issuances and settlements (net)	20,000	92,000	112,000
Balance, end of year	$125,000	$1,082,000	$1,207,000
The amount of total gains or losses for the period included in changes in net assets attributable to the change in unrealized gains or losses relating to assets still held at the reporting date	$40,000	$(50,000)	$(10,000)

Gains and losses (realized and unrealized) included in changes in net assets for the period above are reported in net appreciation in fair value of investments in the Statement of Changes in Net Assets Available for Benefits.

E. Guaranteed Investment Contract With National Insurance Company

In 20X0, the plan entered into a benefit-responsive guaranteed investment contract with National Insurance Company (National). National maintains the contributions in a general account. The account is credited with earnings on the underlying investments and charged for participant withdrawals and administrative expenses. The guaranteed investment contract issuer is contractually obligated to repay the principal and a specified interest rate that is guaranteed to the plan.

Because the guaranteed investment contract is fully benefit-responsive, contract value is the relevant measurement attribute for that portion of the net assets available for benefits attributable to the guaranteed investment contract. The guaranteed investment contract is presented on the face of the statement of net assets available for benefits at fair value with an adjustment to contract value in arriving at net assets available for benefits. Contract value, as reported to the plan by National, represents contributions made under the contract, plus earnings, less participant withdrawals and administrative expenses. Participants may ordinarily direct the withdrawal or transfer of all or a portion of their investment at contract value.

There are no reserves against contract value for credit risk of the contract issuer or otherwise. The fair value of the investment contract at December 31, 20X1 and 20X0 was $1,082,000 and $1,040,000, respectively. The crediting interest rate is based on a formula agreed upon with the issuer, but it may not be less than 4 percent. Such interest rates are reviewed on a quarterly basis for resetting.

Certain events limit the ability of the plan to transact at contract value with the issuer. Such events include the following: (1) amendments to the plan documents (including complete or partial plan termination or merger with another plan), (2) changes to the plan's prohibition on competing investment options or deletion of equity wash provisions, (3) bankruptcy of the plan sponsor or other plan sponsor events (for example, divestitures or spin-offs of a subsidiary) that cause a significant withdrawal from the plan, or (4) the failure of the trust to qualify for exemption from federal income taxes or any required prohibited transaction exemption under ERISA. The plan administrator does not believe that any events which would limit the plan's ability to transact at contract value with participants are probable of occurring.

The guaranteed investment contract does not permit the insurance company to terminate the agreement prior to the scheduled maturity date.

Average yields:	20X1	20X0
Based on actual earnings	4.68%	4.90%
Based on interest rate credited to participants	4.68%	4.90%

F. Certificates of Deposit

Certificates of deposit at December 31, 20X1 and 20X0 consist of amounts on deposit at banks or savings and loan associations, with interest rates ranging from 5.4 percent to 9.1 percent, with maturities of three months or less. These deposits include $400,000 and $500,000 which are in excess of federally insured limits at December 31, 20X1 and 20X0, respectively.

G. Plan Termination

Although it has not expressed any intent to do so, the company has the right under the plan to discontinue its contributions at any time and to terminate the plan subject to the provisions of ERISA. In the event of plan termination, participants will become 100 percent vested in their accounts. Any unallocated assets of the plan should be allocated to participant accounts and distributed in such a manner as the company may determine.

H. Tax Status

The IRS has determined and informed the company by a letter dated August 30, 20XX, that the plan and related trust are designed in accordance with applicable sections of the Internal Revenue Code (IRC). Although the plan has been amended since receiving the determination letter, the plan administrator and the plan's tax counsel believe that the plan is designed and is currently being operated in compliance with the applicable requirements of the IRC and therefore believe that the plan is qualified and the related trust is tax-exempt.

Accounting principles generally accepted in the United States of America require plan management to evaluate tax positions taken by the plan and recognize a tax liability (or asset) if the organization has taken an uncertain position that more likely than not would not be sustained upon examination by the [identify applicable taxing authorities]. The plan administrator has analyzed the tax positions taken by the plan, and has concluded that as of December 31, 20X1, there are no uncertain positions taken or expected to be taken that would require recognition of a liability (or asset) or disclosure in the financial statements. The plan is subject to routine audits by taxing jurisdictions; however, there are currently no audits for any tax periods in progress. The plan administrator believes it is no longer subject to income tax examinations for years prior to 20XX.

I. Reconciliation of Financial Statements to Form 5500

The following is a reconciliation of net assets available for benefits per the financial statements at December 31, 20X1 and 20X0 to Form 5500:

	20X1	20X0
Net assets available for benefits per the financial statements	$9,818,000	$8,541,000
Amounts allocated to withdrawing participants	(50,000)	(35,000)
Net assets available for benefits per the Form 5500	$9,768,000	$8,506,000

The following is a reconciliation of benefits paid to participants per the financial statements for the year ended December 31, 20X1, to Form 5500:

Benefits paid to participants per the financial statements	$1,050,000
Add: Amounts allocated to withdrawing participants at December 31, 20X1	50,000
Less: Amounts allocated to withdrawing participants at December 21, 20X0	(35,000)
Benefits paid to participants per Form 5500	$1,065,000

Amounts allocated to withdrawing participants are recorded on the Form 5500 for benefit claims that have been processed and approved for payment prior to December 31, 20X1, but not yet paid as of that date.

J. Risks and Uncertainties

The plan invests in various investment securities. Investment securities are exposed to various risks such as interest rate, market, and credit risks. Due to the level of risk associated with certain investment securities, it is at least reasonably possible that changes in the values of investment securities will occur in the near term and that such changes could materially affect participants' account balances and the amounts reported in the statement of net assets available for benefits.

III. Illustrations of Financial Statements: Employee Stock Ownership Plan

Exhibit E-7

Employee Stock Ownership Plan
Sponsor Company Stock Ownership Plan
Statements of Net Assets Available for Benefits[1]

| | December 31, | | | | | |
| | 20X2 | | | 20X1 | | |
	Allocated	*Unallocated*	*Total*	*Allocated*	*Unallocated*	*Total*
Assets:						
Investment in Sponsor Company common stock, at fair value	$34,890,000	$57,430,000	$92,320,000	$24,568,000	$47,015,000	$71,583,000
Receivables:						
Employer contributions	—	8,607,000	8,607,000	—	7,062,000	7,062,000
Dividends and interest	570,000	459,000	1,029,000	280,000	3,000	283,000
Cash	156,000	863,000	1,019,000	101,000	448,000	549,000
Total assets	$35,616,000	$67,359,000	$102,975,000	$24,949,000	$54,528,000	$79,477,000
Liabilities:						
Interest payable	—	1,396,000	1,396,000	—	1,033,000	1,033,000
Loan payable	—	73,970,000	73,970,000	—	80,000,000	80,000,000
Total liabilities	—	75,366,000	75,366,000	—	81,033,000	81,033,000
Net assets available (deficit) for plan benefits	$35,616,000	$(8,007,000)	$27,609,000	$24,949,000	$(26,505,000)	$(1,556,000)

The accompanying notes are an integral part of these financial statements.

---

[1] The columns reflected in the example are appropriate for the presentation of a leveraged employee stock ownership plan (ESOP). For a nonleveraged ESOP, the presentation would reflect only the total column without the segregation between allocated and unallocated.

Allocated and unallocated designations distinguish between assets that belong to plan participants and those that are still available as collateral for the ESOP loan. Under the Employee Retirement Income Security Act of 1974 (ERISA), the lender has access to the securities held by the plan, that represent unallocated employer contributions to service the debt, and any earnings on those amounts. Earnings on temporary cash investments also are available to the lender.

An accrued employer contribution for current or future debt service is, therefore, reflected on the Statement of Net Assets Available for Benefits and the Statement of Changes in Net Assets Available for Benefits in the Unallocated column. In contrast, an employer contribution accrued to fund distributions to terminated participants is reflected in the Allocated column.

This distinction is *not* reflected in the participant account balances when reporting to the participant under ERISA. Contributions accrued for future debt service are allocated to the accounts of plan participants.

Exhibit E-8

Sponsor Company Stock Ownership Plan
Statement of Changes in Net Assets Available for Benefits

	December 31, 20X2		
	Allocated	*Unallocated*	*Total*
Investment income:			
Net unrealized appreciation in the fair value of investments	$9,205,000	$15,052,000	$24,257,000
Interest	31,000	58,000	89,000
Dividends	1,380,000	2,184,000	3,564,000
Employer contributions	—	11,524,000	11,524,000
Allocation of 142,000 shares of common stock of Sponsor Company, at fair value	4,637,000	—	4,637,000
	15,253,000	28,818,000	44,071,000
Interest expense	—	5,683,000	5,683,000
Distributions to participants	4,586,000	—	4,586,000
Allocation of 142,000 shares of common stock of Sponsor Company, at fair value	—	4,637,000	4,637,000
Total deductions	4,586,000	10,320,000	14,906,000
Net increase	10,667,000	18,498,000	29,165,000
Net assets (deficit) available for benefits:			
Beginning of year	24,949,000	(26,505,000)	(1,556,000)
End of year	$35,616,000	$(8,007,000)	$27,609,000

The accompanying notes are an integral part of these financial statements.

Exhibit E-9

Sponsor Company Stock Ownership Plan
Notes to Financial Statements
December 31, 20X2

A. Plan Description and Basis of Presentation

The following brief description of the Sponsor Company Stock Ownership Plan (the plan) is provided for general information purposes only. Participants should refer to the plan agreement for complete information.

The Sponsor Company (company) established the Sponsor Company Stock Ownership Plan (plan) effective as of January 1, 20XX. As of January 1, 20XY, the plan was amended and operates, in relevant part, as a leveraged employee stock ownership plan (ESOP), and is designed to comply with Section 4975(e)(7) and the regulations thereunder of the Internal Revenue Code of 1986, as amended (code) and is subject to the applicable provisions of ERISA. The plan is administered by an Employee Benefits Administration Committee comprising up to three persons appointed by the sponsor company's Board of Directors. The trust department of an independent third-party bank is the plan's Trustee.

The plan purchased company common stock using the proceeds of a bank borrowing (see note G) guaranteed by the company, and holds the common stock in a trust established under the plan. The borrowing is to be repaid over a period of ten years by fully deductible company contributions to the trust fund. As the plan makes each payment of principal, an appropriate percentage of stock will be allocated to eligible employees' accounts in accordance with applicable regulations under the IRC. Shares vest fully upon allocation.

The borrowing is collateralized by the unallocated shares of common stock and is guaranteed by the company. The lender has no rights against shares of common stock once they are allocated under the ESOP. Accordingly, the financial statements of the plan as of December 31, 20X2 and 20X1 and for the years ended December 31, 20X2 present separately the assets and liabilities and changes therein pertaining to

    a. the accounts of employees with vested rights in allocated common stock (allocated) and

    b. common stock not yet allocated to employees (unallocated).

Eligibility

Employees of the company and its participating subsidiaries are generally eligible to participate in the plan after one year of service providing they worked at least 1,000 hours during such plan year. Participants who do not have at least 1,000 hours of service during such plan year or are not employed on the last working day of a plan year are generally not eligible for an allocation of company contributions for such year.

Payment of Benefits

Distributions on account of death, disability or retirement are made in a lump sum in the plan year following the event. Distributions for other separations from service commence in the fifth plan year following the separation from service and are made in 5 annual installments. Distributions are made in cash or, if a participant elects, in the form of company common stock plus cash for any fractional share of common stock.

Under the provisions of the plan, the company is obligated to repurchase participant shares which have been distributed under the terms of the plan as long as the shares are not publicly traded or if the shares are subject to trading limitations. During 20X2, the company repurchased from participants XXXX shares at prices determined from the independent appraisal.

Voting Rights

Each participant is entitled to exercise voting rights attributable to the shares allocated to his or her account and is notified by the Trustee prior to the time that such rights are to be exercised. The Trustee is not permitted to vote any allocated share for which instructions have not been given by a participant. The Trustee is required, however, to vote any unallocated shares on behalf of the collective best interest of plan participants and beneficiaries.

Plan Termination

The company reserves the right to terminate the plan at any time, subject to plan provisions. Upon such termination of the plan, the interest of each participant in the trust fund will be distributed to such participant or his or her beneficiary at the time prescribed by the plan terms and the IRC. Upon termination of the plan, the Employee Benefits Administration Committee should direct the Trustee to pay all liabilities and expenses of the trust fund and to sell shares of financed common stock held in the loan suspense account to the extent it determines such sale to be necessary in order to repay the loan.

Participant Accounts

The plan is a defined contribution plan under which a separate individual account is established for each participant. Each participant's account is credited as of the last day of each plan year with an allocation of shares of the company's common stock released by the Trustee from the unallocated account and forfeitures of terminated participants' nonvested accounts. Only those participants who are eligible employees of the company as of the last day of the plan year will receive an allocation. Allocations are based on a participant's eligible compensation, relative to total eligible compensation.

Vesting

If a participant's employment with the company ends for any reason other than retirement, permanent disability or death, he or she will vest in the balances in his or her account based on total years of service with the company. Participants vest 20 percent per year of service and are 100 percent vested after five years of service.

Put Option

Under Federal income tax regulations, the employer stock that is held by the plan and its participants and is not readily tradable on an established market, or is subject to trading limitations includes a put option. The put option is a right to demand that the company buy any shares of its stock distributed to participants for which there is no market. The put price is representative of the fair market value of the stock. The company can pay for the purchase with interest over a period of five years. The purpose of the put option is to ensure that the participant has the ability to ultimately obtain cash.

Diversification

Diversification is offered to participants close to retirement so that they may have the opportunity to move part of the value of their investment in company common stock into investments which are more diversified. Participants who are at least age 55 with at least 10 years of participation in the plan may elect to diversify a portion of their account. Diversification is offered to each eligible participant over a six-year period. In each of the first five years, a participant may diversify up to 25 percent of the number of post-1986 shares allocated to his or her account, less any shares previously diversified. In the sixth year, the percentage changes to 50 percent. Participants who elect to diversify receive a cash distribution.

Participant Accounts and Forfeitures

Employer contributions and plan forfeitures are allocated to each participant's account based upon the relation of the participant's compensation to total compensation for the plan year. Forfeitures of terminated nonvested account balances allocated to remaining participants at December 31, 20X2 and 20X1 totaled $X,XXX and $X,XXX, respectively. Plan earnings are allocated to each participant's account based on the ratio of the participant's beginning of the year account balance to all participants' beginning of the year account balances.

B. Summary of Significant Accounting Policies

Basis of Accounting

The financial statements of the plan are prepared on the accrual basis of accounting.

Use of Estimates

The preparation of financial statements in conformity with accounting principles generally accepted in the United States of America requires management to make estimates and assumptions that affect the reported amounts of assets, liabilities, and changes therein, and disclosure of contingent assets and liabilities. Actual results could differ from those estimates.

Investment Valuation and Income Recognition

The shares of company common stock are valued at estimated fair value. See note F for discussion of fair value measurements.

Dividend income is accrued on the ex-dividend date.

Purchases and sales of securities are recorded on a trade-date basis. Realized gains and losses from security transactions are reported on the average cost method. Net appreciation includes the plan's gains and losses on investments bought and sold as well as held during the year.

Operating Expenses

All expenses of maintaining the plan are paid by the company.

Subsequent Events

The plan has evaluated subsequent events through [*insert date*], the date the financial statements were available to be issued.

C. Tax Status

The IRS has determined and informed the company by a letter dated June 30, 20XX, that the plan is qualified and the trust established under the plan is tax-exempt, under the appropriate sections of the IRC. The plan has been amended since receiving the determination letter. However, the plan administrator and the plan's tax counsel believe that the plan is currently designed and being operated in compliance with the applicable requirements of the IRC. Therefore, they believe that the plan was qualified and the related trust was tax-exempt as of the financial statement date.

Accounting principles generally accepted in the United States of America require plan management to evaluate tax positions taken by the plan and recognize a tax liability (or asset) if the organization has taken an uncertain position that more likely than not would not be sustained upon examination by the [*identify applicable taxing authorities*]. The plan administrator has analyzed the tax positions taken by the plan, and has concluded that as of December 31, 20X1, there are no uncertain positions taken or expected to be taken that would require recognition of a liability (or asset) or disclosure in the financial statements. The plan is subject to routine audits by taxing jurisdictions; however, there are currently no audits for any tax periods in progress. The plan administrator believes it is no longer subject to income tax examinations for years prior to 20XX.

D. Administration of Plan Assets

The plan's assets, which consist principally of sponsor company common shares, are held by the Trustee of the plan.

Company contributions are held and managed by the Trustee, which invests cash received, interest, and dividend income and makes distributions to participants. The Trustee also administers the payment of interest and principal on the loan, which is reimbursed to the Trustee through contributions as determined by the company.

Certain administrative functions are performed by officers or employees of the company or its subsidiaries. No such officer or employee receives compensation from the plan. Administrative expenses for the Trustee's fees are paid directly by the company.

E. Investments

The plan's investments, at December 31, are presented in the following table:

	20X2		20X1	
	Allocated	*Unallocated*	*Allocated*	*Unallocated*
Sponsor Company common stock:				
Number of shares	1,069,000	1,759,000	1,074,000	2,055,000
Cost	$27,014,000	$74,456,000	$29,910,000	$80,000,000
Fair Value	$34,890,000	$57,430,000	$24,568,000	$47,015,000

F. Fair Value Measurements

Financial Accounting Standards Board (FASB) *Accounting Standards Codification* (ASC) 820, *Fair Value Measurements and Disclosures*, provides the framework for measuring fair value. That framework provides a fair value hierarchy that prioritizes the inputs to valuation techniques used to measure fair value. The hierarchy gives the highest priority to unadjusted quoted prices in active markets for identical assets or liabilities (level 1 measurements) and the lowest priority to unobservable inputs (level 3 measurements). The three levels of the fair value hierarchy under FASB ASC 820 are described as follows:

Level 1	Inputs to the valuation methodology are unadjusted quoted prices for identical assets or liabilities in active markets that the plan has the ability to access.
Level 2	Inputs to the valuation methodology include

Level 2 (continued):
- quoted prices for similar assets or liabilities in active markets;
- quoted prices for identical or similar assets or liabilities in inactive markets;
- inputs other than quoted prices that are observable for the asset or liability;
- inputs that are derived principally from or corroborated by observable market data by correlation or other means.

If the asset or liability has a specified (contractual) term, the level 2 input must be observable for substantially the full term of the asset or liability.

Level 3	Inputs to the valuation methodology are unobservable and significant to the fair value measurement.

The asset or liability's fair value measurement level within the fair value hierarchy is based on the lowest level of any input that is significant to the fair value measurement. Valuation techniques used need to maximize the use of observable inputs and minimize the use of unobservable inputs.

Following is a description of the valuation methodologies used for assets measured at fair value. There have been no changes in the methodologies used at December 31, 20X1 and 20X0.

> ***Note:*** Information contained herein for fair value disclosures is based upon information for the Illustrative Financial Statements: Defined Contribution Plans (appendix E) as presented in exhibits E-1–E-3. This illustrative disclosure is not representative of all types of investment securities and does not represent the classification for every instance of such investment securities. It should not be assumed that these methodologies are the only appropriate methodologies for these types of assets. As stated in FASB ASC 820-10-35-5, "The principle (or most advantageous) market (and thus, market participants) should be considered from the perspective of the reporting entity, thereby allowing for differences between and among entities with different activities." Plan sponsors will have to evaluate the appropriate classification for each type of investments securities based upon the plan's portfolio and actual fair valuation techniques used.

The fair value of the sponsor company common stock held by the plan is valued at fair value based upon an independent appraisal. This appraisal was based upon a combination of the market and income valuation techniques consistent with prior years. The appraiser took into account historical and projected cash flow and net income, return on assets, return on equity, market comparables and estimated fair value of company assets and liabilities.

The preceding methods described may produce a fair value calculation that may not be indicative of net realizable value or reflective of future fair values. Furthermore, although the plan believes its valuation methods are appropriate and consistent with other market participants, the use of different methodologies or assumptions to determine the fair value of certain financial instruments could result in a different fair value measurement at the reporting date.

The following table sets forth by level, within the fair value hierarchy, the plan's assets at fair value as of December 31, 20X1 and 20X0:

Practice Tips

The following table illustrates certain disclosure requirements of FASB ASC 820. The disclosures illustrated describe the nature and risks of securities as required by FASB ASC 820-10-50 and are included for illustrative purposes and are NOT intended to represent the ONLY way to disclose such information.

In addition, in January 2010, FASB issued FASB ASU No. 2010-06. FASB ASU No. 2010-06 amends the disclosure requirements of FASB ASC 820 including amendments regarding the level of disaggregation for each class of assets and liabilities. The illustrative financial statements in this appendix have been amended to conform to FASB ASU No. 2010-06, where applicable. The amendments in the level 3 fair value measurement roll forward, related to the separate disclosures requirement of purchases, sales, issuances, and settlements activity are effective for fiscal years beginning after December 15, 2010, and for interim periods within those fiscal years, and therefore these financial statements have not been updated for those amendments. These illustrative financial statements do not contain any transfers between fair value levels and therefore no disclosure has been made. See paragraph 3.22 for the required disclosures.

| | Assets at Fair Value as of December 31 | | | |
| | 20X2 | | 20X1 | |
	Level 3	Total	Level 3	Total
Investment in Sponsor Company common stock	$92,320,000	$92,320,000	$71,583,000	$71,583,000
Total assets at fair value	**$92,320,000**	**$92,320,000**	**$71,583,000**	**$71,583,000**

	Level 3 Assets Year Ended December 31, 20X2
	Investment in Sponsor Company Common Stock
Balance, beginning of year	$71,583,000
Realized gains/(losses)	0
Unrealized gains/(losses) relating to assets still held at the reporting date	24,257,000
Shares distributed to participants	(3,520,000)
Balance, end of year	**$92,320,000**
The amount of total gains or losses for the period included in changes in net assets attributable to the change in unrealized gains or losses relating to assets still held at the reporting date	$24,257,000

Gains and losses (realized and unrealized) included in changes in net assets for the period above are reported in net appreciation in fair value of investments in the Statement of Changes in Net Assets Available for Benefits.

G. Loan Payable

In 20XX, the plan entered into an $80,000,000 term loan agreement with a bank. The proceeds of the loan were used to purchase company's common stock. Unallocated shares are collateral for the loan. The agreement provides for the loan to be repaid over ten years. The fair value of the note payable as of December 31, 20X2 and 20X1 was approximately $77,000,000 and $82,000,000, respectively, determined by using interest rates currently available for issuance of debt with similar terms, maturity dates and nonperformance risk. The scheduled amortization of the loan for the next five years and thereafter is as follows: 20X3—$6,500,000; 20X4—$7,000,000; 20X5—$7,500,000; 20X6—$8,000,000; 20X7—$8,500,000; and thereafter—$36,470,000. The loan bears interest at the prime rate of the lender. For 20X2 and 20X1 the loan interest rate averaged 7.34 percent and 5.12 percent, respectively.

H. Employer Contributions

The company is obligated to make contributions in cash to the plan which, when aggregated with the plan's dividends and interest earnings, equal the amount necessary to enable the plan to make its regularly scheduled payments of principal and interest due on its term loan.

———————————

Appendix F

Illustrative Financial Statements: Employee Health and Welfare Benefit Plans

F.01 These illustrative financial statements were originally derived from AICPA Statement of Position 92-6, *Accounting and Reporting by Health and Welfare Benefit Plans,* which has now been codified in the Financial Accounting Standards Board (FASB) *Accounting Standards Codification* (ASC) 965, *Plan Accounting—Health and Welfare Benefit Plans.* These illustrative financial statements have since been modified to include certain changes necessary due to the subsequent issuance of authoritative guidance. This appendix illustrates certain applications of the provisions of FASB ASC 965 to the annual financial statements of four hypothetical health and welfare benefit plans. They are

a. Allied Industries Health Care Benefit Plan, a multiemployer plan that displays the benefit obligation information in separate financial statements and the retirees contribute a portion of the cost for their medical coverage (exhibits F-1–F-5).

b. Classic Enterprises Benefit Plan, a single-employer plan that displays the benefit obligation information on the face of the financial statements along with the net asset information (exhibits F-6– F-8).

c. C&H Company Welfare Benefit Plan, a plan that includes retiree health benefits that are funded partially through a 401(h) account in the plan sponsor's defined benefit pension plan (exhibits F-9– F-13).

d. Supplemental Unemployment Benefit Plan for Employees of ABC Company Established Pursuant to Agreement with United Workers of America, an employee benefit plan that provides postemployment benefits (exhibits F-14–F-16).

F.02 The plans in exhibits F-1–F-8 have assets in underlying trusts. The plan in exhibits F-1–F-5 pays all benefits directly from plan assets. The plan in exhibits F-6–F-8 obtains insurance for current benefits from its assets. It is assumed that both plans provide health benefits and life insurance coverage to both active and retired participants. Exhibits F-1–F-5 also assume that the plan provides long-term disability benefits and limited coverage during periods of unemployment based on accumulated eligibility credits.

F.03 This appendix also illustrates certain applications of the provisions of FASB ASC 965 that apply to the annual financial statements of a hypothetical health and welfare benefit plan that includes retiree health benefits that are funded partially through a 401(h) account in the plan sponsor's defined benefit pension plan (exhibits F-9–F-13). It illustrates the single line approach to presenting information about the 401(h) account permitted by FASB ASC 965. It does not illustrate other provisions of FASB ASC 965 as well as other FASB ASC topics that might apply in circumstances other than those assumed in the illustration. It also does not illustrate all disclosures required for a fair presentation in conformity with accounting principles generally accepted in the United States of America (U.S. GAAP). The formats presented and the wording of accompanying notes are only illustrative and are not necessarily the only possible presentations. In addition, the illustrative financial statements in this appendix have been amended to conform to FASB ASC 820, *Fair Value Measurements and Disclosures.*[*]

> *Note:* FASB ASC 820 disclosures are limited to the financial instruments contained within this specific example. It is recommended that users consult all the illustrative financial statements within appendixes D–F for FASB ASC 820 examples of different types of financial instruments.

F.04   FASB ASC 965-20-45-1 says that defined-contribution pension plans should report all investments (including derivative contracts) at fair value. However, contract value is the relevant measurement attribute for that portion of the net assets available for benefits of a defined-contribution plan attributable to fully benefit-responsive investment contracts. The statement of net assets available for benefits of the plan should present amounts for (*a*) total assets, (*b*) total liabilities, (*c*) net assets reflecting all investments at fair value, and (*d*) net assets available for benefits. The amount representing the difference between (*c*) and (*d*) should be presented on the face of the statement of net assets available for benefits as a single amount, calculated as the sum of the amounts necessary to adjust the portion of net assets attributable to each fully benefit-responsive investment contract from fair value to contract value. The statement of changes in net assets available for benefits should be prepared on a basis that reflects income credited to participants in the plan and net appreciation or depreciation in the fair value of only those investment contracts that are not deemed to be fully benefit responsive. The examples in this chapter do not contain fully benefit-responsive investment contracts and therefore do not illustrate the provisions of FASB ASC 946, *Financial Services—Investment Companies*.

F.05   The examples do not illustrate other provisions of chapter 4, "Accounting and Reporting by Health and Welfare Benefit Plans," that might apply in circumstances other than those assumed. The format presented and the wording of the accompanying notes are illustrative only and are not necessarily the only possible presentations. Although U.S. GAAP encourages but does not require comparative financial statements, the Employee Retirement Income Security Act of 1974 (ERISA) requires comparative statements of net assets available for benefits. The illustrative financial statements are intended to comply with the requirements of ERISA.

F.06   ERISA and Department of Labor (DOL) regulations require that certain information be included in supplemental schedules, which are not required

---

[*] The illustrative financial statements and footnote disclosures included in this appendix have been updated to reflect the Financial Accounting Standards Board (FASB) *Accounting Standards Codification*™ (ASC) references. However, in FASB's notice to constituents, it suggests the use of plain English in financial statement footnotes to describe broad FASB ASC topic references. They suggest a reference similar to "as required by the *Derivatives and Hedging* topic of the FASB *Accounting Standards Codification*." Entities might consider revising their financial statement references to reflect this plain English referencing, rather than the use of specific FASB ASC references. For specific information on FASB ASC, please see the preface in the guide.

under U.S. GAAP, and reported on by the independent auditor. See appendix A, "ERISA and Related Regulations," for a further discussion of the ERISA and DOL requirements.

F.07 In March 2010, Congress passed two pieces of legislation designed to reform the U.S. health care system. The Patient Protection and Affordable Care Act (Public Law [PL] No. 111-148) was enacted on March 23, 2010, and was quickly followed by the Health Care and Education Reconciliation Act of 2010 (PL No. 111-152), which amended several portions of the first act, as well as added new provisions of its own. One of the goals of the legislation is to reform the health care delivery system to improve its quality while lowering its overall costs.

The health care reform is far reaching and there is much uncertainty as to how health reform measures will impact the way health care entities will deliver services to their patients in the future and how they will be compensated for those services.

CONTENTS

I. Allied Industries Health Care Benefit Plan

Exhibit F-1

ALLIED INDUSTRIES HEALTH CARE BENEFIT PLAN

Allied Industries Health Care Benefit Plan
Statements of Net Assets Available for Benefits
December 31, 20X1 and 20X0

	20X1	20X0
Assets		
Investments, at fair value (see notes 4 and 5)		
U.S. government securities	$5,000,000	$4,000,000
Corporate bonds	2,000,000	1,600,000
Common stocks	1,000,000	600,000
Total Investments	8,000,000	6,200,000
Receivables		
Participating employers' contributions	500,000	430,000
Participants' contributions	100,000	80,000
Accrued interest and dividends	50,000	40,000
Total receivables	650,000	550,000
Cash	140,000	115,000
TOTAL ASSETS	8,790,000	6,865,000
Liabilities		
Due to broker for securities purchased	250,000	240,000
Accounts payable for administrative expenses	25,000	25,000
TOTAL LIABILITIES	275,000	265,000
NET ASSETS AVAILABLE FOR BENEFITS	$8,515,000	$6,600,000

The accompanying notes are an integral part of the financial statements.

Exhibit F-2

Allied Industries Health Care Benefit Plan
Statement of Changes in Net Assets Available for Benefits
Year Ended December 31, 20X1

	20X1
Additions:	
Contributions	
Participating employers	$15,000,000
Participants	3,000,000
Total contributions	18,000,000
Investment income	
Net appreciation in fair value of investments	300,000
Interest	500,000
Dividends	50,000
Total investment income	850,000
Less investment expenses	15,000
Net investment income	835,000
TOTAL ADDITIONS	18,835,000
Deductions	
Benefits paid to participants	
Health care	16,000,000
Disability and death	770,000
Total benefits paid	16,770,000
Administrative expenses	150,000
TOTAL DEDUCTIONS	16,920,000
NET INCREASE DURING YEAR	1,915,000
Net assets available for benefits	
Beginning of year	6,600,000
End of year	$ 8,515,000

The accompanying notes are an integral part of the financial statements.

Exhibit F-3

Allied Industries Health Care Benefit Plan
Statements of Plan's Benefit Obligations
December 31, 20X1 and 20X0

	20X1	20X0
Amounts currently payable		
Claims payable, claims incurred but not reported, and premiums due to insurers	$1,200,000	$1,050,000
Postemployment benefit obligations, net of amounts currently payable		
Death and disability benefits for inactive participants	1,350,000	1,000,000
Postretirement benefit obligations, net of amounts currently payable		
Retired participants	2,000,000	1,900,000
Other participants fully eligible for benefits	4,000,000	3,600,000
Participants not yet fully eligible for benefits	5,000,000	4,165,000
	11,000,000	9,665,000
PLAN'S TOTAL BENEFIT OBLIGATIONS	$13,550,000	$11,715,000

The accompanying notes are an integral part of the financial statements.

Exhibit F-4

Allied Industries Health Care Benefit Plan
Statement of Changes in Plan's Benefit Obligations
Year Ended December 31, 20X1

	20X1
Amounts currently payable	
Balance at beginning of year	$ 1,050,000
Claims reported and approved for payment, including benefits reclassified from benefit obligations	16,920,000
Claims paid	(16,770,000)
Balance at end of year	1,200,000
Postemployment benefit obligations, net of amounts currently payable	
Balance at beginning of year	1,000,000
Increase (decrease) in postemployment benefits attributable to:	
Benefits earned	600,000
Benefits reclassified to amounts currently payable	(450,000)
Interest	90,000
Changes in actuarial assumptions and other actuarial gains and losses	110,000
Balance at end of year	1,350,000
Postretirement benefit obligations, net of amounts currently payable	
Balance at beginning of year	9,665,000
Increase (decrease) in postretirement benefits attributable to:	
Benefits earned	1,150,000
Benefits reclassified to amounts currently payable	(650,000)
Interest	750,000
Plan amendment	(175,000)
Changes in actuarial assumptions and other actuarial gains and losses	260,000
Balance at end of year	11,000,000
PLAN'S TOTAL BENEFIT OBLIGATIONS AT END OF YEAR	$ 13,550,000

The accompanying notes are an integral part of the financial statements.

Exhibit F-5

Allied Industries Health Care Benefit Plan
Notes to Financial Statements

NOTE 1: DESCRIPTION OF PLAN

The following description of the Allied Industries Health Care Benefit Plan (the plan) provides only general information. Participants should refer to the plan agreement for a complete description of the plan's provisions.

General. The plan provides health and other benefits covering all participants in the widgets industry in the Greater Metropolis area. The plan and related trust were established on May 8, 1966, pursuant to a collective bargaining agreement between the Allied Employers' Trade Association and the Allied Union, Local 802. It is subject to the provisions of ERISA, as amended.

Benefits. The plan provides health benefits (medical, hospital, surgical, major medical, and dental), life insurance coverage, long-term disability benefits, and death benefits to full-time participants (with at least 450 hours of work in the industry during a consecutive three-month period) and to their beneficiaries and covered dependents. Retired employees are entitled to similar health benefits (in excess of Medicare coverage) provided they have attained at least age 62 and have 15 years of service with participating employers before retirement.

The plan also provides health benefits to participants during periods of unemployment, provided they have accumulated in the current year or in prior years credit amounts (expressed in hours) in excess of the hours required for current coverage. Accumulated eligibility credits equal to one year's coverage may be carried forward.

Health, disability, and death claims of active and retired participants, dependents, and beneficiaries are processed by the Administrator Group, but the responsibility for payments to participants and providers is retained by the plan.

In 20X1 the board of trustees amended the plan to increase the deductible under major medical coverage from $100 to $300 and to extend dental coverage to employees retiring after December 31, 20X2. The amendment will not affect participating employers' contributions to the plan in 20X2 under the current collective bargaining agreement.

Contributions. Participating employers contribute 5.5 percent of wages pursuant to the current collective bargaining agreement between employers and the union (expiring February 19, 20X5). Employees may contribute specified amounts, determined periodically by the plan's actuary, to extend coverage to eligible dependents. The costs of the postretirement benefit plan are shared by the plan's participating employers and retirees. In addition to deductibles and copayments, participant contributions in the current (and prior, if applicable) year were as follows:

Participants Retiring	20X1 Retiree Contribution	20X0 Retiree Contribution
(1) Pre-1990	(1) None	(1) None
(2) 1990–1994	(2) Retirees contribute 20% of estimated cost of providing their postretirement benefits[†]	(2) Retirees contribute 20% of estimated cost of providing their postretirement benefits
(3) 1995–1999	(3) Retirees pay the cost of providing their postretirement benefits in excess of $200 per month "cap" (approximately 60% of the estimated cost)	(3) Retirees pay the cost of providing their postretirement benefits in excess of $200 per month "cap" (approximately 50% of the estimated cost)
(4) 2000 and after	(4) Retirees pay 100% of estimated cost of providing their postretirement benefits	(4) Retirees pay 100% of estimated cost of providing their postretirement benefits

Other. The plan's board of trustees, as Sponsor, has the right under the plan to modify the benefits provided to active employees. The plan may be terminated only by joint agreement between industry and union, subject to the provisions set forth in ERISA.

NOTE 2: SUMMARY OF ACCOUNTING POLICIES

A. *Use of Estimates.* The preparation of financial statements in conformity with accounting principles generally accepted in the United States of America requires management to make estimates and assumptions that affect the reported amounts of assets, liabilities, benefit obligations and changes therein, IBNR, eligibility credits, claims payable, and disclosure of contingent assets and liabilities. Actual results could differ from those estimates.

B. *Investment Valuation and Income Recognition.* Investments are reported at fair value. Fair value is the price that would be received to sell an asset or paid to transfer a liability in an orderly transaction between market participants at the measurement date. See note 5 for discussion of fair value measurements.

Purchases and sales of securities are recorded on a trade-date basis. Interest income is recorded on the accrual basis. Dividends are recorded on the ex-dividend date. Net appreciation includes the plan's gains and losses on investments bought and sold as well as held during the year.

C. *Postretirement Benefits.* The amount reported as the postretirement benefit obligation represents the actuarial present value of those estimated future benefits that are attributed by the terms of the plan to employees' service rendered to the date of the financial statements, reduced by the actuarial present value of contributions expected to be received in the future from current plan participants. Postretirement benefits include future benefits expected to be paid to or for (1) currently retired or terminated employees and their beneficiaries and dependents and (2) active employees and their beneficiaries and dependents after retirement from service with participating employers. The postretirement

---

[†] Excluding $15 per month per capita increase in 20X1 due to adverse claims experience in 20X0.

benefit obligation represents the amount that is to be funded by contributions from the plan's participating employers and from existing plan assets. Prior to an active employee's full eligibility date, the postretirement benefit obligation is the portion of the expected postretirement benefit obligation that is attributed to that employee's service in the industry rendered to the valuation date.

The actuarial present value of the expected postretirement benefit obligation is determined by an actuary and is the amount that results from applying actuarial assumptions to historical claims-cost data to estimate future annual incurred claims costs per participant and to adjust such estimates for the time value of money (through discounts for interest) and the probability of payment (by means of decrements such as those for death, disability, withdrawal, or retirement) between the valuation date and the expected date of payment.

For measurement purposes, a 9.5 percent annual rate of increase in the per capita cost of covered health care benefits was assumed for 20X2; the rate was assumed to decrease gradually to 8.0 percent for 20X7 and to remain at that level thereafter. These assumptions are consistent with those used to measure the benefit obligation at December 31, 20X1.

The following were other significant assumptions used in the valuations as of December 31, 20X1 and 20X0.

Weighted-average discount rate	8.0%—20X1; 8.25%—20X0
Average retirement age	60
Mortality	RP 2000 Mortality Table

The foregoing assumptions are based on the presumption that the plan will continue. Were the plan to terminate, different actuarial assumptions and other factors might be applicable in determining the actuarial present value of the postretirement benefit obligation.

D. *Other Plan Benefits.* Plan obligations at December 31 for health claims incurred by active participants but not reported at that date, for accumulated eligibility of participants, and for future disability payments to members considered permanently disabled at December 31 are estimated by the plan's actuary in accordance with accepted actuarial principles. Such estimated amounts are reported in the accompanying statement of the plan's benefit obligations at present value, based on an 8.0 percent discount rate. Health claims incurred by retired participants but not reported at year end are included in the postretirement benefit obligation.

E. *Subsequent Events.* The plan has evaluated subsequent events through [*insert date*], the date the financial statements were available to be issued.

NOTE 3: BENEFIT OBLIGATIONS

The plan's deficiency of net assets over benefit obligations at December 31, 20X1 and 20X0, relates primarily to the postretirement benefit obligation, the funding of which is not covered by the contribution rate provided by the current bargaining agreement. It is expected that the deficiency will be funded through future increases in the collectively bargained contribution rates.

The weighted-average health care cost-trend rate assumption (see note 2B) has a significant effect on the amounts reported in the accompanying financial statements. If the assumed rates increased by 1 percentage point in each year, it would increase the obligation as of December 31, 20X1 and 20X0, by $2,600,000 and $2,500,000, respectively.

NOTE 4: INVESTMENTS

The plan's investments are held by a bank-administered trust fund. During 20X1 the plan's investments (including investments bought, sold, and held during the year) appreciated in value by $300,000, as follows:[‡]

	20X1	20X1	20X0
	Net Increase (Decrease) in Value During Year	Fair Value at End of Year	Fair value at End of Year
U.S. government securities	$200,000	$5,000,000	$4,000,000
Corporate bonds	—	2,000,000	1,600,000
Common stocks	100,000	1,000,000	600,000
	$300,000	$8,000,000	$6,200,000

The fair value of individual investments that represent 5 percent or more of the plan's net assets are as follows:

	20X1	20X0
Commonwealth Power Co., 9.0% bonds due 2014 ($500,000 face amount)	$475,000	$450,000
ABC Company common stock (2,000 shares)	500,000	450,000
U.S. Treasury bond, 8.5% due 20X6 ($360,000 face amount)		350,000

NOTE 5: FAIR VALUE MEASUREMENTS

Financial Accounting Standards Board (FASB) *Accounting Standards Codification* (ASC) 820, *Fair Value Measurements and Disclosures*, provides the framework for measuring fair value. That framework provides a fair value hierarchy that prioritizes the inputs to valuation techniques used to measure fair value. The hierarchy gives the highest priority to unadjusted quoted prices in active markets for identical assets or liabilities (level 1 measurements) and the lowest priority to unobservable inputs (level 3 measurements). The three levels of the fair value hierarchy under FASB ASC 820 are described as follows:

[‡] See note 5 for discussion of fair value measurements.

Level 1	Inputs to the valuation methodology are unadjusted quoted prices for identical assets or liabilities in active markets that the plan has the ability to access.
Level 2	Inputs to the valuation methodology include • quoted prices for similar assets or liabilities in active markets; • quoted prices for identical or similar assets or liabilities in inactive markets; • inputs other than quoted prices that are observable for the asset or liability; • inputs that are derived principally from or corroborated by observable market data by correlation or other means. If the asset or liability has a specified (contractual) term, the level 2 input must be observable for substantially the full term of the asset or liability.
Level 3	Inputs to the valuation methodology are unobservable and significant to the fair value measurement.

The asset or liability's fair value measurement level within the fair value hierarchy is based on the lowest level of any input that is significant to the fair value measurement. Valuation techniques used need to maximize the use of observable inputs and minimize the use of unobservable inputs.

Following is a description of the valuation methodologies used for assets measured at fair value. There have been no changes in the methodologies used at December 31, 20X1 and 20X0.

> **Note:** Information contained herein for fair value disclosures is based upon information for the Illustration of Financial Statements: Allied Industries Health Care Benefit Plan (appendix F) as presented in exhibits F-1–F-5. This illustrative disclosure is not representative of all types of investment securities and does not represent the classification for every instance of such investment securities. It should not be assumed that these methodologies are the only appropriate methodologies for these types of assets. As stated in FASB ASC 820-10-35-5, "The principle (or most advantageous) market (and thus, market participants) should be considered from the perspective of the reporting entity, thereby allowing for differences between and among entities with different activities." Plan sponsors will have to evaluate the appropriate classification for each type of investments securities based upon the plan's portfolio and actual fair valuation techniques used.

U.S. Government securities and common stock: Valued at the closing price reported in the active market in which the individual security is traded.

Corporate bonds: Certain corporate bonds are valued at the closing price reported in the active market in which the bond is traded. Other corporate bonds traded in the over-the-counter market and listed securities for which no sale was reported on the last business day of the plan year are valued at the average of the last reported bid and asked prices. For certain corporate bonds that do not have an established fair value, the plan's board of trustees have established a fair value based on yields currently available on comparable securities of issuers with similar credit ratings.

The preceding methods described may produce a fair value calculation that may not be indicative of net realizable value or reflective of future fair values. Furthermore, although the plan believes its valuation methods are appropriate and consistent with other market participants, the use of different methodologies or assumptions to determine the fair value of certain financial instruments could result in a different fair value measurement at the reporting date.

The following table sets forth by level, within the fair value hierarchy, the plan's assets at fair value as of December 31, 20X1 and 20X0:

Practice Tips

The following table illustrates certain disclosure requirements of FASB ASC 820. The disclosures illustrated describe the nature and risks of securities as required by FASB ASC 820-10-50 and are included for illustrative purposes and are NOT intended to represent the ONLY way to disclose such information.

In addition, in January 2010, FASB issued Accounting Standards Update (ASU) No. 2010-06, *Fair Value Measurements and Disclosures (Topic 820): Improving Disclosures about Fair Value Measurements*. FASB ASU No. 2010-06 amends the disclosure requirements of FASB ASC 820 including amendments regarding the level of disaggregation for each class of assets and liabilities. The illustrative financial statements in this appendix have been amended to conform to FASB ASU No. 2010-06, where applicable. The amendments in the level 3 fair value measurement roll forward, related to the separate disclosures requirement of purchases, sales, issuances, and settlements activity are effective for fiscal years beginning after December 15, 2010, and for interim periods within those fiscal years, and therefore these financial statements have not been updated for those amendments. These illustrative financial statements do not contain any transfers between fair value levels and therefore no disclosure has been made. See paragraph 4.38 for the required disclosures.

	Assets at Fair Value as of December 31, 20X1			
	Level 1	*Level 2*	*Level 3*	*Total*
U.S. government securities	$5,000,000	—	—	$5,000,000
Corporate bonds:				
Aaa credit rating	250,000	—	—	250,000
Aa credit rating	—	$1,750,000	—	1,750,000
Total corporate bonds	250,000	1,750,000	—	2,000,000
Common stocks:				
Consumer goods	450,000	—	—	450,000
Information technology	350,000	—	—	350,000
Other	200,000	—	—	200,000
Total common stocks	1,000,000	—	—	1,000,000
Total assets at fair value	$6,250,000	$1,750,000	—	$8,000,000

Assets at Fair Value as of December 31, 20X0

	Level 1	Level 2	Level 3	Total
U.S. government securities	$4,000,000	—	—	$4,000,000
Corporate bonds·				
Aaa credit rating	225,000	—	—	225,000
Aa credit rating	—	$1,375,000	—	1,375,000
Total corporate bonds	225,000	1,375,000	—	1,600,000
Common stocks:				
Consumer goods	270,000	—	—	270,000
Information technology	210,000	—	—	210,000
Other	120,000	—	—	120,000
Total common stocks	600,000	—	—	600,000
Total assets at fair value	$4,825,000	$1,375,000	—	$6,200,000

NOTE 6: TAX STATUS

The Trust established under the plan to hold the plan's assets is intended to qualify pursuant to Section 501(c)9 of the Internal Revenue Code (IRC), and, accordingly, the Trust's net investment income is exempt from income taxes. The Trust has obtained a favorable tax determination letter from the IRS, and the plan sponsor believes that the Trust, as amended, continues to qualify and to operate in accordance with applicable provisions of the IRC.

Accounting principles generally accepted in the United States of America require plan management to evaluate tax positions taken by the plan and recognize a tax liability (or asset) if the organization has taken an uncertain position that more likely than not would not be sustained upon examination by the [identify the taxing authorities]. The plan administrator has analyzed the tax positions taken by the plan, and has concluded that as of December 31, 20X1, there are no uncertain positions taken or expected to be taken that would require recognition of a liability (or asset) or disclosure in the financial statements. The plan is subject to routine audits by taxing jurisdictions; however, there are currently no audits for any tax periods in progress. The plan administrator believes it is no longer subject to income tax examinations for years prior to 20XX.

NOTE 7: RECONCILIATION OF FINANCIAL STATEMENTS TO FORM 5500

The following is a reconciliation of net assets available for benefits per the financial statements to the Form 5500:

	December 31,	
	20X1	20X0
Net assets available for benefits per the financial statements	$8,515,000	$6,600,000
Benefit obligations currently payable (health claims, death and disability benefits)	1,200,000	1,050,000
Net assets available for benefits per the Form 5500	$7,315,000	$5,550,000

The following is a reconciliation of benefits paid to participants per the financial statements to the Form 5500:

	Year ended December 31, 20X1
Benefits paid to participants per the financial statements	$16,770,000
Add: Amounts currently payable at December 31, 20X1	1,200,000
Less: Amounts currently payable at December 31, 20X0	(1,050,000)
Benefits paid to participants per the Form 5500	$16,920,000

Amounts currently payable to or for participants, dependents, and beneficiaries are recorded on the Form 5500 for benefit claims that have been processed and approved for payment prior to December 31, but not yet paid as of that date.

NOTE 8: RISKS AND UNCERTAINTIES

The plan invests in various investment securities. Investment securities are exposed to various risks such as interest rate, market, and credit risks. Due to the level of risk associated with certain investment securities, it is at least reasonably possible that changes in the values of investment securities will occur in the near term and that such changes could materially affect the amounts reported in the statement of net assets available for benefits.

The actuarial present value of benefit obligations is reported based on certain assumptions pertaining to interest rates, health care inflation rates and employee demographics, all of which are subject to change. Due to uncertainties inherent in the estimations and assumptions process, it is at least reasonably possible that changes in these estimates and assumptions in the near term would be material to the financial statements.

II. Classic Enterprises Benefit Plan

Exhibit F-6

CLASSIC ENTERPRISES BENEFIT PLAN
Classic Enterprises Benefit Plan
Statements of Benefit Obligations and Net Assets Available for
Benefits
December 31, 20X1 and 20X0

	20X1	20X0
BENEFIT OBLIGATIONS (see note 3)		
Amount due insurance companies	$1,200,000	$1,000,000
Postretirement benefit obligations	11,000,000	9,665,000
Total benefit obligations	12,200,000	10,665,000
NET ASSETS		
Assets		
Investments at fair value (see notes 4 and 5)		
U.S. government securities	$5,000,000	$4,000,000
Corporate bonds	2,000,000	1,600,000
Common stocks	1,000,000	600,000
Total investments	8,000,000	6,200,000
Receivables		
Sponsor's contributions	500,000	430,000
Participants' contributions	100,000	80,000
Accrued interest and dividends	50,000	40,000
Total receivables	650,000	550,000
Cash	75,000	60,000
Insurance premium deposits	65,000	55,000
TOTAL ASSETS	8,790,000	6,865,000
Liabilities		
Due to broker for securities purchased	250,000	240,000
Accounts payable for administrative expenses	25,000	25,000
TOTAL LIABILITIES	275,000	265,000
NET ASSETS AVAILABLE FOR BENEFITS	8,515,000	6,600,000
EXCESS OF BENEFIT OBLIGATIONS OVER NET ASSETS AVAILABLE FOR BENEFITS	$3,685,000	$4,065,000

The accompanying notes are an integral part of the financial statements.

Exhibit F-7

Classic Enterprises Benefit Plan
Statement of Changes in Benefit Obligations and Net Assets Available for Benefits
Year Ended December 31, 20X1

	20X1
Net Increase in Benefit Obligations	
Increase (Decrease) during the year attributable to:	
Benefits earned and other changes	$1,510,000
Additional amounts payable to insurance company	200,000
Plan amendment	(175,000)
	1,535,000
Net Increase in Net Assets Available for Benefits	
Additions	
Contributions	
Sponsor	15,000,000
Participants	3,000,000
Total contributions	18,000,000
Investments income	
Net appreciation in fair value of investments	300,000
Interest	500,000
Dividends	50,000
	850,000
Less investment expenses,	15,000
Net investment income	835,000
TOTAL ADDITIONS	18,835,000
Deductions	
Insurance premiums paid for health benefits, net of experience-rating adjustments of $250,000 for 20X0 received in 20X1	16,035,000
Insurance premiums paid for death benefits	780,000
	16,815,000
Administrative expenses	105,000
TOTAL DEDUCTIONS	16,920,000
NET INCREASE	1,915,000
Decrease in excess of benefit obligations over net assets available for benefits	(380,000)
Excess of benefit obligations over net assets available for benefits	
Beginning of year	4,065,000
End of year	$3,685,000

The accompanying notes are an integral part of the financial statements.

Exhibit F-8

Classic Enterprises Benefit Plan
Notes to Financial Statements

NOTE 1: DESCRIPTION OF PLAN

The following description of the Classic Enterprises Benefit Plan (the plan) provides only general information. Participants should refer to the plan agreement for a complete description of the plan's provisions.

General. The plan provides health and death benefits covering substantially all active and retired employees of Classic Enterprises (the Sponsor). It is subject to the provisions of ERISA, as amended.

Benefits. The plan provides health benefits (medical, hospital, surgical, major medical, and dental) and death benefits to full-time employees of the Sponsor (with at least 1,000 hours of service each year) and to their beneficiaries and covered dependents. Retired employees are entitled to similar health and death benefits provided they have attained at least age fifty-five and have at least ten years of service with the Sponsor.

Current health claims of active and retired participants and their dependents and beneficiaries are provided under group insurance contracts with ABC Carrier, which are experience rated after the anniversary dates of the policies (generally March 31). Death benefits are covered by a group-term policy with DEF Carrier.

Contributions. The Sponsor's policy is to contribute the maximum amounts allowed as a tax deduction by the IRC. Under present law, the Sponsor is not permitted to deduct amounts for future benefits to current employees and retirees.

Employees and retirees may contribute specified amounts, determined periodically by the plan's insurance companies, to extend coverage to eligible dependents.

In 20X1 the plan was amended to increase the deductible under major medical coverage from $100 to $300 and to extend dental coverage to employees retiring after December 31, 20X1. The amendment is not expected to significantly affect the Sponsor's contribution to the plan in 20X2.

Other. Although it has not expressed any intention to do so, the Sponsor has the right under the plan to modify the benefits provided to active employees, to discontinue its contributions at any time, and to terminate the plan subject to the provisions set forth in ERISA.

NOTE 2: SUMMARY OF ACCOUNTING POLICIES

A. *Use of Estimates.* The preparation of financial statements in conformity with accounting principles generally accepted in the United States of America requires management to make estimates and assumptions that affect the reported amounts of assets, benefit obligations and changes therein, IBNR, eligibility credits, claims payable, liabilities and disclosure of contingent assets and liabilities. Actual results could differ from those estimates.

B. *Investment Valuation and Income Recognition.* The plan's investments are stated at fair value. Fair value is the price that would be received to sell an asset or paid to transfer a liability in an orderly transaction between market participants at the measurement date. See note 5 for discussion of fair value measurements.

Purchases and sales of securities are recorded on a trade-date basis. Interest income is recorded on the accrual basis. Dividends are recorded on the ex-dividend date. Net appreciation includes the plan's gains and losses on investments bought and sold as well as held during the year.

C. *Plan Benefits.* The postretirement benefit obligation (see note 3) represents the actuarial present value of those estimated future benefits that are attributed to employee service rendered to December 31. Postretirement benefits include future benefits expected to be paid to or for (1) currently retired employees and their beneficiaries and dependents and (2) active employees and their beneficiaries and dependents after retirement from service with the Sponsor. Prior to an active employee's full eligibility date, the postretirement benefit obligation is the portion of the expected postretirement benefit obligation that is attributed to that employee's service rendered to the valuation date.

The actuarial present value of the expected postretirement benefit obligation is determined by an actuary and is the amount that results from applying actuarial assumptions to historical claims-cost data to estimate future annual incurred claims costs per participant and to adjust such estimates for the time value of money (through discounts for interest) and the probability of payment (by means of decrements such as those for death, disability, withdrawal, or retirement) between the valuation date and the expected date of payment.

For measurement purposes at December 31, 20X1, a 9.5 percent annual rate of increase in the per capita cost of covered health care benefits was assumed for 20X2; the rate was assumed to decrease gradually to 8.0 percent for 20X7 and to remain at that level thereafter. These assumptions are consistent with those used to measure the benefit obligation at December 31, 20X0.

The following were other significant assumptions used in the valuations as of December 31, 20X1 and 20X0.

Weighted-average discount rate	8.0%
Average retirement age	60
Mortality	1971 Group Annuity Mortality Table

The foregoing assumptions are based on the presumption that the plan will continue. Were the plan to terminate, different actuarial assumptions and other factors might be applicable in determining the actuarial present value of the postretirement benefit obligation.

D. *Subsequent Events.* The plan has evaluated subsequent events through [*insert date*], the date the financial statements were available to be issued.

NOTE 3: BENEFIT OBLIGATIONS

Health costs incurred by participants and their beneficiaries and dependents are covered by insurance contracts maintained by the plan. It is the present intention of the Sponsor and the plan to continue obtaining insurance coverage for benefits. As stated in note 1, the Sponsor is not permitted under present tax law to deduct amounts for future benefits (beyond one year). Insurance premiums for future years in respect of the plan's postretirement benefit obligation will be funded by Sponsor contributions to the plan in those later years.

The postretirement benefit obligation at December 31, 20X1 and 20X0, principally health benefits, relates to the following categories of participants (including their beneficiaries and dependents):

	20X1	20X0
Current retirees	$3,900,000	$3,500,000
Other participants fully eligible for benefits	2,100,000	2,000,000
Participants not yet fully eligible for benefits	5,000,000	4,165,000
	$11,000,000	$9,665,000

The health care cost-trend rate assumption (see note 2B) has a significant effect on the amounts reported. If the assumed rates increased by 1 percentage point in each year, that would increase the obligation as of December 31, 20X1 and 20X0, by $2,600,000 and $2,500,000, respectively.

NOTE 4: INVESTMENTS

The plan's investments are held by a bank-administered trust fund. During 20X1, the plan's investments (including investments bought, sold, and held during the year) appreciated in value by $300,000, as follows:[II]

	20X1		20X0
	Net Increase (Decrease) in Value During Year	Fair Value at End of Year	Fair Value at End of Year
U.S. government securities	$200,000	$5,000,000	$4,000,000
Corporate bonds	—	2,000,000	1,600,000
Common stocks	100,000	1,000,000	600,000
	$300,000	$8,000,000	$6,200,000

The fair value of individual investments that represent 5 percent or more of the plan's net assets are as follows:

	20X1	20X0
Commonwealth Power Co., 9.0% bonds due 2014 ($500,000 face amount)	$475,000	$450,000
ABC Company common stock (2,000 shares)	500,000	450,000
U.S. Treasury bond, 8.5% due 20X6 ($360,000 face amount)		350,000

NOTE 5: FAIR VALUE MEASUREMENTS

Financial Accounting Standards Board (FASB) *Accounting Standards Codification* (ASC) 820, *Fair Value Measurements and Disclosures*, provides the

---

[II] See note 5 for discussion of fair value measurements.

framework for measuring fair value. That framework provides a fair value hierarchy that prioritizes the inputs to valuation techniques used to measure fair value. The hierarchy gives the highest priority to unadjusted quoted prices in active markets for identical assets or liabilities (level 1 measurements) and the lowest priority to unobservable inputs (level 3 measurements). The three levels of the fair value hierarchy under FASB ASC 820 are described as follows:

Level 1	Inputs to the valuation methodology are unadjusted quoted prices for identical assets or liabilities in active markets that the plan has the ability to access.
Level 2	Inputs to the valuation methodology include

- quoted prices for similar assets or liabilities in active markets;
- quoted prices for identical or similar assets or liabilities in inactive markets;
- inputs other than quoted prices that are observable for the asset or liability;
- inputs that are derived principally from or corroborated by observable market data by correlation or other means.

If the asset or liability has a specified (contractual) term, the level 2 input must be observable for substantially the full term of the asset or liability.

Level 3	Inputs to the valuation methodology are unobservable and significant to the fair value measurement.

The asset or liability's fair value measurement level within the fair value hierarchy is based on the lowest level of any input that is significant to the fair value measurement. Valuation techniques used need to maximize the use of observable inputs and minimize the use of unobservable inputs.

Following is a description of the valuation methodologies used for assets measured at fair value. There have been no changes in the methodologies used at December 31, 20X1 and 20X0.

Note: Information contained herein for fair value disclosures is based upon information for the Illustration of Financial Statements: Classic Enterprises Benefit Plan (appendix F) as presented in exhibits F-6–F-8. This illustrative disclosure is not representative of all types of investment securities and does not represent the classification for every instance of such investment securities. It should not be assumed that these methodologies are the only appropriate methodologies for these types of assets. As stated in FASB ASC 820-10-35-5, "The principle (or most advantageous) market (and thus, market participants) should be considered from the perspective of the reporting entity, thereby allowing for differences between and among entities with different activities." Plan sponsors will have to evaluate the appropriate classification for each type of investment securities based upon the plan's portfolio and actual fair valuation techniques used.

U.S. Government securities and common stock: Valued at the closing price reported in the active market in which the individual security is traded.

Corporate bonds: Certain corporate bonds are valued at the closing price reported in the active market in which the bond is traded. Other corporate bonds traded in the over-the-counter market and listed securities for which no sale was reported on the last business day of the plan year are valued at the average of the last reported bid and asked prices. For certain corporate bonds that do not have an established fair value, the plan's board of trustees have established a fair value based on yields currently available on comparable securities of issuers with similar credit ratings.

The preceding methods described may produce a fair value calculation that may not be indicative of net realizable value or reflective of future fair values. Furthermore, although the plan believes its valuation methods are appropriate and consistent with other market participants, the use of different methodologies or assumptions to determine the fair value of certain financial instruments could result in a different fair value measurement at the reporting date.

The following table sets forth by level, within the fair value hierarchy, the plan's assets at fair value as of December 31, 20X1 and 20X0:

Practice Tips

The following table illustrates certain disclosure requirements of FASB ASC 820. The disclosures illustrated describe the nature and risks of securities as required by FASB ASC 820-10-50 and are included for illustrative purposes and are NOT intended to represent the ONLY way to disclose such information.

In addition, in January 2010, FASB issued Accounting Standards Update (ASU) No. 2010-06, *Fair Value Measurements and Disclosures (Topic 820): Improving Disclosures about Fair Value Measurements*. FASB ASU No. 2010-06 amends the disclosure requirements of FASB ASC 820 including amendments regarding the level of disaggregation for each class of assets and liabilities. The illustrative financial statements in this appendix have been amended to conform to FASB ASU No. 2010-06, where applicable. The amendments in the level 3 fair value measurement roll forward, related to the separate disclosures requirement of purchases, sales, issuances, and settlements activity are effective for fiscal years beginning after December 15, 2010, and for interim periods within those fiscal years, and therefore these financial statements have not been updated for those amendments. These illustrative financial statements do not contain any transfers between fair value levels and therefore no disclosure has been made. See paragraph 4.38 for the required disclosures.

Assets at Fair Value as of December 31, 20X1

	Level 1	Level 2	Level 3	Total
U.S. government securities	$5,000,000	—	—	$5,000,000
Corporate bonds:				
Aaa credit rating	250,000	—	—	250,000
Aa credit rating	—	$1,750,000	—	1,750,000
Total corporate bonds	250,000	1,750,000	—	2,000,000
Common stocks:				
Consumer Goods	450,000	—	—	450,000
Energy	350,000	—	—	350,000
Other	200,000	—	—	200,000
Total common stocks	1,000,000	—	—	1,000,000
Total assets at fair value	$6,250,000	$1,750,000	—	$8,000,000

Assets at Fair Value as of December 31, 20X0

	Level 1	Level 2	Level 3	Total
U.S. government securities	$4,000,000	—	—	$4,000,000
Corporate bonds:				
Aaa credit rating	225,000	—	—	225,000
Aa credit rating	—	$1,375,000	—	1,375,000
Total corporate bonds	225,000	1,375,000	—	1,600,000
Common stocks:				
Consumer Goods	270,000	—	—	270,000
Energy	210,000	—	—	210,000
Other	120,000	—	—	120,000
Total common stocks	600,000	—	—	600,000
Total assets at fair value	$4,825,000	$1,375,000	—	$6,200,000

NOTE 6: TAX STATUS

The Trust established under the plan to hold the plan's net assets is qualified pursuant to Section 501(c)9 of the IRC, and, accordingly, the Trust's net investment income is exempt from income taxes. The Sponsor has obtained a favorable tax determination letter from the Internal Revenue Service and the Sponsor believes that the Trust, as amended, continues to qualify and to operate as designed.

Accounting principles generally accepted in the United States of America require plan management to evaluate tax positions taken by the plan and recognize a tax liability (or asset) if the organization has taken an uncertain position that more likely than not would not be sustained upon examination by the [identify the taxing authorities]. The plan administrator has analyzed the tax positions taken by the plan, and has concluded that as of December 31,

20X1, there are no uncertain positions taken or expected to be taken that would require recognition of a liability (or asset) or disclosure in the financial statements. The plan is subject to routine audits by taxing jurisdictions; however, there are currently no audits for any tax periods in progress. The plan administrator believes it is no longer subject to income tax examinations for years prior to 20XX.

NOTE 7: RECONCILIATION OF FINANCIAL STATEMENTS TO FORM 5500

The following is a reconciliation of net assets available for benefits per the financial statements to the Form 5500:

	December 31,	
	20X1	*20X0*
Net assets available for benefits per the financial statements	$8,515,000	$6,600,000
Amounts due to insurance companies	1,200,000	1,000,000
Net assets available for benefits per the Form 5500	$7,315,000	$5,600,000

The following is a reconciliation of insurance premiums paid for participants per the financial statements to the Form 5500:

	Year ended December 31, 20X1
Insurance premiums paid per the financial statements	$16,815,000
Add: Amounts due insurance companies at December 31, 20X1	1,200,000
Less: Amounts due insurance companies at December 31, 20X0	(1,000,000)
Insurance premiums paid to participants per the Form 5500	$17,015,000

NOTE 8: RISKS AND UNCERTAINTIES

The plan invests in various investment securities. Investment securities are exposed to various risks such as interest rate, market, and credit risks. Due to the level of risk associated with certain investment securities, it is at least reasonably possible that changes in the values of investment securities will occur in the near term and that such changes could materially affect the amounts reported in the statements of net assets available for benefits.

The actuarial present value of benefit obligations is reported based on certain assumptions pertaining to interest rates, health care inflation rates and employee demographics, all of which are subject to change. Due to uncertainties inherent in the estimations and assumptions process, it is at least reasonably possible that changes in these estimates and assumptions in the near term would be material to the financial statements.

III. C&H Company Welfare Benefit Plan

> *Note:* The following illustrative health and welfare plan financial statements are not representative of a complete set of financial statements and notes thereto.

Exhibit F-9[#]

C&H Company Welfare Benefit Plan
Statement of Net Assets Available for Plan Benefits

	December 31,	
	20X1	*20X0*
Assets		
Investments, at fair value:		
U.S. government securities	$5,000,000	$4,000,000
Corporate bonds	2,000,000	1,600,000
Common stocks	1,000,000	600,000
Total investments	8,000,000	6,200,000
Net assets held in C&H Company defined benefit plan—restricted for 401(h) account (notes A and E)	1,072,000	966,000
Receivables		
Employer contribution	500,000	430,000
Employee contributions	100,000	80,000
Accrued interest and dividends	50,000	40,000
Total receivables	650,000	550,000
Cash	110,000	115,000
Total assets	9,832,000	7,831,000
Liabilities		
Due to broker for securities purchased	250,000	240,000
Accounts payable for administrative expenses	25,000	25,000
Total liabilities	275,000	265,000
Net assets available for plan benefits	$9,557,000	$7,566,000

The accompanying notes are an integral part of the financial statements.

[#] The illustrative financial statements example is from FASB ASC 965, *Plan Accounting—Health and Welfare Benefit Plans*.

Exhibit F-10#

C&H Company Welfare Benefit Plan
Statement of Changes in Net Assets Available for Plan Benefits

	For the Year Ended December 31, 20X1
Additions	
Contributions	
Employer contributions	$15,000,000
Employee contributions	3,000,000
Total contributions	18,000,000
Investment income	
Net appreciation in fair value of investments	300,000
Interest	500,000
Dividends	50,000
Total investment income	850,000
Less investment expense	15,000
Net investment income	835,000
Net increase in 401(h) account (Note E)	106,000
Total additions	18,941,000
Deductions	
Benefits paid directly to participants:	
Health care	16,000,000
Disability and death	770,000
Total benefits paid	16,770,000
Administrative expenses	180,000
Total deductions	16,950,000
Net increase during the year	1,991,000
Net assets available for benefits:	
Beginning of year	7,566,000
End of year	$ 9,557,000

The accompanying notes are an integral part of the financial statements.

See footnote # in exhibit F-9.

Exhibit F-11[#]

C&H Welfare Benefit Plan
Statement of Benefit Obligations

	For the Year Ended December 31,	
	20X1	*20X0*
Amounts currently payable to or for participants, beneficiaries, and dependents		
Health claims payable	$ 1,100,000	$ 975,000
Death and disability benefits payable	100,000	75,000
Total amounts currently payable	1,200,000	1,050,000
Other obligations for current benefit coverage, at present value of estimated amounts		
Claims incurred but not reported	425,000	390,000
Long-term disability benefits	925,000	610,000
Total other obligations for current benefit coverage	1,350,000	1,000,000
Total obligations other than postretirement benefit obligations	2,550,000	2,050,000
Postretirement benefit obligations		
Current retirees	3,900,000	3,500,000
Other participants fully eligible for benefits	2,100,000	2,000,000
Other participants not yet fully eligible for benefits	5,000,000	4,165,000
Total postretirement benefit obligations	11,000,000	9,665,000
Total benefit obligations	$13,550,000	$11,715,000

The accompanying notes are an integral part of the financial statements.

[#] See footnote [#] in exhibit F-9.

Exhibit F-12[#]

C&H Company Welfare Benefit Plan
Statement of Changes in Benefit Obligations

	For the Year Ended December 31, 20X1
Amounts currently payable to or for participants, beneficiaries, and dependents	
Balance, beginning of year	$ 1,050,000
Claims reported and approved for payment	16,930,000
Claims paid (including disability)	(16,770,000)
Claims paid through 401(h) account (note E)	(10,000)
Balance, end of year	1,200,000
Other obligations for current benefit coverage, at present value of estimated amounts	
Balance, beginning of year	1,000,000
Net change during year:	
Long-term disability benefits	315,000
Other	35,000
Balance, end of year	1,350,000
Total obligations other than postretirement benefit obligations	2,550,000
Postretirement benefit obligations	
Balance, beginning of year	9,665,000
Increase (decrease) during the year attributable to:	
Benefits earned and other changes	1,250,000
Plan amendment	(175,000)
Changes in actuarial assumptions	260,000
Balance, end of year	11,000,000
Total benefit obligations, end of year	$ 13,550,000

The accompanying notes are an integral part of the financial statements.

[#] See footnote [#] in exhibit F-9.

Exhibit F-13

C&H Welfare Benefit Plan
Notes to Financial Statements

NOTE A: 401(H) ACCOUNT

Effective January 1, 20X0, the [company's defined benefit pension plan] was amended to include a medical-benefit component in addition to normal retirement benefits to fund a portion of the postretirement obligations for retirees and their beneficiaries in accordance with Section 401(h) of the IRC. A separate account has been established and maintained in the [defined benefit pension plan] for such contributions. In accordance with IRC Section 401(h), the plan's investments in the 401(h) account may not be used for, or diverted to, any purpose other than providing health benefits for retirees and their beneficiaries. The related obligations for health benefits are not included in the [defined benefit pension plan's] obligations in the statement of accumulated plan benefits but are reported as obligations in the financial statements of the [health and welfare benefit plan].

NOTE E: 401(H) ACCOUNT

A portion of the plan's obligations are funded through contributions to the company's [defined benefit pension plan] in accordance with IRC Section 401(h). The following table presents the components of the net assets available for such obligations and the related changes in net assets available.

Net Assets Available for Postretirement
Health and Welfare Benefits in 401(h) Account

	December 31,	
	20X1	20X0
Investments at fair value:		
U.S. government securities	$140,000	$150,000
Money market fund	900,000	800,000
	1,040,000	950,000
Cash	20,000	10,000
Employer's contribution receivable[1]	20,000	15,000
Accrued interest	7,000	6,000
Total assets	1,087,000	981,000
Accrued administrative expenses	(15,000)	(15,000)
Net assets available	$1,072,000	$966,000

---

[1] A receivable from the employer must meet the requirements of FASB ASC 960-310-25-2.

Changes in Net Assets in 401(h) Account

	For the Year Ended December 31, 20X1
Net appreciation in fair value of investments:	
U.S. government securities	$10,800
Interest	80,200
	91,000
Employer contributions	40,000
Health and welfare benefits paid to retirees	(10,000)
Administrative expenses	(15,000)
Net increase in net assets available	$106,000

NOTE H: RECONCILIATION OF FINANCIAL STATEMENTS TO FORM 5500[2]

The following is a reconciliation of net assets available for benefits per the financial statements to the Form 5500:

Net assets available for benefits per the financial statements	$9,557,000
Claims payable	(1,200,000)
Net assets held in defined benefit plan—401(h) account	(1,072,000)
Net assets available for benefits per Form 5500	$7,285,000

The following is a reconciliation of claims paid per the financial statements to the Form 5500:

Claims paid per the financial statements	$16,770,000
Add: Amounts payable at December 31, 20X1	1,200,000
Less: Amounts payable at December 31, 20X0	(1,050,000)
Claims paid per Form 5500	$16,920,000

The following is a reconciliation of total additions per the financial statements to the Form 5500:

Total additions per financial statements	$18,941,000
Less: Net increase in 401(h) net assets available	(106,000)
Net additions per Form 5500	$ 18,835,000

---

[2] The reconciliation of amounts reported in plan financial statements to amounts reported in Form 5500 is required by the Employee Retirement Income Security Act of 1974.

IV. Supplemental Unemployment Benefit Plan for Employees of ABC Company Established Pursuant to Agreement With United Workers of America Statements of Net Assets Available for Benefits

Exhibit F-14

Supplemental Unemployment Benefit Plan for Employees of ABC Company Established Pursuant to Agreement With United Workers of America Statements of Net Assets Available for Benefits December 31, 20X1 and 20X0

	20X1	20X0
Assets		
Investments	$10,605	$80,750
Cash and cash equivalents	1,025	19,400
Accrued interest receivable	100	125
TOTAL ASSETS	11,730	100,275
Liability		
Accrued investment trustee fees	265	265
NET ASSETS AVAILABLE FOR BENEFITS	$11,465	$100,010

The accompanying notes are an integral part of the financial statements.

Exhibit F-15

**Supplemental Unemployment Benefit Plan for
Employees of ABC Company Established Pursuant to
Agreement With United Workers of America
Statement of Changes in Net Assets Available for Benefits
Year Ended December 31, 20X1**

Additions:	
Contributions	$1,366,065
Interest income	1,960
TOTAL ADDITIONS	1,368,025
Deductions:	
Benefit payments	1,455,460
Investment trustee fees	1,110
TOTAL DEDUCTIONS	1,456,570
NET DECREASE DURING THE YEAR	(88,545)
Net assets available for benefits	
Beginning of year	100,010
End of year	$11,465

The accompanying notes are an integral part of the financial statements.

Exhibit F-16

Supplemental Unemployment Benefit Plan for Employees of ABC Company Established Pursuant to Agreement with United Workers of America
Notes to Financial Statements

NOTE 1: DESCRIPTION OF PLAN

In connection with a negotiated contract, the Supplemental Unemployment Benefit Plan for Employees of ABC Company Established Pursuant to Agreement With United Workers of America (the plan) provides for payment of supplemental unemployment benefits to covered employees who have completed two years of continuous service. Payments are made to (a) employees on layoff and (b) certain employees who work less than 32 hours in any week. The following description is provided for general information purposes. The plan document should be referred to for specific information regarding benefits and other plan matters.

NOTE 2: SUMMARY OF ACCOUNTING POLICIES

Basis of Accounting. The financial statements of the plan are prepared on the accrual basis of accounting.

Investment Valuation and Income Recognition. Investments are reported at fair value. Fair value is the price that would be received to sell an asset or paid to transfer a liability in an orderly transaction between market participants at the measurement date. See note 4 for discussion of fair value measurements.

Purchases and sales of securities are recorded on a trade-date basis. Interest income is recorded on the accrual basis.

Use of Estimates. The preparation of financial statements in conformity with GAAP requires management to make estimates and assumptions that affect the reported amounts of assets and liabilities and disclosure of contingent assets and liabilities at the date of the financial statements and the reported amounts of revenues and expenses during the reporting period. Actual results could differ from those estimates.

Benefit Obligations. The plan's obligation for accumulated eligibility credits is discounted using a weighted-average assumed rate of 7.5 percent.

Subsequent Events. The plan has evaluated subsequent events through [*insert date*], the date the financial statements were available to be issued.

NOTE 3: FUNDING AND OPERATION OF THE PLAN

Funding of the Plan. Contributions funded by ABC Company, the plan's sponsor, pursuant to the plan are invested in assets held in a trust fund (the Fund). General Bank, the trustee of the Fund (the Trustee), invests the Fund's money as set forth in the plan document. Investments consist of money market funds and are reported in the accompanying financial statements at fair value. Interest income from investments is recognized when earned.

Administration. The ABC Company Benefit Plan Administrative Committee has responsibility for administering the plan. The ABC Company Benefit Plan

Asset Review Committee has responsibility for the management and control of the assets of the Trust.

Benefits Under the Plan. The plan provides for the payment of weekly and short-week supplemental unemployment benefits. The benefits payable are reduced by any state unemployment benefits or any other compensation received. Also, a "waiting-week" benefit of $100 will be payable if a participant fails to receive a state unemployment benefit solely because of the state's waiting-week requirement. Benefits paid for any week for which the employee received state unemployment benefits are limited to $180. Benefits paid for all other weeks are limited to $235. The plan provides for a possible reduction of weekly benefits for employees with less than twenty years of service based upon a percentage determined generally by dividing the net assets of the plan, as defined in the plan document, by the "maximum financing" (see "ABC's Obligations Under the Plan"). Employees earn one-half credit unit for each week in which hours are worked or, in some situations, in which hours are not worked (vacation, disability, serving on grievance committee, and so on) up to a maximum of fifty-two credit units for employees with less than twenty years of service and 104 credit units for employees with twenty or more years of service. Generally, one credit unit is canceled for each weekly benefit paid and one-half credit unit is canceled for each short-week benefit paid.

ABC's Obligations Under the Plan. The "maximum financing" of the plan at any month end is the lesser of (a) the product of $.40 and the number of hours worked by covered employees during the first twelve of the fourteen months next preceding the first day of the month and (b) 100 times the sum of the monthly benefits paid for the sixty of the preceding sixty-two months divided by sixty. ABC's monthly contribution to the plan is computed as the lesser of (a) the product of $.175 and the number of hours worked by covered employees in the month and (b) the amount that, when added to the net assets of the plan, as defined by the plan document, as of the end of the preceding month, will equal the "maximum financing." In addition, ABC contributes an income security contribution of $.25 per hour worked by covered employees in the month. In the event of a plan deficit, ABC intends to make sufficient contributions to fund benefits as they become payable.

The following tables present the components of the plan's benefit obligations and the related changes in the plan's benefit obligations.

Benefit Obligations
December 31, 20X1 and 20X0

	20X1	*20X0*
Accumulated eligibility credits and total benefit obligations	$1,107,777	$1,095,620

Changes in Benefit Obligations
Year Ended December 31, 20X1

Benefit obligations, beginning of year	$1,095,620
Benefits earned	1,390,330
Interest	77,287
Claims paid	(1,455,460)
Benefit obligations, end of year	$1,107,777

Plan Expenses. ABC bears all administrative costs, except trustee fees, that are paid by the plan.

NOTE 4: FAIR VALUE MEASUREMENTS

Financial Accounting Standards Board (FASB) *Accounting Standards Codification* (ASC) 820, *Fair Value Measurements and Disclosures*, provides the framework for measuring fair value. That framework provides a fair value hierarchy that prioritizes the inputs to valuation techniques used to measure fair value. The hierarchy gives the highest priority to unadjusted quoted prices in active markets for identical assets or liabilities (level 1 measurements) and the lowest priority to unobservable inputs (level 3 measurements). The three levels of the fair value hierarchy under FASB ASC 820 are described as follows:

Level 1	Inputs to the valuation methodology are unadjusted quoted prices for identical assets or liabilities in active markets that the plan has the ability to access.
Level 2	Inputs to the valuation methodology include • quoted prices for similar assets or liabilities in active markets; • quoted prices for identical or similar assets or liabilities in inactive markets; • inputs other than quoted prices that are observable for the asset or liability; • inputs that are derived principally from or corroborated by observable market data by correlation or other means. If the asset or liability has a specified (contractual) term, the level 2 input must be observable for substantially the full term of the asset or liability.
Level 3	Inputs to the valuation methodology are unobservable and significant to the fair value measurement.

The asset or liability's fair value measurement level within the fair value hierarchy is based on the lowest level of any input that is significant to the fair value measurement. Valuation techniques used need to maximize the use of observable inputs and minimize the use of unobservable inputs.

Following is a description of the valuation methodologies used for assets measured at fair value. There have been no changes in the methodologies used at December 31, 20X1 and 20X0.

Note: Information contained herein for fair value disclosures is based upon information for the Illustration of Financial Statements: Supplemental Unemployment Benefit Plan for Employees of ABC Company (appendix F) as presented in exhibits F-14–F-16. This illustrative disclosure is not representative of all types of investment securities and does not represent the classification for every instance of such investment securities. It should not be assumed that these methodologies are the only appropriate methodologies for these types of assets. As stated in FASB ASC 820-10-35-5, "The principle (or most advantageous) market (and thus, market participants) should be considered from the perspective of the reporting entity, thereby allowing for differences between and among entities with different activities." Plan sponsors will have to evaluate the appropriate classification for each type of investment securities based upon the plan's portfolio and actual fair valuation techniques used.

The plan's investments consist of shares of a money market portfolio which is valued using amortized cost which approximates fair value.

The preceding methods described may produce a fair value calculation that may not be indicative of net realizable value or reflective of future fair values. Furthermore, although the plan believes its valuation methods are appropriate and consistent with other market participants, the use of different methodologies or assumptions to determine the fair value of certain financial instruments could result in a different fair value measurement at the reporting date.

The following table sets forth by level, within the fair value hierarchy, the plan's assets at fair value as of December 31, 20X1 and 20X0:

Practice Tips

The following table illustrates certain disclosure requirements of FASB ASC 820. The disclosures illustrated describe the nature and risks of securities as required by FASB ASC 820-10-50 and are included for illustrative purposes and are NOT intended to represent the ONLY way to disclose such information.

In addition, in January 2010, FASB issued Accounting Standards Update (ASU) No. 2010-06, *Fair Value Measurements and Disclosures (Topic 820): Improving Disclosures about Fair Value Measurements.* FASB ASU No. 2010-06 amends the disclosure requirements of FASB ASC 820 including amendments regarding the level of disaggregation for each class of assets and liabilities. The illustrative financial statements in this appendix have been amended to conform to FASB ASU No. 2010-06, where applicable. The amendments in the level 3 fair value measurement roll forward, related to the separate disclosures requirement of purchases, sales, issuances, and settlements activity are effective for fiscal years beginning after December 15, 2010, and for interim periods within those fiscal years, and therefore these financial statements have not been updated for those amendments. These illustrative financial statements do not contain any transfers between fair value levels and therefore no disclosure has been made. See paragraph 4.38 for the required disclosures.

	Assets at Fair Value as of December 31, 20X1			
	Level 1	Level 2	Level 3	Total
Money market portfolio	$10,605	—	—	$10,605
Total assets at fair value	$10,605	—	—	**$10,605**

	Assets at Fair Value as of December 31, 20X0			
	Level 1	Level 2	Level 3	Total
Money market portfolio	$80,750	—	—	$80,750
Total assets at fair value	$80,750	—	—	**$80,750**

NOTE 5: TAX STATUS

The plan obtained its latest determination letter in 1990, in which the Internal Revenue Service stated that the plan, as then designed, was in compliance with the applicable requirements of the IRC. The plan has been amended since receiving the determination letter. Plan management and plan's tax counsel believe that the plan is currently designed and being operated in compliance with the applicable requirements of the IRC. Therefore, no provision for income taxes has been included in the plan's financial statements.

Accounting principles generally accepted in the United States of America require plan management to evaluate tax positions taken by the plan and recognize a tax liability (or asset) if the organization has taken an uncertain position that more likely than not would not be sustained upon examination by the [identify the taxing authorities]. The plan administrator has analyzed the tax positions taken by the plan, and has concluded that as of December 31, 20X1, there are no uncertain positions taken or expected to be taken that would require recognition of a liability (or asset) or disclosure in the financial statements. The plan is subject to routine audits by taxing jurisdictions; however, there are currently no audits for any tax periods in progress. The plan administrator believes it is no longer subject to income tax examinations for years prior to 20XX.

NOTE 6: TRANSACTIONS WITH PARTIES IN INTEREST

ABC provides to the plan certain accounting and administrative services for which no fees are charged.

NOTE 7: TERMINATION OF THE PLAN

Under certain conditions, the plan may be terminated. Upon termination, the assets then remaining should be subject to the applicable provisions of the plan then in effect and should be used until exhausted to pay benefits to employees in the order of their entitlement.

NOTE 8: RISKS AND UNCERTAINTIES

The plan invests in various investment securities. Investment securities are exposed to various risks such as interest rate, market, and credit risks. Due to the level of risk associated with certain investment securities, it is at least reasonably possible that changes in the values of investment securities will occur in the near term and that such changes could materially affect the amounts reported in the statement of net assets available for benefits.

The actuarial present value of benefit obligations is reported based on certain assumptions pertaining to interest rates, health care inflation rates and employee demographics, all of which are subject to change. Due to uncertainties inherent in the estimations and assumptions process, it is at least reasonably possible that changes in these estimates and assumptions in the near term would be material to the financial statements.

Appendix G

Consideration of Fraud in a Financial Statement Audit[1]

G.01 As discussed in chapter 5, "Planning and General Auditing Considerations," of this guide, during the planning and performance of an audit, you may identify information that indicates the presence of one of the three conditions of the fraud triangle (incentive or pressure, opportunity, and attitude or rationalization). These conditions or events are referred to as *fraud risk factors*. Fraud risk factors do not necessarily indicate the existence of fraud; however, they often have been present in circumstances where fraud exists.

G.02 AU section 316, *Consideration of Fraud in a Financial Statement Audit* (AICPA, *Professional Standards*), provides fraud risk factor examples that have been written to apply to most enterprises. The purpose of this appendix is to provide examples of fraud risk factors specific to employee benefit plans and other conditions that may indicate the presence of a material misstatement due to fraud. Remember that fraud risk factors are only one of several sources of information you consider when identifying and assessing risk of material misstatement due to fraud.

G.03 The fraud risk factors that follow include interpretations of some of the AU section 316 example risk factors tailored to employee benefit plans. The fraud risk factors in this appendix should be used to supplement, but not replace, the example risk factors included in AU section 316. (It is a companion to but not a substitute for the guidance in the section.)

G.04 One of the key changes to audit practice that AU section 316 sought to impose was a better linking of auditor response to identified fraud risk factors. To help you develop more effective audit programs, this appendix also contains example audit procedures you may perform in response to specifically identified risks. Like the fraud risk factors and conditions, those procedures supplement the responses already described in AU section 316.

G.05 Two types of fraud are relevant to the auditor's consideration: fraudulent financial reporting and misappropriation of assets. For each of these types of fraud, the risk factors are further classified based on the three conditions generally present when material misstatements due to fraud occur: incentives or pressures, opportunities, and attitudes or rationalizations. Although the risk factors cover a broad range of situations, they are only examples and, accordingly, the auditor may wish to consider additional or different risk factors. Also, the order of the examples of risk factors provided is not intended to reflect their relative importance or frequency of occurrence. The following list should be used in conjunction with AU section 316 because not every example risk factor in AU section 316 has been tailored, interpreted, or reprinted here and some of the example risk factors not reprinted may be applicable to the engagement.

---

[1] This appendix is based on material from the AICPA publication *Fraud Detection in a GAAS Audit—SAS No. 99 Implementation Guide*.

Part 1: Fraudulent Financial Reporting

G.06 An auditor's interest specifically relates to fraudulent acts that cause a material misstatement of financial statements. Some of the following factors and conditions are present in entities where specific circumstances *do not present a risk of material misstatement*. Also, specific controls may exist that mitigate the risk of material misstatement due to fraud, even though risk factors or conditions are present. When identifying risk factors and other conditions, you should assess whether those risk factors and conditions, individually and in combination, present a risk of material misstatement of the financial statements.

A. Incentives or Pressure

1. Financial stability or profitability is threatened by economic, industry, or entity operating conditions, such as (or as indicated by) the following:

    a. Significant declines in customer demand and increasing business failures exist in either the industry or the economy in which the entity operates.

    　i. The plan sponsor is in an industry that is declining in stability, which could lead to difficulties in meeting financial commitments to the plan, including contributions or debt repayments, or both (leveraged employee stock ownership plan).

    b. The plan holds employer securities and the employer is in an industry in which the value of the securities is subject to significant volatility or is not readily determinable.

    c. Plan sponsor or plan restructuring (for example, layoffs, spin-offs, business combinations, and bankruptcy).

    d. Severely deteriorating financial condition or the threat of regulatory intervention of the plan.

    e. The plan has limited investment options or the plan has invested significantly in employer securities or other employer assets (for example, real estate).

2. Excessive pressure exists for management to meet the requirements or expectations of third parties due to the following:

    a. Senior management of the plan sponsor appoints itself trustee of the plan and uses that position to benefit the plan sponsor, for example, uses the plan's money to do speculative investing or to support the entity through buying employer assets.

B. Opportunities

1. The nature of the industry or the entity's operations provides opportunities to engage in fraudulent financial reporting that can arise from the following:

    a. Significant related-party transactions not in the ordinary course of business or with related entities not audited or audited by another firm.

      i. Indications of significant or unusual parties-in-interest transactions not in the ordinary course of operations.

     ii. Excessive or unusual transaction or prohibited party in interest transactions with the plan sponsor or administrator.

2. Internal control components are deficient as a result of the following:

    a. Inadequate monitoring of controls, including automated controls and controls over interim financial reporting.

       i. Failure by management to have adequate valuations performed, including actuarial valuations and valuations of real estate partnerships and other hard-to-value plan assets.

      ii. The plan administrator lacks an understanding of the major regulations that govern the plans (that is, Employee Retirement Income Security Act of 1974 [ERISA] and the Internal Revenue Code [IRC]).

    b. Unusually high levels of participant complaints and corrections to account balances or plan records.

    c. Lack of qualified service provider organization or change in service provider.

C. Attitudes or Rationalizations

Risk factors reflective of attitudes or rationalizations by board members, management, or employees that allow them to engage in or justify fraudulent financial reporting, or both, may not be susceptible to observation by the auditor. Nevertheless, the auditor who becomes aware of the existence of such information should consider it in identifying the risks of material misstatement arising from fraudulent financial reporting. For example, auditors may become aware of the following information that may indicate a risk factor:

1. Management displaying a significant disregard for regulatory authorities.

    a. Management displaying a significant disregard toward compliance with ERISA and IRC and Department of Labor (DOL) regulations.

    b. The plan administrator or trustees have been investigated by the DOL or IRS for fiduciary violations in operating the plan.

2. Lack of management candor in dealing with plan participants, claimants, actuaries, and auditors regarding decisions that could have an impact on plan assets, including restructuring or downsizing arrangements.

3. The plan has participated in a voluntary compliance program in conjunction with the IRS or DOL (such participation could be an indication of ineffective management of the plan or controls over the plan).

4. Named fiduciary not actively involved in the plan's activities.

5. High level of plan participant complaints.

D. Auditor Responses

In addition to the sample responses presented in AU section 316, an auditor in an employee benefit plan audit engagement may want to consider the following responses:

- *Investment results.* Obtain the requisite investment information directly from the plan trustee, and obtain the same information from the party named as having discretion to make investment decisions, such as the plan administrator, the plan's investment committee, or the plan's investment adviser (the directing party), and review and reconcile the directing party's reports (investment position and activity) with those of the trustee.

- *Claim reserves.* Confirm, with third parties, the historical and statistical information that is being used to prepare the reserves. Review the qualifications of the individuals preparing the reserves.

- *Procedures.* Apply the following procedures to fully understand a party in interest transaction:[2]

    — Confirm transaction amount and terms, including guarantees and other significant data, with the other party or parties to the transaction.

    — Inspect evidence in possession of the other party or parties to the transaction.

    — Confirm or discuss significant information with intermediaries, such as banks, guarantors, agents, or attorneys, to obtain a better understanding of the transaction.

    — Refer to financial publications, trade journals, credit agencies, and other information sources when it is believed that unfamiliar customers, suppliers, or other business enterprises with which material amounts of business have been transacted may lack substance.

    — With respect to material uncollected balances, guarantees, and other obligations, obtain information about the financial capability of the other party or parties to the transaction. Such information may be obtained from audited financial statements, unaudited financial statements, income tax returns, and reports issued by regulatory agencies, taxing authorities, financial publications, or credit agencies. The auditor should decide on the degree of assurance required and the extent to which available information provides such assurance.

---

[2] See chapter 11, "Party in Interest Transactions," of this guide for further audit guidance.

- For single employer plans, obtain the most recent financial statements of the plan sponsor and review for indicators of financial difficulties. For multiemployer plans, obtain an understanding of the industry.

Part 2: Misappropriation of Assets

G.07 An auditor's interest specifically relates to fraudulent acts that cause a material misstatement of financial statements. Some of the following factors and conditions are present in entities where specific circumstances *do not present a risk of material misstatement*. Also, specific controls may exist that mitigate the risk of material misstatement due to fraud, even though risk factors or conditions are present. When identifying risk factors and other conditions, you should assess whether those risk factors and conditions, individually and in combination, present a risk of material misstatement of the financial statements.

G.08 Risk factors that relate to misstatements arising from misappropriation of assets are also classified along the three conditions generally present when fraud exists: incentives or pressures, opportunity, and attitudes or rationalizations. Some of the risk factors related to misstatements arising from fraudulent financial reporting also may be present when misstatements arising from misappropriation of assets occur. For example, ineffective monitoring of management and weakness in internal control may be present when misstatements due to either fraudulent financial reporting or misappropriation of assets exists. The following are examples of risk factors related to misstatements arising from misappropriation of assets.

A. Opportunities

1. Inadequate internal control over assets may increase the susceptibility of misappropriation of those assets. For example, misappropriation of assets may occur because of the following:

    a. Inadequate segregation of duties related to benefit payments, contributions, investment transactions, and loans or independent checks.

        i. No independent records of the plan are maintained to enable the plan administrator to periodically check the information to the custodian.

    b. Inadequate management oversight of employees responsible for assets.

        i. Lack of review of investment transactions by trustees, sponsors, or investment committees.

        ii. Lack of independent preparation and review of reconciliations of trust assets to participant accounts or accounting records of the plan.

    c. Inadequate system of authorization and approval of transactions.

        i. Insufficient approval over transactions with parties-in-interest that could lead to prohibited transactions.

    d. Lack of timely and appropriate documentation of transactions, for example, credits for merchandise returns.

    i. Trustee does not prepare required supplemental information (for example, historical cost records not maintained).

  e. Lack of controls surrounding benefit payments, including the termination of payments in accordance with plan provisions.

  f. Lack of appropriate segregation of plan assets from the sponsor's assets or inappropriate access to plan assets by plan sponsor.

  g. Statement on Auditing Standards (SAS) No. 70, *Service Organizations* (AICPA, *Professional Standards*, AU sec. 324),[3] as amended, report indicates a lack of controls at an outside service provider.

  h. Use of service provider that does not provide a SAS No. 70 report.

  i. Unreconciled differences between net assets available for benefits per the trustee or custodian records and the recordkeeping amounts for a defined contribution plan (unallocated assets or liabilities).

B. Auditor Responses

In addition to the sample responses presented in AU section 316, an auditor in an employee benefit plan engagement may want to consider the following responses:

- Review reconciliations of the assets held by the trust with participant records throughout the year. Review any reconciling adjustments for propriety.

- Review the account activity for participants who have access to plan assets or assist in administering the plan.

- The auditor may have concluded that a risk of material misstatement exists with regard to a lack of a qualified outside service provider acting as trustee or custodian, or both, for plan assets. In these instances, the auditor should physically inspect assets and examine other evidence relating to ownership. In addition, the fair value of investments should be tested by reference to market quotations or other evidence of fair value in accordance with AU section 342, *Auditing Accounting Estimates* (AICPA, *Professional Standards*).

- The auditor may have concluded that a risk of material misstatement exists with regard to unreconciled differences between net assets available for benefits per

---

[3] The Auditing Standards Board has issued Statement on Standards for Attestation Engagements (SSAE) No. 16, *Reporting on Controls at a Service Organization* (AICPA, *Professional Standards*, AT sec. 801), which will replace the guidance contained in AU section 324, *Service Organizations* (AICPA, *Professional Standards*), for a service auditor when reporting on controls at an organization that provides service to user entities when those controls are likely to be relevant to user entities' internal controls over financial reporting. It is effective for service auditors' reports for periods ending on or after June 15, 2011. Early implementation is permitted; therefore, if adopting SSAE No. 16 early, refer directly to the standard as certain guidance in this guide may not be applicable. Also, refer to the preface of this guide for additional information about the changes related to Statement on Auditing Standards No. 70, *Service Organizations* (AICPA, *Professional Standards*, AU sec. 324).

the trustee or custodian records and the recordkeeping amounts for a defined contribution plan. If the trustee or custodian records are higher than the recordkeeping totals (excluding accrual adjustments), an unallocated asset exists that should be allocated to participant accounts. If the trustee or custodian records are lower than the recordkeeping totals (excluding accrual adjustments), plan assets may have been misappropriated requiring further investigation by the auditor (for example, reconciliation of monthly trustee or custodian activity to the recordkeeper).

- The auditor may have concluded that a risk of material misstatement exists with regard to remittance of employee contributions for a defined contribution plan with a sponsor experiencing cash flow problems. In this instance, the auditor may perform a reconciliation of the total employee contributions per the payroll register to the recordkeeping report for the year. In addition, the auditor may select certain months to test for the timely remittance of employee contributions in accordance with regulations.

- The auditor may have concluded that a risk of material misstatement exists with regard to expenses being paid by an overfunded defined benefit plan on behalf of an underfunded plan. In this instance, the auditor might select expense amounts paid by the overfunded plan and trace them to specific invoices noting that the expense pertained to the proper plan. Alternatively, the auditors could also ask to review expense invoices pertaining to the underfunded plan paid by the entity to make sure the overfunded plan did not pay them.

- Review the timeliness of contributions from the plan sponsor throughout the year.

- Compare cancelled checks to disbursement records. When benefits are paid by check disbursements, compare the signature on the canceled check to participant signatures on other employee documents.

- Confirm benefit payments with participants or beneficiaries.

- Confirm medical bills directly with service providers.

- Review plan expenses to ensure that the plan is not paying for expenses that the employer should be paying for.

Fraud Examples

G.09 Listed subsequently are actual instances of fraudulent activity on employee benefit plan engagements. They are presented to help auditors become better acquainted with fraudulent activities. Although none of these particular examples resulted in a material misstatement of the financial statements, similar fraudulent activity at other benefit plans may cause a material misstatement of the financial statements, depending on the circumstances.

- A pension plan notifies participants who have reached the age of 70 and a half that they must under law take their distributions from the plan. An employee of the entity is responsible for notifying the participants and providing distribution forms. The completed forms are provided to a supervisor for approval and submitted to the insurance company (custodian) for payment. For all participants reaching the age of 70 and a half, the employee decides to forge the distribution forms and not notify the participants of the distributions. The forged forms are provided to the supervisor, who approves them and the insurance company is directed to make lump sum distributions via wire transfers into an account set up with the employee's name as a relative for the beneficiary. The fraud continues for several months until a participant notifies the supervisor that he would like to receive his distribution, and the supervisor notices that a lump sum was already distributed.

- A long-time employee at an entity is responsible for reporting loan repayments (for loans not paid off by automatic payroll deduction) to the recordkeeper by providing copies of the face of the repayment checks to the recordkeeper. The employee is also a participant in the plan and currently has a $20,000 loan from her account. The employee decides to take a second loan but under plan provisions cannot do it until her first loan is paid off. The employee makes out a check to pay off the $20,000 loan from her personal account and provides a copy of the check to the recordkeeper. A second loan of $25,000 is taken out for the employee. However, the first loan is never paid off because the employee never deposits the $20,000 check into the plan. Cash reconciliations continually show immaterial unreconciled items that are not followed up timely and the fraud is not discovered for months.

- An entity has two defined benefit plans; one is overfunded and one is underfunded. In past years, administrative expenses were paid from each plan's assets; however, this year the entity decides it will pay the expenses for the underfunded plan. The overfunded plan continues to pay its own expenses. Due to an administrative error, the overfunded plan ends up paying the expenses for both plans. When management discovers this fact, a decision was made to reimburse the plan that paid the expenses because it is fully funded.

- Continuation of pension benefits to a deceased participant. A participant dies but his relatives or other persons do not report his death in order to continue receiving his pension checks.

- A health and welfare supervisor submits phony claims using the names of the plan participants who have the same last name as he or she does. The checks are diverted to the supervisor before they can be mailed to the plan participant in question.

Appendix H

Accounting and Disclosure Requirements for Single Employer and Multiemployer Employee Benefit Plans Related to the Medicare Prescription Drug, Improvement and Modernization Act of 2003

This appendix reproduces two Technical Questions and Answers (TIS) sections from the AICPA publication *Technical Practice Aids* on accounting and disclosures for single employer and multiemployer employee benefit plans related to the Medicare Prescription Drug, Improvement and Modernization Act of 2003:

- TIS section 6931.05, "Accounting and Disclosure Requirements for **Single-Employer Employee Benefit Plans** Related to the Medicare Prescription Drug, Improvement and Modernization Act of 2003" (AICPA, *Technical Practice Aids*)
- TIS section 6931.06, "Accounting and Disclosure Requirements for **Multiemployer Employee Benefit Plans** Related to the Medicare Prescription Drug, Improvement and Modernization Act of 2003" (AICPA, *Technical Practice Aids*)

TIS section 6931.05, "Accounting and Disclosure Requirements for Single-Employer Employee Benefit Plans Related to the Medicare Prescription Drug, Improvement and Modernization Act of 2003"

Inquiry—On December 8, 2003, the president signed into law the Medicare Prescription Drug, Improvement and Modernization Act of 2003 (the act) for employers that sponsor postretirement health care plans that provide prescription drug benefits. The act introduces a prescription drug benefit under Medicare (Medicare Part D) as well as a federal subsidy to sponsors of retiree health care benefit plans that provide a benefit that is at least actuarially equivalent to Medicare Part D.1. FASB ASC 715-60 and FASB ASC 740-10 address the issue of whether an employer that provides postretirement prescription drug coverage should recognize the effects of the act on its accumulated postretirement benefit obligation (APBO) and net postretirement benefit costs and, if so, when and how to account for those effects. FASB ASC 715-60 and FASB ASC 740-10 say that the APBO and net periodic postretirement benefit costs should reflect the effects of the act. FASB ASC 715-60 and FASB ASC 740-10 do not address accounting for the subsidy by health and welfare benefit plans.

For a single-employer health and welfare benefit plan, should the effects of the plan sponsor's (employer's) Medicare prescription drug subsidy (Medicare subsidy) be taken into consideration when calculating the health and welfare plan's postretirement benefit obligation?

Reply—No, the effects of the employer's Medicare subsidy should not be reflected in the plan's obligations. The primary objective of the financial statements of a health and welfare benefit plan is to provide financial information that is useful in assessing the plan's present and future ability to pay its benefit obligations when due. The Medicare subsidy amount is paid to the plan sponsor and does not flow into the plan. The plan sponsor is not required to use the subsidy amount to fund the postretirement benefits and may use the subsidy for any valid business purpose. As a result, the Medicare subsidy does not reduce the amount of benefits that need to be covered by plan assets and future employer contributions. Therefore, the APBO, without reduction for the Medicare subsidy, is a more meaningful measure of the benefits. Further, the information necessary to calculate the gross measure should be readily available for sponsors who are subject to income taxes, because those plan sponsors should maintain gross and net measures of the APBO in order to properly account for income taxes under FASB ASC 740.

Disclosures

The plan should disclose the following:

a. The existence of the act

b. The fact that the APBO and the changes in the benefit obligation do not reflect any amount associated with the Medicare subsidy because the plan is not directly entitled to the Medicare subsidy

c. Until the plan sponsor (employer) is able to determine whether benefits provided by its plan are actuarially equivalent to Medicare Part D.1, that the employer is not able to determine whether the benefits provided by its plan are actuarially equivalent to Medicare Part D.1. If the plan sponsor (employer) has included the effects of the Medicare subsidy in measuring its APBO and changes in benefit obligation, the plan should disclose the fact that the amount of the APBO differs from that disclosed by the plan sponsor (employer) because the plan sponsor's amounts are net of the Medicare subsidy.

TIS section 6931.06, "Accounting and Disclosure Requirements for Multiemployer Employee Benefit Plans Related to the Medicare Prescription Drug, Improvement and Modernization Act of 2003"

Inquiry—On December 8, 2003, the president signed into law the Medicare Prescription Drug, Improvement and Modernization Act of 2003 (the act) for employers that sponsor postretirement health care plans that provide prescription drug benefits. The act introduces a prescription drug benefit under Medicare (Medicare Part D) as well as a federal subsidy to sponsors of retiree health care benefit plans that provide a benefit that is at least actuarially equivalent to Medicare Part D.1. FASB ASC 715-60 and FASB ASC 740-10 address the issue of whether an employer that provides postretirement prescription drug coverage should recognize the effects of the act on its accumulated postretirement benefit obligation (APBO) and net postretirement benefit costs and, if so, when and how to account for those effects. FASB ASC 715-60 and FASB ASC 740-10 say that the APBO and net periodic postretirement benefit costs should reflect the effects of the act. FASB ASC 715-60 and 740-10 do not address accounting for the subsidy by multiemployer health and welfare benefit plans or by the sponsors or participating employers of those plans.

For multiemployer health and welfare benefit plans, should the effects of the Medicare prescription drug subsidy (Medicare subsidy) be taken into consideration when calculating the health and welfare plan's postretirement benefit obligation?

Reply—Yes, the multiemployer plan's benefit obligations should be reduced by the effects of the Medicare subsidy because the multiemployer plan trust receives the subsidy amount directly and not the individual employers. Because the primary objective of the financial statements of a health and welfare benefit plan is to provide financial information that is useful in assessing the plan's present and future ability to pay its benefit obligations when due, and because the Medicare subsidy amount flows into the multiemployer plan trust, the APBO net of the Medicare subsidy is a more meaningful measure of those benefits.

Disclosures

Until the multiemployer plan is able to determine whether benefits provided by its plan are at least actuarially equivalent to Medicare Part D.1, the plan should disclose the following in the notes to its financial statements:

    a. The existence of the act

    b. The fact that measures of the APBO and changes in the benefit obligation do not reflect any amount associated with the subsidy because the plan is unable to conclude whether the benefits provided by the plan are actuarially equivalent to Medicare Part D under the act.

If the multiemployer plan has included the effects of the Medicare subsidy in measuring its APBO and changes in the benefit obligation, the plan should disclose the following:

    a. The existence of the act

    b. The reduction in the APBO for the subsidy related to benefits attributed to past service

    c. The effect of the subsidy on the changes in the benefit obligation for the current period

    d. An explanation of any significant change in the benefit obligation or plan assets not otherwise apparent in the other disclosures

    e. The gross benefit payments (paid and expected, respectively) including prescription drug benefits, and separately the gross amount of the subsidy receipts (received and expected, respectively)

———————————

Appendix I

Schedule of Changes Made to the Text From the Previous Edition

As of January 1, 2011

This schedule of changes identifies areas in the text and footnotes of this guide that have changed since the previous edition. Entries in the following table reflect current numbering, lettering (including that in appendix names), and character designations that resulted from the renumbering or reordering that occurred in the updating of this guide.

Reference	Change
Preface	Updated.
Paragraph 1.01	Updated.
Former footnote 1 in paragraph 1.03	Deleted.
Footnote 1 in paragraph 1.03	Added for clarification.
Footnote ‡ in paragraph 1.04	Revised.
Paragraph 1.09	Revised to reflect the guidance contained in the Financial Accounting Standards Board (FASB) *Accounting Standards Codification*™ (ASC).
Footnote 2 in paragraph 1.17	Added for clarification.
Paragraph 2.04	Revised to reflect changes to provisions of the Employee Retirement Income Security Act of 1974 (ERISA); footnote 2 added to reflect changes to provisions of ERISA.
Paragraphs 2.06–.08, footnote 4 in paragraph 2.07, and paragraph 2.12	Revised to reflect the guidance contained in FASB ASC.
Former footnote * to heading before paragraph 2.16	Deleted.
Paragraph 2.16	Revised to reflect the guidance contained in FASB ASC.
Former paragraph 2.17	Deleted to reflect the issuance of FASB Accounting Standards Update (ASU) No. 2010-06, *Fair Value Measurements and Disclosures (Topic 820): Improving Disclosures about Fair Value Measurements*.

(continued)

Reference	Change
Former footnote † to heading before paragraph 2.17	Deleted.
Footnote * to heading before paragraph 2.18	Added.
Footnote 7 to heading before paragraph 2.18	Added for clarification.
Paragraphs 2.18–.19	Added to reflect the issuance of FASB ASU No. 2010-06.
Footnote 8 in paragraph 2.19	Added for clarification.
Footnote * in paragraph 2.19	Added.
Paragraphs 2.20–.22	Added to reflect the issuance of FASB ASU No. 2010-06.
Footnote 10 in paragraph 2.26	Added for clarification.
Paragraph 2.27	Revised for clarification.
Former footnote ‡ in paragraph 2.28	Deleted.
Paragraphs 2.29–.30	Revised to reflect the issuance of FASB Statement No. 166, *Accounting for Transfers of Financial Assets—an amendment of FASB Statement No. 140.*
Footnote 11 in paragraph 2.33, paragraph 2.37, and paragraphs 2.39–.44	Revised to reflect the guidance contained in FASB ASC.
Footnote 14 in paragraph 2.46	Added to reflect the issuance of FASB ASU No. 2009-06, *Income Taxes (Topic 740)—Implementation Guidance on Accounting for Uncertainty in Income Taxes and Disclosure Amendments for Nonpublic Entities.*
Former footnote ‖ in paragraph 2.46	Deleted.
Footnote † in paragraph 2.46	Added to reflect the issuance of FASB ASU No. 2010-09, *Subsequent Events (Topic 855): Amendments to Certain Recognition and Disclosure Requirements.*
Paragraph 2.47	Added for clarification.
Footnote ‡ in paragraph 2.48	Added.
Former footnote # in paragraph 2.48	Deleted.
Former paragraphs 2.46–.47	Deleted to reflect the issuance of FASB ASU No. 2010-06.

(continued)

Reference	Change
Former footnote ** in former paragraph 2.47	Deleted.
Footnote 18 in paragraph 2.50	Added to reflect the issuance of Technical Questions and Answers (TIS) section 1800.05, "Applicability of Fair Value Disclosure Requirements and Measurement Principles in Financial Accounting Standards Board (FASB) *Accounting Standards Codification* (ASC) 820, *Fair Value Measurements and Disclosures*, to Certain Financial Instruments" (AICPA, *Technical Practice Aids*).
Footnote † in paragraphs 2.61 and 2.62	Added.
Paragraphs 3.06 and 3.08	Revised to reflect changes to provisions of ERISA.
Paragraphs 3.10 and 3.15	Revised to reflect the guidance contained in FASB ASC.
Former footnote † to heading before paragraph 3.19	Deleted.
Paragraph 3.19	Revised to reflect the guidance contained in FASB ASC.
Former paragraph 3.20	Deleted to reflect the issuance of FASB ASU No. 2010-06.
Former footnote ‡ to heading before paragraph 3.20	Deleted.
Footnote † to heading before paragraph 3.21	Added.
Footnote 4 to heading before paragraph 3.21	Added for clarification.
Paragraph 3.21	Added to reflect the issuance of FASB ASU No. 2010-06.
Paragraph 3.22	Added to reflect the issuance of FASB ASU No. 2010-06; footnote 5 added for clarification.
Footnote † in paragraph 3.22	Added.
Paragraphs 3.23–.25	Added to reflect the issuance of FASB ASU No. 2010-06.

(continued)

Reference	Change
Paragraphs 3.27 and 3.35	Revised to reflect the issuance of FASB ASU No. 2010-25, *Plan Accounting—Defined Contribution Pension Plans (Topic 962): Reporting Loans to Participants by Defined Contribution Pension Plans (a consensus of the FASB Emerging Issues Task Force)*.
Former footnote ‖ in paragraph 3.36	Deleted.
Paragraphs 3.37–.39	Revised to reflect the issuance of FASB Statement No. 166.
Heading before paragraph 3.42 and paragraph 3.42	Added to reflect the issuance of FASB ASU No. 2010-25.
Footnote ‡ in paragraph 3.42	Added.
Paragraph 3.44	Revised to reflect the guidance contained in FASB ASC; footnote 7 added to reflect the issuance of TIS section 6931.03, "Should the Sale of Real Estate Investments Held by Employee Benefit Plans Be Treated as Discontinued Operations?" (AICPA, *Technical Practice Aids*).
Footnote 11 in paragraph 3.50	Added to reflect the issuance of FASB ASU No. 2009-06.
Former footnote # in paragraph 3.50	Deleted.
Footnote ‖ in paragraph 3.50	Added.
Paragraph 3.51	Added for clarification.
Footnote # in paragraph 3.52	Added.
Former footnote ** in paragraph 3.52	Deleted.
Former paragraphs 3.48–.49	Deleted to reflect the issuance of FASB ASU No. 2010-06.
Former footnote †† in former paragraph 3.49	Deleted.
Footnote 15 in paragraph 3.54	Added for clarification.
Footnote 16 in paragraph 3.54	Added to reflect the issuance of TIS section 1800.05.
Footnote ‖ in paragraphs 3.57 and 3.58	Added.
Paragraph 3.61	Revised for clarification.

(continued)

Reference	Change
Paragraph 3.65	Added to reflect the issuance of Field Assistance Bulletin No. 2009-02, *Annual Reporting Requirements for 403(b) Plans.*
Footnote 1 in paragraph 4.15	Added to reflect the issuance of TIS section 6931.12, "Accounting and Disclosure Requirements for Health and Welfare Plans Related to the COBRA Premium Subsidy Included in the American Recovery and Reinvestment Act of 2009" (AICPA, *Technical Practice Aids*).
Paragraph 4.27	Revised to reflect changes to provisions of ERISA.
Former footnote ‡ to heading before paragraph 4.35	Deleted.
Paragraph 4.35	Revised to reflect the guidance contained in FASB ASC.
Former paragraph 4.36	Deleted to reflect the issuance of FASB ASU No. 2010-06.
Former footnote ‖ to heading before paragraph 4.36	Deleted.
Footnote ‡ to heading before paragraph 4.37	Added.
Footnote 11 to heading before paragraph 4.37	Added for clarification.
Paragraph 4.37	Added to reflect the issuance of FASB ASU No. 2010-06.
Former paragraph 4.38	Deleted to reflect the issuance of FASB ASU No. 2010-06.
Paragraph 4.38	Added to reflect the issuance of FASB ASU No. 2010-06.
Footnote 12 in paragraph 4.38	Added for clarification.
Footnote ‡ in paragraph 4.38	Added.
Paragraphs 4.39–.41	Added to reflect the issuance of FASB ASU No. 2010-06.
Footnote 14 in paragraph 4.44	Added to reflect the issuance of TIS section 6930.02, "Defined Benefit Plan Measurement of a Life Insurance Policy" (AICPA, *Technical Practice Aids*).
Former footnote # in paragraph 4.53	Deleted.

(continued)

Reference	Change
Paragraphs 4.54–.56	Revised to reflect the issuance of FASB Statement No. 166.
Paragraph 4.63	Revised for clarification; footnote 16 added to reflect the issuance of TIS section 6931.03.
Footnote 35 in paragraph 4.91	Added to reflect the issuance of FASB ASU No. 2009-06.
Former footnote ** in paragraph 4.91	Deleted.
Footnote ‖ in paragraph 4.91	Added.
Paragraph 4.92	Added for clarification.
Footnote # in paragraph 4.93	Added.
Former footnote †† in paragraph 4.93	Deleted.
Former paragraphs 4.90–.91	Deleted to reflect the issuance of FASB ASU No. 2010-06.
Former footnote ‡‡ in former paragraph 4.91	Deleted.
Footnote 38 in paragraph 4.94	Added to reflect the issuance of TIS section 1800.05.
Footnote ‖ in paragraphs 4.97 and 4.98	Added.
Footnote 1 in paragraph 5.14	Added to reflect the issuance of Statement on Standards for Attestation Engagements (SSAE) No. 16, *Reporting on Controls at a Service Organization* (AICPA, *Professional Standards*, AT sec. 801).
Exhibits 5-1 and 5-2	Revised for clarification.
Footnote † in paragraph 5.18	Added.
Exhibit 5-5	Revised to reflect the issuance of Statement on Auditing Standards (SAS) No. 115 *Communicating Internal Control Related Matters Identified in an Audit* (AICPA, *Professional Standards*, AU sec. 325); footnote 9 revised for clarification.
Paragraph 5.68	Revised for clarification.
Footnote 3 to heading before paragraph 6.13	Added to reflect the issuance of SSAE No. 16.

(continued)

Reference	*Change*
Former footnote † in paragraph 6.13	Deleted.
Footnote 5 in paragraph 6.28	Revised for clarification.
Chapter 7 title	Revised to reflect the issuance of FASB ASU No. 2010-25.
Footnote 6 in paragraph 7.19	Added to reflect the issuance of SSAE No. 16.
Paragraph 7.22	Revised to reflect the guidance contained in FASB ASC.
Paragraphs 7.32–.34	Added for clarification.
Former footnote 13 in paragraph 7.55	Deleted for clarification.
Heading before paragraph 7.57 and paragraph 7.57	Revised to reflect the issuance of FASB ASU No. 2010-25.
Paragraph 7.58	Revised to reflect the issuance of FASB ASU No. 2010-25; footnote † added; former footnote 14 deleted for clarification.
Paragraph 7.59	Revised to reflect the guidance contained in FASB ASC.
Paragraphs 7.60–.63	Added for clarification.
Paragraph 7.68	Revised to reflect the issuance of FASB ASU No. 2010-25.
Paragraph 8.05	Added for clarification.
Footnote 1 in paragraph 9.04	Added to reflect the issuance of SSAE No. 16.
Paragraph 9.07	Added for clarification.
Footnote 1 in paragraph 10.03	Added to reflect the issuance of SSAE No. 16.
Paragraphs 10.11 and 10.19	Revised for clarification.
Footnote * in paragraph 11.07	Added.
Footnote 1 in paragraph 12.01	Revised for clarification.
Paragraph 12.03	Revised for clarification; footnotes 2 and 4 added for clarification.
Paragraph 12.04	Revised for clarification.
Paragraph 12.06	Added for clarification.
Paragraph 12.07	Revised for clarification; former footnote † deleted.
Former footnote ‡ in paragraph 12.08	Deleted.

(continued)

Reference	Change
Paragraph 12.09	Revised for clarification; footnote 5 added to reflect the issuance of TIS section 9110.17, "Application of Financial Accounting Standards Board (FASB) *Accounting Standards Codification* 740-10 (previously, FASB Interpretation No. 48, *Accounting for Uncertainty in Income Taxes*) to Other Comprehensive Basis of Accounting Financial Statements—Recognition and Measurement Provisions" (AICPA, *Technical Practice Aids*).
Paragraph 12.10	Added to reflect the guidance contained in FASB ASC; footnote 7 added for clarification; footnote 8 added to reflect the issuance of TIS section 5250.15, "Application of Certain FASB Interpretation No. 48 (codified in FASB ASC 740-10) Disclosure Requirements to Nonpublic Entities That Do Not Have Uncertain Tax Positions" (AICPA, *Technical Practice Aids*).
Paragraph 12.16	Revised for clarification.
Footnote † in heading before paragraph 12.19	Added.
Former footnote ‖ in paragraph 12.19	Deleted.
Footnote 9 in paragraph 12.19	Added to reflect the issuance of TIS section 8700.01, "Effect of FASB ASC 855 on Accounting Guidance in AU Section 560" (AICPA, *Technical Practice Aids*).
Exhibit 12-1	Updated for clarification.
Footnote 26 in paragraph 12.33	Added for clarification.
Footnote ** in heading before paragraph 12.36	Added to reflect the issuance of SAS No. 118, *Other Information in Documents Containing Audited Financial Statements* (AICPA, *Professional Standards*, AU sec. 550).
Former footnote ‖ in paragraph 13.09	Deleted.
Footnote ‖ in paragraph 13.09 and footnote # in paragraph 13.11	Added.

(continued)

Reference	Change
Paragraphs 13.43–.44	Revised for clarification.
Appendix A	Revised to reflect changes to provisions of ERISA and other related regulations.
Appendix B	Footnote * revised.
Appendix C	Revised to reflect the issuance of FASB Statement No. 166.
Appendix D	Revised for clarification; revised to reflect the guidance contained in FASB ASC; revised to reflect the issuance of FASB ASU No. 2010-06 and TIS section 5250.15.
Appendix E	Revised for clarification; revised to reflect the guidance contained in FASB ASC; revised to reflect the issuance of FASB ASU No. 2010-06, TIS section 5250.15, and FASB ASU No. 2010-25.
Appendix F	Revised for clarification; revised to reflect the guidance contained in FASB ASC; revised to reflect the issuance of FASB ASU No. 2010-06 and TIS section 5250.15.
Former appendix G	Deleted.
Appendix G	Revised for the passage of time.
Glossary	Updated.
Index	Updated.

Glossary

The following terms can be found in the Financial Accounting Standards Board (FASB) *Accounting Standards Codification* (ASC) glossary:

accumulated eligibility credits. Plan participants may qualify for a benefit in which eligibility credits or hours accumulate and result in the plan covering payment of insurance premiums or benefits for a period of time for those participants who have accumulated a sufficient number of such credits or hours to be eligible for the credits. Eligible participants are provided with insurance coverage during periods of unemployment, when employer contributions to the plan would not otherwise provide coverage or benefits. The accumulated eligibility credits are sometimes referred to as bank of hours.

accumulated plan benefits. Future benefit payments that are attributable under the provisions of an employee benefit plan to employees' service rendered to the benefit information date. Accumulated plan benefits comprise benefits expected to be paid to (*a*) retired or terminated employees or their beneficiaries, (*b*) beneficiaries of deceased employees, and (*c*) present employees or their beneficiaries.

actuarial asset value. A value assigned by an actuary to the assets of a plan generally for use in conjunction with an actuarial cost method.

actuarial cost method. A recognized actuarial technique used for establishing the amount and incidence of employer contributions or accounting charges for pension cost under a pension plan.

actuarial present value of accumulated plan benefits. The amount as of a benefit information date that results from applying actuarial assumptions to the accumulated plan benefits, with the actuarial assumptions being used to adjust those amounts to reflect the time value of money (through discounts for interest) and the probability of payment (by means of decrements such as for death, disability, withdrawal, or retirement) between the benefit information date and the expected date of payment.

administrative service arrangement. In an administrative service arrangement, the plan retains the full obligation for plan benefits. The plan may engage an insurance entity or other third party to act as the plan administrator. The administrator makes all benefit payments, charges the plan for those payments, and collects a fee for the services provided.

allocated contract. A contract with an insurance entity under which related payments to the insurance entity are currently used to purchase immediate or deferred annuities for individual participants.

annuity contract. A contract in which an insurance entity unconditionally undertakes a legal obligation to provide specified pension benefits to specific individuals in return for a fixed consideration or premium. An annuity contract is irrevocable and involves the transfer of significant risk from the employer to the insurance entity. Annuity contracts are also called **allocated contracts**.

benefit information. The actuarial present value of accumulated plan benefits.

benefit information date. The date as of which the actuarial present value of accumulated plan benefits is presented.

benefit-responsive investment contract. A contract between an insurance entity, a bank, a financial institution, or any financially responsible entity and a plan that provides for a stated return on principal invested over a specified period and that permits withdrawals at contract value for benefit payments, loans, or transfers to other investment options offered to the participant by the plan. Participant withdrawals from the plan are required to be at contract value.

benefit security. The plan's present and future ability to pay benefits when due.

benefits. Payments to which participants may be entitled under an employee benefit plan, including pension benefits, death benefits, and benefits due on termination of employment (further industry-specific information provided in the following list of terms.)

contract value. The value of an unallocated contract that is determined by the insurance entity in accordance with the terms of the contract.

contributions receivable. Amounts due, as of the date of the financial statements, to the plan from employers, participants, and other sources of funding. They include amounts due pursuant to firm commitments, as well as legal or contractual requirements.

contributory plan. A pension plan under which participants bear part of the cost.

defined benefit pension plan. A pension plan that specifies a determinable pension benefit, usually based on factors such as age, years of service, and salary. This includes plans that may be funded pursuant to periodic agreements that specify a fixed rate of employer contributions (for example, a collectively bargained multiemployer plan). For example, this includes plans that prescribe a scale of benefits and experience indicates or it is expected that employer contributions are or will be periodically adjusted to enable such stated benefits to be maintained. Further, a plan that is subject to the Employee Retirement Income Security Act of 1974 and considered to be a defined benefit pension plan under the Act is a defined benefit pension plan.

defined contribution plan. A plan that provides an individual account for each participant and provides benefits that are based on (a) amounts contributed to the participant's account by the employer or employee, (b) investment experience, and (c) any forfeitures allocated to the account, less any administrative expenses charged to the plan.

employee. A person who has rendered or is presently rendering service.

employee stock ownership plan (ESOP). An employee stock ownership plan is an employee benefit plan that is described by the Employee Retirement Income Security Act of 1974 and the Internal Revenue Code of 1986 as a stock bonus plan, or combination stock bonus and money purchase pension plan, designed to invest primarily in employer stock. Also called an employee share ownership plan.

fair value. The price that would be received to sell an asset or paid to transfer a liability in an orderly transaction between market participants at the measurement date.

fully insured experience-rated arrangement. In a fully insured experience-rated arrangement, specified benefits are paid by the insurance entity that assumes all the financial risk. Contract experience is monitored by the insurance entity. Contract experience may or may not include the experience of other similar contract holders. To the extent that benefits incurred plus risk charges and administration costs are less than premiums paid, the related plan is entitled to an experience-rating refund or dividend. If the total of benefits incurred, risk charges, and administrative costs exceeds premiums, the accumulated loss is generally borne by the insurance entity but may be carried over to future periods until it has been recovered. The related plan often has no obligation to continue coverage or to reimburse the carrier for any accumulated loss, although there are certain types of contracts that require additional payments by the plan.

fully insured pooled arrangement. In a fully insured pooled arrangement, specified benefits are covered by the insurance entity. The insurance entity pools the experience of the plan with that of other similar businesses and assumes the financial risk of adverse experience. In such an arrangement, a plan generally has no obligation for benefits covered by the arrangement other than the payment of premiums due to the insurance entity

funding agency. An organization or individual, such as a specific corporate or individual trustee or an insurance entity, that provides facilities for the accumulation of assets to be used for paying benefits under a plan; an organization, such as a specific life insurance entity, that provides facilities for the purchase of such benefits.

funding policy. The program regarding the amounts and timing of contributions by the employer(s), participants, and any other sources (for example, state subsidies or federal grants) to provide the benefits a pension plan specifies.

general account. An undivided fund maintained by an insurance entity that commingles plan assets with other assets of the insurance entity for investment purposes. That is, funds held by an insurance entity that are not maintained in a separate account are in its general account.

health and welfare benefit plan. A plan that provides (a) medical, dental, visual, psychiatric, or long-term health care; certain severance benefits; life insurance; accidental death or dismemberment benefits; (b) unemployment, disability, vacation or holiday benefits; and (c) other benefits such as apprenticeships, tuition assistance, day-care, dependent care, housing subsidies, or legal services benefits.

insurance contract. A contract in which an insurance entity unconditionally undertakes a legal obligation to provide specified benefits to specific individuals in return for a fixed consideration or premium. An insurance contract is irrevocable and involves the transfer of significant risk from the employer (or the plan) to the insurance entity.

investment fund option. An investment alternative provided to a participant in a defined contribution plan. The alternatives are usually pooled fund vehicles, such as (a) registered investment companies (meaning, mutual

funds), (b) commingled funds of banks, or (c) insurance entity pooled separate accounts providing varying kinds of investments, for example, equity
funds and fixed income funds. The participant may select from among the
various available alternatives and periodically change that selection.

minimum premium plan arrangement. In a minimum premium plan arrangement, specified benefits are paid by the insurance entity. The insurance contract establishes a dollar limit, or trigger point. All claims paid by
the insurance entity below the trigger point are reimbursed by the plan to
the insurance entity. The insurance entity is not reimbursed for benefits
incurred that exceed the trigger point. This type of funding arrangement
requires the plan to fund the full claims experience up to the trigger point.
Minimum premium plan arrangements may have characteristics of both
self-funded and fully insured experience-rated arrangements.

multiemployer plan. A pension or postretirement benefit plan to which two
or more unrelated employers contribute, usually pursuant to one or more
collective-bargaining agreements. A characteristic of multiemployer plans
is that assets contributed by one participating employer may be used to
provide benefits to employees of other participating employers since assets
contributed by an employer are not segregated in a separate account or
restricted to provide benefits only to employees of that employer. A multiemployer plan is usually administered by a board of trustees composed
of management and labor representatives and may also be referred to as
a joint trust or union plan. Generally, many employers participate in a
multiemployer plan, and an employer may participate in more than one
plan. The employers participating in multiemployer plans usually have a
common industry bond, but for some plans the employers are in different
industries and the labor union may be their only common bond. Some multiemployer plans do not involve a union. For example, local chapters of a
not-for-profit entity may participate in a plan established by the related
national organization.

multiple-employer plan. A pension plan maintained by more than one employer but not treated as a multiemployer plan. Multiple-employer plans
are not as prevalent as single-employer and multiemployer plans, but some
of the ones that do exist are large and involve many employers. Multiple-
employer plans are generally not collectively bargained and are intended
to allow participating employers, commonly in the same industry, to pool
their assets for investment purposes and reduce the costs of plan administration. A multiple-employer plan maintains separate accounts for each
employer so that contributions provide benefits only for employees of the
contributing employer. Some multiple-employer plans have features that
allow participating employers to have different benefit formulas, with the
employer's contributions to the plan based on the benefit formula selected
by the employer.

net asset information. Information regarding the net assets available for
benefits.

net assets available for benefits. The difference between a plan's assets
and its liabilities. For purposes of this definition, a plan's liabilities do not
include participants' accumulated plan benefits.

noncontributory plan. A pension plan under which participants do not make
contributions.

nonvested benefit information. The actuarial present value of nonvested accumulated plan benefits.

participant. Any employee or former employee, or any member or former member of a trade or other employee association, or the beneficiaries of those individuals, for whom there are accumulated plan benefits.

participating contract. An allocated contract that provides for plan participation in the investment performance and experience (for example, mortality experience) of the insurance entity.

participation right. A plan's right under a participating insurance contract to receive future dividends or retroactive rate credits from the insurance entity.

pension benefits. Periodic (usually monthly) payments made to a person who has retired from employment.

pension fund. The assets of a pension plan held by a funding agency.

pension plan. See **defined benefit pension plan**.

plan administrator. The person or group of persons responsible for the content and issuance of a plan's financial statements in much the same way that management is responsible for the content and issuance of a business entity's financial statements.

postretirement benefits. All forms of benefits, other than retirement income, provided by an employer to retirees. Those benefits may be defined in terms of specified benefits, such as health care, tuition assistance, or legal services, that are provided to retirees as the need for those benefits arises, such as certain health care benefits, or they may be defined in terms of monetary amounts that become payable on the occurrence of a specified event, such as life insurance benefits.

reporting date. The date of which information regarding the net assets available for benefits is presented.

retired life fund. That portion of the funds under an immediate participation guarantee contract that is designated as supporting benefit payments to current retirees.

separate account. A special account established by an insurance entity solely for the purpose of investing the assets of one or more plans. Funds in a separate account are not commingled with other assets or the insurance entity for investment purposes.

service. Periods of employment taken into consideration under a pension plan.

single employer plan. A pension plan that is maintained by one employer.

sponsor. In the case of a pension plan established or maintained by a single employer, the employer; in the case of a plan established or maintained by an employee organization, the employee organization; in the case of a plan established or maintained jointly by two or more employers or by one or more employers and one or more employee organizations, the association, committee, joint board of trustees, or other group of representatives of the parties who have established or who maintain the pension plan.

stop-loss insurance arrangement. In a stop-loss insurance arrangement, a plan's obligation for any plan participant's claims may be limited to a fixed dollar amount, or the plan's total obligation may be limited to a maximum percentage (for example, 125 percent) of a preset expected claims level. These arrangements are commonly used with administrative service arrangements. The insurance entity assumes the benefit obligation in excess of the limit. Stop-loss insurance arrangements may have characteristics of both self-funded and fully insured arrangements.

supplemental actuarial value. The amount assigned under the actuarial cost method in use for years before a given date.

tax position. A position in a previously filed tax return or a position expected to be taken in a future tax return that is reflected in measuring current or deferred income tax assets and liabilities for interim or annual periods.

unallocated contract. A contract with an insurance entity under which related payments to the insurance entity are accumulated in an unallocated fund to be used to meet benefit payments when employees retire, either directly or through the purchase of annuities. Funds in an unallocated contract may also be withdrawn and otherwise invested.

vested benefit information. The actuarial present value of vested accumulated plan benefits.

vested benefits. Benefits that are not contingent on an employee's future service.

The following is a list of additional terms that have been used in this guide:

403(b) plan. A 403(b) plan is a retirement savings arrangement sponsored by certain not for profit organizations (such as hospitals and private colleges) and pubic schools. They are defined contribution plans with individual salary deferral limits that are similar, but not identical to, 401(k) programs.

accrued experience-rating adjustments. The refund at the end of the policy year of the excess of premiums paid over paid claims, reserves required by the insurance entity, and the insurance entity's retention (fee).

act. The Employee Retirement Income Security Act of 1974.

benefits. Payments to which participants may be entitled under an employee benefit plan, including pension benefits, disability benefits, death benefits, health benefits, and benefits due on termination of employment. (Defined in the FASB ASC glossary, as presented in the first section of this glossary.)

cash balance plan. A defined benefit plan that maintains hypothetical accounts for participants. The employer credits participants' accounts with a certain number of dollars each plan year and promises earnings at a specified rate. Interest in the account balance is credited at a stated rate which may be different from the plan's actual rate of return.

cash-or-deferred arrangement (Section 401(k) plan). A plan that may be incorporated into a profit-sharing or stock bonus plan (a few pre-ERISA money purchase pension plans also incorporate cash-or-deferred arrangements). Under such an arrangement, a participant is permitted to elect to receive amounts in cash or have them contributed to the plan as employer contributions on the participant's behalf.

CFR. Code of Federal Regulations.

COBRA. Continuation of benefits provided by health and welfare plans upon termination of employment through the Consolidated Omnibus Budget Reconciliation Act.

common or commingled trust. A trust for the collective investment and reinvestment of assets contributed from employee benefit plans maintained by more than one employer or a controlled group of corporations that is maintained by a bank, trust entity, or similar institution that is regulated, supervised, and subject to periodic examination by a state or federal agency.

deposit administration contract (DA). A type of contract under which contributions are not currently applied to the purchase of single-payment deferred annuities for individual participants. Payments to the insurance entity that are intended to provide future benefits to present employees are credited to an account. For investment purposes, the monies in the account are commingled with other assets of the insurance entity. The account is credited with interest at the rate specified in the contract; it is charged with the purchase price of annuities when participants retire and with any incidental benefits (death, disability, and withdrawal) disbursed directly from the account.

directed trust. An arrangement in which the trustee acts as custodian of a plan's investments and is responsible for collecting investment income and handling trust asset transactions as directed by the party named as having discretion to make investment decisions, such as the plan administrator, the plan's investment committee, or the plan's investment advisor.

discretionary trust. An arrangement in which the trustee has discretionary authority and control over investments and is authorized by the plan or its investment committee to make investment decisions.

eligible compensation. Various aspects of compensation (for example, base wages, overtime, and bonuses) as specified by the plan document that are considered in the calculation of plan contributions for defined contributions plans and in the determination of benefits in a defined benefit plan.

ERISA. The Employee Retirement Income Security Act of 1974.

ERISA plan. A plan that is subject to ERISA.

Form 5500. A joint-agency form developed by the IRS, Department of Labor, and Pension Benefit Guaranty Corporation, which may be used to satisfy the annual reporting requirements of the Internal Revenue Code and Titles I and IV of ERISA.

frozen plan. See **wasting trust**.

full-scope audit. An audit of the financial statements of an employee benefit plan in accordance with generally accepted auditing standards.

guaranteed investment contract (GIC). A contract between an insurance entity and a plan that provides for a guaranteed return on principal invested over a specified time period.

IBNR. Claims incurred by eligible participants but not yet reported to the plan.

immediate participation guarantee contract (IPG). A type of contract under which contributions are not currently applied to the purchase of single-payment deferred annuities for individual participants. Payments to the insurance entity that are intended to provide future benefits to present employees, plus its share of the insurance entity's actual investment income, are credited to an account. The insurance entity is obligated to make lifetime benefit payments to retired employees.

individual separate account. A separate account in which only one plan participates. Also referred to as a separate-separate account.

insured plan. A plan funded through an insurance contract.

investment unit. See **unit of participation**.

Keogh plan. Also called an HR 10 plan, any defined benefit or defined contribution plan that covers one or more self-employed individuals.

limited-scope audit. An audit in which ERISA allows the plan administrator to instruct the auditor not to perform any auditing procedures with respect to information prepared and certified by a bank or similar institution, or by an insurance carrier that is regulated, supervised, and subject to periodic examination by a state or federal agency.

master trust. A combined trust account made up of assets of some or all of the employee benefit plans of an entity that sponsors more than one plan or a group of corporations under common control. Each plan has an undivided interest in the assets of the trust, and ownership is represented by a record of proportionate dollar interest or by units of participation.

modified cash basis of accounting. Cash basis financial statements that adjust securities investments to fair value.

money purchase pension plan. A defined contribution plan under which employer contributions are based on a fixed formula that is not related to profit and that is designated as a pension plan by the plan sponsor.

named fiduciary. The individual responsible for the operation and administration of a plan including the identification of a plan administrator; usually an officer or other employee of the plan sponsor who reports to the plan sponsor's board of directors or management.

omnibus account. An institutional account, often in the name of a custodian bank or an investment advisor, in which transactions are effected on behalf of a number of beneficial owners.

participant directed investment programs. A plan provides for participant-directed investment programs if it allows participants to choose among various investment alternatives. The available alternatives are usually pooled fund vehicles, such as registered investment companies or commingled funds of banks, that provide varying kinds of investments-for example, equity funds and fixed income funds. The participant may select among the various available alternatives and periodically change that selection.

party in interest. A fiduciary or employee of the plan, any person who provides services to the plan, an employer whose employees are covered by the plan, an employee association whose members are covered by the plan, a person who owns 50 percent or more of such an employer or employee association, or relatives of such person just listed.

PBGC. The Pension Benefit Guaranty Corporation.

pension equity plan. A defined benefit plan under which a participant is credited with points based on age, service or both. On termination of employment, a participant's final average compensation is multiplied by his or her accumulated points to determine a hypothetical account balance which normally may be distributed as a lump sum or converted to an annuity.

plan allocation. The allocation of the net assets available for benefits (or plan assets) for defined contribution plans to individual participant accounts according to procedures set forth in the plan instrument or in a collective bargaining agreement.

pooled separate account. A separate account in which several plans participate.

prior service costs. See **supplemental actuarial value.**

profit-sharing plan. A defined contribution plan that is not a pension plan (as defined in the Internal Revenue Code) or a stock bonus plan. Employer contributions may be discretionary or may be based on a fixed formula related to profits, compensation, or other factors. Before 1987, contributions had to be made from the plan sponsor's current or accumulated profits. This requirement is no longer in effect. A profit-sharing plan must be designated as such in the plan document.

prohibited transaction. A transaction between a plan and a party in interest that is prohibited under Section 406(a) of ERISA.

rollover. The transfer of contributions into a qualified defined contribution plan from another qualified plan or from an individual retirement account.

self-directed plan. A defined contribution plan in which the participant authorizes specific investment transactions, such as purchases and sales of specific common stocks or bonds. A self-directed plan does not provide predetermined investment fund options.

self-funded plan. A plan funded through accumulated contributions and investment income.

separately managed accounts. Accounts at trust entity or similar institution consisting of individual plan assets that are managed by an investment manager specifically for the plan.

simple plan. Also referred to as a Savings Incentive Match Plan for Employees is a tax-favored retirement plan available to employers that have no more than 100 employees who earned more than $5,000 or more in compensation during the preceding calendar year. The employer's only required contribution is dollar-for-dollar matching contribution of 3 percent of employee's compensation or a limited profit-sharing type contribution. Employer contributions are fully vested at all times.

split-funded plan. A plan funded through a combination of accumulated contributions and investment income and insurance contracts.

stock bonus plan. A defined contribution plan under which distributions are normally made in stock of the employer, unless the distributee elects otherwise.

synthetic guaranteed investment contract. An investment contract that simulates the performance of a traditional guaranteed investment contract through the use of financial instruments.

target benefit plan. A form of money purchase pension plan under which the employer's annual contribution on behalf of each participation is the actuarially determined amount required to fund a target benefit established by a plan formula. The target benefit is usually based on compensation and length of service. For some target benefit plans, the substance of the plan may be to provide a defined benefit.

tax credit employee stock ownership plan. A profit-sharing or stock bonus plan established before 1987 that satisfies the requirements of Section 409 of the Internal Revenue Code. The sponsor of such a plan is allowed a tax credit, rather than a deduction, for its contributions. Before 1982 these plans were commonly known as TRASOPs (for Tax Reduction Act Stock Ownership Plan), and the maximum allowable credit was based on the plan sponsor's investments that qualified for the investment tax credit. In 1982 TRASOPs were succeeded by Payroll Stock Ownership Plans (PAYSOPs), under which the credit was based on the plan sponsor's payroll.

third-party administrator (TPA). A party unrelated to the plan who contracts to be responsible for plan administration.

thrift plan. A profit-sharing or stock bonus plan under which participants make after-tax employee contributions that are usually matched, in whole or in part, by employer contributions.

unfunded plan. A plan whereby benefits are paid directly from the general assets of the employer or the employee organization that sponsors the plan.

unit of participation. An undivided interest in the underlying assets of a trust.

unrelated business taxable income (UBTI). Gross income derived from an unrelated trade or business that is regularly carried on, less allowable deductions directly connected with the trade or business.

unrelated trade or business. Any trade or business regularly carried on by the trust or by a partnership of which the trust is a member.

wasting trust. A plan under which participants no longer accrue benefits but that will remain in existence as long as necessary to pay already-accrued benefits.

Index

_____